Trade and Environment Governance at the World Trade Organization Committee on Trade and Environment

Global Trade Law Series

VOLUME 53

Series Editors

Prof. Ross P. Buckley, King & Wood Mallesons Professor of International Finance Law, Faculty of Law, University of New South Wales, Sydney, Australia
Prof. Andreas R. Ziegler, Faculty of Law, Criminal Sciences, and Public Administration, University of Lausanne, Switzerland

Introduction and Contents/Subjects

The *Global Trade Law Series* addresses key issues in international trade law. It covers a broad range of topics, including WTO dispute settlement, free trade agreements, investment law and arbitration, export control, and compliance with international trade obligations.

Objective & Readership

The volumes published in this series are aimed at offering high-quality analytical information and practical solutions, for practitioners, policy makers and academics.

Frequency of Publication

2-3 new volumes published each year.

The titles published in this series are listed at the end of this volume.

Trade and Environment Governance at the World Trade Organization Committee on Trade and Environment

Manuel A.J. Teehankee

Wolters Kluwer

Published by:
Kluwer Law International B.V.
PO Box 316
2400 AH Alphen aan den Rijn
The Netherlands
E-mail: international-sales@wolterskluwer.com
Website: lrus.wolterskluwer.com

Sold and distributed in North, Central and South America by:
Wolters Kluwer Legal & Regulatory U.S.
7201 McKinney Circle
Frederick, MD 21704
United States of America
Email: customer.service@wolterskluwer.com

Sold and distributed in all other countries by:
Air Business Subscriptions
Rockwood House
Haywards Heath
West Sussex
RH16 3DH
United Kingdom
Email: international-customerservice@wolterskluwer.com

ISBN 978-94-035-2202-9

e-Book: ISBN 978-94-035-2204-3
web-PDF: ISBN 978-94-035-2210-4

In loving memory of my parents, Claudio and Pilar,
with gratefulness for their nurturing, inspiration and confidence.

Table of Contents

Preface

Of Sisyphus and Yu Gong Yi Shan

The gods had condemned Sisyphus to ceaselessly rolling a rock to the top of a mountain, whence the stone would fall back of its own weight. They had thought with some reason that there is no more dreadful punishment than futile and hopeless labor. … I leave Sisyphus at the foot of the mountain! One always finds one's burden again. But Sisyphus teaches the higher fidelity that negates the gods and raises rocks. He too concludes that all is well. This universe henceforth without a master seems to him neither sterile nor futile. Each atom of that stone, each mineral flake of that night filled mountain, in itself forms a world. The struggle itself toward the heights is enough to fill a man's heart. One must imagine Sisyphus happy.

Albert Camus, 1942

There were two high mountains between Jizhou in the north and Heyang in the south. One was called Taihang Mountain and the other Wangwu Mountain. Just to the north of the mountains lived an old man called Yu Gong who was nearly 90 years old. With the two high mountains just in front of his house, he and his family had to walk a long way around the mountains whenever they had something to do on the other side of the mountains.

One day, Yu Gong called all his family together to discuss about moving the two mountains so that they can have a direct route to the south of Yuzhou reaching the bank of the Han River. His wife said, "An old man like you cannot even move a small hill, not to mention the two high mountains. Even if you can, where can you throw so much earth and stone?" The Bohai Sea is big enough to contain all the earth and stone, said everyone.

So it was decided. His children started to dig the mountains, led by the old man Yu Gong. Even their neighbor's son joined in. From winter through summer, the workers only returned home once. A man named Zhi Sou (literally "wise old man") who lived in Hequ, near a bend of the Yellow River saw them working and tried to stop them, saying, "You are so silly! You're so old and weak that you can't even take away the grass and trees. How can you move the high mountains?"

"You're wrong," Yu Gong said with a long sigh. "Look, my sons can continue my work after my death. When my sons die, my grandchildren will continue. So generation after generation, there's no end. But the mountains can't grow higher. Do you still say I can't move them away?" Zhi Sou was speechless.

Later the Heaven God, upon learning of Yu Gong's story, was greatly moved by his sincerity. He then ordered two sons of Kua Eshi, a god of great strength, to carry the two high mountains away. One was put east of Shuozhou and the other south of Yongzhou. From that time onwards, no mountain stood between the south of Jizhou and the southern bank of the Han River.

Yu Gong Yi Shan from the Lie Zi, *circa* 400 B.C.

The World Trade Organization (WTO) commenced its operations as a new international organization (IO) in January 1995. At the very first WTO General Council's meeting held on January 31, 1995, the Committee on Trade and Environment (the *CTE*) was formally created with its first chairman being appointed in the person of Ambassador Juan Carlos Sanchez Arnau of Argentina, who would convene its first meeting on February 16, 1995.[a]

The CTE already had its roots in its predecessor, known as the Working Group on Environmental Measures and International Trade (*GEMIT*), established by the General Agreement on Tariffs and Trade (GATT) in November 1971.[b] Expectations had always run high on what the GATT or its successor, the WTO, could contribute to the quest for effective global governance in the field of environmental protection; to trade experts, this expectation was welcomed with a mix of caution and willingness. In both instances, in 1971, and again in 1994, the creation of the GEMIT, and later the CTE, were closely linked to then-current global events in the field of environment advocacy,

a. The General Council was acting pursuant to a GATT Ministerial Decision calling on the new WTO to establish the CTE, Ministerial Decision on Trade and Environment, MTN.TNC/MIN (94)/1/Rev.1, adopted by ministers at the meeting of the Uruguay Round Trade Negotiations Committee in Marrakesh, April 14, 1994, 1867 U.N.T.S. 133 (I-31874, 1995), on the occasion of the Marrakesh Agreement Establishing the World Trade Organization, 33 I.L.M. 1267 (1994). *See generally* WTO CTE, Summary of Activities of the Committee on Trade and Environment (1995), WT/CTE/W/17 (December 12, 1995).

b. *See* GATT, Trade and Environment, Factual Note by the Secretariat, L/6896 (September 18, 1991).

particularly in relation to preparations for the Stockholm 1972 United Nations (UN) Conference on the Human Environment and the preparations for, and implementation of the Rio Earth Summit in 1992.

This book was initially motivated by my chairing the CTE (in regular and Special Session) from 2007 to 2011, triggering an interest in the committee's history with the question in mind of identifying the contributions of the CTE to improving trade and environment global governance. It can, therefore, be viewed as an attempt to evaluate and understand the historical performance and work of the CTE as an institution and as an IO, promoting both trade and environment policy objectives.

To a legal practitioner as myself, more inclined to measuring performance through the lens of results, outputs, deliverables, bills or laws passed, and cases won or lost, the natural question was whether there was any advantage or public good that could be derived from the years of work that international practitioners, bureaucrats like myself, and secretariat teams had devoted to the subject, despite the cold fact that there remains no actual new rule or treaty law to speak of that the CTE can lay claim to as evidence of norm creation or international law (IL) formulation. Hence, inspired by the reference to Sisyphus, pre-Camus, and like Zhi Sou, the interlocutor of Yu Gong, my study sought to know the existential meaning or value of all the CTE activity and documentation over the last two decades, hoping it can be more than a lot of *sound and fury*.[c]

Over the course of writing this book, however, which required a detailed examination of the specific work outputs of the CTE, and the repetitive proceedings and recorded minutes, including pre-CTE GATT materials, and some pre-GATT historical records, the superficiality of seeking only hard results and outputs became evident. The main focus of this book evolved naturally towards a more nuanced and contextualized approach at assessing the work processes and deliberations of the CTE, as part of the general evolution of the trade, development, and environment legal and policy regimes. With that, the focus also shifted towards a greater understanding of how particular objectives and specific mechanisms are underpinned by particular policy agendas, biases, movements, or trends in the domestic, regional and international fora concerned.

This is not unique to the CTE, and the assessment approaches suggested or derived in this book could be useful as well in approaching the work of other international cooperation fora that are prone to generating work outputs similar to the CTE that are not delivered as binding new rules or treaties. Of course, not all rules or norms are subject to reform or change; some are clearly meant to remain constant

c. Beyond Camus, or a Dilbert comic spoof of work at the WTO, one can always obtain some poetic solace from the famous lines of Macbeth's Act 5, Scene 5, 23-28:

> Out, out, brief candle!
> Life's but a walking shadow, a poor player,
> That struts and frets his hour upon the stage,
> And then is heard no more. It is a tale
> Told by an idiot, full of sound and fury,
> Signifying nothing.

anchors to the very basic system it underpins. So in trade, development and environment, the basic anchor in a rules-based system, i.e., of promoting fair and open markets, has remained constant, and the role of that constant aids in providing a stable grounding for the competing forces at play and to balance the conflicting interests and occasional tensions between the different policy regimes, and their respective immediate or medium-term objectives.

However, there are two divergent theoretical frameworks underpinning the international rules-based system. One frame is biased towards a singular solution approach of unified governance and harmonization, sometimes described as *Leviathan* or *Hobbesian* in tone; the other or counter-trend attempts to find localized or regionalized solutions, that is perhaps best inspired by Elinor Ostrom's work espousing alternative models for governing the commons as discussed below.[d]

The CTE in the WTO provides a particular example of that tension between a globalized or a localized approach to addressing particular challenges and problems, and the availability of approaches that are shades of grey in between. With these frameworks, it is hoped that this book can contribute to a better understanding and appreciation of the role of the CTE in the continuing dialogue on how to best *govern the commons* through approaches that can engender best practices in the formulation of globalized, regional or localized trade and environment norms, rules and policies.

M.A.J.T.

d. Elinor Ostrom, *Governing the Commons: The Evolution of Institutions for Collective Action* at pp. 8 et seq. (1990) (*Leviathan as the "only" way*).

List of Abbreviations

AB	Appellate Body of the World Trade Organization DSB
AJIL	American Journal of International Law
APEC	Asia Pacific Economic Forum
Art.	Article
ASEAN	Association of Southeast Asian Nations
Basel Convention	Convention on the Control of Transboundary Movements of Hazardous Wastes and Their Disposal, signed in Basel on 22 March 1989
BTA	Border Tax Adjustment
BYIL	British Yearbook of International Law
CBD	Convention on Biological Diversity
CEC	Commission for Environmental Cooperation (NAFTA)
CERDS	Charter of Economic Rights and Duties of States
CFC/HCFC	Chlorofluorocarbon/Hydrofluorocarbons
CHM	Common Heritage of Mankind
CITES	Convention on International Trade in Endangered Species
CSD	Commission for Sustainable Development
CTD	Committee on Trade and Development
CTE	Committee on Trade and Environment
CTE(1-10)	CTE Work Agenda by number (1-10)
CTESS	Committee on Trade and Environment sitting in Special Session
CTS	Council for Trade in Services

DDA	Doha Development Agenda
DNA	Designated National Authority
DSB	Dispute Settlement Body
DSU	Dispute Settlement Understanding
EC/EU	European Communities/European Union
EDB	Environmental Database
EEZ	Exclusive Economic Zone
EGS	Environmental Goods and Services
EJIL	European Journal of International Law
EPPs	Environmentally Preferable Products
ER	Environmental Review
ESIL	European Society of International Law
EST	Environmentally Sound Technologies
ETC	Environmental Taxes and Charges
EU/EC	European Union/European Communities
FAO	Food and Agriculture Organization
FLEGT	Forest Law Enforcement, Governance and Trade
GAL	Global Administrative Law
GATS	General Agreement on Trade in Services
GATT	General Agreement on Tariffs and Trade
GC/GGC	Global Commons/Governing the Global Commons
GEF	Global Environment Facility
GEMIT	Group on Environmental Measures and International Trade
GEN	Global Eco-labelling Network
GMOs	Genetically Modified Organisms
GPA	Government Procurement Agreement
GSP	Generalized System of Preferences
HDI	Human Development Index
HSAP	Hydropower Sustainability Assessment Protocol
ICCAT	International Commission for the Conservation of Atlantic Tunas
ICJ	International Court of Justice
ICTSD	International Centre for Trade and Sustainable Development
IEA	International Environmental Agreement
IFF	Intergovernmental Forum on Forests
IGO	Intergovernmental Organization
IILM	Informal International Lawmaking

IIPPM	Informal International Public Policy Making
IL	International Law
IL-IR	International Law—International Relations
IMF	International Monetary Fund
IO	International Organization
IPCC	Intergovernmental Panel on Climate Change
IPR	Intellectual Property Rights
IR	International Relations (Political Science)
IRPTC	International Register of Potentially Toxic Chemicals
ISO	International Organization for Standardization
ITC	International Trade Centre
ITQs	Individual Transferable Quotas
ITTO	International Tropical Timber Organization
JIEL	Journal of International Economic Law
JPAC	Joint Public Advisory Committee
JWT	Journal of World Trade
Kyoto Protocol	Protocol to the United Nations Framework Convention on Climate Change, signed in Kyoto on December 11, 1997
LDCs	Least Developed Countries
MDGs	Millennium Development Goals
MEA	Multilateral Environmental Agreement
MFN	Most Favored Nation
MNC	Multinational Corporation
Montreal Protocol	Protocol to the Vienna Convention for the Protection of the Ozone Layer on Substances That Deplete the Ozone Layer, signed in Montreal on September 16, 1987
MSME/SME	Micro, Small and Medium Enterprises
NAAEC	North American Agreement on Environmental Cooperation
NAFTA	North American Free Trade Agreement
NEM	National Environmental Measures/Domestic Environmental Measures
NGOs	Nongovernmental Organizations
NIEO	New International Economic Order
NTB	Non-Tariff Barriers
NTMs	Non-Tariff Measures

OECD	Organization for Economic Cooperation and Development
Paris	Paris Agreement
PCIJ	Permanent Court of International Justice
POPs	Persistent Organic Pollutants
PPM	Process and Production Methods
Prin.	Principle
PSNR	Permanent Sovereignty over Natural Resources
Rio Declaration	United Nations Declaration on Environment and Development, signed in Rio de Janeiro on June 14, 1992
Rio + 20 Conference	United Nations Conference on Sustainable Development, held in Rio de Janeiro on June 20-22, 2012
RTA	Regional Trade Agreement
S&D, SDT	Special and Differential Treatment (for Developing Countries)
SCM Agreement	Agreement on Subsidies and Countervailing Measures
SCTE	Subcommittee on Trade and Environment
SMGP	Single Market Green Products
SPS	Sanitary and Phytosanitary Measures
STCs	Specific Trade Concerns
STO	Specific Trade Obligation
TBT	Technical Barriers to Trade
TiSA	Trade-in Services Agreement
TNC	Trade Negotiations Committee
TPRM	Trade Policy Review Mechanism
TRIPS	Trade-Related Aspects of Intellectual Property Rights
TRN	Transgovernmental Regulatory Networks
UN	United Nations
UNCCD	United Nations Convention to Combat Desertification
UNCED	United Nations Conference on Environment and Development, held in Rio de Janeiro on June 3-14, 1992
UNCHE	United Nations Conference on the Human Environment, held in Stockholm on June 5-16, 1972
UNCLOS	United Nations Convention on the Law of the Sea

UNCTAD	United Nations Conference on Trade and Development
UNDP	United Nations Development Program
UNEP	United Nations Environment Program
UNFCCC	United Nations Framework Convention on Climate Change
UNGA	United Nations General Assembly
UNIDO	United Nations Industrial Development Organization
UNTS	United Nations Treaty Series
UR	Uruguay Round
USTR	United States Trade Representative
VCLT	Vienna Convention on the Law of Treaties
VCPOL	Vienna Convention on the Protection of the Ozone Layer, signed in Vienna on March 22, 1985
WCO	World Customs Organization
WIPO	World Intellectual Property Organization
WSSD	World Summit on Sustainable Development, held in Johannesburg from August 26 to September 4, 2002
WTO	World Trade Organization
YBEEL	Yearbook of European Environmental Law

Acknowledgments

This book, which focuses on the twenty-five years of work at the WTO Committee on Trade and Environment and the fifty-year evolution of the Trade, Development and Environment governance regimes, would not have been possible but for the kindness, inspiration and support of many mentors, colleagues, and friends, and the institutions that I have been part of through the years both before and during the years of work that were needed to complete this book project.

Without in any way attempting to pass on responsibility for any errors or incoherence of methodology to any of them, first and foremost, I would like to acknowledge with sincere gratitude my academic guides and mentors: Professor Joost Pauwelyn, who was among the first to encourage me to write on trade and environment based on my experience as chair of the CTE, while cautioning me as well to keep a level of detachment necessary for the academic rigor of the project; Professor Liliana Andonova, for her guidance on the IO performance perspectives for global governance; Professor Jorge Viñuales for his insights on the intersection of environment and investment law; and Professor Peter van den Bossche, for his profound and in-depth expertise on all things WTO. I am deeply indebted as well to the late Professor John Jackson, who had started me on the path of studying the GATT at the University of Michigan in Ann Arbor (as a Dewitt Scholar), and who to this day remains a role model of intellectual leadership coupled with calm introspection and humility. I cannot also fail to acknowledge the influence and inspiration I have derived from the works of Elinor Ostrom, Konrad von Moltke and Steve Charnovitz. I thank as well the Graduate Institute and the Center for Trade and Economic Integration, together with the incomparable IHEID library for hosting me as a research fellow that made my *sabbatical* most agreeable and fulfilling. I hold many happy memories of my interactions with CTEI co-director, Professor Richard Baldwin, Dr. Theresa Carpenter, Professor Gabrielle Marceau, Angelica Zaninelli, and all my fellow research colleagues, allowing me to test and share ideas, whilst making lifelong friends in the process. Similarly, special words of thanks to WTO Deputy Director General, Harsha Vardhana Singh, for endorsing my first research fellowship with the Centre for Global Agreements Legislation and Trade (GALT) at The Energy Research Institute (TERI) in New

Delhi India. TERI and GALT enabled me to do preliminary research on the economics of natural resources and to benefit from the knowledge and experience of various specialist colleagues, including the late Dr. Rajendra Kumar Pachauri, former Chairman of the Intergovernmental Panel on Climate Change, Dr. Ligia Noronha, Dr. Leena Srivastava and Nitya Nanda. I am very grateful as well to Mahesh Sugathan for assisting me in crafting the *triple win matrix tool* to measure the pros and cons of certain proposed environmental goods for liberalization, and to Martin Berger for diligent research on public international law issues. Rishab Raturi and Allan Revote contributed much appreciated assistance and patience in retrieving and reviewing countless historical documents, extracts, original source materials, and exchanging insights and ideas.

On the practice and actual negotiations side, I could not have written this book or been able to speak on the topic without the invaluable guidance and experience of the CTE and CTESS Secretariat at the WTO Trade and Environment Division: then Director Vesile Kulacoglu, Vivien Liu, and of course, Ludivine Tamiotti, co-lead author of the seminal WTO and UNEP 2009 joint report on *Trade and Climate Change*. I also have to fully acknowledge the contribution and professionalism of the many WTO Member delegations and experts at the CTE and CTESS. Their interventions, insights, questions and proposals served to become my best guide and teacher in learning the intricacies of the issues and concerns in the trade and environment sphere. I also acknowledge the support and friendship of the WTO as an institution and all my ambassador colleagues, from all regional groupings, including our close-knit ASEAN Committee in Geneva. Without their trust and confidence, I would not have had the privilege and opportunity to chair the CTE and CTESS and participate in the intense *Green Room* deliberations, led at the time by Director General, Pascal Lamy. I am also grateful to the current WTO Director General, Roberto Azevêdo, for his leadership with UNEP Executive Director Achim Steiner in organizing the expert-rich program commemorating the 20th anniversary of the CTE in April of 2015.

My academic journey began in the Philippines teaching international law and trade law at the Ateneo de Manila Law School, where I first co-taught international economic law with Dean Sedfrey Candelaria. I am therefore most grateful to Dean Candelaria and my students throughout the years. Equally, I owe a debt of gratitude to the public and high authorities I serve, my home office at the Department of Foreign Affairs, the OUIER (Office of the Undersecretary for International Economic Relations), the Foreign Service Institute, and certainly to the camaraderie and support I received from our TCWM (Technical Committee on WTO Matters). It has been fulfilling to work with the three TCWM chairs, Dr. Thomas G. Aquino, Adrian S. Cristobal, Jr. and currently Dr. Ceferino S. Rodolfo. My sincere gratitude must be made to the team of professionals at the Philippine Mission to the WTO in Geneva, both during my first tour of duty and at present.

Finally, I have to express appreciation to the team at Kluwer Law International for agreeing to publish this book in such an efficient and seamless manner, to my good friend Dr. Joachim Monkelbaan, author of *Governance for the Sustainable Development*

Goals, for guiding me through the publication process and providing valuable comments and peer review suggestions, to my dear family and friends, and to the Almighty, for all the special blessings and joys this project has brought along the way.

M.A.J.T.

Geneva
May 14, 2020

26 June 2009: At the launch of the WTO/UNEP Report on Trade and Climate Change, WTO Director-General Pascal Lamy (center) is accompanied on the podium by (from left to right) UNEP Executive Director Achim Steiner, Ambassador Peter Black of Jamaica, Committee on Trade and Environment Chair Ambassador Manuel Teehankee of the Philippines and Minister Counsellor Søren Kragholm of Denmark.

Introduction and Overview of Chapters

Development involves a progressive transformation of economy and society. ... The integration of economic and ecological factors into the law and into decision making systems within countries has to be matched at the international level. ... sustainable development requires the unification of economics and ecology in international relations

Gro Harlem Brundtland
Our Common Future 1987

Humans have a more complex motivational structure and more capability to solve social dilemmas than posited in earlier rational-choice theory. Designing institutions to force (or nudge) entirely self-interested individuals to achieve better outcomes has been the major goal posited by policy analysts for governments to accomplish for much of the past half century. Extensive empirical research leads me to argue that instead, a core goal of public policy should be to facilitate the development of institutions that bring out the best in humans.

Elinor Ostrom
Nobel Prize Lecture 2009

Part I: Chapters 1 to 3, the Conception, Work Mandate and Theories of the CTE

Chapter 1 covers the roots, context and prehistory for the formation of the *CTE*, and the lead-up to the drafting of the GATT 1994 Decision that has served as the organic act for the CTE up to this day. An overview of the work of the CTE would be incomplete without reviewing the work of its predecessor, the *GEMIT* and the contemporaneous context of the times that led to an initial contemplation of a specific organ for discussing environmental concerns within the GATT. These developments occurred with the backdrop of the Stockholm and Rio Conferences, the formation of the North American Free Trade Agreement (NAFTA), and the GATT disputes on *Tuna Dolphin*. This prehistory of the CTE provides us with ample historical perspectives and leads to the well-deserved appreciation for the work of experts and writers whose thoughts remain relevant to this day.

Chapter 2 provides a snapshot of the formal ten-point work mandate and program of the CTE, grouped into the five thematic areas of work, namely, (i) Norm Hierarchy and Specific Trade Obligations (STOs) in multilateral environmental agreements (MEAs) (CTE 1,5,10), (ii) Transparency (CTE 2, 4), (iii) Carbon, standards and eco-labelling (CTE 3a, 3b), (iv) market access issues (CTE 6, (Doha Development Agenda) DDA 31iii), and (v) the special issues of domestically prohibited goods (DPGs), trade-related aspects of intellectual property rights (TRIPS) and Services (CTE 7, 8, 9). Grouping into these five areas are strictly for the convenience and manageability of the discussions, and the actual work and documents in the CTE do have overlapping discussions, but in general, they all fall back in classification to the formal ten-point work agenda. Chapter 2 also provides the basic introduction to the structure of the committee and its deliberations, the workings of the secretariat and the chair processes, and the organization of the official committee documents that have served to preserve the record and details of the discussions at the committee level, spanning over twenty-five years of work of the WTO CTE relating to the interface of trade, environment and development governance policies and practices.

More importantly, Chapter 2 describes the key outputs of the CTE, which, in effect, define the CTE's contribution to trade and environment governance and policy practices in the five thematic work areas. Of significance in the examination of the volumes of documents of the CTE, is the fact that certain output documents of the CTE, such as the Environmental Databases (EDBs) or the Environmental Reviews (ERs), are now taken for granted as part of the regular tool kits of the community of experts. Absent the work outputs and reports of the CTE, the depth of knowledge on matters such as STOs in MEAs would be nowhere near the level where they are today. As already mentioned, these key outputs or work products of the CTE do not amount to binding new rules but are posited to be valuable in the context of the theoretical, analytical frameworks proposed by this book, which are contained in Chapter 3.

Chapter 3 provides the theoretical frames to better understand the raison d'etre of the CTE, namely, (a) the International Law-International Relations (IL-IR) dynamic theory of evolving a rules-based approach to trade and environment governance, (b) encouraging economic cooperation, coordination and experience sharing, among WTO members that can lead to informal rulemaking and a potential rule by professionals and experts, and (c) the community-based, localized or decentralized governance of the commons which is the alternative to singular globalized rulemaking by state actors, IOs, experts and/or transnational regulatory networks.

Chapter 3, therefore, provides the analytical framework by which the key outputs and processes engendered by and in the CTE can be better understood, appreciated and assessed as positive contributions to the evolution of global, regional and local governance of the trade and environment commons. From a pure positive law theory perspective, there is no delivery or contribution, as of yet, by the CTE to new rules or treaty laws. Therefore, the three theoretical frames provide the contextual tools for understanding this very lack of delivery of hard rules or positive laws by the CTE, while providing a mechanism for assessing the work outputs of the CTE.

Part II: Chapters 4 to 6, the Specific Work Areas of the CTE and Application of the Theoretical Frameworks

Chapter 4 reviews the substantive work of the CTE in the areas of understanding the interface of trade rules and environmental policy making. The chapter deals with the essential issue of the hierarchy of norms between different policy regimes and institutions; issues of dispute resolution and mechanisms; the identification of STOs in MEAs; and understanding the relationship between trade and environment, the WTO and MEAs, and their secretariats.

Highlighted as well in this chapter is the importance of the theoretical framework of increased international coordination, cooperation, and the use of transparency mechanisms. Among the major outputs of the CTE that contribute to this framework would be the STO inventory, the annual EDBs and the recurring ERs that increase transparency and enhance expert and technical capacities.

The chapter is organized by the two thematic areas of interface and coordination under the CTE mandates under agenda items 1, 5 and 10, and the utilization of transparency tools under agenda items 2 and 4.

Chapter 5 deals with the special thematic areas covered by the CTE mandates under work agenda items 3a, 3b, 7, 8 and 9, relating to Carbon, Standards, Eco-labelling, DPGs, TRIPS, and Services. These are highly specialized topics that attract the theoretical frame of increased capacity, transparency and expert and technical work that is required, but the intensity of debate and resistance to consensus also highlights the essential roadblock of crafting centralized, singular or globalized solutions to what is also seen as essentially more localized environmental and industrial policy issues.

The outputs in this area have brought expert and secretariat knowledge to WTO members, their officials and constituents, and the public at large, and enabled greater levels of study and analysis of the narrow and specific problem areas that are not necessarily in need of a solution or a specific measure but rather arriving at a common knowledge base for further dialogue on the thematic issues concerned. In this area, the importance of the 2009 Joint WTO - United Nations Environment Program (UNEP) Climate Change Report, and the seminal work of the Secretariat in Special Study No. 4, as well as the other specialized reports each relating to DPGs, the Convention on

Biodiversity (CBD) and Services as contributions to the knowledge base available to WTO Members have to be emphasized and appreciated.

Chapter 6 deals with the mandate on market access under the CTE work agenda item 6, the DDA negotiating mandate under paragraph 31(iii), and the Triple-Win Mandate for Trade, Development and the Environment, a concept of potentially achieving a negotiating outcome that is simultaneously beneficial for the three policy regimes. In this chapter, analysis and review of the various member proposals and modalities for enhancing market access in environmental goods and services (EGS) is attempted, with the aid of a triple-win matrix tool devised to test the *triple-win* elements, derived from paragraph 32(i) of the Doha Declaration.

The various theories and frameworks all play a role in the evaluation and understanding of the work of the CTE in the market access area. The work has resulted in concrete draft modalities and a reference universe of goods identified for increased market access concessions. However, given the difficulty of achieving a consensus on market access, there were also attempts to develop alternative modalities and measures that are localized, regional or plurilateral, or could lead to an exercise of variable geometry.[1]

Part III: Conclusions, Epilogue, Bibliography and Appendices

In the concluding sections, a summary and integration of my findings and conclusions are made, together with key insights and highlights of the work of the CTE, and some documentary annexes that aid in the appreciation of the work of the CTE.

There are key lessons to be learned from the application of the theoretical frameworks to the work of the CTE, with the recommendation for a more pragmatic approach and an update of the work mandate of the CTE to fit more into the current state of governance theory for trade and environment issues.

Though the negotiations and attention of the public remain focused on market access issues for environmental goods, the mandate and history of the CTE show that market access negotiations were not part of the original 1994 work plan of the CTE. Market access does remain, both in general and as a negotiating mandate, as one item out of the ten-point work program of the CTE. Therefore, the benchmark for the success or failure of the CTE as an institution will necessarily have to be based on an evaluation of the complete ten-point work program and the functioning of the CTE mechanisms and processes in these ten areas of its work mandate.

Among my conclusions, certainly, there ought to be an effort to increase awareness of the different thematic work areas of the CTE and the theoretical frameworks that enhance trade and environment governance through increased technical expertise, cooperation and coordination among WTO members and their constituents. This will allow the evolution of globalized trade and environment

1. Several attempts have been made to find alternatives to the consensus rule of decision-making and allow for differentiated responsibilities and levels of concessions and commitments within the WTO System. *See generally*, "Results Oriented Institution Decision-Making and Variable Geometry" *in Report by the Consultative Board to the Former Director General Supachai Panitchpakdi* (Peter Sutherland et al. (eds.)) (2004); Andrew Cornford, *Variable Geometry for the WTO: Concept and Precedents* (UNCTAD Discussion Papers No. 171, May 2004).

governance mechanisms, while at the same time enabling and empowering stakeholders to devise localized or regional approaches and solutions for environmental issues that relate to their own communitarian commons and *common-pool resources* (CPRs). Evolving rule-based policy solutions for the global commons is actually the exception rather than the rule, as, frequently, it is the regional and localized commons or CPRs that are in greater need of attention, preservation, and protection than the global one.

At the same time, the greatest CPR within the *global commons* remains readily available and plentiful. I refer to the great pool of human talent, knowledge, and our own innate ability, as stakeholders, to share stories and experiences, common sense and goodwill, that could enable the CTE to be among the "institutions that bring out the best in humans"[2] and, from there, we could be closer to formulating a trade and environment system of governance that we can all be proud of.

2. Elinor Ostrom, *Beyond Markets and States: Polycentric Governance of Complex Economic Systems*, Nobel Prize Lecture at p. 435 (2009).

Part I The Conception, Areas of Work and Theories of the CTE

CHAPTER 1
The Prehistory of the CTE (1971-1994)

§1.01 THE ROOTS OF THE CTE: THE 1971 GEMIT (NOVEMBER 9, 1971)

In the lead-up to the convening of the United Nations Conference on Humans and the Environment (UNCHE) and the Stockholm Declaration of 1972, the GATT regime was consulted and asked to contribute its views, and this led to the first trade *cum* environment group within the GATT system to be established on November 9, 1971. The fifteen-member group was to serve only as an ad hoc working group and was to be known as the *GEMIT*. As reflected in the GATT Council Decision:[3]

> The CONTRACTING PARTIES
>
> Noting that efforts at the national or international level to control pollution and to protect human environment can have important consequences for international trade;
>
> Desiring to cooperate in this sphere with a view to contributing to the effective operation of the General Agreement and the attainment of its objectives;
>
> Bearing in mind the provisions of the General Agreement;
>
> Recognizing that in appropriate cases it may be desirable that contracting parties examine between themselves the possible effects on the operation of the General Agreement of *measures to control pollution and protect human environment* and that such examinations should be fruitful if they are undertaken at the appropriate time;
>
> Desiring to establish appropriate and flexible procedures which would facilitate consultations between contracting parties;
>
> Decide to establish a Group whose main functions would be:

3. GATT Council, Minutes of the Meeting of November 9, 1971, C/M/74 (November 17, 1971), at pp. 4-5; *see also* GATT Council, Industrial Pollution Control, November 9-10, 1971, C/W/194/Rev.1 (November 9, 1971); GATT Council, Minutes of the Meeting held in the Palais des Nations, Geneva, on October 6-7, 1971, C/M/73 (October 19, 1971); GATT Secretariat, Industrial Pollution Control and International Trade, L/3538 (June 9, 1971).

1. to examine upon request any specific matters relevant to the *trade policy aspects of measures to control pollution and protect human environment* especially with regard to the application of the provisions of the General Agreement taking into account the particular problems of developing countries
2. to report on its activities to the Council.
   Membership [15]: Argentina, Austria, Brazil, Canada, European Communities, India, Israel, Japan, Korea, Nigeria, Nordic Countries, Switzerland, United Kingdom, United States, Yugoslavia.

In adopting the November 9, 1971 decision, the delegates of the United States (U.S.) and the United Kingdom cautioned on the potential for overlapping work with other international bodies while developing countries already raised their concerns over the possible use of environmental policy and border taxes against their export interests:[4]

> Measures taken by industrialized countries in order to prevent pollution (such as special legislation or taxes) might not only hamper international trade in general but have negative effects on exports of developing countries ... environmental measures should not create new trade barriers.

The creation of the GEMIT was rooted in a seminal GATT document (*L/3538, June 9, 1971*),[5] entitled *Industrial Pollution and International Trade*, that had been sought and been contributed to the UNCHE on the specific issue of *externalities* related to pollution control and trade obligations of GATT parties:[6]

> The deterioration of the natural environment caused by industrial production processes is *an instance of "social cost"* [note 1: This notion, and the related one of "external diseconomies," goes back to the analysis by A.C. Pigou (The Economics of Welfare, first edition printed in 1920) distinguishing private and social net products, and classifying the instances in which the two may diverge. One such instance may be that "one person A, in the course of rendering some service, for which payment is made, to a second person B, incidentally also renders services or disservices to other persons ... of such a sort that payment cannot be exacted from the benefited parties or compensation enforced on behalf of the injured parties." In this paper environment pollution is viewed in exactly these terms: as an unintended by-product of services which are in demand. The extensive literature which had grown on these foundations, particularly, in the postwar period, was most recently reviewed by E.J. Isham in "The Postwar Literature on Externalities: An Interpretative Essay," Journal of Economics Literature, March 1971, (Vol. IX, No. 1), pp. 1-28.]
>
> Since the economic concept of "cost" implies quantification, until recently pollution would be more fittingly described as an instance of social disutility—a vague largely psychological cost borne in some way by the community at large. The fact

4. GATT Secretariat, Industrial Pollution Control and International Trade, L/3538 (June 9, 1971) at pp. 3-4.
5. In the minutes of the meeting of November 9, 1971 establishing the GEMIT, the header of agenda item 3 explicitly refers to the background document L/3538; *see* GATT Secretariat, Industrial Pollution Control and International Trade, L/3538 (June 9, 1971).
6. GATT Secretariat, Industrial Pollution Control and International Trade, L/3538 (June 9, 1971) at p. 3.

> that the community now wants to do something about environment means that the cost which pollution represents must be made explicit, i.e., quantified and charged to someone.
>
> The purpose of this analysis is neither to estimate the various elements of this cost, nor to explore in institutional detail the various possible ways of defraying it ... this paper will trace out in the most general terms the impact of various types of action that could be taken with respect to pollution control (henceforth abbreviated to P.C) by the industrialized societies on the international competitive position of individual industries affected, and hence on future development of international trade. It will then explore the extent to which the 78 nations which are contracting parties to GATT are free to act in this area consistently with the obligations they have assumed with respect to promotion of international trade on a non-discriminatory basis.

This GATT expert contribution (*GATT L3538 (1971)*) officially transmitted to the Stockholm Conference is instructive in that it is the first example of primary materials, originally restricted and now publicly available, that constituted highly expert work output on the interface of trade and environment issues, and which today would be classified as expert interdisciplinary information exchange and coordination. Such expert work outputs are, and could be, or ought to be, identified as among key concrete benefits and contributions that should be taken into account in assessing the work and functions of the CTE.

GATT L3538 (1971) predates GEMIT's establishment by five months and, in sending the report to Mr. Maurice Strong, the secretary-general of the Stockholm Conference, GATT, as an institution, was elucidating in detail on an expert economic and technical issue relating to the imperatives of quantifying pollution control costs as an *externality* that impacts the natural environment and that should be factored in by economic and trade experts in their respective policy regimes. *GATT L3538 (1971)*, therefore, provides the seed and the intellectual *point of conception* from which everything else in this book follows.

The conclusions of the *GATT L3538 (1971)* foreshadow the GATT debates on process and production methods (*PPMs*) and also expresses the concerns of the trade economists on the potential political economy risks of overreaching in the areas of PPMs or the imposition of environmental standards, and which would increasingly be a subject of advocacy, outside of the GATT. There were voices that were calling for stricter product and production standards, e.g., the *World Charter for Nature* of 1982,[7] and the highly successful Vienna Convention for the Protection of the Ozone Layer (VCPOL) and its Montreal Protocol that were passed in 1985 and 1987 with strict trade bans to enforce the reduction of CFCs and HCFCs (Chlorofluorocarbon/ Hydrofluorocarbons) to protect the earth's stratosphere.

---

7. Article 21 (b) of the World Charter for Nature mandates the "establishment of standards for products and manufacturing processes that may have adverse effects on nature, as well as agreed methodologies for assessing these effects." UN General Assembly, World Charter for Nature, A/RES/37/7 (October 28, 1982); UN General Assembly, World Charter for Nature, G.A.Res.37/7,U.N.GAOR, 37th Sess. Supp. No. 51, at 17, U.N.Doc. A/37/51 (1982); 22 I.L.M. 455 (1983).

The European Communities (the "EC/EU")[8] would take a gradually stronger position at the GATT as regards the application of the principle of *polluter pays* as its preferred policy response to the issue of *externalities* relating to industrial pollution costs:[9]

> The representative of the *European Communities* said that until the environment issue was brought into the GATT and there was a mechanism to deal with the problem, he was compelled to speak in the Council. *The environment was becoming a priority issue for the Community and its members.* The Community wanted this priority to be clearly understood and, if possible, shared by all contracting parties. *In the area of environmental policy, the Community was moving towards the application of the principle that polluters should pay.* It also wanted priority given to preventive action, taking into account the conditions of the environment in various regions and reserving particular attention to international aspects of the environment. The Community intended to act as a pilot by diversifying and ensuring consistency and efficiency in environmental policies, thus strengthening even further the rules and regulations, which had to be supplemented. He conceded that this might seem strange in times of deregulation, but as there were still no rules in this area, that phase had first to be gone through. [emphasis added].

With the 1972 Stockholm Declaration over, the GEMIT went into hibernation, and the GATT went back to its usual ways. Nearing twenty years post-Stockholm (*twenty seems to be the environment regime's favored number, Stockholm 1972, Rio 1992, Rio 2012*), the GATT, in the midst of its Uruguay Round (UR), was called to participate again and contribute to the then-upcoming Rio Summit in 1992.

§1.02 THE 1991 GEMIT/GEMIT PART 2

In the lead-up to the United Nations Conference on Environment and Development (UNCED) or the 1992 *Earth Summit,* Austria, European Free Trade Association (EFTA) member, along with Switzerland and the Nordic Countries, lobbied in the GATT on the need to deliberate on environment and trade issues in a dedicated group.

These European (EFTA and the Nordics) nations had submitted in December of 1990 the first draft of a GATT Ministerial Statement on Trade and Environment that would serve as the foundational paper for the eventual 1994 Decision establishing the CTE:[10]

> STATEMENT ON TRADE AND THE ENVIRONMENT
>
> (Made by ministers convened in Brussels on December 3-7 1990
>
> to conclude the Uruguay Round of Multilateral Trade Negotiations.)

8. As contained in the abbreviations section, the common references of EC or EU will be utilized throughout to refer interchangeably to the European Communities or the European Union, with best efforts being made to refer to the contemporaneous context of the submission or document.
9. GATT Council, Minutes of Meeting of April 24, 1991, C/M/249 (May 22, 1991) at p. 28.
10. *See* GATT Trade Negotiations Committee, Communication from Austria, Finland, Iceland, Norway, Sweden and Switzerland, MTN.TNC/W/47 (December 3, 1990).

RECOGNIZING that the environment provides a necessary basis for life and health, and for sustainable economic and social development;

TAKING INTO ACCOUNT the growing importance of environmental issues, and that most Contracting Parties have adopted national policies to protect the environment and to preserve natural resources;

RECALLING the *importance of international cooperation on environmental issues with global implications and the need to intensify such cooperation*;

RECOGNIZING that *sustainable development requires the implementation of both environmental, economic and trade policies to foster sound growth and efficient resource allocation*;

NOTING that environmental policy measures may have trade effects; that *trade and environmental policies need to be mutually supportive*; and that every effort should be made to increase their combined effectiveness;

RECALLING the provisions of the General Agreement, and that issues relating to the environment have been discussed in several negotiating groups within the Uruguay Round;

DECLARE

that priority attention should be devoted to interlinkages between trade policy and environmental policy, and for that purpose requires the CONTRACTING PARTIES to:

(a) *undertake a study on the relationships between environmental policies and the rules of the multilateral trading system*;
(b) consider the implications of preparatory work for the 1992 United Nations Conference on Environment and Development, and the possibility of submitting a GATT contribution to that Conference;
(c) *convene in 1991 the GATT Working Group on Environmental Measures and International Trade under an updated mandate* to be decided by the Council of the GATT, in order to provide Contracting Parties with a forum for these issues.

[*emphasis added*].

As provided in action item (c) in the draft ministerial statement above, Austria had proposed the convening of the GEMIT *with an updated mandate* in order for GATT to properly address trade and environmental issues and contribute to the UNCED, as it had done for the UNCHE in Stockholm.[11]

[A] Article XX Put to the Test

[1] The Clash of Trade and Environment Norms: The Tuna Dolphin Factor (1991)

The overall growth of environmental treaty activity and the GATT Council deliberations relating to the activation and re-convening of the *1971 GEMIT* with an updated

11. *Id.* at ¶(c); *see also* GATT Council, Minutes of Meeting of April 24, 1991, C/M/249 (May 22, 1991) at p. 28.

trade and environment agenda would be part of the backstage activity for the first public clash of liberal trade norms with environmental policy priorities.

In November 1990, the month before the Europeans had submitted their GEMIT proposal, Mexico had already sought GATT consultations against the U.S. to counter what it believed to be the encroachment or overreach into trade rules by the U.S. through domestic actions against its exports of tuna to the U.S.

In the famed *Tuna Dolphin I* (DS 21 1991), Mexico questioned the GATT-consistency of the U.S. *Marine Mammal Protection Act of 1972*. At the February 6, 1991 GATT Council meeting, the agenda items on *United States Tuna*, and the *Trade and Environment* proposal of Austria were respectively *Agenda items 9 and 10*, and they became major items of discussion among the GATT Council members, with the minutes reflecting the fact that these two items took up half of the deliberation time and the pages of the minutes.[12]

The linkage of the two problems was apparent in the statement of the EC as regards the Mexican agenda item 9:[13]

> The representative of the European Communities said this case seemed to raise important questions of principle which would come up in a broader context in item 10 [Trade and Environment] of the agenda.

The quiet backroom world of the GATT in lakeside Geneva would never be the same after *September 3, 1991*. The Mexico-established legal panel (DS 21 1991) refused to apply the exceptions of *GATT Article XX* and ruled that the U.S. could not impose a trade embargo on dolphin-harming tuna imports.[14] It was a public relations landmine, and this became the public face of the group of law and trade economics bureaucrats in Geneva at a time when there was a sweeping political change with the newly elected Clinton-Gore administration signaling a new U.S. attitude and readiness to sign the *1992 Rio Declaration* on Environment and Development at the 1992 Rio Earth Summit, along with other positive developments on the environmental governance front.

For sure, *Tuna Dolphin* had sent a discordant, though not legally founded, the impression that interests representing the *wealth of nations, a.k.a.*, business and trade norms could threaten years of work of interest groups representing the interests of an *ecology and health of nations a.k.a.* environment norms. There were vivid images being fostered that American consumers were less than unwittingly killing dolphins

12. GATT Council, Minutes of Meeting of February 6, 1991, C/M/247 (March 5, 1991) at pp. 16-30.
13. *Id.* at p. 18.
14. *See* GATT Panel Report, United States Restrictions on Imports of Tuna, DS21/R (BISD 39S/155) (not adopted September 3, 1991) (chairing the panel was the commercial affairs delegate of Hungary, Andras Szepesi, a Swiss economist delegate, Rudolf Ramsauer, and Uruguayan diplomat, Elbio Rosseli (later Ambassador to the United Nations and currently serving as Chairperson in the nine panels (DS 544, DS 547, DS 548, DS 550, DS 551, DS 552, DS 554, DS 556 and DS 564) established to hear complaints against the United States' *Section 232 measures* relating to certain steel and aluminium products). The insiders appointed as GATT Panelists often hail from being former GATT ambassadors or diplomats. *Tuna Dolphin I* had as panelist diplomats who were likely unaware of the bond that the American voting public had to animal causes, with popular television series such as *Flipper* and *Lassie* ruling the airwaves throughout the decade of the 1950s and 1960s. No American public official would countenance the perception of causing in the slightest any harm to dolphins.

through their consumption of imported tuna. To this day, the word *Tuna Dolphin* represents a *terme d'art* for the dangers of trade norm supremacy.

The EU would later compound the problem by filing its own case against the U.S. (derisively known as the *son of Tuna Dolphin*), causing concern to its own environmental constituents and further driving the public against a by then less-obscure GATT in Geneva.[15] The public arena clash of environment and trade norms reached its apex in the public eye when the successor institution to the GATT, the WTO, ruled through a panel in 1997 that Europe's own embargo of Hormone-fed beef to be illegal (the *Beef Hormone Case DS 26/ DS 48 (1998)*). The trade norm supremacy problem had now crossed the Atlantic, this time providing imagery of European consumers being force-fed American hormone-laden beef.[16]

The trade and environment norms issues were legally joined, and, as is often the case, the two leading governments, the U.S. and the EU, would find themselves on both sides of the same coin. For the Americans, they wanted a trade to rule supreme to permit beef exports to Europe, but at the same time, they wanted the environment to rule supreme at home to ban imports of dolphin-harming tuna. The Europeans wanted a trade to rule for their tuna exports (hence, *son of Tuna Dolphin*), and environment and health to rule at home to reject imports of hormone-bearing beef.[17]

In fairness to trade norm advocates, GATT 1947s Article XX all-important *chapeau* had a long tradition of great importance, with its textual history being traced back to the *chapeau* of Article 4 of the *1927 Convention for the Abolition of Import and Export Prohibitions and Restrictions,*[18] to wit:

> The following classes of prohibitions and restrictions are not prohibited by the present Convention, on condition, however, that they are not applied in such a manner as to constitute *a means of arbitrary discrimination* between foreign countries where the same conditions prevail, or *a disguised restriction on international trade*:...
>
> 4. Prohibitions or restrictions imposed for the protection of public health or for the protection of animals or plants against disease, insects and harmful parasites.

While certainly acknowledging the health and environment exception, international contracting parties, the states signatories, and their trade experts had always

15. *See* GATT Panel Report, United States Restrictions on Imports of Tuna, DS29/R (not adopted June 16, 1994). *Tuna Dolphin II (son of) (DS 29 1994)* was chaired by retired GATT ambassadors George A. Maciel (Brazil) and Alan Oxley (Australia) and the late Austrian delegate Winfried Lang (later to serve as Ambassador to Switzerland).
16. Certainly, a serious public relations concern had arisen, with the environment advocates moving from raising the concerns of potential harm to *delphinus delphis* to one involving *homo sapiens*—in the public perception, the question arises as to how much lower could trade go!.
17. *See Tuna Dolphin I (DS 21 1991); see also Tuna Dolphin II (DS 29 1994); see further* WTO Panel Reports, EC Measures Concerning Meat and Meat Products (Hormones), WT/DS26/R/USA; WT/DS48/R/CAN (August 18, 1997, adopted February 13, 1998), as modified by WTO Appellate Body, WT/DS26/AB/R; WT/DS48/AB/R (February 13, 1998) (DSR 1998: I, 135; DSR 1998: II, 235: DS 1998: III, 699).
18. Convention for the Abolition of Import and Export Prohibitions and Restrictions, Geneva, November 8, 1927, 97 L.N.T.S. 393; also available in 25 (No. 3) American Journal of International Law Supplement: Official Documents (July 1931) 121-145; http://www.jstor.org /stable/2213116 (accessed on November 30, 2019).

been wary of any overreach of any measures that could negate the vital postwar (both World War I and World War II) accomplishment of embodying in international law (IL) the assurances to states, in the interest of peace and avoiding the necessity of wars, the fullest possible openness of trade relations and avoiding discriminatory commercial relations. As emphasized in the words of an earlier 1923 Convention: "equitable treatment of commerce must be observed to the utmost possible extent."[19]

[2] The 1991 GEMIT: An Updated Three-Point Work Agenda

It was in this background of increased international consciousness of the importance of environmental treaty making, following the success of the Montreal Protocol, an upcoming Earth Summit, and a discordant high profile public media clash of trade and environment norms leading to greater scrutiny of GATT Article XX, that the convening of GEMIT was forged and approved on October 8, 1991, with an expanded three-point work agenda, explicitly changing its nature from a fifteen-member group to an open-ended format allowing all GATT parties to participate in its work:[20]

> Mr. Carlisle, Deputy Director General, said that in consultations held on 16 September and 2 October it had been agreed that:
>
> 1. The 1971 Group on Environmental Measures and International Trade would be convened;
> 2. The Group would have, for the present, the following *three items* as its agenda:
>   (a) *trade provisions contained in existing multilateral environmental agreements (e.g. the Montreal Protocol on Substances that Deplete the Ozone Layer, the Washington Convention on International Trade in Endangered Species and the Basel Convention on the Control of Transboundary Movements of Hazardous Wastes and their Disposal) vis-à-vis GATT principles and provisions;*
>   (b) *multilateral transparency of national environmental regulations likely to have trade effects;*
>   (c) *trade effects of new packaging and labeling requirements aimed at protecting the environment.*
>
> ...
>
> 4. The Group would be open-ended, i.e., open to any contracting party which wished to participate.

It was a major step for the GATT, from the 1971 GEMIT, a fifteen-member working group with a single issue work agenda, and single document background note, citing Pigou's 1920 externalities theory in *GATT L3538 (1971)*, to a dedicated *committee of the whole* that would confront the trade and environment nexus head-on along with an updated three-point agenda.

19. *See* Article 17, International Convention relating to the Simplification of Customs Formalities, Geneva, November 3, 1923, 30 L.N.T.S. 371. Grateful acknowledgment is made to Professor Steve Charnovitz for citing these early conventions, and providing the author with copies, during his lectures and visit to Geneva for the 20th anniversary year celebrations of the CTE in 2015 at the WTO; *see also* Steve Charnovitz, *The Path of World Trade Law in the 21st Century* (World Scientific Studies in International Economics 2015).
20. GATT Council, Minutes of the Meeting of October 8, 1991, C/M/252 (November 4, 1991) at pp. 24-25.

To allow the re-convening of the GEMIT, it is interesting to observe, from the primary source documents, that the complex dynamics within the GATT, and the *North-South* divide, required numerous hours of work for delegations to prepare their statements and points of view for a full structured debate on the issue that is captured in the *Minutes of the Meetings of May 29-30, 1991* of the GATT Council. Moreover, it required that the Secretariat prepare an extensive 94-page background note for the members/contracting parties (GATT, *Trade and Environment, L/6896 (1991)*.[21]

Annex V of *GATT L/6896 (1991)* provides another foundational root of current CTE practice. This 1991 document contains the first listing and monitoring of national environmental measures (NEMs) that are now regularly captured as part of the future ten-point work agenda of the CTE (Agenda Item 4), known as the EDB (*CTE see e.g. EDB-1 TO EDB-18 (2002-19)*). The EDB was most recently issued in November of 2019.[22] Annex V, therefore, provides historical evidence of the important role of the predecessor 1971 GEMIT in establishing early on pre-CTE, certain traditions, procedures and technical work outputs that remain of great value today to the transnational network of policy experts and officials of WTO members. Additionally, it foreshadows the essential technical contributions and the role of the CTE and its secretariat in the broader overall interface between the trade, development and environment community.

[3] The 1991 GEMIT: Meetings and Work Outputs (October 1991 to January 1994)

For twenty-eight months, there would be increased and unprecedented activity in the dedicated sessions and debates in the GEMIT that would yield some 600 pages of additional reference studies and meeting minutes prepared by the GATT Secretariat. To this day, the expert outputs of the GEMIT remain relevant and form the foundation of the early technical work relating to the eventual trade and environment work program of the CTE that was to be established by the GATT and WTO Councils in 1994 and 1995.

To give a flavor of the intensity of the GEMIT work, there would be a total of thirteen meetings conducted under the Chairmanship of Japanese Ambassador Hidetoshi Ukawa commencing from November 1991 through January of 1994.

By the last meeting of the GEMIT in 1994, the proposed *GATT Ministerial Statement on Trade and Environment* (prepared originally in 1990 for the then expected earlier closure of the UR) had been transformed to a draft GATT Ministerial Decision that would refer to the new WTO General Council the task of establishing a standing

---

21. *See* GATT Council, Minutes of the Meetings of May 29-30, 1991, C/M/250 (June 28, 1991); GATT Secretariat, Trade and Environment, Factual Note by the Secretariat, L/6896 (September 18, 1991).
22. Reading Annex V of GATT L/6896 (1991) does not bring feelings of finding historical curiosities of things past, but rather engenders feelings of sensing the present in the past (or shades of experiencing that movie, *Back to the Future*), *see* GATT Secretariat, Trade and Environment, Factual Note by the Secretariat, L/6896 (September 18, 1991) at p. 85. The latest version of this output, WTO Environmental Database for 2018, demonstrates the technical outputs of the CTE that may have value to the transnational network of experts and capital officials, WTO CTE, Environmental Database for 2018, Note by the Secretariat, WT/CTE/EDB/18 (November 12, 2019).

CTE, and this *side decision*[23] of the UR was to be the de-constructed source of the ten-point work program of the CTE and remains to this day the work program of the CTE, as will be discussed in the next chapter on the work proper of the CTE.

One can see in tabular form the subject matters of the working documents that were generated either by delegation experts or were background notes prepared by the GATT Secretariat for the GEMIT in Table 1.1.

Table 1.1 GATT Period GEMIT Work Outputs

No.	*Date issued*	*Document*	*Pages*	*Document Description*
1	April 29, 1992	TRE/W/1	7	Trade Provisions Contained in MEAs
2	September 4, 1992	TRE/W/2	5	Agenda Item 2: Multilateral Transparency of National Environmental Regulations
3	September 29, 1992	TRE/W/3	41	Agenda Item 3: Packaging and Labelling Requirements
4	November 16, 1992	TRE/W/4	7	Multilateral Transparency of National Environmental Regulations likely to have Trade Effects
5	November 17, 1992	TRE/W/5	10	European Community Submission on "The GATT and the Trade Provisions of Multilateral Environmental Agreements"
6	December 11, 1992	TRE/W/6	7	U.S. submission on "Environmental Packaging and Labelling Activities in the United States"
7	March 3, 1993	TRE/W/7	4	Agenda Item 2: Multilateral Transparency of National Environmental Regulations likely to have Trade Effects
8	March 10, 1993	TRE/W/8	6	New Zealand submission on "Agenda Item 1: Trade Provisions Contained in Existing MEAs vis-à-vis GATT Principles and Provisions"

23. Steve Charnovitz writes that the formation of a standing CTE was resisted and not contemplated by developing countries at the time of the conclusion of the UR and that the CTE could have been dissolved after it had performed its first reporting function at the first Ministerial Conference of the WTO in 1996. *See* Steve Charnovitz, *A Critical Guide to the WTO's Report on Trade and Environment*, 14 Ariz. J. Int'l & Comp. L. 370, at 370 (1997).

No.	*Date issued*	*Document*	*Pages*	*Document Description*
9	March 10, 1993	TRE/W/9	6	Agenda Item 3: Trade Effects of New Packaging and Labelling Requirement aimed at Protecting the Environment
10	March 17, 1993	TRE/W/10	14	Agenda Item 2: Multilateral Transparency of National Environmental Regulations likely to have Trade Effects
11	June 9, 1993	TRE/W/11	4	Poland submission on "Ecological Labelling and Utilization of used Packaging in Poland"
12	June 14, 1993	TRE/W/12	7	Agenda Item 3: Packaging and Labelling Requirements
13	June 29, 1993	TRE/W/13	9	The Trade Effects of Environmental Measures
14	July 21, 1993	TRE/W/14 COM.TD/W/503	13	UNCED Follow-up: Results of the First Session of the Commission on Sustainable Development and other Related Activities
15	July 23, 1993	TRE/W/15	25	Germany submission on "The Packaging Ordinance and International Trade"
16	September 2, 1993	TRE/W/16	3	Agenda Item 1: Trade Provisions contained in Existing MEAs vis-à-vis GATT Principles and Provisions
17	September 7, 1993	TRE/W/17	7	Agenda Item 1: Trade Provisions Contained in Existing MEAs vis-à-vis GATT Principles and Provisions
18	October 1, 1993	TRE/W/18	7	Agenda Item 1: Trade Provisions Contained in Existing MEAs vis-à-vis GATT Principles and Provisions
19	October 1, 1993	TRE/W/19	17	Austria submission on "GATT and International Environmental Agreements (IEAs)"
20	January 11, 1994	TRE/W/20	16	Border Tax Adjustments (BTAs)
21	January 17, 1994	TRE/W/21	3	Unnecessary Obstacles to International Trade

[4] The Contemporaneous Events Predating the CTE's Establishment

The Ministerial Decision calling for the establishment of the CTE was influenced greatly by contemporaneous events such as the Rio Conference, the *Tuna Dolphin* case, and the foremost question of there being a simmering and perceived conflict of norms between trade and environment policies, rules and priorities. The objective of the CTE was: "to coordinate the policies in the field of trade and environment."[24]

To achieve this objective of *coordination*, along with all the qualifying language of the decision, the committee possesses only *two* powers in its capacity as a subsidiary body of the WTO General Council, to wit,

(i) to *identify* the connectivity and interaction of trade and environment measures in order to promote sustainable development, and

(ii) to *recommend or propose* the modification of any WTO rules in order to promote the mutual supportiveness of trade and environment measures while balancing the need to avoid protectionist pressures.[25]

It is important then to understand the circumstances leading to the work mandate of the CTE, which, as is often and will often be pointed out, was developed in an ad hoc manner. Given that the would-be CTE's core objective is the coordination, and its authority is limited to identification and the making of recommendations or proposals, all of these foundational elements, by necessity and consistency with its purpose, the committee was essentially a forum for informed debate on how trade and environment measures are interlinked, and how they were to be coordinated in order to avoid, address or minimize regulatory and norms conflict.

The CTE has therefore been given various monikers, from being a *talk-shop* to a brainstorming forum or incubator for new ideas, but, all in all, its organic terms of reference provides only a weak tool for governments to achieve a coordinated approach to trade and environment measures, absent a clear mandate through a specific organic agreement, as is present for other trade committees, such as the Technical barriers to trade (TBT) or Sanitary and phytosanitary measures (SPS) committees, and specific implementation functions as would be apt if there were specific tasks to be undertaken that would ensure enforcement of trade measures in support of environment and development objectives.

In any event, so as not to belabor the point, it also becomes of significance to its foundation to revisit the evolution of its mother organization, the WTO, as a successor entity to the GATT, with a firmer grounding on sustainable development objectives.[26]

---

24. Ministerial Decision on Trade and Environment, MTN.TNC/MIN (94)/1/Rev.1, adopted by ministers at the meeting of the Uruguay Round Trade Negotiations Committee in Marrakesh, April 14, 1994, 1867 U.N.T.S. 133 (I-31874, 1995), as part of the Final Act and Texts of the Marrakesh Agreement Establishing the World Trade Organization, 33 I.L.M. 1267 (1994) at ¶5.
25. *Ibid., see also* UN General Assembly, Agenda 21: Program of Action for Sustainable Development, A/Conf.151/26 (June 14, 1992).
26. The prior GATT was not always seen as prioritizing issues of environment or development. *See, e.g.*, Steve Charnovitz, *The WTO's Environmental Progress*, 10(3) J. Int'l Econ. L. 685 (2007), for a brief discussion of the GATT-era attitude and the relevant provisions relating to exceptions for environmental matters; *see also* Michael M. Weinstein and Steve Charnovitz, *The Greening of the*

The *Preamble* of the 1994 treaty establishing the WTO according to the Appellate Body in *US Shrimp*[27] explicitly acknowledged "the objective of sustainable development":

> *Recognizing* that their relations in the field of trade and economic endeavor should be conducted with a view to raising standards of living, ensuring full employment and a large and steadily growing volume of real income and effective demand, and expanding the production of and trade in goods and services, while allowing for *the optimal use of the world's resources in accordance with the objective of sustainable development, seeking both to protect and preserve the environment and to enhance the means for doing so* in a manner consistent with their respective needs and concerns at different levels of economic development.[28]

Many writers have underscored the pivotal role that these few words in the Preamble have played in guiding the work of the new WTO, as a post-GATT institution, to be more sensitive to issues of social development and environmental issues, areas previously reserved to other specialist IOs.[29]

Accompanying the *Preamble* and agreements establishing the WTO was a ministerial decision directing the WTO General Council to establish a CTE; this decision to establish the CTE is also referred to in the *Rio Declaration and Agenda 21*. It further establishes the crossover of the trading system into sustainable development and environmental preservation objectives. The decision affirmed that "there should not be, nor need be, any policy contradiction between upholding and safeguarding an open, non-discriminatory and equitable multilateral trading system on the one hand, and acting for the protection of the environment, and the promotion of sustainable development on the other."[30]

Since the founding charter of the CTE refers to the key 1992 events, it bears also revisiting the *Rio Declaration* and Agenda 21:

> Principle 11
>
> States shall enact effective environmental legislation. Environmental standards, management objectives and priorities should reflect the environmental and development context to which they apply. Standards applied by some countries may be

---

WTO, 80 Foreign Aff. 147 (2001) available at: http://www.foreignaffairs.com/articles/57426/michael-m-weinstein-and-steve-charnovitz/the-greening-of-the-wto (accessed on November 30, 2019).

27. WTO Appellate Body, United States Import Prohibition of Certain Shrimp and Shrimp Products, WT/DS58/AB/R, (November 6, 1998) at ¶129; (DSR 1998:VII, 2755).
28. Marrakesh Agreement Establishing the World Trade Organization, April 15, 1994, 1867 U.N.T.S. 154, 33 I.L.M. 1144.
29. *See generally* Steve Charnovitz, *The WTO's Environmental Progress*, 10 J. Int'l Econ. L. 685 (2007); *see also* Michael M. Weinstein and Steve Charnovitz, *The Greening of the WTO*, 80 Foreign Aff. 147 (2001).
30. Ministerial Decision on Trade and Environment, MTN.TNC/MIN (94)/1/Rev.1, adopted by ministers at the meeting of the Uruguay Round Trade Negotiations Committee in Marrakesh, April 14, 1994, Marrakesh Agreement Establishing the World Trade Organization, 33 I.L.M. 1267 (1994).

> inappropriate and of unwarranted economic and social cost to other countries, in particular developing countries.[31]
>
> Principle 12
>
> States should cooperate to promote a supportive and open international economic system that would lead to economic growth and sustainable development in all countries, to better address the problems of environmental degradation. Trade policy measures for environmental purposes should not constitute a means of arbitrary or unjustifiable discrimination or a disguised restriction on international trade.
>
> Unilateral actions to deal with environmental challenges outside the jurisdiction of the importing country should be avoided. Environmental measures addressing transboundary or global environmental problems should, as far as possible, be based on an international consensus.[32]

Agenda 21 was even more direct in its call for action from the trade regime to serve the interests of sustainable development and the environment, though it must be noted that the contributions to Agenda 21 were sourced from the CTE's predecessor, the GATT/GEMIT. Certain specific provisions of *Agenda 21 Chapter 2* are highlighted here, in that they required a clear policy formulation as well as action from the GATT trade regime:[33]

> ***Agenda 21, Chapter 2***
>
> *Program Areas*
>
> B. Making trade and environment mutually supportive
>
> 2.19. *Environment and trade policies should be mutually supportive. ....*
>
> 2.20. International cooperation in the environmental field is growing, and *in a number of cases, trade provisions in multilateral environment agreements have played a role in tackling global environmental challenges. Trade measures have thus been used in certain specific instances, where considered necessary, to enhance the effectiveness of environmental regulations for the protection of the environment.* ... .
>
> Objectives
>
> 2.21. Governments should strive to meet the following objectives, through relevant multilateral forums, *including GATT [WTO]*, UNCTAD and other international organizations:
>
> (a) To make international trade and environment policies mutually supportive in favor of sustainable development;
> (b) *To clarify the role of GATT [WTO],...* in dealing with trade and environment-related issues, *including, where relevant, conciliation procedure and dispute settlement;...*

31. UN Rio Declaration on Environment and Development, Jun. 13, 1992, 31 I.L.M. 874, at prin. 11; U.N. GAOR, 46th Sess. Agenda Item 21, UN Doc. A/Conf. 151/26 (1992).
32. *Id.* at prin. 12.
33. UN General Assembly, Agenda 21: Program of Action for Sustainable Development, A/Conf.151/26 (June 14, 1992); U.N. GAOR, 46th Sess. Agenda Item 21, UN Doc. A/Conf. 151/26 (1992).

> *Developing an environment/trade and development agenda*
>
> 2.22. *Governments should encourage GATT [WTO],* ... to examine, in accordance with their respective mandates and competences, the following propositions and principles:
>
> (a) *Elaborate adequate studies for the better understanding of the relationship between trade and environment for the promotion of sustainable development;*
> (b) Promote a *dialogue between trade, development and environment communities;*
> (c) In those cases when trade measures related to environment are used, ensure transparency and compatibility with international obligations;
> (...)
> (j) *Develop more precision, where necessary, and clarify the relationship between GATT [WTO] provisions and some of the multilateral measures adopted in the environment area;*
> (...)
> (l) Ensure that environmental policies provide the appropriate legal and institutional framework to respond to new needs for the *protection of the environment that may result from changes in production and trade specialization.*

These provisions in Agenda 21 would all play a role in the formulation of the GATT GEMIT response embodied in the work program of the future CTE, as referred to in the side decision establishing the CTE.

The only direct legally binding textual response after all these years, and the de facto conflict of laws clause, of the WTO, apart from judicial pronouncements, to the environment regime, are Articles XX(b) and XX(g) of GATT 1994 and its *chapeau:*[34]

> *GATT 1994 Article XX*
>
> *General Exceptions*
>
> Subject to the requirement that such measures are *not applied in a manner which would constitute a means of arbitrary or unjustifiable discrimination* ..., or *a disguised restriction on international trade,* nothing in this Agreement shall be construed to prevent the adoption or enforcement by any contracting party of measures:
>
> (b) necessary to protect human, animal or plant life or health;
> (g) relating to the conservation of exhaustible natural resources if such measures are made effective in conjunction with restrictions on domestic production or consumption.

These twin provisions contained in Article XX are the exact same text of GATT 1947, and have been, since 1927, limited and restricted in use by the qualifier in the chapeau to the effect that the measures do not constitute a "means of arbitrary or unjustifiable discrimination." These exceptions were intended to allow environment policy makers the necessary leeway to ensure domestic environmental measures could

34. GATT 1994, Article XX, Marrakesh Agreement Establishing the World Trade Organization, April 15, 1994, 1867 U.N.T.S. 190, 33 I.L.M. 1153, 1867 U.N.T.S. 190; GATT, October 30, 1947, 61 Stat. A-11, 55 U.N.T.S. 194, at Article XX; *see also* Jan Klabbers, *Jurisprudence in International Trade Law—Article XX of GATT*, 26 J. World Trade 63 (1992).

not be negated by liberal trade policy obligations, while also providing trade policy makers with the counterpart assurance (embodied in the *chapeau*) that environmental policy measures would not be used as a tool for *disguised trade protectionism*.

GATT Article XX was therefore fully preserved and re-enacted in the Marrakesh Agreement as GATT 1994, and would, in conjunction with the developments and contributions of the GEMIT to UNCED/Rio 1992, provide the context by which international trade and environmental governance had become irretrievably intertwined.

The calls of the times and Agenda 21 required a greater sensitivity from the trade regime community to assure coherence between market openings and economic growth mandates and effective domestic regulations geared towards environmental values priorities, but this would be slow in coming given the established nature of the trade regime from 1947.

The creation of the CTE was a side decision as already discussed earlier, and did not actually provide specific implementation responsibilities to the CTE, or for the trade regime of the WTO in general. What followed then from 1994 was a quite challenging period for the integration of trade and environment policy objectives, and it became more of a conflict, quite contrary to the calls for coherence and active supportiveness mandated in the Earth Summit and the Agenda Chapter 21 Chapter 2.

The challenging period would find no mechanism for resolving the cross-regime conflict of norms relating to trade and environment, and what resulted was the need to have the WTO's judicial organ, the Appellate Body fill in this gap. The Appellate Body acted not only as an interpreter of trade policy instruments but also as a broader guardian and interpreter of trade, environment and sustainable development policy for the international community of nations, taking into account international norms and agreements beyond the WTO agreements.

This is partly due, by default, to the absence of similar authoritative organs in the non-trade policy fields, which could fill the demand for providing the means to reconcile legal norms where conflict is present or could be perceived to be present, between these intersecting policy areas.

[B] The Contemporaneous Compromise Reached in the NAFTA Context

On another front, in an RTA perspective, on a regional level, a similar conundrum was present for the U.S., Canada and Mexico partnership. As can be seen, a solution to the norm conflict was achieved among a sub-set of three nations, which it is submitted was a more coordinated and satisfactory solution.

To fully understand the rationale for the establishment of the CTE, one would have to take a step back and examine how the exact same contextual problem was handled during the passage of the NAFTA in 1993, amid the public calls and concerns that sought to prevent U.S. congressional ratification of the NAFTA. From the IL-IR frame, though particularly a U.S. concern, in all instances, what happens to a major treaty in Washington, D.C. has far-reaching consequences on the IL-IR front.

[1] The NAFTA Solution: The NAAEC/CEC

It is instructive then at this point in understanding the prehistory of the CTE to review and examine the evolution in NAFTA. Through deft work by a bipartisan set of policy makers during the first years of the Clinton-Gore administration, they were able to manage a transformation of the perceived trade and environment conflict — from policy makers confrontation to a relationship of constructive, albeit, cautious, cooperation and coordination, and perhaps, even more significantly, to one with established institutional and legal mechanisms that cater to the specific environment and trade, and the co-relative science and policy, issues from an empirical and good governance angle.

Given the scrutiny and unprecedented reaction by technocrats and civil society, in the U.S. and beyond, to the *Tuna Dolphin I* ruling, the *new generation* leadership under *Clinton-Gore*, was faced with a dilemma on how to abide by its political commitment to passing the Republican administration's landmark free trade agreement (NAFTA), and the UR treaty as well, that would establish the WTO. The solution conceived by policy leaders, and one might say rooted in the so-called interdisciplinary network of experts, if one were to adopt that frame, involved three elements, all linked to a stand-alone side agreement, named the *North American Agreement on Environmental Cooperation* (the NAAEC).[35]

The first element was to incorporate a commitment to *sustainable development* in the NAFTA preamble, along with language that provisions that reinforced domestic environmental regulatory sovereignty, so that NAFTA members would:

> UNDERTAKE [their trade obligations] in a manner consistent with environmental protection and conservation;
>
> PRESERVE their flexibility to safeguard the public welfare;
>
> STRENGTHEN the development and enforcement of environmental laws and regulations.

The second element was the political agreement rapidly reached (albeit with Mexican reservations) for a limited environmental norm supremacy clause. The *Tuna Dolphin* ruling, though not adopted by the GATT, was deemed untenable and could not be risked or countenanced in the NAFTA context. There were more *tuna dolphin*-related measures being implemented under the Marine Mammal Protection Act of 1972 and other laws being passed.[36] To pass NAFTA, a clear-cut *subordination clause* was needed showing trade norms to be inferior in hierarchy to certain specified MEAs:

35. For a full discussion *see* Steve Charnovitz, *The NAFTA Environmental Side Agreement: Implications for Environmental Cooperation, Trade Policy, and American Treaty Making*, 8 Temp. Int'l & Comp. L.J. 257 (1994).

36. *See* for full text, United States Department of Commerce, National Ocean and Atmospheric Administration, available at: http://www.nmfs.noaa.gov/pr/laws/mmpa/text.htm (accessed on December 15, 2012); for an elaboration of the tuna dolphin issue from a scientific viewpoint, *see also* National Oceanic and Atmospheric Administration, The Tuna Dolphin Issue, available at: http://swfsc.noaa.gov/textblock.aspx?Division=PRD&ParentMenuId=228&id=1408 (accessed on November 28, 2019). A series of other United States legislation relate to the Dolphin

Article 104(1) Relation to Environmental and Conservation Agreements

In the event of any inconsistency between this Agreement and the specific trade obligations set out in [5 MEAs],[37] *such obligations shall prevail to the extent of the inconsistency*, provided that where a Party has a choice among equally effective and reasonably available means of complying with such obligations, the Party chooses the alternative that is the least inconsistent with the other provisions of this Agreement.

Finally, the third element was that NAAEC be designed to establish comprehensive institutional mechanisms and governance procedures to ensure environmental priorities supremacy, or trade, and environment norm coherence. These mechanisms that operate through to today were to be established through a cabinet-level *Commission for Environmental Cooperation* (CEC), and a fifteen-member *Joint Public Advisory Committee* (JPAC) with five members each coming from each NAFTA member, and a central secretariat based in Montreal.

A review and closer examination of these three elements, working together as a NAAEC/CEC institutional framework, shows that the interplay of the whole mechanism goes well beyond the NAFTA Article 104 supremacy clause and expands and strengthens the regulatory prerogatives of environmental agencies towards a broader environment norm supremacy.

It does so by reverse logic. NAAEC Article 37 does disavow any extraterritorial enforcement measures, but significantly, nothing else in NAAEC prohibits or discourages it. Moreover, Article 37 implies environmental regulatory and enforcement supremacy in the domestic or national (not being an extraterritorial act) context, thereby affirming fully the right of the U.S. to enforce domestic embargos or trade bans on environmental grounds.

This is significant in contrast to the discussions that followed relating to the creation of the CTE and its mandate, as well as the deliberations in relation to GATT 1994 Article XX, which curiously also happens to be phrased in the same fashion

Protection Consumer Information Act of 1990, 16 U.S.C. 1361-1370 (104 Stat. 4465) (protection of dolphins when harvesting tuna with purse seine nets, labelling standards for tuna products); the International Dolphin Conservation Act of 1992, 16 U.S.C. 1361 (106 Stat. 3425) (requiring studies in the eastern Gulf of Mexico); and the International Dolphin Conservation Program Act of 1997, 16 U.S.C 1361-1370 (111 Stat. 1122) (amending the 1990 law, changing labelling standards and the definition of "dolphin safe," codifying the *Declaration of Panama* on establishing a fishing program for catching yellow-fin tuna with the legal use of purse seine nets while limiting dolphin mortality) available at: http://www.fws.gov/laws/lawsdigest/DOLPHIN.HTML (accessed on November 29, 2019).

37. The five agreements specifically named in NAFTA were: (a) the Convention on International Trade in Endangered Species of Wild Fauna and Flora, March 3, 1973, (b) the Montreal Protocol on Substances that Deplete the Ozone Layer, September 16, 1987, (c) the Basel Convention on the Control of Transboundary Movements of Hazardous Wastes and Their Disposal, March 22, 1989, (d) the Agreement Between the Government of Canada and the Government of the United States of America Concerning the Transboundary Movement of Hazardous Waste, October 28, 1986, and (e) the Agreement Between the United States of America and the United Mexican States on Cooperation for the Protection and Improvement of the Environment in the Border Area, August 14, 1983, *see* North American Free Trade Agreement, December 17, 1992, 32 I.L.M. 289, at Chapter 1, Article 104 and Annex 104.1.

utilizing the same reverse logic, as Article 37. Both clauses are quoted below for comparative reference:

> Article 37: Enforcement Principle
>
> *Nothing in this Agreement shall be construed to empower a Party's authorities to undertake environmental law enforcement activities in the territory of another Party.*
>
> Article XX: Exceptions
>
> *..., nothing in this Agreement [the GATT] shall be construed to prevent the adoption or enforcement by any contracting party of measures: ...*
>
> (b) *necessary to protect human, animal or plant life or health; ...*
> (g) *relating to the conservation of exhaustible natural resources if such measures are made effective in conjunction with restrictions on domestic production or consumption. ... .*

Article XX will be further discussed in relation to the work of the CTE, but for now, it is important to note: what is *not to be construed*, in both institutional situations, are the very measures and effects so desired and contemplated. In other words, what is *not to be construed* in Article 37, *empowering of extraterritorial environmental enforcement*, and what is *not to be construed* in Article XX, *prevention of environmental measures*, are precisely desired, contemplated and expected by and from the respective institutions. It may take a second reading, but that seems to be the import of both negative provisions and is akin to the result of creating a double negative assertion.

NAAEC then achieves its desired environmental preferences by incorporating additional provisions, which, when taken together, a compound in force to affirm absolute territorial superiority and sovereignty, while imposing soft law imperatives for proxy rules creation and enforcement action by a partner government within its own territory, as well as through further soft obligations requiring *remedies access* and *remedies creation* across borders and jurisdictions, with further provisions to permit the cabinet-level CEC to issue recommendations for the passage of new or missing environmental rules.[38]

To cite some concrete environmental governance and cooperation mandates, the NAAEC, in part borrowing from the *Rio Declaration Principles*, directs, inter alia, *the protection of wild flora and fauna, the use of economic instruments for the efficient*

38. *See* full text of North American Agreement on Environmental Cooperation, September 14, 1993, 32 I.L.M. 1482, at Articles 5, 6 and 7. ("NAAEC") For example, NAAEC provides:

> Article 5(2): Each party shall ensure that judicial, quasi-judicial or administrative enforcement proceedings are available under its law to sanction or remedy violations of its environmental laws and regulations. ... Sanctions and remedies ... shall ... take into consideration the nature and gravity of the violation, any economic benefit derived from the violation by the violator, the economic condition of the violator, ... include compliance agreements, fines, imprisonment, injunctions, the closure of facilities, and the cost of containing or cleaning up pollution.
>
> Article 6: Private Access to Remedies 1. Each Party shall ensure that interested persons may request the Party's competent authorities to investigate alleged violations of its environmental laws and regulations and shall give such requests due consideration in accordance with law.

achievement of environmental goals (embargoes and import bans),[39] and expectation of *high levels of environmental protection and compliance to effectively enforce environmental laws and regulations through appropriate governmental action*,[40] including the mandated use of a whole array of American-crafted/originated regulatory measures by the partner governments (Mexico and Canada, for example), such as those enumerated in Article 5(1), quoted below, illustrating the great detail and specificity of NAAEC regulatory enforcement measures contemplated:

> Article 5: Government Enforcement Action
> 1. With the aim of achieving high levels of environmental protection and compliance with its environmental laws and regulations, each Party shall effectively enforce its environmental laws and regulations through appropriate governmental action, subject to Article 37, such as:
>   (a) appointing and training inspectors;
>   (b) monitoring compliance and investigating suspected violations, including through on-site inspections;
>   (c) seeking assurances of voluntary compliance and compliance agreements;
>   (d) publicly releasing non-compliance information;
>   (e) issuing bulletins or other periodic statements on enforcement procedures;
>   (f) promoting environmental audits;
>   (g) requiring record keeping and reporting;
>   (h) providing or encouraging mediation and arbitration services;
>   (i) using licenses, permits or authorizations;
>   (j) initiating, in a timely manner, judicial, quasi-judicial or administrative proceedings to seek appropriate sanctions or remedies for violations of its environmental laws and regulations;
>   (k) providing for search, seizure or detention; or
>   (l) issuing administrative orders, including orders of a preventative, curative, or emergency nature.[41]

[2] The CEC Administrative and Institutional Mandate

Institutionally, a three-nation Commission on Environmental Cooperation (CEC) was established. It was composed of cabinet rank officials, which interestingly provided a governance tool in the field of international cooperation by seeking higher levels of enforcement *via* the creation of expectations that the creation of the CEC represented. As further elaborated below, the NAFTA parties agreed to the public clamor to make environmental concerns a primary policy concern with the promise of enforceability.

A review of the NAAEC and the activities and reports of the CEC confirm the intent to establish a system of governance of a *public-private* character, which has

39. *Id.* NAAEC at Articles 2(1)(f) et seq. *See also* Article 2(3) encouraging the use of counterpart export bans to match import bans which to Mexico's relief was negotiated to apply only to pesticides and toxic substances.
40. This is reflected in Article 3 which, while recognizing that individual NAFTA members may set their own levels of protection but in the same article sets the level as "high."
41. NAAEC at Article 5. *See also* NAAEC at Articles 2, 6 and 7. The whole panoply of domestic environmental regulatory measures appears to be mentioned and integrated in NAAEC. There are more, and more, and even more provisions, in the NAAEC.

become a mainstream practice for the U.S. and other developed nations on environmental protection issues. The functions mandated for the CEC were of a very comprehensive and broad nature. An examination of the source documents and the resulting work and reports of the CEC testify to influence of the *Rio Principles* and *Agenda 21*. It also signifies the entry and mainstreaming of environmental governance best-practice concepts that were close to then-Vice President Gore's remit in the U.S. administration.[42]

To cite and illustrate the mainstreaming impact of the NAAEC, the CEC, among many others (again the list goes much longer), was empowered to:[43]

- serve as a forum for the discussion of environmental matters within the scope of this Agreement [NAAEC];
- promote and facilitate cooperation between the Parties with respect to environmental matters;
- develop recommendations regarding:
  - pollution prevention techniques and strategies;
  - the use of economic instruments for the pursuit of domestic and internationally agreed environmental objectives;
  - scientific research and technology development in respect of environmental matters;
  - promotion of public awareness regarding the environment;
  - transboundary and border environmental issues, such as the long-range transport of air and marine pollutants.

A further review of the original documents of NAAEC, along with research on the drafting history of NAAEC and the examination of CEC's detailed official reports and materials, could yield useful analysis.[44] A wealth of expert data, reports on public consultations, studies, and scientific reports and statistics are reflected in the annual reports of the CEC.[45]

---

42. In giving him the 2007 Nobel Prize, the organization attributes to VP Gore: "*As early as in 1992, the year when he was elected Vice President of the United States, Gore was making himself known as a highly environment-conscious politician, among other things through his book Earth in the Balance: Forging a New Common Purpose, in which he took up the problem of global warming. Having lost the presidential election in 2000, he decided to use his influence to increase public awareness in the United States and other countries of the seriousness of the environmental situation. This goal he well-nigh achieved by means of his documentary film An Inconvenient Truth (2006).*" Nobelprize.org. Nobel Media AB 2014, available at: http://www.nobelprize.org/nobel_prizes/peace/laureates/2007/gore-facts.html (accessed on November 30, 2019).
43. *See generally* NAAEC, September 14, 1993, 32 I.L.M. 1482.
44. For purposes of examining the historical evolution of mainstreaming into the multilateral context the interagency practice of the United States government, it is interesting to view the original documents; and the first council meeting record, along with more recent records, and they appear to follow a routine of rotating meetings among the NAAEC members that can include ministerial meetings in exotic Mexican cities to conference call records. The documents can be accessed at the website of the Commission for Environmental Corporation, available at: http://www.cec.org/Page.asp?PageID=1226&SiteNodeID=207 (accessed on November 29, 2019).
45. *See*, for example, there are project summaries relating to climate change, ecosystems and green growth, available at: http://www.cec.org/Page.asp?PageID=924&SiteNodeID=1008 (accessed January 6, 2014); or public studies and consultations on lead batteries available at the website

[3] Observations on NAAEC/CEC

It is interesting, therefore, to note from the foregoing that what the negotiators of the U.S. focused on, and achieved, was the task of imposing, not so much on their Canadian or Mexican counterparts, but rather on themselves, soft obligations that expressly mentioned and mandated the panoply of domestic measures (conveniently as well as incidentally implemented and enforced by U.S. federal and state jurisdictions and, in essence, not imposing on them any additional treaty-based regulatory burdens). This strategy afforded U.S. domestic law measures a mantle of international obligation and legitimacy, being specifically required pursuant to an international multilateral treaty commitment, *ergo*, less prone to a claim of domestic overreaching, or international norms inconsistency should they be considered an exercise of unilateral enforcement.[46]

The level of interagency engagement that can be observed as being performed in the U.S. governmental context appears to have been incorporated in the NAAEC/CEC multilateral sphere and represents a shift to mainstreaming and harmonizing governance and transparency procedures and mechanisms that are designed to specifically address environmental norms and objectives on a day-to-day basis, while allowing increased process interactions with environmental constituents, within and outside government.

In some form or manner, the foregoing observations are consistent with the refusal of the U.S. to affirm or consent to the legitimacy or enforceability of the *Tuna Dolphin* ruling. With the three elements of the NAAEC/CEC solution acting together, (i) the preambular commitment to *sustainable development*, (ii) the clear hierarchy or environment norm supremacy in NAFTA Article 104, and (iii) the extensive administrative and institutional mechanisms established by NAAEC, aided in part by the timing of the 1991 *Tuna Dolphin* ruling and the 1992 Rio Declaration, the outcome in the NAAEC context has been to galvanize and crystallize the strengthening, mainstreaming and expanding of environmental governance and enforcement mechanisms.[47]

§1.03 THE GATT TRADE SUPREMACY NORM AND THE EMERGING CTE

Following the entry into force of NAFTA on January 1, 1994, enabled in part by the signing of NAAEC in August of 1993, the other major trade agreement that needed

of the Commission for Environmental Corporation at: http://www.cec.org/content/hazardous-trade (accessed January 6, 2014).

46. *See*, e.g., in the investment and environment arena, Jorge E. Viñuales, *Foreign Investment and the Environment in International Law* at pp. 185, 248-249 (2012) (relevant authorities would be well advised to spell out the link between the measure and the State's obligations under international law; useful to strengthen the link between the domestic measure and the host-State's international environment obligations).
47. Each of the GATT *Tuna Dolphin* rulings themselves (absent the reverse consensus rule in later years at the WTO) was not, and could not be, adopted absent United States consent. *See Tuna Dolphin (DS 21 1991); Tuna Dolphin II (DS 29 1994)*.

passage in 1994 would be the UR agreements that would pave the way for the creation of the WTO. As with NAAEC/CEC forming part of the solution to the passage of NAFTA, there was a similar need to fashion a solution to address trade and environment conflict of norms in time for the planned entry into force of the WTO within a year of NAFTA (January 1, 1995).

Again like NAFTA, there would be as well three elements to the conceived solution, linked as well to a side agreement, in this case, a *side decision* creating the CTE:

(i) the preambular commitment to sustainable development;
(ii) a more nuanced fixing of a relationship, in lieu of a hierarchy or superiority of norms, though through this implicating a preference for trade norms; and
(iii) the establishment of institutional mechanisms, albeit feebler and with less institutional or mandate clarity.

[A] Element 1: Sustainable Development and the Preamble

The first element, similarly to NAFTA, added language to the *Preamble* of the 1994 Agreement Establishing the WTO that, in the words of the Appellate Body in *US Shrimp*[48] explicitly acknowledged "the objective of sustainable development":

> *Recognizing* that their relations in the field of trade and economic endeavour should be conducted with a view to raising standards of living, ..., while allowing for *the optimal use of the world's resources in accordance with the objective of sustainable development, seeking both to protect and preserve the environment and to enhance the means for doing so* in a manner consistent with their respective needs and concerns at different levels of economic development.[49]

With this addition, environment objectives were officially adopted as a crossover value to the old GATT club, and a new era of environmental progress, as one writer has termed it, was in the offing.[50] Much has been written through the analysis and review of WTO case law, as well as within these case decisions, on the impact that this addition and refinement to the preamble has given leeway or guidance to future decisions of WTO panels or the Appellate Body.[51]

---

48. WTO Appellate Body, United States Import Prohibition of Certain Shrimp and Shrimp Products, WT/DS58/AB/R (November 6, 1998) at ¶ 129 (DSR 1998: VII, 2755).
49. Marrakesh Agreement Establishing the World Trade Organization, April 15, 1994, 1867 U.N.T.S. 190, 33 I.L.M. 1153, 1867 U.N.T.S. 190. *See also* for a further discussion of the history of environment issues at the GATT and the WTO, Steve Charnovitz, *The WTO's Environmental Progress*, 10 J. Int'l Econ. L. 685 (2007); *see also* Michael M. Weinstein and Steve Charnovitz, *The Greening of the WTO*, 80 Foreign Aff. 147 (2001).
50. *See* Steve Charnovitz, *WTO's Environmental Progress*, J. Int'l Econ. L. 10(3) (2007).
51. *See, e.g.*, *United States Shrimp (DS58 1998)*; *see* Robert Howse, *The Appellate Body Rulings in the Shrimp-Turtle Case: A New Legal Baseline for the Trade and Environment Debate*, 27 Colum. J. Envtl. L. 491 (2002); *see also* Howard Chang, *Toward a Greener GATT: Environmental Trade Measures and the Shrimp-Turtle Case*, 71 S. Cal. L. Rev. 31 (2000).

[B] Element 2: The Setting of the Mutually Supportive Standard

De Facto Trade Norm Preference

The second element, as contained in a GATT *Ministerial Decision on Trade and Environment (April 14, 1994)*, was a stand-alone annex to the Final Act Embodying the UR documents known as *the Marrakesh Agreements*.[52] It established the first precept through an existentialist official denial:

> there should not be, nor need be any policy contradiction between upholding and safeguarding an open, non-discriminatory and equitable multilateral trading system on the one hand, and acting for the protection of the environment, and the promotion of sustainable development on the other.[53]

This would, therefore, be in stark contrast to the NAFTA approach with Article 104 signed and in force just months before this decision of GATT Ministers, expressly providing for environment norm supremacy in a regional free trade setting.

There was no GATT acknowledgment that any conflict of norms problem existed despite the clear overhanging presence of *Tuna Dolphin* and *son of Tuna Dolphin*—though not legally binding as un-adopted GATT reports. Through this fiction of non-existence, a nuanced hierarchy and preference of norms were established, but in favor of trade, without calling it trade superiority.

It becomes even clearer from the mandated *trade and environment work program* that, among others, the structural design of the CTE, from an environmental protection standpoint, again in contrast to the NAAEC, was very weak and merely intended only "to identify the relationship between trade measures and environment measures."

The decision *notes* the Rio Declaration on Environment and Development and Agenda 21, but in the same breath rather than provide clear guidance on achieving the goals of *Rio. Agenda 21*, again in contrast to the NAFTA model, adopts a quite the opposite approach of breathing trade and protectionism fears as the main concern, and upheld these concerns as equal, if not superior norms.[54]

Citing the 1993 GATT work program on trade and environment, which operated on the premise of requiring vigilance towards any negative effects that might arise from environment measures taking the form of trade measures, if potentially discriminatory or protectionist. The decision set as a term of reference, the need for receiving:

52. Ministerial Decision on Trade and Environment, MTN.TNC/MIN (94)/1/Rev.1, adopted by ministers at the meeting of the Uruguay Round Trade Negotiations Committee in Marrakesh, April 14, 1994, 33 I.L.M. 1267 (1994); and Marrakesh Agreement Establishing the World Trade Organization, April 15, 1994, 1867 U.N.T.S. 154, 33 I.L.M. 1144.
53. Ministerial Decision on Trade and Environment, MTN.TNC/MIN (94)/1/Rev.1, adopted by ministers at the meeting of the Uruguay Round Trade Negotiations Committee in Marrakesh, April 14, 1994, as part of the Marrakesh Agreement Establishing the World Trade Organization, 1867 U.N.T.S. 133 (I-31874, 1995), 33 I.L.M. 1267 (1994).
54. *See also* discussions above, regarding the major members' twofold position as regards trade norms prevailing for their export interests. It might also be noted that NAFTA/ NAAEC was being handled closely by the Clinton-Gore new administration officials in order to assure passage of NAFTA.

recommendations on whether any modifications of the provisions of the multilateral trading system are required, compatible with the open, equitable and non-discriminatory nature of the system, as regards, in particular:

- the need for rules to enhance positive interaction between trade and environmental measures, for the promotion of sustainable development, with special consideration to the needs of developing countries, in particular, those of the least developed among them;
- the avoidance of protectionist trade measures, and the adherence to effective multilateral disciplines to ensure responsiveness of the multilateral trading system to environmental objectives set forth in Agenda 21 and the Rio Declaration, in particular, Principle 12; and
- surveillance of trade measures used for environmental purposes, of trade-related aspects of environmental measures which have significant trade effects, and of effective implementation of the multilateral disciplines governing those measures.

Departing from the NAFTA model, and consistent with the dual interests of major trading members on the importance of preserving trade norms as a check on attempts to protect against any of their export interests on environmental grounds, no environmental supremacy is provided, and institutional preference for the protection of trade norms is established with the aim of allowing mutual supportiveness and non-conflict, which in essence affirms a temporary or status quo trade norm supremacy until changes are required or made to the existing rules.

[C] Element 3: Institutional Mechanisms

The third element, akin to the NAAEC/CEC, and having as its aim, "making international trade and environmental policies mutually supportive," was the formulation of the ten-point work mandate of the CTE, which was briefly covered earlier and discussed in more detail in parts B and C. The work plan would permit the CTE to conduct a very broad program that would have a range, not limited to the norms and hierarchy debate, but involve diverse issues related to environmental issues such as eco-labelling, climate change, environmental taxes and charges, the interface and information exchanges with MEAs, as well as joint studies and reports with MEAs, and the analysis and compilation of data, as well as technical assistance and capacity building for developing and least developed countries (LDCs).

Similar to NAAEC/CEC, the work of the CTE has generated a wealth of information and reports that reflect perspectives, policy debates, information exchange and capacity building work of the CTE, as an institution, which while not having a direct impact on the norms and hierarchy debate, nevertheless all play a role towards the desired levels of transparency and governance processes that enable environment constituents to have a voice towards the resolution, or airing, of trade and environment issues as they arise or occur.

§1.04 THE CTE IN THE MIDST OF CONFLICTING REGIME NORMS

The beginnings of the CTE are subject to many monographs, journal articles, and chapters of treatises. Konrad von Moltke's Graduate Institute 1996 monograph *The WTO and the Environment: What Must Change in the WTO*[55] had already expressed disappointment about the early work at the CTE. Von Moltke (1996) identifies early on the problem—a problem that underlies the current research project's attempt to formulate a metric and objective standard or measure by which policy makers could engage in some intelligible discourse—that the negotiators and advocates in the CTE were from different policy regimes and were speaking completely different languages from different vantage points and values:

> Trade and environment regimes respond to a different hierarchy of values, which are reflected in different structures ....[56]

Watson (2013) and McCormick (2006) also highlight these contrasts of values and perspectives, as my own personal experiences as chair confirm as well,[57] that the triple win mandate, while acknowledged, signified very different things to different negotiators, experts or audiences. Under such conditions, the engagements in discourse were challenging and less fruitful, despite the common aspirations and shared forum at the CTE.

Steinberg (1997)[58] highlighted the difficulty of the CTE delivering results or consensus in the changed landscape (post-GATT) among members of varying levels of development and varying negotiating priorities. He saw more promise in regional trade regimes or negotiations among more developed economies or similar levels of development, and also saw environment benefiting from the drive towards higher levels of development, indirectly supporting the Kuznets curve thesis, that the 1999 *WTO Study no. 4*[59] in some measure attempted to temper.

Von Moltke (1996) posits that with the treaty establishing the WTO, the GATT-era *members only* trade club had become a true transnational governance organization

55. Konrad Von Moltke, *The World Trade Organization and the Environment: What Must Change* at p. 1 (1996).
56. *Id.* at p. 18.
57. *See*, e.g., Green Room (September 15, 2009) discussions relating to the progress of CTESS item. Certain developing members emphasized the need for concessions in environmental goods and services tariff reduction to be based on request and offer modalities, and linkage to progress in NAMA and Agriculture in order to assure a benefit to development, while others viewed greater volumes of trade in EGS were a benefit in and of themselves as to afford a benefit to trade environment and development. Chair's Notes (author's file, *Green Room Senior Officials Week* September 15-22, 2009).
58. Richard H. Steinberg, *Trade-Environment Negotiations in the EU, NAFTA, and WTO: Regional Trajectories of Rule Development*, 91(2) AJIL 231 (1997).
59. Håkan Nordström and Scott Vaughan, *Special Studies No. 4: Trade and Environment* (1999) available at: http://www.wto.org/english/res_e/reser_e/special_studies_e.htm (accessed on November 30, 2019); *see also* commentary, Steve Charnovitz, *World Trade and the Environment: A Review of the New WTO Report*, 12 Geo. Int'l Envtl. L. Rev. 523 (1999-2000).

with constitutional mandates, and had shifted fundamentally from *traits-contracts* to *traits-lois*.[60]

The three policy regimes of trade, environment, and development in and of themselves have broad coverage and laudable individual objectives and tools that are of course not limited to the present nexus discussions, and these impact much on the challenge of approaching the nexus from a strict nexus perspective:

- trade and economics have a profound and the most mature set of intellectual principles and an established and respected hierarchy of experts and policy leaders;
- development policy regime objectives are post-colonial in age and maturity while standing on the highest level of the moral ground in its aspiration that science and economics theory should in fact speedily achieve social justice and poverty eradication for the planet and all its citizens;
- the environment regime, advocating the respect for *third-generation* rights that will protect and preserve the environment and intergenerational equity, contains and attempts to blend all the aspirations of past, present, and future that in physical and historical terms relate to values that pre-date, coincide and are certainly more profound and richer in texture and broader in scope than the trade and development regimes put together—it, therefore, attempts a claim at pre-eminence that is naturally resisted by the other regimes.

The approach to this conundrum of conflicting norms, values and perceptions, leads in many directions. Pauwelyn (2003) provides the leading treatise on the subject of conflict of norms in the WTO context,[61] and on the conflict of norms between the WTO and MEAs. It can provide the current research project a frame by which the treatment of norm conflict-resolution proposals at the CTE discussed in the thematic Part III can be approached. Pauwelyn observes on the MEA issue, the absence of conflict rules save for the preamble, and as discussed above, the de facto rules under GATT Article XX, and the rather *playing it safe* attitude of the drafters of both the WTO agreements and MEAs:[62]

> This [CTE] mandate has, so far, not resulted in any explicit conflict rules ... drafters of MEAs did not include a conflict clause ...could be interpreted in both ways: (i) the drafters wanted to make sure that the GATT was left unaffected, ... or, in contrast (ii) the drafters wanted to make sure that the new MEA would be effective and not be nullified by the earlier GATT ...

60. *See*, e.g., Von Moltke (1996) *The World Trade Organization and the Environment*; Alexandre Kiss, "The International Protection of the Environment" *in The Structure and Process of International Law: Essays in Legal Philosophy, Doctrine and Theory* (St. J. Ronald MacDonald and Douglas Johnston (eds.)) (1983).

61. Joost Pauwelyn, *Conflict of Norms in Public International Law: How WTO Law Relates to Other Rules of International Law* (2003); *see also* John H. Jackson, *Restructuring the GATT System* (1990).

62. *See* Pauwelyn (2003) *Conflict of Norms* at pp. 350-351.

The CTE was, therefore, born in such a context of a dramatic historical ferment in the three policy regimes of trade, development and environment, and originating its work program in the program of action of Agenda 21. It is important then to obtain a fuller understanding of the work of the CTE that the policy tools and benchmarks of each of the three regimes be also more fully understood.

In the succeeding two chapters, we proceed to discuss from a neutral perspective the organization, the agenda items, mandate and areas of work of the CTE, and the potential theoretical frame of analysis by which one could constructively identify a role for the mass of knowledge and expertise and work that the CTE has generated.

CHAPTER 2

The Areas of Work of the CTE

§2.01 INTRODUCTION TO THE CTE's MANDATED 10 POINT WORK PROGRAM AND FIVE THEMATIC AREAS)

Further to the WTO General Council formally establishing the CTE at its first meeting on January 31, 1995, the CTE would, in turn, adopt its ten-point work program at its first meeting on February 16, 1995, based on the mandate contained in the April 14, 1994 GATT *Ministerial Decision on Trade and Environment*.[63]

It will be immediately evident, in parsing out the work of the CTE that, like its predecessor, its creation was ad hoc and provisional, and accompanied by the hesitant acquiescence of the trade governance community. The decision to establish the CTE was not part of the Marrakesh Treaty or one of the "covered agreements" of the WTO that form the volumes that were acceded to by the incoming members of the WTO. This explains in part the less than ideal structuring of the ten-point work program of the CTE, which was never formulated as a formal mandate or official work program under a constitutional charter or organic mandate but was based on a General Council decision, as is the case with other committees that are implementing bodies of a covered agreement, e.g., the TBT or SPS committees.

So figuring out the mandated work areas of the CTE starts off like a jigsaw puzzle, and even the numbering of the ten-point agenda work program items remains nebulous and gray, and become firm only through the customary practice and the passage of time. While some items appear to have already outlived their usefulness, they remain part of the CTE tradition and remain on the standing agenda. As already mentioned in the prior chapter, the mandate on trade and environment started with just one agenda item in 1971 in the GATT-era GEMIT, then it was expanded to three items in 1991,[64] and with the establishment of the CTE in 1995, the work program had evolved to

63. Ministerial Decision on Trade and Environment, MTN.TNC/MIN (94)/1/Rev.1 (April 14, 1994); 1867 U.N.T.S. 133 (I-31874, 1995), 33 I.L.M. 1267, *see also* Annex A.
64. *See generally* Part I of this book.

become a ten-point agenda, sourced from the wording of the 1994 Ministerial Decision on Trade and Environment.

The first chair of the CTE, Ambassador Sanchez, in his first summary of the activities of the CTE, in WT/CTE/W/17, December 12, 1995, noted that the CTE work agenda was subject to review by the middle of 1996 after the CTE would have had its first year of operation:

> In order to establish *a more focused* but well balanced work program, the Chairman submits the following proposals:
>
> (a) *to keep all items on our agenda,* but to move, whenever possible, from the discussion of agenda items to the analysis of those issues identified during the debate as the core of each item and, to that end, to organize our future work programme on the basis of the proposal submitted below;
> (b) to continue the process of analysis of these issues *until May 1996, when a new review of the work programme will take place;*
> (c) the list of issues identified next to each item is not necessarily exhaustive. Once the discussion of the identified issues is carried out by the Committee, Members would be free to raise other related issues under each agenda item at the same meeting.

To this day, regrettably, the failure to revise or refine the work program remains a major inefficiency of the CTE, and it is one of the recommendations of this book that the CTE work program ought to be updated and modernized. The CTE, which as mentioned, was not a standing body of the WTO, but rather was created by Ministerial Decision. It could have expired or faded away, but it ended up continuing its work by an ad hoc extension of its life, by the action of the first-ever WTO Ministerial Conference (MC1) held in Singapore in 1996, Ministerial Conference (1st Session Singapore December 9-13, 1996), Ministerial Declaration, WT/MIN (96)/DEC; 36 I.L.M. 218 (1997), which, in retrospect, failed to do anything to refine the work program:

> Re: Trade and Environment
> 16. The Committee on Trade and Environment has made an important contribution towards fulfilling its Work Programme ... has been examining and will continue to examine, *inter alia,* the scope of the complementarities between trade liberalization, economic development and environmental protection. ... further work needs to be undertaken on all items of its agenda, as contained in its report ... and therefore direct the Committee to carry out its work, reporting to the General Council, under its existing terms of reference.

The CTE numbering of the work agenda items follows the original numbering by the first chair of the CTE, Ambassador Sanchez of Argentina, as reported in his first and second reports on CTE work for 1995 and 1996 (*see Summary of Activities of the CTE (1995),* WT/CTE/W/17, December 12, 1995; CTE 1996 Report, WT/CTE/1, November 12, 1996). The CTE ten-point mandate would be supplemented and enhanced in 2001 with the Doha Ministerial Declaration that had specific instructions for the work of the

CTE. The first two chair reports, together with 1994, 1996, and 2001 Ministerial documents, in legal effect, constitute the ad hoc organic charter of the CTE (see Annex 1).

Table 2.1 constitutes the CTE Work Program Guide with the work agenda numbering system, and the CTE numbering becomes significant throughout this book and in the functioning and organizational efficiency of the CTE since they serve as the basis for the CTE secretariat, chairs, members documentation, summaries, and deliberations. The CTE Work Program Guide also indicates the chapters of this book, specifically Chapters 4, 5 and 6, that specifically discuss the relevant or specific CTE agenda item. As will be evident in the following pages, the 10 point work program items of the CTE are then further grouped into five thematic areas that are, in turn, captured in discussions in the mentioned chapters. A chapter guide follows Table 2.1 for ease of reference.

Table 2.1 CTE Work Program Guide

No.	*1994 CTE*	*2001 DDA CTE CTESS*	*Chapter/Section Treatment*
1	[1] the relationship between the provisions of the multilateral trading system and trade measures for environmental purposes, including those pursuant to multilateral environmental agreements;	**[DDA1 CTESS 1/5]** ***Par 31 (i)*** the relationship between existing WTO rules and specific trade obligations set out in multilateral environmental agreements (MEAs). The negotiations shall be limited in scope to the applicability of such existing WTO rules as among parties to the MEA in question. The negotiations shall not prejudice the WTO rights of any Member that is not a party to the MEA in question;	Chapter 4
2	[2] the relationship between environmental policies relevant to trade and environmental measures with significant trade effects and the provisions of the multilateral trading system;	**[DDA4 CTE2/4]** ***Par 32 (i)*** the effect of environmental measures on market access, especially in relation to developing countries, in particular the least-developed among them, and those situations in which the elimination or reduction of trade restrictions and distortions would benefit trade, the environment and development; **[DDA7 CTE2 CTESS]** ***Par 33.*** We recognize the importance of technical assistance and capacity building in the field of trade and environment to developing countries, in particular the least-developed among them. We also encourage that expertise and experience be shared with members wishing to perform environmental reviews at the national level.	Chapter 4
3	[3] the relationship between the provisions of the multilateral trading system and: 3a charges and taxes for environmental purposes;	**[DDA3a CTESS Rules]** ***Par 31*** . . . We note that fisheries subsidies form part of the negotiations provided for in paragraph 28;	Chapter 5
3	3b requirements for environmental purposes relating to products, including standards and technical regulations, packaging, labelling and recycling;	**[DDA6 CTE3b]** ***Par 32*** *(iii)* labelling requirements for environmental purposes.	Chapter 5
4	[4] the provisions of the multilateral trading system with respect to the transparency of trade measures used for environmental purposes and environmental measures and requirements which have significant trade effects;	*See DDA 4 / 7 in CTE2/4 above*	Chapter 4
5	[5] the relationship between the dispute settlement mechanisms in the multilateral trading system and those found in multilateral environmental agreements;		Chapter 4

No.	*1994 CTE*	*2001 DDA CTE CTESS*	*Chapter/Section Treatment*
6	[6] the effect of environmental measures on market access, especially in relation to developing countries, in particular to the least developed among them, and environmental benefits of removing trade restrictions and distortions;	**[DDA3 CTESS 6]** ***Par 31 (iii)*** the reduction or, as appropriate, elimination of tariff and non-tariff barriers to environmental goods and services.	Chapter 6
7	[7] the issue of exports of domestically prohibited goods,		Chapter 5
8	that the Committee on Trade and Environment will consider the . . . [8] the relevant provisions of the Agreement on Trade-Related Aspects of Intellectual Property Rights as an integral part of its work, within the above terms of reference,	**[DDA5 CTE8]** ***Par 32 (ii)*** the relevant provisions of the Agreement on Trade-Related Aspects of Intellectual Property Rights; and	Chapter 5
9	that the Committee on Trade and Environment will consider the [9] work program envisaged in the Decision on Trade in Services and the Environment		Chapter 5
10	[10] to invite the Sub-Committee of the Preparatory Committee, and the Committee on Trade and Environment when it is established, to provide input to the relevant bodies in respect of appropriate arrangements for relations with inter-governmental and non-governmental organizations referred to in Article V of the WTO.	**[DDA2 CTESS 10]** ***Par 31 (ii)*** procedures for regular information exchange between MEA Secretariats and the relevant WTO committees, and the criteria for the granting of observer status;	Chapter 4

Each of the ten work agenda items, the three chapters, and the five thematic areas are grouped together as follows.

Table 2.2 The Book Chapters of the CTE Work Program Guide

Chapter 4	***Trade and Environment Interface, Cooperation, Coordination and Transparency***
Section a.	CTE/CTESS 1/5/10—MEAs relationship and STOs in MEAs; and legal implications
Section b.	CTE 2/4—transparency of trade measures used for environmental purposes; environmental policies with trade effects;[65]
Chapter 5	***Special Issues of Carbon, Standards, Eco-labelling, DPGs, TRIPS, Services***
Section a.	CTE 3a—charges and taxes for environmental purposes; (with DDA par. 31 cross-reference to fisheries subsidies rules negotiations)
	CTE 3bi—environmental requirements relating to products, including PPMs, and standards and technical regulations;
	CTE 3bii—packaging, labelling, and recycling;
Section b.	CTE 7/8/9—special issues of exports of domestically prohibited goods; Trade-Related Aspects of Intellectual Property Rights; and Environmental Services
Chapter 6	***Market Access for Environmental Goods and the Triple-win Mandate***
Section a.	CTE 6—Market Access issues
Section b.	CTE 6/DDA 31iii—The Triple-win

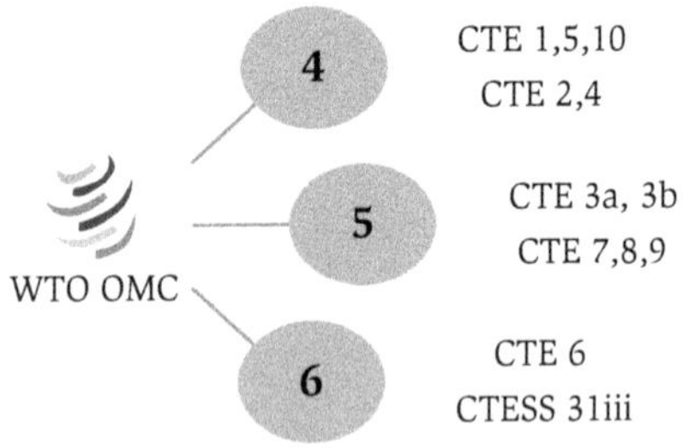

65. CTE 2 relating to environmental policies as a general matter appears to be overlapping with various agenda items. The appropriate treatment of CTE 2 will have to be subject to further refinement and study, and at present, it has been categorized as overlapping with CTE 1 and CTE 4. Hopefully the research is successful in parsing this work item further to allow a fuller understanding of the intent of the original drafters.

[A] CTE and CTESS Documentation System

As seen and mentioned in the prior chapter, the GEMIT had set the procedures for the future CTE work, and the GATT Council had required, pursuant to an Association of Southeast Asian Nations (ASEAN) proposal, that the Secretariat prepare a ninety-four-page background note (GATT, *Trade and Environment*).[66] This Secretariat note provided the foundation of current CTE practice, and the Annex thereto contains the first listing and monitoring of NEMs that are now regularly captured in the CTE Agenda 4 work output known as the EDB.[67]

Following the GEMIT's traditions, the CTE and the transitional SCTE (Subcommittee on Trade and Environment of the Preparatory Committee for the Establishment of the WTO) generated meetings and documentation, though, at a slower pace, that has yielded for the CTE and SCTE some 7,000 pages of minutes and working documents, exclusive of internal notes, supplemental records, and informal transcripts.

After 2001, the CTE would be called to assemble in Special Session (the CTESS (Committee on Trade and Environment sitting in Special Session)) as part of the Doha round of trade negotiations under the WTO Trade Negotiating Committee, and this work would generate as well a substantial amount of work documentation and proposals nearing 4,000 pages. Table 2.3 gives a summary of the available work documents on trade and environment at the CTE, which acts as the successor custodian of its predecessor's documents as well.

Table 2.3 Summary of Trade and Environment Documents: GEMIT, SCTE, CTE, CTESS (Exclusive of Internal Notes and Non-papers)

Document Series	*Page Count*
GEMIT (1971 to 1994)	811
SCTE (1994)	241
CTE (1995 to present)	7,521
CTESS (2001 to present)	3,775
Total	**12,348**

These documents are instrumental to evaluate and examine the work of the CTE, and they provide a rich source of historical narrative and sense of the evolution of the CTE as a body, as well as its component parts. The statements made by delegations, and the particular nuances and priorities of the various positions of delegations involved in the processes, demonstrate as well the interactions of various interest groups and policy regimes in the CTE's work.

66. *See* GATT Council, Minutes of the Meetings of May 29-30, 1999, C/M/250 (June 28, 1991); GATT Secretariat, Trade and Environment, Factual Note by the Secretariat, L/6896 (September 18, 1991).
67. WTO CTE, Environmental Database for 2018, WT/CTE/EDB/18 (November 12, 2019) is the latest version of this output and demonstrates the technical outputs of the CTE that may have value to the transnational network of experts and capital officials.

Based on the practice of the CTE, the work agenda items numbered 1 (on the relationship of MEA provisions in general), 5 (on MEA provisions in relation to the WTO dispute settlement mechanisms) and 10 (on relations with other IOs and coordination with MEA secretariats) (hereinafter for convenience referred to as CTE 1, 5, 10) are discussed together in CTE meetings.

The general agenda items as derived from the organic mandates of the CTE found in the 1994 Decision and paragraphs 31-33 of the Doha Ministerial Declaration provide a structure by which all the work of the CTE may be organized and understood, and allows the result to be organized according to the specific agenda item or negotiating area.

§2.02 THE CTE AND CTESS

As mentioned, the CTE meets in two iterations or capacities, and this explains the various types of meetings and documentation, with the CTE meeting in regular session and the CTESS having the nomenclature when it meets as a Doha Round negotiating committee. *See* Figure 2.1.

The CTE meetings take place at least twice a year, with the sole exception of 2008 when only one meeting took place at the CTE Regular Session. The frequency of CTESS meetings was inconsistent in terms of documentation but also occurred more frequently than CTE Regular meetings when negotiations were actively being pursued. The lacuna in the documentation for the CTESS was due to the negotiating nature or mode of the discussions, which required that many of the CTESS meetings to be informal in nature, variable in configuration, and discussions either being confidential, un-recorded or held without minutes.

Table 2.4 shows the number of documented meetings at the CTE Regular and CTESS from 1995 till 2017. CTESS is marked in red and entered into existence in 2001. The trend demonstrates the decline in the number of official meetings from 1995 till 2017.

Table 2.4 Summary of Meetings of the CTE and CTESS

Year	*No. of Meetings CTE*	*No. of Meetings CTESS*
1995-2001	28	NA
2002-2010	21	21
2011-2014	9	2
2015-2018	6	1

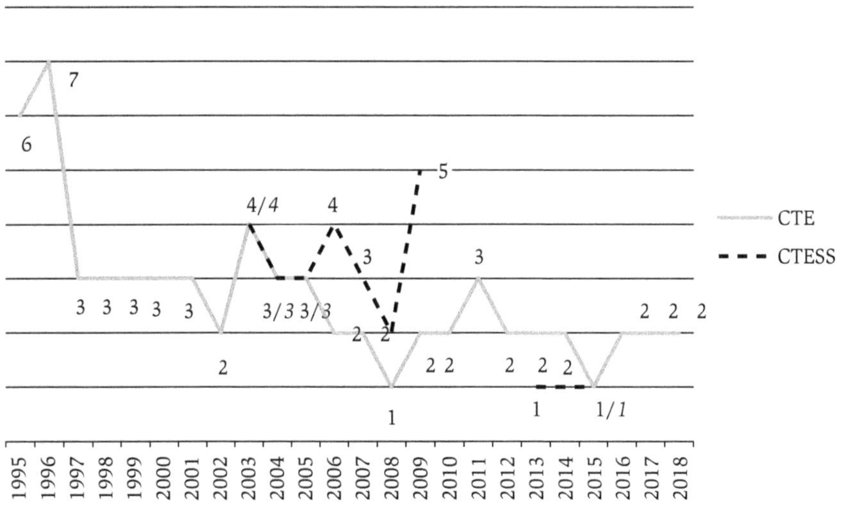

Source: Summary of Reports of CTE and CTESS from 1995 till 2018.

CTE 3a on taxes and charges indirectly covers fisheries subsidies by the cross-reference in DDA paragraph 31 that "fisheries subsidies form part of the negotiations provided for in paragraph 28." Moreover, paragraph 33 of the Doha Ministerial Conference also included cross-cutting trade-related technical assistance and special and differential treatment issues. (Figure 2.1).[68]

The CTE Regular session has been functioning since the inception of the WTO, and a total of 545 submissions have been made to it. The CTESS commenced only in 2002, with a total of 229 submissions being made.

68. *See* ¶¶ 28 *et. seq.*, WTO Ministerial Conference (4th Session Doha November 9-14, 2001), Ministerial Declaration, WT/MIN (01)/DEC/1 (November 20, 2001).

Figure 2.1 Coverage Areas of the CTE/CTESS

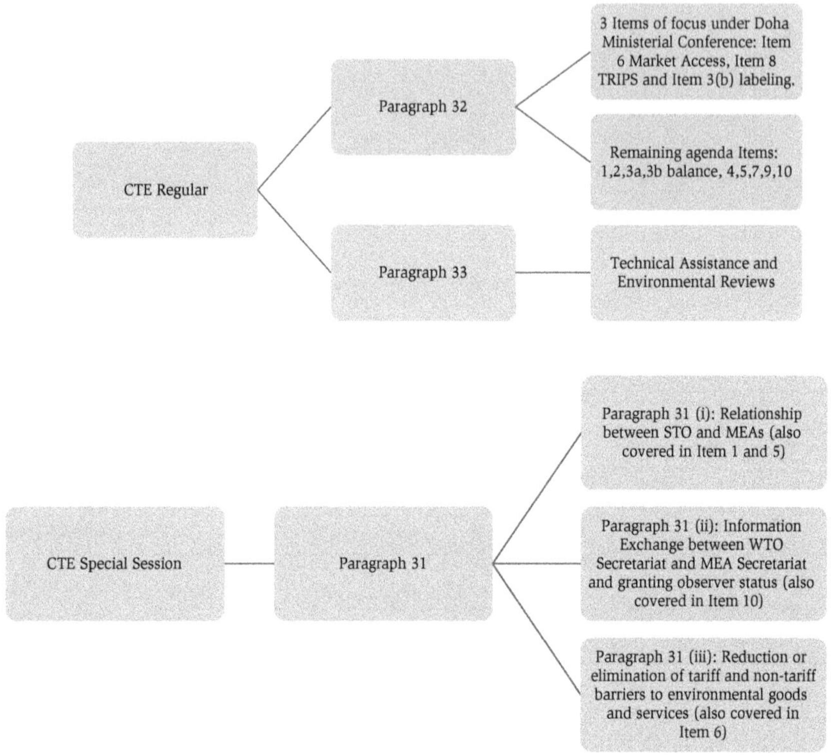

These submissions have primarily been made by three participants: Members, WTO Secretariat, and official representatives of other IOs. Collectively, these 774 documents form the historical narrative of the discussions at the CTE and CTESS and also present themselves as a repository of information for future negotiations.

As shown in Figure 2.2, the CTE Secretariat has devised a system by which all the documents of the CTE and CTESS are listed and regularly updated and indexed. Figure 2.2 provides a general picture of the structure and document codes referred to in the document lists of the CTE, which are available online. These two separate CTE lists constitute the essential guide and index by which one can find all the official CTE Member submissions and documentation.

Figure 2.2 CTE and CTESS Documents Lists

(1) CTE List of Documents, WT/CTE/INF/5/Rev.12), February 29, 2016; and
(2) CTE in Special Session, (CTESS) List of Documents, Revision (TN/TE/INF/4/Rev.16), May 3, 2013.

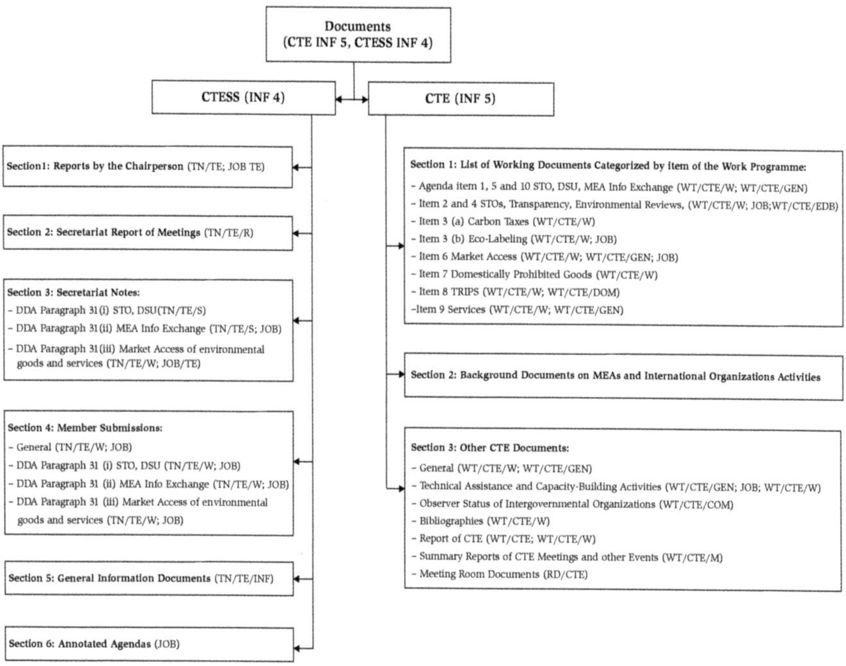

GUIDE TO CTE DOCUMENTS AND CODES

A. CTE DOX
1. WT/CTE (Annual Reports)
2. WT/CTE/COM
3. WT/CTE/EDB (Environmental Database)
4. WT/CTE/GEN
5. WT/CTE/M (Summary Reports of CTE meetings)
6. WT/CTE/W
7. JOB or JOB/TE*
8. RD/CTE* (Room Documents)

B. CTESS DOX
1. TN/TE (Chair Reports)
2. TN/TE/INF (Information Documents)
3. TN/TE/R (Summary Reports of CTESS meetings)
4. TN/TE/S
5. TN/TE/W
6. JOB or JOB/TE*

*Member Documents Limited Access

Utilizing the latest versions of these CTE and CTESS master lists provide an essential tool for analyzing and reviewing the CTE work program.

In reviewing the work and discussions at the CTE, it will be useful to keep in mind the specific dynamics of the information exchange and related meetings and deliberations of the CTE, and these would not be limited in scope to CTE meetings of member delegations, and their national experts and negotiators, which is the member-driven portion, but also the professional and administrative workings of the WTO's and CTE division's administrative infrastructure as an international professional organization. There would also be the factor of informal exchanges that take place among delegates and experts that are further discussed in the chapter on theoretical approaches.

§2.03 THE CTE THEMATIC AREAS AND THEIR KEY WORK OUTPUTS

CTE 1, 5, 10; CTESS (i), (ii)): Norm Coherence and Norm Conflict and the CTE
Agenda Items 1, 5 and 10

Mandate under 1994 Decision and 2001 Ministerial Declaration
Item 1: *The relationship between the provisions of the multilateral trading system and trade measures for environmental purposes, including those pursuant to multilateral environmental agreements*
Item 5: *The relationship between the dispute settlement mechanisms in the multilateral trading system and those found in multilateral environmental agreements*
Item 10: *Input to the relevant bodies in respect of appropriate arrangements for relations with intergovernmental and non-governmental organizations referred to in Article V of the WTO*
Paragraph 31(i) and (ii): *With a view to enhancing the mutual supportiveness of trade and environment, we agree to negotiations, without prejudging their outcome, on:*

(i) *the relationship between existing WTO rules and specific trade obligations set out in multilateral environmental agreements (MEAs). The negotiations shall be limited in scope to the applicability of such existing WTO rules as among parties to the MEA in question. The negotiations shall not prejudice the WTO rights of any Member that is not a party to the MEA in question;*
(ii) *procedures for regular information exchange between MEA Secretariats and the relevant WTO committees, and the criteria for the granting of observer status.*

Outcome Documents for Items 1, 5 and 10:

1. Matrix on Trade-Related Measures Pursuant to Selected Multilateral Environmental Agreements ("STO Inventory"), WT/CTE/W/160/Rev.8 (2000-2017).
2. Compliance and Dispute Settlement Provisions in the WTO and in Multilateral Agreements, WT/CTE/W/191 (2001).
3. GATT/ WTO Dispute Settlement Practice relating to GATT Article XX, Paragraphs (b), (d) and (g), WT/CTE/W/203 (2002).
4. MEA Information Session on Technical Assistance, Capacity Building and Enhancing Information Exchange, WT/CTE/W/209 (2002).
5. Draft Decision on Trade and Environment, TN/TE/20 (Annex 2) (2011).
6. 1999 WTO Special Studies No. 4.

A total of 215 documents were analyzed to draw a narrative of the discussions that took place at the CTE Regular and CTE Special Session. Of these, 9 non-papers were introduced at the CTE, 10 were proposals made at the CTE by Members, 10 were submissions and notes by WTO Secretariat, 6 were submissions by MEA Secretariats, 10 were annual secretariat reports and 59 were summary reports of meetings which included Members verbal interventions. Further, 43 documents submitted to CTESS under paragraph 31(i) of Doha declaration as proposals by Members, 11 submissions by the WTO Secretariat, 3 general submissions of paragraph 31(i) of Doha declaration, 23 summary reports by the WTO Secretariat and 20 reports by the Chairperson of CTESS were analyzed. Further, 3 documents submitted under item 10 were also analyzed along with 11 Member Proposals under paragraph 31(ii) of the Doha Declaration (Table 2.5).

Table 2.5 Summary of Documentation: CTE 1/5/10 and DDA31(i)(ii)

Number of Documents	*Kind of Documents*	*Forum*
9	Non-Papers (Members)	CTE
10	Proposals by Members	CTE
10	WTO Secretariat Submissions and Notes	
6	Submissions by MEA Secretariat	CTE
10	Annual Reports	CTE
59	Summary Reports	CTE
43	Proposals by Members	CTESS
11	WTO Secretariat Submissions and Notes	CTESS
3	Member Submissions to paragraph 31(i) of Doha Declaration	CTESS
11	Member Submissions to paragraph 31(ii) of Doha Declaration	CTESS
23	Summary Reports	CTESS
20	Reports by Chairperson	CTESS
Total: 215		

Item 1 of the CTE work program deals with the issues related to trade measures that are to be applied unilaterally by WTO Members to address environmental problems that lie outside their national jurisdiction.[69] Item 5 examines the relationship between the dispute settlement mechanisms in the multilateral trading system and those found in MEAs. Both items 1 and 5 were subject as well of and subsumed by the DDA paragraph 31(ii) mandate.

Item 10 was already being discussed pre-1995 in informal consultations under both the SCTE of the WTO Preparatory Committee and the CTE and at informal and

69. WTO CTE, Report (1996) of the Committee on Trade and Environment, WT/CTE/1 (November 12, 1996).

formal meetings of the CTE. This led to the early grant of observer status to fourteen intergovernmental organizations (IGOs), which was later confirmed by the General Council of the WTO.

§2.04 KEY OUTPUT IN THE 2011 DRAFT DECISION

While negotiations have risen and ebbed through the years, the last set of negotiations in 2011 culminated in embodying some guidance in a draft Decision on Trade and Environment (CTE Decision II). The draft decision was annexed to the latest report of the chair of the special session presented on April 21, 2011,[70] along with all the other reports of the Doha negotiating group chairs (collectively known as the Easter 2011 Package). The consensus draft also reflected and confirmed the agreement not to agree on defining the term *STO* as contained in an MEA, with members agreeing *not* to attempt a prescriptive or static definition of *STOs*, but rather have a common reference paper often referred to as the *STO Inventory*.[71] More detail is provided on this in Chapter 4 discussions.

CTE 2 and 4: Transparency, EDBs and Environment Reviews:

Agenda Items CTE 2, 4

Item 2: *The relationship between environmental policies relevant to trade and environmental measures with significant trade effects and the provisions of the multilateral trading system.*
Item 4: *The provisions of the multilateral trading system with respect to the transparency of trade measures used for environmental purposes and environmental measures and requirements which have significant trade effects.*
Paragraph 33 of Doha Ministerial Meeting: *We recognize the importance of technical assistance and capacity building in the field of trade and environment to developing countries, in particular the least-developed among them. We also encourage that expertise and experience be shared with members wishing to perform environmental reviews at the national level. A report shall be prepared on these activities for the Fifth Session.*

Output for Item 2:

1. List of Environmental Reviews ("Notifications"), WT/CTE/W/245 (2007-2008)

Output for Item 4:

2. Environmental Database, CTE Environmental Database (EDB 1996-2018),
3. Latest version, WT/CTE/EDB/18 (November 12, 2019)

CTE 2 deals with the relationship between, *firstly*, the environmental policies relevant to trade and, *secondly*, environmental measures which may have significant trade effects and its relationship with the multilateral trading system. CTE 4, on the

70. WTO CTESS, Report by the Chairman Ambassador Manuel A.J. Teehankee to the Trade Negotiations Committee, TN/TE/20 (April 21, 2011).
71. WTO CTESS, Matrix on Trade Measures Pursuant to Selected Multilateral Environmental Agreements *(STO Inventory)*, WT/CTE/W/160/Rev.8 (October 9, 2017); *see also* first original version, WT/CTE/W/160 (September 19, 2000).

other hand, is designed to ensure transparency for domestic trade measures used for environmental purposes and/or environmental measures and requirements having significant trade effects. This endeavor seeks to avoid WTO non-compliant barriers to trade, which, in turn, results in dispute avoidance and strengthening the global trading system. CTE 2 has also been a subject of DDA paragraph 33.

In reviewing the records for these agenda items, there were 116 documents summarized as follows:

Table 2.6 CTE 2, CTE 4 Documentation

Number of Documents	*Kind of Documents*	*Forum*
10	Proposals by Members	CTE
35	WTO Secretariat Submissions and Notes	CTE
2	Submissions by MEA/IOs Secretariat	CTE
10	Annual Reports	CTE
59	Summary Reports	CTE
Total: 116		

Both items 2 and 4 cover the relationship between environmental policies at a domestic level and ensuring the transparency of these policies. There were intensive discussions of these work topics during the early years, and it led to the development of two important policy tools and work outputs, the Listing of ERs, and the annual EDB, which are further discussed in Chapter 4 and below in the Summary of Key Outputs of the CTE.

CTE 3a, 3b: Carbon, Border Taxes, Standards, and Eco-Labelling

Agenda Item 3(a) and 3(b)

Item 3(a): *The relationship between the provisions of the multilateral trading system and charges and taxes for environmental purposes.*
Item 3(b): *The relationship between the provisions of the multilateral trading system and (b) requirements for environmental purposes relating to products, including standards and technical regulations, packaging, labelling and recycling*
Paragraph 32(iii) of Doha Mandate: *We instruct the Committee on Trade and Environment, in pursuing work on all items on its agenda within its current terms of reference, to give particular attention to (...) (iii) labelling requirements for environmental purposes.*

Output Documents for Item 3(a) and 3(b):

1. Negotiating History of the Coverage of the Agreement on Technical Barriers to Trade with Regard to Labelling Requirements, Voluntary Standards, and Processes and Production Methods Unrelated to Product Characteristics, WT/CTE/W/10; G/TBT/W/11 (1995)
2. Taxes and Charges for Environmental Purposes—Border Tax Adjustment Report, WT/CTE/W/47
3. Information Relevant to the Consideration of the Market Access effects of Eco-Labelling Schemes, WT/CTE/W/150 (2000)
4. 2009 WTO UNEP Climate Change Report (26 June 2009)
5. Eco-Labelling: Overview of Current Work in Various International Fora, JOB/TE/9 (2010)

The CTE discussion on CTE 3 involved a high level of expertise, and highly specialized knowledge that ranged from carbon and border taxes, standards, eco-labelling, and clearly was a productive area with the Secretariat generating a number of work outputs that would be of great utility to many delegations and trade and environment policy makers and researchers.

The expertise of, and the ability to source expertise by, the Secretariat was certainly a highlight, and the generation of work outputs was certainly Secretariat-led. The documentation review shows that the CTE is able to act as a forum for reporting and the sharing of information and expertise from experts, MEAs, and delegations. The level of discussions could be said to be a prime example of the CTE fulfilling its role of increasing the capacity and the exchange of ideas between and among the trade and environment policy regimes.

In the discussions and work under CTE 3a and CTE 3b, a good number of reports were generated of a highly specialized nature, and in total, ninety-six documents were generated (Table 2.7).

Table 2.7 CTE 3a, 3b Documentation

Number of Documents	*Kind of Documents*	*Forum*
15	Proposal by Members	CTE
10	WTO Secretariat Submissions and Notes	
2	Submissions by International Organization for Standardization (ISO)	CTE
10	Annual Reports	CTE
59	Summary Reports	CTE
Total: 96		

Among the notable outputs as a result of these agenda items would be the special reports generated on the interface of trade and climate change, as well as what was initially a contentious issue of border taxes, PPMs, and eco-labelling. Much progress can be observed as to the level of cooperation and information exchange at the CTE in relation to improving transparency and coordination in the field of environment-related labelling and standards.

CTE 6 / DDA 31iii—Market Access and Environmental Goods and the Triple-win
CTE 6, DDA31 (iii), DDA32(i)

Item 6: *The effect of environmental measures on market access, especially in relation to developing countries, in particular to the least developed among them, and environmental benefits of removing trade restrictions and distortions.*
Paragraph 31 (iii) of Doha: *With a view to enhancing the mutual supportiveness of trade and environment, we agree to negotiations, without prejudging their outcome, on:*

(iii) *the reduction or, as appropriate, elimination of tariff and non-tariff barriers to environmental goods and services.*

Paragraph 32 of Doha: *We instruct the Committee on Trade and Environment, in pursuing work on all items on its agenda within its current terms of reference, to give particular attention to:*

(i) *the effect of environmental measures on market access, especially in relation to developing countries, in particular the least-developed among them, and those situations in which the elimination or reduction of trade restrictions and distortions would benefit trade, the environment and development*

Output of Item 6:

1. Environmental Requirements and Market Access: Recent Work in OECD and UNCTAD, WT/CTE/W/244 (2006)
2. Revision of the synthesis of submissions on Environmental Goods TN/TE/W/63, JOB(07)/137 (2007)
3. Draft Decision, Annex II on Structure and the Outcome Environmental Goods Coverage Under Paragraph 31(iii), Annex II, TN/TE/20 (2011)
4. Compilation of submission under paragraph 31(iii) of Doha Pursuant to the CTESS Work Programme, JOB/TE/3/Rev.1 (2011)

This has become a key area of contention in the CTE and CTESS. The narrative of these discussions, as covered in Chapter 6, relate to 285 documents, 43 of which were proposals by Members, 23 WTO Secretariat submissions, 16 submissions by IO/MEA Secretariats. There were also 78 proposals by WTO Members in the CTESS (Table 2.8).

Table 2.8 CTE 6, DDA 32i, 31iii Documentation

Number of Documents	*Kind of Documents*	*Forum*
43	Proposals by Members	CTE
23	WTO Secretariat Submissions and Notes	CTE
16	Submissions by IO/MEA Secretariat	CTE
10	Annual Reports	CTE
59	Summary Reports	CTE
78	Proposals by Members under paragraph 31(iii) of Doha Declaration	CTESS
13	WTO Secretariat Submissions and Notes	CTESS
23	Summary Reports	CTESS
20	Report by Chairperson	CTESS
Total: 285		

CTE 6 had been originally crafted to allow WTO members to "*talk-shop*" on how environmental measures could affect market access, especially in relation to developing countries and LDCs. The nature of discussions and the mandate of the CTE shifted significantly when actual trade negotiations for market access was mandated in DDA 32(i) and DDA 31(iii).

CTE 7, 8, 9: Special Issues DPGs, TRIPS, Services

Agenda Items 7, 8 and 9

Item 7: *The issue of exports of domestically prohibited goods.*
Item 8: *Relationship between the Environment and Agreement on Trade-Related Aspects of Intellectual Property*
Item 9: *The work programme envisaged in the Decision on Trade in Services and the Environment*
Paragraph 31(iii) of Doha Declaration: *With a view to enhancing the mutual supportiveness of trade and environment, we agree to negotiations, without prejudging their outcome, on:*

(iii) *the reduction or, as appropriate, elimination of tariff and non-tariff barriers to environmental goods and services.*

Paragraph 32(2) of Doha Declaration: *We instruct the Committee on Trade and Environment, in pursuing work on all items on its agenda within its current terms of reference, to give particular attention to:*

(ii) *the relevant provisions of the Agreement on Trade-Related Aspects of Intellectual Property Rights*

Output Documents:

1. Domestically Prohibited Goods: Assessment of the Product Coverage in Specific International Instruments, WT/CTE/W/29 (1996); see also WT/CTE/W/43 (1997).
2. The Relationship between the Convention on Biological Diversity (CBD) and the Agreement on the Trade-Related Aspects of Intellectual Property Rights (TRIPS); with focus on Article 27.3(B), WT/CTE/W/125 (1999).
3. Discussion Paper on the Environmental Effects of Services Trade Liberalization, WT/CTE/W/218 (2002).

CTE 7, 8 and 9, as in the case of CTE 3, dealt with highly technical and expert special topics that required the secretariats certain delegations to take the lead in the discussions. Item 7 covered the topic of DPGs; CTE 8 covered the TRIPS Agreement and the environment, and CTE 9 covered services. A total of 104 documents related to these topics and the discussions on environmental services were also discussed briefly at the CTESS. DPGs relate to banned or severely restricted goods on the domestic market of the exporting country because they are determined to present risks for human, animal or plant life or health, or the environment, but which may nevertheless be exported (Table 2.9)[72]

72. Tina Winquist, *Trade in Domestically Prohibited Goods* at p. 1 (1999) available at: http://www.iisd.org/sites/default/files/publications/viet_dpg.pdf (accessed on November 20, 2019).

Table 2.9 CTE 7, 8, 9 Documentation

Number of Documents	*Kind of Documents for items 7, 8 and 9*	*Forum*
11	Proposals by Members	CTE
13	WTO Secretariat Submissions and Notes	
11	Submissions by MEA/IO Secretariat	CTE
10	Annual Reports	CTE
59	Summary Reports	CTE
23	Summary Reports	CTESS
20	Reports by Chairperson	CTESS
Total number of documents: 147		

Historically, the issue of DPGs was first discussed in the 1980s during the GATT and has since been deliberated upon at length. The 38th Session of GATT Contracting Parties, in 1982, decided that:[73]

> to the maximum extent feasible, notify GATT of any goods produced and exported by them but banned by their national authorities for sale on their domestic markets on grounds of human health and safety.

The issue of DPGs has remained unresolved at the CTE since 1996, but the Secretariat Paper has widely been considered as a tangible outcome.

Item 8, on the relationship between the CBD and the TRIPS Agreements, was the subject of much debate in the discussions that took place from 1995 till 2000. These discussions assumed a clear divide between developed and developing WTO Members. Canada, Switzerland, and the U.S. considered TRIPS Agreement and CBD to be mutually supportive, whereas Brazil, India, and Pakistan considered the issue to be discussed at the TRIPS Council, where they sought to modify the agreement so as to provide increased patent rights related to biological materials and traditional knowledge.

The CTE's Agenda Item 9 on Services appears intangible when linked with the environment. However, on closer inspection, the production, distribution, and consumption of various services have ecological footprints. For example, transportation services are major contributors to greenhouse gases and air pollution. Also, tourism services, if left unchecked, could destroy sensitive ecosystems. Services such as water distribution and sanitation can assist in achieving sustainable development. Thus, the regulation of services could contribute to sustainable development.

73. GATT Council Document, BISD-29S/19 (1982); *see also* WTO CTE, A Review of the Information Available in the World Trade Organization on the Export of Domestically Prohibited Goods, Note by the Secretariat, WT/CTE/W/43 (April 22, 1997).

§2.05 SUMMARY OF KEY CTE's WORK OUTPUTS

Not counting other important reports and CTE work, I have identified twenty key CTE work output documents, which are briefly summarized below.

CTE 1, 5 and 10 Work Outputs

(1) **WTO Special Studies Number 4, 1999:** The WTO Special Studies Number 4 report was published in 1999 and has been extensively used by trade delegations. This report notes that while the multilateral trading system has been blamed for the slowness in the political process to produce an outcome on trade and environment, it recommends that in the mandate of the CTE potential contributions can be sought through reducing subsidies that harm the environment, including energy, agricultural and fishing subsidies. The study also notes that another "more obvious" opportunity would be to reduce or eliminate tariffs on environmental goods, technologies, and services.

(2) ***MEA Information Session on Technical Assistance, Capacity Building and Enhancing Information Exchange*, WT/CTE/W/209 (2002):** The Secretariats of UNEP and WTO jointly prepared this note at their own initiative to list of the trade-related technical assistance and capacity building activities and information exchange between WTO, UNEP, and MEAs such as Convention on International Trade in Endangered Species (CITES) and CBD Secretariats. This document is a direct output result of the discussions that were taking place under items 1, 5 and 10, and paragraph 31(i) of the Doha Declaration.

(3) ***Matrix ("STO MEA Inventory") on Trade-Related Measures Pursuant to Selected MEAs*, WT/CTE/W/160/Rev.8 (2000-2017):** This comprehensive document provides detailed information on trade-related measures pursuant to selected MEAs. The first version was released by the Secretariat in 2000, and the report has undergone several revisions. Prepared in consultation with several MEA Secretariats, this document presents updated information on happenings in MEAs and "contains specific information on the trade-related measures of each MEA, including any requirements or restrictions on imported or exported products or trade in transit." Further, the document provides information on technology transfer and technical assistance under the provisions of the MEA and lists out mechanisms for non-compliance with a party. This document is a result of the prevailing lack of clarity over the relationship between WTO and MEAs during early discussions. After the issuance of this document, and complemented by information exchange mechanisms developed by the WTO and MEA Secretariats, most of the concerns of Members about the impending collision of two disciplines of trade and environment are abated.

(4) ***Compliance and Dispute Settlement Provisions in the WTO and in MEAs***, WT/CTE/W/191 (2001): CTE 5 called for discussion of MEAs and the dispute settlement mechanism. This paper was prepared as a response to requests made by Members to the WTO Secretariat in February 2010 and was prepared in cooperation with the UNEP and MEA Secretariats. It details all the compliance and dispute settlement provisions in the WTO and MEAs. It also examines the compliance and dispute settlement systems in selected MEAs as well as the WTO to note the similarities and differences. Based on this paper, Members reinforced their views that while the multilateral trading system and the MEA universe were premised on different legal and policy orientations, both paths sought to pursue the same shared goal of sustainable development and environmental protection. One of the primary differences between the two regimes that were noted through this paper was that MEAs preferred a compliance-based approach whereas WTO—aiming at securing the stability of the multilateral trading system—considered settling disputes in a time-bound manner.

(5) ***GATT/WTO Dispute Settlement Practice Relating to GATT Article XX, Paragraphs (b), (d) and (g)***, WT/CTE/W/203 (2002): In 1996 and 1997, the Secretariat had responded to members requests on a compilation and discussion of GATT and WTO dispute settlement practice that related to the environmental exceptions embodied in GATT Article XX. The updated Secretariat Note prepared in 2002 has provided members and practitioners a very useful reference report on the interplay of environment norms and exceptions embodied in Article XX while preserving the requirements of the chapeau relating to disguised trade protectionist measures that have retained its relevance through the years and been integral to the discussion on the discussions on MEA and WTO norm coherence and conflict.

(6) ***Draft Decision on Trade and Environment*****, TN/TE/20 (2011), Annex II:** The draft decision was an annex to the report of the Chairperson of CTESS dated April 21, 2011.[74] The draft decision presents the evolution of the debates between MEAs and the multilateral trading system. Admittedly, this is still considered as "work in progress," but one bracketed portion of the draft would attempt to anchor achieving coherence of norms to treaty interpretation principles, including *pacta sunt servanda*:

> [Noting that the Vienna Convention on the Law of Treaties states that every treaty in force is binding upon the parties to it and must be performed by them in good faith;]
> [Recognizing that both MEAs and the WTO Agreement are instruments of international law of equal standing between parties to the agreements,

74. WTO CTESS, Report by the Chairman Ambassador Manuel A.J. Teehankee to the Trade Negotiations Committee, TN/TE/20 (April 21, 2011) at p. 5.

and that all provisions under international law should be implemented harmoniously and in good faith;][75]

CTE 2 and 4 Work Outputs

(7) ***Environmental Database (EDB)*, WT/CTE/EDB/18 (1996-2018):** The Annual WTO EDB is an acknowledged major policy tool developed as a direct output of CTE 4. It is an electronic database that acts as a repository for information on national environment-related measures notified under WTO Agreements, environment-related provisions of notified Regional Trade Agreements (RTAs), and national environment-related measures or programs, mentioned in Trade Policy Reviews (TPRs) on an annual basis. The database was a result of a realization by Members that no single collection point for all environmental measures existed in the WTO. This database is updated annually with new features and is used by Members in their preparation for meetings and other related policy work.

(8) ***List of ERs*, WT/CTE/W/245 (2007-2008):** The CTE List of ERs is another policy tool that was a direct work output of CTE 2 discussions, and also referred to in paragraph 33 of the Doha Ministerial Declaration. This document provides a list of various trade-related ERs and impact assessments that have been carried out on an annual basis. These include projects under multilateral trade liberalization initiatives, regional or bilateral trade liberalization initiatives, and domestic projects. ERs are the result of a proposal made by several Members, including the U.S., to initiate a platform where Members shared the experiences of trade liberalization and its effects on the environment. This has now become standard practice in the WTO, and Members are often quoted in summary reports appreciating this practice of sharing ERs.

CTE 3a 3b Work Outputs

(9) ***WTO UNEP Report on Trade and Climate Change*, 2009:** The WTO UNEP Report was an important publication that shifted the debate at the WTO on the intersection between trade and climate change. It shares perspectives on the science and economics of climate change, the efforts to mitigate climate change made at a multilateral level, and the national climate change policies. The report indicated that liberalizing global trade and combating climate change could be mutually supportive towards realizing a low carbon economy. The report noted that rising incomes resulting from trade liberalization could change social dynamics and aspirations. As a result, wealthier communities can demand higher environmental

75. *Id.* at p. 7.

standards. Further, the report also reviewed taxes and emission trading systems as tools to reduce greenhouse gas emissions.

(10) ***Negotiating History of the Coverage of the Agreement on TBT with Regard to Labelling Requirements, Voluntary Standards, and Processes and Production Methods Unrelated to Product Characteristics*, WT/CTE/W/10; G/TBT/W/11 (1995):** This note was prepared upon request by Members who sought clarity on the issue of eco-labelling but understanding the negotiating history that covered both the Tokyo and the UR negotiations. The note also detailed provisions of the TBT Agreement regarding its coverage of labelling requirements, PPMs unrelated to product characteristics, and voluntary standards. All three of these topics were intensely debated at the CTE. Part 1 of the report summarized the relevant legal provisions regarding labelling requirements. Part 2 addressed the disciplines in the TBT Agreement regarding the different types of standardizing bodies such as the central, local, regional, and nongovernmental bodies. Part 3 discussed in detail the coverage of PPMs in the TBT Agreement. The report noted that:

> Standards that are based on processes and production methods (PPMs) related to the characteristics of a product are clearly accepted under the TBT Agreement, subject to them being applied in conformity with its substantive disciplines. The negotiating history suggests that many participants were of the view that standards based, *inter alia*, on PPMs unrelated to a product's characteristics should not be considered eligible for being treated as being in conformity with the TBT Agreement.

While the report did not clarify unrelated PPMs, it clearly set aside doubts amongst Members about the applicability of WTO law on related PPM methods.

(11) ***Taxes and Charges for Environmental Purposes—BTA*, WT/CTE/W/47 (1999):** The "Border Tax Report" for environmental taxes was issued by the WTO Secretariat upon request by Members who had several questions related to domestic taxation policies and its effect on WTO law. The *raison d'etre* for this discussion is that several Members—mostly developed—were in favor of implementing a taxation policy that would promote environmentally friendly products. This comprehensive report provided Members with a clear understanding of the various policy instruments that are available to address environmental problems. It further discussed "wider economic and trade implications of eco-taxes and eco-charges and provided an overview of WTO provisions and dispute settlement practice pertaining to the application of domestic taxes and charges to traded goods."

(12) ***Information Relevant to the Consideration of the Market Access Effects of Eco-Labelling Schemes,* WT/CTE/W/150 (2000):** This document is a response to a request made by the CTE to the Secretariat to prepare an up-to-date document detailing market access effects of eco-labelling. Eco-labelling was another vigorously contested topic with many developing Members claiming that eco-labels presented a de facto barrier to trade, especially for small- and medium-sized enterprises (SMEs). The note provided detailed factual information on the principle eco-labels that were present in the market based on criteria such as geographical distribution and number of eco-labels in existence. It also provided a compilation of environmental labels and marks notifications that were made under the TBT Agreement. Furthermore, it discussed relevant literature on ecolabels and discussed the relevant ecolabels that existed in the market at the time.

(13) ***Eco-Labelling: Overview of Current Work in Various International Fora,* JOB/TE/9 (2010):** The document, dated 1997, provided a broad overview of all the work that was taking place in various international fora on eco-labelling and environmental labelling. It provided Members with an update on the work that was being undertaken in other IOs or bodies such as the Food and Agriculture Organization (FAO), International Organization for Standardization (ISO), Organization for Economic Cooperation and Development (OECD), United Nations Conference on Trade and Development (UNCTAD), and United Nations Environment Programme (UNEP). For example, FAO was undertaking work on specific kinds of ecolabels that were designed for the fisheries sector, whereas UNCTAD had undertaken work on sustainability claims. It noted that the work that was being carried out sought to improve general understanding of environmental labels, their scope, and the impact on consumers, market access, and the environment. It also informed Members about the development of standards and guidelines to enhance the quality and efficiency of ecolabels. The document is often used by Members as a reference point when discussing eco-labels.

CTE 6 Market Access Work Outputs

(14) ***Environmental Requirements and Market Access: Recent Work in OECD and UNCTAD,* WT/CTE/W/244 (2006):** This document, while not a direct output, is an important reference of recent studies on environmental requirements and market access undertaken by the OECD and UNCTAD. It highlights key points that were subsequently discussed in the CTE with regard to market access. It identifies market access difficulties faced by developing country exporters as well as developing country responses to environmental requirements. It also addresses the market access-related difficulties faced by developing countries at the national and multilateral levels.

(15) ***Revision of the synthesis of submissions on Environmental Goods (TN/TE/W/63)*, JOB (07)/137 (2007):** This document is a compilation of all the discussions that took place in the CTESS on paragraph 31(iii) of the Doha Declaration that aimed at reducing or eliminating tariffs and non-tariff barriers to EGS. This document sets out the potential deliverables of a triple-win outcome for trade, environment, and development. It also lists the approaches to the mandate under paragraph 31(iii). Further, the document lists out proposals on special and differential treatment and a compilation of the list of goods that Members have proposed under this paragraph during the negotiations.

(16) ***Annex II on Structure of the Outcome Environmental Goods Coverage under Paragraph 31(iii)*, TN/TE/20 (2011):** This draft decision is also an annex to the report by the Chairperson of CTESS dated April 21, 2011. The decision mentions the reference universe of all the environmental goods that Members identified in their proposals. Further, this draft decision also presents potential structures of the outcome on coverage. It specifically lists out the hybrid approach, requests and offers approach, environmental projects approach, alpha-beta combined approach, and the common lists approach.

(17) ***Compilation of Submissions under paragraph 31(iii) of Doha Pursuant to the CTESS Work Program*, JOB/TE/3/Rev.1 (2011):** This document lists out all the proposals made by Members under DDA paragraph 31(iii).

CTE 7, 8 and 9 Work Outputs

(18) ***DPGs: Assessment of the Product Coverage in Specific International Instruments*, WT/CTE/W/29 (1996):** The report was prepared after Members had requested for "additional information regarding existing international instruments relevant in the field of domestically prohibited goods (DPGs), with a view to facilitating identification of possible gaps in the product coverage." This report provided Members with a detailed survey of product coverage and information exchange mechanisms that existed in other international fora. Several Members had requested that DPGs be dealt with in a more specific and technical forum. The report details four broad categories of potential DPGs, which include chemicals such as pesticides and fertilizers, pharmaceutical products, consumer products, and hazardous wastes. It also specifies the international instruments operated by specialized UN agencies that oversee the international governance of these DPGs. These agencies came into force after the issue of DPGs was first raised at the GATT in 1982.

(19) ***The Relationship between the Convention on Biological Diversity (CBD) and the Agreement on the TRIPS; with Focus on Article 27.3 (B)*, WT/CTE/W/125 (1999)** The "CBD Report" was issued by the WTO

Secretariat as a factual paper that discussed the relationship between the CBD and the TRIPS Agreement. The discussions on this relationship, until the issuance of this report, had been quite contentious. A clear gap had developed with no clear demarcation between developed and developing Members' interests. The report provided an overview of existing international instruments relevant to plant variety protection and introduced information provided by WTO Members to the TRIPS Council on their sui generis systems. The report concludes with examples of domestic legislation enacted to implement the CBD in Members. This report provided clarity to the Members on the relationship between the CBD and TRIPS Agreement. Eventually, the discussions moved forward at the TRIPS Council. This is an item that could be ripe for dropping from the CTE work program.

(20) ***Discussion Paper on the Environmental Effects of Services Trade Liberalization*, WT/CTE/W/218 (2002):** The WTO Secretariat prepared a background document on the effects of services trade liberalization on the environment.[76] This was an exploratory paper that studied the potential effects of services liberalization on tourism, land freight transport (interurban), and environmental services. This document did not yield any output to the discussions since it only briefly considered the horizontal issues of how to assess the environmental effects of services trade liberalization. However, it did set the tonality of subsequent discussions and was used as a reference tool by Members when more specific negotiations took place under the CTESS.

These work outputs have not as of yet led to actual new rules, though in some instances, over time they have evolved into practice, such as the practice of information exchanges and coordination, and could arguably be thought of as evolving into soft law or best practices, that could eventually lead to new rules. These outputs are, of course, subject of further discussion in the succeeding chapters on the suggested applicable theoretical frameworks in Chapter 3 and the more detailed review of the work of the CTE in Chapters 4-6. Table 2.10 provides an easy reference guide to the twenty Key CTE Work Outputs.

76. WTO CTE, Discussion Paper on the Environmental Effects of Services Trade Liberalization, Note by the Secretariat, WT/CTE/W/218 (2002).

Table 2.10 CTE CTESS Key Work Outputs

Output No.	*First Publication Date*	*Document Codes*	*Output Document Title*	*Agenda Number*	*2nd Agenda Number*	*Page Count*
1	January 1, 1999	WTO	WTO Special Studies No. 4 Trade and Environmental (a key study updating the prior 1991 GEMIT Note on Trade and Environment)	1	5, 6	109
2	September 19, 2000	WT/CTE/W/160 (Rev 1 to Rev 8, 2001, 2003, 2005, 2007, 2011, 2013, 2015, 2017)	CTE Matrix on Trade-Related Measures Pursuant to Selected MEAs ("STO Inventory")	1		193
3	March 8, 2002	WT/CTE/W/203	WTO Secretariat Note on GATT/ WTO Dispute Settlement Practice Relating to GATT Article XX, paragraphs (b), (d), and (g)	1		48
4	June 6, 2001	WT/CTE/W/191 (2001)	WTO UNEP Joint Note on Compliance and Dispute Settlement Provisions in the WTO and in MEAs	1		27
5	June 5, 2002	WT/CTE/W/209 (2002)	MEA Information Session on Technical Assistance, Capacity Building and Enhancing Information Exchange (Inputs from WTO, UNEP, and MEA Secretariat)	1		12
6	April 21, 2011	TN/TE/20 (April 21, 2011), Annex I	CTESS Draft Ministerial Decision on Trade and Environment (2011)	1	5	10
7	June 4, 2007	WT/CTE/W/245 (2007-2008)	List of ERs ("Notifications")	2		8
8	August 29, 1995	WT/CTE/W/10; G/TBT/W/11 (1995)	CTE TBT Note on Negotiating History of the Coverage of the Agreement on TBT with Regard to Labelling Requirements, Voluntary Standards, and Processes and Production Methods Unrelated to Product Characteristics	3	3b	54
9	May 2, 1997	WT/CTE/W/47 (1997)	CTE Note on Taxes and Charges for Environmental Purposes—BTA	3	3a	21
10	June 29, 2000	WT/CTE/W/150 (2000)	CTE Note on Information Relevant to the Consideration of the Market Access effects of Eco-Labelling Schemes	3	3b	15
11	June 26, 2009	WTO UNEP	2009 WTO UNEP Climate Change Report	3		194
12	September 29, 2010	JOB/TE/9 (2010)	CTE Note on Eco-labelling: Overview of Current Work in Various International Foras	3	3b	5

Output No.	*First Publication Date*	*Document Codes*	*Output Document Title*	*Agenda Number*	*2nd Agenda Number*	*Page Count*
13	April 29, 1997	WT/CTE/EDB/1 to 18 (2001-2018); WT/CTE/W/46, 77, 118, 143, 195 (1996-2000)	EDB (for years 1996-2018; and formal EDB Series 2001-2019) (publication dates 1997-2019)	4		18
14	December 8, 2006	WT/CTE/W/244 (2006)	CTE Note on Environmental Requirements and Market Access: Recent Work in OECD and UNCTAD	6		14
15	September 17, 2007	JOB (07)/137 (2007)	CTESS Revision of the Synthesis of Submissions on Environmental Goods in TN/TE/W/63, 17 November 2005	6		35
16	April 21, 2011	TN/TE/20 (2011), Annex II	CTESS Annex II on Structure of the Outcome Environmental Goods Coverage Under paragraph 31(iii)	6		33
17	April 21, 2011	TN/TE/20 (2011), Annex IIA; JOB/TE/3 (March 22, 2010); JOB/TE/3/Rev.1 (January 5, 2011)	CTESS Reference Universe of Environmental Goods: Official Harmonized System Description (Based on Compilation of Submissions under paragraph 31(iii) of Doha relevant to the CTESS Work Program, JOB/TE/3 (March 22, 2010); JOB/TE/3/Rev.1 (January 5, 2011)	6		128
18	May 14, 1996	WT/CTE/W/29 (1996)	CTE Note on Item 7: DPGs, Assessment of the Product Coverage in Specific International Instruments ("DPG Report")	7		14
19	October 5, 1999	WT/CTE/W/125 (1999)	CTE Note on the Relationship between the Convention on Biological Diversity (CBD) and the Agreement on the TRIPS; with focus on Article 27.3 (B)	8		33
20	October 3, 2002	WT/CTE/W/218 (2002)	CTE Note on Items 6 and 9, Discussion Paper on the Environmental Effects of Services Trade Liberalization	9		12
Total						1,064

CHAPTER 3

Theories of Trade and Environment Governance

At the end of the day, the balancing between trade and environmental objectives will involve difficult choices, which will have economic consequences. Until the CTE becomes more "action-oriented" towards dealing with what are key political choices, it cannot be expected that it will be the forum where these issues are ultimately resolved.[77]

Richard Tarasofsky in 1999

I think it's important to reason from first principles rather than by analogy. The normal way we conduct our lives is we reason by analogy. We are doing this because it's like something else that was done, or it is like what other people are doing. Slight iterations on a theme ... "first principles" is a physics way of looking at the world. What that really means is that you boil things down to the most fundamental truths and then reason up from there. That takes a lot more mental energy.[78]

Elon Musk, Forbes Man of the Year 2013

77. Richard Tarasofsky, "The WTO Committee on Trade and Environment: Is it Making a Difference?" *in The Max Planck Yearbook of United Nations Law* (Jochen Frowein and Rüdiger Wolfrum (eds.)) pp. 471-488, at 488 (1999).
78. *See* Foundation 20, Elon Musk Interview, available at: https://www.youtube.com/watch?v=L-s_3b5fRd8 (accessed on November 30, 2019); for relevant transcript *see also* First Principles: The Building Blocks of True Knowledge, Farnam Street Blog, available at: https://fs.blog/2018/04/first-principles/#_ftn7 (accessed on November 30, 2019).

§3.01 THE NEED FOR A THEORETICAL FRAMEWORK

In the previous chapter, we went through the gamut of the prehistory and conception of the CTE, the basic structure of the CTE's ten-point agenda and mandate, and the system and structure of the CTE documentation and processes. This all provides the backdrop of the CTE's work and debates, the substance of which will be discussed in detail in the following Chapter 4 through Chapter 6. This chapter provides the three theoretical frameworks or lenses that could assist in evaluating, understanding and appreciating, all the work documentation and efforts that have been, and are being, put into the CTE, CTESS, and other related WTO committees and working groups.[79]

Given the ad hoc nature and history of the CTE work agenda, a key purpose of having an analytical frame would also lead to the ability to both understand better the thematic work areas of the CTE work agenda as well as suggest more targeted reforms for modernizing the CTE mandate or modernizing of the CTE mandate. After all, as detailed in Chapter 2, the ad hoc work agenda that was first conceived in 1971 for the predecessor GEMIT, in conjunction with the seminal Report on Industrial Pollution and Control (citing the 1920 Pigou theory of externalities and social costs of pollution) has only slightly been updated and expanded in three instances, in 1991, 1994 and 2001.

While there is much literature on IO performance, and methodologies for evaluating institutional quality, which is useful and partially utilized in this book, an obstacle for the CTE work processes being properly appreciated, is again due to its ad hoc and inter-regime or interdisciplinary nature. The CTE is a creature that straddles the policy regimes of trade and environment governance, and for some, it is even straddling three policy regimes if development is to be counted as a stand-alone policy regime, as many would posit.

For this book, it is submitted that an assessment of the CTE's work and performance, would not be feasible without developing some frame or lens by which the evaluation is to be made. Even more significant, a frame of assessment would assist greatly if the goal were to provide some basis of fashioning reforms or even a fundamental re-think and update of its two-decade-old ten-point work agenda.

While these theoretical approaches are only tools for analysis and understanding of the ongoing work of the CTE, as well as methods of applying first principles thinking, the use of these analytical frames is significant and serves the dual purpose of:

(a) aiding practitioners and policy researchers in better understanding the different components of work of the CTE under the various thematic areas to allow a more coherent and objective evaluation and appreciation of the work processes and outputs to enable better functional utilization of the said work outputs of the CTE by the various policy experts, negotiators and concerned community with interface with the CTE; and

79. These documentation and efforts emanate not only from the WTO membership and their experts and officials from capital and in Geneva but also from the intergovernmental organizations and the sixteen MEA's that have presented and participated in the sessions of the CTE.

(b) guiding the CTE, and the experts and administrators within the WTO, the Ministers and member governments of the WTO to which it is ultimately accountable, as well as to the overseers and constituents of the CTE outside the WTO, in fashioning an updated, modernized mandate for the CTE.

We can already conclude from the CTE work outputs described in Chapter 2 that much has been accomplished by the CTE, albeit in varying degrees of completion, in respect of its various work mandates, especially for example, in terms of the inter-agency and intergovernmental coordination and exchange, and rendering available to the universe of policy experts the latest catalogs of NEMs as well as maintaining a knowledge base of STOs in MEAs. Also evident is the level of expert discussions on potential work in the areas of services, DPGs, TRIPS, carbon taxation, climate goods, and subsidy regulations.

At the outset, it is noted, as already mentioned in the introduction, that negative perceptions and prejudgments of the work of the CTE do prevail in the sense of its having failed in its work.[80] Such perceptions certainly further motivate the need for defining the appropriate analytical perspectives as an objective evaluation would vary depending on the thematic area of work being reviewed. This will be evident in the discussions and review of CTE work detailed in Chapters 4 through 6, on the different areas of work of the CTE, necessitating the utilization of varying theoretical approaches or frameworks. This is required given the distinctive and differing nature and purposes of the ten-point work agenda of the CTE or the applicable thematic areas of work. It is submitted that it will be difficult to have a singular frame of reference for the differing types of activities or objectives of the CTE as contained it its work program. At the same time, it is also submitted that, with the use of the appropriate theoretical lens in accordance with the specific thematic area or objective, the appreciation and evaluation of the CTE processes, as well as fashioning reforms or formulating an updated mandate for the CTE, becomes more facile and productive to the evaluator or policy expert.

There necessarily are distinct strands of thinking and metrics for appreciating the work done to date by the CTE. While these strands do come from differing vantage points, they greatly assist in the overall understanding, as well as the fashioning of reforms or formulation of an updated mandate for the CTE and creating benchmarks for the performance and work of the CTE today and going forward. Part of the question relates to how the frame is to be set for the mentioned three generalized work categories of the CTE, i.e.:

(i) the primary work on regime norms interface and conflict, as well as inter-regime coordination and cooperation;
(ii) primary or secondary R&D for new, evolving or highly specialized or technical expert issues; and

80. *See*, e.g., Vol Molkte (1996); Steve Charnovitz, *The WTO's Environmental Progress*, 10(3) J. Int'l Econ. L. 685 (2007); Michael M. Weinstein and Steve Charnovitz, *The Greening of the WTO*, 80 Foreign Aff. 147 (2001).

(iii) the work relating to economic and commercial issues of market access improvements and trade enhancing/restricting modalities.

Before discussing in detail the different theoretical approaches to trade and environment governance at the CTE, Table 3.1 provides a graphic reference point for the three theoretical lenses that this book utilizes, as discussed below in evaluating and understanding the CTE work.

Simply as a mnemonic for identifying easily the analytical frame one ought to be utilizing, in a particular instance, one can place oneself temporarily (*în sens virtuelle*) in the mind of one's preferred political philosopher, with each frame necessarily having an assigned ideological patron or muse. The key approach or root of the first is necessarily classical positive law theory, IL-oriented, and hence, Westphalian, with the primary actors being states and governments, and philosophically attuned to the Hobbesian or Hardin's perspective of the need for a *global rule of law* for preventing the tragedy of the commons. The muse for this would be Leviathan or some such other symbol.

The muse for the second approach, a lens that maintains up to a point and only if convenient, its central or core state actor orientation, resurrects an ancient sage in the person of Plato together with his theories of the ideal Republic, having a sage/philosopher based sovereignty.

Table 3.1 Table of Governance Theories/Approaches

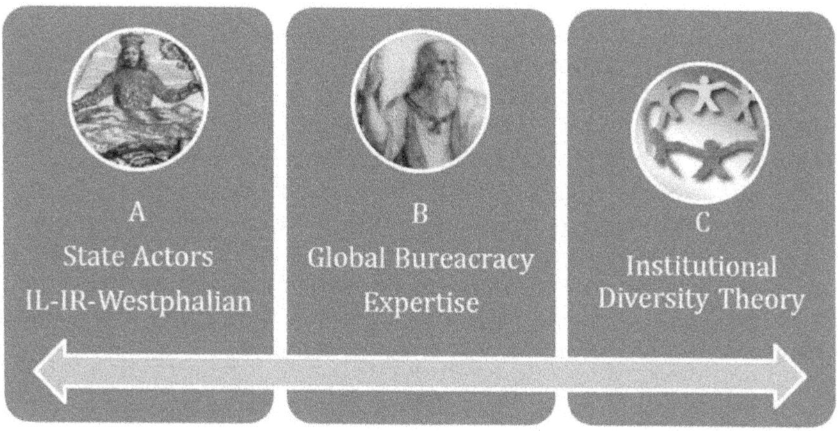

	Lens A	*Lens B*	*Lens C*
Basic Theory	Global IL-IR Rulemaking Policy Coordination Cooperation	Managerial, Experts, Transgovernmental Regulatory Networks (TRNs), Guaranteed Access Levels (GALs)	Institutional Diversity
Key Players, Constituents	State Actors, Governments, IOs, Secretariats, TRNs	Bureaucrats, Secretariats, TRNs, Managers, Experts	Communities, Local Authorities, CPRs
Key Principles	Rule of Law, Norm Creation, Policy Regimes, Global Governance, Harmonization, Formal / Informal Law and Policy Making	Global Knowledge and Expertise, Technical Capacity, Best Practices, Experience Sharing,	Self-Governance, Non-Experts, Institutional Diversity, Regional, Transfer of Technology
CTE Work Areas	(Chapter 4) CTE 1, 2, 4, 5, 10	(Chapter 5) CTE 3a, 3b, 7, 8, 9	(Chapter 6) CTE 6, 31iii
Secondary CTE Work	CTE 3a, 3b, 7, 8, 9 CTE 6	CTE 1, 2, 4, 5, 10 CTE 6	CTE 1, 2, 4, 5, 10 CTE 3a, 3b, 7, 8, 9
Scope of Work	Trade and Environment Interface, Norms Hierarchy, Transparency, MEA Secretariats, Information Exchange, Policy Formulation and Coordination	Specialized Expert Regulations, Carbon, Climate, Border Taxes, DPGs, TRIPS/CBD, Services	Market Access Issues and Modalities and Environment Measures with Market Mechanisms

The muse could well be Confucius or the *Système Grands Ecoles* of France or any other philosophical system, that while still preserving its state-centered approach, emphasizes knowledge, credentials, and expertise as the ultimate best solution for also avoiding a *tragedy of the commons*. The modern-day manifestation of this theory would be the international civil service of the UN and the WTO, where there is a constant search for the best talents and the most knowledgeable in the relevant fields of expertise, and the use of *Green Rooms* or *back rooms* and the propagation of Transnational Regulatory Networks (TRNs) and Global Administrative Law (GAL) practitioners.

The third approach would be an anti-theory approach up to a point, while at the same time providing a contrary more positive view of the fundamental nature of man and mankind as not pre-destined to ruin or to self-interest. Lens C finds its modern-day muse in the Nobel laureate Elinor Ostrom and her community-based decentralized *non-Washington consensus* approach to trade and environment governance and policy making. Immanuel Kant may provide some initial inspiration as many have attributed to him the seeds of the more modern IL concept of the common heritage of mankind (*CHM*). While many thinkers would co-opt Kant and the *CHM* towards achieving a single unitarian global governance system, espoused and promoted by the two earlier theoretical approaches, Lens C focuses on the decentralized regional or community-based decision-making process that is captured by Elinor Ostrom's theories.

The following three sections of this chapter discuss the literature relevant to the CTE and the three mentioned frameworks. As a general *caveat*, it must be kept in mind that as tools for analysis, the concepts and ideas do overlap among the differing frameworks. All of them have a common public policy or public good in mind of improving trade and environment interface and governance, with not a single one of the three theories superior to the others, as their applicability or relevance would depend in large part on the CTE function or objective in question.

§3.02 THE LENS OF AN INTERNATIONAL RULE OF LAW

> *Each man is locked into a system that compels him to increase his herd without limit—in a world that is limited. Ruin is the destination toward which all men rush, each pursuing his own best interest in a society that believes in the freedom of the commons. Freedom in a commons brings ruin to all.*
>
> Garret Hardin
> Tragedy of the Commons
>
> *...in the first place, I put for a general inclination of all mankind, a perpetual and restless desire of power after power, that ceaseth only in death. ... During the time men live without a common power to keep them all in awe, they are in that condition called war; and such a war, as if of every man, against every man.*
>
> Thomas Hobbes
> Leviathan 1651

The first framework certainly provides the classic legal positivist approach, together with the IL and International Relations (IR) perspectives of power, leverage, and centralized rulemaking. In utilizing this frame for the CTE, there are nuances of the theory that allow some leeway for deriving benefits from the work done and the outputs generated to date, such as the STOs inventory and other transparency mechanisms that are essential building blocks for policymaking and policy coordination. This is especially so in the realm of the hierarchy of norms and trade and environment policy regime conflicts.

From the primary theoretical perspective, there are two sub-strands of thinking that, while heading towards contrary assessments, equally encourage a review of the primary sources of CTE materials. First, and quite credibly, is the considered view that the physical evidence of zero treaty or new rules having resulted from the CTE leaves little room but to logically deduce that the 1994 decision creating the CTE was a failure; and the only thing worse than failure is the second failure of not learning from the first one. Confirming this negative assessment requires, in any case, a study of the body of work of the CTE.

As illustrated by the work by Barrett (2003), Levy (1993, 1995) and others, there are a wealth of studies on failures and deficiencies in environmental treaty-making, and that these studies of failures in treaty and rulemaking can be good sources of lessons as are certainly the successes such as the Montreal Protocol.[81] It had already been recommended by several writers in 1996 when the first WTO Ministerial Conference was considering whether to continue with its work, that the CTE be abolished as in their view, the CTE had failed to achieve any of its objectives.[82]

The challenge will lie in how much coherence and consistency can be gleaned from the over 12,000 or so pages of CTE and GEMIT documentation while at the same time keeping a strong guard on the importance of deriving value from already existing

81. There are many studies on environmental treaty making and documented studies on the various subjective theories on criteria and formulae, not least of which is the contrast often made between the Montreal and Kyoto Protocols. Most interesting and relevant would be the approaches that deal with a theory on the evolution of international cooperation as part of a process of strategic environmental treaty making. *See*, e.g., Scott Barrett, *Environment and Statecraft: The Strategy of Environmental Treaty Making* (2006) where he observes that treaty failures might create incentives for negotiating the next treaty and to seek treaty success. *See also generally* Marc A. Levy, "International Cooperation to Combat Acid Rain" *in Green Globe Yearbook of International Cooperation on Environment and Development* (Helge Ole Bergesen, Georg Parmann, and Øystein B. Thommessen (eds.)) (1995); Andrew Linklater, *Men and Citizens in the Theory of International Relations*, 2nd edn. (1990); and Mark A. Levy, "European Acid Rain: The Power of Tote-Board Diplomacy" *in Institutions for the Earth: Sources of Effective International Environmental Protection—Global Environmental Accord: Strategies for Sustainability and Institutional Innovation* (Peter M. Haas, Robert O. Keohane, and Marc A. Levy (eds.)) 75 (1993).

82. To do so could be more of the same and of no value. As already advocated in 1996 by one commentator: "The CTE is a waste of time and money and threatens to stand in the way of real environment progress." *See*, Steve Charnovitz, *A Critical Guide to the WTO's Report on Trade and Environment*, 14 Ariz. J. Int'l & Comp. L. 370, at 370 (1997). My only concern on taking this approach would be the difficulty of confirming the conclusion absent a fairly comprehensive study—it is similar to the conundrum that "*only by going to hell can one finally say in fact that there is no hell*" and if it happens to in fact exist, well there is the *catch 22*, one is stuck there unless there is a way to go to hell and back, as some theorists would attempt to opine (if that makes sense at all). In any event, it *is a catch 22* situation—one simply has not choice in scientific research to attempt to verify the two propositions, which, require the road to be taken of examining the work of the CTE.

written accounts or studies that focus specifically on the work of the CTE. Among these would be the early work conducted by Charnovitz (1997 and 1999) and Tarasofsky (1999) when both writers lamented the lack of positive contributions by the CTE and, in Charnovitz's case, advocating for the abolition of the CTE or changing its work mandate to make it more balanced.[83] These assessments are based on the first few years' works of the CTE, which makes them valuable reference benchmarks in examining whether the later work of the CTE provided any additional value as to render these early criticisms of the CTE less valid today.

The second sub-strand of the general positive law theory perspective involves the interface of IL with IR perspectives of institution-building and evolutionary rule and policymaking. Of relevance is the IL and IR and regime/institutional-building theorist approach in Steinberg's seminal work on *Trade-Environment Negotiations in the EU, NAFTA and WTO: Regional Trajectories of Rule Development*,[84] which, taken together with the work of Barrett (2003), provides great insight on the importance of power politics and financial incentives as key factors to ensure successful environmental treaty negotiations and the attainment of global environmental governance goals.[85]

McCormick (2006)[86] and Watson (2013)[87] provide more recent studies and treatment of the work at the CTE with their own recommendations on the need for improved procedures and changes to the work mandate of the CTE, which are considered in the conclusions of this book. McCormick pointedly recommends a review and updating of the CTE work program, including a more interactive and reflexive structure, taking into account the already existing information exchanges with MEAs, an approach, and recommendations well-supported by the current preliminary results and findings in this book.[88]

[A] The IL-IR Institutional Theories Context

Hence in the call for openness and *first principles*, the interdisciplinary approach could assist in providing the general approach to the study. Of course, much has been written on the evolving or already evolved, *international law of cooperation* and the fusion of IL and IR approaches in the field of trade, development, and environmental governance since these three policy regimes are well-suited to engage in quite apt rational-choice

83. *Ibid.*; and *see generally* Richard Tarasofsky, "The WTO Committee on Trade and Environment: Is it Making a Difference?" *in The Max Planck Yearbook of United Nations Law* (Jochen Frowein and Rüdiger Wolfrum (eds.)) 471-488, at 488 (1999).
84. Richard H. Steinberg, *Trade-Environment Negotiations in the EU, NAFTA, and WTO: Regional Trajectories of Rule Development*, 91(2) AJIL 231 (1997).
85. *See also*, on the importance of financial incentives in treaty ratification and accession, Andrew Pfluger, *Why the Montreal Protocol Is Not a Template for Multilateral Environmental Agreements: An Examination of why China and India Ratified*, 43 Middle States Geographer 96 (2010).
86. Rachel McCormick, *A Qualitative Analysis of the WTO's Role on Trade and Environment Issues*, 6(1) Global Envtl. Pol. 102 (2006).
87. *See generally* Chapter 6 titled "Environment under the WTO and the CTE", James J.R. Watson, *The WTO and the Environment* (2013).
88. Rachel McCormick, *A Qualitative Analysis of the WTO's Role on Trade and Environment Issues*, 6(1) Global Envtl. Pol. 102, at 121 (2006).

game theoretics, in order to achieve the tenuous common objective of an effective system of global governance.

Andonova and Elsig (2010) and Pauwelyn et al. (2012) discuss the growth of Informal International Public Policy Making (IIPPMs) and the levels of informal rulemaking as part of evolving international governance mechanisms.[89] More recently, Elsig, Hoekman and Pauwelyn concluded that a “more holistic approach allows understanding the multitude of objectives an organization such as the WTO can serve and also sends a warning signal to having unrealistic expectations about the role of international institutions.”[90]

Table 3.2, which is based on their findings, discusses the IL-IR disciplines, as well as the economic/trade policy regime perspectives, and the key objectives of each discipline in the functioning of the WTO.[91]

Table 3.2 Elsig, Hoekman and Pauwelyn (2017) Table of Disciplinary Objectives

Discipline	*Key Objectives*
IR	Rule of law against abuse of power
IR	Integrating emerging powers
IR	Performance in times of distress
IR	LDC Integration
IR	Enforcement/dispute settlement
Economics	Reducing trade barriers and agreeing to policy discipline
Economics	Avoiding protectionism during economic crisis
Economics	Increasing trade, integration and specialization
Economics	Enforcement of commitments
IL	Case-specific compliance
IL	Primary norm compliance
IL	Embeddedness effectiveness-direct effect
IL	Norm development

89. Liliana Andonova and Manfred Elsig, *Informal International Public Policy Making—A Conceptual View from International Relations* (Centre for Trade and Economic Integration 2010) available at: https://repository.graduateinstitute.ch/record/11747/?ln=en (accessed on November 30, 2019).
90. Manfred Elsig, Bernard Hoekman and Joost Pauwelyn, *Thinking about the Performance of the World Trade Organization: A Discussion Across Disciplines* (2016); *see also* Manfred Elsig studying the WTO system from Principal-Agent lens in Manfred Elsig, *The World Trade Organization at Work: Performance in a Member-Driven Milieu*, 5 Rev. Int. Organ 345-363 (2010).
91. Manfred Elsig, Bernard Hoekman and Joost Pauwelyn, *Thinking about the Performance of the World Trade Organization: A Discussion Across Disciplines*, EUI Working Papers, RSCAS 2016/13, 2016 at p. 16. *See also* Manfred Elsig, Bernard Hoekman and Joost Pauwelyn, “Thinking about the Performance of the World Trade Organization: A Discussion Across Disciplines” *in Assessing the World Trade Organization, Fit for Purpose?* (Manfred Elsig, Bernard Hoekman and Joost Pauwelyn (eds.)) 12 (2017).

Furthermore, Bernstein has argued that "[On] the one hand, social structure may legitimize forms of governance that may not coincide with what many environmentalists view as optimal ecologically, while on the other hand, non-state governance systems with a greater direct ability to tap into ecological and social concerns of core constituencies also face more stringent 'democratic' legitimacy demands."[92]

As a general matter, IR institutionalist theory has been the most accessible and constructive bridge between the realm of lawyers and political scientists for trade and environment governance. Haas, Keohane, and Levy (1993) tackle the issue of the *Sources of Effective International Environmental Protection* directly.[93] As observed by Keohane's since 1984,[94] in theory, states are still central actors but have been acting out of their rational self-interest in expanding cooperation. Coupling with this trend of cooperation has been the more humble approach of modern international legal scholars as to the role of law, and the rule of law, in global governance theory, as exemplified by Aceves (1997) and Slaughter (1997, 2004, 2011, 2013).[95]

These frameworks are useful in viewing the work of the CTE through the IR-IL lens of governance[96] through, and by, rational self-interested coordination, cooperation, and capacity building by state actors, national officials, and the increased use and dependence on technical expertise and networks of experts of both national governments, and in IOs. This aspect of the IL-IR perspective overlaps greatly with Lens B, but the emphasis and focus of the use of experts in this IL-IR framework maintain a strong rule and policy formulation objective, which distinguishes it from the managerial and rule by experts paradigm, that is more focused on managing results rather than formulating rules.

92. Steven Bernstein, *Legitimacy in Intergovernmental and Non-State Global Governance*, 18(1) Rev. Int'l Pol. Economy 43 (2011).

93. *See generally* Peter M. Haas, Robert O. Keohane, and Marc A. Levy, *Institutions for the Earth: Sources of Effective International Environmental Protection—Global Environmental Accord: Strategies for Sustainability and Institutional Innovation* (1993).

94. Robert O. Keohane, *After Hegemony: Cooperation and Discord in the World Political Economy* (1984).

95. William J. Aceves, *Institutionalist Theory and International Legal Scholarship*, 12(2) Am. U. Int'l L. Rev. 227 (1997); *see also* Anne-Marie Slaughter, *A New World Order* (2004); Anne-Marie Slaughter, *The Real New World Order*, 76 Foreign Aff. 183 (1997); and Anne-Marie Slaughter, "International Relations, Principal Theories" *in The Max Planck Encyclopedia of International Law* (RüdigerWolfrum (ed.)) at p. 1 (2011). *See also* Chapter 6 titled "Who is Who" and Chapter 7 titled "Negotiating Agreements" *in* Daniel Bodansky, *The Art and Craft of International Environmental Law* (2011).

96. Abraham Newman and David Zaring, "Regulatory Networks: Power, Legitimacy, and Compliance" *in Interdisciplinary Perspectives on International Law and International Relations: The State of the Art* (Jeffrey L. Dunoff and Mark A. Pollack (eds.)) (2013); *see also* Ian Johnstone, "Lawmaking by International Organizations: Perspectives from IL-IR Theory," Kal Raustiala, "Institutional Proliferation and the International Legal Order;" Daniel Bodansky, "Legitimacy in International Law and International Relations;" *in International Law and International Relations: The State of the Art* (Jeffery L. Dunoff and Mark A. Pollack (eds.)) at pp. 293-320; 321-342; pp. 266 –292 (2013).

Under the current framework and perspective, binding rules are the primary objective and are essential, even if they go the long route of varying stages of informal rulemaking. It is widely acknowledged that only through the foundations of binding treaty agreements can the next phase (*post hegemony*) of cooperation and coordination have the contextual strength to be of use to IL-IR theoreticians.

As stated succinctly by Keohane, Haas and Levy (1993):[97]

> [we] conclude that most effective institutions penetrate the state politically to a high degree ... outside the formal institutional apparatus. Indeed, intergovernmental organizations can be expected to be more effective as catalysts for transnational networks of nongovernmental networks and transgovernmental linkages among sympathetic governmental bureaucracies, than as independent actors.

Hard law and soft law are often considered in understanding and describing the nature of various international agreements. This is also true for IEAs. The basic characteristic that separates hard law from soft law is that hard law has specific binding obligations, whereas soft law is not legally binding or the obligations are flexible and lacking specificity. The term "soft law" could be considered paradoxical since laws are inherently authoritative, prescriptive, and binding in nature. Soft law originates when drafters introduce flexibility to texts, which include no set standard for compliance.[98] This leaves room for states to use their discretion and, thus, decisions can be taken through multilateral environment agreements (MEAs), which do not result in legal obligations.[99] Notably, the concept of soft law in international environmental law is the same as that within the realm of public IL. Therefore, the Stockholm Declaration of 1972, in adopting the *UN Conference on the Human Environment,* helped shape a normative framework of common principles for conservation and enhancement of the human environment.[100]

[B] The Role of the Evolution of Environment Law

In 1972, governments gathered for the *United Nations Stockholm Conference on the Human Environment* and established the UNEP, ushering in the modern era of international environmental law. Several important IEAs have since then been concluded by states. The subject matter and embedded legal and policy tools of many of these agreements are quite distinct not just from the previous IEAs but also from each

97. Peter M. Haas, Robert O. Keohane, and Marc A. Levy, *Institutions for the Earth: Sources of Effective International Environmental Protection: Global Environmental Accord: Strategies for Sustainability and Institutional Innovation)* at p. 24 (1993).
98. *See generally* Dinah L. Shelton, *Soft Law in Handbook of International Law* (2008) at pp. 1-4.
99. Gregory Shaffer and Mark Pollack, *Hard vs. Soft Law: Alternatives, Complements and Antagonists in International Governance*, 94 Minn. L. Rev. 709 (2010).
100. *See generally* Chapter 12 titled "Intergenerational Equity: A Legal Framework for Global Environmental Change," in Edith Brown Weiss, *Environmental Change and International Law: New Challenges and Dimensions* (1992).

other.[101] Present-day agreements are diverse in nature, text, and structure—seeking to control pollution, conserving habitats, and protecting global commons such as the ozone layer. For example, some agreements focused primarily on scientific research and monitoring of environmental issues so as to reduce certain identified pollutants while others required a reduction in pollutant emissions.

The interpretation of sources of IL was also strengthened with the introduction of the Vienna Convention on the Law of Treaties (VCLT) in 1969 and jurisprudence laid out by various international tribunals and the International Court of Justice (ICJ). Further, during this period, globalization also witnessed a proliferation of norms due to the introduction of non-state actors and individuals in the rulemaking process. This, along with the development of ILs and norms, capacity building and financing tools, and enhanced scientific networks, laid the foundation for a specialized discipline called environmental governance. Moreover, overlaps between different legal regimes, which are now entrenched in the firmament of public IL, such as the overlap between international environmental law and international economic law, have become common.

The CTE, in its initial discussions, actively debated the consequences of this overlap and for both the first and second frameworks, a great influence on the approaches to trade and environment governance is the great success and growth of MEAs entering into force, and this has given the lens of positive law and rulemaking a primary objective of trade and environment governance.

In sum, the first lens of traditional rulemaking becomes the main framework and metric when dealing with the areas of work of the CTE as it relates to the interface between trade and environment policy and issues related to the agenda work items under CTE 1, 5, 10 and CTE 2 and 4, which are covered in Chapter 4.

In the field of expert matters covered by Chapter 5, where the issues focus on the work of the CTE to increase capacity and knowledge on specialized topics, the influence or importance of this lens of rulemaking or treaty-making becomes less pronounced.

The lens of traditional rulemaking asserts itself again in Chapter 6, where CTE 6 and DDA 31iii issues are covered relating to improving market access. The importance of the formulation of new market access rules or trade modalities becomes evident in the desire to implement incentives or disincentives to promote environmental objectives. There is, however, great tension with the third lens (see section 3.04), as will be seen in the discussions in Chapter 6.

101. Carolyn Fischer, Sandra Hoffman and Yutaka Yoshino, *Multilateral Trade Agreements and Market-Based Environmental Policies* 2002).

§3.03 THE LENS OF THE RULE OF THE MANAGERS AND EXPERTS (TRNs, GAL)

Until philosophers are kings, or the kings and princes of this world have the spirit and power of philosophy, and political greatness and wisdom meet in one, and those commoner natures who pursue either to the exclusion of the other are compelled to stand aside, cities will never have rest from their evils — nor the human race, as I believe — and then only will this our State have a possibility of life and behold the light of day.

Plato, The Republic (c.375 B.C.)

The second theoretical framework arises from a more pragmatic approach to trade and environment governance, which involves a non-legal and non-traditional governance perspective as regards the inner workings of the WTO and its infrastructure of committees. The theory would seek to objectively assess the value and the nature of the contributions of the CTE and its performance as an institution in the context of the overall results and progress made in increasing expertise. It would appreciate the overall level of the administrative and expert ranks of trade and environment professionals and attaining influence towards promoting certain trade and environment principles and objectives. For example, Lang and Scott (2009),[102] posit in their piece *The Hidden World of WTO Governance* that there is more to the WTO than seeking binding, enforceable governance rules through the dispute settlement mechanism. Lang and Scott recommend (given difficulties besetting the Doha Round) on focusing instead on the "administrative hinterland"[103] and on the hidden functioning of these committees:

> [If there is] a broader shift in the role of the WTO, from a forum for the creation and enforcement of binding legal commitments to an institution for the supervision, monitoring, and management of (certain aspects of) the international trading system, then it is a relatively urgent task to build better maps and create thicker descriptions of what is going on within the administrative infrastructure of the WTO. The work of these committees, it should be acknowledged, is mundane: it is primarily concerned with the administration of trade agreements, deliberately eschews matters of high politics, is frequently technical, and is hardly noticed among most scholars of international organizations. But this is of course why we have chosen to study them—in our view, it is precisely on the basis of this ordinary world of apparently mundane activity, on the day-to-day interactions which together constitute the practice of governing, that we ought to build our understanding of what global governance is and ought to be.

Lang and Scott use three structural frameworks derived from trends in IL and IR institutional theories rooted in the rise of TRNs, global administrative law, and the emergence of a "managerialist" ethos in IL.

102. Andrew Lang and Joanne Scott, *The Hidden World of WTO Governance*, 20 Eur. J. Int'l L. 575 (2009).
103. *Id.* at 576.

The focus of the initial work of Lang and Scott were the work of the CTS (Council for Trade in Services) and the SPS Committee. They identify trends in the workings of these committees as aiding in areas such as norm elaboration, a shared and common knowledge base, rules harmonization, and a process of information exchange and coordination.

Horn, Mavroidis and Wijkstrom (2013), more recently, sought to illuminate us on the inner workings and hidden value of these administrative, coordinative and information gathering and exchange functions of the TBT and SPS committees of the WTO with a specific focus on the practice of raising specific trade concerns (STCs) in these committees. Horn, Mavroidis and Wijkstrom argue that these informal interactions play a larger role than perceived, by ensuring smoother trading relations and preventing trade frictions from requiring higher-level legal remedies through the formal dispute settlement mechanisms of the WTO.[104]

Ala'i (2008), in turn, emphasizes the rise of the regulatory state and the global regulatory, administrative regime, and the role of international obligations of transparency and good governance from a legal perspective.[105] She observes an evolving entrenchment of the obligation as a principle of WTO dispute settlement. Ala'i theorizes that the hortatory principles of transparency and good governance evolve to be universally required and enforceable tenets under WTO rules. It would be good to examine the value of information exchange carefully, coordination, and technical expert functions of WTO standing committees as these practices, as posited by the frameworks of Lang and Horn et al., could lead to the formulation of soft law and more standardized best practices.

In this context, the conversation on the research on the inner workings of the WTO encourages the work of examining in greater depth the work of the CTE and the GEMIT, and their underlying infrastructure, including its networking interface with MEA regimes. There could certainly be rich texture, as well as inevitable mundane-ness and repetition.

[A] The Managerial Model (Cooperation, Experts and Problem Solving)

Chayes & Chayes introduced the managerial model. This model relies on a "cooperative, problem-solving approach."[106] According to Chayes & Chayes, there are three primary reasons why states comply with IL.[107] *First*, upon compliance with an agreed international standard, a State does not need to calculate its costs and benefits after making the decision. More often than not, bureaucracies of states are inclined to follow

104. Henrik Horn, Petros Mavroidis and Erik N. Wijkstrom, *In the Shadow of the DSU, addressing Specific Trade Concerns in the WTO SPS and TBT Committees*, 47(4) J. World Trade 729 (2013).
105. Ala'i, Padideh. "From the Periphery to the Center? The Evolving WTO Jurisprudence on Transparency and Good Governance." Journal of International Economic Law 11 (2008): 779–802.
106. Abram Chayes and Antonia Handler Chayes, *The New Sovereignty: Compliance with International Regulatory Agreements* (1995).
107. Andrew T. Guzman, *A Compliance-Based Theory of International Law*, 90 Cal. L. Rev. 1823, at 1830 (2002).

the rule of law.[108] *Second*, since agreements are consent-based, it is assumed that they serve the interest of all participating states. States only enter into agreements that are in their interests. Treaties are not fixed. Rather, they are the objects of bargains and negotiation between states. Those negotiating on behalf of states are likely to be also responsible for enforcement and, therefore, will be mindful of the potential long-term implications for the State.[109] *Third*, legal norms constrain states. This is why states take care while negotiating international agreements.[110] Less effort would be put in negotiating international agreements if states did not believe that agreements would be enforced.

Chayes & Chayes also present three reasons for potential non-compliance with international agreements. *First*, ambiguity in treaty language can reflect a lack of political consensus for specific obligations. Paradoxically, a complicated treaty can also create an aura of ambiguity. Both these situations can test the acceptable limits of the treaty language. *Second*, many international agreements require the establishment of a domestic regulatory body that can oversee the functioning of the legislation in question. However, states that lack resources to implement such mechanisms are not in compliance with the agreement. This is particularly true for technical areas such as the environment. *Third*, many agreements are designed to govern State behavior over a long period of time. Therefore, it is important to note that what may seem to be non-compliance might actually be the first step in what eventually becomes a series of agreements leading to compliance.[111]

The *Managerial Model* is called as such because it introduces management tools such as transparency, reporting, verification and monitoring, dispute resolution, and capacity building—all of which are aimed at encouraging compliance.[112] The core principle of this model is the emphasis on the interdependence of the community of states. Koh has noted that this model encourages compliance for fear of loss of reputation and not of sanction.[113] While sound when describing the matrix of coordination agreements, the managerial model is useful but not complete, and it is discussed more in line with its complementarity to the other sub-strands that lie at the foundation of our second theoretical frameworks, such as the growth of networks of experts and managers.

Lang and Scott also cited in their 2009 paper the rise of *managerialism* in international lawmaking. According to them, the colonization of international politics by professional experts and the technical nature of the ensuing discussions introduce

108. Abram Chayes and Antonia Handler Chayes, *On Compliance*, 47(2) Int'l Org. 175, at 178 (1993).
109. *Id.* at 179-185.
110. *Id.* at 185-187.
111. *See generally* Andrew T. Guzman, *A Compliance-Based Theory of International Law*, 90 Cal. L. Rev. 1823, at 1830 (2002).
112. *See generally* Abram Chayes, Antonia Handler Chayes and Ronald B. Mitchell, "Managing Compliance: A Comparative Perspective" *in Engaging Countries: Strengthening Compliance with International Environmental Accords* (Edith Brown Weiss and Harold Jacobson (eds.)) at p. 39 (1998).
113. Harold Hongju Koh, *Why Do Nation Obey International Law?* 106 Yale L. J. 2555, at 2636 (1997).

a more dynamic aspect where traditional political processes are replaced by more technocratic and precise discussions. This process has also been cited by Koskenniemi[114] as a type of "deformalization" within international institutions that could lead to alternative formulations of global rules.

The mindset of a manager would, according to this theory, move in parallel with, and could at times whelm, the more formal process-based directives generally used for administration of international problems. As Lang and Scott note, "the result is a movement towards technocratic, expert-oriented forms of governance, through the transnational consolidation of global professional cultures and transnational networks of expertise common to specific functional issue areas."[115]

The experts are known to be held together by shared knowledge. They have a common way of analyzing problems and coming out with solutions. They also generally share similar professional training.[116] Unlike conventional politics, the primary role played by actors according to this model relates to "the knowledge that they create, disseminate, and deploy, and in the shared vocabularies which structure their thought and action." Therefore, socialization plays an important role in maintaining a common framework of norms. Furthermore, Lang and Scott observe that power is exercised on the basis of professional or scientific techniques. This exercise of power works through persuasion and deployment of information and knowledge via particular cultures of rationality. These networks are oriented to finding solutions to a given problem through cooperation and not political contest. In one sense, larger questions of global governance are debated within the context of the question at issue and the specialist knowledge and professional discipline required.

Lang and Scott also note that there is deep skepticism about the entrenchment of expert networks. They quote Kennedy, who argued that only marginal opportunities for political contestation exist with the increase in such experts in rulemaking.[117] Because of this, there are often concerns about the ways in which the expert rules disguise political choices. They reason that: "[A]s a result, much work in this line is oriented precisely towards reopening space for politics within domains of apparently technical decision-making, and countering the self-presentation of expert decisions as 'determined, rather than free'." Networks created under the managerial model focus its attention, creating the foundational norms of international economic governance, unlike more politically conventional means such as negotiations and judicial decision-making.

Lang and Scott probe the functioning of WTO Committee work and compare it to the managerial governance method. In particular, they raise three questions. *First*, are

114. Martti Koskenniemi, *Global Governance and Public International Law*, 37(3) Kritische Justiz 241, at 245-249 (2004); *see also* Nico Krisch, "Weak as Constraint, Strong as Tool: The Place of International Law in US Foreign Policy" *in Unilateralism and US Foreign Policy International Perspectives* (David M. Malone (ed.)) at p. 49 (2003).
115. *Lang and Scott Hidden World of WTO Governance (2009)* at 611.
116. *Ibid.*
117. *Ibid.* citing David Kennedy, *Challenging Expert Rule: The Politics of Global Governance*, 27 Sydney J Int'l L 5, at 6 (2005) and David Kennedy, *The Politics of the Invisible College: International Governance and the Politics of Expertise*, 5 Eur. Hum. Rts. L. Rev. 463 (2001).

WTO Committees contributing to the managerial approach for the governance of international trade? *Second*, what are the effects of the managerial models on the authority and influence of experts within global governance? *Third*, what role do these practices play in the creation, maintenance, and evolution of forms of knowledge which structure the deployment of political powers in international life? After assessing the work of the Trade in Services Committee, Lang and Scott noted that the committee has acted as a venue for information exchange. The knowledge produced in this committee came by way of either Member's narration of their experiences in liberalizing its services economy or through formal presentations by the OECD and UNCTAD. They further noted that: "information exchange programs, mechanisms of peer review, workshops and seminars, and other activities described earlier demonstrate the increasing integration of the committee system, and the trade regime more generally, into existing networks of knowledge dissemination."[118] Besides this, Lang and Scott argued that Members also looked to expert communities for guidance for ambiguous legal concepts and normative questions. They agree that a more detailed account of professional know-how cultures is transforming the modalities of global governance.

[B] Global Administrative Law

The idea of global administrative law is coherent with the view of global regulatory governance. In this model, different levels of regulations are not separated as local, national, international laws and private standard settings, but much rather seen as a global administrative space that includes international institutions and transnational networks. These networks also include domestic administrative bodies operating within international regimes. This theory of global administrative law is different from the conventional understanding of IL, which is considered to be the law regulating conduct between states. Global administrative law, or GAL, does not make a distinction between international and domestic actors. According to Kingsbury:[119]

> In a world that is increasingly occupied by transnational private regulators, hybrid bodies such as public-private partnerships involving states or interstate organizations, national public regulators whose actions have external effects but may not be controlled by the central executive authority, informal interstate bodies with no treaty basis (including "coalitions of the willing"), and formal interstate institutions (such as those of the United Nations) affecting third parties through administrative-type actions. A lot of the administration of global governance is highly decentralized and not very systematic. Some entities are given roles in global regulatory governance, which they may not wish for or be particularly designed or prepared for. For instance, national courts may find themselves reviewing the acts of international, transnational and especially national bodies that are in effect administering decentralized global governance systems, and in some cases, the national courts themselves form part not only of the review but of the practical administration of a global governance regime.

118. *Lang and Scott Hidden World of WTO Governance (2009)* at 612.
119. Benedict Kingsbury, *The Concept of "Law" in Global Administrative Law*, 20(1) Eur. J. Int'l L. 23, at 25 (2009).

The emergence of GAL is directly proportionate to the increase in the reach and forms of transnational governmental regulation and its administration.[120] This takes place in the field of security, environmental protection, banking and finance, telecommunication, and trade in goods and services, to name a few. It is premised upon the assumption that isolated national regulatory authorities cannot effectively address several of the abovementioned global problems. As a result, various transnational systems of regulation have been established through treaties which shift the regulatory decision-making to a global level.[121]

According to Stewart and Badin, WTO offers examples of GAL since it includes:[122]

> the development of mechanisms for transparency, participation, and reason-giving in the internal administrative decision-making processes of global regulatory bodies; the absorption of global administrative law norms in states' domestic administrative structures and procedures; and the legal issues presented by increasingly close linkages among different global regulatory institutions.

The WTO has imposed strong requirements of transparency, participation, reason-giving, and review on members' domestic administrative bodies in order to protect foreign nations and economic actors against local regulatory protectionism and to secure intellectual property rights (IPR).[123] These domestic bodies form the distributed administration of the global trade regime. These GAL requirements have had a significant impact on domestic administration in many countries. GAL also finds potential for development in the TBT and SPS Agreements, which provide a presumptive legal "safe harbor" for members against challenges to domestic regulatory measures that have been based on international standards adopted by other global bodies.[124] Here, GAL issues are, at present, only incipient yet potentially significant. If the WTO, through its administrative and dispute settlement bodies, were to condition recognition of other global bodies' regulatory standards upon their observance of GAL norms of transparency, participation, and reason-giving, that would help to ensure that the standards to be accorded recognition are well informed and reflect a fair consideration of the interests at stake. Stewart and Badin note that "such a development, which would involve horizontal review by one global regulatory body of another's standards and procedures, would manifest the 'inter-public' character of global administration and law and create a platform for the further diffusion of GAL norms throughout the global administrative space."[125]

---

120. *Ibid.*
121. Benedict Kingsbury, Nico Krisch and Richard B. Steward, *The Emergence of Global Administrative Law, Introduction: The Unnoticed Rise of Global Administrative Law,* 68 L. & Contemp. Probs. 15, at 16 (2005).
122. Richard Stewart and Michelle Ratton-Sanchez Badin, *The World Trade Organization and Global Administrative Law* at p. 2 (Institute for International Law and Justice 2009).
123. *Ibid.*
124. *Id.* at pp. 2-3.
125. *Id.* at p. 2.

[C] Transgovernmental Regulatory Networks (TRNs)

Lang and Scott note that concerns are often accompanied by the rise of TRNs. This is because these networks seem to bypass traditional accountability mechanisms. Slaughter aptly defines the crux of the issue—the primary actors of TRNs are no longer always viewed as accountable to governments back in the Capital.[126] In studying the role of WTO committees in the development of TRNs, three questions were raised by Lang and Scott. *First*, who participates in the activities of these committees? *Second*, what kinds of accountability mechanisms were in place? *Third*, to what extent did this "hidden world" of WTO governance parallel the shadowy world of TRNs?

International or transnational cooperative initiatives amongst national regulators have been studied by IL and IR scholarship since the 1990s. Around that time, the Basel Committee adopted an international accord on bank capital adequacy, and IEAs were being negotiated, both of which included networks of domestic environmental and banking regulators.[127] A detailed theoretical structure introducing principle characteristics of these transnational networks was proposed by Raustiala and Zaring. According to them, the primary players in negotiating international cooperative agreements in transnational regulatory networks were not states but national regulatory authorities of these states.[128] These regulatory authorities did not have any legal personality beyond those that were conferred upon it by the states that hosted them. According to Verdier, they function:[129]

> by consensus without formal voting procedures, their membership is selective, and despite recent efforts at greater transparency, many of their important meetings and negotiations are kept secret until the resulting document is released.

Verdier further notes that the guidelines that they promulgate have no international legal status. They do not create obligations at IL and do not require domestic ratification procedures as treaties. Lastly, these networks do not formally monitor the implementation of their decisions or provide dispute resolution procedures. Raustiala argues that the rise of transnational regulatory networks (TRNs) through international cooperation among national regulatory agencies was a direct result of technological innovation, expansion of domestic regulation, and economic globalization.[130] One major development in TRNs has been the rise of transnational networks between cities

126. *See generally* Anne-Marie Slaughter, *The Accountability of Government Networks*, 8(2) Ind. J. Global Legal Stud. 347 (2001).
127. *See generally* Pierre-Hugues Verdier, *Transnational Regulatory Networks and Their Limits*, 34 Yale J. Int'l L. 114 (2009).
128. *Id.*, at 118 quoting Kal Raustiala, *The Architecture of International Cooperation: Transgovernmental Networks and the Future of International Law*, 43 Va. J. Int'l. L. 1 (2002-2003); *see also* David Zaring, *International Law by Other Means: The Twilight Existence of International Financial Regulatory Organizations*, 33 Tex. Int'l. L. J. 281 (1998).
129. Pierre-Hugues Verdier, *Transnational Regulatory Networks and Their Limits*, 34 Yale J. Int'l L. 118 (2009).
130. *Id.* at p. 119.

for environmental (mostly climate change) and sustainability matters.[131] Climate action by states and cities has been accelerated in the U.S. in particular as the federal government pulled out of the Paris Climate Agreement. Equally important was the crystallization of environmental issues, which required scientific know-how generally present in specialized environmental agencies. According to Zaring, regulators could also use these networks to free themselves from domestic constraints and pursue self-regarding aims.[132]

Lang and Scott note that the GATT and WTO systems have created "a governmental network of the second kind."[133] This includes a "relatively close-knit community of trade negotiators and governmental officials with a defined 'ethos,' a sense of common purpose, broadly shared normative commitments, and common ways of defining and analyzing problems."[134] In one sense, WTO Committees, according to Lang and Scott, represent one kind of social space in which shared ideas are enunciated, deliberated, and disseminated. An example is the Information Exchange program, which is conducted by the CTS, where common ways of describing or quantifying existing domestic challenges are shared by Members. The forum also functions as a platform for norm formulation and crystallization. Certain ambiguous WTO legal texts are discussed by Members, which ultimately lead to a degree of normative convergence. Moreover, activities in these committees have resulted in newer forms of TRNs. For example, the SPS Committee provides a forum for food safety regulators to exchange information and discuss common problems. According to Lang and Scott, this is in line with Zaring's description of TRNs being a "conduit for ongoing flexible relationships."[135] Notably, this relationship differs from different committees. For example, the SPS Committee has more direct participation of regulators when compared to the Services Committee.

The study by Lang and Scott has also provided support to Raustiala's proposition that formal treaty regimes need not be understood as alternatives to TRNs, but rather lead to the creation of such networks. Further, it has identified two models of interaction between WTO Committees and existing TRNs:[136]

> First, as our case studies illustrate, there are clearly occasions on which these committees act as conduits for the importation of policy ideas and forms of analysis from these networks to the trade community—another element, in other words, of a transgovernmental network's mechanism for the broad dissemination of common regulatory ideas and practices. In this model, interactions between

131. *Ibid.*; *see* Kal Raustiala, *The Architect of International Cooperation: Transgovernmental Networks and the Future of International Law*, 43 Va. J. Int'l. L. (2002). *See also* Wolfgang Haupt and Alessandro Coppola, *Climate Governance in Transnational Municipal Networks: Advancing a Potential Agenda for Analysis and Typology,* 11 (2) Int'l J. Urb. Sust. Dev. 123 (2019).
132. Pierre-Hugues Verdier, *Transnational Regulatory Networks and Their Limits*, 34 Yale J. Int'l L. 119 (2009); *see also* David Zaring, *International Law by Other Means: The Twilight Existence of International Financial Regulatory Organization*, 33 Tex. Int'l L.J. 281 (1998).
133. *Lang and Scott Hidden World of WTO Governance (2009)* at 604.
134. *Ibid.*
135. *See* David Zaring, *International Law by Other Means: The Twilight Existence of International Financial Regulatory Organizations*, 33 Texas Int'l L.J. 281 (1998).
136. *Lang and Scott Hidden World of WTO Governance (2009)* at 605.

formal regimes and networks can, to some extent, transform the former so that they take on some characteristics of networks as sites of learning and socialization. Secondly, we also saw the way that the international trade regime can actively support and encourage ongoing standard-setting efforts within transgovernmental networks.

[D] The Role of GATT Experts in the Success of the Montreal Protocol

Touched upon as well in the earlier section, there is also utility in studying the dynamics of the work of the CTE and the available literature on environmental treaty case studies. The trade and environment dialogue and establishment of the CTE was a result of multiple parallel developments at a time when great strides were being made in the area of environmental treaty-making. Much has been written on the approaches to environmental treaty-making and the successes and failures of various attempted solutions. One universally cited success story is the 1985 VCPOL and its 1987 Montreal Protocol.

A key feature in the history of how the Montreal Protocol came to be an environmental success story was the role of trade measures being agreed upon early in the negotiations as a viable and essential tool in the toolbox of implementation and enforcement for the reduction of harmful CFCs, HCFCs and related substances that were damaging the earth's stratospheric ozone layer. In particular, Article 4 of the protocol provided for an absolute trade ban of trade with non-parties:[137]

> Article 4:
> 1. As of 1 January 1990, each party shall ban the import of the controlled substances in Annex A from any State not party to this Protocol. ...
> 2. As of 1 January 1993, each Party shall ban the export of any controlled substances in Annex A to any State not party to this Protocol ... .

The literature would point to the GATT secretariat as having contributed, albeit implied by some accounts to be unintentional, to the final agreement to the inclusion of the said legally binding trade-restrictive provisions. According to Richard Benedick,[138] the chief U.S. negotiator:

> the EC Commission and U.K. representatives blocked further discussion of trade *until a legal expert from the General Agreement on Tariffs and Trade (GATT) secretariat could advise on the permissibility of such measures under existing international law.* The tactic backfired when the expert affirmed that trade restrictions were allowable under article XX of GATT, as they could be considered "necessary to protect human, animal, or plant life or health" and "relating to

137. UN Montreal Protocol on Substances that Deplete the Ozone Layer, September 16, 1987, 1522 U.N.T.S. 3.
138. Richard Elliot Benedick, *Ozone Diplomacy: New Directions in Safeguarding the Planet* (1998); *see also* Scott Barrett, *Climate Change and International Trade: Lessons on Their Linkage from International Environmental Agreements* at pp. 8-9 (2010) available at: https://repository.graduateinstitute.ch/record/296909?ln=en (accessed on November 30, 2019) (*citing* Stephen O. Andersen and K. Madhava Sarma, *Protecting the Ozone Layer: The United Nations History* (2002)).

conservation or exhaustion of exhaustible natural resources." *From this point on, a consensus inexorably grew that such measures were indispensable to the protocol's effectiveness.*

The point of the story for purposes of the current framework is to highlight the importance of experts and their roles in the dynamic of international treaty and rules negotiations, be they in the environmental governance area or in trade and development issues, and certainly, in the work mandate of the CTE.

Another example of such technical and cross-organization and cross-sector sharing of ideas and expertise would be the 2009 joint UNEP and WTO CTE Report on Trade and Climate Change that had a role in establishing a *clear enough* nexus for trade negotiators and delegates in the trade and climate change area in order to shift the level of engagement on trade and climate change at the CTE and which was formally launched at a special meeting of the WTO on June 26, 2009.[139] A section of the study focuses on these types of special expert reports that are generated from time to time.

If one is to report and evaluate the work of the CTE, research might be useful on the specific dynamics of the information exchange and related meetings and deliberations of the CTE, and these would not be limited in scope to CTE meetings of member delegations, and their national experts and negotiators. Part of the dynamic involves the professional and administrative workings of the CTE's secretariat and administrative infrastructure, and non-documented or un-captured exchanges that take place among diplomats, specialist delegates, international civil servants, internal and external organization experts, MEA representatives, Nongovernmental Organizations (NGOs), among others and more, that are of a reflexive or informal nature but could be part of the process of building TRNs with a common knowledge or technical expertise base.

In this regard, the evaluation and review of CTE documentation would also find relevant the reference to available internal notes and records, e.g., notes taken by meeting chairs, secretariat or delegation personnel, so-called non-papers, and drafts of proposals, conversations, interviews and recollections of meetings and negotiating sessions in informal and open-ended mode, press reports, informal recordings, and transcripts. Such material may aid, as well as muddle, the efforts towards creating the *thicker descriptions*, referred to by Lang and Scott (2009) of the mundane day-to-day process and work of governance by cooperation, coordination, and technical assistance among internal and external networks.[140]

139. The Secretariats of both the UNEP and WTO CTE worked hand in hand in delivering and drafting the special study which was launched by the top level officials of both organizations at the WTO on June 26, 2009. *See* WTO UNEP, *Trade and Climate Change Report (2009)* (2009); *see also* WTO Media releases, available at: http://www.wto.org/english/news_e/pres09_e/pr559_e.htm (accessed November 30, 2019).

140. Among the aids to obtain these thicker descriptions will be the resort to off the record interviews as well as internal notes and records of chairs on file with the author and others. Non-papers are what are commonly referred to as unofficial submissions and floating of ideas papers which have some value in the general appreciation of the processes of negotiating and drafting texts. *See also* Peter M. Haas, Robert O. Keohane, and Marc A. Levy, *Institutions for the Earth: Sources of Effective International Environmental Protection: Global Environmental Accord: Strategies for Sustainability and Institutional Innovation* at p. 24 (1993); Andrew Lang

Gutner also poses the issue of evaluating performance not only based on results but also on the quality of the process.[141] This is of particular significance, such as in the NAFTA/NAAEC context, where the process leads the way rather than insisting on an established hierarchy. The factors for IO Performance evaluation are important tools for potentially guiding in the reform and update of the CTE's work mandate and procedures. The use of this second theoretical framework becomes most prevalent and appropriate in Chapter 5, where the CTE work areas focus on specialist topics under agenda items CTE 3, 7, 8 and 9.

§3.04 THE THEORY OF INSTITUTIONAL DIVERSITY AND DECENTRALIZED GOVERNANCE: COMMON-POOL RESOURCES CPRs, GOVERNING THE COMMONS

> *Unfortunately, many analysts—in academia, special-interest groups, governments, and the press—still presume that common-pool problems are all dilemmas in which the participants themselves cannot avoid producing suboptimal results, and in some cases disastrous results.*
>
> Elinor Ostrom
> Governing the Commons 1990
>
> *For peace to reign on Earth, humans must evolve into new beings who have learned to see the whole first ... the Right, which the human species have in common to the surface of the earth, into a means for social intercourse.*
>
> Immanuel Kant
> Perpetual Peace 1795

Elinor Ostrom's work (1989, 1990) of managing the commons by developing community-based institutions serves as a cornerstone of inspiration for original ideas that the CTE might be able to utilize and, at the same time, as a frame by which the work of the CTE may be viewed as well. Ostrom's diversity thesis is a key lens in the IR Institutional theory perspective that will be relevant to the issues of trade and environment governance.[142] The theme of decentralization and the related literature that flows from Ostrom's work could be of some guidance as in the work of Breton et al. (eds.) (2007).[143]

Unlike Lang and Scott's legalistic approach to central governance, Elinor Ostrom's paradigm-shifting research on decentralization in community-based governance illustrated surprising applicability in explaining how community-based governance around the world sustained operational performance over long periods of time.

---

and Joanne Scott, *The Hidden World of WTO Governance*, 20 Eur. J. Int'l L. 575, at 604 (2009); and Abraham Newman and David Zaring, "Regulatory Networks: Power, Legitimacy, and Compliance" *in Interdisciplinary Perspectives on International Law and International Relations: The State of the Art* (Jeffrey L. Dunoff and Mark A. Pollack (eds.)) at p. 244 (2013).

141. *See generally* Tamar Gutner and Alexander Thompson, *The Politics of IO Performance: A Framework*, 5 (3) Rev. Int'l Org. 227 (2010) available at: https://link.springer.com/article/10.1007/s11558-010-9096-z (accessed on November 30, 2019).
142. *See generally* Ostrom (1990) *Governing the Commons*.
143. Albert Breton, et al., *Environmental Governance and Decentralisation* (2007).

Ostrom posed the question of how certain communities' institutional arrangements evaded the depletion of natural resources in a structured manner with a developed culture of sustainability, yet maintaining profitability. What organizational structure prevents herders from increasing their flocks to maximize their profits when the increased amount of sheep in the meadows results in overgrazing, which subsequently negatively affects every herder's profitability and future sustainability of the resources? Thus, the CPR deteriorates and as Hardin explains in his seminal work "Tragedy of the Commons": "each man is trapped into a system that compels him to increase his herd without limit—in a world that is limited."[144]

Consequently, this leads to the vicious cycle of mismanagement and overexploitation, which, in turn, leads to irreversible environmental degradation. Therefore, the "tragedy" in this behavior is that the actors exploiting CPRs are actually not behaving in self-interest in perpetuity. In the alternative, if actors work with each other, then they could establish a symbiotic system of beneficiaries of all stakeholders involved as well as a protection of the CPR itself. Hardin did not believe that such a degree of self-organization was possible and proposed two polarizing solutions: either establish private property over CPRs or establish the authority of a Leviathan central power posed by Hobbes. Ostrom, however, challenged the polarized solutions by rejecting the Leviathan approach of Hardin to attempt to answer the question of why certain communities do not overexploit natural resources. What is proposed is that the particularities of each individual CPR demand a more nuanced analysis in understanding how to minimize the risk of the individual's exponential and unsustainable use of the CPR.

According to Ostrom, the appropriators of the commons ought to be provided with considerable involvement in the creation of congruent rules governing the institution in order to be effective. Introducing a centralized state authority bears the risk of oversimplifying the issues at hand and simultaneously fails to recognize the idiosyncrasies of the particular CPR. One can purport to suggest that a centralized system can provide the simplest solution to address all the various institutions created by different communities. Ostrom does not consider a simple solution utilitarian. On the contrary, society and people are complex in all parts; therefore, to provide a simple solution to a complex problem is not a good idea as appealing minimalism may be.

Ostrom is of the view that involving the appropriators becomes imperative because they have generally developed an internal complex structure over a significant period of time, if not over generations, where trials and errors have developed resilience and robustness within the institutions themselves. Substituting these internal rules and norms by inexperienced decision-makers in a centralized setting risks simplification and disturbance of the internal checks and balances that operate. Although Ostrom does have a tendency to reject simplifications and generalizations, she does nonetheless embark on identifying underlying commonalities that could explain why certain CPR institutions operate successfully around the world. Ostrom argued that effective self-organizing actors and sustainably managed CPRs that ensure

144. *See generally* Gareth Hardin, *Tragedy of the Commons*, 162 Sci. 1243 (1968).

benefit to commons as well as the future generations of actors not only exist in theory but also in practice, in which communities have managed to establish rules that are congruent with the specific conditions operating in that particular environment. During her time, Ostrom examined several CPR institutions and environments to dissect the common grounds to conceptualize some principles.[145]

Although the case studies conducted consisted of a variety of institutions across the world, dealing with a myriad of CPR, each creating own local rules to administer the resources prudently, Ostrom had identified the underlying commonalities considered essential to robust CPR management listing the eight principles for the governance of CPRs. She presented these eight principles in her Nobel Prize lecture, and as being based on studies "by scholars who assessed the relevance of the principles as explanation of success or failure of diverse common-pool resources."[146]

Ostrom included in her Nobel lecture the listing of successful CPR governance design principles, which is reproduced *in toto* in Table 3.3.

145. Ostrom (1990) *Governing the Commons* at p. 61.

146. Ostrom (2009) *Beyond Markets and States* at p. 422, also available at: https://www.nobelprize.org/uploads/2018/06/ostrom_lecture.pdf (accessed on November 30, 2019). See, Cox, M., G. Arnold, and S. Villamayor-Tomás, *A review of design principles for community-based natural resource management*, 15(4) Ecology and Society 38 (2010), available at: http://www.ecologyandsociety.org/vol15/iss4/art38/ (accessed on November 30, 2019).

Table 3.3 Elinor Ostrom Design Principles (1990/2009)

Ostrom Design Principles for CPR Governance
1A. ***User Boundaries:*** *Clear and locally understood boundaries between legitimate users and nonusers are present.*
1B. ***Resource Boundaries:*** *Clear boundaries that separate a specific common-pool resource from a larger social-ecological system are present.*
2A. ***Congruence with Local Conditions:*** *Appropriation and provision rules are congruent with local social and environmental conditions.*
2B. ***Appropriation and Provision:*** *Appropriation rules are congruent with provision rules; the distribution of costs is proportional to the distribution of benefits.*
3. ***Collective-Choice Arrangements:*** *Most individuals affected by a resource regime are authorized to participate in making and modifying its rules.*
4A. ***Monitoring Users:*** *Individuals who are accountable to or are the users monitor the appropriation and provision levels of the users.*
4B. ***Monitoring the Resource:*** *Individuals who are accountable to or are the users monitor the condition of the resource.*
5. ***Graduated Sanctions:*** *Sanctions for rule violations start very low but become stronger if a user repeatedly violates a rule.*
6. ***Conflict-Resolution Mechanisms:*** *Rapid, low-cost, local arenas exist for resolving conflicts among users or with officials.*
7. ***Minimal Recognition of Rights:*** *The rights of local users to make their own rules are recognized by the government.*
8. ***Nested Enterprises:*** *When a common-pool resource is closely connected to a larger social-ecological system, governance activities are organized in multiple nested layers.*
Source: Originally *Table 3.1* in Elinor Ostrom's *Governing the Commons (1990)*, at p.90, as modified by Ostrom in her 2009 Nobel Prize Lecture. *Beyond Markets and States*, at p. 422, citing updates by Cox, Arnold, and Villamayor-Tomas (2009).

Understanding the operational use and limits of the design principles can provide a gamut of robustness in analyzing institutional arrangements. One example includes studies conducted by Fehr and Leibbrandt (2008), who conducted an experiment on public goods with fishermen harvesting fish using an "open access" inland lake in Brazil:[147]

> They found that a high percentage (87 percent) of fishers contributed in the first period of the field experiment and that contributions leveled off in the remaining periods. Fehr and Leibbrandt examined the mesh size of the nets used by individual fishermen and found that those who contributed more in the public goods experiment used nets with bigger mesh sizes. Larger mesh sizes allow young fish to escape, grow larger, and reproduce at a higher level than if they are caught when they are still small. In other words, cooperation in the field experiment was consistent with observed cooperation related to a real CPR dilemma. They conclude that "the fact that our laboratory measure for other-regarding preferences predicts field behavior increases our confidence about the behavioral relevance of other-regarding preferences gained from laboratory experiments."

The premise upon which Ostrom's principles are grounded is that the behavior of an individual is affected by the "context in which different interactions take place rather than being simply a result of individual differences."[148] It is upon this assumption that Ostrom's theory diverges from traditional game theory. The concept of the individualist approach is replaced by a polycentric approach in which the decision-making system is formally independent. An example of this was when Ostrom, in 1965, studied the water service industry in California, U.S., and noted that despite the presence of various public and private agencies, a productive way of organizing water resources without any hierarchy was demonstrated—a polycentric approach. Further, Ostrom's approach notes that there is an assumption that individuals have complete information about actions available to them. Through this, the individuals identify the likely strategies to be adopted. This information can be gathered in various ways, such as heuristic processes learned over time. Besides this, Crawford and Ostrom studied that individuals also learn norms such as the positive or negative valuation related to specific actions such as the consequences of lying. Moreover, "it is not only that individuals adopt norms but also that the structure of the situation generates sufficient information about the likely behavior of others to be trustworthy reciprocators who bear their share of costs." This indicates that individuals can move beyond the "presumption that rational individuals are helpless in overcoming social dilemma situations."[149]

Ostrom also notes the six factors are key to assessing micro-situational levels of analysis. *First*, communication is feasible with a full set of participants. *Second*, the reputation of participants is known. "It is likely that knowing the past history of participants who might not be personally known prior to the interaction, increases the

147. Ostrom (2008) *Beyond Markets and States* at p. 426 citing the work of Fehr et.al. in Ernst Fehr and Andreas Leibbrandt, *Cooperativeness and Impatience in the Tragedy of the Commons* (2008).
148. *Id.* at 431.
149. Ostrom (2008) *Beyond Markets and States* at p. 432.

likelihood of cooperation."[150] *Third*, whether the marginal per capital return is high or low. Based on this, each participant knows the contributions that they need to make. *Fourth*, "entry or exit capabilities. If participants can exit the situation at low cost, this gives them the opportunity not to sucker … ." In other words, cooperators may leave if their cooperation is not reciprocated. *Fifth*, participants anticipate more earnings through cooperation over a long period of time rather than a short period of time. *Sixth*, "while external sanctions or imposed sanctioning systems may reduce cooperation, when participants themselves agree to sanctioning system they frequently do not need to use sanctions at a high volume and net benefits can be improved substantially."

Ostrom contends that building trust and developing institutional rules are central to resolving social dilemmas. However, simplistic policy prescriptions provided by policy analysts do not reflect this. Ostrom gave the example of Individual Transferable Quotas (ITQs), which is often recommended as a policy prescription for all resources such as fisheries. She noted that while several such systems were working successfully, it did involve several years of "hard work by fishers involved as well as the government officials." Ostrom at her Prize Lecture of December 8, 2009, encapsulates her call for a more positive view of humankind's ability to rise to the challenge of cooperative governance and puts into question the premises of both the school of Leviathan and the Experts (Hobbes and Hardin):[151]

> The most important lesson for public policy analysis derived from the intellectual journey I have outlined here is that humans have a more complex motivational structure and more capability to solve social dilemmas than posited in earlier rational-choice theory. Designing institutions to force (or nudge) entirely self-interested individuals to achieve better outcomes has been the major goal posited by policy analysts for governments to accomplish for much of the past half century. Extensive empirical research leads me to argue that instead, a core goal of public policy should be to facilitate the development of institutions that bring out the best in humans. We need to ask how diverse polycentric institutions help or hinder the innovativeness, learning, adapting, trustworthiness, levels of cooperation of participants, and the achievement of more effective, equitable, and sustainable outcomes at multiple scales.

[A] Examples of Robustness in Practice

In the Swiss village of Törbel, legal documents traced back as far as 1224 provide insight into the communal tenure and the specific rules and regulations drafted by the villagers to govern the five types of communally owned types of property. The regulations set forth provisioned for clearly defined boundaries of the communally owned property limited to the citizens of Törbel. The entire commune was governed by a sophisticated set of rules addressing the numbers of cattle allowed onto the grazelands to the shares owned in the cooperative and the local official who was authorized to levy fines on those individuals who transgressed the rules of the commune. Incentivizing an effective monitoring system, the local official kept half of

150. For the quoted phrases, *see* Ostrom (2008) *Beyond Markets and States* at pp. 432-433.
151. Ostrom (2008) *Beyond Markets and States* at p. 435.

the sum of the fines for himself. Congruent rules were created governing the appropriation levels and the accessibility to the CPR. Determinative factors include a number of animals that can be fed during the winter, the amount of meadowland owned by the farmer, the production of hay by the farmer, the value of the land owned in the valley, the number of shares owned in the cooperative. Also, all the decisions made in relation to the CPR are taken by the appropriators themselves. The institution of the village of Törbel was considered by Ostrom of robust nature.[152]

Another case study was conducted by Ostrom on the irrigation systems (*zanjera*) in the Ilocanos area of Ilocos Norte in the Philippines. Similarly, to the village of Törbel, the irrigators utilizing the irrigation systems all have responsibilities and obligations clearly set out. Each member of the zanjera was provided with an "atar," equaling a membership. The *atar* allowed a member to cast a vote in the organization. It also spells out a variety of obligations attached to the atar, such as repair and upkeep of the irrigation system. Each atar-holder was obliged to contribute one day's work of labor per work season. With the atar, a member was accredited to elect a maestro for the positions of CEO, secretary, treasurer, etc. The zanjera also consists of irrigation community officers that are supposed to motivate and incentivize each member to make active contributions to the maintenance work. The inherent issue with the irrigation system is the distribution of water. Naturally, the members located near the head of the system can more easily draw water from the system, while those individuals allocated at the end of the system are essentially dependent on a well-maintained system. To ensure that each member would contribute to the maintenance work, the supervising community officers were allotted as a form of compensation, a parcel of land at the tail end. Without a well-managed irrigation system, the parcels would not be fruitful. The community officers would thus be incentivized to more effectively carry out their mandates or else they would be directly affected by their inactions.[153]

The ingenuity and entrepreneurship of the irrigators and their ability to self-organize solved the risk of the tragedy of the commons. By organizing themselves to understand the specific issues at hand, their "savoir-faire" could more effectively address the particularities of the irrigation system in the Philippines in ways that a centralized agency could not, due to lack of experience and insight.

As Ostrom-inspired John Stossel phrased it:

> *There is no reason to believe that bureaucrats and politicians, no matter how well-meaning, are better at solving problems than the people on the spot, who have the strongest incentive to get the solution right.*[154]

The above cases have illustrated some multifaceted CPR institutions across the world which have all endured the test of time and developed robustness and effectiveness to ensure the vitality of the resources for future generations. Although the

152. Ostrom (1990) *Governing the Commons* at pp. 61-65.
153. Ostrom (1990) *Governing the Commons* at pp. 82-88.
154. John Stossel, A Nobel Prize for Showing That Freedom Works, Reason.com, 22 October 2009, available at: https://reason.com/2009/10/22/a-nobel-prize-for-showing-that/ (accessed on 30 November 2019).

institutions themselves differ in types, there are common similarities that unite them. There is a continuity that has persevered over a long period of time, where the institutions have existed and remained solid and without radical change. Individuals have relied on future generations to inherit the property owned in the community and not only maintained its sustainability, but invested in ensuring the vitality of the resources will benefit their successors. This culture has developed due to the shared communal values and unity in a historical context. Consequently, the individual reputation becomes an integral part of the community where honest dealings and proper behavior form part of the community norm. For emphasis, it should be noted that commonly shared traits in all of the cases have been the homogenous properties of the communities. Individuals have tended to share ethnicity, race, knowledge, skills, ownership of the resources, and been absent of factors that could easily cause a divide among themselves. Of course, Ostrom also acknowledged that not all institutions pass the test of robustness. Several examples are considered fragile or even failures based on the design principles and institutional performances, and this is detailed in her masterwork entitled Governing the Commons, and her Table 5.2 of Design Principles and Institutional Performance, reproduced here as Table 3.4.

Table 3.4 Ostrom (1990) Governing the Commons, Table 5.2 at p. 180

	Table 5.2. Design Principles and Institutional Performances								
Site	*Clear Boundaries & Memberships*	*Congruent Rules*	*Collective-Choice Arenas*	*Monitoring*	*Graduated Sanctions*	*Conflict-Resolution Mechanisms*	*Recognized Rights to Organize*	*Nester Units*	*Institutional Performance*
Torbel, Switzerland	yes	yes	yes	yes	yes	Yes	yes	NR[a]	robust
Japanese mountain villages	yes	yes	yes	yes	yes	yes	yes	yes	robust
Valencia, Murcia, & Orihuela, Spain	yes	yes	yes	yes	yes	yes	yes	yes	robust
Raymond, West, & Central basins (current)	yes	yes	yes	yes	yes	yes	yes	yes	robust
Alicante, Spain	yes	yes	yes	yes	yes	yes	yes[b]	Yes	robust
Bacarra-Vintar, Philippines	yes	yes	yes	yes	yes	yes	yes	yes	robust
Alanya, Turkey	no	yes	weak	yes	yes	weak	weak	NR	fragile
Gal Oya, Sri Lanka	yes	yes	yes	yes	c	weak	weak	yes	fragile
Port Lameron, Canada	yes	Yes	weak	yes	yes	yes	no	no	fragile
Bay of Izmir & Bodrum, Turkey	no	no	no	no	no	no	weak	no	failure
Mawelle, Sri Lanka	no	yes	no	yes	yes	no	no	no	failure

	Table 5.2. Design Principles and Institutional Performances								
Site	*Clear Boundaries & Memberships*	*Congruent Rules*	*Collective-Choice Arenas*	*Monitoring*	*Graduated Sanctions*	*Conflict-Resolution Mechanisms*	*Recognized Rights to Organize*	*Nester Units*	*Institutional Performance*
Kirindi Oya, Sri Lanka	yes	no	no	no	no	no	no	no	failure
Raymond, West, & Central basins (earlier)	no	no	no	no	no	yes	yes	no	failure
Mojave groundwater basing	no	no	yes	no	no	yes	yes	no	failure

[a] NR: Not relevant.
[b] With two major exceptions, from 1739 to 1840 and 1930 to 1950.
[c] Missing information.

Without delving into each of these sites, certain aspects can be noted that have a direct correlation to Ostrom's design principles. When an institution lacks any, or several, of the design principles, there is an overwhelming risk of fragility, as illustrated in the cases of Port Lameron, Canada; Bay of Izmir & Bodrum, Turkey; and the Mojave groundwater basins.

The common denominators in these cases are a failure to adhere to all of the seven principles, eight in larger-scale enterprises. In the cases of the two fisheries in Turkey, compared to Törbel, where the latter was considered homogenous, the Turkish fisheries consisted of divergent interests among the different actors. Overcoming the conflicting self-interest demanded considerable financial resources. Without a cost-effective monitoring and enforcement system where enforceable contracts can be reached, the rate of success of self-organization is overwhelmingly low, according to Ostrom's theories.[155]

In sum, Ostrom won the Nobel Prize in 2009 for her having "challenged the conventional wisdom by demonstrating how local property can be successfully managed by local commons without any regulation by central authorities or privatization,"[156] and it is to her credit that one owes the third analytical framework for appreciating the work of the CTE. The work of the CTE has demonstrated a resistance to singular global regulation in favor of more localized solutions rooted in communities or the CPRs stakeholders themselves.

The Ostrom-ian Lens provides an influential perspective on the deliberations and work of the CTE in its thematic area on market access covered by CTE 6 and DDA 31iii, as reviewed and to be discussed in Chapter 6. It could also provide a framework of analysis for more recent developments demonstrating resistance to globalized or

155. Ostrom (1990) *Governing the Commons* at pp. 173-181.
156. "Elinor Ostrom—Facts." Nobelprize.org. Nobel Media AB 2014. Web. June 9, 2017, at http://www.nobelprize.org/nobel_prizes/economic-sciences/laureates/2009/ostrom-facts.html.

multilateral solutions in favor of more custom-tailored solutions that address in more localized fashion environmental issues and problems, such as can be seen in recent trade and environment developments with the recent U.S. actions on the Trans-Pacific Partnership (TPP) and the Paris Agreement.[157]

§3.05 PART I: SUMMATION

In concluding this chapter on the theoretical frameworks, and the Part I of this book on the basic framework of the CTE Work and Structure, it would be good to keep in mind these background discussions on the prehistory of the CTE, dating back to the Stockholm Declaration, the ad hoc work structure of the CTE with its expanded ten-point agenda, and the corresponding twenty CTE work outputs that have been generated, and the context or perspectives of the three analytical, theoretical frameworks, in evaluating the worth or a waste of time expended at the CTE.

A sober review and assessment would need to be based on both a constructive as well as a critical approach, and in proposing improvements or refinements of the work of the CTE, one cannot merely attempt to do more of what has already been done before or recycling the prior work as the basis of the future.[158]

To do and learn by analogy is, of course, acceptable and much easier, but it cannot be the only way if one is to provide some added value. Hopefully, the review and study of the CTE work and deliberations can become more than a mass of discussions with the aid of the foundations provided in this Part I, and a reading of the same can ideally lead to having both an objective and pragmatic perspective of the years of work of the CTE, enabling one to call a spade a spade, while also being wide open to other approaches and perspectives, if not original and more creative ideas, given that the path of all policy makers and of mankind, in general, is merely a gradual attempt towards the improvement of governance that necessitates in many instances trial and error, and successes and failures. With the goal of improved trade and environment governance at the WTO and the CTE, Part II deals with the comprehensive work that has taken place in the CTE on its 10-point work mandate.

---

157. *See* United States, Office of the United States Trade Representative, *Press Release: The United States Officially Withdraws from the Trans-Pacific Partnership*, January 30, 2017, available at: https://ustr.gov/about-us/policy-offices/press-office/press-releases/2017/january/US-Withdraws-From-TPP (accessed on November 30, 2019); *see also* United States Department of State, *Press Statement: On the U.S. Withdrawal from the Paris Agreement*, November 4, 2019, available at: https://www.state.gov/on-the-u-s-withdrawal-from-the-paris-agreement/ (last accessed on November 6, 2019). *See further* as a commentary on how the private sector initiatives rather than government initiatives should be primary actions, available at, CNBC News, *Trump May Be the Best Thing That Ever Happened to the Planet*, June 5, 2017, available at: https://www.cnbc.com/2017/06/05/trump-paris-accord-exit-is-actually-good-for-planet-commentary.html (last accessed on November 6, 2019).
158. Einstein, or whoever said it, said it best: insanity can be defined as doing exactly as one has always done while expecting a different result. *See* Peter Baskerville, updated May 11, 2017, available at: https://www.quora.com/Did-Einstein-really-define-insanity-as-doing-the-same-thing-over-and-over-again-and-expecting-different-results (accessed on November 30, 2019); *see also* Quote Investigator, March 23, 2017, available at: https://quoteinvestigator.com/2017/03/23/same/ (accessed on November 30, 2019).

Part II
The Work of the CTE

Developing an environment, trade and development agenda
2.22. Governments should encourage [WTO],... to examine, ... the following propositions and principles:

(j) Develop more precision, where necessary, and clarify the relationship between [WTO] provisions and some of the multilateral measures adopted in the environment area;

(k) Ensure public input in the formation, negotiation and implementation of trade policies as a means of fostering increased transparency in the light of country-specific conditions;

Agenda 21 (1992)

INTRODUCTORY SECTION TO PART II

As mentioned in Part I, this Part II consists of three chapters, each providing a broad overview and flavor of the years of work of the CTE in the five thematic areas concerned as grouped from the 1994 ten-point work program.

The CTE was originally envisioned to be an interdisciplinary forum, a "talk-shop," a brainstorming and debating society, where the views on trade, development and environment policies and governance mechanisms, as well as the needed technical and organizations interface among these policy regimes could be discussed and fleshed out.

Absent some theoretical frame and a clear picture of the historical process that led to the end results that served as the key work products of the CTE, also summarized in Chapter 2, the historical review of all these debates at the CTE could easily leave a reader to wonder how so much work and talk could be expended in the halls of the CTE.

However, if one keeps in mind the continuum of the evolution of trade and environment policy and governance, and utilize the most appropriate theoretical lens for the discussions to be reviewed, one can then have a better understanding and appreciation of the essential roles the CTE, as well as the GEMIT, its predecessor, both had, in evolving and converging the understanding among the various levels of governance, from the state actors, to the experts and bureaucracy, and to the constituents and communities themselves, of the salient issues that constitute rational trade and environment policy and governance formulation. In this context, or in the separate lenses and frames, then the discussions, debates, submissions, proposals, meetings, and the refrains of the said discussions, debates, submissions, proposals, meetings, and needless to say further and sometimes endless refrains, of the same, have some color of value by contributing to the eventual *modus vivendi* that has been reached between the trade and environmental law and policy communities.

In tackling the agenda items of the CTE in Chapter 4, there is no avoidance of having to use the classic IL-IR lens of formal and informal rulemaking, as well as the legal issues arising due to the potential conflict and hierarchy of norms. The output documents do show for Chapter 4, the beginnings of new rules, or adoption of informal traditions and best practices that will be familiar to IL and IL-IR theorists. New rules were mandated for some of the areas covered by Chapter 4, including the discussion of the dispute settlement mechanisms in the WTO and in MEAs, and the popular and specialized issue of STOs in MEAs.

In all this, the appropriate theoretical framework remains the continuing process of formulating new rules or the harmonization or reconciliation of trade and environment norms, rules and policies, in order to assure the continued mutual supportiveness of trade and environment policies.

While no new rules as of yet were passed for CTE 1, 5, and 10, the evolved practice and understandings did result in a draft ministerial decision as part of the key outputs of the CTE, and, which are actually in part in effect as evolving consuetude. Of note as well, is that the work output of the STO Inventory has become a handy reference for both CTE practitioners and beyond. The work items CTE2 and CTE4 are part of Chapter 4 coverage. Under these work items, actual policy tools have been generated by the CTE in terms of EDB and the ERs. These are seen as useful and acknowledged as positive work outputs of the CTE.

As described in Chapter 5, where the topics are highly technical and it being crystal clear that no mandate for negotiations towards new rules is involved, the important roles of the Secretariat and the experts have blossomed. There, the import and relevance of the historical discussions will have greater value to the technical and expert community of managers, TRNs and Global Administrative Law (GALs), rather than to the Hobbesian community of rule and policy makers. The output of the CTE in this area is considered laudable and allows for the greater level of knowledge and informed idea exchanges among trade and environment policy makers, secretariats and administrators. Of particular noteworthiness is the shifting of the conversation in the area of trade and climate change, as well as in the greater understanding of border taxes and eco-labelling standards. The specialized topics on DPGs, TRIPS, and Services, while having achieved certain work outputs, have become less of a priority and are probably ripe for retirement from the CTE work agenda or appropriate for referral to other WTO bodies.

In Chapter 6, all three theoretical frameworks coincide and become active and applicable. Despite appealing to all theories, and generating proposals and approaches from all perspectives, there remains a stalemate in the work of the CTE in the area of negotiating new market access commitments. However, the active work and dialogue have also led to substantial work outputs of the CTE as well as a higher level of specific negotiations focused on the elusive *triple-win* concept mandated by paragraph 32(i) of the DDA.[159]

The review of the history of the CTE 6 work in Chapter 6 is recommended across all the three theoretical frames or biases covered by Chapter 3 and becomes instructive in engendering further interaction and creativity among the trade and environment governance community toward formulating an updated work program for market access and the potential modalities to incentivize environment-friendly trade or trade-friendly environmental measures.

159. *See* WTO, Ministerial Declaration of November 14, 2001, WTO Ministerial Conference (4th Session Doha November 9-14, 2001), Ministerial Declaration, WT/MIN (01)/DEC/1 (November 20, 2001) at ¶ 32 (i) which states "[...] *those situations in which the elimination or reduction of trade restrictions and distortions would benefit trade, the environment and development.*"

CHAPTER 4

Interface, Coordination and Transparency

§4.01 CTE 1, 5, 10—NORM HIERARCHY, STOs, DSU, MEAs

Mandate under 1994 Decision and 2001 Ministerial Declaration

Item 1: The relationship between the provisions of the multilateral trading system and trade measures for environmental purposes, including those pursuant to multilateral environmental agreements

Item 5: The relationship between the dispute settlement mechanisms in the multilateral trading system and those found in multilateral environmental agreements

Item 10: Input to the relevant bodies in respect of appropriate arrangements for relations with intergovernmental and non-governmental organizations referred to in Article V of the WTO

Paragraph 31(i) and (ii): With a view to enhancing the mutual supportiveness of trade and environment, we agree to negotiations, without prejudging their outcome, on:

(i) the relationship between existing WTO rules and specific trade obligations set out in multilateral environmental agreements (MEAs). The negotiations shall be limited in scope to the applicability of such existing WTO rules as among parties to the MEA in question. The negotiations shall not prejudice the WTO rights of any Member that is not a party to the MEA in question;

(ii) procedures for regular information exchange between MEA Secretariats and the relevant WTO committees, and the criteria for the granting of observer status.

Key Output Documents for Items 1, 5 and 10:

1. Matrix on Trade-Related Measures Pursuant to Selected Multilateral Environmental Agreements ("STO Inventory"), WT/CTE/W/160/Rev.8 (2000-2017).
2. Compliance and Dispute Settlement Provisions in the WTO and in Multilateral Agreements, WT/CTE/W/191 (2001).
3. GATT/ WTO Dispute Settlement Practice relating to GATT Article XX, Paragraphs (b), (d) and (g), WT/CTE/W/203 (2002).
4. MEA Information Session on Technical Assistance, Capacity Building and Enhancing Information Exchange, WT/CTE/W/209 (2002).
5. Draft Decision on Trade and Environment, TN/TE/20 (Annex I) (2011).
6. WTO Special Studies No. 4 (1999)

The establishment of the WTO and the CTE coincided with a period of time of great discourse on the conflict of norms and of laws between trade and environment law regimes.[160] One can confidently say that the *coordination* work items (CTE 1, 5, 10) on the trade-environment regimes interface, or the WTO-MEA relationships, are the most developed and mature of all the work areas of the CTE over its twenty years of existence, and in fact, the work in these areas were subject of GATT and GEMIT work as well. As discussed in more detail in Chapter 1, the GEMIT had already begun its work on these issues with secretariat studies generated on its own agenda work item 1 (TRE/W/1, TRE/W/16, TRE/W/17, and TRE/W/18),[161] which corresponds to CTE Agenda Work Items 1 and 2, as well as the CTESS work item DDA paragraph 31(i) and (ii), not to mention its being subject of the pre-GEMIT GATT Document L/6896 of September 18, 1991.

For purposes of the analyses, there were essentially two phases, first, from 1994 to 2001, then followed by the Doha Round mandate, from 2002 through to the Easter package of 2011.[162] These two phases set the frame that resulted in concrete work output and a draft ministerial decision relating to coordination of trade and environment, and prospectively only the second decision since the very first decision on trade and environment in 1994.[163]

A total of seventeen proposals and submissions during the first phase of the debate, from 1995 to 2001, relating to materials received from the inception of the Committee until ministers in Doha referred this agenda item as a negotiating item under the Doha round, which was equivalent to referring the matter, if in the domestic context, to the legislative or rulemaking arm of government. During the Doha round/negotiating phase (2002-2011), a total of fifty-three proposals and submissions were received on this Agenda item (which includes a limited number of some eleven co-related proposals and submissions on the matter of coordination and exchanges of information with MEAs).

In sum, there are some seventy source documents to consider. They cover a long period of time since many of them are overlapping or repeat prior ideas or proposals, as well as relate to some proposals superseding earlier ones when coming from the

160. *See* Jorge Vinuales, "The Environment Breaks into Investment Disputes" *in International Investment Law* (Marc Bungenberg, Jörn Griebel, Stephan Hobe, and August Reinisch (eds.)) at p. 1714 (2012), also available online at: http://ssrn.com/abstract=2125209 (accessed November 29, 2019).

161. *See* GATT GEMIT, Trade Provisions contained in Multilateral Environmental Agreements, TRE/W/1 (April 29, 1992); GATT GEMIT, Agenda Item 1: Trade Provisions Contained in Existing Multilateral Environmental Agreements vis-à-vis GATT Principles and Provisions, TRE/W/16 (September 2, 1993); GATT GEMIT, Agenda Item 1: Trade Provisions Contained in Existing Multilateral Environmental Agreements vis-à-vis GATT Principles and Provisions, TRE/W/17 (September 7, 1993); GATT GEMIT, Agenda Item 1: Trade Provisions Contained in Existing Multilateral Environmental Agreements vis-à-vis GATT Principles and Provisions, TRE/W/18 (October 1, 1993).

162. Annex I titled "Draft Ministerial Decision on Trade and Environment" in the CTESS Chairman's Report at WTO CTESS, Report by the Chairman Ambassador Manuel A.J. Teehankee to the Trade Negotiations Committee, TN/TE/20 (April 21, 2011) at p. 7.

163. A discussion of the MEAs relationship to the WTO is aided by the discussion of the history of the NAFTA/NAAEC side agreement in Chapter 1.

same delegation. These proposals provide a rich source of reading on matters that have been much discussed in trade and environment writings or other fora, some already moot, while others remaining relevant.[164]

Item 1 of the CTE work program dealt with the issues related to trade measures that are to be applied unilaterally by WTO Members to address environmental problems that lie outside a member's national jurisdiction.[165] The item was mandated to assess the relationship between the provisions of the multilateral trading system and trade measures for environmental purposes, including those pursuant to MEAs. In turn, the CTE was, in 1994, tasked with the role of examining existing and emerging rules under WTO law and its relationship with MEAs. It had to assess whether there was any requirement to expand the scope of WTO rules to accommodate these MEAs and, if so, then under what circumstances and through which available means.[166] Notably, WTO rules already provide scope for the use of trade measures for environmental purposes. These provisions, enshrined in Article XX of GATT, aimed at ensuring that Members can enforce measures for the protection of their environmental resources while safeguarding the rights of other WTO Members against arbitrary or unjustifiable discrimination and disguised restrictions on trade.[167] Moreover, while MEAs are based on international consensus and are widely viewed by the international community as the best way of coordinating policy action to tackle global environmental problems, WTO rules are applicable when trade measures pursuant to MEAs can affect WTO Members rights and obligations.

Item 5 examined the relationship between the dispute settlement mechanisms in the multilateral trading system and those found in MEAs. There were primarily two issues that needed to be discussed under this item. *First*, whether the issue of the competent forum needed to be examined to understand where a dispute arising between two WTO Members over a trade measure applied pursuant to an MEA would be dealt with; and *second*, was there a requirement to increase the scope of institutional cooperation in relation with environmental expertise in dispute settlement proceedings. Item 5 was initially discussed as a stand-alone item for discussion at the CTE. However, the item began being discussed in conjunction with Item 1 towards the end of 1996. Both items 1 and 5, were absorbed as part of the Doha Declaration mandate through paragraph 31(ii).

Item 10 was discussed as part of informal consultations under both the SCTE of the WTO Preparatory Committee and the CTE and at informal and formal meetings of the CTE. It was a discussion through this item that led to observer status being granted on an ad hoc basis to fourteen IGOs. This was later confirmed by the General Council

164. For documents relating to the CTESS, *see* WTO CTESS, Committee on Trade and Environment Special Session (CTESS) List of Documents, Note by the Secretariat, TN/TE/INF/4/Rev.16 (May 3, 2013); *see also* for documents relating to the CTE WTO, Committee on Trade and Environment (CTE) List of Documents, Note by the Secretariat, WT/CTE/INF/5/Rev.12 (February 29, 2016).
165. WTO CTE, Report (1996) of the Committee on Trade and Environment, WT/CTE/1 (November 12, 1996).
166. *Id.* at ¶¶ 5-11.
167. *See*, e.g., *Id.* at ¶ 7.

of the WTO. This item also sought to improve the transparency of the WTO's work in the area of trade and environment, given that public awareness and increase in public access of information through the de-restriction of WTO working documents would benefit NGOs and the public at large, thereby increasing the WTO's legitimacy.

[A] CTE 1, 5

The WTO Secretariat prepared a note dated March 10, 1995, which highlighted developments regarding the interplay between trade measures and MEAs.[168] This note was built on significant pre-existing work that was conducted by its predecessor, the GEMIT. Notably, the GEMIT had based its work around the results of the then recently concluded UNCED, also referred to as the *Rio de Janeiro Earth Summit*, which had endorsed efforts to foster international cooperation as the most effective manner to address global and transboundary problems.[169] Given that MEAs were a direct result of cooperative multilateral solutions, they were widely recognized in a positive light by the multilateral trading system.[170] Further, the note analyzed 180 MEAs that were negotiated until 1995 and found that only eighteen MEAs included trade-related provisions.[171] As a consequence, only a limited range of trade measures would have to be considered in the context of rulemaking for the global trading system.[172] Moreover, there was a growing perception that trade measures could facilitate the achievement of the environmental objectives of MEAs. Therefore, Members wanted to ensure that the rules of the international trading system coexisted with multilateral environmental objectives.

Parallel to the discussions on item 1, the delegate of Chile presented a paper that opened discussions on item 5.[173] Item 5 dealt with dispute settlement mechanisms in MEAs and WTO. The Chile paper compared procedural aspects of the United Nations Convention on the Law of the Sea (UNCLOS) 1982, which, in Section 6 of Part XI, recognized the competence of WTO GATT. Specifically, the Chile paper noted that UNCLOS provided for:[174]

> (i) a dispute between parties regarding a purely technical, scientific or legal matter to be resolved by the dispute settlement mechanisms in Part XV of the Convention; and (ii) a dispute over matters concerning production policy in the international seabed, in particular subsidies and restrictive trading practices to be submitted to the WTO dispute settlement mechanisms.

The paper further established that several MEAs included trade-related provisions. Nigeria contended that it was unnecessary to link WTO Dispute Settlement

168. WTO CTE, Approaches to the Relationship Between the Provisions of the Multilateral Trading System and Trade Measures Pursuant to Multilateral Environmental Agreements, Note by Secretariat, WT/CTE/W/4 (March 10, 1995).
169. *Id.* at ¶ 2.
170. *Ibid.*
171. *Ibid.*
172. *Ibid.*
173. WTO CTE, Communication from Chile, WT/CTE/W/2 (February 16, 1995).
174. *Id.* at pp. 2-3.

Understanding (DSU) with MEAs despite the lack of a central international environmental dispute institution.[175]

Argentina stated that environmental disputes could be burdensome to the WTO Dispute Settlement Body (DSB) and sought to introduce two general principles as guidance in case of any such dispute: *first*, WTO Members would only utilize the DSB if all other mechanisms for resolving disputes are exhausted; and, *second*, environmental aspects of the dispute should be settled in specific environmental forums.[176]

The representative of *Hong Kong, China,* noted that it was beyond the task of WTO to address the MEA dispute settlement mechanism or its improvement.[177] Around the time of the Singapore Ministerial Conference, item 5 was effectively subsumed as part of item 1, given that the discussions on both items largely overlapped.

[B] CTE 10 and Interface with MEAs and NGOs

Article V of the Marrakesh Agreement Establishing the WTO deals with the relationships between the WTO and other organizations.[178] Article V(1) of the agreement states that the General Council of the WTO will make appropriate arrangements for effective cooperation with IGOs that have responsibilities related to those of the WTO. Article V(2) of the agreement makes arrangements for consultation and cooperation with NGOs that are concerned with matters related to the WTO.

Discussions at the CTE, particularly in relation to items 1, 5 and 10, necessarily included other IGOs such as Secretariats of MEAs. Pending a decision by the General Council on the formulating criteria for observer status for IGOs, the CTE, in 1996, extended observer status on an ad hoc basis to fourteen IGOs.[179] The criteria were formulated when the General Council, on July 18, 1996, adopted the Decision on "Observer status for international IGOs in the WTO."[180]

The limited discussions of this item continued from 2001 onwards, with only two submissions being made at the CTE. One of the submissions was a joint submission by

175. WTO CTE, Approaches to the Relationship Between the Provisions of the Multilateral Trading System and Trade Measures Pursuant to Multilateral Environmental Agreements, Note by Secretariat, WT/CTE/W/4 (March 10, 1995).
176. WTO CTE, Report of the Meeting Held on April 6, 1995, WT/CTE/M/2 (May 8, 1995) at ¶¶ 51-53.
177. *Id.* at ¶ 45.
178. Article V of the Marrakesh Agreement Establishing the World Trade Organization, April 15, 1994, 1867 U.N.T.S. 190, 33 I.L.M. 1153, 1867 U.N.T.S. 190.
179. WTO General Council, Rules of Procedures for Sessions of the Ministerial Conference and Meeting of the General Council, WT/L/161 (July 25, 1996).The IOs are: United Nations (UN), the United Nations Conference on Trade and Development (UNCTAD), the World Bank, the International Monetary Fund (IMF), the United Nations Environment Program (UNEP), United Nations Development Program (UNDP), Commission for Sustainable Development (CSD), the Food and Agriculture Organization (FAO), the International Trade Centre (ITC), the Organization for Economic Cooperation and Development (OECD), and the European Free Trade Association (EFTA), the UN Industrial Development Organization (UNIDO), the World Customs Organization (WCO), and the International Organization for Standardization (ISO).
180. WTO General Council, Procedures for the Circulation and De-restriction of WTO Documents, Decision Adopted by the General Council on July 18, 1996, WT/L/160/Rev.1. (July 26, 1996).

the WTO, UNEP and MEA Secretariats discussing technical assistance, capacity building, and enhancing information exchange. This document provided information on all the work that was being done with regard to trade measures in environment agreement in the WTO, UNEP, CITES, Basel Convention, United Nations Framework Convention on Climate Change (UNFCCC), CBD, International Tropical Timber Organization and the UNCLOS.[181] The other submission was a note by the WTO Secretariat on technical assistance and capacity building activities. This document demonstrated the list of technical assistance activities organized by WTO that was conducted on trade and environment in 2002.[182] Besides this, no other discussion on CTE 10 (agenda item 10) took place at the CTE.

§4.02 THE GENERAL APPROACHES TO THE RELATIONSHIP OF THE WTO MULTILATERAL TRADING SYSTEM AND MEAs

Two parallel narratives developed as a consequence of the MEA WTO Norm Coherence discussions. One narrative considered the GATT/WTO multilateral trading system to co-exist with and complement the MEAs whilst the other sought to accommodate provisions of MEAs in the multilateral trading system. Further, two concerns also developed from the discussions. *First*, would trade provisions of those eighteen MEAs and future MEAs with trade-related provisions apply separately to non-parties or countries that did not join the MEA? *Second*, would trade measures applied to protect environmental resources that did not fall within the national jurisdiction of one or more WTO Members, nor necessarily affect their own environment solely, be protected under either WTO law or the MEAs?[183]

In reconciling these potentially conflicting obligations between WTO laws with MEAs, two approaches were considered by WTO Members. The first approach, also known as the *ex ante* approach, would involve negotiation of a collective interpretation or an amendment to the general exceptions in Article XX of GATT. As per the *ex ante* approach, a set of criteria would be established regarding trade measures taken pursuant to MEAs that would be required to be met in order to be granted an exception. Besides *ex ante*, the CTE also considered introducing the *ex post* approach for discussion. This approach would rely on a case-by-case granting of waiver based on Article XXV: 5 of GATT and would require approval by a two-thirds majority of the votes cast. At the time, the CTE also noted that the *ex ante* and *ex post* approaches were

181. WTO CTE, MEA Information Session on Technical Assistance, Capacity Building and Enhancing Information Exchange—Input from the World Trade Organization, UNEP and MEA Secretariats, WT/CTE/W/209 (June 5, 2002).
182. WTO CTE, Technical Assistance and Capacity Building Activities in 2002—Paragraph 33, WT/CTE/W/216 (September 30, 2002).
183. *See generally* WTO CTE, Approaches to the Relationship Between the Provisions of the Multilateral Trading System and Trade Measures Pursuant to Multilateral Environmental Agreements *(WTO CTE Approaches Paper WT/CTE/W/4 1995)*, Note by Secretariat, WT/CTE/W/4 (March 10, 1995) at ¶ 3; *see also* WTO CTE, Matrix on Trade-Related Measures Pursuant to Selected Multilateral Environmental Agreements, Note by the Secretariat, WT/CTE/W/160/Rev.8 (October 9, 2017).

neither mutually exclusive, nor did they exclude the possibility of other proposals emerging in the future works.

The *ex ante* approach was premised on three primary considerations.[184] *First,* that the target for collective interpretation is the application of trade measures to WTO Members who are not a party to a specific MEA. *Second,* that the WTO should limit its competence to clarifying the scope for using trade measures within the framework of MEA. *Third,* that justification for trade measures must be clearly related to the environmental objectives of an MEA so as not to go beyond the necessary threshold to achieve the environmental goals enshrined in MEAs. Besides this, the note also clarified that an *ex ante* approach would have to be based on specific criteria that would determine whether the trade measures taken pursuant to an MEA are WTO consistent.[185] According to the note, the formulation of such criteria would be developed after examining various underlying concepts and principles.

The second approach, referred to as the *ex post* approach, envisages the granting of a waiver under Article XXV: 5 for MEAs on a case-by-case basis.[186] This approach builds on the view that the GATT already provides considerable scope for using trade measures for environmental purposes.[187] Further, it reflects doubts that trade measures which would exceed the limitations of existing provisions are likely to prove efficient or effective policy tools for use in MEAs as well as concerns about disturbing the balance of rights and obligations conferred by the GATT on its contracting parties. Recourse to the waiver provisions of Art XXV could be taken when doubts exist regarding the compatibility of trade measures in MEAs with the provisions of the GATT.

Besides *ex ante* and *ex post* approaches, some Members also revealed a preference for a combination of both. Austria suggested two approaches.[188] *First,* it proposed introducing an "understanding" concerning the application of trade measures so as not to create unnecessary barriers to trade. *Second,* it recommended incorporating a NAFTA-type clause that would allow provisions of certain existing MEAs to take precedence over WTO provisions.[189]

In a submission, New Zealand identified two areas where a dispute between MEAs and trade measures could arise.[190] *First,* when the use of trade measures to help protect environmental resources do not fall within the national jurisdiction of the country imposing the measure, nor necessarily affect solely or directly its own

184. *WTO CTE Approaches Paper WT/CTE/W/4 1995* at ¶¶ 3-4.
185. *Id.* at ¶ 11.
186. *Id.* at ¶ 5.
187. GATT GEMIT, Agenda Item 1: Trade Provisions Contained in Existing Multilateral Environmental Agreements vis-vis GATT Principles and Provisions, TRE/W/18 (October 1, 1993) at ¶¶ 8-11; *see generally WTO CTE Approaches Paper WT/CTE/W/4 1995.*
188. GATT GEMIT, GATT and International Environmental Agreements (IEAs) (Submission by Austria), TRE/W/19; *see also WTO CTE Approaches Paper WT/CTE/W/4 1995* at ¶ 19.
189. *Ibid.*
190. WTO CTE, Item 1: The Relationship Between the Provisions of the Multilateral Trading System and Trade Measures for Environmental Purposes, Including Those Pursuant to Multilateral Environmental Agreements (MEAs) (Submission by New Zealand), WT/CTE/W/20 (February 15, 1996).

environment. This type of action would invoke the application of Article III of GATT, which deals with non-discrimination between like products of domestic and foreign origin and Art XI of GATT, which concerns itself with prohibiting quantitative restrictions on trade. *Second*, when countries implement the discriminatory application of trade measures, including trade provisions from MEAs. This possible conflict would breach Article I of GATT, which safeguards the most favored nation (MFN) obligations.

The first WTO Ministerial Conference was set to take place in Singapore in December 1996. By now, the discussion relating to the relationship of MEAs and the multilateral trading system had been assimilated and assessed for both its veracity and potential. Views of Members were further informed by jurisprudence set out by the panel and Appellate Body in the *United States—Standards for Reformulated and Conventional Gasoline* on the interpretation of Article XX of GATT. This is demonstrated by the fact that most delegations considered that the provisions of Article XX of GATT did not permit Members to impose unilateral trade restrictions. Further, numerous proposals were also made that aimed at blocking Members from implementing these unilateral trade restrictions.

Interestingly, while many Members actively made proposals and discussed additional provisions needed with WTO law to prevent conflicts between MEAs and the multilateral trading systems, other Members did not hold the same view. India proposed that existing GATT provisions were sufficiently detailed to deal with any such potential conflict.[191] Other Members posited various benefits and negatives of both *ex ante* and *ex post* approaches.

Proposals and discussions in the CTE testify to some Members' views that MEAs based on international consensus was the best way of coordinating policy action to tackle global and transboundary environmental problems. Some Members also contended that WTO has no competence on matters of environmental policy but, rather, concerned itself with trade measures pursuant to MEAs that can affect the rights and obligations of WTO Members. Therefore, Members went to the Singapore Ministerial Conference with fractured views regarding the relationship between the multilateral trading system and MEAs.

After the Singapore Ministerial Conference, the discussions on the relationship between MEAs and WTO were limited to communications by MEAs secretariats and notes by the WTO Secretariat discussing recent developments.[192] However, in October 2000, New Zealand, once again, reignited the debate at the CTE on the relationship between the multilateral trading system and MEAs. It contended that trade measures would continue to be a feature of some MEAs and reasoned that the relationship

191. WTO CTE, Non-Paper by India (July 23, 1996) as cited in WTO CTE, Report (1996) of the Committee on Trade and Environment, WT/CTE/1 (November 12, 1996).
192. Some of the MEA Secretariats included Convention on Biological Diversity (CBD), Montreal Protocol on Substances that Deplete the Ozone Layer (Montreal Protocol), Global Environment Facility (GEF), United Nations Framework Convention on Climate Change (UNFCCC), Stockholm Convention on Persistent Organic Pollutants (POPs), United Nations Convention to Combat Desertification (UNCCD), Minamata Convention on Mercury, Convention on International Trade in Endangered Species of Wild Flora and Fauna (CITES), Latin American Economic System (SELA). *See*, e.g., UNEP, Minamata Convention on Mercury, Protecting Human Health and the Environment, Meeting on October 16, 2013, RD/CTE/25 (October 22, 2013).

between such agreements and the WTO rules needed clarification. Noting that the potential range of conflict between MEAs and WTO law was "tightly circumscribed."

Several countries supported New Zealand's approach to introducing a consultative mechanism system. Mexico and India acknowledged that trade measures were not the best solution for resolving environmental problems and that a consultative mechanism should be included in MEAs so as to generate obligations for MEA Parties. However, other WTO Members noted that New Zealand's proposal was not suited to resolving disputes between MEAs and the multilateral trading system. For instance, Brazil asked whether the proposal was aimed to resolve disputes at a bilateral or multilateral level. It also expressed concern about the introduction of such a mechanism into the WTO system.

[A] The 2001 CTE Note on WTO and MEA Dispute Settlement Provisions

In 2001, the WTO Secretariat, in cooperation with UNEP and MEA Secretariats, prepared a background note, which, along with another important background note in 2002 (that built on the earlier discussions on GATT and WTO dispute settlement rulings from 1996 and 1997) would become a pair of key work outputs of the CTE, as identified in the introduction to this section and in Chapter 2.[193] The 2001 CTE Note (on WTO and MEA Dispute Settlement Provisions) contrasted and cataloged all the compliance and dispute settlement provisions in the WTO and MEAs, while the 2002 CTE Note (on GATT/WTO Dispute Settlement Practice) cataloged and discussed the GATT and WTO rulings relating to the environment-related exceptions contained in Article XX (b), (d) and (g). These two key work outputs that were secretariat-led while being member-driven has provided trade and environment policy makers and researchers a relevant tool for understanding the key drivers of WTO and MEA dispute settlement mechanisms.

According to the 2001 CTE Note, the two regimes (WTO and MEAs) emphasized different approaches to securing compliance with their respective agreements. MEAs were tailored to reflect differing environmental, economic, social, institutional, and technological factors. For instance, they could seek to regulate trade in a particular category of products, such as wildlife. Or they could protect the domestic environment of states from harmful substances such as hazardous wastes. Some MEAs were even designed to protect the global commons, such as the global climate and the ozone layer. Therefore, compliance and dispute settlement mechanisms in MEAs were shaped and determined by the character of the underlying problem that they sought to address. On the other hand, the dispute settlement mechanism of the WTO aimed at providing security and predictability to the multilateral trading system in a timely and predictable manner. The note also reasoned that failure by a State to comply with its

193. WTO CTE, Compliance and Dispute Settlement Provisions in the World Trade Organization and in Multilateral Environmental Agreements, Note by the WTO and UNEP Secretariats, WT/CTE/W/191 (June 6, 2001); WTO CTE, GATT/World Trade Organization Dispute Settlement Practice Relating to GATT Article XX, Paragraphs (b), (d) and (g), WT/CTE/W/203 (March 8, 2002).

treaty obligations in MEAs could potentially harm the environment as well as the interest of states. This failure was often due to the lack of capacity of the State. As a result, MEA work focused more on assisting Parties to remain in compliance with environmental policy priorities rather than on resolving conflicts between participating Members. This is demonstrated by the fact that not a single dispute settlement mechanism in MEAs had been invoked until 2001. The WTO, on the other hand, focused on a more legalistic approach to resolving conflicts if consultations failed. This was to protect the interest of traders and businesses of Members. In other words, the WTO dispute settlement mechanism relied on strict timetables and binding judicial settlement; MEAs relied on facilitation for compliance.

The 2001 CTE Note suggested that a way to reduce potential tension between the two regimes and enhance implementation of WTO Agreements would be to focus less on judicial settlement of disputes and more on mediation, conciliation, technical assistance, and capacity building.[194] Similar conclusions were reached in discussions that took place in the UNEP High-Level Meeting on "Developing Mutually Supportive Trade and Environment Policies" in Berlin, Germany (March 20-22, 2001)[195] and the UNEP Meeting on "Compliance, Enforcement and Dispute Settlement in Multilateral Environmental Agreements and the WTO in Geneva," Switzerland (June 26, 2001).[196] Reactions to the 2001 CTE note were mixed, and the records and minutes show varying views among the CTE delegations.

[B] The 2002 CTE Note on GATT/WTO Article XX Dispute Settlement Practice and Related CTE Discussions

While debating the implications of trade and environment norm coherence and disputes, WTO delegations had also sought the assistance of the CTE Secretariat to catalog and summarize the dispute settlement rulings of GATT and WTO panels relating to the Article XX environmental exceptions found in paragraphs (b), (d) and (g).[197] This resulted in the CTE Secretariat preparing another key output that eventually resulted in the 2002 CTE Note on Article XX Dispute Settlement Practice, and which provides to this day a convenient reference tool on the GATT and WTO rulings and their significance to trade and environment policy coherence and coordination.

As discussed in Chapter 1, the *Tuna Dolphin* case played a prominent role in the early development of the trade and environment debate. *Tuna Dolphin* and *US Shrimp* (or *Shrimp–Turtle)* would feature prominently in the CTE discussions as reflected both in the 2002 CTE Note and in the CTE discussions themselves. The evolution of the 2002 CTE Note provides ample basis of the positive influence of member discussions occurring in the CTE, and this can be observed as the 2002 CTE Note underwent

194. *Id.* at ¶ 144.
195. WTO CTE, UNEP High-Level Meeting on Developing Mutually Supportive Trade and Environment Policies—Berlin, WT/CTE/W/198 (June 25, 2001).
196. WTO CTE, UNEP Meeting on Compliance, Enforcement and Dispute Settlement in Multilateral Environmental Agreements and the WTO, WT/CTE/W/199 (July 20, 2001).
197. WTO CTE, Report of the Meeting Held on May 21-22, 1997, WT/CTE/M/14 (June 25, 1997) at ¶ 105.

revisions over a period of time that reflected the debates at the CTE, and as it was later consolidated from earlier versions dating from 1997 and 1998.[198] Over the same period, the CTE Secretariat also prepared a useful reference bibliography on academic articles on trade and environment to assist delegations in developing a greater understanding of the relationship between trade and environmental issues.[199]

To illustrate some examples where WTO or GATT disputes did figure as well in the discussions at the CTE: in 1995, the EC had proposed the possibility of including an additional paragraph (k) to be inserted in GATT Article XX in order to make explicit reference to MEAs, and even suggested that, in the event that an MEA-based trade measure was challenged by a non-party, the WTO panel could adopt the three-step approach as was taken in *Tuna–Dolphin;*[200] in 1996, Korea had questioned whether compliance costs relating to market access was appropriately analyzed and whether the compliance costs were as insignificant as the CTE Secretariat note seemed to suggest;[201] in 1998, Korea stated that "[t]he WTO *Shrimp–Turtle* Panel Report reinforced Korea's conviction that unilateral trade measures to address environmental problems enforced extra-jurisdictionally should be avoided."[202]

Similarly, during discussions relating to the development of standards, in 1998, New Zealand contended that implementing voluntary instruments such as standards could have a serious impact on trade if they were designed and developed using incorrect criteria, and suggested introducing the concept of equivalence for voluntary standards, an idea which New Zealand had suggested was supported by the Appellate Body Report in *US Shrimp*.[203] In 2000, Switzerland had submitted a paper which presented the idea that MEAs and WTO rules were mutually supportive,[204] and suggested that the Appellate Body decision in *US Shrimp* confirmed this understanding

198. WTO CTE, GATT/ WTO Dispute Settlement Practice Relating to Article XX, Paragraphs (b), (d) and (g) of GATT, WT/CTE/W/53 (July 30, 1997); WT/CTE/W/53/Rev.1 (October 26, 1998); WT/CTE/W/203 (March 8, 2002).
199. *See* WTO CTE, Selective Bibliography on Trade and Environment, WT/CTE/W/49 (May 16, 1997) and WT/CTE/W/49/Add.1 (October 7, 2002).
200. According to the EC, the three-step approach as developed by the panel in *Tuna Dolphin* which would apply to the hypothetical would be as follows: *first*, the panel would review whether the measure at issue would fall within the MEA; *second*, the panel would examine the "necessity" for the measure to achieve the environmental objective infixed in the MEA; and *third*, the panel would test the whether the measure met the requirements of the *chapeau* to Article XX of GATT. *See* WTO CTE, Report of the Meeting Held on October 26-27, 1995, WT/CTE/M/5 (November 30, 1995) at ¶¶ 19-20; subsequently, the EC also presented a non-paper dated July 23, 1996. This non-paper was discussed by the representative of the EC at the CTE meeting held between July 24-25, 1996, *see* WTO CTE, Report of the Meeting Held on July 24-25, 1996, WT/CTE/M/11 (August 25, 1996).
201. WTO CTE, Report of the Meeting Held on March 25-26, 1996, WT/CTE/M/8 (April 11, 1996) at ¶ 12; WTO CTE, The Effects of Environmental Measures on Market Access Especially in Relation to Developing Countries in Particular to the Least Developed Amongst Them, Note by the Secretariat, WT/CTE/W/26 (March 26, 1996) at ¶¶ 11-12.
202. WTO CTE, Report of the Meeting Held on July 23-24, 1998, WT/CTE/M/18 (August 10, 1998) at ¶ 25.
203. WTO CTE, Report of the Meeting Held of October 26-27, 1998, WT/CTE/M/19 (November 30, 1998) ¶ 18.
204. WTO CTE, The Relationship Between the Provisions of the Multilateral Trading System and the Multilateral Environmental Agreements (Submission by Switzerland), WT/CTE/W/139 (June 8, 2000).

by indicating that the words of Article XX of GATT 1994 "[...] must be read by a treaty interpreter in the light of contemporary concerns of the community of nations about the protection and conservation of the environment."[205] However, in subsequent meetings at the CTE, some Members raised concerns about Switzerland's arguments. *Hong Kong, China*, in particular, had countered the reasoning offered by Switzerland by noting that *US Shrimp* dealt with unilateral trade action and not the relationship between MEAs and WTO rules.[206] India endorsed the *Hong Kong, China*, position by noting that Switzerland's reliance on only one aspect of the *Shrimp–Turtle* dispute was an oversimplification of the issues tackled in the dispute.[207]

§4.03 THE DOHA ROUND MANDATE

By late 2001, paragraph 31 of the Doha Declaration of November 14, 2001, provided the mandate to pursue negotiations without prejudging their outcome with regard to the relationship between existing WTO rules and STOs set out in MEAs. As detailed in Chapter 2, this led to negotiations that would now take place on two-tracks—at the special session and the regular CTE meetings. At the CTE regular session, the discussions on the relationship between MEAs and the multilateral trading system declined with submissions limited to background papers made by the UNEP[208] and CITES[209] secretariats.

The discussion on MEAs and STOs shifted to the negotiations on a concrete outcome at the CTESS. The representative of the Philippines contended that negotiations under paragraph 31(i) needed to identify MEAs containing STOs on the basis of *common but differentiated responsibilities* and S&D treatment.[210] The EU proposed identifying, by way of negotiation, different STOs, while Australia argued that the negotiations were not needed to clarify the WTO-MEA relationship. Norway argued that the mandate excluded certain controversial aspects of the WTO-MEA relationship, while Canada observed that the word "specific" indicated that the trade measure

205. *United States Shrimp (DS58 1998) at* ¶ 129.
206. WTO CTE, Report of the Meeting Held of July 5-6, 2000, WT/CTE/M/24 (September 19, 1999) at ¶ 12; subsequently, Switzerland submitted another paper to the Committee on Trade and Environment clarifying the relationship between the WTO and Multilateral Environmental Agreements, *see* WTO CTE, Clarification of the Relationship Between the WTO and Multilateral Environmental Agreements (Submission by Switzerland), WT/CTE/W/168 (October 19, 2000).
207. WTO CTE, Report of the Meeting Held of July 5-6, 2000, WT/CTE/M/24 (September 19, 1999) at ¶ 14.
208. WTO CTE, Statement by the UNEP at the Regular Session of the Committee on Trade and Environment of October 8, 2002—Items 1 and 5, WT/CTE/GEN/4 (November 20, 2002); *see also* WTO CTE, Enhancing Synergies and Mutual Supportiveness of MEAS and the WTO—A Synthesis Report, Contribution by UNEP, WT/CTE/W/213 (June 12, 2002).
209. *See generally* UNEP, Decision on Economic Incentives and Trade Policy, Economic Incentives and Trade Policy CITES Papers, available at: https://cites.org/sites/default/files/eng/dec/valid13/E13-Dec.pdf (accessed on November 30, 2019).
210. WTO CTESS, Summary Report on the First Meeting of the Special Session Held on March 22, 2002, TN/TE/R/1 (April 19, 2002) at ¶ 16.

needed to be explicitly provided in the MEA and not simply a measure that was adopted by the Conference of Parties.

Switzerland had presented two submissions on the issue of MEAs[211] and reiterated its position that the principle of mutual supportiveness of the two international regimes should be upheld. In sum, the post-Doha discussions had commenced with delegations offering differing views on the interpretation of STOs and the context surrounding paragraph 31(i) of the Doha mandate.

Over the next two years, two central themes that were discussed in detail during discussions at the CTESS were primarily definitional in character—what constituted an STO? And what was an MEA? However, it was broadly understood that many delegations participating had agreed that the so-called STO Inventory, another key output of the CTE, the *Matrix on Trade Measures Pursuant to Selected MEAs* could serve as the basis for further discussions at the CTESS.[212] In terms of substantive discussions, it was noted that what constituted STOs for some WTO Members were not necessarily perceived as STOs by other WTO Members.[213]

Notably, discussions on STOs and MEAs were specific in nature. Take, for example, the definition of the term STOs in papers submitted by China[214] and Chinese Taipei.[215] Members argued that STOs included treaty texts, amendments, and Conference of the Parties (COP) decisions; however, China also introduced "level of authoritativeness" in its design structure, which differed from the proposal submitted by Chinese Taipei.[216]

In the months leading up to the Hong Kong Ministerial Conference that was scheduled for December 2005, little progress was registered in the rulemaking work item under DDA 31(i). Some delegations such as Switzerland and the EU had voiced skepticism regarding the current procedural practice adopted in the CTESS of sharing national experiences, and they questioned the practical benefit of the same under DDA

---

211. WTO CTE, The Relationship Between the Provisions of the Multilateral Trading System and Multilateral Environmental Agreements (Submission by Switzerland), WT/CTE/W/139 (June 8, 2000); *see also* WTO CTE, Clarification of the Relationship Between the WTO and MEA (Submission by Switzerland), WT/CTE/W/168 (October 19, 2000).
212. WTO CTE, Matrix on Trade Measures Pursuant to Selected MEAs, Note by the Secretariat, WT/CTE/W/160/Rev.1 (June 14, 2001); WTO CTESS, Summary Report on the Fifth Meeting of the Committee on Trade and Environment in Special Session, TN/TE/R/5 (April 14, 2003); *see also* WTO CTESS, Compilation of Submissions under Paragraph 31(i) of the Doha Declaration, Note by the Secretariat, TN/TE/S/3 (January 31, 2003).
213. WTO CTESS, The Relationship Between MEAS and World Trade Organization Agreements: Set Out in MEAs (Submission by the European Communities), TN/TE/W/31 (May 14, 2003).
214. WTO CTESS, Identification of Multilateral Environmental Agreements (MEAs) and Specific Trade Obligations (STOs) (Submission by Separate Customs Territory of Taiwan, Penghu, Kinmen and Matsu), TN/TE/W/35 Rev.1 (July 3, 2003).
215. WTO CTESS, The Relationship Between WTO Rules and Specific Trade Obligations Set Out in MEAs (Submission by Separate Customs Territory of Taiwan, Penghu, Kinmen and Matsu), TN/TE/W/36 (July 3, 2003).
216. WTO CTESS, Summary Report on the Seventh Meeting of the Committee on Trade and Environment in Special Session, Note by the Secretariat, TN/TE/R/7 (August 1, 2003).

31(i), with Switzerland inviting delegations to explain "how experience-based discussions could lead to an operational result so that Members could start working on finding common ground on this issue."[217]

§4.04 REFLECTIONS ON CTE 1, 5 AND 10: APPROACHES TO NORM CONFLICTS, THE WTO–MEA INTERFACE

In the NAAEC/CEC context, there was a relatively binary choice of the supremacy of one or the other, the trade and environment discussion before the CTE was not as clear-cut. Traditional conflict of law norms would apply the three principles of *lex superior, lex specialis,* and *lex posterior* to classify the problem.[218] While not directly apt to the current situation, where the CTE is the forum to receive and deliberate on proposals under CTE 1, on how to "define a relationship," the main question lies on resolving differences of perspectives between two administrative and regulatory regimes and sets of the norm—that of trade and environment.

For structure, "conflict of law" approaches are helpful in categorizing the proposals relating to that which we have been calling a norm preference or inclination. As mentioned earlier, Pauwelyn (2003) provides a comprehensive legal approach to the methods by which conflict of norms could be addressed by state parties,[219] and the following groups of proposals do not attempt to follow the legal analysis strictly but are a simplified structure by which to understand their perspective or vantage points.

[A] Trade Norms Preferred (*Lex Superior*)

In this category, the proposal based approach to trade norms are the more desirable and reliable regime, and that, in no case should they be deemed as inferior to environmental norms. The results would range from discouraging the use of trade measures altogether as an environmental tool, or the need for a case-by-case waiver to permit the use of trade measures as environmental policy or regulatory tool. ASEAN's or *Hong Kong, China*'s early proposals on the need for applying for WTO waivers could be categorized as belonging to this general approach that affirms the superiority and priority of WTO as an institution for any issue relating to trade measures in all forms.[220]

217. WTO CTESS, Summary Report on the Fourteenth Meeting of the Committee on Trade and Environment in Special Session, Note by the Secretariat, TN/TE/R/14 (February 9, 2006).
218. *See*, Pauwelyn (2003) *Conflict of Norms* at 327-439, 489 for a comprehensive dissertation on the legal sequencing procedures for conflicts resolution; *see also* Jorge E. Viñuales, *Foreign Investment and the Environment in International Law* at pp. 140-148 (2012).
219. Pauwelyn (2003) *Conflict of Norms* at p. 489.
220. *See* WTO CTE, The Relationship Between the Provisions of the Multilateral Trading System and Trade Measures for Environmental Purposes Including Those Pursuant to Multilateral Environmental Agreements (MEAs) (Proposal from ASEAN), WT/CTE/W/39 (July 24, 1996).

[B] Trade Norms Less Preferred (Lex Inferior)

In this approach, the grounding is on the need to respect and promote environmental objectives and leans to supporting a presumption in favor of environmental norm supremacy, akin to the NAFTA Article 104 model. While no direct references to a strong environment norm supremacy are proposed, the approach has resulted in various ranges of proposals that would shift the burden of proof or provide a presumption of validity in favor of the environmental measure, and include certain less norm specific results such as referrals or deferral approaches. The Swiss and EU proposals would provide good examples of this category.[221]

[C] No Hierarchy and No Hierarchy Plus

The overwhelming number of proposals lean towards the absence of any preference and affirm the absence of any hierarchy or single solution, and the results would range from requiring a case-by-case analysis of the situation, the non-derivation of a standard rule, to increased dialogue, coordination and information exchanges between the WTO and MEAs, as well as between government agencies dealing with trade and environment issues. We could sub-categorize these latter more detailed proposals as the No Hierarchy Plus approach.

It may also be instructive to get a flavor of the other concerns and issues raised by reviewing the first Annual Report (1996) of the CTE, WT/CTE/1 (November 12, 1996) if only to get a flavor of the wide range of ideas that were floated and today mostly abandoned. As the Chair reports in parts of the 1996 report:

> 7. Most of the delegations which intervened in the debate on this issue stated that they consider that the provisions of GATT Article XX do not permit a Member to impose unilateral trade restrictions that are otherwise inconsistent with its WTO obligations for the purpose of protecting environmental resources that lie outside its jurisdiction. For them, a renewed commitment needs to be taken by WTO Members to avoid using trade measures unilaterally for that purpose, and numerous proposals have been made in the CTE to that effect. Another view is that there is nothing in the text of Article XX which indicates that it only applies to policies to protect animal or plant resources or conserve natural resources within the territory of the country invoking the provision. A number of Members noted that there were differing views as to what constituted "unilateralism."
> 8. MEAs based on international consensus are viewed by the international community as the best way of coordinating policy action to tackle global and transboundary environmental problems cooperatively. The WTO has no competence in the area of environmental matters per se, but it is concerned with trade measures applied pursuant to MEAs which can affect WTO Members' rights and obligations. Of the many MEAs currently in effect, only

221. *See*, e.g., WTO CTE, Resolving the Relationship Between WTO Rules and Multilateral Environmental Agreements (Submission by the European Community), WT/CTE/W/170 (October 19, 2000); *see also* WTO CTE, Clarification of the Relationship Between the WTO and Multilateral Environmental Agreements, WT/CTE/W/168 (October 19, 2000).

> about 20 contain trade provisions. There are considerable differences between the trade provisions of different MEAs, in particular the kinds of trade measures that MEA Parties are authorized or required to apply and the conditions pursuant to which the measures are taken. No GATT or WTO trade dispute has arisen so far over the use of trade measures applied pursuant to an MEA. Nevertheless, doubts have been expressed by some WTO Members about the WTO consistency of certain trade measures applied pursuant to some MEAs, in particular discriminatory trade restrictions applied by MEA Parties against non-parties that involve extra-jurisdictional action. For some, the uncertainty these doubts create for WTO Members and for the negotiators of MEAs makes clarification of the relationship between WTO provisions and these trade measures desirable.

The offshoot of the wider range of discussions on MEAs and STOs in MEA's resulted, as has been highlighted previously, in a policy tool known as the *STO Inventory, Matrix on Trade-Related Measures Pursuant to Selected Multilateral Environmental Agreements.* This illustrates a solid CTE institutional output that assists in a concrete manner CTE delegates in their work and analysis of governance approaches to trade and environment issues.[222] The CTE tradition of extracting and examining trade measures in MEAs dates back to the GEMIT and the technical work contained in annexes III and IV of L/6896 (September 18, 1991), and, also, e.g., TRE/W/16 (*Secretariat note on Trade Provisions contained in Existing Multilateral Environmental Agreements vis-à-vis GATT Principles and Provisions*, September 2, 1993).[223]

§4.05 THE EASTER PACKAGE AND 2011 DRAFT DECISION

By 2010, the discussions at the CTESS had resulted in the identification of at least five issues, where convergence was possible based on recorded observations of the author as CTESS Chairman at the time:[224]

> *First*, many delegations considered the process of national experience sharing beneficial to the discussions under paragraph 31(i) of the Doha declaration.
> *Second*, several delegations had, on an illustrative basis, identified STOs in MEAs. Through this exercise, several common features for understanding STOs were identified though some delegations were in favor of avoiding prescriptive language for defining STOs.
> *Third*, with regard to dispute settlement procedures, which is also item 5 of the original CTE work program, several concerns regarding the use of MEA expertise in WTO disputes was raised. The Chairperson noted that further engagement on this topic was needed.

222. *See* WTO CTE, WTO CTESS, Matrix on Trade Measures Pursuant to Selected Multilateral Environmental Agreements, WT/CTE/W/160/Rev.8; TN/TE/S/5/Rev.6 (October 9, 2017).
223. *See generally* discussions in Chapter 1.
224. WTO CTESS, Report by the Chairman Ambassador Manuel A.J. Teehankee to the Trade Negotiations Committee TNC Stocktaking Exercise, TN/TE/19 (March 22, 2010).

Fourth, the importance of technical assistance and capacity building was iterated by many delegations. This issue could also support the development dimension of trade and environment negotiations.

Finally, several delegations were exploring the general principles governing the WTO-MEA relationship and more discussions were needed to get clarity for an outcome in this area.

The work of the CTESS had intensified in terms of textual submissions which resulted in the areas of convergence and what would be included in the "Easter Package" of 2011.[225] Included in the 2011 Easter Package was the draft Ministerial Decision on Trade and Environment and which was based on a proposal by the U.S.[226]

This draft proposed the enhancement of cooperation between MEAs and WTO and encouraged enhanced coordination at the domestic level among relevant government agencies when negotiating, implementing, and applying WTO rules and STOs set out in MEAs. The draft-text also indicated that delegations discussed dispute settlement and capacity building.[227] However, the presence of many square brackets—a simple grammatical tool used to highlight divergence during textual negotiations—indicated that WTO Members were of different minds on these issues.[228]

While negotiations had risen and ebbed through the years, the last set of negotiations during the period 2010 to 2011 culminated on embodying some guidance in a draft Decision on Trade and Environment (CTE Decision II). The draft decision was annexed to the latest report of the chair of the special session that was presented on April 21, 2011,[229] along with all the other reports of the Doha negotiating group chairs (collectively known as the Easter 2011 Package). The draft decision provides a snapshot of where the debate has evolved towards and it, of course, remains a work in progress and is annexed at the end of this section as one of the key outputs for the work agenda item CTE 1, 5 and 10 as well as under the DDA mandate under paragraph 31(i) and (ii).

One bracketed portion of the draft would attempt to anchor achieving coherence of norms to treaty interpretation principles, including *pacta sunt servanda*:

> [Noting that the Vienna Convention on the Law of Treaties states that every treaty in force is binding upon the parties to it and must be performed by them in good faith;]
>
> [Recognizing that both MEAs and the WTO Agreement are instruments of international law of equal standing between parties to the agreements, and that all

225. "Easter Package" was a term used for documents and reports that were compiled by Chairs of Committees in 2010 and 2011, and reported to the TNC in Easter of 2011, *see generally* at WTO, *WTO Annual Report 2012* at p. 22 (2012).
226. WTO CTESS, Draft Decision for an Outcome under Doha Paragraphs 31(i) and 31(ii) (Communication from the United States), TN/TE/W/78 (February 14, 2011).
227. *Ibid.*
228. Office of the United States Trade Representative, 2011 Annual Report of the President of the United States on the Trade Agreements Program at p. 13, available at: https://ustr.gov/sites/default/files/FULL%20REPORT%20-%20PRINTED%20VERSION.pdf (accessed on November 30, 2019).
229. WTO CTESS, Report by the Chairman Ambassador Manuel A.J. Teehankee to the Trade Negotiations Committee, TN/TE/20 (April 21, 2011).

provisions under international law should be implemented harmoniously and in good faith.][230]

The issue of interpretative techniques is an important tool that can be used for norm coherence and preferred norms. As one writer has expressed:

> [s]ubsequent *practice establishing the agreement of the parties under Article 31(3)(b) need not be by every party; the practice need only be accepted by all, and the acceptance can be tacit. MEAs containing trade restrictions provide an example of such subsequent practice. From the early 1970s, when CITES was drafted and adopted, to the present, when it and other major MEAs with trade restrictions have attained close to universal membership, the vast majority of GATT parties have negotiated, signed, and ratified the MEAs without contemporary claims by other GATT parties that the trade restrictions violate GATT. While "negative practice"—i.e., "the absence of action which would have been expected had a certain interpretation of a treaty been the correct one"—should be carefully employed, when coupled with such a long-standing positive practice, there can be little doubt that GATT parties have accepted the MEAs as consistent with GATT. This practice has specific implications for Article XX, as the only GATT provision whose interpretation can avoid conflicts with the MEAs.*[231]

The consensus reflects the agreement to disagree, or not to agree, as it remains difficult to define what an *STO* in an MEA is. The premise of any decision will, therefore, be based founded on Members avoiding a prescriptive definition of *STOs* in MEAs, taking into account the useful CTE Secretariat compilation of *STOs* in MEAs.[232] Argentina, together with Australia, contributed much through joint submissions.[233]

The progress of discussions and the extensive work performed at the committee through the years could, on an illustrative basis, provide examples of what trade-related measures in MEAs might constitute an STO, such as for example the obligation to ban or regulate the import or export of certain products in the context of the Montreal Protocol.[234] Language in the draft CTE Decision II reflects the observation of Members that "an STO set out in an MEA is understood to be one that requires an MEA party to take, or refrain from taking, a particular trade action," while discussions on the same cover as well the issue of whether broader trade actions might also be included in the scope of discussions.[235]

On the negotiations for facilitating information exchange with MEAs, which is incorporated in the draft outcome, members have had a long history of agreeing to the

---

230. *Id.* at p. 3.
231. John H. Knox, *The Judicial Resolution of the Conflicts Between Trade and the Environment*, 28 Harv. Envtl. L. Rev. 1, at 68 (2004).
232. *See* WTO CTE, WTO CTESS, Matrix on Trade Measures Pursuant to Selected Multilateral Environmental Agreements, WT/CTE/W/160/Rev.8; TN/TE/S/5/Rev.6 (October 9, 2017).
233. *See* WTO CTESS, Proposal for an Outcome on Trade and Environment Concerning Paragraph 31(i) of the Doha Ministerial Declaration (Submission from Australia and Argentina), TN/TE/W/72/Rev.1 (May 7, 2007).
234. *Id.* at p. 59.
235. WTO CTESS, Annex I of the Draft Ministerial Decision on Trade and Environment at WTO CTESS, Report by the Chairman Ambassador Manuel A.J. Teehankee to the Trade Negotiations Committee, TN/TE/20 (April 21, 2011) at p. 7; *see also* at note 11 of said Annex I citing Japan's position pursuant to its non-paper (March 21, 2011) for a broader reference to "trade-related action" as covering *obligation de résultat*.

importance of cooperation and collaboration among the WTO and MEA secretariats in order to enhance the mutual supportiveness of trade and the environment,[236] while also adding that coordination at the domestic level among relevant government agencies when negotiating or implementing WTO rules as well as when negotiating and implementing STOs set out in MEAs ought to be encouraged.[237] There is likewise a provision for continuing the sharing of domestic experiences by members as part of the agenda of the CTE on trade and environment. Other aspects of the draft decision relate to the grant of observer status to MEAs.[238] The emerging points of consensus affirm what is already, to a great extent, current practice in the committee and among the secretariats of the WTO and MEAs.

[A] Technical Assistance and Capacity Building

In the area of technical assistance and capacity building, highlighted in paragraph 33 of the Doha Ministerial Declaration, there still remains some work for developing countries to obtain full consensus from their developed partners. The Africa Group and the African, Caribbean and Pacific (ACP) Group of States proposed that the outcome enhance technical assistance to developing countries relating specifically to the implementation of STOs set out in MEAs and provide for a group of experts on trade and environment to be elected periodically by the CTE who would be "available on a priority basis to least developed and developing countries as a complement to existing technical assistance mechanisms."[239]

[B] Summation CTE 1, 5, 10

In sum, much work has been done on CTE 1, 5 and 10. While a draft decision has been made available, to this date, no progress has been made to move forward on the same, but in the context of Lens A of both hard and soft law, as well as informal rulemaking, for all intents and purposes, the draft decision is already effectively in practice. The draft decision is reproduced in whole in Section 4.7 at the end of this chapter.

In the larger scheme of things, the trade and environment divide triggered by *Tuna Dolphin I* went directly to the question of societal preferences and the very tricky issue of the level of intent: is protectionist effect to be treated the same way as

236. *Id. see*, e.g., ¶¶ 2, 5(b).
237. *Id.* at ¶ 1.
238. *Id.* at ¶ 5(a).
239. This was presented by the Africa Group in WTO CTESS, Proposal for the Establishment of a Group of Experts on Trade and Environment (Submission by the African Group), JOB (08)/38 (May 8, 2008); *see also* ACP Group in WTO CTESS, Proposals for Elements of a Decision of the Ministerial Conference on Trade and Environment, JOB/TE/14 (March 7, 2011); an additional element on which no consensus has been reached, which is not an issue for developing countries, relates to the proposals of the European Union and Switzerland on the handling of potential disputes. These are subject of paragraph 5(e) of the draft CTE Decision II and Annex I.B of the 2011 Chairman Report, *see* Annex I to the Draft Ministerial Decision on Trade and Environment at WTO CTESS, Report by the Chairman Ambassador Manuel A.J. Teehankee to the Trade Negotiations Committee, TN/TE/20 (April 21, 2011) at p. 13.

protectionist impact or effect. To trade lawyers, there is hardly a difference; to judicial legal experts, they will tell you the jurisprudence and theory turn on very fine distinctions between effects and intent, which almost erase the distinction or intertwine them to such an extent that it would be very difficult to tell the difference.

However, to society and to lawyers at large, and more specifically to the environmental community of NGOs and legal advocates, there remains a crucial difference, bordering on right and wrong, and the need to reflect social and political preferences and choices that ought not to be second-guessed or lightly overturned when there is a textually demonstrable commitment of discretion and a mandate to achieve a certain result through command and control mechanisms, the traditional environmental toolkit and measure.

The history of the trade and environment norms divide, whether in the NAAEC/CEC or WTO CTE context, do not yield much in terms of new legal rules or theories. However, one can daresay that evolution towards certain levels of hierarchy, coherence or preferences has occurred in no small measure due to the institutional mechanisms for debate, expertise and data and information gathering, and a forum for the exchange of ideas and generation of new ideas such as for coordination mechanisms, all appropriately officially recorded and subject to good governance interagency and cross-sector standards on a national and international level.

In the end, institutional mechanisms and processes are representative of basic due process, both on a procedural and on a substantive basis. The ability and availability of development and environmental interests and constituents to be heard by institutional mechanisms and bureaucracies in the trade regime, and vice versa, and to allow access to specialized expertise and specialized organizations, and an exchange of ideas with official records and reporting that accumulate knowledge and experiences over time are key elements in the evolution of norms coherence and norms preferences being achieved with less conflict and sacrifice of one value over another.

§4.06 CTE 2, 4: TRANSPARENCY, EDBs AND ENVIRONMENT REVIEWS

Item 2: *The relationship between environmental policies relevant to trade and environmental measures with significant trade effects and the provisions of the multilateral trading system.*
Item 4: *The provisions of the multilateral trading system with respect to the transparency of trade measures used for environmental purposes and environmental measures and requirements which have significant trade effects.*
Paragraph 33 of Doha Ministerial Meeting: *We recognize the importance of technical assistance and capacity building in the field of trade and environment to developing countries, in particular the least-developed among them. We also encourage that expertise and experience be shared with members wishing to perform environmental reviews at the national level. A report shall be prepared on these activities for the Fifth Session.*

Output for Item 2:

1. List of Environmental Reviews ("Notifications"), WT/CTE/W/245 (2007-2008)

Output for Item 4:

2. Environmental Database, WT/CTE/EDB/1-WT/CTE/EDB/18 (2002-2018)

Item 2 of the CTE deals with the relationship between, *firstly*, the environmental policies relevant to trade and, *secondly*, environmental measures that had significant trade effects, and its relationship with the multilateral trading system. This broad mandate had been designed to act as a net that covered all environmental policies that have not been discussed under any other item of the work program. Similarly, item 4 of the CTE aims at ensuring transparency for trade measures used for environmental purposes and/or environmental measures and requirements having significant trade effects. This endeavor seeks to avoid WTO non-compliant barriers to trade, which, in turn, results in dispute avoidance and strengthening the global trading system. After the Doha Ministerial Meeting, item 2 was captured under paragraph 33 of the Doha Declaration.

Both items 2 and 4 discussed the relationship between environmental policies at a domestic level and ensuring the transparency of these policies. During the initial years of the WTO, discussions under these items were diverse and robust in substantive content. This was, perhaps, because delegations anticipated discord between the multilateral trading and environmental regimes and their application in domestic policy. What is also evident from the ensuing decline in discussions from 1995 till 2016 under both items is that delegations recognized that discussions on these items were unlikely to progress beyond that scope of discussions that had already taken place. This was despite the fact that item 2 of the original agenda items were subsumed under paragraph 33 of the Doha declaration.

The discussions in items 2 and 4 were relatively linear once the contours for discussion of the items were defined. For instance, under item 2, it was the U.S.'s proposal for Delegations to share their national experiences of introducing environmental policies and its effects on trade that initiated the process of sharing national experiences. While this suggestion was introduced under item 2, delegations also discussed their national experiences under other items as well—in particular, under item 6. This practice created an environment for delegations to constructively share their views, opinions, and learn from the methods used by the presenting Member. Another example of delegations' proposal shaping the agenda of an item was when *Hong Kong, China*, proposed the introduction of a database that was to be maintained by the WTO Secretariat under item 4 of the CTE agenda. Both the sharing of national experiences and the creation and maintenance of a database capturing domestic environmental measures with potential effects on trade are concrete outcomes from discussions that took place at the CTE.

In terms of work output, the CTE, through member involvement and expert work of the Secretariat, can be said to have delivered on its mandate and made positive contributions to the knowledge base and toolkits for policy makers and WTO delegations to benefit from the work done so far.

[A] CTE 2

Item 2 of the CTE had a broad mandate of assessing relationships between environmental policies relevant to trade and environmental measures, which had significant trade effects on the multilateral trading systems. This is indicative of the discussions that took place in the initial years. Delegations discussed a variety of topics such as property rights, tradeable emission permits, fiscal instruments, emission taxes, financial subsidies and bonds, and deposit refund system as possible issues that could be discussed under this item. Traction was gained, in particular, with regard to discussions on environmental subsidies under the Subsidies and Countervailing Measures (SCM Agreement). More specifically, Article 8.2 of the SCM Agreement relating to the identification of non-actionable subsidies was discussed in detail.[240] This category of subsidies was applicable provisionally for a period of five years and was set to end on December 31, 1999, but could be extended by consensus of the SCM Committee pursuant to Article 31 GATT. Some WTO Members were of the opinion that environmental subsidies may differ from more traditional forms of production subsidies but could still influence price and producers' incomes. However, since no consensus was reached at the SCM Committee, the provision expired on December 31, 1999, and no subsequent discussions on subsidies took place at the CTE under this item.

Two years later, in January 2003, Canada became the first country to present conclusions from its environmental assessments.[241] The two main findings were, *first*, that the environmental impact of agricultural production changes resulting from trade liberalization in agriculture would likely be minimal, and *second*, the overall economic impact of the negotiations would not significantly impact the environment for non-agricultural market access. Later, the European Commission (EC) made a presentation of their practice of requiring *sustainability impact assessments* (SIAs) for entering into trade agreements such as with MERCOSUR,[242] the U.S.,[243] New Zealand,[244] and the Dominican Republic[245] discussed its recent activities in assessments on its trade agreements, placing emphasis on the environmental aspects of the agreements. However, after this, there were no further discussions on this item with delegations demonstrating their national environmental assessment at the CTE under other items such as discussions on combating illegal logging or illegal, unreported and unregulated (IUU) fishing.[246]

240. WTO CTE, Report (1996) of the Committee on Trade and Environment, WT/CTE/1 (November 12, 1996).
241. WTO CTE, Initial Environmental Assessment: Trade Negotiations in the World Trade Organization, WT/CTE/W/221 (January 24, 2003).
242. WTO CTE, Sustainability Impact Assessment of Trade Agreements: Making Trade Sustainable?—DG Trade Seminar in Brussels (Submission by European Communities under Paragraph 33), WT/CTE/W/224 (February 21, 2003).
243. WTO CTE, Paragraph 33 of the Doha Declaration (Submission by the United States), WT/CTE/W/227 (April 29, 2003).
244. WTO CTE, Report of the Meeting Held on September 29, 2010, WT/CTE/M/50 (November 2, 2010) at ¶¶ 2-11.
245. *Id.* at ¶ 31.
246. *See generally* WTO CTE, Report of the Meeting Held on October 6, 2015, WT/CTE/M/60 (March 16, 2016).

[B] CTE 4

Between 1992 and 1994, the GEMIT had discussed the subject of transparency regularly.[247] However, no definitive conclusions had been drawn from its work.[248] Yet, there was a common understanding that several points relating to transparency would be discussed in future work. These points were broadly divided into three issues: *first*, to analyze the possibility of certain trade measures that could escape transparency mechanism because they are either not subject to substantive GATT/WTO disciplines or because those disciplines are not adequately linked to transparency requirements; *second*, to assess the extent to which measures are captured by the transparency requirements and, if need be, to recalibrate these requirements; and *third*, to study the compliance levels of GATT/WTO transparency requirements.[249]

Several narratives developed from ensuing discussions. From the proposals and interventions of many delegations, it was clear that the purpose of this item was to ensure trade measures taken for environmental purposes should be transparent so as to avoid unnecessary trade restrictions.[250] Some delegations believed that this would also present important information to producers about overseas market access opportunities and restrictions.[251] Many delegations were also of the view that proposed transparency requirements of trade-related environmental measures should not be more onerous than other measures affecting trade. Nevertheless, the CTE's Annual Report of 1996 noted that delegations felt it was important to examine whether any categories of trade-related environmental measures escaped WTO transparency mechanisms.[252]

Some WTO Members noted that the degree of transparency—be it *ex ante* or *ex post* notification—should correlate with the potential significance of a measure's trade. Other WTO Members felt that transparency mechanisms would increase overall costs and, therefore, assessment should be made on a case-by-case basis. *Hong Kong, China* suggested the establishment of inquiry points that would facilitate WTO Members' access to information about these measures.[253] Brazil noted that trade-related environment measures did not fall within the purview of TBT and SPS inquiry points.

In response, some WTO Members proposed a centralized collection point in the WTO for trade-related environmental measures, to which other Members proposed a database.[254] It was decided that this proposed database would include the nature and

247. WTO CTE, Report of the Meeting Held on December 14, 1995, WT/CTE/M/6 (January 17, 1996).
248. WTO CTE, Item 4: The Provisions of the Multilateral Trading with Respect to the Transparency of Trade Measures, WT/CTE/W/5 (March 23, 1995).
249. *Ibid.*
250. WTO CTE, Report (1996) of the Committee on Trade and Environment, WT/CTE/1 (November 12, 1996).
251. *See*, e.g., *Id.* at ¶¶ 65, 77.
252. *Id.* at ¶ 83.
253. WTO, Non-paper by *Hong Kong, China* (May 28, 1996) as cited in WTO CTE, Report (1996) of the Committee on Trade and Environment, WT/CTE/1 (November 12, 1996).
254. *See generally* WTO CTE, Central Registry of Notifications (CRN), Note by the Secretariat, WT/CTE/W/34 (August 5, 2007).

title of the measure, objective, product coverage, relevant WTO and MEA provisions, and description of how the measure operates and comments on its trade effects. There was a convergence for the establishment of a database, which was welcomed by most WTO Members, and the WTO Secretariat was mandated with the task of setting up this database.[255] Some WTO Members raised more fundamental questions about the difficulty in defining the term "environment" in an operational manner for the WTO.[256] Elaborating further, these delegations noted that many trade-related measures were associated with various public policy objectives, and it is possible that environmental or conservational aims may be ancillary policy characteristics in the measure.

Subsequently, the WTO Secretariat, mindful of the concerns raised by delegations, created what we have described already as one key policy tool and output of the CTE, the CTE annual EDB. As of 2008, for example, 3,636 documents were issued with respect to notifications submitted by Members under WTO law, of which 12.2% were environment-related.[257] These notifications were divided into two categories. The first category either explicitly referred to the environment was: (a) Annex 2 paragraph 12 of the Agreement on Agriculture, (b) Article 5 paragraph 2 of the SPS Agreement, (c) Articles 2 and 5 of the TBT Agreement, (d) Article XIV (b) of General Agreement on Trade in Services (GATS), (e) Article 27.2 of the TRIPS Agreement and (f) Article XX (b) of GATT 1994.[258] The second category included notifications that were not primarily environment-related but contained a reference to environment-related aspects. According to the database, most of the notifications were either SPS or TBT Agreement related.

After much debate, the annual EDB has become a fixture of the work of the CTE and a useful policy tool for delegates and trade and environment practitioners. The later versions of the EDB are made available in database-friendly formats and demonstrates the technical outputs of the CTE performed in conjunction with other divisions and work areas of the WTO. See, EDB for 2018, WT/CTE/EDB/18 (November 12, 2019).

255. Several discussions regarding the content and selection process of the database took place between 1997 and 1999.
256. WTO CTE, Report (1996) of the Committee on Trade and Environment, WT/CTE/1 (November 12, 1996).
257. WTO CTE, Environmental Database for 2008, WT/CTE/EDB/8 (October 4, 2010).
258. *Ibid.*

§4.07 KEY OUTPUT RELATED TO CTE 1, 5, 10

DRAFT MINISTERIAL DECISION ON TRADE AND ENVIRONMENT
[DISCUSSION DRAFT ONLY CITATIONS OMITTED]
[Extract from Annex I, Report of the Chair, TN/TE/20 (21 April 2011)]

Ministers,

Recalling that:

- Paragraph 31(i) of the Doha Ministerial Declaration called for negotiations on the relationship between existing WTO rules and specific trade obligations (STOs) set out in multilateral environmental agreements (MEAs) and stated that the negotiations were to be limited in scope to the applicability of such existing WTO rules as among parties to the MEA in question, and were not to prejudice the WTO rights of any Member that is not a party to the MEA in question;

- Paragraph 31(ii) of the Doha Ministerial Declaration called for negotiations on procedures for regular information exchange between MEA secretariats and the relevant WTO committees, and the criteria for the granting of observer status; and

- Pursuant to Paragraph 32 of the Doha Ministerial Declaration, the outcome of negotiations carried out under Paragraphs 31(i) and 31(ii) was to be compatible with the open and non-discriminatory nature of the multilateral trading system, not to add to or diminish the rights and obligations of Members under existing WTO Agreements, in particular the Agreement on the Application of Sanitary and Phytosanitary Measures, nor alter the balance of these rights and obligations, and was to take into account the needs of developing and least developed countries;

Affirming our commitment to the objective of sustainable development, as stated in the Preamble to the Marrakesh Agreement Establishing the World Trade Organization (WTO Agreement), and our conviction as stated in Paragraph 6 of the Doha Ministerial Declaration that the aims of upholding and safeguarding an open and non-discriminatory multilateral trading system, and acting for the protection of the environment and the promotion of sustainable development can and must be mutually supportive;

Recalling also the 1994 Marrakesh Ministerial Decision on Trade and Environment which considered that there should not be, nor need be, any policy contradiction between upholding and safeguarding an open, non-discriminatory and equitable multilateral trading system on the one hand, and acting for the protection of the environment, and the promotion of sustainable development on the other;

[*Noting that the Vienna Convention on the Law of Treaties states that every treaty in force is binding upon the parties to it and must be performed by them in good faith;*] [*Recognizing that both MEAs and the WTO Agreement are instruments of international law of equal standing between parties to the agreements, and that all provisions under international law should be implemented harmoniously and in good faith;*]

Committed to ensure coherence between international trade and environmental law in a mutually supportive way in order to continue to improve the architecture of international law to better cope with future challenges in an ever more interlinked world;

Reaffirming that MEAs constitute the response of the international community to environmental problems and play an instrumental role in reinforcing the individual and collective actions of all Members;

Recognizing the importance of technical assistance and capacity building in the field of trade and environment to developing countries, in particular, the least developed among them;

Noting the important work undertaken in the Committee on Trade and Environment in Special Session (CTESS) on Paragraphs 31(i) and 31(ii) of the Doha Ministerial Declaration;

Considering observations of Members in the CTESS that:

- A specific trade obligation (STO) set out in a multilateral environmental agreement (MEA) is understood to be one that requires an MEA Party to take, or refrain from taking, a particular trade action [a trade-related action];

- The relationship between WTO rules and STOs set out in MEAs is working well, and no formal disputes in the WTO have arisen challenging the implementation of an STO set out in an MEA;

- Until now STOs among parties to MEAs have not been contested in the WTO and should a situation arise of a WTO Member bringing such cases before the WTO, WTO rules would be applicable: observing also that STOs that are multilaterally negotiated, between parties and specific in nature are unlikely to be challenged in the WTO;

- Efforts undertaken by Members at the domestic level to coordinate the views of all relevant government agencies and stakeholders when negotiating and implementing STOs [as well as WTO rules] [, and also at the international level in terms of coordination between various governmental bodies and international organizations when addressing WTO matters related to MEAs,] have been helpful to enhancing the mutual supportiveness of trade and the environment;

- Sharing of domestic experiences in the CTESS in negotiating and implementing STOs [as well as WTO rules] has provided useful insight into ways in which Members can work to promote mutually supportive trade and environment policies;

- Several features in the design of STOs set out in MEAs have contributed to the positive relationship between such obligations and existing WTO rules such as, careful tailoring of STOs to meet a particular environmental objective, clarity of scope and application of STOs, certain procedures laid out in the MEA that rely on objective criteria and scientific input to make decisions, and other built in procedures in the MEA for changes to its scope that are inclusive, transparent and appropriately flexible;

Ministers,

With a view to enhancing the mutual supportiveness of trade and the environment, hereby *decide* as follows:

1. Members are encouraged to coordinate at the domestic level among relevant government agencies [and with international organizations] when negotiating and implementing WTO rules and when negotiating and implementing STOs set out in MEAs, and to share domestic experiences in this regard in the Committee on Trade and Environment (CTE) [, with a view to ensuring coherence/compatibility with rights and obligations arising from WTO Agreements and from STOs in MEAs].

2. The WTO Secretariat, on behalf of the CTE, shall:

   (a) cooperate and collaborate with MEA secretariats, including through: increased information exchange; as appropriate, document sharing and preparation; and enhanced trade and environment-related technical assistance and capacity building activities, particularly those related to the implementation of STOs set out in MEAs;

   (b) Facilitate appropriate access by MEA secretariats to derestricted WTO documents on a reciprocal basis and make information from MEA secretariats available to WTO Members, including through the use of indexing and internet-based tools. Access to derestricted WTO documents by MEA secretariats shall be facilitated in accordance with the General Council Decision of 14 May 2002 on Procedures for the Circulation and Derestriction of WTO Documents (WT/L/452).

3. While affirming that requests for observer status of international intergovernmental organizations are subject to the criteria and procedures set out in Annex 3 of the Rules of Procedure for Sessions of the Ministerial Conference and Meetings of the General Council (WT/L/161) the CTE shall, when examining requests for observer status from MEA secretariats, have particular regard to the following:

   (a) the relevance of the MEA's scope of work to the Committee as well as the relevance of the Committee's scope of work to the MEA;

   (b) the MEA secretariat's participation in the CTE and its prior contribution to WTO work, including workshops, capacity building activities and preparation of documents, and/or the mutual benefit that may accrue to the

Committee and the MEA from the MEA secretariat's participation in meetings of the CTE.

4. The CTE shall grant observer status to MEA secretariats that have applied for such status in the Committee and have met the criteria set out in paragraph 3 above;

The CTE shall grant observer status to the secretariats of the following MEAs, recognizing that all have applied for such status and have met the criteria and procedures set out in Annex 3 of the Rules of Procedure for Sessions of the Ministerial Conference and Meetings of the General Council: *(i) Basel Convention on the Control of Transboundary Movements of Hazardous Wastes and their Disposal; (ii) International Tropical Timber Organization; (iii) Montreal Protocol on Substances that Deplete the Ozone Layer; and (iv) Rotterdam Convention on the Prior Informed Consent Procedure for Certain Hazardous Chemicals and Pesticides in International Trade.*

5. The CTE shall:

(a) provide a forum to continue to share experiences of individual Members pursuant to paragraph 1 of this Decision with a view to enhancing the mutual supportiveness of trade and the environment;

(b) hold information exchange sessions with MEA secretariats on a regular basis. The sessions will provide an opportunity for two-way information exchanges between MEA and WTO secretariats and their respective memberships on topics of common interest;

(c) oversee the provision and, as necessary, the development of technical assistance activities by the WTO Secretariat focused on the implementation of STOs set out in MEAs, drawing on the WTO Secretariat's knowledge of provisions of the WTO Agreement, as well as the relevant MEA secretariat's knowledge of particular STOs. The Committee shall ensure that such activities draw on experiences and expertise shared in the Committee on Trade and Environment pursuant to this Decision, and take into account, *inter alia*, the following important objectives:

(i) maintenance of the independence of the respective secretariats;

(ii) avoidance of duplication of resources and efforts; and

(iii) consideration of developing countries, and in particular the least developed among them, as recipients of technical assistance.

[(d) [Establish][Provide for the establishment of] a group of [2] experts on trade and environment to be elected [every three years] by the CTE based on criteria to be determined by the Committee, who shall be available on a priority basis to least developed countries and developing countries as a complement to existing technical assistance mechanisms of the WTO.]

[(e) Provide for a flexible and expeditious procedure of a conciliatory and non-adjudicatory nature to assist Members with [potential] differences regarding the relationship between existing WTO rules and specific trade obligations of multilateral environmental agreements, through the offices of its Chair or a Friend of the Chair agreed upon by the parties.]

CHAPTER 5

Carbon, Eco-Labelling, DPGs, TRIPS, Services

§5.01 CARBON TAXES, CLIMATE, STANDARDS, ECO-LABELLING

CTE 3a, 3b, CTESS 32iii

CTE 3a, 3b

Item 3(a): *The relationship between the provisions of the multilateral trading system and charges and taxes for environmental purposes.*
Item 3(b): *The relationship between the provisions of the multilateral trading system and (b) requirements for environmental purposes relating to products, including standards and technical regulations, packaging, labelling and recycling*
DDA Paragraph 32(iii):
32. We instruct the Committee on Trade and Environment, in pursuing work on all items on its agenda within its current terms of reference, to give particular attention to: …
(iii) labelling requirements for environmental purposes.

Key Output Documents for Item 3(a) and 3(b):

1. Negotiating History of the Coverage of the Agreement on Technical Barriers to Trade with Regard to Labelling Requirements, Voluntary Standards, and Processes and Production Methods Unrelated to Product Characteristics, WT/CTE/W/10; G/TBT/W/11 (1995)
2. Taxes and Charges for Environmental Purposes—Border Tax Adjustment Report, WT/CTE/W/47 (2 May 1997)
3. Information Relevant to the Consideration of the Market Access effects of Eco-Labelling Schemes, WT/CTE/W/150 (2000)
4. 2009 WTO UNEP Climate Change Report (26 June 2009)
5. Eco-Labelling: Overview of Current Work in Various International Fora, JOB/TE/9 (29 September 2010)

For these special issues covered by CTE 3, 7, 8 and 9, the mandate of the CTE was clearly exploratory and designed to increase knowledge, expertise, and technical knowledge in the specific areas or issues identified in the 1994 work program. The lens of hard or positive law theory would not be immediately appropriate, though it remains part of the context, in that all study and knowledge gathering could, in the end, lead to new rules, or the clarification of existing rules, especially in the field of potential conflict with existing trade and/or environment policies. The main theoretical frame of positive rulemaking would also remain relevant where there may be evolving soft law or best practices evolving into customary rules.

However, most of the discussions under this chapter are best approached from the lens of enabling or increasing the expertise and knowledge for the secretariats of IOs, and the international and national bureaucracies and the CTE as well, as an institution. No negotiations were mandated though there was a Doha Ministerial instruction under paragraph 32(iii) that would focus further work on studying "labeling requirements for environmental purposes."

Based on the mandate to study and discuss these areas, one can generally evaluate that the results of the technical and specialized work of the CTE in these areas met with success and that the outputs were useful and complementary to the CTE. The discussions on the special issues of climate and carbon taxes were indeed among the highlights of the work of the CTE. The dissonance or sense occasionally felt of some frustration, is not due to the CTE not doing its work under the mandates of CTE 3, 7, 8, and 9, but rather the general condition, sometimes complained of, in Lens 2. With increased expertise, there is a great temptation to prescribe new rules or provide guidance from the perspective of the experts, or for the administrators to assume greater management discretion.

In these instances, there can be tension arising when the *Transnational Regulatory Networks (TRNs), managers, or experts* potentially go beyond their administrative sphere and into the realm of the delegations' political discretion. The other source of tension arises when members or governments themselves use their own expert base, through the *TRNs* to guide the secretariat and other members towards the establishment or formulation of new rules or practices that match the particular member's inclination or perception of the appropriate policy mix or governance measures. These are, of course, beyond the CTE's mandate given that in this area, as of now, no negotiations are mandated. However, within the general mandate of the CTE, there is the general option to propose areas for rules formulation, and in this context, preparatory work can be quite helpful and essential for advocates of the potential new rules.

§5.02 CTE 3A: CARBON AND BORDER TAXES, CLIMATE CHANGE

Item 3a seeks to analyze the potential effects of environmental taxes on trade, and the important issue of taxes at the border. The discussions include the effects of environmental taxes on the valuation of tradeable environmental products for tax purposes.

Delegations based their discussion on debating general economic principles and the potential effectiveness of levying environmental taxes and charges.

The narrative of the discussion for this item was not smooth, but in the end, part of the breakthrough was building up enough knowledge and expertise to have a more holistic discussion among the trade and environment policy makers. The trend would suffer peaks and troughs, with the Copenhagen Accord and later the Paris Climate Agreement making these agenda work items more acceptable and popular.

At the time the CTE was established in 1995, the UNFCCC had been signed at the Rio Earth Summit, and it was expected that there would be a necessary intersection of work between the WTO and the UNFCCC, as had happened with success with the Montreal Protocol where trade enforcement was a key feature.

[A] The 2009 WTO UNEP Report on Trade and Climate Change

A time marker, in what is concededly a still continuing transition, would be the CTE's deliberations during its July 10, 2009 meeting where the committee agreed to commence discussions directly on the topic of the inter-relationship of trade and climate change, and developments in other for a.[259] The CTE also agreed to have further informal sessions on the findings of the WTO UNEP Report on *Trade and Climate Change*, which had at the time just been formally presented on June 26, 2009, at the Centre William Rappard by the WTO Director General Pascal Lamy and UNEP Executive Director Achim Steiner.[260]

The WTO UNEP report is noteworthy in breaking the resistance through the early years of the CTE to tackle head-on issues on climate change and potential carbon taxes. The report is also complimented as a worthy CTE work output for being able to articulate in as simple terms as possible to the trade and environment community the theoretical and scientific nexus between trade policy, trade measures, and climate issues.

The WTO UNEP Report provided a significant and helpful political communication tool by explaining in layman's terms, or in translation to, as one would say, *ordinary English*, how trade volumes, economic activity, and accumulated carbon were seen as interlinked by the scientific and environmental community. The report demonstrated how trade, in theory, could lead to greater or lesser greenhouse gas emissions through the *scale*, *composition*, *technique*, and *direct* effects.[261]

The "scale" effect refers to the impact on greenhouse gas emissions from the increased output of economic activity resulting from freer trade. The general presumption is that trade opening will increase economic activity and hence energy use.

---

259. WTO CTE, Report (2009) of the Committee on Trade and Environment, WT/CTE/16 (October 30, 2009) at ¶¶ 14-15; WTO CTE, Report of the Meeting Held on July 10, 2009, WT/CTE/M/47 (August 31, 2009) at ¶¶ 69-103.
260. WTO UNEP *Trade and Climate Change Report (2009)*; *see also* WTO Media releases, available at: http://www.wto.org/english/news_e/pres09_e/pr559_e.htm (accessed November 30, 2019).
261. *Id.* at pp. 48 et seq. (Part II: Trade and Climate Change Theory and Evidence).

Everything else being equal, this increase in the scale of economic activity and energy use will lead to higher levels of greenhouse gas emissions.

The "composition" effect refers to the way that trade liberalization changes the mix of a country's production towards those products where it has a comparative advantage. This re-allocation of resources within a country is how trade improves economic efficiency. The effect on greenhouse gas emissions will depend on the sectors in which a country has a comparative advantage. The composition effect will result in less greenhouse gas emissions if the expanding sectors are less energy-intensive than the contracting sectors. Whether the composition effect results in higher or lower greenhouse gas emissions is, therefore, difficult to predict in advance.

Trade opening can lead to improvements in energy efficiency—the "technique" effect—so that the production of goods and services generates less greenhouse gas emissions. This decline in emission intensity can come about in two ways. First, freer trade will increase the availability and lower the cost of *environmentally friendly* goods, services and technologies.

Since the scale and technique effects tend to work in opposite directions, and the composition effect depends on the comparative advantage of countries, the overall impact of trade on greenhouse gas emissions cannot be determined in advance. It will depend on the magnitude or strength of each of the three effects. (WTO UNEP Trade and Climate Change Report (2009))

Finally, there are the "direct" effects of trade on Greenhouse Gas (GHG) emissions—for example, originating from transport that is required for the trade.

While no negotiations were mandated or linked to the work under CTE 3a or 3b, it becomes evident in the CTE discussions that there are parallel events and activities in the CTE 6 market access mandate as well as in the CTE 1.5.10 hierarchy and interface of norms mandate covered by the other work program areas. It will, therefore, be necessary to keep in mind the context of parallel negotiations or discussions overlapping with the areas of discussion in this chapter, particularly including the agenda item on market access.

[B] Carbon-Related Charges and Taxes

These provisions mandating the CTE to deal with charges and taxes had served as the basis for work dealing with BTAs related to carbon. The early history of the committee displayed a sharp divide between (i) members wishing to directly discuss climate change mitigation and adaptation issues as against (ii) members believing it was not within the mandate of or useful to the CTE's work. There was not a clear *developed-developing* countries divide on this issue, though it can be said that the EU and its members were more inclined to the former position and developing countries, including the main emerging developing countries as well as a major developed member, were more inclined towards the latter.[262] More recently, the committee has shifted

262. *See generally* CTE Minutes and Reports, e.g., WTO CTE, Report (1996) of the Committee on Trade and Environment, WT/CTE/1 (November 12, 1996); WTO CTE, Report (2007) of the

towards accepting that climate and carbon are part of the issues under the CTE work programs.

The issue of carbon adjustments at the border had been a sensitive topic in the CTE. It relates directly to the legal question of the WTO consistency of additional costs and taxes being imposed at the border to address climate change mitigation and carbon leakage issues. There is also the related question of arriving at an objective or universal basis for such carbon adjustments. The literature is rich in the potential inconsistency of border charges and taxes with: GATT Article I (MFN), Article II (violation of bindings), Article III (national treatment and like product/PPM issues), and Article XI (quantitative restriction prohibitions).[263]

Border tax adjustments (BTAs)

An important source of political opposition to measures aimed at reducing emissions of GHGs arises from concerns over their negative effects on the competitiveness of domestic firms. Politicians and industry fear that imports from countries without similar regulations can gain cost-of-production advantages over domestic goods. With many of the major economies of the world contemplating unilateral action to restrict their carbon emissions (while continuing to pursue coordinated multilateral action), a parallel concern that arises is that of carbon leakage, whereby domestic reductions in emissions are partially or wholly counterbalanced by increased emissions elsewhere in the world. Various adjustments have been proposed, both in the academic literature and in draft climate legislation, including levying a border tax or requiring importers to surrender a quantity of carbon permits.

Collectively, these kinds of adjustments are often referred to as border tax adjustments (BTAs) or border carbon adjustments (BCAs).

The dual issues of carbon leakage and competitiveness (energy-intensive domestic industries facing stiffer competition because of cost increases) have been central considerations in the design of flanking policies. Among the most common types are unilateral measures applied to imports — generally, either import taxes or requirements that importers surrender carbon permits. In recent years, other ideas have emerged on ways in which such measures could be designed to minimise adverse trade effects, and some commentators have proposed alternatives to measures applied on imports, such as voluntary export restraints.

From: Condon and Ignaciuk, 2013 https://www.oecd-ilibrary.org/fr/trade/border-carbon-adjustment-and-international-trade_5k3xn25b386c-en

Among the studies, the mentioned WTO UNEP report had explained that among the policy options being considered in the UNFCCC context were the measurement of embodied carbon in products and the imposition of carbon adjustments or charges at the border. Border measures were discussed as potentially subject of conflict with, or exceptions to, certain WTO rules, and it was this portion of the report that had attracted

Committee on Trade and Environment, WT/CTE/14 (December 4, 2007); WTO CTE, Report (2008) of the Committee on Trade and Environment, WT/CTE/15 (December 10, 2008); WTO CTE, Report (2009) of the Committee on Trade and Environment, WT/CTE/16 (October 30, 2009).

263. Patrick Low, Gabrielle Marceau and Julia Reinaud, *The Interface Between the Trade and Climate Change Regimes: Scoping the Issues* (2011), for a comprehensive discussion of the World Trade Organization legal provisions.

some controversy and debate at the July 10, 2009 meeting.[264] China and India, for example, had raised concerns that border measures and taxes were anti-competitive and unilateral, and contrary to the mandate of seeking a multilaterally agreed and coordinated approach to carbon leakage; and the concern was raised that the report could be read as providing a green light on the WTO consistency or validity of such border measures under certain conditions.[265]

Significantly on this topic, Singapore formally tabled on March 30, 2011, a paper on *Promoting Mutual Supportiveness between Trade and Climate Change Mitigation Actions: Carbon-Related Border Tax Adjustments* [BTAs] which was discussed on July 6, 2011.[266] Singapore clarified that it was seeking to increase awareness of BTA proposals tabled at the UNFCCC negotiations and not to propose any rules in the WTO.

According to Singapore, many discussions in these negotiations included a trade-angle which could possibly interface with WTO rules. The primary focus of this paper was to raise awareness among trade experts at the CTE on the use of carbon BTAs as an example of trade-related proposals tabled at UNFCCC. Another ancillary objective of the paper was to facilitate dialogue in the WTO to promote mutual supportiveness between trade rules and climate measures. This, Singapore reasoned, would ensure that trade-related climate initiatives were consistent with WTO rules and would not raise barriers to trade. The paper recalled that no discussions on the item took place since the run-up to the 1996 Singapore Ministerial Conference. However, it also reminded Members that the CTE had noted that:[267]

> [...] scope exists under the WTO provisions for Member governments to apply environmental charges and taxes. The CTE has undertaken so far a preliminary examination of some of these issues under the item. Further work on this item is needed.

Singapore urged Members to build on existing work and requested the CTE to prepare a compilation on three issues: *first*, the role of BTA in addressing competitiveness and leakage concerns; *second*, application of BTA in a WTO consistent manner; and *third*, usefulness of developing a set of multilaterally agreed guidelines to pre-empt the abuse of BTAs.[268]

China agreed with the main thrust of Singapore's paper.[269] However, it also disagreed on two broad issues. *First*, BTAs were not consistent with Article I and III of GATT 1947, nor could they be justified under Article XX of GATT 1947. *Second*, China

264. WTO UNEP *Trade and Climate Change (2009)* at Part IV.A.2 (Border Measures) at pp. 98 et seq.
265. *Ibid.*
266. WTO CTE, Promoting Mutual Supportiveness between Trade and Climate Change Mitigation Actions—Carbon-Related Border Tax Adjustments (Communication from Singapore), WT/CTE/W/248 (March 30, 2011); *see also* WTO CTE, Report (2011) of the Committee on Trade and Environment, WT/CTE/18 (November 21, 2011); and WTO CTE, Report of the Meeting Held on July 6, 2011, WT/CTE/M/52 (September 6, 2011) at ¶¶ 50-93.
267. *Ibid.*
268. WTO CTE, Promoting Mutual Supportiveness Between Trade and Climate Change Mitigation Actions—Carbon-Related Border Tax Adjustment (Communication from Singapore), WT/CTE/W/248 (March 30, 2011) at p. 4.
269. WTO CTE, Report of the Meeting Held on July 6, 2011, WT/CTE/M/52 (September 6, 2011) at ¶ 55.

supported the view that a multilateral climate agreement should first be agreed before discussing how the multilateral trade rules could be justified.

Saudi Arabia argued that the UNFCCC should have exclusive jurisdiction for any discussions relating to climate change.[270] Speaking on developing country issues specifically, Saudi Arabia said that "any discussion of this issue in the CTE could be used to justify the imposition of border measures, which would disadvantage developing country Members." India, while supporting Singapore's view that climate change needed global solutions, also felt that WTO was not the correct forum to engage in such discussions.[271] India commented that "WTO-inconsistent trade measures would reduce development prospects for developing countries." India also asked why Singapore would introduce the subject for discussion at the CTE though Singapore had clearly indicated that it did not intend to bring UNFCCC negotiations to the WTO. Australia also agreed that UNFCCC was the competent body to deal with a legally binding agreement on climate change.[272] New Zealand noted that carbon BTAs would be difficult to design or effectively enforce in a WTO-consistent manner.[273] It further noted that there was a risk that the imposition of BTAs could prompt retaliatory trade measures, which would affect international trade. The representative of Argentina also strongly criticized the paper and summarized developing county concerns.[274]

During the first three years of the CTE, there were robust discussions on different facets of item 3(a). Amongst these, the most prominent was the legality of eco-tax measures in light of the GATT rules on BTAs and the effect of eco-tax measures on non-product related PPMs. For more than a decade after this, discussions on the item were sparse and lacking substantial proposals. In March 2011, Singapore introduced a paper that discussed trade, climate change, and the role of carbon taxes. This paper sparked an intense debate with many Members marking reservations to Singapore's conclusion that carbon BTAs are GATT consistent. However, with no subsequent submission, discussions related to the item declined post Singapore's submission again. Nevertheless, issues related to this item overlap with market access, which is in item 6 of the CTE work program, and several Members have made submissions under this item under paragraph 32(i) of the Doha Declaration.

The relationship between the multilateral trading system and charges and taxes for environmental purposes can, in simpler terms, be rephrased as WTO consistency of environmental tax adjustments at the border. Seeking clarity, WTO Members examined the application of BTA rules to environmental taxes and charges. According to the 1996 Report of the CTE, WTO Members presented diverging views on the potential trade effects of levying environmental taxes and charges on imports and providing rebates on exports for correcting consumption and production externalities.[275] For these discussions, Members used the 1970 Report of the GATT Working Party as a

270. *Id.* at ¶ 56.
271. *Id.* at ¶ 59.
272. *Id.* at ¶ 70.
273. *Id.* at ¶ 67.
274. *Id.* at ¶ 72.
275. WTO CTE, Report (1996) of the Committee on Trade and Environment, WT/CTE/1 (November 12, 1996) at pp. 14-15

point of reference to assess the treatment of environmental taxes and charges under BTA provisions.[276] This report stated that BTA provisions were based on the concept of trade neutrality and applied the destination principle. Further, the report recommended that certain taxes not levied directly on products were ineligible for BTA, whereas those directly levied would be considered eligible for tax adjustment. Put differently, the 1970 GATT Working Party concluded that the application of BTA was possible for taxes which were imposed directly on a product. These taxes were WTO-consistent as long as MFN and national treatment obligations were respected.. Switzerland said that the use of eco-taxes was efficient and innovative. However, the delegate of Switzerland cautioned Members to recall WTO rules before the eco-tax measure is applied.[277]

WTO Members also presented views on the application of BTA to environmental taxes or charges applied to non-product-related PPMs. One WTO Member contended that BTA would apply solely to taxes levied on products or product-related PPMs. Some WTO Members such as Switzerland noted that the application of BTA on PPMs would be complicated given that PPMs are domestic by definition and would negatively affect exclusively domestic producers as well. Contrary to Switzerland's position, Canada enunciated that its concern with eco-tax on PPMs was grounded in the presumption that measures aimed at the local environment would negatively impact the production stage in export countries because of the application of non-product related PPM standards.[278] Some WTO Members even suggested that environmental taxes and charges should be accorded different treatment under WTO rules than normal fiscal measures. Despite conflicting views, the CTE, by November 1996, had recognized that scope existed under WTO provisions for WTO Members to apply environmental charges and taxes. This was based on a preliminary examination undertaken by the CTE.[279]

Further, some WTO Members made reference to the Agreement on SCM when discussing the likely treatment of a rebate for exported products of indirect environmental taxes on non-product-related PPMs in excess of tax rebate on a "like" product when sold for domestic production. In particular, provisions listed under "prohibited subsidies" in Article 2 and Annex I of the SCM Agreement and the "Guidelines on Consumption of Inputs in the Production Process" in Annex II were discussed in detail.[280]

From 2002 till 2010, there were no direct submissions or statements related to item 3(a). In 2002, Saudi Arabia, which was then an observer at the WTO, said that

276. *Id.* at ¶¶ 49-54, citing Report of the Working Party (Border Tax Adjustments) (2 December 1970), L/3464, BISD 18S/97-109.
277. WTO CTE, Report of the Meeting Held on October 26-27, 1995, WT/CTE/M/5 (November 30, 1995) at pp. 17-18 (paras. 62 - 67).
278. WTO CTE, Report of the Meeting Held on October 26-27, 1995, WT/CTE/M/5 (November 30, 1995).
279. Id. at para. 62. WTO CTE Report (1996) of the Committee on Trade and Environment, WT/CTE/1 (November 12, 1996), at para. 53.
280. One WTO Member noted that energy taxes would be covered by Footnote 61 of the SCM Agreement whereas another reasoned that physical incorporation would be the basis for application of BTA; *see generally* WT/CTE/1 (November 12, 1996), at para. 53.

WTO Members were imposing high taxes on imported commodities such as oil from developing countries to promote environmental protection.[281] The representative of Saudi Arabia said that a paper on this issue would be submitted to the CTE.[282] The representative of Venezuela agreed with Saudi Arabia and contended that unjustifiably high taxes on petrochemicals were being implemented by several WTO Members. Kuwait also stated that it did not favor fiscal policies to fulfill climate change obligations such as taxes and subsidies laid down under the Kyoto Protocol.[283]

In 2013, Australia presented its Clean Energy Future Package. This was an economy-wide carbon pricing mechanism designed to reduce Australia's carbon emissions in line with international commitments. Saudi Arabia argued that carbon pricing could be a disguised restriction to trade. Moreover, it noted that this issue should be discussed at the UNFCCC and not the WTO.[284]

With no further discussions on this topic, two things were clear. *First*, that there was no consensus amongst WTO members—developed and developing countries alike—on the compatibility of BTAs since 1996. *Second*, emerging views on the appropriate forums for discussion were forming, and UNFCCC was largely identified as that forum. Yet, this statement only holds steady with the introduction of a caveat: Members were constantly testing the limits to which the CTE could be used to discuss the issue. For instance, Australia, who felt that the issue raised by Singapore should be dealt with at the UNFCCC, was, in turn, told by Saudi Arabia that the CTE was not the correct forum to present its experience on carbon pricing mechanisms.[285]

In sum, with Members presenting ideas from policy experts, the CTE gradually became more open to potential rulemaking, with no prejudice to the necessity of a ministerial mandate. Within its *talk-shop* mandate (as opposed to a rulemaking committee) and in the theoretical frame of increasing knowledge, there was a healthy discussion which a strict rules-inclined policy maker would probably find exasperating.

However, to bureaucrats, experts, and academic researchers, these meetings with lively discussions would certainly make their day and fit well into the mode of specialization and justify the continued existence of their respective divisions. The question is whether the brainstorming and expert and technical output and capacities of the CTE could be more formalized for better availability to policy makers. Similar discussions relating to the building of the knowledge base in the area of environmental policy, as well as the conundrum of institutionalizing or preserving said knowledge,

281. WTO CTE, Report of the Meeting Held on March 21, 2002, WT/CTE/M/29 (May 7, 2002) at p. 18.
282. Later, in 2010, Saudi Arabia made a proposal on Technology Dissemination dealing indirectly with subsidies and incentives. *See generally* WTO CTE, Technology Dissemination (Communication by the Kingdom of Saudi Arabia), WT/CTE/W/247 (October 29, 2010); *see also* WTO CTE, Report of the Meeting Held on June 5, 2013, WT/CTE/M/55 (August 16, 2013).
283. WTO CTESS, Summary Report on the Third Meeting of the Committee on Trade and Environment Special Session, TN/TE/R/3 (October 31, 2002).
284. WTO CTE, Report of the Meeting Held on June 5, 2013, WT/CTE/M/55 (August 16, 2013) at pp. 11-12.
285. *Id.* at p. 12.

would also be experienced in the other areas of discussion, such as in the areas of eco-labelling and standards.

[C] Technical Assistance, Technologies and Expertise Sharing

Paragraph 33 of the Doha Ministerial Declaration had provided additional areas for the committee to examine, namely, (i) the importance of technical assistance and capacity building to benefit developing countries, and (ii) expertise and experience be shared with members wishing to perform ERs at the national level.

In terms of experience sharing, and quite specific to the issue of the correlation between trade and climate change mitigation, the CTE did have an occasion to benefit from the assessment shared by Korea on their Free Trade Agreement (FTA) with the US. Korea reported to the committee specifically that their FTA was evaluated, among other impacts, in respect of air pollutants, and that their studies projected a decrease of air pollutants by 0.35%.[286] Necessarily, these types of assessments are difficult to model and establish for many developing countries, and the UNEP representative at the same meeting highlighted the challenges and capacity building opportunities for developing countries to do reliable ERs of trade agreements.[287]

§5.03 CTE 3B: LABELLING

Labelling is one of the subjects assigned to the CTE. It is part of an item 3b on the committee's work program in which the committee is assigned to consider the relationship between the provisions of the WTO's agreements and the requirements governments make for products in order to protect the environment. In addition to labelling, this includes standards and technical regulations, and packaging, and recycling requirements.

In 2001, the Doha Ministerial Conference made this an issue of special focus for the regular CTE (i.e., the regular committee sessions that are not part of the Doha Round negotiations). (*See* paragraph 32(iii) of the Doha Declaration.) The use of ecolabels (i.e., labelling products according to environmental criteria such as energy efficiency) is increasing. Concerns have been raised about the growing complexity and diversity of environmental labelling schemes. One reason for this complexity is that ecolabels emanate from both top-down (government-regulated and mandatory) and bottom-up (voluntary and driven by civil society or industry) initiatives. Labelling that is based on life cycle analysis, which looks at a product's environmental effects from the first stages of its production to its final disposal, can be particularly complex. These requirements could create difficulties for developing countries to comply with eco-labelling schemes, and particularly SMEs in export markets.

---

286. WTO CTE, Report of the Meeting Held on June 5, 2013, WT/CTE/M/55 (August 16, 2013) at ¶ 103.
287. WTO CTE, Report of the Meeting Held on May 2, 2007, WT/CTE/M/44 (June 13, 2007) at ¶¶ 106 et seq.

These same schemes could be misused to protect domestic producers. For this reason, the schemes should not discriminate between countries and should not create unnecessary barriers or disguised restrictions on international trade.

A particularly thorny issue in the eco-labelling debate has been the use of criteria linked to processes and production methods (PPMs). WTO Members agree that countries are within their rights under WTO rules to set criteria for the way products are produced if the production method leaves a trace in the final product; for example, cotton is grown using pesticides, leaving pesticide residue in the cotton itself. In that case, there are more obvious distinctions between products that are produced in a more environmentally friendly manner and those products that are not.

However, WTO Members disagree about discriminatory measures based on "unincorporated PPMs" (or "non-product related PPMs"), i.e., PPMs which leave no trace in the final product. For example, one cannot tell whether a table has been produced from sustainably managed wood by simply looking at it. The key question is: are these measures consistent with WTO agreements? Many countries argue that measures that discriminate between products based on unincorporated PPMs, such as some ecolabels, should be considered inconsistent with WTO agreements.

[A] CTE 3b: Eco-Labelling – Developing Country Concerns

In the discussion, developing country members voiced concerns about the proliferation of labels, certificates and schemes. While ecolabels can be used to foster compliance with environmental goals and policies, they can also raise market access barriers for many developing country exporters due to the lack of transparency and coherence, or the diversity of deferring requirements. While some concordance in standards was developing as private organizations responsible for voluntary standards signed MRAs with other similar organizations based in different countries, the international regime was still largely in disarray. This brought with it a potentially onerous burden on exporters, particularly from developing countries to enter foreign markets given that voluntary labelling schemes were de facto mandatory. Whilst, none of these issues were resolved per se, the CTE provided a platform where governments could debate the contours of these labelling schemes and their impact on market access.

A key point of reference in this item was the TBT Agreement and its relationship with eco-labelling/environmental labelling schemes/programs. The GEMIT had undertaken considerable empirical work on this issue, having covered eco-labelling, environmental packaging, and waste handling requirements. Also, discussions on eco-labelling were enriched by presentations of several existing schemes at a joint-informal session of the CTE and TBT committee. It was Canada that opened discussions on this item in 1995 by noting that four aspects should be considered when considering eco-labelling: transparency, government participation, life-cycle analysis (LCA), and work in other fora.[288] In particular, Canada underscored the importance of transparency and observed that the application of TBT transparency provisions could address some substantive concerns.[289] However, the representative also noted that eco-labelling, in contrast to other labelling programs, was largely based on non-product related PPMs because of the extensive use of LCA. As a result, the Canadian delegation proposed extending TBT disciplines to non-product related PPMs, which, according to Canada, was, in its present form, not sufficient to deal with it.[290] With Canada setting the tone for the discussion, the CTE provided a forum for debating the topical issues that item 3b sought to cover.

At the CTE, members were able to present eco-labelling schemes that had been implemented in their jurisdictions. These presentations illustrated a variety of approaches that had been adopted by WTO Members. Chile presented the Chilean Ozone Seal of Approval System.[291] The Czech Republic presented its national eco-labelling program, which applied equally for domestic as well as imported products.[292] The EU (European Communities/EC at the time) explained the Ecolabel Award which entered into force on March 23, 1992, as having a twofold objective of promoting products with reduced environmental impact over their entire life cycle and providing consumers with better information on environmental impact products, and that EU members had already implemented voluntary market-led eco-labelling schemes. These included Germany, the Netherlands, France, Spain, Austria, and Sweden. Canada described its eco-labelling scheme and stated that four aspects should be considered when implementing eco-labelling regimes: transparency, government participation, LCA, and work in other fora.[293] Other countries that discussed their eco-labelling regulations were the U.S. and the Nordic Countries, including Norway, Sweden, Iceland, and Finland, which called their policy the "Nordic Swan." Interestingly, *Nordic Swan* was the first eco-labelling regime to have been implemented when it was passed in November 1989 by the Nordic Council of Ministers.[294]

Many WTO Members noted that a deeper analysis of eco-labelling schemes was required to determine its effectiveness as a policy instrument for environmental

288. WTO CTE, Report of the Meeting Held on October 26-27, 1995, WT/CTE/M/5 (November 30, 1995) at pp. 18-19.
289. *Id.* at p. 20.
290. *See generally* WTO Committee on Technical Barriers to Trade, Draft Minutes of the Meeting Held on October 20, 1995, G/TBT/W/55 (November 22, 1995).
291. This scheme was created after the *Montreal Protocol to Protect the Ozone Layer* entered into force. According to the scheme, an ecological label was given to all products that did not damage the ozone layer or did not contain ozone depleting substances. Companies that either did not use ozone depleting substances or reconverted their traditional technology so as not to contribute to ozone depletion participated in the scheme; *see also* WTO CTE, Report of the Meeting Held on June 5, 2013, WT/CTE/M/55 (August 16, 2013) at pp. 2-3.
292. 141 ecolabels granted to twenty-one firms of which four firms were German, three were Italian and one was British. Note also, that Czech Republic was formed from erstwhile Czechoslovakia and became a Member of the European Union on May 1, 2004, *see Id.* at pp. 2-3.
293. WTO CTE, Report of the Meeting Held on October 26-27, 1995, WT/CTE/M/5 (November 30, 1995).
294. *See generally* WTO CTE, Report of the Meeting Held on June 5, 2013, WT/CTE/M/55 (August 16, 2013); *see also* Nordic Eco-labelling, The History of Nordic Eco-labelling, available at: www.nordic-ecolabel.org/about/history/ (accessed on November 30, 2019).

protection, particularly in view of their potentially trade-distorting nature. These Members saw eco-labelling as an important cornerstone of Agenda 21. They were concerned that successful eco-labelling schemes would influence consumer behavior and could significantly affect market access. Other Members expressed doubts about eco-labelling becoming a significant force in the market. They noted that only twenty schemes were implemented globally. Some Members even questioned why the CTE had spent a large amount of time discussing these schemes, given the small number of eco-labelling schemes in operation. They noted that existing eco-labelling schemes were "overwhelmingly voluntary" in nature, thereby allaying concerns of their potential trade-restricting effects.

The main concerns of developing countries were the potential negative impact on their market access for their exports to developed economies, such as difficulties in complying with standards based on non-product-related PPMs, or the impact on small firms for whom difficulties would arise in obtaining and adapting the required technology. Other concerns related to multiple criteria-based schemes and programs which would inevitably reflect the environmental conditions, preferences, and priorities prevailing in that domestic market. This would result in creating market access difficulties and make it onerous on overseas suppliers that operate in different environmental conditions. According to these Members, such schemes would increase costs to producers who would have to adjust their products to meet the criteria of their export markets. In examining the relationship between the TBT Agreement and eco-labelling schemes, two points need to be discussed: *first*, the application of the notification and other transparency provisions of the TBT Agreement related to eco-labelling standards; and, *second*, the applicability of the provisions of the TBT Agreement to voluntary eco-labelling schemes based, *inter alia*, on criteria of non-product related PPMs.

With regard to the first issue, it is a widely held view that full transparency is important to mitigate potential trade disputes. Transparency provisions would also increase the legitimacy of such schemes and programs. WTO Members recalled that the TBT Committee had decided that mandatory labelling requirements were subject to notification provisions of Article 2.9 of the TBT Agreement.[295] Some WTO Members also considered that voluntary eco-labelling standards were subject to the transparency provisions of the Code of Good Practices for the Preparation, Adoption, and the Application of Standards of the TBT Agreement.[296] Other WTO Members argued that such interpretation was erroneous. With regard to the second issue, many delegations presented their interpretation of the negotiating history of the TBT Agreement, which, according to them, did not legitimize the use of measures based on non-product-related PPMs. The United Arab Republic of Egypt raised an objection to extend the scope of the

295. WTO Committee on Technical Barriers to Trade, Decisions and Recommendations Adopted by the Committee since January 1, 1995, G/TBT/1/Rev.3 (March 28, 1996).
296. *See* Annex 3 of the Agreement on Technical Barriers to Trade, 1868 U.N.T.S.120.

TBT Agreement through the CTE's work on eco-labelling so as to permit the use of standards based on non-product-related PPMs.[297]

In the specific areas of product requirements relating to carbon footprint labelling and standard-setting, and with the increased interest in discussing the impact of labelling, the work and discussions in the committee increased in frequency with the CTE meetings going beyond the usual one or two meetings per year.[298] In the 2009 report of the CTE, developing countries raised their concern about "unilateral voluntary carbon footprint labelling schemes, believing that these schemes were not based on life cycle analysis and lacked consistency."[299] In 2010, the discussions on carbon footprint and labelling as it related to market access concerns heated up with this topic being discussed in detail during the four meetings of the committee, including an information session devoted to *Product Carbon Footprint and Labelling Schemes*.[300] Developing countries, such as China, Argentina, Saudi Arabia, Turkey and Colombia, speaking on the issue of market access and carbon footprint labelling requirements, expressed their concerns on the difficulty of determining an objective basis for a product's carbon footprint. These members argued that this would only provide further grounds for concerns that carbon-related standards, whether voluntary or government-imposed, could be used as a means for restricting trade or exports, particularly from developing countries.[301]

As summed up succinctly in the 2010 report of the committee, members across the board expressed a clear interest in the topic, particularly as regards:

> the competitiveness implications of these schemes for domestic industry; the cost and market access impact of these schemes for developing countries and small and medium-sized enterprises (SMEs), especially in the context of multiple, overlapping schemes and standards; the potential non-neutrality of carbon footprint methodologies; the lack of a uniform methodology for calculating carbon footprints; the risk of discrimination on the basis of non-product related processes and production methods (PPMs); the role of carbon footprint for identifying emissions "hotspots" in the production process; and the relevance of the TBT Agreement to this discussion.[302]

297. Egypt Non-paper, June 18, 1996, as cited in footnote 47 of WTO CTE, Report (1996) of the Committee on Trade and Environment, WT/CTE/1 (November 12, 1996).
298. Formal meetings were held on February 17, 2010, September 29, 2010 and November 9, 2010, and informal meetings took place on February 17, 2010, July 2, 2010 and September 29, 2010. *See* WTO CTE, Report (2010) of the Committee on Trade and Environment, WT/CTE/17 (November 30, 2010).
299. WTO CTE, Report (2009) of the Committee on Trade and Environment, WT/CTE/16 (October 30, 2009) at ¶ 4.
300. *See* WTO CTE, Summary Report of the Meeting Held on February 17, 2010, WT/CTE/M/49/Add.1 (May 28, 2010).
301. *See* WTO CTE, Report of the Meeting Held on February 17, 2010, WT/CTE/M/49 (April 7, 2010), specifically deliberating on the Information Session on Product Carbon Footprint and Labelling Schemes held in the morning of February 17, 2010 at ¶ 9 (Saudi Arabia), ¶ 10 (India), ¶ 14 (Colombia), ¶¶ 15-17 (Argentina), ¶ 20 (Turkey) and ¶ 22 (China).
302. WTO CTE, Report of the Meeting Held on February 17, 2010, WT/CTE/M/49 (April 7, 2010) at p. 7.

The main concerns of developing countries, even in areas of other environmental standards, such as for organic agriculture, related to these standards operating as an additional technical barrier to trade on exports of developing countries. Even back in 2007, the delegation of China and India had already voiced serious concerns in the committee meetings about the increasing use of environment-related product requirements and standards:[303]

> [India] said that ... since governments had no role in setting private standards, these standards were not notified to the TBT Committee. Second, on market access, private standards inclined to fragment the market, since each private buyer had its own standard, it became burdensome for producers to cater to different standards under the same production facility.
>
> China said that in recent years, environmental requirements had posed serious challenges to developing countries' exports, including those from China. Three trends could be observed on new environmental requirements. First, they tended to relate to processes and production methods (PPMs) rather than end products. They usually targeted sectors and products that developed countries had stopped producing, but of trade interests to developing countries. Finally, these new requirements prepared by one country could create a domino effect encouraging other countries to follow, which in turn would increase the difficulties faced by developing countries.

There was also work in 2007 at the committee related to a voluntary labelling scheme for energy efficiency called "Energy Star" as a contribution to the effort to mitigate the effects of climate change through the increased use of more energy-efficient appliances. This certainly directly involved the climate change mandate of mitigation under the rubric of the UNFCCC. There was a form of intergovernmental coordination on voluntary standards between standard-setting agencies among partner countries; for example, there was cooperation between the U.S. Environmental Protection Agency (EPA) and China's Standards and Certification Centre.[304]

[B] Eco-Labelling: WTO Members' Views and Proposals

In October 2002, Switzerland requested for a common understanding of the qualifying elements of eco-labelling schemes.[305] It contended that such an understanding could lead to significant facilitation of discussions at the CTE. It also queried whether the contour of the term "eco-labelling" included mandatory environmental labelling schemes or whether it was only limited to those labelling schemes that were voluntary in nature. It stated that since the Doha mandate specifically referred to "labelling requirements for environmental purposes," subsequent discussions in the CTE should

303. WTO CTE, Report of the Meeting Held on May 2, 2007, WT/CTE/M/44 (June 13, 2007) at ¶¶ 27-30.
304. WTO CTE, Report of the Meeting Held on May 2, 2007, WT/CTE/M/44 (June 13, 2007) at ¶¶ 69-72.
305. WTO CTE, Labelling for Environment Purposes (Submission by Switzerland), WT/CTE/W/219 (October 14, 2002).

not be limited to voluntary schemes but must also include mandatory labelling schemes.[306]

The EU submitted a proposal in June 2002 that dealt with labelling requirements.[307] It demonstrated similar views to those made by Switzerland about the benefits and potential challenges associated with labelling. It proposed that the TBT Committee should hold an informal workshop which CTE members could attend. This would, according to the EU, enhance synergies between the ongoing works on labelling in Committees and fora at the WTO. After all, paragraph 32 of the Doha Ministerial Declaration instructed the "Committee on Trade and Environment ... to give particular attention to: ... (iii) labeling requirements for environmental purposes." It also noted that facilitating technical assistance was the key to addressing developing country concerns on labelling.[308] Further, the EU/EC requested the CTE to analyze all notifications relating to labelling in the TBT Committee and also to provide an overview of developing country technical assistance relating to labelling.

The EU observed that labelling schemes that promoted environmental objectives had increased considerably since discussions on the topic began at the WTO in 1995.[309] Further, it listed developing countries that had introduced voluntary eco-labelling schemes based on LCA, including the Republic of Korea, China, India, Brazil, Thailand, Indonesia and Malaysia.[310] The EU observed that implementation of eco-labelling schemes could have consequences for international trade and should be applied in a transparent manner. Therefore, the EU opined that CTE discussions should be grounded on five principles. *First*, the use of voluntary eco-labelling schemes based on LCA contributed to achieving environmental objectives. *Second*, such schemes would provide an opportunity for developing countries to enter markets where environmental considerations were important. *Third*, the use of voluntary eco-labelling schemes based on LCA was legitimate and within the rights and obligations of WTO Agreements. *Fourth*, developing country governments needed to be supported to access operations of such schemes. And *fifth*, these schemes should reflect the principles embedded in the TBT Code of Good Practice.[311]

Canada had actively participated in discussions on eco-labelling. In its interventions, it had noted that in recent years, the number of labelling proposals notified and adopted by WTO Members increased significantly. While it was difficult to estimate with precision the impact these measures had on trade, Canada stated that there was strong evidence that certain labelling measures had affected the international flow of goods. In a submission dated June 2003, Canada stated that the TBT Agreement applied to all labelling measures that fit the definition of either a technical regulation or a

306. *Id.* at p. 1.
307. WTO CTE, Labelling for Environment Purposes (Submission by EC), WT/CTE/W/208 (June 3, 2002).
308. *Id.* at p. 2.
309. WTO Committee on Technical Barriers to Trade, Minutes of the Meeting of November 10-11, 2011, G/TBT/M/55 (February 9, 2002).
310. WTO CTE, Labelling for Environment Purposes (Submission by EC), WT/CTE/W/208 (June 3, 2002), at pp. 10-17.
311. *Id.* at ¶¶ 286, 291.

standard, except those governed by disciplines in the SPS Agreement. Canada, thus, saw no rationale in re-negotiating existing rules. Canada also reasoned that WTO Members would need to—at the outset—distinguish between mandatory measures and voluntary measures. In doing so, Canada encouraged Members to explore two sequential questions relating to necessity and design. *First*, relating to necessity, Canada stated that the following questions be asked:[312]

> What is the problem or risk to be addressed? Is the labelling proposal necessary to fulfill a legitimate objective? Does the proposal have to be in the form of a technical regulation? Are there other equally effective options? This includes discussion on whether the technical regulation option can meet a "least trade restrictive" or "no more trade restrictive than necessary" test while achieving the objective; and whether the proposal would discriminate amongst '*like products*.'

Second, with regard to the design of the measure, Canada proposed that Members deliberate whether:[313]

> [...] labelling measures in the form of technical regulations are deemed necessary and considered the best option for achieving a given legitimate objective, then there needs to be further consideration on methodology and transparency when establishing criteria for the labelling measure. (e.g., is the criteria being proposed more onerous than necessary to meet the objective? Is the process to establish the criteria inclusive and transparent?)

According to Canada, eco-labelling was a topic that needed further discussion and stated that the TBT Committee should take "strong interest" in the discussions related to eco-labelling. This is because labelling for environmental purposes such as non-product related PPM labelling presented a more complicated scenario than a regular labelling regime.

To recall, until now, different Members had different interpretations of the applicability of the TBT Agreement and its application in labelling schemes. In 2002, the EU presented a paper on labelling in which it was noted that labelling, while less restrictive than many regulatory measures, could significantly impact trade.[314] As a result of its implementation, developing country exporters could face problems related to compliance. The paper reiterated that the most debated issue was that of non-product-related PPMs. There were two primary issues that the EU paper sought to highlight: *first*, the role of international standards for labelling and, *second*, developing country concerns. With regard to international standards, the paper noted that labelling had significant potential to facilitate trade if these standards were harmonized. According to the EU, Members should discuss ISO standards for voluntary eco-labelling at the CTE to gain an understanding of its implications. Regarding developing country concerns, the paper noted that "CTE could look at ways of ensuring

312. WTO Committee on Technical Barriers to Trade, Labelling and Requirements of the Agreement on Technical Barriers to Trade (Communication from Canada), G/TBT/W/174 (March 12, 2002) at p. 3.
313. *Ibid*.
314. WTO CTE, Report of the Meeting Held on June 13-14, 2002, WT/CTE/M/30 (September 11, 2002).

timely information on proposed or existing labeling schemes; the facilitation of compliance with labeling requirements; and the promotion of participation in international standard-setting."[315] The EU paper also set out two specific ideas as future plans of action. *First*, the EU suggested that a TBT Secretariat paper with a descriptive analysis of the primary areas of discussions should be distributed to Members. This, according to the EC, would provide an overview of the state of play of discussions on labelling at both WTO and other international fora. Discussions based on this paper would be relevant to the CTE as well. *Second*, the EU supported a proposal for the TBT Committee to organize an informal workshop on labelling. This, according to the EU, would assist the CTE in finalizing its report on paragraph 32(ii) of the Doha declaration for the 5th Ministerial Meeting in Cancun, Mexico.

Switzerland commented that while the TBT Committee dealt with labelling, in general, the CTE needed to focus its attention on eco-labelling, in particular.[316] For this, Switzerland proposed the initiation of discussions that would assist in defining the term eco-labelling and identifying pertinent rules of WTO agreements that would be applicable.[317] Further, the delegate of Switzerland stressed that the CTE needed to intensify its work on environmental labelling in line with the Doha mandate and proposed a three-step approach.[318] *First*, Switzerland noted that the CTE should identify a common understanding of the notion of eco-labelling, which would account for various types of labelling schemes, be they mandatory or voluntary. *Second*, upon conclusion of such identification, Switzerland proposed the need to identify STCs relevant to environmental labelling. To this end, Switzerland suggested that the WTO Secretariat be asked to update its overview on the notifications filed within the TBT Committee with regard to environmental labelling.[319] *Third*, based on the conclusion of these processes, the CTE could make recommendations on necessary actions that could be taken as part of the Doha mandate.[320]

Contrary to the views espoused by the EU and Switzerland, Australia remained convinced that WTO disciplines were adequate to deal with eco-labelling.[321] The U.S. also considered the possibility of recommending discussions on eco-labelling in terms of general labelling discussions at the TBT Committee.[322] Brazil asserted that the Doha declaration did not clearly assign the task of progressing work on environmental

315. WTO CTE, WTO Committee on Technical Barriers to Trade Labelling (Submission by the European Communities), WT/CTE/W/212; G/TBT/W/175 (June 12, 2002).
316. WTO CTE, Report of the Meeting Held on June 13-14, 2002, WT/CTE/M/30 (September 11, 2002) at p. 22.
317. *Id.*, at pp. 22-23.
318. WTO CTE, Report of the Meeting Held on October 8, 2002, WT/CTE/M/31 (December 2, 2002) at p. 23.
319. *Ibid.*
320. WTO CTE, Report of the Meeting Held on October 8, 2002, WT/CTE/M/31 (December 2, 2002) at pp. 1-4.
321. WTO CTE, Report of the Meeting Held on October 8, 2002, WT/CTE/M/31 (December 2, 2002) at p. 7.
322. In response, EC stated that there was a "slight sloppiness in language" of the delegates of US and Australia. *See* WTO CTE, Report of the Meeting Held on February 14, 2003, WT/CTE/M/32 (March 4, 2003) at p. 14.

labelling to the CTE.[323] The delegate of Brazil categorically noted that the words "progress" mentioned in the Doha declaration did not reflect any prioritization of eco-labelling and other issues mentioned in the Doha declaration over the ten items that were to be discussed under the original CTE mandate. Nevertheless, it seems that the delegate may have interpreted the proposals of EU/EC and Switzerland to indicate that the thrust of discussions at the CTE should be focused on eco-labelling, as it did note the importance and proliferation of eco-labelling which needed to be discussed. Canada took a position that was quite different from Brazil. It stated that the CTE should be a forum for discussion of non-product related PPM.[324]

In 2003, the representative of the EU voiced concern that the success of the TBT workshop on eco-labelling held in October 2003 should not preclude discussions at the CTE.[325] Moreover, the EU introduced several proposals for preparation in the run-up to the Cancun Ministerial Conference. *First*, it noted that a study of existing eco-labelling schemes should be made to review how they could foster trade in environmentally friendly products. *Second*, it observed that there should be an increase in the exchange of information on relevant activities related to eco-labelling amongst Members. *Third*, it encouraged Members to ensure that the eco-labelling regimes were administered in a non-protectionist manner.[326] The EU's views were supported by Indonesia and Switzerland. In response, Brazil noted that while paragraph 32(iii) of the Doha declaration was mandated to CTE, it felt that this item should best be discussed at the TBT Committee. Australia, India, the U.S., Thailand, and several other Members supported Brazil's views.[327]

The EU, then, presented an informal room document entitled "Trade as an Environmental Policy Tool" which was prepared by the Global Eco-labelling Network (GEN). GEN was open to government, semi-governmental, or private bodies that administered eco-labels.[328] The paper provided a practical approach to the issues with respect to eco-labelling and focused on possible ways to improve or create market access. The delegation of the EU stated that they found it necessary "to push the CTE debate into the practical domain in order to exploit market opportunities which eco-labels might provide."[329] Later, the EU noted that the evolution of the discussions

323. This was the conclusion that was drawn by the proposal made by Switzerland, *see* WTO CTE, Labelling for Environment Purposes (Submission by Switzerland), WT/CTE/W/219 (October 14, 2002).
324. WTO CTE, Report of the Meeting Held on February 14, 2003, WT/CTE/M/32 (March 4, 2003) at p. 4.
325. WTO CTE, Report of the Meeting Held on October 28, 2003, WT/CTE/M/35 (November 19, 2003).
326. WTO CTE, Report of the Meeting Held on April 20, 2004, WT/CTE/M/36 (May 19, 2004) at p. 4.
327. *Ibid.*
328. WTO CTE, Report of the Meeting Held on October 14, 2004, WT/CTE/M/38 (December 20, 2004) at p. 14.
329. WTO CTE, Report of the Meeting Held on October 14, 2004, WT/CTE/M/38 (December 20, 2004) at p. 14.

unfolding under this item needed to be re-visited. It summed up the discussion as follows:[330]

> the Committee had shifted five years ago from a debate on voluntary and mandatory labels and how these came under TBT rules to, lately, a debate focusing on market access issues. The EC was proactive in the discussion on labelling, no longer because it wished to secure WTO compatibility of certain aspects of labelling, since the question of whether or not these labels could exist was no longer disputed. Instead, the question was how to avoid their negative impacts on market access.

With the exception of Colombia arguing for assisting developing countries to implement paragraph 31(iii) of Doha declaration,[331] the CTE was only used by Members as a platform for discussing labelling standards. This trend began with the U.S. that presented the U.S. Energy Star Product Labelling[332] and Australia discussed the mandatory energy efficiency labels implemented domestically.[333]

Discussions at the CTE between 2011 and 2016 largely resonated with four guiding principles that WTO Members considered essential with regard to eco-labelling. *First*, eco-labels must be compatible with WTO law. The Saudi Arabian delegation, in particular, contended that labelling requirements for environmental purposes had to be consistent with the TBT Agreement. *Second*, eco-labelling requirements should not cause any distortion to trade. *Third*, the development of eco-labels had to be carried out in a transparent and inclusive manner. And *fourth*, capacities of developing countries had to be taken into account.

Chile initiated the discussion on eco-labelling in 2011.[334] It explained that while there was no general policy on eco-labelling in the country in the 1990s, some individual initiatives had been developed. The majority of these schemes were voluntary and developed by the private sector. However, in 2005, Chile introduced a national energy efficiency labelling program. The implementation of these policies was gradual and began with light bulbs and refrigerators and then proceeded to cover microwaves and TVs. The EU also provided an update on the pilot phase of the EU Single Market for Green Products (SMGP) in 2015.[335] SMGP was a voluntary scheme that aimed at enhancing the availability of comparable and reliable information on the environmental impacts of products and organizations.[336] This scheme sought to

330. WTO CTE, Report of the Meeting Held on July 6, 2005, WT/CTE/M/40 (November 2, 2005) at pp. 9-10.
331. WTO CTE, Report of the Meeting Held on November 20, 2009, WT/CTE/M/48 (December 12, 2010) at ¶ 12.
332. WTO CTE, Report of the Meeting Held on November 30, 2007, WT/CTE/M/45 (December 9, 2008) at ¶ 21.
333. WTO CTE, Report of the Meeting Held on November 3, 2008, WT/CTE/M/46 (December 12, 2009) at ¶ 41.
334. WTO CTE, Report of the Meeting Held on July 6, 2011, WT/CTE/M/52 (September 6, 2011) at ¶ 4.
335. WTO CTE, Report of the Meeting Held on October 23, 2014, WT/CTE/M/58 (March 23, 2015) at ¶¶ 1.1-1.3.
336. *Id.*, at ¶ 31.

simplify labelling requirements to reduce EU and non-EU operators' costs and enhance consumer trust.

Singapore also presented its environment-related labelling schemes.[337] With the three-fold objective of educating consumers to make informed decisions, promoting energy efficiency and introducing environmental awareness, Singapore had introduced six eco-labelling schemes beginning with its Mandatory Energy Labelling Scheme of 2008 which was administered to encourage consumers to purchase energy-efficient products by rating goods based on their energy efficiency. Another example was Chinese Taipei presenting its Green Mark Program.[338] This voluntary and private standard was launched in 1992 and has since been issued to nearly 6,000 products. The presentation also highlighted the process of signing MRAs with other private eco-labelling schemes such as TerraChoice of Canada, Green Seal of the US, Living Planet of Ukraine and the Philippines Center for Environmental Protection and Sustainable Development Inc.[339] This was the first instance where some efforts to introduce coherence in eco-labelling standards was demonstrated.

Later, in 2015, China presented its Environmental Labelling Program.[340] The program aimed at inspiring enterprises to manufacture and produce goods in an environmentally friendly way. It also sought to enhance the competitiveness of environmentally friendly products. Life cycle assessment (LCA) methodology was used to quantify environmental friendliness. Till 2015, China reported that ninety-seven categories of products had been certified which included automobiles, electronic products and textiles. Of note, printing services were also cited as having received a form of environmental certification. This provides a good and rare example of CTE discussions that tackle both CTE 3b and CTE 9 of the CTE dealing with services between 1995 and 2001.

[C] Summation on Eco-Labelling

In sum, the CTE work in these areas were both intensive and constructive and would provide great opportunities for experience sharing and yield a greater understanding of the various issues of concern to the trade and environment governance advocates. This ranged from the advocacy of utilizing trade measures to further environment objectives and the opposite concern that the concerns of the developing country be also addressed regarding the trade-impacting effects of eco-labelling.

In the end, a great amount of documentation and meetings on the issues of labelling were generated by the CTE. Apart from member delegations providing information and proposals, the CTE is credited with having generated three key reference outputs in the form of secretariat notes on eco-labelling spanning almost fifteen years of work from 1995 to 2009:

337. WTO CTE, Report of the meeting Held on November 9, 2010, WT/CTE/M/51 (May 31, 2011) at ¶¶ 22-33.
338. *Id.*, at ¶¶ 36-38.
339. *Id.*, at ¶ 38.
340. WTO CTE, Report of the meeting Held on November 9, 2010, WT/CTE/M/51 (May 31, 2011).

(1) *Negotiating History of the Coverage of the Agreement on TBT with Regard to Labelling Requirements, Voluntary Standards, and Processes and Production Methods Unrelated to Product Characteristics*, WT/CTE/W/10; G/TBT/W/11 (1995);
(2) the *Information Relevant to the Consideration of the Market Access effects of Eco-Labelling Schemes*, WT/CTE/W/150 (2000); and
(3) *Eco-Labelling: Overview of Current Work in Various International Fora*, JOB/TE/9 (2009).

It becomes evident that confining the workings of the WTO to the IL-IR positive rule formulation lens (Lens A) would unfairly evaluate the value of the endeavors of the CTE covered by this chapter relating to highly specialized topics that are in the nature of information exchange and gathering of greater knowledge and technical proficiency on the subject area, and are for further research and analysis purposes.

Special topics discussions, while also policy-oriented, are more technical in focus, and do not address rulemaking directly. Admittedly, they could nevertheless become a stepping stone for trade and environment policy and rulemaking. However, the work itself is more akin to the processes of legislative study and inquiry, to allow various constituents to make their views known and also to test the ripeness of the ideas and the fertility of the soil for possible seed-planting. They are not directly focused on rulemaking in the short- or medium-term time frame.

There is also the dimension of the administrative and regulatory networks, the TRNs and secretariat exchanges, which are more akin to the executive branch interface among various agencies of a federal or national government.

The tenor of the exchange of experiences on border taxes and eco-labelling just reviewed are not designed to create, set or encourage new norms, but instead provide other Members with information and insights on recent or potential best practices, and are aimed at providing advice and recommendations, or toolkits for implementation and for the regular interface among government administrators and international civil service counterparts.

All these are relevant for trade and environment governance development but again are not directly rulemaking in nature. There are benefits to having thematic issues become subject of focused discussions as they could lead to deeper analysis and knowledge on the subject matter, such as when the CTE discussions did lead to requests for greater studies on the effects of potentially trade-restrictive policies, and issues with *standards* or *labelling* compliance. These are not legal issues, but operational problems and by shedding light on these issues in a forum with experts and bureaucrats, they have the effect of enhancing trade and environment governance through the means of greater cooperation, coordination and technical assistance. These means are essential for creating robust and viable domestic institutions that are coherent for both the domestic and international administration of existing trade and environment policies.

Considering Lens B, as the focal theoretical framework for this chapter's coverage of the CTE 3, 7, 8, 9 work areas, and as pointed out by Lang and Scott, as well as Chayes & Chayes, and discussed in Chapter 3, meetings of experts lead to problem-solving approaches and their primary focus could lead to more in-depth analysis of global trade and environment-specific issues. Such meetings fulfill the need for a forum where member delegations and specialists and officials from the capital are able to share their experiences and concerns on particular topics. It is important though to improve the processes of the CTE in this area to make clear the distinctions between on the one hand the work on the thematic area of norms conflicts and actual coherence and policy interface issues which are more law-oriented (as in CTE 1, 5, 10 and CTE 2, 4) and, on the other hand, the specialized areas that required technical expertise and increasing the knowledge among the bureaucracy (CTE 7, 8, 9).

§5.04 CTE 7, 8, 9: SPECIAL ISSUES DPGs, TRIPS, SERVICES

Item 7: *The issue of exports of domestically prohibited goods.*
Item 8: *Relationship between the Environment and Agreement on Trade-Related Aspects of Intellectual Property*
Item 9: *The work programme envisaged in the Decision on Trade in Services and the Environment*
Paragraph 31(iii) of Doha Declaration: *With a view to enhancing the mutual supportiveness of trade and environment, we agree to negotiations, without prejudging their outcome, on:*

(iii) *the reduction or, as appropriate, elimination of tariff and non-tariff barriers to environmental goods and services.*

Paragraph 32 (2) of Doha Declaration: *We instruct the Committee on Trade and Environment, in pursuing work on all items on its agenda within its current terms of reference, to give particular attention to:*

(ii) *the relevant provisions of the Agreement on* Trade-Related Aspects of Intellectual Property Rights

Key Output Documents:

1. Domestically Prohibited Goods: Assessment of the Product Coverage in Specific International Instruments, WT/CTE/W/29 (1996); see also WT/CTE/W/43 (1997).
2. The Relationship between the Convention on Biological Diversity (CBD) and the Agreement on the Trade-Related Aspects of Intellectual Property Rights (TRIPS); with focus on Article 27.3(B), WT/CTE/W/125 (1999).
3. Discussion Paper on the Environmental Effects of Services Trade Liberalization, WT/CTE/W/218 (2002).

CTE 7, 8 and 9 continue the work on specialized topics, and these three agenda items focus on the very specific technical issues of DPGs; the TRIPS Agreement; and environmental services. The work outputs provide knowledge and technical updates and are useful to experts and the administrative bureaucracy.

[A] CTE 7: DPGs

DPGs are products which are banned or severely restricted on the domestic market of the exporting country because they are determined to present risks for human, animal or plant life or health, or the environment, but which may nevertheless be exported.[341] According to Winquist, DPGs fall into four general categories: chemicals (including pesticides and fertilizers), pharmaceutical products, consumer products and hazardous wastes.[342] Several developing countries and LDCs did not have the technical knowledge to deal with the import controls of DPGs and sought to utilize the CTE as a forum for further discussion.

Historically, the issue of DPGs was first discussed in the 1980s during the GATT and has since been deliberated upon at length. The 38th Session of GATT Contracting Parties, in 1982, decided that:[343]

> to the maximum extent feasible, notify GATT of any goods produced and exported by them but banned by their national authorities for sale on their domestic markets on grounds of human health and safety.

As a result, the Notification System on the Export of DPGs came in to effect in 1983 and was functional until 1990. During this period, a total of fifty notifications were received of which thirty-six notifications dealt with general prohibitions of export of DPGs whereas the remaining fourteen mentioned specific DPGs.[344] Furthermore, by way of a decision dated 1989, a *Working Group on the Export of Domestically Prohibited Goods and Other Hazardous Substances* was established. The issue of exports of DPGs was of particular concern to many developing and least developed countries. DPGs covered those products whose sale and use are banned or severely restricted domestically on the grounds that they presented a danger to human, animal, plant life or health or the environment[345] but are, nonetheless, permitted to be exported. The CTE discussions noted that there were four broad categories of potential DPGs which can be identified as chemicals (including pesticides and fertilizers), pharmaceutical products, consumer products and hazardous wastes.[346]

The *GATT Working Group* produced a "draft *Decision on Trade in Banned or Severely Restricted Products and Other Hazardous Substances*." However, a consensus

341. Tina Winquist, *Trade in Domestically Prohibited Goods* (IISD 1999) at p. 1, available at: http://www.iisd.org/sites/default/files/publications/viet_dpg.pdf (accessed on November 30, 2019).
342. *Id.*, at pp. 1-3.
343. GATT Ministerial Work, *Export of Domestically Prohibited Goods*, BISD 29S/19 (1982).
344. WTO CTE, A Review of the Information Available in the World Trade Organization on the Export of Domestically Prohibited Goods, Note by the Secretariat, WT/CTE/W/43 (April 22, 1997) at ¶ 2.
345. WTO CTE, A Review of the Information Available in the World Trade Organization on the Export of Domestically Prohibited Goods, Note by the Secretariat, WT/CTE/W/43 (April 22, 1997) at ¶ 7; *see also* WTO CTE, Item 7: Domestically Prohibited Goods, Assessment of the Product Coverage in Specific International Instruments, Note by the Secretariat, WT/CTE/W/29 (May 14, 1996).
346. *Ibid.*

to adopt the decision could not be reached.[347] Since then, several new international agreements and conventions dealing with the monitoring and control of trade in certain domestically produced goods entered into force whilst others were in the process of being negotiated. This included the Basel Convention on the Control of Transboundary Movements of Hazardous Wastes and their Disposal and the draft Protocol on Liability and Compensation for Damage Resulting from Transboundary Movement of Hazardous Wastes and their Disposal.[348] It was agreed by WTO Members that multilateral rules on exports of DPGs should primarily be developed through these environmental instruments. Detailed discussions on DPGs were held in the CTE in February 1995. At that time, several WTO Members reiterated concerns over the shortcomings of multilateral mechanisms to ensure full transparency of trade in DPGs. Later that year, Nigeria and Senegal jointly proposed the establishment of a technical sub-group within the CTE, which would report the progress of such discussions to the CTE. This group, as envisioned in the proposal, would discuss WTO Member's concerns and reach mutually agreeable solutions to issues of DPGs.[349]

In April 1997, a note by the WTO Secretariat assessed information that was already available with the WTO on trade-related environmental measures which relate to trade in DPGs.[350] For this, the Secretariat gathered data from SPS and TBT notification systems and the mentioned GATT-era DPG notification system, and the CTE noted that the TBT and SPS notification systems were not designed to address exports and were, thus, not a useful data source. It further noted that while the DPG notification system of the GATT-era was the most useful tool to collect data on DPGs, it suffered from three inter-related problems: *first*, the inadequate definition of product coverage; *second*, the fact that other international instruments have started addressing

347. *See* GATT GEMIT, Report by the Chairman of the Working Group on Domestically Prohibited Goods and Other Hazardous Substances, L/6872 (July 2, 1991).
348. According to the CTE note dated March 31, 1995, there are fourteen agreements related to DPGs. This includes six legally binding international Montreal Protocol On Substances That Deplete the Ozone Layer, UNEP, 1989; Basel Convention on the Control of Transboundary Movements of Hazardous Wastes and their Disposal, UNEP, 1992; Convention Concerning Safety in the Use of Chemical at Work, ILO, 1990; 1988 Convention Against Illicit Traffic in Narcotic Drugs and Psychotropic Substances, UN, 1990; 1971 Convention On Psychotropic Substances, UN, 1976; 1961 Single Convention on Narcotics, UN, 1994, as Amended by 1072 Protocol, 1975. It also includes 1 legally binding plurilateral agreement which is the Decision Concerning the Control of Transfrontier Movements of Wastes Destined for Recovery Operations, OECD, 1992. Further, it includes voluntary international instruments such as the Amended London Guidelines for the Exchange of Information on Chemicals in International Trade, UNEP, adopted 1989; Code of Ethics on International Trade in Chemicals, UNEP, 1994; International Code of Conduct on the Distribution and Use of Pesticides, FAO, 1985; Certification Scheme on the Quality of Pharmaceutical Products Moving in International Trade, WHO, 1975. Lastly, there is one voluntary plurilateral instrument which is the Decision-Recommendation in the OECD Notification System on Consumer Safety Measures, OECD, 1989. For more information, *see* WTO CTEA Description of International Agreements and Instruments Dealing with Trade in Domestically Prohibited Goods and Other Substances, Note by the Secretariat, WT/CTE/W/6 (March 31, 1995).
349. WTO CTE, Communication from the Delegations of Nigeria and Senegal—Domestically Prohibited Goods, WT/CTE/W/11 (September 14, 1995).
350. WTO CTE, A Review of the Information Available in the WTO on the Export of Domestically Prohibited Goods, Note by the Secretariat, WT/CTE/W/43 (April 22, 1997).

DPGs; and, *third*, a limited response from Contracting Parties. This finding can be highlighted as one of the CTE's contributions to the DPG knowledge base, and can be counted as an additional work output of the CTE in this area, in addition to the 1996 Secretariat Note *Domestically Prohibited Goods, Assessment of the Product Coverage in Specific International Instruments* (the 1996 DPG Report).[351]

Despite Nigeria and Senegal's joint request in 1995 indicating that they were hoping for this issue to be discussed in the Singapore Ministerial Declaration, no consensus was reached amongst Members. Discussions soon digressed to other items on the CTE agenda. Bangladesh, in 2000, submitted four recommendations on the issue of exports of DPGs. *First*, it noted that CTE should recommend WTO Members to notify DPG exports in the area of consumer products. *Second*, it recommended that each WTO Member should have necessary domestic health and environmental standards and regulations in place for the management of imports of DPGs. *Third*, it requested that CTE should consider preparing a study on export on domestically prohibited consumer products and their possible effects on human health and the environment. And, *fourth*, it observed there should be a platform for sharing of information on DPGs among developing and developed countries.[352]

Egypt, India, and *Hong Kong, China* agreed with Bangladesh that technical assistance was necessary. Switzerland said that it was interesting to note that while DPGs cause problems to the domestic environment and economy, yet the focus of discussion at the CTE should be DPGs not covered by any other instrument. Subsequently, the Secretariat agreed that it would prepare a report on the export of DPGs and focus on gaps in coverage of other international instruments.[353] However, no subsequent discussions on the item took place.

In 2001, the Secretariat of the UN made a presentation at the CTE on the UN *Consolidated List of Products Whose Consumption and/or Sale Have Been Banned, Withdrawn, Severely Restricted or Not Approved by Governments*. This list has often been regarded as the primary source of information for governments when considering regulatory action. Senegal welcomed the presentation by the UN and encouraged efforts to ensure that the UN List was made readily available to developing countries. It noted that DPGs were traded—often illegally—and caused serious problems in developing countries. India suggested that the List should be widely disseminated through the internet. The EU also supported India's suggestion. Gambia and Benin also noted that DPGs could potentially cause dangers in agricultural or consumer products.[354]

351. WTO CTE, Item 7: Domestically Prohibited Goods, Assessment of the Product Coverage in Specific International Instruments, Note by the Secretariat, WT/CTE/W/29 (May 14, 1996).
352. WTO CTE, Trade in Domestically Prohibited Goods, Submission by Bangladesh, WT/CTE/W/141 (June 15, 2000).
353. WTO CTE, Report of the Meeting Held on July 5-6, 2000, WT/CTE/M/24 (September 19, 2000) at ¶¶ 41-42, 55.
354. WTO CTE, United Nations Consolidated List of Products whose Consumption and/or Sale Have Been Banned, Withdrawn, Submission by the UN Secretariat, WT/CTE/W/194 (June 26, 2001).

[B] CTE 8: TRIPS/CBD

CTE 8 mandated the discussion of the relationship between the Agreement on TRIPS (TRIPS Agreement) and the environment. TRIPS Article 27.2 is the only provision in the TRIPS Agreement that makes explicit reference to the environment:[355]

> Members may exclude from patentability inventions, the prevention within their territory of the commercial exploitation of which is necessary to protect order *public* or morality, including to protect human, animal or plant life or health or to avoid serious prejudice to the environment, provided that such exclusion is not made merely because the exploitation is prohibited by their law.

Based on this paragraph, the CTE trade and environment policy focus was three-fold:

(i) the generation of, access to, and transfer of, environmentally sound technologies (EST);
(ii) indigenous and traditional knowledge; and
(iii) the relationship of the TRIPS Agreement with certain MEAs containing Intellectual Property Right (IPR) provisions.

The CTE discussions involved Members' questions on the lack of specific mechanisms to achieve objectives such as sustainable development and environmental protection and issues relating to the effective implementation of the TRIPS Agreement, possibly leading to the transfer of ESTs, which, in turn, could lead to enhancing environmental protection. Promoting EST had been discussed in various international environmental fora, including Agenda 21 of the CBD. In assessing TRIPS relation with ESTs, the twofold purpose of IPR protection and promoting ESTs was also highlighted in a 1996 WTO Secretariat paper:[356]

> [...] a combination of well-functioning IPR system and appropriate price signals in the market, which direct research and development effort to [ESTs] can play a major role in developing the technologies that will respond to environmental problems.

Some WTO Members noted that the machinery to implement this intricate balance already existed in the text of Article 7 of the TRIPS Agreement. Article 7 lists out the aims and objectives of the agreement based on the principles of "mutual advantage of producers and users" and "in a manner conducive to social and economic welfare." These discussions were pertinent since ESTs could potentially raise tensions between the objectives of promoting technological innovation and transfer of technology. The CTE note of 1996 recognized that in the event of tension because of these objectives, a number of provisions including those on compulsory licensing and

355. *See* Article 27.2, Agreement on Trade-Related Aspects of Intellectual Property, 1869 U.N.T.S. 299.
356. WTO CTE, Factors Affecting Transfer of Environmentally Sound Technology, WT/CTE/W/22 (February 21, 1996) at ¶ 2.

control of anti-competitive practices could provide the appropriate balance in light of Article 7 of the TRIPS Agreement.[357]

Some WTO Members also noted that patent systems are known to encourage inventors to disclose new technology. According to them, patents provided protection to foster a culture of innovation. Transferring of technology could only take place if the invention existed. They argued that Article 29 of the TRIPS Agreement established an obligation on WTO Members to require patent applicants to disclose the invention. In many jurisdictions, patent terms ended eighteen months after they were filed. Post the patent protection period, the invention would be accessible to the public. This obligation to disclose, according to the Members, held important consequences for the transfer and access to ESTs since the disclosed invention would fall into the public domain and be freely available to all. Some Members also recalled that existence of an intellectual property (IP) regime is:[358]

> [...] only one of the factors which supports technology transfer; others are economic and political stability in the country of destination, the level of infrastructure and availability of skilled labour, access to financial resources, as well as domestic policies concerning investment, market access, services and environmental regulation which play a more direct role in technology transfer.

Despite the protections enshrined in the text of TRIPS Agreement, some WTO Members felt that the utility of environmentally sound technologies (ESTs) could be questioned if it was not disseminated and widely used. These Members believed that additional rules might be necessary to limit the discretionary power of owners of ESTs for better accessibility to the technologies. Others observed that IPR protection would increase costs of EST technology which would be a concern to small and medium enterprises (SMEs) in developing countries. India focused on the need to encourage global use of ESTs and associated products through easy access and widespread dissemination under "fair and most favorable terms." These terms, according to India, could be re-interpreted as "preferential and non-commercial" in nature. It suggested that compulsory licensing provisions under Article 31 and the terms of protections in TRIPS Agreement Article 33 should be examined in a way that it encourages transfer of EST&Ps. India also suggested that obligations be imposed on IP owners of EST&Ps through TRIPS Agreement to sell technology upon demand to any interested party under "fair and most favorable terms."

Responses to India's submission were mixed. Many WTO Members considered that there was no need to undertake such a reconciliation. They noted that problems arising from the dissemination of EST&Ps did not relate to proprietary technology but, much rather, occurred as a result of impediments to foreign investment and trade in such products. Some Members expressed concern about the negative effects of some technologies on the environment. These technologies—also referred to as Environmentally Unfriendly Technologies—included genetically modified organisms (GMOs). Some WTO Members also voiced concerns over ethical, moral and religious conflicts in

357. *Id.* at ¶ 16.
358. *Id.* at ¶ 5.

patenting microorganisms, genes, genetic material and genetically-engineered crops and plants. Other Members felt that patenting life forms could lead to biodiversity loss and create environmental and development problems. In response, other Members noted that Article 27.2 and 27.3 of TRIPS Agreement were adequate to address problems in the area. They also noted that national health and safety standards embedded in MEAs that would offer additional protection and that providing remedies to resolving ethical, moral and religious problems are not in the WTO's working mandate.

Other aspects of the TRIPS Agreement relating to indigenous and traditional knowledge were also discussed at the CTE: *first*, the recognition of the intellectual contributions made by indigenous peoples and local communities; *second*, the contribution of municipalities and communities through the conservation and provision of genetic resources in their natural state. The discussions on traditional knowledge were rich in texture, and debates were lively. Delegations were able to use the CTE again as a forum for their proposals and ideas on how to best protect indigenous genetic resources.

As an example, Peru would use the CTE as a forum to present its experience of protecting traditional knowledge and access to genetic resources. Describing itself as a country with a "great wealth of genetic resources, biological diversity and hydrological resources,"[359] Peru explained that it had taken practical measures to utilize this potential wealth by introducing legislation that focused on conservation of the environment and regulating access to genetic resources which reflected the ratification of various international treaties that it had signed. For example, it expounded the principles enshrined in the proposed Protection Regime for the Collective Knowledge of Indigenous Peoples. This regulation established a sui generis system which sought to provide adequate protection to those possessing traditional knowledge. The proposed regime recognized ownership of indigenous people and associated rights over their traditional knowledge as well as their right to decide on how it should be used. In describing the legislative framework implemented at a domestic and regional level, such as the Andean Common System for Access to Genetic Resources, Peru urged the international community to recognize that traditional knowledge would provide economic benefits to those possessing it. Such recognition would also limit misappropriation and unauthorized exploitation of the knowledge.[360] Peru had made its submission on October 27, 2000, but with no mandate for rules formulation, in the six years since the issues had first been debated in the CTE, no consensus was arrived at on any of the proposed solutions to the concerns that were raised.

The relationship between the TRIPS Agreement and MEAs that cover IP rights—in particular, the CBD—was also debated at the CTE. The objectives of the CBD, as stated in Article 1 of CBD, are the conservation of biological diversity, sustainable use of its components, and the fair and equitable sharing of the benefits

359. WTO CTE, Peru's Experience of the Protection of Traditional Knowledge and Access to Genetic Resources, WT/CTE/W/176 (October 27, 2000).
360. *Ibid.*

arising out of the utilization of genetic resources. Principles of the CBD are enshrined in Article 3 of the CBD and states that:[361]

> States have, in accordance with the Charter of the United Nations and the principles of international law, the sovereign right to exploit their own resources pursuant to their own environmental policies, and the responsibility to ensure that activities within their jurisdiction or control do not cause damage to the environment.

As noted by the CTE on May 20, 1997, IPRs under the CBD proved to be a sensitive issue during the negotiation stage of the CBD. The Third Conference of the Parties, which took place in November 1996, recognized that:[362]

> [...] further work [was] required to help develop a common appreciation of the relationship between intellectual property rights and the relevant provisions of the Agreement on Trade-related Aspects of Intellectual Property Rights and the Convention on Biological Diversity, in particular on issues relating to technology transfer and conservation and sustainable use of biological diversity and the fair and equitable sharing of benefits arising out of the use of genetic resources including the protection of knowledge, innovations and practices of indigenous and local communities embodying traditional lifestyles relevant for the conservation and sustainable use of biological diversity.

Parties to the CBD examined the role of IPR protection in the conservation and sustainable use of biological diversity. However, there were divergent views as to whether IPR protection encouraged conservation and sustainable use of biodiversity since this could, both, encourage the development of environmentally friendly products or favor "monoculture of propriety crop varieties or inappropriate use of pesticides."[363] These diverging views permeated into the discussions that were taking place at the CTE. Access to the transfer of technology was seen as playing an important part in the conservation and sustainable use of biological diversity. Here too, conflicts arose. A CTE note dated June 8, 1995, stated that the most difficult issues that were raised during the CBD negotiations concerned access to transfer of technology.[364]

Certain provisions of the TRIPS Agreement are relevant to matters that were raised during the CBD. These include Articles 7, 8.1, 27.2, 27.3 (b), 29, 30, 31 and 40 of the TRIPS Agreement. Article 7 lists out the intricate balance between the producer and user of technological knowledge. Article 8.1 states that while formulating or amending laws and regulations, Members can adopt measures to protect public health and nutrition. Article 27.2 enables Members to exclude patenting of inventions which could seriously prejudice the environment. Article 27.3(b) makes explicit reference to the protection of plant varieties. It stipulates that new plant varieties do not need to be protected by patent, but Members who choose to exclude them from patent protection

361. Article 3 of the Convention on Biological Diversity, 1760 U.N.T.S. 79; 31 I.L.M. 818 (1992).
362. UN Convention on Biological Diversity, Conference of Parties Decision III/17, UNEP/CBD/COP/DEC/III/9 (1996) available at: https://www.cbd.int/decision/cop/?id=7113 (accessed on November 30, 2019).
363. WTO CTE, The Convention on Biological Diversity and the Agreement on Trade-Related Aspects of Intellectual Property Rights, WT/CTE/W/50 (May 20, 1997).
364. WTO CTE, Environment and TRIPS, WT/CTE/W/8 (June 8, 1995).

are required to provide for effective sui generis systems. Article 29 details disclosure requirements of patent applications. Article 30 states that Members may provide limited exceptions to exclusive rights conferred by a patent, provided that such exceptions do not unreasonably conflict with a normal exploitation of the patent. Article 31 enlists uses other than those allowed under Article 30 of the right holder of IP right. Article 40 deals with the control of anti-competitive practices in contractual licenses.

In a submission made to the CTE on September 29, 1997, India noted that Article 15 of the CBD obliged parties to the CBD to take necessary measures to share in a fair and equitable way the results of research and development from commercial and other utilization of genetic resources.[365] However, India stated that the TRIPS Agreement did not deal with the fair and equitable sharing of benefits. According to it, the TRIPS Agreement and the CBD represented two significantly separate multilateral approaches to the utilization of living resources. This is because the TRIPS Agreement promoted technological innovation by "ensuring certainty of intellectual property protection and of world markets for at least some biotechnological inventions [...]."[366] On the other hand, the CBD facilitated "access to living resources as well as the equitable sharing of the benefits of such use."[367]

India would, therefore, suggest the reconciliation of the provisions of the TRIPS Agreement and the CBD. *First*, it recommended the introduction of a clause on the patent application in Article 29 of the TRIPS Agreement, which would mention the origin of biological/genetic resources and indigenous/traditional knowledge used in the biotechnological invention. *Second*, it noted the lack of prior informed consent of the country of origin and the knowledge holder of the biological raw material that was to be used for the patent. According to India, the scenario that would unfold if such a provision was introduced would be as follows:[368]

> [...] if any inventor wants to develop such biological materials for commercial purpose, he or she would have to get prior consent of the country as well as the owner and, if required by such owner, enter into agreements with the country of origin.

Third, India recommended the introduction of a Material Transfer Agreement for inventors desirous of using biological material and Transfer of Information Agreement for inventions based on indigenous or traditional knowledge.[369]

The U.S. raised several points against India's proposal. It asserted that "truly" traditional and indigenous knowledge is already in the public domain and would not meet the standards of patentability specified under Article 27.1 of the TRIPS Agreement. It also noted that the TRIPS Agreement was concluded after the CBD and had

365. WTO CTE, Cluster on Market Access, the Relationship Between the TRIPS Agreement and the Convention on Biodiversity (Communication from India), WT/CTE/W/65 (September 29, 1997).
366. *Id.* at ¶ 12.
367. *Ibid.*
368. *Id.* at ¶ 14.
369. *Id.* at ¶ 13.

accounted for discussions that had taken place in the CBD. India argued that negotiations on the TRIPS Agreement hadn't changed much since the so-called *Dunkel* "draft"[370] of December 1991.[371]

A quick recap would demonstrate that most of the questions that were raised at the CTE in 1995 remained unresolved by the end of 2001. There was no consensus amongst Members on the issues that were being debated. Some considered it contradictory to introduce changes to the TRIPS Agreement, which could diminish incentives to develop and disseminate ESTs. Some suggested that ESTs should not be sought through the TRIPS Agreement but through relevant MEAs. Others suggested increased cooperation between the TRIPS Agreement and MEAs containing IPR-related obligations.

On the specific focus of the relationship between the TRIPS Agreement and the environment, in February 2001, Brazil introduced a paper on the review of Article 27.3(b) of the TRIPS Agreement.[372] More specifically, Brazil wanted to discuss the relationship between the TRIPS Agreement and the CBD. Brazil was of the opinion that Article 27.3(b) of the TRIPS Agreement should preserve Member's flexibility to exclude plants and animals from patentability. Brazil noted that its domestic legislation excluded all or part of plants and animals, except transgenic microorganisms, from patentability. This was subject, however, to three requirements—novelty, inventive step and industrial application. But, as Brazil noted:[373]

> [...] there is evidence that patent offices in some developed countries do not necessarily follow such a policy and they tend to accept overly broad claims on genetic resources that could lead to the grant of patents with a broad scope.

According to Brazil, such "broad patents" over microorganisms could pose problems since loose criteria to establish novelty, inventive step and the industrial application would undermine the patent system as a whole. This would result in conflict with the CBD. Article 16.5 of CBD states:

> The Contracting Parties, recognizing that patents and other intellectual property rights may have an influence on the implementation of this Convention, shall cooperate in this regard subject to national legislation and international law in order to ensure that such rights are supportive of and do not run counter to its objectives.

This, read with Article 15 of CBD, which gives sovereign rights to states over their natural resources including access to genetic material, would conflict with the "broad patent" interpretation of Article 27.3(b) of the TRIPS Agreement. Brazil considered that TRIPS and CBD should be mutually supportive and promote the sustainable use of

370. The Dunkel "draft" from the GATT Secretariat was the draft final act embodying the results of the Uruguay Round of Multilateral Trade Negotiations. *See* Craig Van Grasstek, *The History and Future of the WTO* at p. 46 (2013).
371. WTO CTE, Cluster on MEAs (Response of India to Comments by United States), WT/CTE/W/65, WT/CTE/W/85 (July 7, 1998).
372. WTO CTE, Review of Article 27.3(b) (Communication from Brazil), WT/CTE/W/186 (February 12, 2001).
373. *Ibid.*

natural resources. Broad patents over microorganisms, plants and animals would result in monopoly rights for the patent's subject matter. Brazil narrated its example of the *ayahuasca* vine, which was a native plant in the Amazonian rainforest and was used by thousands of indigenous peoples for religious ceremonies. A patent of this vine using a broad patent definition would result in restricting the economic benefits of such resources. Brazil also reported India's experience with cases of patents claimed over turmeric, *karela, basmati rice* and the *neem* tree.[374] To avoid further conflicts between CBD and the TRIPS Agreement, Brazil proposed an amendment to Article 27.3(b) to include requirements of identification of the source of genetic material, related traditional knowledge used to obtain the material, evidence of fair and equitable sharing and evidence of prior informed consent from the Government or indigenous community for the exploitation of the subject matter of the patent.[375]

The EU, then the EC, which has often been a *demandeur* for many issues related to IP including geographical indications, supported Brazil's proposal, acknowledging a link between the TRIPS Agreement and MEAs, such as the CBD. Further, the EU noted that international action to protect traditional knowledge was necessary. India, too, agreed that Article 27.3(b) should preserve Members' flexibility to exclude the patentability of plants and animals. It further noted that a precise definition of the term "microorganism" is needed to determine the scope of patentability under Article 27.3(b) of the TRIPS Agreement. Cuba also supported the conclusions of Brazil's paper, as did Kenya.

The U.S. described a system of contracts that protected the sovereign rights to provide access to genetic resources or to traditional knowledge. According to the U.S., contract obligations established the rights and obligations of all parties prior to granting any access to genetic resources and could also include benefit-sharing clauses.[376] In 2002, India noted that the Doha declaration had provided the mandate to examine the relationship between the TRIPS Agreement and the CBD.[377]

The representative of India noted that while the CBD and the TRIPS Agreement were mutually supportive, conflicts between the two could arise at the implementation stage in cases where patents were claimed over genetic resources that were protected by the CBD. Further, the delegate noted:[378]

> Currently, the TRIPS Agreement allowed Members to provide patents over genetic resources (plants, animals and microorganisms). The Agreement, however, contained no provisions preventing a person from claiming patent rights in one country over genetic resources that were under the sovereignty of another country. In particular, the TRIPS Agreement contained no provisions allowing a Member to enforce fair and equitable sharing of benefits from the patenting of its own genetic

374. WTO CTE, WTO Council for Trade-Related Aspects of Intellectual Property Rights, Protection of Biodiversity and Traditional Knowledge (Submission by India), WT/CTE/W/156; IP/C/W/198 (July 14, 2000).
375. WTO CTE, Review of Article 27.3(b) (Communication from Brazil), WT/CTE/W/186 (February 12, 2001).
376. WTO CTE, Report of the Meeting Held on June 13-14, 2002, WT/CTE/M/30 (November 11, 2002) at ¶¶ 13-15.
377. *Id.* at ¶ 7.
378. *Ibid.*

> resources abroad. In the absence of clear provisions providing for a mutually supportive relationship of the TRIPS Agreement with Members' obligations under the CBD, the implementation of the former could allow for acts of biopiracy and thus result in systemic conflicts with the CBD. It was India's view that to avoid conflicts in the implementation, an amendment of the TRIPS Agreement to accommodate some essential elements of the CBD would be necessary.

India also noted that several developing countries had proposed amendments to the TRIPS Agreement so as to require applicants for a patent relating to biological materials or to traditional knowledge to, *first*, disclose the source and country of origin of the biological resource and of the traditional knowledge used in the invention; *second*, give evidence of prior informed consent through approval of authorities under the relevant national regimes; and *last*, give evidence of fair and equitable benefit sharing under the relevant national regimes.

This, according to India, was in line with the provisions of the CBD and recommendations of the *Bonn Guidelines on Access to Genetic Resources and Fair and Equitable Sharing of the Benefits Arising Out of Their Utilization.*[379] As a solution, India recommended the inclusion of such provisions as an amendment to the TRIPS Agreement, which—it argued—would prevent systemic conflicts with the CBD arising from the implementation of the TRIPS Agreement. While India's proposal was supported by several Members, including Brazil, other Members such as the Czech Republic "was convinced that there was no legal conflict between the TRIPS Agreement and the CBD." According to the Czech Republic:[380]

> [...] the CBD recognized the patentability of products issued from genetic resources and the TRIPS Agreement set the minimum standards of intellectual property rights protection, including patents. From this point of view, the Czech Republic supported the opinion of some Members of the WTO that both the TRIPS Agreement and the CBD had to be implemented in a mutually supportive way. To achieve this goal, effective cooperation among relevant WTO bodies and the CBD was necessary, and technical assistance provided to developing countries was of high importance.

In 2003, the EU submitted a paper in the TRIPS Council,[381] which reviewed the relationship between the TRIPS Agreement and the CBD, especially regarding traditional knowledge. The delegate of the EU also presented the same paper at the CTE Regular sessions but clarified that the purpose of such introduction was not with the intent of distracting ongoing negotiations at the TRIPS Council but to encourage Members to make a note of the points mentioned in the paper.[382]

379. *See generally* UN Convention on Biological Diversity, Bonn Guidelines on Access to Genetic Resources and Fair and Equitable Sharing of the Benefits Arising out of their Utilization, CBD Conference of Parties 6 Decision VI/24, UNEP/CBD/COP/6/20 (2002) available at: https://www.cbd.int/abs/bonn/ (last accessed on November 30, 2019).
380. WTO CTE, Report of the Meeting Held on June 13-14, 2002, WT/CTE/M/30 (November 11, 2002) at ¶¶ 27-28.
381. WTO Council for Trade-Related Aspects of Intellectual Property Rights, Review of Article 27.3(b) (Communication by the European Communities and their Members), IP/C/W/383 (October 17, 2002).
382. WTO CTE, Report of the Meeting Held on April 20, 2004, WT/CTE/M/36 (May 19, 2004).

Through this concept paper, the EU discussed a number of pertinent issues.[383] *First*, as regards Article 27.3(b) of the TRIPS Agreement, the EU stated that it saw no reason to amend this article. According to it, Article 27.2 of the TRIPS Agreement, which deals with the exclusion from patentability, and Article 27.1 of the TRIPS Agreement, which lays out the patentability criteria already provided sufficient flexibility to modulate patent protection. *Second*, the paper addressed the relationship between the TRIPS Agreement and the CBD. The EU stated that there was no legal conflict or incompatibility between the two agreements. However, the EU did recognize that the implementation of the two legal orders could raise questions. Mitigating this could only take place if the agreements were interpreted in a mutually supportive manner. Besides this, the EU also stressed that sound regulation (through either legislation or administration) would be essential for the benefit-sharing aspects of the CBD. This, according to the EC, would guarantee the legal security to the rights of providers of genetic resources. Furthermore, the paper discussed the protection of traditional knowledge. The EU believed that the TRIPS Council should consider preventive approaches to ensure that no misappropriation of traditional knowledge should take place. This, according to the EU, would catalyze benefit sharing that resulted from its use. The EU also stressed that if any innovation were to take place based on traditional knowledge, then it would be important to ensure that the traditional knowledge holders shared benefits through the derived innovation. Moreover, the EU supported further work on the development of an international sui generis model for legal protections. This work should take place at the World Intellectual Property Organization (WIPO).

India stated that it did not share some of the views expressed by the EU. It also stressed that it would be important to disclose the source of the country of origin of the biological resource and the traditional knowledge used in the invention. Peru also stated that it agreed with some aspects of the EU's submission.[384] However, it stated that the requirement to disclose information for traditional knowledge needed to be compulsory and not voluntary. Brazil and Australia agreed that the TRIPS Council was the appropriate forum for ongoing discussions. Japan noted that the harmonized system for the protection of breeder rights' was already established in the International Union for the Protection of New Varieties of Plants (UPOV) system.[385]

In 2004, members of the CBD Secretariat made a presentation at the CTE after several countries, including Brazil, Ecuador and India, endorsed the relevance of the CBD secretariat's work on the CTE's mandate. After the CBD secretariat made a

383. WTO, Council for Trade-Related Aspects of Intellectual Property Rights, Review of Article 27.3(b) (Communication from the European Communities and their Members), IP/C/W/383 (October 17, 2002).

384. A similar point was also raised in the Council for Trade-Related Aspects of Intellectual Property Rights. *See generally* WTO Council for Trade-Related Aspects of Intellectual Property Rights, Minutes of Meeting Held in the Centre William Rappard on October 25-26 and 28, November 29 and December 6, 2006, IP/C/M/49 (October 31, 2006).

385. UPOV provides for a right to restrict breeder's rights. *See generally* International Convention for the Protection of New Varieties of Plants Convention 1991 Act of December 2, 1961, as revised in Geneva on November 10, 1972, October 23, 1978 and March 19, 1991, 815 U.N.T.S. 89 (UPOV Convention).

presentation in December 2004, Colombia noted that the discussion under paragraph 32(ii) should cover the question of how trade and IP had an impact on natural resources and related knowledge.[386]

Subsequently, in 2005, Colombia supported the proposal made by India, Brazil and the other delegations, which sought an amendment to the TRIPS Agreement. This would require patent applicants to disclose: the source and country of origin of any biological resources or traditional knowledge used in inventions; evidence of prior informed consent from the competent authority in the country of origin; and evidence of fair and equitable appropriate benefit-sharing arrangements.[387] Norway, too, informed the CTE in 2005 about its proposal to amend the TRIPS agreement so as to include an obligation to disclose the source of genetic resources and traditional knowledge in patent applications.[388] The delegate noted that disclosure requirements would contribute to reducing the risk of wrongful patents. In this regard, Norway shared the views of India, Brazil and other Members that a disclosure requirement would improve the TRIPS agreement. However, Norway stressed that it was important that a disclosure requirement was put in place in a manner that maintained the integrity of the patent system.[389]

Discussions on the different aspects of the environment and its relationship with the TRIPS Agreement effectively stopped at the CTE and CTESS after 2008. In fact, there were only two instances where issues related to the TRIPS Agreement were raised. *First*, when the representative of the UNEP informed the CTE that the European Patent Office, the International Centre for Trade and Sustainable Development (ICTSD), and UNEP had examined the role of IPRs in the transfer of clean energy technologies. This study, which was released on September 30, 2010, analyzed key clean energy technologies and their applications, including a survey of related licensing practices. No responses by WTO Members were documented.[390] *Second*, the delegation of Egypt, in 2013, stressed the importance of IPR and noted that further discussion on this topic was warranted at the CTESS. However, it did not clarify any specific issues that it wanted to discuss and merely stated that "[a] related proposal was being prepared by his delegation in collaboration with other like-minded Members, and would be shared in the near future."[391] No such submission has as of yet been made as of January 2017.

386. WTO CTE, Report of the Meeting Held on June 21, 2004, WT/CTE/M/37 (July 13, 2004).
387. WTO CTE, Report of the Meeting Held on October 11, 2005, WT/CTE/M/41 (November 30, 2005).
388. *Ibid.*
389. WTO General Council, WTO Trade Negotiations Committee, WTO Council for Trade-Related Aspects of Intellectual Property Rights, The Relationship Between the TRIPS Agreement (Communication from Norway), WT/GC/W/566; TN/C/W/42; IP/C/W/473 (June 14, 2006).
390. WTO CTE, Report of the Meeting Held on November 9, 2010, WT/CTE/M/51 (May 31, 2011).
391. WTO CTE, Report of the Meeting Held on November 13, 2012, WT/CTE/M/54 (March 15, 2013) at ¶ 1.71.

[C] CTE 9: Environmental Services

Services appear intangible when linked with the environment. However, on closer inspection, the production, distribution, and consumption of various services have ecological footprints. For example, transportation services are major contributors to greenhouse gases and air pollution. Also, tourism services, if left unchecked, could destroy sensitive ecosystems. On the other hand, services such as water distribution and sanitation can assist in achieving sustainable development. Thus, the regulation of services would substantially contribute to sustainable development.

In 1995, there were few rules governing how domestic government-regulated services. International trade—with the exception of the EU—created rules that dealt exclusively with goods. However, with the signing of NAFTA in 1994 and the GATS in 1995, this trend began to change. The scope of the GATS is quite large. It applies to all governmental measures, be they national or sub-national, which affect trade in services. The primary principles governing the GATS are non-discrimination, market access, the prohibition of monopolies and ban on performance requirements. Given its unique scheduling geometry, Members have an opportunity to protect non-conforming measures when making service commitments but creating a list of carve-outs. While these carve-outs could be protectionist, it would take incredible, arguably unrealistic, amount of foresight to carve-out what measure might be needed to respond to future environmental challenges. Furthermore, if challenged, then it is likely for the dispute settlement mechanism to consider this carve-out to be more trade restrictive than necessary.

On March 1, 1995, the CTS adopted a decision that created the foundation for discussions on the relationship between environment and the GATS. The decisions that CTS adopted:[392]

> [...] acknowledged that measures necessary to protect the environment may conflict with the provisions of the [GATS] Agreement; and noting that since measures necessary to protect the environment typically have as their objective the protection of human, animal or plant life or health, it is not clear that there is a need to provide for more than is contained in paragraph (b) of Article XIV [of the GATS].

Thus, CTS requested the CTE to examine and report the relationship between services trade and the issues relating to the environment, including sustainable development (and not on the effect of the environment on trade in services, such as ecotourism).[393] The CTE note on the relationship between GATS and the environment dated June 1995 studied the negotiating history of the GATS. According to the note, a small number of delegations, in 1991, proposed that the GATS should provide a specific reference to the possibility of suspending obligations in order to protect a Member's own environment. However, other delegations argued that environmental concerns were adequately covered under Article XIV (b), which refers to measures "necessary to

392. WTO Council for Trade in Services, Decision on Trade in Services and the Environment, S/L/4 (April 4, 1995).
393. WTO CTE, Environment and Services, WT/CTE/W/9 (June 8, 1995) at footnote n. 6.

protect human, animal or plant life or health." In fact, with the passing of time, most delegations had agreed that Article XIV (b) covers the environment towards the end of the negotiations. Yet, a few delegations felt that this article did not cover all aspects of environmental concern, such as maintenance of the landscape in the countryside. Therefore, it was decided that a working program on environment and trade in services would be set up to examine the relationship between the two and its effects on sustainable development. As regards what services could be considered when discussing its relationship with the environment, the CTE note provided four examples that demonstrated the complementarities between the provision of a service and another product:[394]

(1) service trade not involving any complementary use of any products, e.g., advice on environmental standards on environmental law, or on environmental information and data;
(2) service trade that facilitates the provision of another product, e.g., repair and maintenance or installation of machinery that produces an environmentally friendly product, development of environmentally friendly design standards, or transport of environmentally friendly products to another market;
(3) service trade that facilitates the provision of another product, e.g., repair and maintenance or installation of machinery that produces an environmentally friendly product, development of environmentally friendly design standards, or transport of environmentally friendly products to another market;
(4) service being embodied in a good, e.g., a computer program for environment-related activities contained in a computer diskette or a video film containing instructions regarding environmental safety.

These examples demonstrate the level of complexity in assessing services trade and the environment. As a result, most of the discussions on this topic were largely exploratory in nature. Also, services, unlike goods, are non-polluting since they are intangible in nature per se. Nonetheless, a careful analysis was called upon to distinguish environmental measures applied directly to trade in services.

WTO Members also discussed the relationship between Article XIV (b) of GATS and the environment. They noted that Article XIV (b) of GATS contains very similar language to Article XX (b) of GATT.[395] Therefore, some WTO Members were of the opinion that an assessment under Article XIV (b) of GATS should be considered only after progress has been made with regard to discussions on MEAs and the multilateral trading system. Other Members recalled that GATS was still evolving and included certain concepts that did not exist in GATT. Therefore, these Members cautioned against an automatic juxtaposition of jurisprudence.

Some Members suggested that progress on this topic should be made in conjunction with the discussions taking place in Item 1. On the other hand, other Members felt that progress in assessing the relationship between GATS and MEAs could be made

394. *Ibid.*
395. *Ibid.*

independently of progress in Item 1. It was also suggested that an analysis could be made that would study the relationship between Article VI of GATS dealing with domestic regulation and trade measures applied pursuant to MEAs dealing with services trade such as the *Basel Convention on the Control of Transboundary Movements of Hazardous Wastes and Their Disposal of 1978* and the Montreal Protocol. This view found merit in a CTE note, which stated that since "investigating, identifying and avoiding environmental harm"[396] requires access to, or provision of, services which have a positive impact on the environment. Such services can also facilitate the achievement of environmental objectives listed in the MEAs. However, until the end of 2000, no further work was conducted regarding the aforementioned discussions.

The U.S. introduced another facet to the discussions when it discussed the global economic and environmental benefits of liberalizing environmental services.[397] It defined environmental services as those services that generated revenue by fees for a service related to a project which benefits the environment. According to the U.S.' submission dated 1997, the environmental service industry supplied pollution control, reduction, clean-up and waste handling services. The submission concluded that trade liberalization in the environmental services sector would yield environmental and economic benefits through improved market access.[398] Three years later, in 2000, an information note by the OECD Secretariat circulated in the CTE posited a similar "win-win outcome" for liberalizing environmental services.[399]

The Secretariat released a discussion paper on *Environmental Effects of Services Trade Liberalization* in October 2002 studying tourism, land freight transport, and environmental services after being requested by Members to prepare a background note. Markedly, this paper did not assess the environmental effects of services trade liberalization, but the focus of the paper was to establish:[400]

> [...] a strong link between services liberalization and the environment may not be sector specific but depends also on a chain of causation that runs from liberalization to development and from development to environment.

The CTE Services Paper, which is a key output of the work done under CTE 9, acknowledged that attributing potential environmental effects from the liberalization of trade in services may be difficult to assess. This is because it is difficult to distinguish environmental effects attributed to services trade in contrast with those that arose from factors other than services trade. The paper deduced that one method of measuring the

396. WTO CTE, Environment and Services, WT/CTE/W/9 (June 8, 1995) quoting David Hunter, Julia Sommer and Scott Vaughan, *Concepts and Principles of International Environmental Law: An Introduction, Environment and Trade* at p. 15 (1994).
397. *See generally* USTR, US Proposals for Liberalizing Trade in Services Executive Summary, (July 1, 2002).
398. WTO CTE, Liberalization of Trade in Environmental Services and the Environment, Contribution by the United States, WT/CTE/W/70 (November 21, 1997).
399. WTO CTE, Environmental Goods and Services: An Assessment of the Environmental, Economic and Development Benefits of Further Globalization, Note by the OECD Secretariat, WT/CTE/W/172 (October 20, 2000).
400. WTO CTE, Discussion Paper on Environmental Effects of Services Trade Liberalization, Note by the Secretariat, WT/CTE/W/218 (October 3, 2002); *see* also, discussion of CTE Agenda Item 9 in Part I, Chapter 2.

effects of services trade on the environment was to measure the environmental impact associated with the consumption of the goods for which service is being provided. Therefore, in considering the environmental effects of services trade liberalization, effects arising from supply and consumption of associated goods must be accounted for.

Further, the CTE Services paper reasoned that tourism could contribute to sustainable development. After all, "damage done to the very environment which is often at the heart of the tourists' attraction will, at the end of the day, affect the viability of the sector in the long term."[401] The report further noted that tourism had relatively high levels of commitments under GATS. Yet, the need for flexibility to address environmental concerns was recognized in the schedules of some of the Members. For example, Kenya upheld the right of Members in GATS to use the necessary flexibility to pursue legitimate policy objectives such as encouragement of ecotourism for sustainable development in its proposal on services.[402] The CTE Services paper further noted that ample information was available for studying the negative environmental effects resulting from transport. However, it was difficult to establish whether this negative correlation was due to services trade liberalization or because of overall economic growth. The CTE Services Paper also cited a report of the Norwegian government that stated, "the likelihood of negative environmental effects resulting from the ongoing rounds of negotiations 'seems small'", referring to an assessment on environmental consequences of trade liberalization in the transport sector.[403]

Regarding environmental services, the paper argued that by its very nature, environmental services had a positive effect on the environment. This is because the service provided was about delivering improved environmental quality such as clean water, reduced wastage and recycling. Therefore, the paper noted that the reduction of barriers to such trade would be intrinsically positive to environmental protection.

According to the delegation of Saudi Arabia, the WTO Secretariat had erred in identifying the transportation sector as an example in this paper. It recalled that *Agenda 21*, to which the paper had made reference, contained more than thirty-three sectors—all of which were equally important. Switzerland, which had made the original request to the WTO Secretariat for the paper, said that the note would serve as a useful tool for future work. The EU was of the opinion that it was too early for substantial deliberations on the paper. Venezuela noted that CTE would, in the future, need to address the issue of subsidies in the area of environmental services.[404]

On April 29 and 30, 2003, Hamid Mamdouh, the Director of WTO Trade in Services Division, made a statement at the CTE. In this statement, information was

401. *Ibid.*
402. WTO Council for Trade in Services Special Session, Negotiating Proposal (Communication from Kenya, Negotiating Proposal), S/CSS/W/109 (September 26, 2001).
403. *See* WT/CTE/W/218 (October 3, 2002), ¶26 citing at fn. 12: Miljøkonsekvenseravmer liberal handel med transporttjenester, *Notat 92/01*, Econ Senter for økonomiskanalyse, Oslo, March 2002. Note that this study is mostly in Norwegian. However, it contains an English summary, and available from the Norwegian Ministry of Foreign Affairs, and also at: http://www.lindhjem.info/N92-01%20IPE.pdf (last accessed on November 30, 2019).
404. WTO CTE, Report of the Meeting Held on October 8, 2002, WT/CTE/M/31 (December 2, 2002).

provided to WTO Members about the discussions on environmental services taking place in the services negotiations. According to the statement:[405]

> Services Sectoral Classification List (MTN.GNG/W/120) developed during the Uruguay Round, and largely based on the United Nations Provisional Central Product Classification (CPC), the environmental services sector includes: (A) sewage services (CPC 9401); (B) refuse disposal services (CPC 9402); (C) sanitation and similar services (CPC 9403); and (D) other environmental services. Although the "other" category does not refer to any CPC item, it presumably includes the remaining elements of the CPC environmental services category, *i.e.* cleaning of exhaust gases (CPC 9404), noise abatement services (CPC 9405), nature and landscape protection services (CPC 9406), and other environmental protection services not included elsewhere (CPC 9409). This List has been used by many Members in their schedules of specific commitments.

It was noted that environmental services was a sector where most trades took place through commercial presence (Mode 3) along with the accompanying presence of natural persons (Mode 4). It further noted that cross-border trade (Mode 1) and consumption abroad (Mode 2) were of limited relevance but could offer supporting services. Further, it was noted that at the services negotiations, some WTO Members, including the U.S., the EU and Switzerland, proposed the identification of services that were not environmental per se but nonetheless important to the provision of environmental services. These services included engineering and research and development (R&D). This exercise was proposed to be undertaken besides the identification of "core" environmental services. Notably, proposals by the U.S.,[406] the EU,[407] Canada,[408] Switzerland,[409] Australia,[410] Colombia[411] and Cuba[412] shared the premise that increased liberalization in environmental services could play a positive role in improving environmental protection and human health. This assumption was made with the introduction of a caveat that appropriate domestic regulatory instruments are in place, and stress the potential for "win-win" situations, especially for developing countries.

The U.S. had asked whether any delegation in the services' negotiation raised questions regarding the environmental implications of the negotiations on Article VI:4

405. WTO CTE, Environmental Issues Raised in the Services Negotiations, Statement by Mr. A. Hamid Mamdouh—April 30, 2003—Paragraph 51, WT/CTE/GEN/11 (April 16, 2003).
406. WTO, Council for Trade in Service Special Session, Communication from the United States—Environmental Services, S/CSS/W/25 (December 18, 2000).
407. WTO, Council for Trade in Services Special Session, Communication from the European Communities and their Members—GATS 2000: Environmental Services, S/CSS/W/38 (December 22, 2000).
408. WTO, Council for Trade in Services Special Session, Communication from Canada, Initial Negotiating Proposal on Environmental Services, S/CSS/W/51(March 14, 2001).
409. WTO, Council for Trade in Services Special Session, Communication from Switzerland—GATS 2000: Environmental Services, S/CSS/W/76 (May 4, 2001).
410. WTO General Council, Preparations for the 1999 Ministerial Conference, Focus and Priorities of the New Round of Services Negotiations, Communication from *Hong Kong, China*, S/C/W/112 (June 22, 1999).
411. WTO, Council for Trade in Services Special Session, Communication from Colombia, Negotiating Proposal on Environmental Services, S/CSS/W/121 (March 22, 2002).
412. WTO, Council for Trade in Services Special Session, Communication from Cuba, Negotiating Proposal on Environmental Services, S/CSS/W/142 (March 22, 2002).

of GATS, which dealt with domestic regulations.[413] This was because negotiations on Article VI:4 of GATS focused on transparency and the necessity test; both topics were debated with intensity at the CTE. In particular, the U.S. queried if potential negative or positive environmental effects on necessity were apparent from discussions in the services negotiations.

In response to the question posed by the delegation of the US, the WTO Secretariat noted, "without making a judgmental answer," that it was possible that negotiations under Article VI:4 of GATS could affect environmental services. The necessity test stated that measures relating to qualification requirements, licensing requirements, and technical standards should not constitute an unnecessary barrier to trade. However, the Secretariat stated that the imposition of such measures could be aimed at protecting the environment. Therefore, the Secretariat concluded that the extent of necessity to impose such measures would need to be assessed in order to serve as a legitimate environmental protection policy objective or an unnecessary barrier to trade in services.

Venezuela, once again, pointed out that subsidies could distort a level-playing field. The WTO Secretariat responded that no specific work on subsidies in environmental services was undertaken. Canada, the EU and Egypt presented their views on the relationship of the environment in services negotiations. Canada, in particular, encouraged WTO Members who had not already done so to make commitments in environmental service areas for all modes of service delivery. The EU stated that regulations needed to accompany services trade liberalization in order to benefit economic growth, environmental protection and sustainable development.[414]

Two years later, in October 2005, the report of the Chairperson of the Special Sessions of the CTS reported that twenty-one offers had been made in the environmental services sector as of July 2005.[415] Of these, seven offers were made by developed economies, and fourteen offers were made by developing countries. There were no further discussions on environmental issues in services negotiations subsequent to the update by the WTO Secretariat in October 2005.

After the 2001 Doha Ministerial Meeting, services were captured under paragraph 31(iii) of the Doha Declaration. Members agreed that the paragraph 31(iii) mandate on liberalizing services would be shifted to the Council for Trade in Services Special Session (CTSSS) with the CTESS maintaining a monitoring role in examining the definitional aspects and scope of environmental services.

After initial progress at the CTESS, the work stalled—possibly with discontented *demandeurs* of services deciding to negotiate the Trade in Services Agreement (TiSA),[416] a plurilateral services agreement with like-minded Members. Another reason

413. WTO CTE, Environmental Issues Raised in the Services Negotiations, Statement by Mr. A. Hamid Mamdouh—April 30, 2003—Paragraph 51, WT/CTE/GEN/11 (April 16, 2003).
414. WTO CTE, Report of the Meeting Held on April 29, 2003, WT/CTE/M/33 (May 21, 2003).
415. WTO, Council for Trade in Services Special Session, Report by the Chairman to the Trade Negotiations Committee, TN/S/23 (November 28, 2005).
416. The TiSA, in negotiation since 2012, seeks to liberalize trade in services by way of the plurilateral route to pursue deeper service-sector liberalization. *See generally* on the current status of TiSA negotiations, Mathew Oxenford, Rethinking the WTO's Role in a Digital, Divided

was that the classification of environmental services was based on the 1991 Services Sectoral Classification List,[417] which outlined environmental services into four categories, which included sewage, refuse disposal, sanitation and "other" environmental services. However, some Members like the EU argued that this classification did not reflect the realities of the market.[418] The WTO Secretariat provided various background papers to aid in the environmental negotiations, as did the UNCTAD Secretariat, which submitted a paper on developing countries developing their environmental service sector.[419] Despite this, no further discussion on the role of services and the environment was made, and this topic before the CTE and CTESS had come to a pause.

§5.05 CTE 7, 8, 9 FUTURE WORK

The work outputs and the results of the CTE work on the specialized topics under CTE 7, 8, and 9 relating to DPGs, TRIPS and Services are evidently less satisfactory than the work on the special topics under CTE 3a and 3b relating to climate and border taxes or environmental charges, and the issues of standards and eco-labelling. This is because they fall short of providing a platform for the managers, experts, secretariats, TRNs and GALs to have constructive and fulfilling information sharing and idea exchanges that could lead to better and potential best practices or that member delegations could report or apply for purposes of improving trade and environment policy implementation and formulation. There is also a need for coherence and avoidance of duplication for discussions that might be the subject of parallel or more appropriate focus of other WTO bodies such as the TRIPS Council or the CTS.

The work of the CTE in these areas remained consistent and coherent with the legally mandated areas of work under CTE 7, 8 and 9, and the work performed did create further technical knowledge and understanding of the specific and specialized topics covered. The work outputs relating to CTE 7, 8 and 9 do not generate policy toolkits that could be useful for policy makers or policy implementers, much less as aids to potential rulemaking. Unless there is some well-defined updated guidance, both from the political and policy expert context, on the further objectives that the CTE could accomplish in these areas, these work areas are ripe for closure or referral to other bodies at the WTO or outside the WTO.

It is suggested that a serious review of the CTE mandates in these three areas be made, and a definition of the short- and medium-objectives for these topics be formulated if more work is to be expected in these areas. Another administrative

---

World, Chatham House: Royal Institute of International Affairs (2019) available at: https://www.chathamhouse.org/expert/comment/rethink-wto-s-role-digital-divided-world (accessed on November 30, 2019); *see also* Juan Marchetti and Martin Roy, *The TiSA Initiative: An Overview of Market Access issues* (2013).

417. WTO, Services Sectoral Classification List, MTN.GNS/W/120 (July 10, 1991).
418. WTO Committee on Specific Commitments, Communication from the European Communities and their Members, Classification Issues in the Environmental Sector, S/CSC/W/25 (September 28, 1999).
419. WTO CTE, UNCTAD Expert Meeting on Strengthening Capacities in Developing Countries to Develop Their Environmental Services Sector, Communication from UNCTAD, WT/CTE/W/96 (August 3, 1998).

technique that could come in handy would be to provide for a ministerial instruction with sunsetting provisions for these areas of work that no longer require further focus, as the sunset period allows for a smooth transition and closing report to be made on the special topic.

One topic of particular importance that the CTE has started to discuss is the circular economy and trade. Over the last few years, a marked shift has been taking place as a linear focus on producing, using, and discarding products is slowly being replaced. Instead, under a circular economy model, societies are looking at solutions that maximize resource efficiency and minimize waste across product life cycles and the economy as a whole. One additional driver behind the circular economy concept is the long-term supply of and access to natural resources, such as rare earth minerals, for example.[420] Once the security of supply is at stake, this will focus attention on both circular economy solutions and related trade elements—the risk of export restrictions increases. At the same time, extracting secondary materials becomes more viable and interesting, driving new technological developments.

The circular economy goes to the heart of how we produce and consume. Many countries, such as China, Finland, France, India, and the Netherlands, have adopted national circular economy roadmaps and implementation plans.[421]

In a recently delivered speech, on November 25, 2019, at a workshop organized by the governments of China, Morocco and Sri Lanka at the WTO, Director General Roberto Azevêdo highlighted the growing interest among WTO Members in the cross-border implications of plastic pollution, the role international cooperation, and circular economy. Roberto Azevedo stated:[422]

> Some members have raised the cross-border implications of plastics pollution here at the WTO. Over the past three years, plastic pollution has repeatedly figured in the Committee on Trade and the Environment. Members have discussed their domestic policies to address plastics pollution, measures to prevent marine pollution, and trade in waste that contains plastics. And I understand plastic use may come up in the discussion on the circular economy planned for this week's CTE.

420. *See generally* China Measures Related to the Exportation of Rare Earths, Tungsten, and Molybdenum, WT/DS431/R; WT/DS432/R; WT/DS433/R (March 26, 2014, adopted August 29, 2014); China Measures Related to the Exportation of Rare Earths, Tungsten, and Molybdenum, WT/DS431/AB/R; WT/DS432/AB/R; WT/DS433/AB/R (August 7, 2019, adopted August 29, 2014); *see also* Manuel A.J. Teehankee, *The WTO China Raw Materials Case: Re-Igniting the Debate on Coherence and Conflict between Free Trade Theory and Resource Economics* 6 Teri GALT 10 (2012).

421. *See*, e.g., World Bank, *Developing Circular Economy in China: Highlights and Recommendations* (2008).

422. *See* Roberto Azevedo, Speech: Members have the Opportunity to Address Global Plastic Pollution at the WTO, November 25, 2019, available at: https://www.wto.org/english/news_e/spra_e/spra295_e.htm (accessed on November 30, 2019); CTE, Report of the Meeting Held on November 30, 2018, WT/CTE/M/66 (March 22, 2019); *see also* Alan Wolff, Speech: WTO Can Play a Role in Supporting a Circular Economy, November 25, 2019, available at: https://www.wto.org/english/news_e/news19_e/ddgaw_25nov19_e.htm (accessed on November 30, 2019).

However, the circular economy neither starts nor ends at national borders or company walls. This is where trade comes into the picture, and as an example, when in 2017, China notified the WTO of its trade ban on certain plastics and waste products, it was objected to by the U.S.[423] The EU has also announced a trade ban on ten single-use plastic products from 2021.[424] We may have national circular economy strategies, but they exist in the context of a global economy and international value chains, as well as within our sole earth with its limited resources and planetary boundaries.

As the circular economy becomes more mainstream, what it actually means—and what it means for trade—needs to be clarified. Circularity is about material cycles and systemic change, and as such needs to be analyzed at the global level, including the flow of natural resources, products, and services, and the energy that fuels our economies. In a nutshell, there is a need to consider the circular economy transition from the perspective of global value chains and trade rules. There should be collaboration and cooperation among WTO members in problem-solving mode, which can complement and supplement national and domestic strategies rather than create new barriers and obstacles that could cause transition imbalances and instability in the general global recycling sectors and lead to unintended consequences.

Indeed, the CTE could appropriately serve as a proper forum for emerging global environmental concerns apart from the work it has undertaken in the specialized areas of DPGs, TRIPS, the CBD, and Environmental Services. However, the CTE needs must be provided with a clearer Ministerial Mandate that includes the securing of greater technical expertise in its Secretariat for it to meaningfully contribute to the global governance challenges facing the trade and environment regimes.

Absent such a clear mandate and the provision of greater technical and expert support, I posit that these functions of CTE 7, 8 and 9 should be sunsetted or in the alternative updated to take into account current and emerging trends, including on the impact of trade bans, the global plastics issues, and the diverse issues relating to the circular economy and equitable access to natural resources trade.

---

423. *See* China's notification imposing an import ban on certain kinds of plastic items, WTO Committee on Technical Barriers to Trade, Notification (China), G/TBR/N/CHN/1211 (July 18, 2017); *see also* United States' response to China's notification at WTO Committee on Technical Barriers to Trade, China—Chinese Environmental Protection Control Standards for Imported Solid Waste as Raw Materials (Statement by the United States to the Committee on Technical Barriers to Trade), G/TBT/W/468 (March 27, 2018).

424. European Commission, Communication on a European Strategy for Plastics in a Circular Economy, COM (2018) 28 final (January 16, 2018); *see also* WTO CTE, Circular Economy in the European Union: Achievements under the 2015-2019 Circular Economy Action Plan (Submission by the EU), RD/CTE/164 (November 25, 2019); WTO CTE, Circular Economy and the WTO (Submission by the United States), RD/CTE/153 (November 19, 2019),

CHAPTER 6

Market Access and the Triple-win Mandate

there should not be, nor need be, any policy contradiction between upholding and safeguarding an open, non-discriminatory and equitable multilateral trading system on the one hand, and acting for the protection of the environment, and the promotion of sustainable development on the other

Ministerial Decision on Trade and Environment
Marrakesh, April 14, 1994

32. We instruct the Committee on Trade and Environment, ... to give particular attention to: (i) the effect of environmental measures on market access and those situations in which the elimination or reduction of trade restrictions and distortions ***would benefit trade, the environment and development.***

Ministerial Declaration
Doha, November 14, 2001

§6.01 INTRODUCTORY SECTION ON THE MARKET ACCESS WORK OF THE CTE

At the core of the decision establishing the WTO CTE in 1994 was the fundamental principle of the WTO for promoting a fair and open global economy through a rules-based global governance system, and the very *raison d'etre* for having such an institution combines *the triple-win* goal of promoting development and social justice, first of all, growing trade volumes, and environmental protection and sustainable development, as expressed succinctly in this sequence in the preamble of the Marrakesh Treaty:

> Recognizing that their relations in the field of trade and economic endeavour should be conducted with a view to raising standards of living, ensuring full employment and a large and steadily growing volume of real income and effective demand, and expanding the production of and trade in goods and services, while allowing for the optimal use of the world's resources in accordance with the objective of sustainable development, seeking both to protect and preserve the environment and to enhance the means for doing so in a manner consistent with their respective needs and concerns at different levels of economic development.[425]

While it is acknowledged that as part of the service to humankind, when GATT was established, uppermost in the minds of the statesmen and founders of the GATT was the urgent need to avoid for all time the necessity, and tragedy, of war, by assuring global society that markets would be open and fair. Only by assuring that markets are open can economies then prosper and work together in economic cooperation. This is the basic theory by which trade and open markets contribute to global peace, security and peace.

As we have seen in the review of the nine agenda items out of the ten-point work program of the CTE, there are positive and excellent evaluations on certain of the CTE work areas, as in the mandates for transparency, international cooperation and coordination, as well as, in increasing expert knowledge and bureaucratic team building and interface, so that the environment policies and priorities are respected and fostered. However, what does it all mean to the citizens of the world and to the business and industrial sectors; among the ten-point work program areas of the CTE, *where is the beef*? Which agenda item provides the real opportunity for trade and development, and increased livelihoods and rising incomes?

Even if the CTE was mandated to be a forum or a *talk-shop* that can lead to greater coordination and cooperation, not all the *talk-shops* in the world can make up for the lack of some tangible and practical results that can translate to economic and business gains and profits for constituents and stakeholders. Evidently, therefore, there is still the last key work area and mandate of the CTE under agenda item 6 of its work program, and subject of this last substantive chapter.

The market access negotiating mandate for the CTE and CTESS was part of the broad spectrum of goals proclaimed as the DDA and is more particularly contained in paragraphs 31(iii) and 32(i) of the Doha Ministerial Declaration of 2001, which directly co-relates to the original 1994 CTE Decision mandate for work on agenda item 6 (CTE 6) for studies of the "environmental benefits of removing market access restrictions and distortions."

In the previous two chapters where the various thematic work areas of CTE were discussed, one could derive that one or two of the three theoretical frameworks could be applied as benchmarks or measures for evaluating the work of the CTE as an IO or institution of global governance. However, in the case of the market access work theme, all the lenses or theories are fully active and applicable and inspired in part by the trade and environment governance partnership that led to the success in other

425. Preamble of the Marrakesh Agreement Establishing the World Trade Organization, Marrakesh Agreement Establishing the World Trade Organization, 33 I.L.M. 1267 (1994).

MEAs such as the Montreal Protocol. Market access, therefore, becomes a focus of the Lens A IL-IR Leviathan visionaries of global governance and the rule of law for the common good. Lens B Policy specialists and experts who engender the global civil service and bureaucracy of MEA secretariats and transgovernmental regulators with their ability to build global networks of professional and talented service providers, within and without national and international government agencies, and with their combined expertise are well placed to guide the optimal levels of market openings. Lens C enthusiasts will see the need to interact with academia and think tanks, with specialists of economics and environmental science, and with local and regional governance mechanisms, in order to ensure that market openings take into account the self-governance mechanisms for CPRs and the regional diversity of resources.

In the work area of market access, the promise remains that the constituents and advocates of excellence in trade and global environment governance ought to be able to deliver some new rules and policies that will lead to practical outcomes that improve the welfare of the CTE constituents and serve the ends of trade and sustainable development.

In addition, the CTE's market access work is informed by and complemented by all the other CTE work generated in the other mandated thematic areas, such as the work done on identifying STOs in MEAs, as well as the knowledge and experience obtained from the prior work of the GEMIT, which were previously covered in Chapters 4 and 1, respectively, as well as early work of the CTE in discussing agenda item 6 on the co-relation or effects of environmental measures on market access, relating to the four original sectors of agriculture, fisheries subsidies, energy and forestry (see this volume's Annex 2 summary of CTE6 Sectoral Discussions).

Market Access, and market opportunities, therefore, is the area, elusive as it has been, that remains of great interest to governments and state actors, multinational enterprises, rural development enthusiasts, environmental business enterprises, traditional and renewable energy companies, and the theoreticians from all the three lenses discussed in Chapter 3.

As mentioned, it was paragraph 32(i) of the Doha Ministerial Declaration that mandated delivery of *triple-win* outcomes through market access and market openings. In reviewing the work of the CTE and CTESS in the work area of CTE 6, the focus is on the shape and structure of the negotiated potential outcomes which are captured among the key CTE work outputs for the CTE 6 market access agenda item, as well as understanding the proposals and modalities approaches for the negotiations, and the substantive meaning and objectives of achieving a market access *triple-win for trade, development and the environment.*

§6.02 CTE 6 / CTESS 31III / DDA 32I

Item 6: *The effect of environmental measures on market access, especially in relation to developing countries, in particular to the least developed among them, and environmental benefits of removing trade restrictions and distortions.*
DDA 31iii: 31. *With a view to enhancing the mutual supportiveness of trade and environment, we agree to negotiations, without prejudging their outcome, on:*

(iii) *the reduction or, as appropriate, elimination of tariff and non-tariff barriers to environmental goods and services.*

DDA 32i: *32. We instruct the Committee on Trade and Environment, in pursuing work on all items on its agenda within its current terms of reference, to give particular attention to:*

(i) *the effect of environmental measures on market access, especially in relation to developing countries, in particular the least-developed among them, and those situations in which the elimination or reduction of trade restrictions and distortions would benefit trade, the environment and development;*

Key Output Documents for Item 6:

1. Environmental Requirements and Market Access: Recent Work in OECD and UNCTAD, WT/CTE/W/244 (2006)
2. Revision of the synthesis of submissions on Environmental Goods TN/TE/W/63, JOB(07)/137 (2007)
3. Draft Decision, Annex II on Structure and the Outcome Environmental Goods Coverage Under Paragraph 31(iii), Annex II, TN/TE/20 (2011)
4. Compilation of submission under paragraph 31(iii) of Doha Pursuant to the CTESS Work Programme, JOB/TE/3/Rev.1 (2011)

[*Plurilateral Environmental Goods Discussions (APEC, EGA, Coalitions of the Willing)*]

Paragraph 31(iii) of the Doha Ministerial Declaration became the first concrete mandate of the CTE/CTESS to engage positively to formulate new market access opportunities and rules and modalities for improving market access for Environmental Goods and Services (EGS).[426]

As part of the DDA single undertaking, the CTE/CTESS (or collectively CTE) commenced meetings in the negotiating format of the CTESS that involved many informal and small group interactions. The CTESS would generate at least four key work outputs from 2006 through to 2011. These outputs evolved to give concrete shape to what an environmental goods agreement would look like, and like the draft decision discussed in Chapter 4 relating to the mandate for CTE 1, 5, and 10, much of the drafts have become effective in practice.

For easy reference, one can refer to Annex II and Annex II.B to the 2011 CTESS Chairman's report of April 21, 2011, *see* this volume's ***Annex 3*** *(the Full Chair Report)*,

426. WTO Ministerial Conference (4th Session Doha November 9-14, 2001), Ministerial Declaration, WT/MIN(01)/DEC/1 (November 20, 2001) provides that "[w]ith a view to enhancing the mutual supportiveness of trade and environment, we agree to negotiations, without prejudging their outcome, on:... (iii) the reduction or, as appropriate, elimination of tariff and non-tariff barriers to environmental goods and services."

which reflected the state of play of the market access negotiations at the time, and which remains the framework for the market access discussions.

In the context of the exchange of ideas and knowledge, the sources of the structure and the suggested tariff modalities have, in certain instances, contributed to the negotiations happening multilaterally within and outside the WTO. The Asia-Pacific Economic Cooperation forum (APEC), for one, has adopted tariff cuts for many of the goods or HS lines listed in the Reference Universe or the Sample Core List of Environmental Goods.[427]

From very early on, developing countries had a foundational divide with their developed counterparts on the market access focus of the CTESS DDA paragraph 31(iii). I suggest that the three theoretical frameworks were all at work in the market access negotiations resulting in the battle between a singular global structure and mechanism for trade and environment governance, with the Ostrom-ian school pitted against the two other frameworks seeking a rational, unified framework in the traditional sense of obtaining consensus and agreement as had been successfully done both for the WTO treaty as well as the great leaps forward in the environmental treaty context.

The main thrust of the argument of developing countries is that, in order to be faithful to the mandate of sustainable development (paragraph 6 of the Doha Declaration) and the *triple win* concept enunciated in paragraph 32, the outcome ought to be more than the reduction of tariffs and non-tariff barriers, and any outcome should demonstrate a clear environmental and developmental benefit. This has been the clarion call from countries, led by India and Argentina, who proposed the project or integrated approach whereby concessions would be on a project by project basis. This foundational approach led, in the early years, to the immense debate and scrutiny accorded to every tariff line in order to hurdle the so-called *single-use* green credentials of any particular product.[428]

427. APEC List of Environmental Goods, Annex C, APEC Leaders Declaration (2012), available at: https://www.apec.org/Meeting-Papers/Leaders-Declarations/2012/2012_aelm/2012_aelm_annexC.aspxs ; https://www.apec.org/Press/News-Releases/2016/0128_EG.aspx ; http://www.apec.org/Groups/Committee-on-Trade-and-Investment/APEC-Economies-Implementation-Plans.aspx; see also Rene Vossenaar, The APEC List of Environmental Goods: An Analysis of the Outcome and Expected Impact (2013) available at: https://www.greengrowthknowledge.org/resource/apec-list-environmental-goods-analysis-outcome-expected-impacts; https://www.ictsd.org/sites/default/files/downloads/2013/06/the-apec-list-of-environmental-goods.pdf; Rene Vossenaar, Reducing Import Tariffs for Environmental Goods: The APEC Experience (2016) available at: https://www.ictsd.org/sites/default/files/research/reducing_import_tariffs_for_environmental_goods_the_apec_experience.pdf.

428. *See* WTO CTESS, Structural Dimensions of the Environmental Project Approach—Submission by India—Paragraph 31(iii), TN/TE/W/54 (July 4, 2005); WTO CTESS, Communication from Cuba—Paragraph 31(iii), TN/TE/W/73 (July 9, 2008); WTO CTE, Elements for Ensuring a Sustainable Development Outcome under Paragraph 31(iii) of the Doha Ministerial Declaration (Submission by the Plurinational State of Bolivia and the Bolivarian Republic of Venezuela), JOB/TE/17 (March 24, 2011); WTO CTESS, Integrated Proposal on Environmental Goods for Development (Submission by Argentina), TN/TE/W/62 (October 14, 2005); WTO CTESS, WTO Negotiations on Environmental Goods and Services—Addressing the Development Dimension for a "Triple Win" Outcome (Communication from China and India), TN/TE/W/79 (April 15, 2011).

The contrast in approach is in no small measure attributable to the strong advocacy led by Brazil[429] (which proposed the request and offer modality) for a mercantilist anchor to the negotiations that would ensure developing countries get compensated for providing further tariff concessions, coupled with the policy space dimension that speaks to developing their national industries in the environmental sector. Necessarily, this runs counter to developed members approaching the problem from a tariff reduction or elimination perspective. As a corollary, developing countries, parallel to their positions in climate change negotiations in the UNFCCC, pushed for making technology sharing and transfer priority elements of the market access negotiations.

As pointed out in a submission titled "The Doha Round and Climate Change," Argentina proposed linking climate change mitigation to the negotiations:

> The WTO negotiations ... should therefore be aimed primarily at facilitating access to goods and services that used in climate change mitigation and adaptation projects ... help to reduce the costs of projects relating to action against climate change, which might help to stabilize greenhouse gas concentrations at a level that would prevent anthropogenic interference with the climate system ... .
>
> The work of the CTESS should therefore be aimed at establishing synergies between the climate change regime and the multilateral trading system, so as to enhance mutual supportiveness between trade liberalization objectives, environmental protection and sustainable development.[430]

Market access has always had strong linkages to the manner in which WTO Members conduct their trade relations. Discussions related to market access become particularly relevant in the context of the environment. This is because WTO Members, in reading the preamble to the Marrakesh Agreement[431] have argued and debated the meaning of "allowing for the optimal use of the world's resources in accordance with the objective of sustainable development" as dependent on members' levels of economic development.

Most of the discussions then that took place in the CTE, particularly in the initial years, made extensive reference to five general principles enshrined in the Rio Declaration. These principles were: *first*, poverty is the basic cause of environmental degradation in many Member economies, and trade can contribute to the eradication of poverty. *Second*, it is not trade but unsustainable production and consumption

429. WTO CTESS, Environmental Goods for Development (Submission by Brazil), JOB(07)/146 (October 1, 2007).
430. WTO CTESS, The Doha Round and Climate Change (Submission by Argentina), TN/TE/W/74 (November 23, 2009) at ¶¶ 2, 4.
431. The Preamble to the Marrakesh Agreement states: "The Parties to this Agreement, Recognizing that their relations in the field of trade and economic endeavor should be conducted with a view to raising standards of living, ensuring full employment and a large and steadily growing volume of real income and effective demand, and expanding the production of and trade in goods and services, while allowing for the optimal use of the world's resources in accordance with the objective of sustainable development, seeking both to protect and preserve the environment and to enhance the means for doing so in a manner consistent with their respective needs and concerns at different levels of economic development." Marrakesh Agreement Establishing the World Trade Organization, 33 I.L.M. 1267 (1994).

processes that are the root of environmental degradation. *Third*, the principle of "common but differentiated responsibility" permits sovereign states the right to make their own judgment on the standards they apply in their territories. *Fourth*, policy measures taken to promote the internalization of environmental costs should not distort international trade and investment. And, *fifth*, Members should promote an open international economic system that would lead to economic growth and sustainable development to combat environmental degradation. The central themes for most of the proposals made by WTO Members were based on or related to these five general principles.

Australia observed that low-income, commodity-dependent countries, and countries that were marginal participants in world trade were more likely confronted with environmental challenges than their counterparts. It suggested that trading partners of these countries should assist in the diversification of export opportunities through the inclusion of higher value-added products. This, according to Australia, could help these countries reduce poverty and protect the environment. In agreeing with Australia, other Members also stated that trade liberalization should be accompanied by technology and financial transfer.

The U.S. argued that economic growth and a strong environmental policy would improve overall environmental quality. It reasoned that opening up of agricultural markets would contribute to the efficient allocation of resources, which, in turn, would contribute to protecting the environment. It further noted that nationally-specific environmental problems should be effectively tackled through domestic environmental policy and not trade restrictions. Many WTO Members agreed that environmental problems should be dealt with at the national level and not through trade-restrictive measures. These discussions are in line with the text of Principle 11 of the Rio Declaration, which states that:[432]

> States shall enact effective environmental legislation. Environmental standards, management objectives and priorities should reflect the environmental and development context to which they apply. Standards applied by some countries may be inappropriate and of unwarranted economic and social cost to other countries, in particular developing countries.

Many Members also contended that unilateral action to protect the environment was unacceptable and would undermine the foundational principle of consensus in the multilateral trading system. They noted that while Members have the responsibility to ensure activities within their jurisdiction, issues such as transboundary harm could only be resolved in a cooperative manner through the negotiation of MEAs. Further, some Members observed that environmental standards differed from one country to another, and trade-related measures should not be coercively applied in an attempt to harmonize these standards. This would, in their opinion, amount to an extra-jurisdictional imposition of environmental standards. In this regard, some Members even recalled the 1995 Report on Trade and Environment to the OECD Council at the

432. UN Rio Declaration on Environment and Development, Jun. 13, 1992, 31 I.L.M. 874, at prin. 11; U.N. GAOR, 46th Sess. Agenda Item 21, UN Doc. A/Conf. 151/26 (1992).

Ministerial Level in which governments agreed the principles in *Agenda 21* would "extend to unilateral import restrictions based on PPM-related requirements."[433]

Some Members suggested protecting the existing market access opportunities. India, for instance, noted that SMEs, which account for a large share of manufactured exports in developing countries, would benefit from protection. In response, many WTO Members contended that existing WTO disciplines such as the TBT and SPS Agreements, the SCM Agreement, the TRIPS Agreement and WTO provisions for special and differential treatment for developing countries were sufficiently competent to safeguard these market access opportunities.

By and large, Members agreed that environmental benefits could accrue in a variety of ways. Some Members considered that removal of trade restrictions on environmentally friendly goods and services would help in protecting the environment. Other Members argued that restricting the transfer of EST would be counterproductive to environmental protection. Still, others contended that trade restrictions and distortions led to the ineffective allocation of resources, which held back income growth in developing countries. Some Members considered that trade liberalization should be complemented with discussions on improving market access, ESTs, finance and capacity building.

After the Doha Ministerial Conference, with the negotiating mandate under paragraph 31(iii), the discussions at the CTESS focused more on the gathering of concrete proposals for an outcome. Members focused their energy on coalescing on common interests. An agreement that sought to eliminate or reduce tariffs on EGS was identified as a possible item to negotiate. However, with this identification came the questions relating to the correct forum for the ensuing negotiations to take place. It was the representative of Peru who argued that negotiations on trade liberalization for goods be undertaken at the Negotiating Group on Market Access for Non-Agricultural Products.[434] According to the representative, the role of the CTE would be to assist in paragraph 31(iii) negotiations. This proposal was supported by Japan, Venezuela, Canada, Singapore, EC, Paraguay, New Zealand and Switzerland.[435] According to these countries, such bifurcation of roles of different committees during paragraph 31(iii) negotiations would lead to avoidance of duplication of work. On the other hand, the Republic of Korea, while agreeing that duplication of work would be counterproductive, argued that the CTESS would have to play a pivotal role in defining environmental goods. In one sense, it can be noted that the Republic of Korea's views were not very different from those of Peru and countries that supported its views— the delegate of the Republic of Korea only reminded Members of CTESS's specialized role.

433. OECD, Report on Trade and Environment to the OECD Council at Ministerial Level (1995) at p. 7; *see also* UN General Assembly, Agenda 21: Program of Action for Sustainable Development, A/Conf.151/26 (June 14, 1992); U.N. GAOR, 46th Sess. Agenda Item 21, UN Doc. A/Conf. 151/26 (1992).
434. WTO CTESS, Summary Report on the First Meeting of the Special Session Held on March 22, 2002, TN/TE/R/1 (April 19, 2002).
435. *Ibid.*

Several submissions made by Members such as New Zealand[436] and the U.S.[437] were based on the cross-cutting work on environmental goods undertaken by the APEC. The Republic of Korea also believed that the work by APEC was a good starting point for further discussion.[438] Other noteworthy proposals included those made by Qatar and Japan. Japan's paper was based on a research paper on environmental goods that was prepared by the OECD Joint Working Group on Trade and Environment dated 2000, whereas the U.S. submission was based on work undertaken by APEC. As a result, the U.S. emphasized the importance of the APEC list since, according to the U.S. delegate, it was a result of highly technical analysis over a period of several years and represented a collaborative effort of several developed and developing countries. While the APEC and OECD lists provided a good starting point, Members could include other environmentally friendly products on the list as well. Some Members such as India and Kenya voiced concerns regarding the OECD list. According to them, the list was not taking into account the concerns of the developing countries.

Seven submissions at the CTESS saw Members proposing an initial list of environmental goods. These Members included Canada,[439] EU,[440] Japan,[441] the Republic of Korea,[442] New Zealand,[443] Qatar,[444] Chinese Taipei,[445] and the U.S.[446] The papers submitted by these Members included various considerations in drawing up the list. This includes, *first*, the reliance on the products' environmental "end use" or "direct use," for example, products used to clean the environment or control pollution (mentioned in the proposals made by Korea, the U.S. and Chinese Taipei). However, Korea and the U.S. noted that product distinction should not be based on PPM criteria. *Second*, other proposals, such as those by New Zealand and the EU, forwarded lists that

436. WTO CTESS, Environmental Goods Paragraph 31(iii) (Submission by New Zealand), TN/TE/W/6 (June 6, 2002).
437. WTO CTESS, Summary Report on the Sixth Meeting of the Committee on Trade and Environment Special Session, TN/TE/R/6 (June 12, 2003).
438. WTO CTESS, Summary Report on the Fifth Meeting of the Committee on Trade and Environment in Special Session, TN/TE/R/5 (April 14, 2003).
439. WTO CTESS, Canada's Initial List of Environmental Goods Paragraph 31(iii) (Submission by Canada), TN/TE/W/50 (June 2, 2005).
440. WTO CTESS, Market Access for Environmental Goods (Communication from the European Communities), TN/TE/W/47 (February 17, 2005).
441. WTO CTESS, Market Access for Non-agricultural Products (Communication from Japan), TN/TE/W/17 (November 20, 2002).
442. WTO CTESS, Initial List of Environmental Goods Proposed (Submission by the Republic of Korea), TN/TE/W/48 (February 18, 2005).
443. WTO CTESS, Environmental Goods (Submission by New Zealand), TN/TE/W/46 (June 6, 2002).
444. WTO CTESS, Negotiations on Environmental Goods (Submission by Qatar), TN/TE/W/19 (January 28, 2003); WTO CTESS, Negotiating Group on Market Access Harmonized System (HS) Classification Codes of Gas-Related Goods (Submission by Qatar), TN/TE/W/27 (April 25, 2003).
445. WTO CTESS, Proposed Initial List of Environmental Goods (Submission by the Separate Customs Territory of Taiwan and Matsu), TN/TE/W/44 (October 7, 2004).
446. WTO CTESS, Liberalizing Environmental Goods in the WTO (Submission by the United States), TN/TE/W/34 (June 19, 2003); WTO CTESS, Market Access for Non-agricultural Products—US Contribution Environmental Goods Modality (Addendum), TN/TE/W/38 (July 7, 2003); WTO CTESS, Negotiating Group on Market Access—Initial List of Environmental Goods (Submission by the United States), TN/TE/W/52 (July 4, 2005).

were based on the treatment of environmentally preferable products (EPPs). New Zealand felt that EPPs should only be based on end use or disposal characteristics, whereas the EU prepared the list by including certain products based on parameters such as environmental performance. Notably, the Republic of Korea proposed a list that was based on the exclusion of EPPs or products based on superior environmental performances.[447] *Third*, some Members, such as the EU, prepared lists based on the contribution of environmental goods to the fulfillment of internationally agreed environmental priorities such as MEAs and Millennium Development Goals (MDGs). Qatar, too, supported this view but was more specific since it identified UNFCCC as the MEA that contributed concrete criteria for identifying environmental goods. *Fourth*, Members such as Japan prepared lists based on wider environmental objectives such as global environmental problems and sustainable use of exhaustible natural resources. *Fifth*, Canada, EU and New Zealand prepared a list of environmental goods when considering the national interest of all Members, including developing country Members. *Last*, the Republic of Korea and New Zealand proposed lists based on different classifications. The Republic of Korea used the product's classifiability under the HS system, whereas New Zealand's list was based on the OECD's definition of environmental industries and APEC's conceptualization of environmental goods.

India, on the other hand, submitted a concept paper that presented the *Environmental Project Approach*. Under this approach, goods and services were to be included in a project that was to be approved by a Designated National Authority (DNA), which every Member must establish. The projects decided by the DNA would include those aimed at meeting national environmental objectives as well as MEAs and could include, *inter alia*, equipment, parts and services, consumables, services, financial aid and transfer of technology. The scope of projects could include air pollution control, waste and waste management, solid waste management, noise abatement and energy saving, to name a few.[448]

Over time, the list approach gained traction amongst Members, and India's proposal was not taken forward mainly due to the technical issue of how tariff lines could be defined on a multilateral basis and on a more or less stable basis. With this clarity, Members debated over the list of goods that should be included to fulfill the *triple win* outcome, which would lead to greater access to technologies and promote development goals. Other Members like Argentina and India argued that preparing a list was not the purpose of negotiations under paragraph 31(iii) mandate, and Members should instead focus attention on the identification of environmental activities that the negotiations should promote.[449] The delegation of India cited examples such as waste water management and soil pollution.

447. WTO CTESS, Liberalizing Environmental Goods in the World Trade Organization (United States), TN/TE/W/34 (June 19, 2003).
448. WTO CTESS, An Alternative Approach for Negotiations under Paragraph 31(iii) (Submission by India), TN/TE/W/51 (June 3, 2005); *see also* WTO CTESS, Synthesis of Submissions on Environmental Goods, Informal Note by the Secretariat, JOB (05)/57/Rev.1. (July 4, 2005).
449. WTO CTESS, Integrated Approach to Paragraph 31(iii) (Submission by Argentina and India), JOB(07)/77 (June 6, 2007).

Furthermore, though the task of developing modalities for paragraph 31(iii) negotiations belonged to the Negotiating Group on Market Access, yet some Members also made proposals for special and differential treatment in these negotiations. For example, Canada, EU, New Zealand, Norway, Singapore, Switzerland and the U.S. had proposed that tariffs should be eliminated "as soon as possible, but no later than 2008 for developed countries and those developing countries declaring themselves in a position to do so. For other developing countries, tariffs should be eliminated by X years thereafter."[450]

Through the years,[451] the negotiations proved contentious, and the North-South divide in the negotiations consisted of failing to agree on a theoretical or foundational methodology (project, list or request and offer) towards agreeing to what product or tariff line would qualify for purposes of tariff and non-tariff barrier elimination or reduction, as well as the developed partners silent approach as regards the issue of technology sharing and transfer that would have addressed certain of the concerns of developing countries.

However, similar to the compromise approach in avoiding a prescriptive definition for STOs in MEAs, members progressed through an intensification of the negotiations under a two-step process guided by the CTESS chair whereby members would instead focus on specific submissions relating (i) to specific tariff lines or products that, on a without prejudice basis, they proposed or considered to be environmentally useful or beneficial;[452] and (ii) to move to text-based proposals on modalities and treatment.[453] On the first part of the process, based on the chair's work program, members' proposals were then categorized, again without prescriptiveness, according to categories that were by consensus agreed to be environmentally beneficial, namely:

(i) *Air Pollution Control*
(ii) *Renewable Energy*
(iii) *Waste Management and Water Treatment*
(iv) *Environmental Technologies*

450. WTO CTESS, Market Access for Non-agricultural Products (Submission by EC, Switzerland, and the United States), TN/TE/W/65 (May 9, 2005).
451. *See generally* WTO CTESS, Committee on Trade and Environment Special Session Chair Reports; *see also* Part II, and *see generally* Werner Corrales, *The EPAs and Sustainable Development: Benchmarks for Pro-Development Monitoring of the Negotiations* (2005); Veena Jha, *Environmental Priorities and Trade Policy for Environmental Goods: A Reality Check* (2008); Lynn Mytelka, *Technology Transfer Issues in Environmental Goods and Services: An Illustrative Analysis of Sectors Relevant to Air Pollution and Renewable Energy* (2007); Rene Vossenaar, *Climate-Related Single-Use Environmental Goods* (2010); Marie Wilke, *Feed in Tariffs for Renewable Energy and WTO Subsidy Rules* (2011); Vicente Paolo Yu III, *WTO Negotiating Strategy on Environmental Goods and Services for Asian Developing Countries* (2007).
452. *See* WTO CTESS, Report by the Chairman Ambassador Manuel A.J. Teehankee to the Trade Negotiations Committee for the Purpose of the TNC Stocktaking Exercise, TN/TE/19 (March 22, 2010); *see also* Committee on Trade and Environment Special Session Chair Reports and the work programs therein (2008, 2009).
453. WTO CTESS, Report by the Chairman, Ambassador Manuel A.J. Teehankee, to the Trade Negotiations Committee for the Purpose of the TNC Stocktaking Exercise, TN/TE/19 (March 22, 2010); and WTO CTESS, Report by the Chairman Ambassador Manuel A.J. Teehankee to the Trade Negotiations Committee, TN/TE/20 (April 21, 2011).

(v) *Carbon Capture and Storage*
(vi) *Others (a catch-all category).*

These categories served to anchor what would eventually be dubbed the *reference universe* of 408 tariff lines at the 6-digit level that members had proposed for coverage or inclusion under the paragraph 31(iii) mandate to reduce or eliminate tariffs and non-tariff barriers.[454] By no means can the *reference universe* be considered an agreed set of goods;[455] however, it provided a frame by which approaches on modalities for coverage and treatment could be discussed and negotiated[456]

The categorization of the discussions aided Members in discussing the various proposals and the potential HS lines to be identified as potentially benefiting from tariff reductions or other market access benefits, as well as, determining which specific goods could be deemed as environmental or beneficial for the environment. It is noted that the use of categories is reminiscent as well of the four sectoral discussions had in the CTE during the early years of the CTE which, while having no market access negotiating mandate, did discuss in general terms the benefits and impact of trade and environment measures being coherent and mutually supportive, a summary of which is annexed herewith in Annex 2 of the book.[457]

With the seminal *WTO UNEP Report on Trade and Climate Change*, subject of the information sharing and exchanges hosted by the CTE in the thematic areas reviewed in Chapter 5, it is noteworthy that discussions on climate and carbon adjustments became open items for negotiation with the categories on air pollution, renewable energy, environmental technologies and carbon capture and storage, and that these items represent over 90% of the tariff lines identified. With the *reference universe* as a frame, the latter part of 2010 saw an intensification of the work of the special session on textual submissions and concrete discussions in various configurations on coverage and treatment, and the matter of technology sharing and transfer.

The overall state of play as of 2011 is reflected in the Chair's report to the Trade Negotiations Committee (TNC) of April 21, 2011, as contained in document TN/TE/20.[458] At the time, the report identified the remaining areas of work on coverage based on all approaches on the table. It was the view at the time that if coverage could be agreed, then the matter of agreeing on particular language could follow, which would relate to (i) the preambular language and triple win concepts; (ii) the treatment of tariffs and non-tariff barriers, including special and differential treatment; and (iii) cross-cutting and development elements.

In terms of negotiation coverage, the intensified work yielded two compromise proposals—a hybrid approach and combined approach—which were put forward in an

454. *See* WTO CTESS, Report by the Chairman Ambassador Manuel A.J. Teehankee to the Trade Negotiations Committee, TN/TE/20 (April 21, 2011) at pp. 18-46.
455. *Ibid.*
456. *Id.* at pp. 18-46.
457. *See* Annex 2, Environment and Trade Sectoral Discussions (Agriculture, Fisheries, Energy, Forestry).
458. *See generally* WTO CTESS, Report by the Chairman Ambassador Manuel A.J. Teehankee to the Trade Negotiations Committee, TN/TE/20 (April 21, 2011).

effort to bridge the various proposals on the table, and that the Chair stated could provide a compromise starting point for structured discussions on coverage.

Similar to the other areas of the negotiations, while the major developing countries (Brazil, China and India) reserved their options, other developing countries coalesced with some developed partners to work on potential compromises. The *Hybrid Approach* was an attempt by the delegations of Australia, Colombia, *Hong Kong, China*, Norway and Singapore to bridge the existing approaches on the table from the request and offer a proposal to the core list approach, and the project or integrated approach. In essence, it adopted the approach that members should agree on a limited core set of tariff lines or products from the *reference universe* which would be mandatory on all members, and this would be complemented by a supplementary or complementary list, as well as by request and offer and project approaches based on the *reference universe*.[459] Annex II.B of the *Chair Report 2011* contains a sample core list that the proponent members had provided as a possible starting point containing twenty-six tariff lines drawn from *the reference universe*.

The Combined Approach was presented by Mexico and Chile.[460] At the core of this compromise, the proposal was the built-in or integration of special and differential treatment in the element of coverage: developed countries would automatically select more lines from the *reference universe* than developing countries, with *alpha* representing the minimum number of lines required from developed countries and *beta* representing the minimum number of tariff lines from developing countries. In all cases, *alpha* would exceed *beta*.

On treatment, as pointed out in the April report, the options presented are limited to the range of tariff cutting options from zero to less than zero, or from formula cuts to more than formula cuts, as well as to options for greater monitoring and transparency when it relates to non-tariff barriers. Special and differential tariff cut proposals, of course, related to lesser cuts and to longer time frames.[461]

However, divergences amongst Members regarding the direction to steer these paragraph 31(iii) discussions remained. The *demandeurs* of a list-based approach including the U.S., Australia, Canada, China, Costa Rica, the EU, *Hong Kong, China*, Japan, Korea, New Zealand, Norway, Singapore, Switzerland and Chinese Taipei, which accounted for 86% of global trade in environmental goods, announced negotiations of a separate environment goods agreement at the World Economic Forum in

459. WTO CTESS, A Hybrid Approach to Liberalization of Environmental Goods under Paragraph 31(iii) (Submission by Australia, Colombia, *Hong Kong, China*, Norway and Singapore), JOB/TE/15 (March 8, 2011); WTO CTESS, Report by the Chairman Ambassador Manuel A.J. Teehankee to the Trade Negotiations Committee, TN/TE/20 (April 21, 2011).

460. WTO CTESS, Combined Approach for Environmental Goods (Submission by Mexico and Chile), JOB/TE/16 (March 11, 2011); WTO CTESS, Combined Approach for Environmental Goods (Submission by Mexico and Chile), JOB/TE/16/Corr.1 (March 21, 2011); and WTO CTESS, Views of the Small Vulnerable Economies on the Negotiation of Paragraph 31(iii) of the Doha Ministerial Declaration (Communication from the Small, Vulnerable Economies), JOB/TE/18 (April 1, 2011).

461. *See* WTO CTESS, Report by the Chairman Ambassador Manuel A.J. Teehankee to the Trade Negotiations Committee, TN/TE/20 (April 21, 2011) at ¶¶ 17 and 18.

Davos in January 2014 and launched these negotiations on July 8, 2014. As mentioned, APEC also proceeded to implement its APEC List of Environmental Goods concessions.

The progress and work outputs then of the CTE on market access are substantial and need only strong political will and consensus to move forward and a greater understanding of the various elements that could provide the triple-win outcome. As negotiations on technical and proposal based submissions have matured, the benchmarks of what a triple-win actually means became a focus of the research towards potentially providing a policy tool or metric for assessing the various proposals made.

§6.03 CTE 6, DDA 321: THE TRIPLE-WIN FOR TRADE DEVELOPMENT AND ENVIRONMENT

The DDA mandate and the triple-win phrase brought about an opportunity to shift the CTE discussions to something more productive and concrete with a focus on a possible market access result. The priority of the analysis in this section is to understand what the phrase ought to mean in policy and implementation terms, and the three lenses or frameworks could aid in certain respects the analysis. Some writings on the importance of generating incentives may prove of some use and need to be considered as a potential area of study.[462] In the end, the purpose of the triple-win analysis and matrix is to find ways forward to enhance the ability of the CTE to implement the mandate of DDA paragraph 32(i) and on the meat of the matter of whether the CTE can, in fact, be an output-oriented member of the trade and environment policy community by delivering on this important mandate of market access for environmental goods. The CTE members had responded positively to the challenge, and a substantial number of proposals were generated in the market access arena. Table 6.1 lists a numerical tally of proposals made by WTO Members before and after 2001.

Table 6.1 CTE Market Access Proposal

	1995-2001	*2002-2012*	*2013-2016*	*Total*
CTE	30	13	0	43
CTESS	NA	82	0	82
				122

Source: Section 1.6, WT/CTE/INF/5/Rev.12, Section 4, TN/TE/INF/4/Rev.16.

The CTE was moving away from talk into the real business of market access modalities, and commercial incentives. The market access proposals and documents are of great importance in that they could allow through a combination of objective and

462. *See generally* Barrett (2006) *Environment and Statecraft*; *see also* Andrew Pfluger, *Why the Montreal Protocol Is Not a Template for Multilateral Environmental Agreements: An Examination of Why China and India Ratified*, 43 Middle States Geographer 96 (2010); *see further* Part I, Chapter 3.

subjective analysis to arrive at some conclusions on the utility of the metric of a *triple-win* to the market access mandate of the CTE.

For this purpose, *a triple win survey matrix* is part of the data collection methodology for this chapter on market access, which required the complete tallying and indexing of all the proposals presented by the WTO members, and to then identify the specific measure or modality being proposed for implementation towards the benefit of the three policy regimes. To enable a better understanding of the proposals, it is vital to know what the modality being proposed by members is and the types of modalities or a mix of them that are feasible or relevant to the triple-win context.

In Table 6.2, a summary of the various types of modalities proposed by the members are listed which total up to some fifteen types of modality proposals, which for purposes of data collation have been categorized into a universe of ten defined and number-coded measures that will be at the core of the proposed trade friendly environmental measure or the eco-friendly trade measure, or the triply beneficial development-oriented measure, that is intended by the proponent to evolve into the potential rulemaking formulation for the EGS negotiations.

The table further shows that the defined ten types of measures can be further generally grouped into three categories:

(1) TMs—Tariff Measures, which WTO experts and trade policy makers would be most familiar with;
(2) NTMs—Non-tariff Measures, which are the current focus of many a negotiation given that tariffs for many items have universally reached the lowest peaks in history; and NTMs range in type from subsidy regulations, state trading preferences or BTAs; and
(3) CCs—Command & Control mechanisms that environmental policy makers, as well as development policy planners, are familiar with.

Table 6.2 Summary of Market Access Modalities

Modality Code No.	*Category*	*Modality-Proposal*	*Proponents CTE DDA 32i*	*CTE6 / 32i*	*Proponents CTESS 31iii*	*31iii*	*31iii*
1	TM	*List Approach*			United States W/38; China W/42; Australia; Colombia; Hong Kong, China; Norway; and Singapore TE/15		
1	TM	*Hybrid Approach*			Australia; Colombia; Hong Kong, China; Norway; and Singapore TE/15; Mexico and Chile TE/16		
1	TM	*Request and Offer*			Brazil JOB(07)/146; JOB(09)/184; US W/38		
1	TM	*Project (Zero Duties per Project Basis)*			India W/60; W/51;W/54; Argentina W/62; Argentina and India JOB(07)/77		
1	TM	*Tariffs (Zero, Reduction or Tariff Peaks or Escalation Elimination)*	Argentina W/24; Australia W/105; Brazil W/98; Japan W/222	9	Brazil JOB TE/6;W/76; Canada JOB (04)/98;W/50;W/50/Rev.1; W/50/Suppl.; W/50; W/165; JOB (06)/140; United States W/38; W/52; JOB(06)/169; JOB (07)/193; JOB(07)/193/Rev.1; W/8;EC W/56; JOB (06/74); (06)/177;W/47; Switzerland JOB(06)/178; JOB(06)/179;TE/5; New Zealand W/49; W/49/Rev1; W/49/Rev2;W/49/Suppl; JOB(06)/170; Saudi Arabia JOB(06)/169; JOB(06)/169/Add.1; JOB(06)/169/Add.2; Chinese Taipei W/41; W/41/Corr1; Peru JOB(07)/161; JOB(09)/177; Argentina W/74; Philippines TE/2; Qatar W/27; W/14; TE/4; Cuba W/73; Korea W/48; Japan JOB(06)/79; W/17;W/17/Corr.1	50	59
2	NTM	*Non-Tariff Measures or Barriers /Licensing, Permitting, Other Regulatory Measures)*	Argentina W/24; Australia W/36; Saudi Arabia W/247; United States W/70; Costa Rica W/202	7	Singapore TE/5; Qatar TE/4;W/27; W/14;Cuba W/55;W/73Peru JOB(09)/177; Saudi Arabia JOB(09)/169; JOB(09)/169/Add.1; JOB(09)/169/Add.2; Brazil TE/6; W/74; Canada W/50/Rev.1; W/50/Supp.1; W/50; W/65; JOB(04)/98; JOB (06)/140; JOB(09)/132; Philippines T/2; EC JOB(06)/70; (06)/77; Switzerland JOB (06)/178; W/57; W/57/Corr.1; JOB (09)/169; United States W/8;Argentina W/74; Japan W17; W/17/Corr.1	45	52

Modality Code No.	*Category*	*Modality-Proposal*	*Proponents CTE DDA 32i*	*CTE6 / 32i*	*Proponents CTESS 31iii*	*31iii*	*31iii*
3	NTM	*State Trading, Financial Incentives, Subsidies Regulation or Monitoring*	Argentina W/24,105; Saudi Arabia W/215; United States W/35; W/36;W/51; New Zealand W/52; European Union W/83; Brazil W/109	19		2	21
4	NTM	*Internal Tax Measures including carbon taxation, Border Tax Adjustments*	Australia W/36; European Union W/83;W/98; Japan W/222	1	Cuba W/73	1	2
5	CC	*Export Restrictions*	Japan W/222	1		1	2
6	CC	*Labelling and Standards Requirements*	Japan W/211	3	Japan W/75; W/74/Add.1; W/74/Add.2	3	6
7	CC	*Technology Diffusion*	Switzerland W/240; India W/177	3	EC JOB (07)/193; JOB (07)/193/Rev.1.	9	12
8	CC	*Coordination, Cooperation and Information Exchange*		21	United States W/34; New Zealand W/6.	18	39
8	CC	*TACB*	European Union W/239		Philippines TE/2; Colombia JOB (06)/149		
9	CC	*Development Incentives (Job Creation, Poverty Alleviation, etc.)*	Argentina W/88; India W/207; Australia W.105	3	Brazil TE/6; Cuba W/73; W/69; Colombia JOB (06)/149; Uruguay W/144; Argentina W/62; Brazil W/59; China W/42	12	15
10	CC	*Resource Allocation, Conservation, Management*	Australia W/36; W/105;United States W/51; New Zealand W/52; Brazil W/109; European Union JOB/TE/27; Japan W/226; W/222; Korea W/175; Iceland W/103	13	Switzerland JOB (06)/178	2	15
				80		**143**	***223***

All of the proposals under agenda Item 6 were contextually submitted, offered or solicited under the rubric of either (a) promoting mutual supportiveness of trade and environment, (b) promoting a double win for trade and environment, or (c) leading to what is now referred to as the Doha-era phrase towards a triple-win for trade, environment and development.[463] It is this last purpose that is most relevant to the interface of interest to this research and to trade and policy governance theory. This triple win mandate and conundrum can be traced back to November 14, 2001, when Ministers in Doha added a phrase to the 1994 original mandate of CTE 6 and when they instructed the CTE under paragraph 32(i):

> in pursuing work on all items on its agenda ... to give particular attention to ... situations in which the elimination or reduction of trade restrictions and distortions *would benefit trade, the environment and development.*

What exactly do the *founding fathers* mean by *triple-win*? Is it a serious mandate or mere disambiguation or palliative, or even a placebo to calm down the *uncalmables*? Is it a *triple-win* for trade values or a *triple-win* for the environment? Why are there references in the literature to *double wins*,[464] and if such *double wins* do happen, which of the three policy values are likely to be left out, or does the mandate contemplate, rather than preclude, outcomes that are useful to one, or two, rather than all, of the policy regimes?

Since the CTE was the result of a bridging exercise, the *triple-win* easily falls within the ambit of negotiation-speak, and has been interpreted to refer to the multiple benefits that ought to accrue by the correct policy measures to the three policy regimes of trade, development and environment, and lead to a gain for:

- the liberal and non-discriminatory trade regime;
- economic development and poverty eradication; and
- environmental protection and sustainability.

Being then a three-regime scenario, there is, therefore, either a requirement of a simultaneous benefit, which is highly unlikely, or a trilateral combination of scenarios as may happen in mathematical and logical combinations, and there happens to be a limited number of variations that can occur for this triple-win.

463. WTO Ministerial Conference (4th Session Doha November 9-14, 2001), Ministerial Declaration, WT/MIN(01)/DEC/1 (November 20, 2001). Its origins can also be argued to be found in the mandate of Chapter 2 of Agenda 21 where it calls for development of an environment, trade and development agenda at paragraphs 2.22 et seq. More likely than not it was coined by a trade negotiator used to the concept of deal-making, a commercial concept not commonly welcome or practiced by the environment regime community.

464. *See* UN General Assembly, Agenda 21: Program of Action for Sustainable Development, A/Conf.151/26 (June 14, 1992); U.N. GAOR, 46th Sess.; *see also* Pascal Lamy, Doha could deliver double win for environment and trade: Speech, Informal Trade Ministers' Dialog on Climate Change, December 9, 2007) available at: http://www.wto.org/english/news_e/sppl_e/sppl83_e.html (November 30, 2019). The origins and organic history of the CTE show that it was meant to address two policy regimes as covered by its nomenclature, and not three policy regimes, until the calls for including development as an equal policy priority arose later and was incorporated in the *Doha Development Agenda*. *Cf.* Agenda 21, which early on since 1992 called for a combination of all three benefits when calling for an environment, trade and development agenda, though one reading for Agenda 21, questions also the sincerity of such a formulation given the discussions and the text itself of Agenda 21 refer to a "trade/environment" or "environment/trade" and development agenda, which can be read to see trade and environment as alternative agendas, as in the success case of the Montreal Protocol.

Such a tri-regime situation could thus result, in theory, in seven end-case permutations, as regards a specific measure or proposed new legal rule that the CTE could suggest or recommend. The first three variations possible would represent potential gains and benefits accruing to a particular policy regime. The next three situations represent twin or alliance-building policy gains between, or for, two of the three regimes and the 7th scenario amounts to the only ideal unique case of a triple-combined simultaneous positive *win* for all the three policy regimes. Statistically, this must not have been the intent of the framers of the triple win phrase and scenario, to make the ideal a quite difficult rarity, to happen only in one in seven situations:

(i) Primarily Trade Growth / Win for Trade.
(ii) Primarily Development / Win for Development.
(iii) Primarily Environmental / Win for Environment.
(iv) Dual Gains for Trade and Development.
(v) Dual Gains for Trade and Environment.
(vi) Dual Gains for Development and Environment.[465]
(vii) *Triple-win for Trade, Development and Environment.*

To be complete, one must also raise the question of the pre-CTE success of the Montreal Protocol, whereby some accounts, was primarily a result of a *single win* for the environment, with a certain loss or negative to trade, given the enforcement of absolute trade bans on CFCs and HCFCs. Would the repeat of such a success based on a loss for trade amount to a barrier to the CTE mandate for a required *triple-win*? The author of course disputes and would disagree with the latter argument, given similar to the fur seal situation, and other success stories of environmental law and environmental action that there are certain un-quantifiables or instances where upholding a societal norm is a priority and not a commercial issue, with the concomitant result of norm upholding often resulting in a post-adjustment re-balancing that benefits all.

The seven permutations and scenarios only serve as a basic frame for soliciting views of specific policy regime experts or leaders on the meaning of a triple-win. In responding to this very specific CTE idiosyncrasy, there are questions on the evaluation mechanism for judging how and whether a specific proposal impacts or contributes to a specific policy regime benefit or to a dual benefit or the mandated *triple-win*? In the end, this is subjective, but as a general rule, the type of modality usually will be able to emphasize the objective that is being promoted. A tariff reduction simply is targeted towards greater trade volumes and, to the extent it also adds benefits of increased job employment, there could be a development gain.

465. This permutation may attract argument as being beyond the ambit or mandate of the CTE, but for purposes of completeness of the research methodology and remaining neutral to the results of the research remains a permutation for now for purposes of the study, even if two possible results may arise which would still have to be explained in the final results (either as an explained absence of this permutation for the reasons to be found, or its remaining as a viable permutation). An early reply to this question, in the negative, might lead to larger problems relating scenarios i, ii, and iii, and the likelihood of a false syllogism at the heart of the founding of Agenda 21, Chapter 2 and the CTE, and it would best be referred to be part of the current research project.

To a trade negotiator familiar with the single undertaking, one of the immediate options is the package approach. Then the package must have something beneficial to each regime, and so a single win measure or modality could be balanced by other modalities or measures so that a balance is reached. But then this makes the triple win more of the same, which is the resort to the usual horse-trading and bargaining that policy makers have objected to as too focused on special interests, and dissipates the interest in the promise of a mutual win for all.

Other research undertaken by authors to date on the work of the CTE will be useful guides.[466] There is also the reference work contained in the WTO's 1999 *Special Study No. 4 on Trade and Environment*,[467] as well as various studies on proposing benchmarks and green indicators from United Nations Development Program (UNDP), UNCTAD and other sources.[468]

Campling and Havice point out the elusiveness of a *triple-win* and that it could lead to the ability of negotiators to turn the laudable objective on its head and prevent any outcome that could be politically sensitive to the negotiator's constituents.[469] Based on the deliberations and the ongoing stagnation, perhaps Campling and Havice have hit the nail on its head.

The use of the triple-win matrix as a policy testing tool becomes more evident by requiring a metric towards exploring alternative methods of assessing how specific measures or modalities could each independently contribute to attaining (i) the trade growth and comparative advantage benefits, (ii) the environmental protection benefits, or (iii) the development and poverty alleviation benefits, that a triple win mandate, all in all, was expected to accomplish.

§6.04 THE DOUBLE WIN CONCEPT FOR TRADE AND ENVIRONMENT

It was at the Earth Summit in Rio de Janeiro, Brazil, in 1992, where the integration across environmental, social and economic strands was first identified as vectors for sustainable development.

---

466. McCormick utilized datasets and findings arising from a focused set of questions to a cross section of 71 interviewees, *see* Rachel McCormick, *A Qualitative Analysis of the WTO's Role on Trade and Environment Issues*, 6 Global Envtl. Pol. 102 (2006); Watson cites McCormick's work, insofar as the book deals with the work of the CTE at Chapter 6, *see* James J/R/ Watson, *Environment under the WTO: Development of Competence Beyond Trade* (2013); *see further* Robert H. Steinberg, *Trade-Environment Negotiations in the EU, NAFTA, and WTO: Regional Trajectories of Rule Development*, 91(2) Am. J. Int'l L. 231 (1997).
467. Håkan Nordström and Scott Vaughan, *Special Studies No. 4: Trade and Environment* (1999) available at: http://www.wto.org/english/res_e/reser_e/special_studies_e.htm (accessed on November 30, 2019).
468. UNDP, *Case Studies of Sustainable Development in Practice: Triple-win for Sustainable Development* (2012) available at: http://www.undp.org/content/undp/en/home/librarypage/poverty-reduction/triple-wins-for-sustainable-development.html (accessed on November 30, 2019); Werner Corrales, *The EPAs and Sustainable Development: Benchmarks for Pro-development Monitoring of the Negotiations* (2005), http://www.stopepa.de/img/A%20EPAs%20and%20Sustainable%20Development%20FINAL.pdf (accessed January 2, 2014).
469. *See generally* Liam Campling and Elizabeth Havice, *Mainstreaming Environment and Development at the World Trade Organization? Fisheries Subsidies, the Politics of Rulemaking, and the Elusive "Triple Win,"* 45 J. Env't & Plan. 835 (2013).

Principle 1 of the Rio Declaration states that human beings are central to concerns of sustainable development and are entitled to a healthy and productive life in harmony with nature. Principle 3 of the declaration states that the right to development must be fulfilled in a manner so as to equitably meet developmental and environmental needs of present and future generations. Principles 6, 7 and 11 discuss the special situations and needs of developing countries—in particular, the least developed and the most environmentally vulnerable communities—and of common but differentiated responsibilities of countries. It also talks about the importance of technological and financial resources to pursue sustainable development goals (SDGs). Principle 8 states that countries should reduce and/or eliminate unsustainable patterns of production and consumption. Principle 10 notes that environmental issues are best dealt with by the participation of all concerned citizens and that all citizens should have appropriate access to information concerning the environment, such as information on hazardous substances. Principle 12 states that countries should cooperate to promote an open international economic system, which would lead to economic growth and sustainable development. The text of Principle 15 entrenches the precautionary principle, stating that countries could implement precautionary approaches to protect their environment. Principles 20, 21 and 22 promote the role of women, youth and indigenous people in achieving sustainable development and environmental management.

Even before the Rio Declaration, the idea of people choosing to live lives they value has permeated into international policy. For instance, the Human Development Report of 1990 introduced the Human Development Index (HDI), which included indicators for decent standards of living, knowledge, and living healthy lives. Later, in 2000, environmental sustainability was listed as a target under the UN Millennium Declaration and the eight Millennium Development Goals (MGDs), which were adopted as a global commitment to reduce extreme global poverty. MDGs 7 is aimed at ensuring environmental sustainability. Goal 7 includes the integration of sustainable development into country policies and seeks to reverse the loss of environmental resources; reduce the loss of biodiversity; aim at reducing the proportion of the population without sustainable access to safe drinking water and sanitation by 50%; and improve the lives of at least 100 million slum dwellers. The MDGs were set to be achieved by 2015 and have now been replaced by an even more ambitious set of targets. These targets are known as the UN SDGs.[470] Environment-related issues underline each of the seventeen SDG goals.

Broadly, trade-related targets and commitments in the SDGs can be grouped as follows:

(1) Cross-cutting targets related to the multilateral trading system. These include references to doubling the exports of LDCs, implementing duty-free quota-free (DFQF) market access for LDC exports, or implementing the new

470. On governance for the SDGs, including a case study on trade, ESTs and the SDGs, *see* Joachim Monkelbaan, *Governance for the Sustainable Development Goals: Exploring an Integrative Framework of Theories, Tools, and Competencies* (2019).

Agreement on Trade Facilitation, reached at the 2013 WTO Ministerial Conference in Bali.

(2) Targets aimed at removing certain trade distortions. These include goal-specific targets aimed at removing agricultural export subsidies and measures with equivalent effect, prohibiting certain kinds of fisheries subsidies that contribute to overcapacity and overfishing, or rationalizing inefficient fossil fuel subsidies that encourage wasteful consumption.

(3) Market access-related targets. References to market access include targets such as doubling the productivity and incomes of small-scale food producers, among others, by improving access to markets, and—more broadly—promoting the integration of developing countries into international value chains to support sustainable development.

(4) Technology diffusion targets. Several targets in the proposed framework—for example, under Goal 6 on water and Goal 7 on sustainable energy—refer to the importance of access to and cooperation in the field of technology in order to support sustainable development objectives.

(5) Trade-related assistance targets. These include goal-specific targets related to capacity building and technical assistance, such as the need to increase support for Aid for Trade under goal 8 on sustainable economic growth and employment.

(6) Illegal extraction and trade in natural resources. Several SDGs include targets related to illegal extraction and trade in natural resources, including protected species.

When considered together, the Rio Declaration, MDGs and SDGs have laid the foundation for the development of a holistic approach to development. Significant progress has been made over the past twenty-six years, and the concept of "triple win" percolated into the WTO through the Doha Ministerial Declaration (*see* figure 6.1).[471]

As mentioned, since the commencement of the Doha Round in November 2001, Members had sought to achieve a triple win at the CTE. Halle breaks down the environmental negotiations mandate into four parts: the relationship between MEAs and trade rules; procedures of information exchange between MEA secretariats; liberalization of trade in EGS; and disciplining subsidies to fisheries. According to him, the latter two were "low-hanging fruits"—good for trade, good for developing countries, and good for the environment—the classic triple-win so dear to the rhetoric of the WTO.[472] Members had sought to enter into trade agreements, which would lower both tariff and non-tariff barriers for EGS. The goal of this endeavor was to liberalize EGS, which would benefit the environment, reduce GHG emissions and improve environmental indicators such as clean air and water quality. Members stated that a successful agreement on EGS would amount to a triple win for WTO Members: a win for the environment, a win for trade and a win for development.

471. Jorge E. Vinuales, *Foreign Investment and the Environment in International Law* at p. 9 (2012).
472. Mark Halle, *Trade and Environment: Looking Beneath the Sands of Doha?* (2006) available at: http://www.iisd.org/pdf/2006/trade_sd_jeepl_2006.pdf (accessed on November 30, 2019).

However, as Wu notes, "the lofty rhetoric soon gave way to the cold realities of the negotiating table."[473] Campling and Havice observe that in the negotiating context, a triple-win is utilized as a political economy tool rather than as a means to a happy mutually beneficial much less a triply beneficial end.[474] Environmental stakes are increasing every day, yet WTO Members were in disagreement regarding what constituted or did not constitute EGS. These fault lines have already been identified and discussed in detail in Chapter 2.

Figure 6.1 A Graphical Representation of Triple-Win Between the Social, Economic and Environmental Dimensions of Sustainable Development

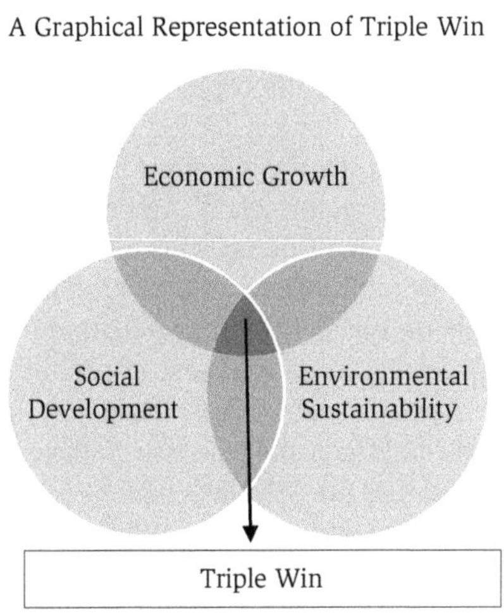

Source: Inspired by the Doha Ministerial Declaration (2001).

§6.05 TRIPLE-WIN DISCUSSIONS AT THE CTE AND CTESS

Triple-win is formally still being perused at the CTE. Members have made several proposals at the CTE and CTESS, which reflected their definitional boundaries or inclinations regarding the *triple-win*. The proposals submitted to the CTESS are particularly relevant since they are within the negotiating mandate of the Doha round. These proposals have included common themes and ideas, as well as diverging views. In 2003, the U.S. submitted a proposal to the CTESS, where one of the first mentions of the triple-win was indirectly made. According to the U.S., members could "realize

473. Mark Wu, *Why Developing Countries Won't Negotiate? The Case of the WTO Environmental Goods Agreement*, 6(1) J. Trade L. & Dev. 93 (2014).
474. Liam Campling and Elizabeth Havice, *Mainstreaming Environment and Development at the World Trade Organization? Fisheries Subsidies, the Politics of Rulemaking, and the Elusive "Triple Win,"* 45 J. Env't. & Plan. 835 (2013).

economic growth and development patterns that are more environmentally sustainable over time" by removing trade barriers and that trade liberalization and environmental protection are mutually supportive. This submission was based on the concept of a triple-win.

Subsequently, several other Members also discussed triple-win. For instance, India, in 2005, noted that the text in paragraph 31(iii) of the Doha declaration was environmental-benefit oriented. According to this submission, the delegation of India was of the view that market access was only a means to the objective of promoting environmentally strong policies and not the objective itself. In the same submission, India also asserted the need to address coherence in trade and environmental policy to promote sustainable development.[475] Argentina also proposed that negotiations under paragraph 31(iii) of the Doha Declaration should result in environmental, trade and developmental benefits for all WTO Members.[476] A joint proposal by China and India dated 2011[477] broadened the ambit of the triple-win to include paragraph 32 of the Doha Declaration also.

This submission emphasized the need to have a triple-win outcome that would benefit trade, environment and development.[478] An earlier joint proposal by Canada, EU, New Zealand, Japan, Norway, the Separate Customs Territory of Taiwan, Penghu, Kinmen and Matsu (Chinese Taipei), Switzerland and the U.S. dated May 2006 which related to environmental goods noted that increased trade in environmental goods would "secure enhanced access at a reduced cost to products and technologies that support all Member's environment objectives, including in particular improving domestic and environmental conditions and resource management."[479] From these and similar submissions, it is clear that the Members had an accepted understanding that "triple win" was inclusive of trade, environment and development.

An analysis of the contents in these proposals also demonstrated the levels of ambition that Members held with regard to triple-win. For example, some Members were of the opinion that triple-win would increase foreign exchange earnings and expand employment and facilitate access to environmental technologies. This, in turn, would stimulate innovation and technology transfer. The EU forwarded the view of rewarding producers in all countries that invested in environmentally friendly technologies and incorporated corporate policies that were environmentally friendly.[480] They also supported the fostering of technological innovation and contended that the

475. WTO CTESS, Structural Dimensions of the Environmental Project Approach (Submission by India), TN/TE/W/54 (July 4, 2005).
476. WTO CTESS, Integrated Proposal on Environmental Goods for Development (Submission by Argentina), TN/TE/W/62 (October 14, 2005).
477. WTO CTESS, WTO Negotiations on Environmental Goods and Services: Addressing the Development Dimension for a "Triple Win" Outcome (Submission by China and India), TN/TE/W/79 (April 15, 2011).
478. WTO CTESS, Market Access for Non-agricultural Products (Submission by EC, Switzerland and the United States), TN/TE/W/65 (May 9, 2006).
479. WTO CTESS, Market Access for Environmental Goods: The Environmental and Development Benefits of Waste Water Management (Submission by EC, Switzerland and the United States), JOB (06)/140 (May 8, 2006).
480. WTO CTESS, Market Access for Environmental Goods (Communication from the European Communities), TN/TE/W/47 (February 17, 2005).

creation of a conducive regulatory environment would make environmental technologies available at less cost to developing countries. This, the EU noted, would assist developing countries in meeting their developmental and environmental objectives. Argentina noted that triple-win could reduce costs of projects relating to actions against climate change, which would help in stabilizing greenhouse gas concentration. The U.S. believed that access to a higher quality of environmental goods at a lower cost would improve the effectiveness of environmental investment programs which would "lead to direct quality of life benefits for citizens in all countries in terms of cleaner environment and indirectly lead to developing greater regulatory capacity in environmental protection."[481]

Some Members, mainly developing countries, made direct mention of the development aspects of a triple-win in their submission. For instance, Brazil noted that improved market access of products of low environmental impacts could assist in poverty alleviation through income generation and job creation for the local population.[482] Brazil, in a subsequent submission, also stated that discussions on trade liberalization should not focus solely on increasing the sales of environmental goods but should also promote the development and participation of environmental goods industries in developing countries as well. The submission noted that:

> A key issue for sustainable development in developing countries is the establishment of industries that do not reproduce the patterns of energy consumption and natural resource depletion of the developed countries. This will only be sustainable if developing countries are allowed to develop the capacity to generate solutions, in terms of environmental goods, that are adapted to local necessities and conditions.[483]

China and India introduced a more specific example in their joint proposal. According to them, access to ESTs was required to address the needs of developing countries. They proposed that financial mechanisms be set in place, which could ensure access to and development of ESTs. This could promote investments in sustainable environmental projects and assist in the development of capacity for producing environmental goods.[484] Argentina also observed that triple-win reflected the development objectives set out in the Marrakesh Agreement and was reaffirmed in the Doha Ministerial Declaration.[485] Some developing countries like Bolivia and Venezuela even introduced the "historical argument" to the debate. They contended

481. WTO CTESS, Negotiating Group on Market Access—Liberalizing Environmental Goods in the WTO (Submission by United States), TN/TE/W/34 (June 19, 2003).
482. WTO CTESS, Environmental Goods for Development (Submission by Brazil), TN/TE/W/59 (July 8, 2005).
483. WTO CTESS, Environmental Goods for Development (Submission by Brazil), JOB(07)/146 (October 1, 2007).
484. WTO CTESS, Integrated Proposal on Environmental Goods for Development (Submission by Argentina), TN/TE/W/79 (October 14, 2005).
485. WTO CTESS, Integrated Proposal on Environmental Goods for Development (Submission by Argentina), TN/TE/W/62 (October 14, 2005).

that developing countries were suffering the most from an environmental crisis that was not historically created by them.[486]

However, it is the submission by the Small, Vulnerable Economies (SVE) Group—a group of countries that account for a small fraction of world trade and which are affected the most by economic uncertainties and environmental shocks—that clearly summarized the development aspect of triple-win:[487]

> [The SVEs] Group is interested in ensuring that any outcome in this negotiation effectively strikes a balance between market access, environmental benefits, and the legitimate objective of our Members to maintain policies that will allow our sustainable development.

Paragraph 32(i) of the Doha Declaration bears repeating again another time as it is the origin of the phrase that has caught the imagination of the CTE community:

> 32. We instruct the Committee on Trade and Environment, in pursuing work on all items on its agenda within its current terms of reference, to give particular attention to:
>   (i) the effect of environmental measures on market access, especially in relation to developing countries, in particular the least developed among them, and those situations in which the elimination or reduction of trade restrictions and distortions *would benefit trade, the environment and development*.

DDA 32(i) is technically not part of the negotiating mandate of DDA 31(iii) but describes the crux of the triple-win principle. This principle has permeated into the meaning of the negotiations mandated by DDA 31(iii) though no direct mention of the principle is made.

For example, paragraph 31(iii) calls for the reduction or elimination of tariffs and non-tariff barriers for EGS. This could be identified as a triple-win since the reduction of tariffs of environmental goods, for example, would promote a cleaner environment, protect trade and create employment if Members wanted to develop technologies that produced environmental goods. Another example of the triple-win, which can be found in early CTE discussions, is under item 6 on fisheries subsidies. Overfishing, as a result of subsidies, can have an adverse effect on the environment. This item also found its way into paragraph 31 but directed the negotiations on fisheries subsidies to take place under the Committee on Rules. A more indirect interpretation of the triple-win can also be found in paragraph 31(i) of the Doha Declaration. This paragraph the examination of the relationship between MEAs and WTO with a view to enhancing mutual supportiveness. Lydgate argues that "mutual supportiveness" echoes other similar statements within the Doha Declaration, which indicate that "there should not be, or need not be" policy contradictions between trade and SDGs.[488]

---

486. WTO CTESS, Elements Ensuring a Sustainable Development Outcome under Paragraph 31(iii) of Doha Ministerial Declaration (Submission by Bolivarian Republic of Venezuela), JOB/TE/17 (March 24, 2011).
487. WTO CTESS, Views of SVE on the Negotiation of Paragraph 31(i) of Doha Ministerial Declaration (Submission by SVE Group), JOB/TE/18 (April 1, 2011).
488. Emily Barrett Lydgate, *Sustainable Development in the WTO: For Mutual Supportiveness to Balancing*, 11(4) World Trade Rev. 621 (2012).

§6.06 TRIPLE-WIN MATRIX AND MODALITIES

The objective perhaps of the matrix and this analysis is to break down the tautological chants of triple-win and to identify what triple-win means for different Members, and perhaps conclude that it cannot become an end and an obstacle in and of itself that it sometimes feels it has become. By making it the objective of the negotiations, the expert dialogue of trade and environment good governance loses teeth and negotiators may, as Campling has warned, avoid negotiations or concessions.

The triple-win cannot evolve to become an end in itself. Every Member could have a different interpretation of a triple-win definition. For instance, it is possible that developing and LDC Members may consider a higher threshold standard of development when compared to developed Members. In turn, developed Members may seek a higher threshold for trade. Also, some Members have higher environmental regulatory standards than others and will consider a proposal to be a triple-win situation in case the environmental standards either meet the threshold of that Member or goes beyond that threshold. Therefore, the interpretation of triple-win is deeply entrenched in subjectivity depending on a Member's economic, environmental, social and political orientation, and could lessen the factors of objectivity and certainty as to the correct or appropriate standard or metric.

This is where the third lens comes in, where Ostrom and the theories of increased criteria and public policy tools are relevant in order to allow the best of each community to bloom towards self-governing CPRs. The triple-win matrix, in this sense, can then serve as a positive policy tool to foster customized solutions and diversified approaches and solutions and avoids the one size fits all conundrum. Ostrom's lens provides a powerful critique of attempting singular solutions to solve a simple community waste management problem.

Similarly, the lens of the experts and TRNs and professional administrative bureaucracy can further enhance the proper contextual meaning of the triple-win to mean a triple-win for coordination and cooperation among the three policy regimes and their professional secretariats. A matrix could therefore serve as a policy tool to decipher from situation to situation, or proposal to proposal, or modality to modality, what exactly are the benefits of a particular measure, and how a triple-win standard at the WTO is more a policy surveying tool, to ensure fact- and metric-based dialog and conversations rather than the circular ones that one often encounters when reviewing the mass of records and minutes and meeting reports of the CTE through the years.

Attached as part of this volume's *Annex 2* is the *triple-win matrix survey* that serves as a snapshot and inventory of all the market access proposals to date, and utilized here to derive notional triple-win scoring for any particular proposal. The more important approach is to use the matrix as a tool to measure the validity of the claimed triple-win of a proposal. The structure of this matrix is designed to assess whether a proposal is a win for trade, a win for development, or a win for the environment. Since there are different normative gradients for each of the three pillars of trade, environment and development, the quantification of the level of wins for each of the three pillars is based on an arbitrary maximum score of three points per policy regime, with an automatic plus one to allow for a maximum score of ten points.

Therefore, if a proposal has a very strong component for environmental development, then that proposal, in theory, could receive a total of three points in the environment metric. Similar to the three lenses discussed in Chapter 3, these are merely guides and not prescriptive methodologies that must be utilized or applied in a particular way. The assessment will necessarily be subjective but having a subjective metric will still require some subjective explanation of the basis for a high or low score, in relation to the objectives of the proposal and the modalities proposed to be used to achieve that objective.

NTMs or barriers have been identified as one of the most prevalent forms of modalities to achieve the triple-win objective. Several Members across the developing-developed Members' divide noted that the reduction or removal of NTMs such as regulations that create unnecessary obstacles to the course of trade would assist in the achievement of triple-wins. Similarly, tariff reduction was also raised as one of the trade-related modalities. Self explanatorily, reduction or elimination of tariffs on environmentally friendly goods and services is beneficial to the achievement of triple-win. DDA paragraph 31(iii) has the same mandate as well. Besides this, internal taxation policies, including those related to carbon taxation, have also been raised as a modality for a triple-win. Tax, unlike a tariff, is unbound, and exporting Members are allowed to set the rate according to the domestic needs.

In earlier CTE discussions, the elimination or regulation of subsidies was also an often-raised potential modality.[489] The submissions with specific modalities relating to subsidies were mostly relating to fisheries, energy, or agriculture.[490]

Of these, fisheries was the most dominant sector where elimination or regulation of subsidies was identified as the modality. However, not all Members were of the same opinion. For instance, Korea, in its submission, had noted that providing subsidies could benefit the fisheries sector of Members.[491] The regulation of state trading was also identified as a modality that could achieve environmental goals.[492] Similarly, Japan contended that export restrictions were also required to be WTO law consistent. In the context of illegal logging, Japan noted that a case could arise where Members had not imposed export restrictions on processed wood products that were made from unprocessed logs, which were subject to an export restriction.[493] Labelling has also been identified as a trade modality. Japan noted that the labelling of products would assist in sustainable forest management programs.[494]

489. WTO CTE, Utilization of Subsidies and Their Positive Role in the Fisheries Sector (Communication from Korea), WT/CTE/W/175 (October 24, 2000).
490. *See* generally Annex 2; WTO CTE, Subsidies in the Fisheries Sector: Update on Recent Work Conducted by New Zealand (Communication from New Zealand), WT/CTE/W/134 (February 24, 2000); WTO CTE, Utilization of Subsidies and Their Positive Role in the Fisheries Sector (Communication from Korea), WT/CTE/W/175 (October 24, 2000).
491. WTO CTE, Utilization of Subsidies and Their Positive Role in the Fisheries Sector (Communication from Korea), WT/CTE/W/175 (October 24, 2000).
492. WTO CTE, Communication from Argentina on Item 6 of the Committee's Work Program, WT/CTE/W/24 (March 20, 1996).
493. WTO CTE, Sustainable Development and the Trade of Forest and Fishery Products (Submission by Japan), WT/CTE/W/222 (February 6, 2003).
494. WTO CTE, Issues on Forestry Products Trade and Environment (Submission by Japan), WT/CTE/W/211 (June 11, 2002).

From a development perspective, three modalities were raised. These included technology diffusion, technical assistance and capacity building and other developmental incentives, such as job creation and poverty alleviation. Technology diffusion would be a key element in the achievement of a triple-win. Sound, environmentally friendly technologies would assist developing and LDC Members to grow their domestic economy to produce products that are environmentally friendly as well as produced in a sustainable manner. A parallel effort to technology diffusion is technical assistance and capacity building. Here, Members that have developed technologies that are environmentally friendly can assist developing and LDC Members to develop the capacity to utilize the technology. Another important modality—which is really an assimilation of various sub-modalities—is development incentives. Development, to developing Members, means job creation, which, in turn, would lead to poverty alleviation. Several proposals made by Members identified this broad vehicle of modalities as a triple-win.

Resource allocation and conservation management is the only environment-oriented modality that could be identified through the submissions made by Members. This included the management of fisheries, forests and other natural resources. Members making proposals that were founded on environmental modalities contended that it was the management of these resources that would benefit both trade and development. This does not, however, preclude the utilization of both traditional development- or trade-type measures towards achieving, for example, environmental ends. Resource management could also benefit from the interdisciplinary learning that the second theoretical framework promotes in the sense that policy experts in one regime could learn a lot from and adopt practices of another regime. For example, the Universal Period Review (UPR) practice in the Human Rights Council was borrowed from the peer review practice of the GATT and the WTO TPRs. Nowadays, the CTE-evolved practice of ERs and the EDB have become regular policy toolkits that aid, in a triple-win fashion, the delegates and capital officials who have to deal with interdisciplinary issues of implementation and monitoring of trade, development and environment concerns and policies.

In sum, while there needs to be concrete progress, it appears that Ostrom's thesis of focusing on more localized and more diverse rules has increasing relevance, with state actors not being as united in pursuing traditional treaty law solutions. This implies that increasing economics, environment, and development issues will require more agile and rapid response mechanisms that can be achieved through devolved governance.

It is hoped perhaps that the assessment of the CTE work areas and, in particular, its progress on the market access mandate can be aided by more processes and procedures that attempt to measure benefits and costs and avoid the paralysis of action. In any event there are indeed trends that require perhaps an Ostrom-ian solution of increasing the capacity of communities and localities, and by extension, developing countries and regions, to no longer await the signal of a singular best practice or a singular best policy prescription, in favor a more responsive, positive, effective adjustment of policy levers to fit the particular objectives that have to be re-evaluated and regularly updated and tested.

The takeaway in terms of the CTE market access work program is that the CTE cannot be static, and there is enough energy among its members to do the right thing if there is continuing dialogue and coordination and cooperation. The problem or silver lining perhaps, with the demise of the Doha round is that it has become clearer, with modern communication technology, increased education, and increased prosperity and development, that much stays the same, and that accountability and responsibility remain the highest tools by which trade and environment rulemaking can be enhanced through more localized and regionalized policy coordination and formulation.

However, localized solutions with strong domestic and international coordination will not add up to the systemic change and impact that is needed for achieving true sustainability. However, recent research (e.g., Hickel and Kiallis, 2019)[495] has examined green growth policies as articulated in major reports by the World Bank, the OECD and the UN Environment Program, and tested the theory against extant empirical evidence and models of the relationship between Gross Domestic Product (GDP) and *materials flows and footprints* and CO_2 emissions.

For *material footprint*, an important question pertains to whether we can achieve absolute decoupling of GDP from resource use. Hickel and Kiallis (2019) show that empirical projections show no absolute decoupling on a global scale, even under highly optimistic conditions. In addition, they suggest that, while some models show that it may be achieved in high-income nations under highly optimistic conditions, this cannot be sustained for the long term given limits to efficiency improvements.

These results assume current levels of GDP growth, of around 2 % to 3 % per year. They consider that it may be feasible to achieve absolute reductions in resource use, with GDP growing at less than 1 % per year. However, to achieve reductions rapid enough to get us down to safe thresholds will require degrowth strategies.

As already previously mentioned, other issues also relate to the emerging issues of the circular economy and the issue of trade in recycled and waste products.

§6.07 RECAP OF THE CTE MARKET ACCESS WORK

Despite the stalemate of environmental goods market access negotiations, it becomes evident that this work area remains the most active and potentially the most promising area for the future work of the CTE.

The concern should be to enable the CTE structure and processes to operationalize the different theoretical frames as most appropriate for the particular functions being conducted by the CTE. There has been good progress at the level of norms interface, coordination and exchange, and for the specialized topics, as well as in the area of CTE 6.

It will be perhaps time in the near future to attempt a formalization of the methodologies of the CTE as an institution in the two specific thematic work areas of norm interface (CTE 1, 2, 4, 5, 10) and special expert issues (CTE 3, 7, 8, 9), as well as to have a holistic analytical frame for the work of the CTE on market access.

495. Jason Hickel and Gorgio Kallis, *Is Green Growth Possible?*, 25(1) New Pol. Economy 1 (2019).

In sum, then the evaluation of the CTE work in market access is of a high mark under the three theoretical lenses, given the progress and outputs to actual legal texts, and structures for market access modalities, and in terms of expertise given the high level of the secretariat and MEA participation in monitoring and reviewing the proposals as well as the reference universe of goods and technologies sought to be part of the coverage on market access.

From the Ostrom-ian lens, as well, the continued stalemate and debates highlight the importance of developing objective criteria and approaches that will determine best or at least provide some expertise and level of objectivity in evaluating if a proposal meets the standard of accomplishing a triple-win for development as well as for trade and environment objectives. This can be a highly localized, regional or subjective exercise, in which not one single solution would fit all situations, and where the objective of the market access work area cannot be simply traditional trade enhancement, but rather there will be a need for more customized and specialized solutions that provide true environment policy value to the constituents of the CTE.

The CTE 6/DDA 32i Work Program

For the regular CTE work under the original 1994 CTE 6 mandate, which do not involve a mandate to negotiate an outcome or new rules, but rather focuses on "the effect of environmental measures on market access" and trade in general, as well as the "environmental benefits of removing trade restrictions and distortions," the discussions were organized around four sectors that impact the environment, and the documentation and meetings of the CTE regular session follow this organizational system.

These are the special sectors of (a) agriculture; (b) fisheries resources; (c) energy, and (d) forestry (see Annex 2). The relevant and latest iteration of the regular CTE list of documents, INF/5/Rev. 12 (Section 1.6) lists all the documentation relating to these sectors under specific subsections as relating to the Agenda Item 6 mandate, which is also subsumed by paragraph 32(i) of the Doha Declaration that mandated attempting to achieve *the triple-win*, already cited above.

It becomes evident that these early discussions were in the nature of debate and elaboration of the benefits or disadvantages of the concept of removing or lessening tariffs or NTMs and fall short of any concrete attempts at increasing market access in environmental goods or services. However, they did aid in a better understanding of the trade and environment linkages, which progressed from discussions to a negotiating mandate granted at the Doha Ministerial Conference.

Therefore, the early discussions in the CTE 6 mandate tend to repeat themselves in the negotiations discussions, and while adding to the knowledge base, the tone of the discussions tend to be in the nature of the specialist discussions that the CTE is known for in its other work areas under CTE 3, 7, 8, and 9. They provide a good background for further work, but I would posit suffer the same low evaluation grade and assessment for actual or concrete results, especially in obtaining greater trade volumes.

The lack of a concrete outcome on market access in any case to date could be frustrating for many delegates and leads as well to a temptation to repeat what *Friends of the Earth* stated prior to the Singapore Ministerial Conference of 1996 when the NGO had learned that the CTE was seeking a renewal or extension of its limited *talk-shop* mandate. As a noted author reported:

> *Friends of the Earth (International), called on the WTO to discontinue the CTE. Friends of the Earth declared: "The CTE is a waste of time and money and threatens to stand in the way of real environmental progress." This position was supported by the Competitive Enterprise Institute (a free market NGO in Washington D.C.). In November 1996, this author recommended that the WTO abolish the CTE or if that were impossible, that the WTO revise its mandate to provide for more balanced discussions.*[496]

The author is highly tempted to adopt the same view when it comes to the evaluation of the work under the CTE 6/DDA 32i market access mandate, given that the discussions to a limited extent also suffer the circular rhythms observed in work conducted in the areas of CTE 7, 8, and 9. However, as noted in the evaluation of CTE 7, 8 and 9, even when dealing with such specialized topics, the CTE did fulfill its mandated tasks. In fact, it is the limited *talk shop* mandate as contained in the 1994 CTE Decision that is at the root of all the mandated sufferance, and not the CTE itself. There is, therefore, room for further discussions towards new market access rules for specific sectors (e.g., energy-related goods and services), which could garner interest from other experts and CTE constituents, provided there is a clarified mandate on the specific output that will be expected of the CTE as regards the energy sector.

Updating the CTE mandate

The negotiating mandate of the CTE and its thematic work on market access towards the *triple-win*, if properly managed under the tutelage of the three theoretical frameworks, could provide an excellent incubator for testing the potential of the CTE for truly providing state of the art trade and environment governance.

With the public, NGOs and private enterprises increasingly sensitive and open to the commercial aspects of environmentally sound projects and trade, there is a sense of optimism in the field of market access. Even the lens of self-regulation provides aid to the formulation of best local practices and the criteria for an enabling regulatory environment, which is still a form of normative creation for guidelines in the field of trade and environment policy making.

With the substantive outputs of the CTE on market access, and the built-in knowledge and experience in the area, the expansion of ideas for the melding of commercial and trade opportunities with projects that enhance the approaches to a constructive triple-win, it is hoped that there is enough material generated by the CTE and CTESS that will allow policy makers, experts and political leaders to evolve an updated mandate for the market access area of work of the CTE.

496. Steve Charnovitz, *A Critical Guide to the WTO Report on Trade and Environment*, 14 Ariz. J. Int'l. & Comp. L. 341, at 370 (1997).

Part III Concluding Section

CHAPTER 7

Conclusion: Evaluation of the WTO CTE

Principle 14
Rational planning constitutes an essential tool for reconciling any conflict between the needs of development and the need to protect and improve the environment.

Principle 25
States shall ensure that international organizations play a coordinated, efficient and dynamic role for the protection and improvement of the environment.

Declaration of the United Nations Conference on the Human Environment
Stockholm, June 16, 1972

§7.01 TRADE AND ENVIRONMENT GOVERNANCE AT THE WTO CTE

IL blossomed after the publication of *Mare Liberum* by Hugo Grotius. Scholars refer to this triggering phenomenon as a *Grotian moment*. Similarly, for international environmental law, the 1972 Stockholm Declaration with its *26 Principles,* is seen as a historic accomplishment that galvanized international environmental treaty making. But post-*Grotian* moments are accompanied by the human momentum, and after the momentum, there will have to be a peak. The peak seems to have been reached, for both environmental treaty making, as well as in the area of trade governance and treaty making.

Before Stockholm, there were 283 MEAs starting with the 1857 *Agreement respecting the regulation of the flow of water from Lake Constance* and post-Stockholm through to 2016, a total of 1,033 MEAs were signed, meaning that 78.49% of all MEAs entered into existence post-Stockholm (*see* figure 7.1). The CTE's creation was part of the post-Stockholm momentum culminating in the decade of the 1990s, when both trade and environment treaty making reached their peak, with the 1992 Rio Declaration, the UNFCCC and the 1994 Marrakesh Treaty establishing the WTO and capping the UR. These were historic high points for the advocates of unified singular global governance.

Figure 7.1 MEA Numbers

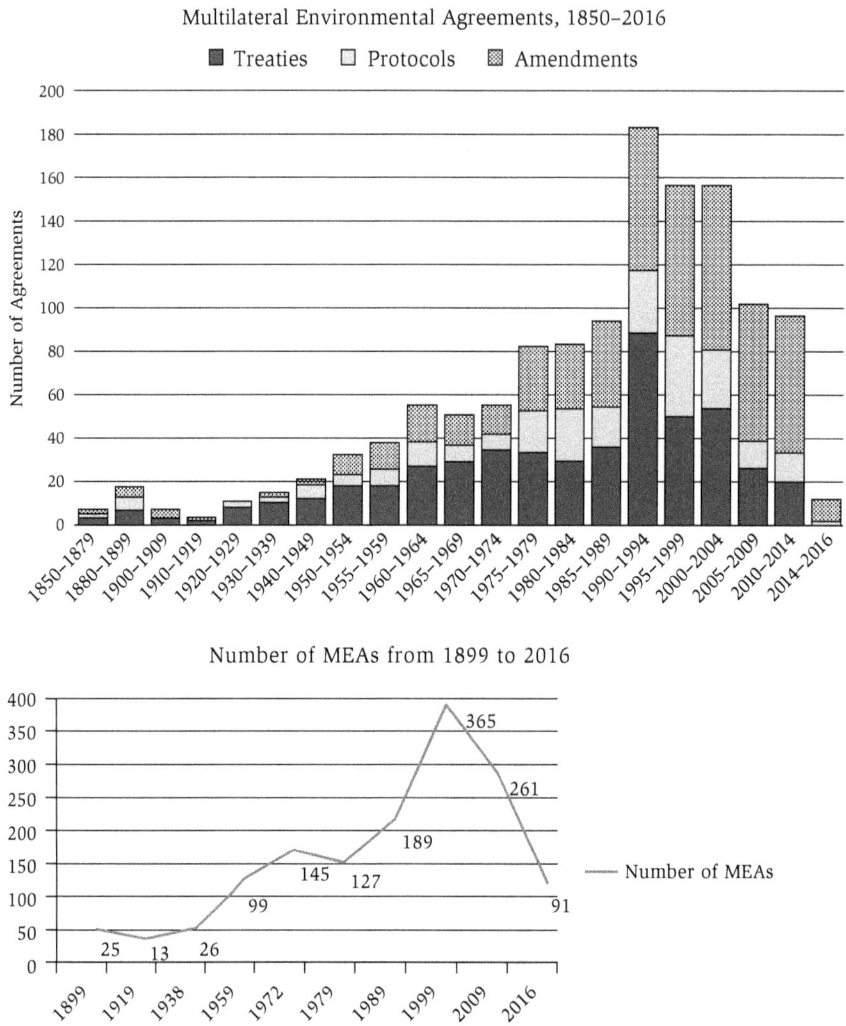

Source: Mitchell, Ronald B. (2017). International Environmental Agreements Database Project, Eugene, Oregon, University of Oregon. http://iea.uoregon.edu (accessed 30 March 2020).

The time has come to buckle down and to do the work. Today we are at an inflection point, post the *Grotian* momentum of enthusiasm for new deals and new agreements. The signs of the times point to pushback against more and more agreements, and more and more treaties, as well as a pushback against globalized harmonized singular approaches to treaty and rulemaking. The goal, at any rate, is not to have new agreements and rules per se, but rather fulfill its mandated functions, serve well the policy directives and objectives, and perhaps do more. Current trends signal a return to a more *rational* and more pragmatic approach requiring diversified, responsive and customized global governance systems, or a more federalized system of international cooperation and coordination that can more nimbly and rapidly address concerns of citizens and constituents demanding more attention to *the local* over *the international,* to *the substance* over *the procedural.*

Stockholm Principle 25 (SP25) should serve as an inspiration to the current and future CTE on the standard expected of interdisciplinary institutional interactions. SP25 commands that state actors (yes, it is directed to the member governments of the WTO) ensure that IOs, or their progeny, like the WTO CTE, must have fully coherent, coordinated and dynamic governance systems and that the CTE "play a coordinated, efficient and dynamic role for the protection and improvement of the environment." *SP25* must share its relevance with *Stockholm Principle 14 (SP14)* that mandates these same CTE members to be pragmatic and use common sense, i.e., *rational* planning mechanisms to tackle and reconcile policy norms conflicts and interface.

In concluding the panoramic review of the CTE, as an IL-IR institution, as a microcosm of its constituent members and its secretariat, as a by-product of its own prehistory and its organic ad hoc mandate, irrespective of the evaluation grades being pass or fail, or with distinction or without, one ought not to avoid having a sense of gratefulness and privilege to have readily on hand the complete CTE/GEMIT work outputs. These outputs contributed to the trade and environment policy community, the official and internal documentation reflecting years of activities, meetings, deliberations, factual and background notes, chair reports, member submissions, proposals, papers and non-papers, presentations, debates, most of which can be traced through the *must read* for any aspiring CTE practitioner, the INF5 and INF4 lists.

[A] The CTE Committee Processes

Members, MEAs, Secretariat Processes

As we have learned from reviewing Chapters 4, 5, and 6, the committee work on the ten-point agenda of the CTE, spanning twenty-one years, from 1995 to 2016, that the deliberations were certainly informative, and allowed for the interaction among members, MEAs, and Secretariats, for regular exchanges of views, and sharing of new and not-so-new ideas. At points, though, these exchanges could also be uninspiring, frequently inconclusive and regularly circular. One can only point to the frank description of Lang & Scott in their review of other WTO committee processes as appropriate in certain instances.[497]

497. Their observations are apt for certain of the CTE discussions: "[t]hese negotiations have been far less successful than had been hoped, at least in terms of the production of agreed rules and texts. They have generated a good deal of activity—meetings, discussion papers, reports, draft texts, and so on—but very little by way of concrete result. The documentary record of the safeguard negotiations, for example, yields a picture of discussions which are largely ungrounded and rudderless, disclosing 'no common basis' on which to draft rules. The subsidy

The subject of the evaluation, though, in this instance, will fall with the CTE membership as they are the main drivers of what is often referred to as a "member-driven organization." The question arises as regards the Members being distracted from focusing on their work at the CTE. Is there a mechanism to ensure the focus of members on the importance and urgency of environmental concerns given that trade negotiations give priority to trade concerns? *SP14* requires some rational planning, and this, in turn, requires a mandated check on the ten-point work program as well as the planning of meeting structure and processes.

While Members did recognize that discussions at the CTE were important and attested to the close linkages between trade and environment, many of the discussions displayed reservations that were either politically motivated or represented long-standing holding positions being repeated. Further, the discussions, with additional focus and mandates, were rendered further complicated with the push for the ill-fated Doha Round, and the CTE was granted a negotiating mandate, along with other instructions, though in the case of the CTE and CTESS, this added some structure to the processes.

The contours of the nebulous "*win-win-win*" or *triple-win* as discussed in Chapter 6 were a source of inspiration, as well as frustration, and while the market access discussions displayed substantial progress and structure, progress towards a concrete outcome was held back, leading a group of like-minded members that accounted for a large share of world trade in environmental goods to move the negotiations outside of the discussions of the CTE, or to voluntary, non-binding cooperation arrangements.

Nevertheless, the interactions at the CTE as a committee and as a constituent body of an IO surely contributed to a deeper discussion of issues relating to trade and the environment. Lang and Scott, as we covered in Chapter 3, point out that WTO Committees can certainly contribute to greater information exchange among IOs and norm elaboration.[498] The CTE, for example, had invited organizations and MEAs such as the UNFCCC, UNEP, World Bank, OECD, CBD and FAO and twenty other international IGOs to be permanent or ad hoc observers at the CTE. This aspect then of the interface relating to other IOs and MEAs has been a very positive aspect of the CTE's committee processes, and are commendable.

Early discussions at the CTE were vibrant and vigorous in their discussions on the relationship between MEAs and the multilateral trading system. Over the years, however, these discussions declined, and again, this is an area where *SP25* and *SP14* should be used to reinvigorate the need for rational planning and scheduling of these information exchanges. Increasing their regularity or instituting a system of thematic updates to allow for focus and specialization and building on prior reports and presentations could enhance the value addition and value preservation of the substantive content of these ideas and information exchanges. Various MEA observers were

---

negotiations have foundered in part because of fundamental disagreements about what kinds of measures should and should not be classified as subsidies." *See* Andrew Lang and Joanne Scott, *The Hidden World of WTO Governance*, 20 Eur. J. Int'l L. 575, at 585 (2009).

498. *Ibid.*

able to and continue to make presentations to update Members on the happenings in various international environmental fora.

Much of the work and output has resulted from the committee processes when the CTE or the WTO Secretariat have been asked to prepare notes or background papers, and these add to the overall work outputs of the CTE as also discussed and evaluated further below. Also notable, and arising from the benefits of the interfaces of the committee processes, are the outputs generated in cooperation with other MEA Secretariats, as in the case of the joint WTO UNEP Report on Climate Change.

The committee processes also encourage Members to share their national experiences, make presentations of successful programs that have been initiated, and share their learning with other WTO Members. As we saw in Chapter 4, many of the discussions at the CTE were based upon these presentations by Members sharing and narrating their *triple-win* experiences or initiatives with respect to eco-labelling. These presentations introduced to other Members the challenges and difficulties that were faced during the processes of implementation and execution of the measures being discussed. Other Members would discuss the presentation, ask questions, make comments, and offer views on the lessons that could be drawn from the WTO Members that shared the experience. This is not to say that discussions at the CTE are politically neutral or without ulterior motives. In the trade regime, motivations are a given and encouraged, and proposals are expected to have economic and commercial value as well as potential mutually beneficial economic activity, in consonance with the core principle of the WTO for advancing open, fair and free economic exchanges.

Member presentations were business-like and tended to highlight compliance with the mandated contours of the *triple-win* or *double win*, as the case may be, and were aimed at shaping future discussions by persuading others of the merits of the suggested practices or technologies. WTO Members with strong industrial interests in utilizing indigenous knowledge for business purposes, for example, extolled universal benefits of unrestricted access to plant genetic sources for food and agriculture at the CTE, and generally, *demandeurs* in negotiations have made presentations that would further interests in their proposals.

Another aspect of the interface among members and other organizations, including secretariats of other WTO committees, that can be observed would be the direct and indirect impact of knowledge creation and knowledge sharing among the professional bureaucracy and the evolvement of best practice procedures. The narrative of discussions drawn out at the CTE, for instance, may have assisted in re-assessing the needs of a WTO Member which would have permeated into concurrent negotiations such as those in the Rules committee (for fisheries subsidies), TBT committee (for labelling requirements) or even in subsequent bilateral trade negotiations. Additionally, many LDCs and other WTO Members with limited capacity have expressed appreciation for presentations made by Members regarding their experiences in implementing domestic legislation that protected the environment and also included a trade aspect. Moreover, international trade negotiations are information intensive.

In that regard, work done by the CTE in collecting data on environment-related trade measures and making them available through the establishment of a database in accordance with Item 4 of the discussions is noteworthy. *Hong Kong, China* and Brazil, in 1996, had pointed out that no information collection point for trade-related environment measures existed in the WTO and that environment-related information fell outside the purview of SPS and TBT inquiry points. This interface and exchanges in the committee processes have led to work outputs or policy tools that can benefit trade and environment governance both within and outside the WTO setting, as with the resulting EDB, and periodic Environment Review (ER) practices that have become solid work outputs of the CTE as well.

These committee processes also promote greater cooperation amongst ministries at the domestic level—in particular between those responsible for trade and environment negotiations—and like other committee processes, they aid in allowing the cross-pollination of ideas and practices among delegations from Members' capitals. As mentioned, there are norm elaboration benefits to the committee processes, as pointed out by Lang & Scott. The committee processes also offer coherence efforts among policy makers. The next section will further explore this topic together with the rulemaking function of the CTE.

[B] The CTE Theories: Law and Policy Interface and Development

As presented in Chapter 3, the work of the CTE can best be understood when keeping in mind the actors and constituents that become factors in the equation depending on the thematic work area or agenda item in play, which are either: (i) member governments, which are the state actors, the high officials, and the law and policy advisers; (ii) the professional bureaucrats and administrators, which include the network of experts (including legal experts) and secretariats, and professional government officials; and (iii) the trade and environment communities, citizens or constituents, which will include the CPR stakeholders, business associations and Multinational corporations (MNCs), Micro, small and medium enterprises (MSMEs) and NGOs. Again, like frames or lenses, they overlap and are only meant to aid in the holistic analysis and evaluation of the functions, processes and outputs of the CTE by adopting distinct perspectives or points of reference.

Lens A: Rule of Law

Acknowledging at the outset the absence of new laws or rules, the assessment is, however, helped in terms of the development of soft law and evolving custom and practice in the fields of MEA exchanges and policy coordination, and the evolved practice and policy toolkits contained in the annual EDB, and periodic Environment Review (ER) mechanisms. These are, therefore, good signs in the field of the traditional lens of rulemaking and global singular governance mechanisms.

In the area of norm elaboration and trade and environment policy coordination, which remains the primary mandate of the CTE, as covered in Chapter 4, the discussions at the CTE have led to more clarity on the relationship between MEAs and the multilateral trading system. Early discussions at the CTE dealt with reconciling potentially conflicting obligations between WTO law and MEAs. Many WTO Members proposed various *ex ante* and *ex post* solutions for certain MEAs that included trade-related provisions so as to pass the test of GATT Article XX. These solutions were based upon the assumption that there was a clear demarcation between public IL and WTO law. However, over time, WTO Members recognized that it was unlikely for these potential conflicts to arise. Their views were strengthened with every passing presentation made at the CTE by Secretariats of these MEAs, which did not report any conflict between MEAs and the multilateral trading system. This perhaps can obtain for the CTE an excellent rating for compliance with *Stockholm Principle 25 (SP25)* mentioned above for achieving coherence and coordination among the various MEAs.

Further, greater cooperation, information exchanges, legal expert briefings amongst delegations, capital officials and national regulators dealing with trade and environment policy coordination, and avoidance of conflict, yielded a gradual evolution that helped clarify the relationship between MEAs and WTO law as well as an acceptance of the wisdom and flexibility afforded by GATT Article XX. The CTE, while not the premier fora, can be said to have provided a platform for the exchanges of views in this regard.

In the area of the mandate for a legal outcome in the market access negotiations, the CTE work resulted in substantial outputs and worked as reflected in the draft structure of modalities and the reference universe of potential environmental goods, which but for the political will being insufficient would have resulted in quite a concrete outcome. In any event, as discussed in Chapter 6, many participants have proceeded to implement the implementation of the tariff cutting modality under alternate or voluntary cooperation fora, such as in APEC. The attempt to establish some criteria or metric for the triple-win, and the matrix analysis tool, could also generate some positive aspects if pursued and utilized as a policy aid.

Lens B: Expert Administration

In the area of developing a knowledge bank and encouraging and building expertise on trade and environment issues, as well as expanding the network of expert professionals, TRNs and GALs that are conversant on the issues, the CTE can be said to have obtained reasonably good results, particularly, as regards the professionalization of the administrative bureaucracy and maintaining secretariat expertise. It cannot be questioned that the CTE remains a repository of the needed knowledge and information, which are easily available for delegations and capital officials who may need assistance on specialized topics. The problem lies, though, with the conversion rate of the expertise into tangible new rules, or into creative and dynamic user-friendly tools, or the actual resolution of issues, or in the alternative, the closure and solution of certain areas.

As mentioned, there were unsatisfactory results and discussions in the areas of CTE 7, 8 and 9 (DPGs, TRIPS/CBD and Environmental Services) as well as in the area of CTE 6 where discussions related to particular areas with no clear objective to be achieved (e.g., carbon emissions, fisheries and forestry). In these areas, a major part of the inefficiency or lackluster compliance with *SP25* is the failure to abide by *SP14* on having some rationality and a master plan for these areas of concern. Dynamism required by *SP25* had not been achieved in these areas.

Another key factor in the negative evaluation would be the overlapping jurisdictions with other IGOs or committees (e.g., DPGs for Basel Convention; carbon dioxide and other greenhouse gases for UNFCCC; TRIPS/CBD for the TRIPS Council or WIPO, etc.). These overlaps and absence of clear ministerial guidance provides fertile ground for the all-too-common specialty of bureaucracies worldwide of *ping-pong'ing* or *passing the baton.*

An area of weakness would be the lack of interface and think tank levels of output that could have been generated, e.g., expert presentations on CPR issues that intersect with trade issues could deliver new strategies for these communities. This could potentially be an area for improvement and growth in the CTE deliberations and melds well with the theory of Elinor Ostrom of allowing greater diversity and building broader technical capacity for governments to assist their CPR stakeholders, and would particularly enhance compliance with both *SP14* and *SP25* requirements of dynamism and effective rational planning.

In the area of secretariat expertise and networking, the CTE has had an excellent record of internal administrative management and knowledge maintenance as mentioned in the committee processes section and evaluation. The questions on TRNs and GAL are relatively benign, and, at this point, given the paucity of the administrative staff, there is probably more room to expand the TRN and GAL capacity of the CTE than to be concerned about its political overreach. As discussed in Chapter 2 and below, the outputs of the CTE and its predecessor, the GEMIT, have been laudable, and strengthening the R&D and think tank capacity of the CTE can only improve efficiency, creativity and coordinative capacity, and enhance the overall need and essentiality of the need to expand rational planning (*SP14*).

Concerns expressed by Lang & Scott and by Zaring, among others, discussed in Chapter 3,[499] should be taken into account and noted. They relate to the fact that TRNs and experts are known to have common approaches to solving problems and have a built-in loyalty to their own rationality, and this may lead to the entrenchment of TRNs, citing Kennedy, who argued that TRNs lessen the need for political contests. In *Rousseau* fashion, there is a perceived danger of "self-presentation of expert decisions as '*determined, rather than free*'."[500] Needless to say that the patron icon of the expert lens B of the expert rule is Plato himself, who, ironically, despite all his wisdom, suffered at the hands of the political overlords (the non-philosopher-kings), whom he spoke against.

Lens C: Diversity and Self-Governance Mechanisms

Since Lens C adopts more of an antithetical approach, its utility may appear obtuse. One example is the generation of work outputs in work items 1, 5, and 10, which are focused on clarifying the differences between the current WTO's legalistic approach to

499. *Lang and Scott Hidden World of WTO Governance (2009)* at 611; *see also* discussion in Chapter 3 at pp. 81. et seq.
500. David Kennedy, *Challenging Expert Rule: The Politics of Global Governance*, 27 Sydney J Int'l L. 5, at 6 (2005); David Kennedy, *The Politics of the Invisible College: International Governance and the Politics of Expertise*, 5 Eur. Hum. Rts. L. Rev. 463 (2001).

dispute settlement and the MEA's facilitating approach to enhance the capacity of compliance of states. The CTE emphasized that in order to enhance compliance with international environmental law, it is important to develop mechanisms in dispute settlement in order to be effective.

The CTE or WTO approach seemed to indicate that another solution would be to engage the two regimes in a merger so as to lessen the tension between them. CTE work was to make the WTO facilitate discussions through less judicially stringent means and instead encourage mediation and conciliation. The approach of the committee cannot, thus, be solely understood in a purely legalistic sense of hard law. What the committee is attempting to do is to find alternative paths to compliance on the international level, and this goes directly to the mandate of *SP25* that there should be a "coordinated, efficient and dynamic role" to be performed by the CTE as an IO body.

Environmental protection and sustainable development of global natural resources do not always benefit from a hard law approach, especially considering the Ostrom-ian communitarianism of international society requiring continuing dialogue on competing scientific, environmental theories. Therefore, given the conflict of norms and differing levels of hierarchy, there is the hesitancy to have a merged legal system or for one policy regime to be adjudged as superior or inferior to the other. An example would be the carbon and climate issue where, for a brief moment, the expectation was again a singular global unitary system, following belatedly on the heels of the nostalgic success of the Montreal Protocol. Under the hard law lens, this was a triumph of good over evil that ought to be the case in all other scientific situations. The Ostrom-ian lens challenges this centralized approach and presumption of rightness very strongly. With recent developments, it seems like Ostrom may have foreshadowed the fate of the Paris Agreement and the important priority concept of each local community, such as California or Ohio, to be making their own decisions with respect to issues of greater importance to them, without of course violating the "do no harm" or precautionary principles. A similar concern against a singular approach or belief by TRNs of their absolute truth was expressed by Lang & Scott and by Kennedy *vis-à-vis* the dangers of resurrecting Plato's expert republic.[501]

As Ostrom notes, sometimes, it is not prudent to utilize centralized governance. Climate science (and its assessments of actual economic impacts of climate change), for example, is still considered an uncertain science by a few states, despite the media or experts, or their political sponsors, regularly pronouncing in the news that certain truths are absolute. In such instances, rather than focusing on the urgent ameliorative measures, valuable time is spent on disputing the certainty of climate change and its predominantly anthropogenic causes.

501. *Lang and Scott Hidden World of WTO Governance (2009)* at 611; David Kennedy, *Challenging Expert Rule: The Politics of Global Governance*, 27 Sydney J. Int'l L. 5, at 6 (2005); David Kennedy, *The Politics of the Invisible College: International Governance and the Politics of Expertise*, 5 Eur. Hum. Rts. L. Rev. 463 (2001).

A polycentric approach to governance ensures the multifaceted management of resources.[502] That said, Ostrom does not believe in a complete absence of centralized governance interference and recognizes that it is essential to provide a structure to the liberalization of community governance. It should not be forgotten that facilitating trade is not merely about treaties and trade rules. The global market is complex in its structure; governments may or may not, in reality, influence markets, depend on resources, governmental policies, enterprises, and economic capacity of the state. Against this background, and the diversity of WTO Members, the CTE undertook a more information-oriented methodology, e.g., by structuring the information flow between Members in order to coordinate policies, practices and know-how of the trade on environmentally sustainable goods and services.

In sum, the core problem identified here is the shift in focus and energies of the governance infrastructure. Like the case of the *triple-win* scenario, the energies of government often focus on determining the criteria or having a rule, rather than the real problem on the ground. Thus, there is an obvious need and priority to empower and aid the communities on the ground to act in their own self-interest to address the problem appropriately.

The Montreal Protocol approach to the unitary global management of trade and environment is still to be considered *novus*. While, eventually, these practices could evolve into a custom or hard law, the rulemaking cannot be the objective of the exercise, nor the identification of which state or expert is right or wrong. The objective should be the availability of a policy framework that is coordinated, dynamic, pragmatic, not overly pedagogical, responsive and agile, to enable the various communities and stakeholders to solve problems when suitable at a localized or regional level in a timely fashion.

In the end, the adjudication of environmental transgressions presumes a compliance ability of Members if it is to be considered to be purposeful. If the international community is to combat successfully, for e.g., carbon accumulation in the global commons, each country ought to be equipped and provided with adequate resources and institutional knowledge in order to effectively address the problem. Since the global commons do not fall within the exclusive jurisdiction of one Member, the administration of these resources cannot be controlled by mere legislative intentions. Information sharing, technical assistance and capacity building all form part of long-term investments to protect long-term financial viability. Members are, therefore, inter-dependent when dealing with the global commons, either on a regional basis or on the global market. Policy making, thus, ought to make sense not merely on a domestic level, but governments will also be more prone to consider policy making of other Members to align itself with best practices. The CTE, therefore, plays a crucial part in the development of robust institutional arrangements that allow for dynamic interaction and rational planning.

502. Elinor Ostrom, *A Polycentric Approach for Coping with Climate Change* (2009) available at: http://documents.worldbank.org/curated/en/480171468315567893/pdf/WPS5095.pdf (accessed on November 30, 2019).

Recap of Theoretical Frames

Table 7.1 provides a modified version of Table 3.1 that recaps the three theoretical perspectives adopted for the assessments and evaluations of the functioning of the CTE in this book. It contains some illustrative suggestions on identified areas of strength and weakness and items that might be ripe for sunsetting.

Table 7.1 CTE Strengths and Weaknesses

	Lens A	*Lens B*	*Lens C*
Basic Theory	Global IL-IR Rule Making Policy Coordination Cooperation	Managerial, Experts, TRNs, GALs	Institutional Diversity
Key Players, Constituents	State Actors, Governments, IOs, Secretariats, TRNs	Bureaucrats, Secretariats, TRNs, Managers, Experts	Communities, Local Authorities, CPRs
Key Principles	Rule of Law, Norm Creation, Policy Regimes, Global Governance, Harmonization, Formal / Informal Law and Policy Making	Global Knowledge and Expertise, Technical Capacity, Best Practices, Experience Sharing,	Self-Governance, Non-Experts, Institutional Diversity, Regional, Transfer of Technology
CTE Work Areas	(Chapter 4) CTE 1, 2, 4, 5, 6, 10 Other Areas	(Chapter 5) CTE 3a, 3b, 6, 7, 8, 9 Other Areas	(Chapter 6) CTE 6, 31iii Other areas
Potential Strong Area	EDB, ERs, Transparency and Coordination, STO Inventory, MEA exchange, Market Access Modalities	Market Access, Eco-labelling, Climate, BTAs, Carbon	Market Access Project Approach, Case to Case Approach, Non-commercial mandate of EGS negotiations
Area for Improvement	Rulemaking, Policy Coherence/Coordination Mechanisms, CTE Work Program Update, rational planning, dynamism	TACB, New Strategies, R&D, CPRs, Environmental Technologies and Finance, CTE Work Program New Topics	CPR interface, RTA, Market Access Issue identification, rational planning, dynamism
Sunset Areas		DPGs, TRIPS, Environmental Services, Fisheries, Forestry	

Lens A—As summarized in Chapter 3, theoretical Lens A focuses on the traditional positive hard law issues and deliverables of the CTE, encouraging closer coordination with members and governments who are the primary actors at the international level thereby promoting a global system of laws and preventing a tragedy of the commons.

Lens B—Rather than placing the rule of law at the center, Lens B leans towards a more pragmatic results-oriented and technocratic-oriented working of the CTE with the same end in view, i.e., of improving governance and attempting to avoid a tragedy of the commons. Problem-solving becomes a key element of the work of the experts and professional managers, and this could certainly aid in the highly technical and scientific areas of work of the CTE. This is also able to manifest itself in the technical and complex studies on the varying sectors or types of environmental goods wherein particular categories are more applicable to particular CPRs, or CPR type situations. More analysis is required on how the CPR approach translates analogously if feasible to the global commons.

Lens C—Lens C contrasts itself fundamentally from the first two lenses by its quasi-rebellious nature and refusal to accept that centralized institutions are most suitable to complex issues. Instead, this Ostrom-ian view asserts that the most effective solution to the governance of CPRs would be through decentralization and by enabling the best responses to manifest themselves at the local level. The manifestation of this lens in the work and outputs of the CTE is not immediately identifiable but can be said to be increasing its influence on the general pushback against singular one size fits all prescriptions and solutions. Lens C could be said to manifest itself in the insistence by some delegations that the outcome of any market access negotiations should satisfy *the triple-win* mandate.

[C] CTE Key Work Outputs

Table 7.2 Tally of Document Outputs

Theme	*Work Area/Theme*	*Work Agenda Item*	*No. Of Outputs*	*Documents*	*Output as % Documents*
A	Norm Coherence	CTE1, 5, 10	6	215	2.79%
A	EDBs ERs	CTE2, 4	2	116	1.72%
Sub-total A	**Policy Interface and Coordination**	**CTE1,2,3,5,10**	**8**	**331**	**2.42%**
B	DPGs, TRIPS, CBD, Services	CTE 7, 8, 9	3	147	2.04%
B	Carbon, BTAs, Eco-labelling, TBTs, Standards	CTE3a, 3b	5	96	5.21%
Sub-total B	**Special Expert Topics / R&D**	**CTE3, 7, 8, 9**	**8**	**243**	**3.29%**
C	**Market Access**	**CTE6, DDA32iii**	**4**	**285**	**1.40%**
		Grand Total	**20**	**859**	**2.33%**

Chapter 2 and Table 2.10 contained therein provides the complete summary of the twenty key CTE work outputs, which were also categorized according to the thematic work areas, as grouped from the ten-point work program. Also discussed are the numbering system and sources of the mandated work item. However, in general, there are three broad categories of work outputs and functions of the CTE. With the availability of the documents generated per agenda item and the identification of the work outputs, basic productivity and efficiency ratio can be generated as provided in Table 7.2. We can see that the expert function of the CTE relating to specialized areas for reporting and discussion covered by CTE 3, 7, 8 and 9 garnered the highest efficiency ratio of 3.29 in terms of the volume of the outputs against the total documents catalogued for the same area. A sub-area of this category, under CTE 3, got the highest rating of 5.21. This is understandable given the high level of outputs and the amount of work dedicated to the topic of climate change, carbon taxes and eco-labelling.

Another area covered obtaining the second-highest ratio of 2.33 was the work delivery for CTE 1, 5, and 10 on the studies on the relationship between trade and environment regimes.

The identification of the twenty key outputs has to be qualified with the fact that there are many other CTE work products and documents that qualify as well to be work outputs that are essential and key, which would then increase the efficiency rating of the CTE. Again, this is but an aid to analysis, and the key work outputs are intended to provide a broad-brush idea of the types of work product that have been generated by the CTE. Further, the process of identifying the key output documents has been influenced by the frequency of citation or practical use of or references made to the document.

To aid in providing some integration insights, one can highlight again some examples of the concrete or practical contributions of the CTE to trade and environment governance and policy making.

In market access, there was a robust delivery of work on the structure of the modalities options and potential coverage through a reference universe based on member proposals. In the area of policy coordination, the STO Inventory provides policy makers with a convenient guide to all the identified STOs in MEAs, while the ER process has become a regular practice within the WTO.

The WTO EDB was prepared as a result of the recommendations of the CTE and now provides a repository for information on national environment-related measures notified under WTO Agreements, environment-related provisions of notified Regional Trade Agreements, and national environment-related measures or programs mentioned in TPRs, on an annual basis. The notifications can be sub-divided into two groups: (i) environmental measures as the principal objective; (ii) environmental-related notifications that do not primarily address environmental protection but consists of environmental elements. The EDB does not merely assist individual Members by providing easily accessible information on all notified environment-related measures but also provides to global policy makers and trade and environment experts and specialists a reference tool and compendium of the universe of regulatory practices in environmental governance. In relation to trade governance, the practice of information compilation and sharing could equally reinforce good practices and promote the resilience of the multilateral trading system by aiding governments to guard against or combat trade-disruptive regulatory measures while aiming to harmonize approaches that fight transboundary environmental harm with non-discriminatory trade measures.

As regards the CTE mandate in each of the specialized topics of DPGs, TRIPS/CBD and Environmental Services, the work outputs consist of specialized reports that are primarily in the nature of comprehensive summaries of the available information and expert perspectives. These documents are relatively less useful as policy tools, but considered less satisfactory than other CTE key outputs and given certain other factors already discussed above; these reports still provide an excellent reference on the specialized topic that would not otherwise be easily available to specialist researchers.

The CTE key outputs are available for all to scrutinize and these all aid in one way or the other to fulfill the mandate of *SP25* for trade and environment policy coordination. As already identified above, there is definitely room for improvement through better structuring of the meetings as well as a full review and revamp of the work program that should already place sunset provisions on the recommended items for closure.

The key output documents of the CTE surely count as contributions to environmental protection, whilst encouraging international trade. It can be said that the CTE has delivered robustly on the thematic areas of work within its mandate. The challenge remains on the conversion factor and rational planning that could be the main focus for the CTE of the future, towards formulating a well-organized new work program that is coherent and simplified with clear objectives and benchmarks for delivering benefits that truly enhance the global governance of trade, development and the environment, and answer the call for coherence, responsiveness and dynamism.

In conclusion, the CTE's history and work since 1995 have been a journey of great expectations rooted in great moments of history, and the progress of humankind in both the economic, developmental and environmental spheres. The momentum has shifted; now is the time for the CTE to seize the moment. While respecting the past, the CTE must break with it to take hold of its own future and claim its destiny to becoming a fully dynamic and efficient governance platform that is able to generate and influence evolving policies and rules for the WTO community and beyond.

Trade rules such as MFN and NT, and GATT Article XX jurisprudence on coherence with environmental or health protections provided they are not disguised protectionist restrictions, have achieved a level of peremptory norm status. Environmental imperatives of late will find it challenging to dislodge the established hierarchy of norms, and the goal should be one of increased coherence, coordination and mutual supportiveness as mandated by the original CTE Decision in 1994.

Triple-win, if used properly as inspiration and an additional aid and not an obstacle, can be useful criteria to enhance the CTE's objectives of dynamic trade and environment policy making and governance, with the caveat that the focus should remain on the delivery of trade and economic benefits to the global community in a manner that is consistent with sustainable development.

No other forum provides such direct influence on and input to the trade and investment community while remaining fully connected with UNEP and the MEA community, through the facility of exchange that has become the tradition of the CTE. The CTE has always been a bridge between the constituents of the trade, development and environment communities, and, in being that bridge, the CTE can play a pivotal role in ensuring that the public good is served and the *global commons* stands ever bountiful.

Epilogue

Of Sisyphus, Yu Gong Yi Shan, and the 363 29s

The power of a theory is exactly proportional to the diversity of situations it can explain.

Elinor Ostrom, Governing the Commons (1990) at p.24

The power of a common vision is incalculable.[503]

Bishnoi Principle 19 [504]
Do not cut green trees, save the environment.

Guru Jambheshwar, ca. 1451

Sar sāntey rūkh rahe to bhī sasto jān.
If a tree is saved even at the cost of one's head, it's worth it.

Amrita Devi, Khejarli, ca. 1730

503. My own derivation as inspired by Peter Senge (The Fifth Discipline: The Art and Practice of the Learning Organization, 1990, rev. 2006) and Stephen Covey (Seven Habits of Highly Effective People, 1989).
504. As with the Rio and Stockholm Declarations, the Bishnoi community in India, founded in the 15th century by Guru Jambheshwar, *ca. 1451*, had identified 29 principles to live by (the tribe's name, Bishnoi, literally means 29). The 1730 martyrdom of 363 Bishnoi community members, led by Amrita Devi, was to uphold *Principle 19: Do not cut the green trees, save the environment.* The icon reproduced above is the Cenotaph at Khejarli, built in memorial to the martyred 363 Bishnoi (29ers) who died in Khejarli, Rajasthan, India.

At the end of this book, I cannot help but feel the dual emotions of completion and that the journey is not yet complete; that more research, analysis or insights ought to have been done. As it is in the beginning, so it is in the end. I was armed with Camus's Sisyphus, and Yu Gong's persistent reply to Yi Shan, characters who have traveled from ancient times to share their message with us today. I thought I would leave behind these strangers along the path of research but they stayed on and their message remains relevant, a message of patience and persistence, and I have added two more messengers, from the Bishnoi who crafted principles to live by well before the messages of Rio and Stockholm, and a modern-day hero in the person of Elinor Ostrom.

I started my trade journey in Ann Arbor with Professor John Jackson, to learn about the GATT, and by some twist of fate I would end up serving in the organization that was then but yet to be born, and also end up chairing what would succeed the then-existing GEMIT that was still in suspended animation at the time. To add to the story, along the path of my research, the earliest legal document on trade relations I encountered dates back to November 3, 1923 that was coincidentally signed in Geneva, the *International Convention relating the Simplification of Customs Formalities*, containing the precursor to GATT Article XX. Later on, a key work output of the CTE would be the compilation of GATT and WTO dispute settlement discussions on GATT Article XX exceptions.

I am not yet convinced, unlike Sisyphus, who was given Camus, and Yu Gong having Yi Shan, that the CTE has found its *contra punto,* which could crystallize its purpose. However, a new decision may make the learning in the CTE evolve into a new structure, and the Ostrom-ian vision may unify the three lenses of the central government, technocratic rule, and localized solutions. I do remain cautiously confident that the CTE will yet achieve an updated work program. Already, through twenty-one years of work on its ad hoc agenda, it was able to fashion a three-prong thematic structure to handle (i) legal norms and hierarchy issues, with appropriate coordination mechanisms; (ii) research and learning on highly technical environmental topics, and last, but not least of all, (iii) market access.

While the Grotian moment of Stockholm has passed and the challenge is not to wait out another wave of enthusiasm, the path ahead has already been set by the coterie of friends history has given us: Sisyphus, Yu Gong and Amrita Devi from circa 1730, the latest persistent one who led 362 other persistent ones to their sacrifice. With the peak of the environmental movement culminating in Rio, and the free trade movement climaxing in Marrakesh, all that remains is the peak of the world's population due to hit us in twenty to thirty years. The development movement peaked as well in 2000 with the establishment of the MDGs, with poverty levels now hitting historic lows, coupled with the universal consensus embodied in the SDGs that global poverty needs to be eradicated by 2030.

Indeed the challenges to trade and environment governance remain and are plentiful but the message I hold dearest is that of Elinor Ostrom, whose model and plan, coupled with our friends of more ancient times who exemplified human commitment, provides us with the vision and pathway forward. In conclusion, I can confidently respond to the basic question raised when I first embarked on this project—was there some existential meaning or value to all the CTE activity and the CTE documentation generated over the last two decades. The key work outputs generated amply demonstrate the relevance and value of all the work and documentation of the CTE as part of the quest for the attainment of a *global good governance of the commons*. And even more relevantly perhaps, they demonstrate the existential persistence of man and woman, no matter the odds, to search for what is at the core right for humankind while facing up to the challenges and inconveniences that the processes of debate and judgment entail.

The future of global governance will be local, and the future of local governance will be global. Such is the conundrum, as it is, and will be, for the *triple-win* for trade, development and the environment. Trade will be environmental and developmental. And the environment will be trade and development, and so on and so forth. This is the promise of the well-oiled machine of coherent, efficient, rational, planned, responsive and dynamic governance that lies at the core of Stockholm Principles 14 and 25.

DOCUMENTARY REFERENCE ANNEXES

Annex 1:	- CTE/CTESS Key Work Outputs - List of Figures and Tables - Organic Documents of the Committee on Trade and Environment
Annex 2:	A. Triple Win Matrix for Proposals under CTE6, DDA 31iii, 32i B. An Overview of CTE6/DDA32i Sectoral Discussions
Annex 3:	WTO CTESS, Report by the Chairman, Ambassador Manuel A. J. Teehankee, to the Trade Negotiations Committee, TN/TE/20, 21 April 2011 - Annex I, Draft Decision on Trade and Environment - Annex II, Structure/Coverage for Environmental Goods, Reference Universe and Sample Core List of Environmental Goods

ANNEX 1

CTE/CTESS Key Work Outputs, List of Tables and Figures, Organic Documents

20 KEY WORK OUTPUTS OF THE CTE

Theme A

Norm Coherence, MEA Exchange, Environmental Reviews, Policy Interface and Coordination

CTE Agenda Items 1, 2, 4, 5, 10

1) WTO Special Studies No.4 Trade and Environmental (a key study updating the prior 1991 GEMIT Note on Trade and Environment)
2) CTE Matrix on Trade-Related Measures Pursuant to Selected Multilateral Environmental Agreements ("STO Inventory"), WTO/CTE/W/160/Rev.1 - WTO/CTE/W/160/Rev.8 (2001-2017).
3) WTO Secretariat Note on GATT/ WTO Dispute Settlement Practice Relating to GATT Article XX, Paragraphs (b), (d), and (g), WT/CTE/W/203 (8 March 2002).
4) WTO UNEP Joint Note on Compliance and Dispute Settlement Provisions in the WTO and in Multilateral Environmental Agreements, WT/CTE/W/191 (6 June 2001).
5) MEA Information Session on Technical Assistance, Capacity Building and Enhancing Information Exchange (Inputs from WTO, UNEP and MEA Secretariat), WT/CTE/W/209 (5 June 2002).
6) CTESS Draft Ministerial Decision on Trade and Environment - Annex I, TN/TE/20 (21 April 2011).
7) List of Environmental Reviews ("Notifications"), WT/CTE/W/245 (4 June 2007).
8) Environmental Database ("EDB") (for years 1996 to 2000; and formal EDB Series 2001 to 2018) (publication dates 1997 to 2019), WT/CTE/EDB/1 - WT/CTE/EDB/18 (*see also* WT/CTE/W/46, 77, 118, 143, 195).

Theme B
Carbon; BTA; Eco-labelling; Standards; DPG; CBD; TRIPS; Services; R&D
CTE Agenda Items 3a, 3b, 7, 8, 9

9) CTE TBT Note on Negotiating History of the Coverage of the Agreement on Technical Barriers to Trade with Regard to Labelling Requirements, Voluntary Standards, and Processes and Production Methods Unrelated to Product Characteristics, WT/CTE/W/10; G/TBT/W/11 (29 August 1995).
10) CTE Note on Taxes and Charges for Environmental Purposes – Border Tax Adjustment, WT/CTE/W/47 (2 May 1997).
11) CTE Note on Information Relevant to the Consideration of the Market Access effects of Eco-Labelling Schemes, WT/CTE/W/150 (29 June 2000).
12) 2009 WTO UNEP Climate Change Report.
13) CTE Note on Eco-Labelling: Overview of Current Work in Various International Foras, JOB/TE/9 (29 September 2010).
14) CTE Note on Item 7: Domestically Prohibited Goods, Assessment of the Product Coverage in Specific International Instruments ("DPG Report"), WT/CTE/W/29 (19 May 1996).
15) CTE Note on the Relationship between the Convention on Biological Diversity (CBD) and the Agreement on the Trade-Related Aspects of Intellectual Property Rights (TRIPS); with focus on Article 27.3 (b), WT/CTE/W/125 (5 October 1999).
16) CTE Note on Items 6 and 9, Discussion Paper on the Environmental Effects of Services Trade Liberalization, WT/CTE/W/218 (3 October 2002).

Theme C
Market Access
CTE6, DDA 31(iii), DDA 32(i)

17) CTE Note on Environmental Requirements and Market Access: Recent Work in OECD and UNCTAD, WT/CTE/W/244 (8 December 2006).
18) CTESS Revision of the Synthesis of Submissions on Environmental Goods in TN/TE/W/63, 17 November 2005, JOB(07)/137 (17 September 2007).
19) CTESS Annex II on Structure of the Outcome Environmental Goods Coverage Under Paragraph 31 (iii), TN/TE/20 (21 April 2011).
20) CTESS Reference Universe of Environmental Goods: Official HS Description (Based on Compilation of Submissions under paragraph 31 (iii) of Doha relevant to the CTESS Work Programme, JOB/TE/3 (22 March 2010); JOB/TE/3/Rev.1 (5 January 2011).

List of Figures and Tables

(Prefix refers to Chapter Number)

Organic Documents of the
Committee on Trade and Environmnet

1. Communication from the Chairman (Peter Sutherland), Trade Negotiations Committee at Official Level (re: Draft Decision on Trade and Environment), MTN.TNC/MIN(94)/1/Rev.1, 11April 1994 (p. 1).

2. Trade and Environment, Decision of 14 April 1994, in Communication from the Chairman, Trade Negotiations Committee at Official Level, MTN.TNC/MIN(94)/1/Rev.1, 11 April 1994, at pp. 4-6; MTN.TNC/W/141, 29 March 1994, at pp.1-3; MTN.TNC/45(MIN), 6 May 1994, Annex II, at pp. 16-18.

3. CTE Work Programme, Annex 1 in Summary of Activities of the Committee on Trade and Environment (1995) Presented by the Chairman, WT/CTE/W/17, 12 December 1995, at pp. 3-8.

4. Paragraph 16, Ministerial Conference (1st Session Singapore 9 - 13 December 1996), Ministerial Declaration, WT/MIN(96)/ DEC (18 December 1996); I.L.M. 218 (1997), at p. 5.

5. Paragraphs 31 – 33, WTO Ministerial Conference (4th Session Doha 9 - 14 November 2001), Ministerial Declaration, WT/MIN(01)/DEC/1 (20 November 2001), at pp. 6-7.

MULTILATERAL TRADE

NEGOTIATIONS

THE URUGUAY ROUND

MTN.TNC/MIN(94)/1/Rev.1
11 April 1994
Special Distribution

(UR-94-0108)

Trade Negotiations Committee
at Official Level

COMMUNICATION FROM THE CHAIRMAN

Revision

The following texts:

— Decision on Acceptance of and Accession to the Agreement Establishing the World Trade Organization (MTN.TNC/W/137);

— Decision on Trade and Environment (MTN.TNC/W/141);

— Decision on Organizational and Financial Consequences flowing from Implementation of the Agreement Establishing the World Trade Organization (MTN.TNC/W/145); and

— Decision on the Establishment of the Preparatory Committee for the World Trade Organization (MTN.TNC/W/142/Rev.1),

were approved by the Trade Negotiations Committee at its meetings at official level on 30 March and 7 April as decisions that would be submitted to the Ministers for adoption at Marrakesh. The rectified text of the Final Act was also approved at the meeting on 30 March, and is being submitted separately for signature by Ministers.

GATT SECRETARIAT

MTN.TNC/MIN(94)/1/Rev.1
Page 4

Trade and Environment

Decision of 14 April 1994

Ministers, meeting on the occasion of signing the Final Act embodying the results of the Uruguay Round of Multilateral Trade Negotiations at Marrakesh on 15 April 1994,

Recalling the preamble of the Agreement establishing the World Trade Organization (WTO), which states that members' "relations in the field of trade and economic endeavour should be conducted with a view to raising standards of living, ensuring full employment and a large and steadily growing volume of real income and effective demand, and expanding the production of and trade in goods and services, while allowing for the optimal use of the world's resources in accordance with the objective of sustainable development, seeking both to protect and preserve the environment and to enhance the means for doing so in a manner consistent with their respective needs and concerns at different levels of economic development,"

Noting:

— the Rio Declaration on Environment and Development, Agenda 21, and its follow-up in GATT, as reflected in the statement of the Chairman of the Council of Representatives to the CONTRACTING PARTIES at their 48th Session in December 1992, as well as the work of the Group on Environmental Measures and International Trade, the Committee on Trade and Development, and the Council of Representatives;

— the work programme envisaged in the Decision on Trade in Services and the Environment; and

— the relevant provisions of the Agreement on Trade-Related Aspects of Intellectual Property Rights,

Considering that there should not be, nor need be, any policy contradiction between upholding and safeguarding an open, non-discriminatory and equitable multilateral trading system on the one hand, and acting for the protection of the environment, and the promotion of sustainable development on the other,

Desiring to coordinate the policies in the field of trade and environment, and this without exceeding the competence of the multilateral trading system, which is limited to trade policies and those trade-related aspects of environmental policies which may result in significant trade effects for its members,

Decide:

— to direct the first meeting of the General Council of the WTO to establish a Committee on Trade and Environment open to all members of the WTO to report to the first biennial meeting of the Ministerial Conference after the entry into force of the WTO when the work and terms of reference of the Committee will be reviewed, in the light of recommendations of the Committee,

— that the TNC Decision of 15 December 1993 which reads, in part, as follows:

"(a) to identify the relationship between trade measures and environmental measures, in order to promote sustainable development;

(b) to make appropriate recommendations on whether any modifications of the provisions of the multilateral trading system are required, compatible with the open, equitable and non-discriminatory nature of the system, as regards, in particular:

— the need for rules to enhance positive interaction between trade and environmental measures, for the promotion of sustainable development, with special consideration to the needs of developing countries, in particular those of the least developed among them; and

— the avoidance of protectionist trade measures, and the adherence to effective multilateral disciplines to ensure responsiveness of the multilateral trading system to environmental objectives set forth in Agenda 21 and the Rio Declaration, in particular Principle 12; and

— surveillance of trade measures used for environmental purposes, of trade-related aspects of environmental measures which have significant trade effects, and of effective implementation of the multilateral disciplines governing those measures;"

constitutes, along with the preambular language above, the terms of reference of the Committee on Trade and Environment,

— that, within these terms of reference, and with the aim of making international trade and environmental policies mutually supportive, the Committee will initially address the following matters, in relation to which any relevant issue may be raised:

— the relationship between the provisions of the multilateral trading system and trade measures for environmental purposes, including those pursuant to multilateral environmental agreements;

— the relationship between environmental policies relevant to trade and environmental measures with significant trade effects and the provisions of the multilateral trading system;

— the relationship between the provisions of the multilateral trading system and:

(a) charges and taxes for environmental purposes

(b) requirements for environmental purposes relating to products, including standards and technical regulations, packaging, labelling and recycling;

— the provisions of the multilateral trading system with respect to the transparency of trade measures used for environmental purposes and environmental measures and requirements which have significant trade effects;

MTN.TNC/MIN(94)/1/Rev.1
Page 6

- the relationship between the dispute settlement mechanisms in the multilateral trading system and those found in multilateral environmental agreements;

- the effect of environmental measures on market access, especially in relation to developing countries, in particular to the least developed among them, and environmental benefits of removing trade restrictions and distortions;

- the issue of exports of domestically prohibited goods,

- that the Committee on Trade and Environment will consider the work programme envisaged in the Decision on Trade in Services and the Environment and the relevant provisions of the Agreement on Trade-Related Aspects of Intellectual Property Rights as an integral part of its work, within the above terms of reference,

- that, pending the first meeting of the General Council of the WTO, the work of the Committee on Trade and Environment should be carried out by a Sub-Committee of the Preparatory Committee of the World Trade Organization (PCWTO), open to all members of the PCWTO,

- to invite the Sub-Committee of the Preparatory Committee, and the Committee on Trade and Environment when it is established, to provide input to the relevant bodies in respect of appropriate arrangements for relations with inter-governmental and non-governmental organizations referred to in Article V of the WTO.

WT/CTE/W/17
Page 3
[12 December 1995]

Annex 1

At its meeting on 16 February 1995, the Committee on Trade and Environment adopted the following schedule of meetings and programme of work:

6-7 April:-	- Item 4: "the provisions of the multilateral trading system with respect to the transparency of trade measures used for environmental purposes and environmental measures and requirements which have significant trade effects" - Item 5: "the relationship between the dispute settlement mechanisms in the multilateral trading system and those found in multilateral environmental agreements" - Item 10: "appropriate arrangements for relations with non-governmental organizations referred to in Article V of the WTO and transparency of documentation"
21-22 June:	- Item 8: "TRIPS" - Item 9: "Services" - Item 2: "the relationship between environmental policies relevant to trade and environmental measures with significant trade effects and the provisions of the multilateral trading system"
Early September:	- Item 6: "the effect of environmental measures on market access, especially in relation to developing countries, in particular to the least developed among them, and environmental benefits of removing trade restrictions and distortions"
Late October:	- Item 1: "the relationship between the provisions of the multilateral trading system and trade measures for environmental purposes, including those pursuant to multilateral environmental agreements" - Item 3: "the relationship between the provisions of the multilateral trading system and: (a) charges and taxes for environmental purposes (b) requirements for environmental purposes relating to products, including standards and technical regulations, packaging, labelling and recycling - Stocktaking and planning program of work for 1995/1996

WT/CTE/W/17
Page 4-5
[12 December 1995]

Annex 2

The Committee on Trade and Environment

The informal consultations made evident the following points:

That the stocktaking is more a process-related exercise than a substance-related analysis and, therefore, the result of this exercise has to be a detailed work programme to advance the CTE mandate, i.e. to produce a report:

(a) identifying the relationship between trade measures and environmental measures in order to promote sustainable development;
(b) making recommendations on whether any modifications to WTO provisions are required, compatible with the open, equitable and non-discriminatory nature of the system; and
(c) complying with the mandate of the Ministerial Decision on Trade in Services and Environment.

In order to establish a more focused but well-balanced work program, the Chairman submits the following proposals:

(a) to keep all items on our agenda, but to move, whenever possible, from the discussion of agenda items to the analysis of those issues identified during the debate as the core of each item and, to that end, to organize our future work programme on the basis of the proposal submitted below;
(b) to continue the process of analysis of these issues until May 1996, when a new review of the work programme will take place;
(c) the list of issues identified next to each item is not necessarily exhaustive. Once the discussion of the identified issues is carried out by the Committee, Members would be free to raise other related issues under each agenda item at the same meeting;
(d) As part of the work programme:
    (i) joint informal meetings of the CTE and the CTBT are envisaged, subject to the agreement of the CTBT, to analyze the applicability of the TBT Agreement to eco-labelling and the possible need for further disciplines for eco-labelling;
    (ii) all other issues identified in the table below and items in the agenda would be discussed in the Plenary but informal open-ended meetings, back to back to the Plenary, would be convened when a detailed analysis of a topic is necessary or a paper on a specific issue is submitted for discussion;
    (iii) some few studies/reports to be prepared by the Secretariat have been suggested in addition to those already in course. The Secretariat is encouraged to continue to cooperate closely with, and to take full advantage of available and forthcoming studies in, UNCTAD, UNEP and other intergovernmental institutions.

WT/CTE/W/17
Page 6
12 December 1995

The Committee on Trade and Environment

Item on the Work Programme	*Issues*	*Studies*	*When to be discussed*
Item one: "The relationship between the provisions of the multilateral trading system and trade measures for environmental purposes, including those pursuant to multilateral environmental agreements"	- ensuring the compatibility of trade measures taken pursuant to MEAs and the WTO - adequacy of WTO transparency mechanisms concerning trade measures included in relevant MEAs - see item 5		26/27 October 95 early February 96 (7/8 February 96) 26/27 October 95 early February 96 (7/8 February 96)
Item three: "The relationship between the provisions of the multilateral trading system and:			
(a)charges and taxes for environmental purposes	- environmental taxes which could be adjusted at the border and their WTO-consistency	- gather information on national environmental taxes for the study	26/27 October 95 early February 96 (7/8 February 96)
(b)requirements for environmental purposes relating to products, including standards and technical regulations, packaging, labelling and recycling"	- applicability of the TBT Agreement to eco-labelling - adequacy, from both the trade and environmental perspectives, of WTO rules regarding eco-labelling and possible need for further disciplines and transparency		Joint Informal Meetings of the CTE + CTBT[****]

[****]Report to the CTE once work is completed.

WT/CTE/W/17
Page 7
12 December 1995

Item on the Work Programme	*Issues*	*Studies*	*When to be discussed*
Item three (b) cont'd	- adequacy, from both the trade and environmental perspectives, of WTO rules regarding packaging, handling, and other environmental regulations, requirements and standards, including the possible need for further disciplines and transparency		26/27 October 95 early February 96 (7/8 February 96)
Item four: "The provisions of the multilateral trading system with respect to the transparency of trade measures used for environmental purposes and environmental measures and requirements which have significant trade effects"	- examination of the proposal that Members should establish environmental enquiry points - see items 1 and 3		14/15 December 95 - item to be revisited in May 96, in order to determine whether and where further gaps in transparency existed
Item five: "The relationship between the dispute settlement mechanisms in the multilateral trading system and those found in multilateral environmental agreements"	- see item 1 - environmental expertise in trade dispute settlement - trade expertise in environmental dispute settlement		early February 96 (7/8 February 95)
Item six: "The effect of environmental measures on market access, especially in relation to developing countries, in particular to the least developed among them, and environmental benefits of removing trade restrictions and distortions"	- the effect of environmental measures on market access - the environmental benefits of removing trade restrictions and distortions, including tariff escalation, subsidies, state trading, excessively high tariffs	- environmental measures on market access and setting up of a mechanism to survey environmental measures	mid March 96 (13/14 March 96) mid March 96 (13/14 March 96)

WT/CTE/W/17
Page 8
12 December 1995

Item on the Work Programme	*Issues*	*Studies*	*When to be discussed*
Item seven: "The issue of exports of domestically prohibited goods"	- DPGs, and whether there is a need for a DPG Agreement		14/15 December 95
Item eight: "Trade-Related Aspects of Intellectual Property Rights and the environment"	- the relationship of the TRIPs Agreement to access to and transfer of technology and the development of environmentally-sound technology - the relationship between the TRIPS Agreement and MEAs which contain IPR-related obligations	- analytical paper on factors affecting transfer of environmentally-sound technology	end April 96 (17/18 April 96) end April 96 (17/18 April 96)
Item nine: "Services and the environment"	- sufficiency of Article XIV of GATS - possible points of contact between relevant MEAs and GATS		early February 96 (7/8 February 96) early February 96 (7/8 February 96)
Item two: "The relationship between environmental policies relevant to trade and environmental measures with significant trade effects and the provisions of the multilateral trading system"			May 96 (21/22 May 96)
Item ten: "Appropriate arrangements for relations with non-governmental organizations referred to in Article V of the WTO and transparency of documentation"			in the CTE[*****]

[*****]Once a decision is adopted by the General Council.

WORLD TRADE ORGANIZATION

[EXTRACT, p. 5]
WT/MIN(96)/DEC
18 December 1996

(96-5316)

MINISTERIAL CONFERENCE
Singapore, 9-13 December 1996

SINGAPORE MINISTERIAL DECLARATION

Adopted on 13 December 1996

Trade and Environment

16. The Committee on Trade and Environment has made an important contribution towards fulfilling its Work Programme. The Committee has been examining and will continue to examine, *inter alia*, the scope of the complementarities between trade liberalization, economic development and environmental protection. Full implementation of the WTO Agreements will make an important contribution to achieving the objectives of sustainable development. The work of the Committee has underlined the importance of policy coordination at the national level in the area of trade and environment. In this connection, the work of the Committee has been enriched by the participation of environmental as well as trade experts from Member governments and the further participation of such experts in the Committee's deliberations would be welcomed. The breadth and complexity of the issues covered by the Committee's Work Programme shows that further work needs to be undertaken on all items of its agenda, as contained in its report. We intend to build on the work accomplished thus far, and therefore direct the Committee to carry out its work, reporting to the General Council, under its existing terms of reference.

World Trade Organization

[EXTRACT, pp. 6-7]
WT/MIN(01)/DEC/1
20 November 2001
(01-5859)

Ministerial Conference
Fourth Session
Doha, 9-14 November 2001

MINISTERIAL DECLARATION

Adopted on 14 November 2001

Trade and Environment

31. With a view to enhancing the mutual supportiveness of trade and environment, we agree to negotiations, without prejudging their outcome, on:
    (i) the relationship between existing WTO rules and specific trade obligations set out in multilateral environmental agreements (MEAs). The negotiations shall be limited in scope to the applicability of such existing WTO rules as among parties to the MEA in question. The negotiations shall not prejudice the WTO rights of any Member that is not a party to the MEA in question;
    (ii) procedures for regular information exchange between MEA Secretariats and the relevant WTO committees, and the criteria for the granting of observer status;
    (iii) the reduction or, as appropriate, elimination of tariff and non-tariff barriers to environmental goods and services.

    We note that fisheries subsidies form part of the negotiations provided for in paragraph 28.
32. We instruct the Committee on Trade and Environment, in pursuing work on all items on its agenda within its current terms of reference, to give particular attention to:
    (i) the effect of environmental measures on market access, especially in relation to developing countries, in particular the least-developed among them, and those situations in which the elimination or reduction of trade restrictions and distortions would benefit trade, the environment and development;
    (ii) the relevant provisions of the Agreement on Trade-Related Aspects of Intellectual Property Rights; and
    (iii) labelling requirements for environmental purposes.

    Work on these issues should include the identification of any need to clarify relevant WTO rules. The Committee shall report to the Fifth Session of the Ministerial Conference, and make recommendations, where appropriate, with respect to future action, including the desirability of negotiations. The outcome of this work, as well as the negotiations carried out under paragraph

31(i) and (ii), shall be compatible with the open and non-discriminatory nature of the multilateral trading system, shall not add to or diminish the rights and obligations of Members under existing WTO agreements, in particular the Agreement on the Application of Sanitary and Phytosanitary Measures, nor alter the balance of these rights and obligations, and will take into account the needs of developing and least-developed countries.

33. We recognize the importance of technical assistance and capacity building in the field of trade and environment to developing countries, in particular the least-developed among them. We also encourage that expertise and experience be shared with Members wishing to perform environmental reviews at the national level. A report shall be prepared on these activities for the Fifth Session.

ANNEX 2

Triple-win Matrix for Proposals under CTE6, DDA 31iii, 32i An Overview of CTE6/DDA32i Sectoral Discussions

Annex 2A: Triple-win Matrix

Row No.	CTE Document Code	Date issued	Topic / Title	Proponent(s)	Proposal and Ratio T, D, E (Strictly must have a T, D an/or E line	Modality Code	T Score (max 3)	E Score (max 3)	D Score (max 3)	Total Score (+1 max 10)	Notes
1	1 List of Working Documents Categorized by Item of the Work Programme										
2	1.6 Item 6 (Paragraph 32(I) of the Doha Declaration): The effect of environmental measures on market access, especially in relation to developing countries, in particular to the least-developed among them, and environmental benefits of removing trade restrictions and distortions										
3	1.6.1 General										
4	JOB/TE/25	11 January 2012	Proposed Outline of a Workshop on Technology Dissemination: Carbon Capture and Storage Technology to be held in Spring 2012	Kingdom of Saudi Arabia	**Proposed Outline of a Workshop on Technology Dissemination: Carbon Capture and Storage Technology to be held in Spring 2012 with the** overall aim of providing a framework for further work under Paragraph 32(I) of the Doha mandate, in the CTE, on technology dissemination, using market access issues related to CCS technology as a starting point. **Trade:** Reduction of non-tariff barriers (NTBs) to technology dissemination would provide a positive signal to the market and enhance deployment of technologies like CCS. **Environment:** Relevance of CCS to address environmental concerns.	8-TACB					
5	WT/CTE/W/247	29 October 2010	Technology Dissemination	Kingdom of Saudi Arabia	**Greater information exchange on addressing NTBs to technology dissemination and country best practices through CTE organised workshops and briefings by external organisations.Trade** - NTMs such as standards and labeling inhibit technology dissemination. Info sharing and exchange allows greater transparancy and avoids trade disruption; **Environment**- avoids conflict of norms with transparency	8-TACB					
6	WT/CTE/W/240	21 October 2004	Market Access via Organic Commodity Chains – The Case of Organic Cotton	Switzerland	**Information-exchange on role of swiss development co-operation through public private partrnerships in** (i) **Trade:** Enabling market access (ii) **Environment:** addressing environmental objectives as well (iii) **Development:** Addressing capacity building needs of local industries in developing countries including through technology-transfer.	7-Technology 8-TACB					
7	WT/CTE/W/239	12 October 2004	Addressing the Concerns of Developing Countries on the Effects of Environmental Measures on Market Access	European Union	**Emphasis on information exchange as a means to address developing country concerns regarding the effects of environmental requirements on market access.Development:**prevents use of environmental requirements to hamper development of developing countries **Environment:** Environmental objectives can still be met.	8-TACB					
8	WT/CTE/W/207	21 May 2002	The Effects of Environmental Measures on Market Access, especially in relation to Developing Countries, in particular the Least-Developed among them – Paragraph 32(I) of the Doha Ministerial Declaration	India	**Emphasis on considering special needs of developing countries in CTE Work programme. Trade:** Consideration of developing country market access interests. **Development:** prevents use of environmental requirements to hamper development of developing countries hrough setting criteria for standard-setting and compliance with environmental measures.	6-Standards					
9	WT/CTE/W/188	25 April 2001	Legitimate Non-Trade Concerns – Item 6 of the Work Programme	Argentina	**Raising three key environmental and social consequences of trade-related restrictions and distortions.Trade: Commitment to achieving substantial and progressive reductions in support and protection in the agricultural sector including tariffs and susbidies. Environment:** Environmental degradation **Developent:**prevents use of environmental requirements to hamper development of developing countries	1-Tariff 3-SMs					
10	WT/CTE/W/177	27 October 2000	The Study of the Effects of Environmental Measures on Market Access	India	**Agenda setting for CTE work. Trade:** Emphasises need to focus on environmental requirements such as eco-labelling and market access in both positive and negative aspects as well as issues such as availability of information, lack of access to technology, TACB and avoiding unilateral standard-setting**. **Development:** prevents use of environmental requirements to hamper development of developing countries	2-NTMs 6-Standards 7-Technology 8-TACB					
11	WT/CTE/W/105	2 February 1999	Trade Liberalization and the Environment – A Positive Agenda for Trade Reform	Australia	**Agenda setting for the CTE to focus its priority on trade reforms that lead to environmental outcomes.Trade:** Removal of trade barriers-tariffs and NTMs. **Environment:** Beneficial impact through reform of subsidies and tariff-peaks and escalation. **Development:** Given the strong links between poverty and environmental degradation in many countries, policies to ensure that resources are directed towards poor communities and that equity considerations are adequately addressed can also be vital components in promoting ecologically sustainable patterns of development.	1-Tariff 2-NTMs 3-SMs 9-Dev					

Row No.	CTE Document Code	Date Issued	Topic / Title	Proponent(s)	Proposal and Ratio T, D, E (Strictly must have a T, D an/or E line	Modality Code	T Score (max 3)	E Score (max 3)	D Score (max 3)	Total Score (+1 max 10)	Notes
1	1 List of Working Documents Categorized by Item of the Work Programme										
2	1.6 Item 6 (Paragraph 32(i) of the Doha Declaration): The effect of environmental measures on market access, especially in relation to developing countries, in particular to the least-developed among them, and environmental benefits of removing trade restrictions and distortions										
12	WT/CTE/W/83	10 June 1998	Comments by the European Communities on the Secretariat's document WT/CTE/W/67	European Union	**Acknowledgement of usefulness of Secretariat working information on 'double-wins' (for trade and environment) of removing trade distortions) with caveat that often trade liberalisation will not automatically lead to such result.Trade** - removal of trade distortions, **Environment** - removal of trade distortions for environmental goods. There is a need for appropriate environmental policies at national level if the benefits of liberalization, including the environmental ones, are to be realized.	10-RACM					
13	WT/CTE/W/82	7 April 1998	Cluster on Market Access	India	**Agenda setting for CTE work:** Facilitating transfer of technology including by imposing obligation on right holders to transfer such technologies at fair and most favourable terms and conditions, upon demand, to any interested party which has an obligation to adopt these under national law of another country (as for instance in the case of mandatory national environmental standards) or under international law (as for instance in MEAs). **Development:** Technology access for developing countries . **Environment:** Better access to environmental technologies	7-Technology					
14	WT/CTE/W/70	21 November 1997	Liberalization of Trade in Environmental Services and the Environment	United States	**Agenda setting for CTE work:**Benefits of liberalising environmental services and complementing it through liberalising trade in environmental goods.**Trade:** Improved market access for ES. **Environment:** Better dissemination of environmental services	1-Tariff 2-NTMs					
15	WT/CTE/W/36	23 July 1996	Trade Liberalization, the Environment and Sustainable Development	Australia	**Agenda setting for CTE work. Trade:** Specifically highlights a number of key issues in the analysis of the relationship between trade liberalization and the environment including specific examples of trade restrictions such as tariffs, NTMs, subsidies and high internal taxes and examples of priority areas.**Environment:** Highlights investment in agricultural research and extension services and the adoption of appropriate domestic policies to secure sustainable resource management **Development:** Emphasies concerns of low-income commodity commodity dependent countries and agricultural trade reform and opportunities for economic diversification of these countries.	1-Tariff 2-NTMs 3-SMs 4-TM					
16	WT/CTE/W/35	23 July 1996	Trade Liberalization and the Environment	United States	**Agenda setting for CTE work programme to identify areas of strong potential win-win situations where win-wins can be achieved. Trade:** Greater market access through addressing distortions like high tariffs, tariff-escalation, subsdlies and policies of State Trading Enterprises. **Environment:** Internalisation of positive and negative environmental externalities. Role for 'positive' environmental subsidies.	1-Tariff 3-SMs 10-RACM					
17	WT/CTE/W/24	20 March 1996	The Environmental Benefits of Removing Trade Restrictions and Distortions, including Tariff Escalation, Subsidies, State Trading, and Excessively High Tariffs	Argentina	**Agenda setting for further CTE work.** CTE should acknowledge**Trade:** Removing barriers and distortions esp subsides affecting trade in Agriculture **Environment:** Identifying negative consequences of trade barriers and distortions for environment.	1-Tariff 2-NTMs 3-SMs					
18	1.6.2 Agriculture										
19	WT/CTE/W/202	8 October 2001	Organic Farming	Costa Rica	**Report on process launched by Inter-American Institute for Cooperation on Agriculture (IICA) and the ICCI-2 project of the Canadian International Development Agency (CIDA) to promote organic agriculture exports from developing countries as well UNCTAD workshop. Highlights role of support in Costa Rica for organic production which benefits indigenous communities and small producers through information, certification and trade promotion assistance Trade:** Promotion of organic agriculture exports **Development:** Benefit to organic agriculture exports and the sector in developing countries. **Environment:** Environmental benefits of promoting organic agriculture.	8-TACB 9-Dev					
20	WT/CTE/W/127	27 October 1999	Chairman's Report on the FAO/Netherlands Conference on the Multifunctional Character of Agriculture and Land	Argentina	**Trade:** Removal of trade-barriers to agricultural products : **Development:** Benefits for sustainable agriculture in developing countries. **Environment:** Beneficial impacts on agriculture of removing trade barriers	8-TACB					

Row No.	CTE Document Code	Date issued	Topic / Title	Proponent(s)	Proposal and Ratio T, D, E (Strictly must have a T, D an/or E line	Modality Code	T Score (max 3)	E Score (max 3)	D Score (max 3)	Total Score (+1 max 10)	Notes
1	1 List of Working Documents Categorized by Item of the Work Programme										
2	1.6 Item 6 (Paragraph 32(i) of the Doha Declaration): The effect of environmental measures on market access, especially in relation to developing countries, in particular to the least-developed among them, and environmental benefits of removing trade restrictions and distortions										
21	WT/CTE/W/109	16 February 1999	The Agriculture Sector: Environmental Benefits of Trade Liberalization	Brazil	To demonstrate the role that trade liberalization plays in the promotion of sustainable development and to emphasise 'win-wins' for trade and the environment. **Trade:** Removal of trade-barriers to agricultural products such as subsidies and ensuring 'non-trade' concerns do not restrict developing country market access. **Development:** Increased agriuclture income and poverty-reduction through better market access. **Environment:** Better market access and revenues helps in freeing up of more resources in devleoping countries for sustainable agriculture.	1-Tariff 3-SMs 9-Dev 10-RACM					
22	WT/CTE/W/107	15 February 1999	Environmental Effects of Trade Liberalization on Agriculture	Japan	**Trade liberalisation byitself cannot cope with market failures. Proposing the examination of appopriate policy measures , taking into account the actual conditions such as the natural conditions of each country and region as well as the different agricultural production methods.** **Environment:** active government intervention required to maintain sustainability and multifinctionality of agriculture.	10-RACM					
23	WT/CTE/W/106	11 February 1999	Agriculture and the Environment – The Case of Export Subsidies	Argentina, Australia, Brazil, Canada, Chile, Colombia, Indonesia, Malaysia, New Zealand, Paraguay, Philippines, Thailand, United States and Uruguay	**Proposing a case for the removal of export subsidies.** **Trade:** Better market access for agricultural products. **Development:** Beneficial impacts on commodity prices leading to less economic instability, lower poverty, less presssure on migration from rural to urban areas and greater food security and for **Environment:** lowered pressure on the environment due to consequent trade and development benefits of removing export subsidies.	3-SMs					
24	WT/CTE/W/100	8 January 1999	Environmental Effects of Trade Liberalization in the Agricultural Sector	Norway	**Emphasises importance of maintaining a minimum level of domestic agricultural production to enable provision of environmentally related public goods. Environment:** Benefit to environment from the maintaining a certain level of domestic agriculture.	10-RACM					
25	WT/CTE/W/97	10 August 1998	Non-Trade Concerns in the Next Agricultural Negotiations	Argentina	**Proposal to eliminate those trade restrictions and distortions esp subsidies that prevent the true production costs from being reflected in the actual price of goods traded and, only then, attempt to counterbalance market failures.** **Trade:** Enhancing market opportunities for countries that cannot afford to subsidize local production **Development:**Reducing rural poverty and increasing food security in developing countries **Environment:** Beneficial effect on environment by reducing over-exploitation	3-SMs					
26	1.6.3 Energy										
27	WT/CTE/W/215	23 September 2002	Energy Taxation, Subsidies and Incentives in OECD Countries and their Economic and Trade Implications on Developing Countries, in particular Developing Oil Producing and Exporting Countries	Kingdom of Saudi Arabia	**Highlights the benefits of removing trade distortions in the energy sector such as energy subsidies and carbon taxes including for oil-exporting countries. Also highlights costs to economies including developing ones from imposition of carbon tax and calls for more appropriate measues based on carbon content.** **Trade:** Safeguards market access for oil-exporting including developing countries and avoid negative impatcs on competitiveness. **Development:**Avoids regressive distibutional impacts of measures such as a carbon tax in countries which rely on fossil-fuels. **Environment:** Removal of coal subsidies enables better reflection of actual pricing and carbon-content with better results for the environment	2-NTMs 3-SMs					

Row No.	CTE Document Code	Date issued	Topic / Title	Proponent(s)	Proposal and Ratio T, D, E (Strictly must have a T, D an/or E line	Modality Code	T Score (max 3)	E Score (max 3)	D Score (max 3)	Total Score (+1 max 10)	Notes
1	1 List of Working Documents Categorized by Item of the Work Programme										
2	1.6 Item 6 (Paragraph 32(I) of the Doha Declaration): The effect of environmental measures on market access, especially in relation to developing countries, in particular to the least-developed among them, and environmental benefits of removing trade restrictions and distortions										
28	WT/CTE/W/185	13 February 2001	Environmentally Harmful and Trade Distorting Measures and Policies in Energy Markets	European Union	**Guidance for CTE work and analysis: Request for revised CTE analysis on trade distortions in the energy sector.** Need to consider more recent data and a broader assessmemnt of measures prevalent in the energy sector and also a more nuanced approach to discern trade-distortive impacts of measures in the sector. Assessment of environmental and climate considerations is important as also recognition of energy as an 'intermediate'good with market failures having an impact on upstream activity.	8-TACB					
29	WT/CTE/W/98	30 September 1998	The Energy Sector – The Case of Alcohol Fuel (Ethanol)	Brazil	**Request for CTE analysis:** how to improve market access for alternative energy sources based on biomass. **Trade:** Improved market access for biomass-based renewanle energy sources such as ethanol.Elimination of trade distortions such as tariffs, internal taxes, domestic and export subsidies. **Development:** Benefits include job creation,diversification of energy sources,development of new car engine technologies and development of environmentally sustainable agricultural production processes **Environment:** Environmental benefits including through better allocation of resources and reduction of health costs related to atmospheric pollution in large urban centers. Facilitating the accomplishment of the climate mitigation commitments undertaken in Kyoto.	1-Tariff 2-NTMs 3-SMs 8-TACB					
30	1.6.4 Fisheries										
31	JOB/TE/27	29 October 2012	Combating Illegal, Unreported and Unregulated (IUU) Fishing: Establishment of a European Union System to Prevent, Deter and Eliminate IUU Fishing – a Global Problem and a Key Challenge for Europe	European Union	**Adoption of EU Framework on Illegal, Unreported and Unregulated (IUU) fishingto ensure full traceability of all marine fishery products traded with the EU.** **Trade:** restricts trade and market access of fishery products to the EU for non-compliant operators **Development:** Helps developing countries and coastal communities heavily dependent on fisheries for their livelihoods. **Environment:** Helps conservation of fish stocks through avoiding illegal fishing	8-TACB					
32	WT/CTE/W/226	24 April 2003	Analysis on the Relationship between Fisheries Subsidies and Over-exploitation of Fisheries Resources	Japan	**Reflection on IUU fishing and provide some analyses on the relationship between fisheries subsidies and over-exploitation, taking into account discussions in international organizations as well as those taking place within WTO. Emphasises need for understanding that impacts of subsidies on resources vary depending on resource status and fishery management regimes. Lack of fisheries management can bring over-capacity even without subsdies. Underlines importance for CTE to continue discussion on possible impacts of fisheries subsidies on resources, taking into account the work of the FAO and OECD.**	3-SMs 10-RACM					
33	WT/CTE/W/222	6 February 2003	Sustainable Development and the Trade of Forest and Fishery Products	Japan	**Linking trade liberalisation in fisheries products to status of fishery resource management.** Certain types of subsidies may be beneficial in this regard. Flexibility in tariff reduction and avoiding zero for zero tariff liberalisation in fisheries.No need to create special disciplines for fisheries sector but there is a need for clarifying and improving disciplines under SCM Agreement. **Trade:** Market access that is responsive to and supportive of sustainable fisheries management and sustainable development. **Environment:** Sustainability of fishery resources **Development:** Technical and financial assistance for fisheries management in develoing countries together with special and differential treatment and consideration of needs of developing and least-devleoped countries.	10-RACM					
34	TN/MA/W/15/Add.1										

Row No.	CTE Document Code	Date issued	Topic / Title	Proponent(s)	Proposal and Ratio T, D, E (Strictly must have a T, D an/or E line	Modality Code	T Score (max 3)	E Score (max 3)	D Score (max 3)	Total Score (+1 max 10)	Notes
1	1 List of Working Documents Categorized by Item of the Work Programme										
2	1.6 Item 6 (Paragraph 32(i) of the Doha Declaration): The effect of environmental measures on market access, especially in relation to developing countries, in particular to the least-developed among them, and environmental benefits of removing trade restrictions and distortions										
35	WT/CTE/W/204	19 March 2002	Fisheries Subsidies – Paragraph 32(i) of the Doha Ministerial Declaration	New Zealand	**Information exchange: Presentation of findings from a University of British Columbia paper that analyse the theoretical impact of subsidies under several conditions of access and management and for several categories of subsidy.** The paper challenge the environmental benefits of certain categories. of subsidy. According to New Zealand, the paper potentially reinforces the case for improving WTO disciplines over subsidies which can be demonstrated to have negative trade impacts. **Trade:** Better market access for fishery products through removal of subsidies. **Development:** Better market access for developing country producers and favourable impact on local fisheries. **Environment:** More sustainable fisheries	8-TACB					
36	WT/CTE/W/175	24 October 2000	Utilization of Subsidies and their positive role in the Fisheries Sector	Korea	**Guidance for CTE work. Proposal highlights positive role that some fisheries subsidies can play in conserving fisheries resources and improving the marine environment in addition to respoinding to needs of fishing communities and increasing fishing incomes. Cautions against avoid rushing to conclusions on the effects of fisheries subsidies without fully considering all relevant factors. Calls for considering the positive and negative effects of fisheries subsidies in a balanced way. Constructive discussions at the CTE requires a comprehensive approach that takes into full account the socio-economic needs of the fishing industry, the unique domestic environment and development needs of countries. Development:** Certain subsidies respond to needs of fishing communities and must be taken into account. **Environment:** Certain subsidies can play a positive role for marine environment.	10-RACM					
37	WT/CTE/W/173	23 October 2000	Japan's basic position on the Fishery Subsidy Issue	Japan	**Guidance for CTE work.** Proposal states there is no clear evidence to show depletion of fish stocks due to fisheries subsidies. **Environment:** Rather it is possible to show depletion of fish stocks due to lack of adequate fishery management including insufficient measures against illegal, unreported and unregulated (IUU) fishing activities. Many factors are involved in fish stocks depletion and CTE needs to consider all factors.FAO may be better placed to undertake technical work and feed results back to the CTE.	8-TACB 10-RACM					
38	WT/CTE/W/154	4 July 2000	Environmentally-harmful and Trade-distorting Subsidies in Fisheries	United States	**Reviews the international debate on the environmental and trade implications of fisheries subsidies and identifies categories of fisheries sector subsidies that are environmentally harmful and that distort trade.Based on this it states that a general consensus is emerging on the need for subsidies reform in the fisheries sector. In particular, there is growing support for the view that certain types of subsidies in fisheries are harmful to resource sustainability and distort trade. Trade:** Fairer market acces for fisheries through subsidy reform. **Development:** Impact on livelihoods and access to fishery resources in developing countries through subsidy reform **Environment:** Greater sustainability and conservation of fish stocks through subsidy reform.	8-TACB 3-SMs					
39	WT/CTE/W/134	24 February 2000	Subsidies in the Fisheries Sector: Update on Recent Work Conducted by New Zealand	New Zealand	**Information exchange and guidng CTE work:** Proposal alludes to ongoing anaylitical work by New Zealand on fisheries subsdiies and welcomes contributions by WTO members and experience sharing in this regard. Emphasises important role of WTO in subsidy reform and considration of new WTO rules given the absence of concerted unilateral action by members to reduce and eliminate fisheries subsidies that adversely impact on trade and sustainable development. **Trade:** Fairer market acces for fisheries through subsidy reform. **Development:** Impact on livelihoods and access to fishery resources in developing countries through subsidy reform **Environment:** Greater sustainability and conservation of fish stocks through subsidy reform.	8-TACB 3-SMs					
40	WT/CTE/W/132	21 February 2000	Fisheries Subsidies and the Environment	Iceland	**Guiding CTE work: Guide for further CTE work on fisheries subsidies based on previous work done and studies presented and request for WTO to conduct a factual study on impacts of fisheries subsidies taking into account (Trade):** trade and trade distortions in the fishing sector,fisheries management,overcapacity and overfishing, **(Environment):** the environmental impacts of fisheries and **(Development)**:the importance of the fisheries sector to the interests of the developing and the least-developed countries.	8-TACB 3-SMs					

Row No.	CTE Document Code	Date issued	Topic / Title	Proponent(s)	Proposal and Ratio T, D, E (Strictly must have a T, D an/or E line	Modality Code	T Score (max 3)	E Score (max 3)	D Score (max 3)	Total Score (+1 max 10)	Notes
1	1 List of Working Documents Categorized by Item of the Work Programme										
2	1.6 Item 6 (Paragraph 32(i) of the Doha Declaration): The effect of environmental measures on market access, especially in relation to developing countries, in particular to the least-developed among them, and environmental benefits of removing trade restrictions and distortions										
41	WT/CTE/W/121	28 June 1999	Benefits of Eliminating Trade Distorting and Environmentally Damaging Subsidies in the Fisheries Sector	New Zealand	**Recommendations for a CTE work programme that would assist in advancing work on fish subsidies** including evaluation of adequacy and implementation of existing subsidy rules and recognition of the fact that the full implementation of the FAO Plan of Action would contribute to important trade, developmental and environmental goals to which WTO and FAO members are committed.	8-TACB 3-SMs					
42	WT/CTE/W/111	11 March 1999	On the Environmental Impact of Fisheries Subsidies – Report by the Icelandic Ministry of Fisheries	Iceland	**Information exchange and guiding CTE work: lays out environmental impact of fisheries subsidies and speculates that given recent estimates of fisheries subsidies asubstantial part of the current overexploitation of the world's fish stocksand habit damage in the oceans is a direct consequence of past and current fisheries subsidies. Environment:**Reduced fishing effort due to subsidy reform, less exploited fish stocks and reduced ocean habitat damage due to reduction in fishing operations.	3-SMs 8-TACB 10-RACM					
43	WT/CTE/W/103	25 January 1999	The Icelandic Fisheries Management System – A Market-driven Sustainable Fisheries Regime	Iceland	**Information exchange and guidng CTE work: Presentation of fisheries management system as implemented in Iceland and its positive impacts on fish stocks and sustainability. Identificiation of overcapacity in global fishing fleet as predominant cause of depletion of fish stocks and lack of rigid fisheries management systems and government subsidies as two contributing factors for overcapacity. Environment:** Proposes elimination of government subsidies as the key single action for positive results towards achieveing sustainable development in fisheries.	3-SMs 8-TACB 10-RACM					
44	and Corr.1	27 January 1999									
45	WT/CTE/W/99	6 November 1998	Comments by the European Communities on the Secretariat's Document WT/CTE/W/80 on Subsidies and Aids Granted in the Fishing Industry	European Union	**Information exchange:** Including higlighting EU participation in the OECD study "Towards sustainable fisheries", as well as in the financing of technical working groups within the FAO, including one on overcapacity in the fisheries sector. Emphasis that subsidies do not necessarily exert increased pressure on fisheries resource and that the overexploitation of stocks is not due to the subsidies regime. **Guidance for CTE work:** It would be interesting to study whetherthe absence of subsidies targeted at adjustment of fishing activity could lead to undesirable overexploitation of fisheries resources.	8-TACB					
46	WT/CTE/W/52	21 May 1997	The Fisheries Sector	New Zealand	**Guidance for CTE work: Considers it timely and appropriate to examine the relationship between trade distortions in the fisheries sector such as tariff escalationa and subsidies and problems of fisheries resource sustainability. Need for review of whether existing WTO rules adequately regulate such subsidies.Environment:**Such an examination will also assist in identifying the expected benefits for the marine environment in removing trade distortions. **Development:** Secure interests of developing countries and safeguard sustainable development.	1-Tariff 3-SMs 8-TACB					
47	WT/CTE/W/51	19 May 1997	Environmental and Trade Benefits of Removing Subsidies in the Fisheries Sector	United States	**Information exchange and guidance for CTE work: Removing subsidies will generatesignificant benefits for trade and the environment. Trade:**Addressing subsidy-induced trade-distortion which affects prices and distorts sources of supply will benefit trade. **Environment:** Will help reflect internal costs and reduce the problems of overcapacity and over fishing, a problem especially acute for developing countries whose economies are less diversified and who are therefore more dependent on export earnings from their natural resources.Certain environmental subsidies can play a positive role in reducing effort and capacity in fisheries such as vessel and fishing permit buybacks to bring vessels out of production; retraining of fishermen stock enhancement and R&D in "clean" harvesting technology	3-SMs 8-TACB					

Row No.	CTE Document Code	Date issued	Topic / Title	Proponent(s)	Proposal and Ratio T, D, E (Strictly must have a T, D an/or E line	Modality Code	T Score (max 3)	E Score (max 3)	D Score (max 3)	Total Score (+1 max 10)	Notes
1	1 List of Working Documents Categorized by Item of the Work Programme										
2	1.6 Item 6 (Paragraph 32(i) of the Doha Declaration): The effect of environmental measures on market access, especially in relation to developing countries, in particular to the least-developed among them, and environmental benefits of removing trade restrictions and distortions										
48	1.6.5 Forestry										
49	WT/CTE/W/233	22 October 2003	Bilateral Cooperation between Japan and Indonesia in Combating Illegal Logging	Japan	**Information exchange and guidance for further CTE work: Presentation on Japan-Indonesia "Joint Announcement" and "Action Plan" on the Cooperation in Combating Illegal Logging and the Trade in Illegally Logged Timber and Wood Products signed on 24 June 2003 as an example of initiatives that contribute to the promotion of global sustainable forest management and environmental protection, while keeping balance with the development of forest products trade. Trade:** Sustainable trade in forestry products **Environment:** Conservation of forestry resources including by restricting trade in illegally harvested timber.	8-TACB 10-RACM					
50	WT/CTE/W/222	6 February 2003	Sustainable Development and the Trade of Forest and Fishery Products	Japan	**Proposes sustainable forest management as the basis for:** **Trade:** Sustainable trade in forestry products. Avoidance of trade liberalisation that leads to forest devastation. **Environment:** Consevaration of forestry resources including through appropriate export restrictions and export taxes.	10-RACM					
51	TN/MA/W/15/Add.1										
52	WT/CTE/W/211	11 June 2002	Issues on Forestry Products Trade and Environment	Japan	**Information exchange and guidance for further CTE work** on trade and forestry issues including on: **Trade:** Examining the role of extending the export restrictions and labelling on forestry products as a conservation tool.**Environment:** Conservation of forestry resources.	5-Export 6-Standards 8-TACB					
53	WT/CTE/W/81	11 March 1998	Forests – A National Experience	Canada	NEED DOC						
54	G/TBT/W/61										

Row No.	CTE Document	Date issued	Topic / Title	Proponent(s)	Proposal - Modality and T, E, D Rationale	Modality Code	T Score (max 3)	E Score (max 3)	D Score (max 3)	Total Score (+1 max 10)	Notes
	4 Submissions by Participants /Members										
1	4.4 Paragraph 31 (iii)										
2	JOB/TE/18	1 April 2011	Views of the Small Vulnerable Economies on the Negotiation of Paragraph 31(iii) of the Doha Ministerial Declaration	Small Vulnerable Economies	**Proposal on negotiating modalities for Para 31 (iii).Any outcome should effectively strikes a balance between market access, environmental benefits and the legitimate objective of SVE Members to maintain policies that will allow sustainable development. Development**: SVEs also require S&DT in line with Para 50 of the Doha mandate which in turn would lead to fulfilment of the sustainable development mandate contained in Para 51. The negotiations should not follow a sectoral, market-access type approach and cannot and shall not adversely affect the flexibilities that have been agreed for SVEs in other negotiating areas of the Doha Development Agenda, such as in NAMA and Agriculture. Proposal also stresses and reiterate the importance of technical assistance, capacity building and transfer of technology.**Environment:** Due recognition should be given to the fact that many developing countries, including SVEs, contribute least to the degradation of the environment, but suffer most of its negative consequences.	7-Technology 8-TACB 9-Dev					
3	JOB/TE/17	24 March 2011	Elements for Ensuring a Sustainable Development Outcome under Paragraph 31(iii) of the Doha Ministerial Declaration	Plurinational State of Bolivia and Bolivarian Republic of Venezuela	**Highlights elements of a sustainable development outcome for the negotiations on paragraph 31(iii) with emphasis on S&DT and greater policy space for developing countries.** That would ensure both the mutual supportiveness between trade and environment and a "triple-win" situation in which environment, development and trade might benefit. **Trade:** Developed countries do not resort to unilateral tariff and non-tariff measures and maintain other policies including susbsidies and standards detrimental to developing countries' trade interests. **Development:** Developed countries to take lead in making commitments under DMD, relaxation or removal of patent and related IPR protection on environmentally sound technologies, creation of technology pools to benefit developing countries, provision for financing and technology transfer and ensuring susbidies provided by developing countries for legitimate development and environmental goals are treated as non-actionable. **Environment:** environment goals should be considered non-actionable. In addition there is need for a peace-clause restraining DSU action against developing country measures take under WTO covered agreements for legitimate environmental policy objectives.	1-Tariff 2-NTMs 3-SMs 6-Standards 7-Technology 9-Dev 10-RACM					
4	JOB/TE/16	11 March 2011	Combined Approach for Environmental Goods	Mexico and Chile	**Proposal for negotiating liberalisation modalities based on overlap between self-selected products among developed and developing countries and others to be based on negotiations following a 'request-offer' approach. Trade:** Greater market access for selected products through reduction or removal of tariffs following Swiss formula. **Development:** S&DT for Developing countries through flexibility of self-selection, requirement to reduce tariffs only by 50percent in addition to NAMA commitment while developed countries reduce tariffs to zero.Longer tariff implementation commitments (10 years) for developing countries compared to developed ones (5 years).	1-Tariff 9-Dev					
5	and Corr.1	21 March 2011									
6	JOB/TE/15	7 March 2011	A Hybrid Approach to the Liberalization of Environmental Goods under Paragraph 31(iii)	Australia; Colombia; Hong Kong, China; Norway; Singapore	**Proposal on negotiating modalities-a hybrid approach to liberalisation of environmental goods based on a 'common-core' list, a complementary self-selected list, a list based on 'request-offer' and unilateral liberalisation for relevant environmental projects. Trade:** Tariff reduction or elimination as appropriate for selected goods. **Development:** S&DT though Longer implementation periods and/or differential tariff-cuts for developing countries, optional participation by LDCs.	1-Tariff					

Row No.	CTE Document	Date issued	Topic / Title	Proponent(s)	Proposal - Modality and T, E, D Rationale	Modality Code	T Score (max 3)	E Score (max 3)	D Score (max 3)	Total Score (+1 max 10)	Notes
	4 Submissions by Participants /Members										
1	4.4 Paragraph 31 (iii)										
7	JOB/TE/13	15 February 2011	Simulation on Tariff Reduction of Proposed Environmental Goods in the Context of NAMA and Paragraph 31(iii) Negotiations	China	**Information Exchange**: Provides results of a simulation of tariff reduction on proposed environmental goods in the context of NAMA and Para 31 (iii) negotiations.	8-TACB					
8	JOB/TE/6	1 July 2010	Environmental Goods and Services, Paragraph 31 (III) – Biofuels	Brazil	**Proposes a strong case for inclusion of biofuels as environmental goods towards achieving a 'triple-win' outcome on trade, development and environment. Trade:** Reduction of tariffs and NTBs on biofuels **Development:** Promoting agro-industrial development without affecting food-security, trigerring inftarsucture development including in transport, generating rural incomes and poverty reduction, co-generation of electricty and use as a fuel for cooking and increased energy security through reduced dependence on oil imports, uses less complicated technology that is easily deployed in developing countries. **Environment:** Reduction in GHG emissions and application in bioplastics, biopolymers and other degradable materials.	1-Tariff 2-NTMs					
9	TN/TE/W/76	30 June 2010	Environmental Goods and Services – Paragraph 31(III) – Special and Differential Treatment	Argentina and Brazil	**Reflecting S&DT principles including in tariff reductions, flexibility of phase-outs and exemptions for developing countries. Trade:** Greater market access for EGS from developing countries **Development:** More ambitious reduction by developed countries for EGS of export interest from developing countries and preseving domestic 'policy space'. Information should be made vailable to enable developing countries to better assess available environmentally sound technologies in a given field	1-Tariff 8-TACB 9-Dev					
10	JOB/TE/5	23 June 2010	Paragraph 31 (iii) of the Doha Ministerial Declaration – Environmental Goods	Singapore	**Proposes 35 products for liberalisation under categories of (i) waste management; (ii) air pollution control; (iii) noise pollution control; (iv) wastewater treatment; (v) environmental monitoring, analysis and analysis equipment; (vi) renewable products and energy sources; and (vii) energy-efficient products. Trade:** Reduction of tariffs and NTBs on identified products. **Environment:** Singapore has included several products related to renewable energy sources relevant to climate-change mitigation.	1-Tariff 2-NTMs					
11	JOB/TE/4	14 June 2010	Continued work under Paragraph 31 (iii) of the Doha Ministerial Declaration	Qatar	**Qatar's list of environmental goods complementing its previous submisison under TN/TE/W/19 and identifying specific tariff lines coded by the six-digit Harmonized System (HS) 2002 and product description of Natural Gas goods** and the components of the technologies using it.**Trade:** Reduction of tariffs and NTBs on identified products. **Environment:** Lower GHG emissions associated with natural gas and related products and relevance to climate-change mitigation.	1-Tariff 2-NTMs					

Row No.	CTE Document	Date Issued	Topic / Title	Proponent(s)	Proposal - Modality and T, E, D Rationale	Modality Code	T Score (max 3)	E Score (max 3)	D Score (max 3)	Total Score (+1 max 10)	Notes
	4 Submissions by Participants /Members										
1	4.4 Paragraph 31 (iii)										
12	JOB/TE/2	16 February 2010	Continued Work Under Paragraph 31 (iii) of the Doha Ministerial Declaration	Philippines	**Philippines' submission of environmental goods with particular emphasis on renewable including solar energy-related parts and components. Trade:** reduction of tariffs and NTBs on proposed products. **Development:** Emphasis on developing countries' capacities to access and use environmental goods ginvolving (i) Common but differentiated responsibilities through S&DT (ii) Addressing NTBs and (iii) Establishment of a viable technology absorption and diffusion mechanisms and the provision of technical assistance and capacity-building relating thereto.**Environment:** Environmental benefit and rationale listed for each of teh submitted products. E.g.;Relevance of renewable including solar energy products to climate-change mitigation.	1-Tariff 2-NTMs					
13	JOB(09)/184	15 December 2009	Scheme for Request and Offer Procedure in Environmental Goods – Non-paper	Brazil	**Submission on negotiating modalities-outlines scheme for request and offer procedure in environmental goods.**	1-Tariff					
14	TN/TE/W/75	27 November 2009	Proposal on Environmental Goods and Services	Japan	**Inclusion of energy-efficient products as environmental goods proposed by Japan to address climate-change mitigation. Trade:** Greater market access for energy-efficient products **Environment:** Climate benefits from reduced use of energy	1-Tariff 2-NTMs					
15	and Add.1	16 February 2010									
16	and Add.2	10 January 2011									
17	JOB(09)/177	27 November 2009	Environmental Goods and Services for Sustainable Development	Peru	**Proposes inclusion of agricultural products such as organic products and traditional products derived from biodiversity, artisanal technologies with low environmental impact etc within a definition of environmental goods** that would (a) be compatible with sustainable development needs of developing countries (b) take into account different levels of social and economic development among Members (c) increase developing countries' participation in the production and international trade of environmental goods and (d) ensure effective environmental benefits. Need to also focus discussions on environmental services such as preservation of river basins, ecotourism services, the prevention of deforestation. **Trade:** Elimination of tariffs and NTBs on organic products. **Development:** Relevance of organic products for incomes and livelihoods; Need to include specific provisions on transfer of clean-technologies. **Environment:** Beneficial impacts of organic agriculture and use of artisanal technologies on environment and biodiversity. Relevance of environmental services to forests and bidoversity protection.	1-Tariff 2-NTMs 7-Technology 10-RACM					
18	TN/TE/W/74	23 November 2009	The Doha Round and Climate Change	Argentina	**Lowering tariffs and NTBs identifed as necessary for national projects including CDM projects under an 'integrated approach' identifying both project categories as well as specific goods and services required for these projects and used for the duration of the projects. Trade:** Greater (though temporary) market access for CDM relevant goods and services.	1-Tariff 2-NTMs					

Row No.	CTE Document	Date issued	Topic / Title	Proponent(s)	Proposal - Modality and T, E, D Rationale	Modality Code	T Score (max 3)	E Score (max 3)	D Score (max 3)	Total Score (+1 max 10)	Notes
	4 Submissions by Participants /Members										
1	4.4 Paragraph 31 (iii)										
19	JOB(09)/169	6 November 2009	Continued Work Under Paragraph 31 (iii) of the Doha Ministerial Declaration	Kingdom of Saudi Arabia	**Saudi Arabia's submission of its list of environmental goods and information exchange note explaining sustainable development benefits related to: carbon capture and storage technologies, or CCS; gas flaring emission reduction technologies and – efficiency technologies. Trade**: Reduction of tariffs and NTBs on proposed goods. Specfcially proposes standards, conformity assessment and certification, labelling schemes as well as Intellectual property for further discussion and elimination. **Environment**: Relevance to climate change mitigation and energy-efficiency	1-Tariff 2-NTMs 6-Standards 7-Technology					
20	and Add.1	15 December 2009									
21	and Add.2	21 July 2010									
22	JOB(09)/132	9 October 2009	Continued Work Under Paragraph 31 (iii) of the Doha Ministerial Declaration	Canada, European Communities, Japan, Korea, New Zealand, Norway, Chinese Taipei, Switzerland, United States	**Submission of a revised 'convergence' list of a products considered by the co-sponsors to: (1) be particularly important – even critical - for environmental protection, and workable from a customs facilitation perspective; (2) have the potential for a high degree of convergence among Members; and (3) serve as a basis for further work and negotiation under paragraph 31 (iii) of the Doha Declaration. Further considerations for negotiating modalities. Trade:** Reduction of tariffs and NTBs for proposed goods. **Development:** S&DT involving longer tariff phase-outs for developing countries. **Environment:** Inclusion of goods considered 'critical' from an environmental perspective with mention of environmental benefits for each item.	1-Tariff 9-Dev					
23			- Non-Paper								
24	TN/TE/W/73	9 July 2008	Paragraph 31 (iii)	Cuba	**Methodology and guidelines for liberalising tariiffs and NTBs on environmental goods based on S&DT principles and measures to facilitate technology transfer. Trade:** Reduction of tariffs and NTBs for goods used exclusively for environmental purposes as well as primary commodities requiring environmental technologies for environmentally-friendly production so as to generate revenues. **Development:** (i)Granting of aid and loans to developing countries by developed ones to facilitate purchase of EGs and implement projects (ii) Reduction in no: of years of patent protection laid down by TRIPS for for goods and procedures for environmental use or having an environmental impact. (iii) Application of tax exemptions and reduction of protection to faciliate export of technologies to developing countries.**Environment**: Ban on export of DPGs, hazadrous waste, export of polluting technologies and industries and recycled or used goods with liitle or no useful shelf life and containing harmful environmental components unless with consent of importing government and accompanied by funding and know-how for modernization.	1-Tariff 2-NTMs 4-TMs 5-Export 7-Technology 8-TACB 9-Dev					

Row No.	CTE Document	Date issued	Topic / Title	Proponent(s)	Proposal - Modality and T, E, D Rationale	Modality Code	T Score (max 3)	E Score (max 3)	D Score (max 3)	Total Score (+1 max 10)	Notes
	4 Submissions by Participants /Members										
1	4.4 Paragraph 31 (iii)										
25	JOB/07)/193/Rev .1	6 December 2007	Proposal for a result under Paragraph 31(iii) of the Doha Ministerial Declaration-Non paper	European Communities and the United States	**Proposes a two-tier result under under DDA para 31 (iii) covering goods and services relevant to climate change mitigation under Tier 1 and negotiate a broader environmental goods and services agreement (EGSA) through market access commitments in a broader set of goods (building on tier 1 commeitments)and services (binding existing commitments and undertaking new commitments in areas where significant impediments remain in a broader set of environmental and climate-related services such as environment, energy, arhcitecture, construction and engineering. Trade:** Elimination of tariffs and NTBs in proposed goods and services **Environment:** Relevance of proposed goods and sevices to climate-change mitigation.	1-Tariff 2-NTMs					
26	JOB(07)/193	4 December 2007		European Communities and the United States							
27	JOB(07)/161	30 October 2007	Environmental Goods and Services for Development – Paragraph 31(iii), and Paragraph 32(i) and (ii)	Peru	**Proposes inclusion and preferential treatment of organic agcricultural products. Trade: Reduction of tariffs and NTBs for organic products. Also pursuant to para 32 iii) of the Doha declaration calls for complusory requirement disclose the origin and source of genetic resources and the related traditional knowledge in the patent system. Development:** Greater market access encourages agricultural producers in developing countries, provides an alternative to help combat drugs and poverty if producers receive better premiums.**Environment:** Helps preserve ecosystems and bidoversity. Compulsory disclosure of patents facilitates access to the CBD.	1-Tariff 2-NTMs					
28	JOB(07)/146	1 October 2007	Environmental Goods for Development	Brazil	**Proposal for negotiating modalities calls for consideration of biofuels as environmental goods , approach liberalisation based on a 'request-offer' approach by members providing scope to consider various types of both agricultural as well as non-agricultural goods, addressing NTBs to organic agriculture and submit a request to Codex Alimentarius to set standards for organic products. Proposal also calls for analysis by CTE of alternative means of promoting technology-transfer. One possibility is the establishment of a mechanism to evaluate the transference of clean technology pertinent to products that might be the object of tariff concessions as a result of CTESS negotiations. Trade:** Greater market access involving tariff and NTB reduction or removal for proposed goods. **Development:** Inclusion of organic agriculture could help alleviate poverty for small farmers. Technology transfer mechanism can promote access to technologies by developing countries. **Environment:** Relevance of biofuels as a cleaner alternative to fossil-fuels.	1-Tariff 2-NTMs 6-Standards 7-Technology					

Row No.	CTE Document	Date issued	Topic / Title	Proponent(s)	Proposal - Modality and T, E, D Rationale	Modality Code	T Score (max 3)	E Score (max 3)	D Score (max 3)	Total Score (+1 max 10)	Notes
	4 Submissions by Participants /Members										
1	4.4 Paragraph 31 (iii)										
29	JOB(07)/77	6 June 2007	Integrated Approach to Paragraph 31(iii)	Argentina and India	**Proposal on negotiating modalities calls for an 'integrated approach' to EGS liberalsiation.** This would involve: (i) Identifying and agreeing on environmental activities of concern to the members (ii) Notifying to the WO a list of public and private entitites that carry out these activities and finalising and further amending the list through negotaitions (iii) grant of preferential tariff and market access treatment to all goods and services imported by these entities. (iv) Put in place post-audit systems to monitor actual use of imported products for the environmental activities. **Trade:** Greater market access for identified products through reduction or elimination of tariffs and NTBs covering both goods and services required by the entities. **Development:** Approach avoids adverse impacts on developing countries in 'dual-use' sectors. S&DT to ensure greater concessions (100% on tariffs) by developed countries with lower preference margin for developing ones.Ensuring technology-transfer for developing countries. **Environment:** Approach ensures that goods and services liberalised actually benefit the environment as compared to 'list approach.'	1-Tariff 2-NTMs 7-Technology					
30	JOB(07)/54	27 April 2007	Continued Work Under Paragraph 31 (iii) of the Doha Ministerial Declaration	Canada, European Communities, Korea, New Zealand, Chinese Taipei, Switzerland, United States	**Submission of a revised 'convergence' set of products. Please see JOB(09)/132**	1-Tariff 2-NTMs					
31			- Non-Paper								
32	JOB(07)/26	6 March 2007	Refinement of Japan's Environmental Goods List	Japan	**Removal of 13 items from Japan's environmental goods list (TN/MA/W/15, TN/TE/W/17) on considerations of practicality.**	1-Tariff 2-NTMs					
33	TN/TE/W/50/Rev. 1	4 July 2006	Canada's List of Environmental Goods	Canada	**List of environmental goods proposed by Canada for trade liberalisation. These include goods relevant to environmental services delivery. Also highlights role of Canadian firms and Canadian technicla assistance in technology diffusion.Trade:** Market access (lowering tariffs and non-tarff barriers for environmental goods). **Development:**Canada has also been mindful of the need to include environmental goods of export interest to developing countries in our own submission to the CTESS and is considering a range of goods for further analysis in Canada.**Environment:** Environmental benefits of market access. Coverage of various sectors such as renewable energy, air-pollution control, solid and hazardous waste managaement etc.	1-Tariff 2-NTMs					
34	TN/TE/W/50/Sup pl.1	1 July 2005									
35	TN/TE/W/50	2 June 2005									
36	TN/TE/W/49/Rev. 2	30 June 2006	Market Access for Environmental Goods: Revised New Zealand List	New Zealand	**Lists of environmental goods propposed by new Zealand for trade liberalisation. Highlights 'double-win' (trade and environment) and 'triple-win' (trade, environment and development aspects of its list. Trade:** Market access (lowering tariffs and non-tarff barriers for environmental goods) .**Development:** Formally outlines in some detail the numerous developmental benefits that it considers can be secured as a consequence ofthe liberalisation of trade in environmental goods. **Environment:** New Zealand has also added an environmental benefits column to	1-Tariff 2-NTMs					
37	TN/TE/W/49/Rev. 1	12 October 2005									
38	TN/TE/W/49/Sup pl.1	16 June 2005									

Row No.	CTE Document	Date issued	Topic / Title	Proponent(s)	Proposal - Modality and T, E, D Rationale	Modality Code	T Score (max 3)	E Score (max 3)	D Score (max 3)	Total Score (+1 max 10)	Notes
	4 Submissions by Participants /Members										
1	4.4 Paragraph 31 (iii)										
39	TN/TE/W/49	26 May 2005			its list to provide succinct explanations of the environmental applications and advantages of all of the products on New Zealand's environmental goods list.						
40	TN/TE/W/69	30 June 2006	The Development Dimension as an Integral Part of the Negotiations on Environmental Goods: The Principle of Special and Differential Treatment	Cuba	**Reflecting 'development dimension' in environmental goods negotiations through appropriate S&DT provisions for developing countries in offensive and defensive aspects of market access. Trade:** Greater market access for EG exports from developing countries. **Development:** S&DT in both defensive (policy space) and offensive aspects of environmental goods so as to refelect development dimension in environmental goods negotiations.	1-Tariff 2-NTMs 9-Dev					
41	TN/TE/W/67	13 June 2006	Environmental Project Approach: Compatibility and Criteria	India	**Granting temporacy market access for environmental goods and services for specific projects. Trade:** Removal of tariffs and NTBs through project Approach.**Development:** Time-bound tempoary liberalisation for environmental goods and services used in designated environmental projects ensures preservation of policy space in 'non-environmental' end-use categories. **Environment:** Market access covers goods and services for specifc clearly identified environmental projects ensuring clear environmental benefits of market access.	1-Tariff 2-NTMs					
42	JOB(06)/177	9 June 2006	Technical Discussions under Paragraph 31(iii) of the Doha Declaration - Products with High Environmental Performance / Low Environmental Impacts - Non-Paper	European Communities	**Proposes products listed in the high environmental performance or low environmental impacts (HEP) category as set out in the EC's submission TN/TE/W/56. HEPs are listed as part of the Environmentally Preferable Products contained in document JOB(06)/162 issued by the WTO Secretariat. Includes eco-labelled products that have a label delivered by an ecolabelling organisation member of the Global Ecolabelling Network (GEN).** HEP category comprises products identified by UNCTAD as those which cause "significantly less 'environmental harm' at some stage of their life-cycle than alternative products that serve the same purpose. **Trade:** Reduction or elimination of tariffs and NTBs on identified products. **Development:** Export interest of many developing countries in identified products. Also helps in development of mult-modal transport systems and energy-efficiency. **Environment:** Range of environmental benfefits identified by product such as prevention of soil eriosion, energy-efficiency etc. Also contributes directly to the delivery of internationally and regionally agreed policy objectives and action plans such as Agenda 21, Johannesburg Plan of Implementation and Kyoto Protocol.	1-Tariff 2-NTMs					

Row No.	CTE Document	Date issued	Topic / Title	Proponent(s)	Proposal - Modality and T, E, D Rationale	Modality Code	T Score (max 3)	E Score (max 3)	D Score (max 3)	Total Score (+1 max 10)	Notes
	4 Submissions by Participants /Members										
1	4.4 Paragraph 31 (iii)										
43	JOB(06)/178	9 June 2006	Technical Discussions under Paragraph 31(iii) of the Doha Declaration - Market Access for Environmental Goods: Cleaner Technology and Products (CTPs) - Non-Paper	Switzerland	**Non-paper on Cleaner Technology and Products (CTPs) relevant to transport to assist technical discussions in the CTESS plus list of proposed CTP products. CTPs are used to improve or adjust production processes or products, so that use of raw materials, energy and natural resources is efficient, with minimum waste or none at all. Trade:** Market access (lowering tariffs and non-tarff barriers for proposed products as well as associated parts and components. **Environment:** Pollution-reducing at source,facilitates recycling and re-use, contributes to goal of Sustainable Transportation listed in Agenda 21 (chapter 9) in case of products listed under categories of such as listed under railways, bicycles and boats. Products are predominantly 'environmental end-use.'	1-Tariff 2-NTMs					
44	JOB(06)/179	9 June 2006	Technical Discussions under Paragraph 31(iii) of the Doha Declaration - Market Access for Environmental Goods: Environmentally Preferable Products (EPPs) - Non-Paper	Switzerland	**Non-paper on Environmentally-preferable products (EPPs) to faciliate technical discussions in the CTESS plus list of proposed EPP products. UNCTAD (1995) described EPPs as products that, from a life-cycle perspective (i.e. production/processing, consumption, waste/disposal), cause significantly less "environmental harm" than alternative products that serve the same purpose. Trade:** Market access (lowering tariffs and non-tarff barriers for proposed products. **Development**: Promotion of trade in natural EPPs offers opportunities to develop a natural-products-based industry through better utilisation of raw material and skills that developing countries are relatively better endowed with. **Environment:** Facilitates more sustainable consumption and production patterns, improving the efficiency and sustainability in the use of resources and by reducing resource degradation, pollution and waste. Examples of specific benefits of listed products include biodegradibility and non-toxicity during use and disposal (e.g natural products like jute, sisal, natural rubber or cork), reduction of indoor air-pollution and better energy efficiency (e.g.cooking devices such as clean stoves and domestic immersion heaters)and minimsiing water-use and avoiding needs for on-site treatment (e.g. waterless urinals and composting toilets).	1-Tariff 2-NTMs					

Row No.	CTE Document	Date issued	Topic / Title	Proponent(s)	Proposal - Modality and T, E, D Rationale	Modality Code	T Score (max 3)	E Score (max 3)	D Score (max 3)	Total Score (+1 max 10)	Notes
	4 Submissions by Participants /Members										
1	4.4 Paragraph 31 (iii)										
45	JOB(06)/170	7 June 2006	Technical Discussions under Paragraph 31(iii) of the Doha Declaration - Market Access for Environmental Goods: The Environmental, Trade and Developmental Benefits of Remediation and Clean-up of Soil and Water - Non-Paper	New Zealand United States	**Non-paper on Environmental, Trade and Developmental Benefits of Remediation and Clean-up of Soil and Water plus list of relevant goods to facilitate technical discussions in the CTE.One definition of the category of remediation and clean-up of soil and water that has been used internationally is "any activity that produces equipment or specific materials to reduce the quantity of polluting materials in soil and water, including surface water, groundwater and seawater. It includes absorbents, chemicals and bio-remediators for cleaning-up as well as cleaning up systems either in situ or in appropriate installations.** **Trade:** Market access (lowering tariffs and non-tarff barriers for proposed products. **Development**: listed products enhances productvity of land a target of 2002 WSSD plan of implementation, promotes access to safer drinking water (WSSD goal). Other development benefits include: • improved quality of life with provision of basic human needs such as water; • reductions in preventable disease and death from inadequate drinking water supply and poor water quality; • healthier environments for people, reducing illness allowing reallocation of medical resources to other priorities; • enhanced and expanded use of land for agriculture and forestry providing additional income earning opportunities and resulting in more and healthier food. In addition developing countries are important suppliers of listed products to New Zealand and many developing countries also enjoy high trade growth rates in many of the listed products. **Environment:** Environmental benefits listed for proposed products and includes reduction of soil and water pollutants. Products included are those with a 'direct	1-Tariff 2-NTMs					
46	JOB(06)/169	6 June 2006	Technical Discussions under Paragraph 31(iii) of the Doha Declaration - Monitoring and Assessment Equipment - Non-Paper		**Non-paper on Monitoring and Assessment equipment to assist technical discussions in the CTE.Monitoring and assessment equipment can be subdivided into three sub-sectors: 1) measuring equipment (e.g., thermometers, equipment for checking pressure, meters for measuring/detecting pollutants); 2) laboratory or processing equipment (e.g., glassware used in hygienic laboratory facilities, mass spectrometers used to detect contaminants in drinking water, and centrifuges used to separate waste and particles from water); and 3) surveying equipment (e.g., instruments for surveying land, generator units and radiation devices used to measure soil density). Trade:** Market access (lowering tariffs and non-tarff barriers for proposed products. **Development:** Access to monitoring data critical in achievement of sustainable development goals. **Environment:** Access to monitoring data critical in achievement of environmental goals. Specific case-studies reveal benefits such as water-conservation, measurement of water and air quality, improve the capacity of regulatory bodies to identify sources of pollution and respond effectively and access to information that coudl be used to channel specific technical and financial assistance requests.	1-Tariff 2-NTMs					

Row No.	CTE Document	Date issued	Topic / Title	Proponent(s)	Proposal - Modality and T, E, D Rationale	Modality Code	T Score (max 3)	E Score (max 3)	D Score (max 3)	Total Score (+1 max 10)	Notes
	4 Submissions by Participants /Members										
1	4.4 Paragraph 31 (iii)										
47	JOB(06)/149	19 May 2006	Paragraph 31(iii) of the DMD – Environmental Goods – Technical discussion meetings in the WTO Committee on Trade and Environment: Priority Categories	Colombia	**To provide input into technical meetings that the CTE-SS chair is holding to examine products relating to the main categories of environmental goods.** Proposal includes criteria to determine goods with "environmental end-use" or having " dual or multiple end-uses." **Environment:** Proposes criteria to define goods with an environmental end-use as: (i) having direct and verifiable environmental application including in meeting MEA objectives (ii) used in environmental control and improvement. Goods withg multiple end-uses have to be linked to a project, programme, plan or system that generates a verifiable environmental benefit, under review by a Designated National Authority, in accordance with internal priorities, policies, programmes and legislation. **Development:** To be considered 'environmental end-use' goods must also comply with sustainable development and poverty objectives fo MEAs and other international instruments. Technology transfer and S&DT should also be included in proposals listing environmental goods for liberalisation. Consequences of addressing NTBs for exports from developing countries also needs to be examined.	8-TACB					
48	JOB(06)/144	15 May 2006	Negotiations on Environmental Goods	Uruguay	**Proposal on modalities to define environmental goods. Proposal calls on competent international organizations, the WTO and the MEAs, should cooperate and coordinate with each other in order to determine what constitutes an environmental good (or service) under the paragraph 31 (iii) mandate. goods deriving from Identified 'environmental activities' that have both environmental and development benefits should be considered environmental goods. National activities should also be 'internationall certified.'** **Trade:** greater market access for goods identified as ' environmental' under proposed approach. **Development**: All activities conducive to the alleviation or eradication of poverty, health programmes, activities that promote sustainable development, and other activities that contribute to overcoming one of the major causes of environmental degradation, namely poverty, would also be considered environmentally relevant. This approach would also be responsive to developing countries' own national plans and projects as well as offensive interests. **Environment:** Environmental activities would consist of activities covered by an MEA and recognized by that MEA through the recognition of the methodologies or	8-TACB					
49	TN/MA/W/70	9 May 2006	Market Access for Environmental Goods	Canada, European Communities, New Zealand, Norway, Singapore, Switzerland and the United States	**Tariff and NTB reduction on environmental goods based on 'list approach' with S&DT for developing countries. Trade:** Market access for environmental goods through reduction or elimination of tariffs and NTBs. **Development:**S&DT in terms of phase-out periods for developing countries.	1-Tariff 2-NTMs					
50	TN/TE/W/65										

Row No.	CTE Document	Date issued	Topic / Title	Proponent(s)	Proposal - Modality and T, E, D Rationale	Modality Code	T Score (max 3)	E Score (max 3)	D Score (max 3)	Total Score (+1 max 10)	Notes
	4 Submissions by Participants /Members										
1	4.4 Paragraph 31 (iii)										
51	JOB(06)/140	8 May 2006	Technical Discussions under Paragraph 31(iii) of the Doha Declaration - Market Access for Environmental Goods: The Environmental and Development Benefits of Waste Water Management and Solid and Hazardous Waste Management Products - Non-Paper	Canada, European Communities, New Zealand, Japan, Norway, Chinese Taipei, Switzerland and the United States	**Non-paper on Environmental and Development Benefits of Waste-Water management and Solid and Hazardous Waste Management Products as well as approaches on "multi-use" goods to facilitate discussions in the CTE-SS. According to co-sponsors substantially increasing market access for appropriate environmental goods through the reduction or, as appropriate, elimination of tariffs and non-tariff barriers will ensure a "win-win-win" outcome for all WTO Members.One definition of the category of waste water management products that has been used internationally is 'equipment or specific materials for the collection, treatment and transport of wastewater and cooling water.' Solid waste management products have been defined as 'equipment or specific materials for the collection, treatment, transport, disposal and recovery of hazardous and nonhazardous solid waste'. Trade:** Market access for environmental goods through reduction or elimination of tariffs and NTBs. **Development:** Improved access to sanitation, safe-water and hygiene, lower disease and mortality rates, improved quality of life and productivity, enhanced environment for toursim and export promotion, job-creation, relief for government budgets, acheievement of goals under the MDGs as well as the WSSD implementation plan. **Environment:** Reduction in or elimination and prevention of soil, air and water pollution.	1-Tariff 2-NTMs					
52	JOB(06)/75	5 April 2006	Technical Discussions under Paragraph 31(iii) of the Doha Declaration - Air Pollution Control - Non-Paper	Chinese Taipei	**Non-paper to facilitate discussions in CTESS on Air-pollution control equipment plus proposed list of 19 items for air-pollution control equipment. Trade:** Reduction or elimination of tariffs and NTBs for proposed products. **Environment:** Removing air-pollutants.	1-Tariff 2-NTMs					
53	JOB(06)/73	3 April 2006	Technical Discussions under Paragraph 31(iii) of the Doha Declaration - Non-Paper	Canada	**Non-paper submitted to stimulate the technical discussion of environmental goods in the context of negotiations under Paragraph 31(iii) of the Doha Declaration.** Application of indicative parameters to determine environmental and non-environmental end-uses to products listed under two categories, i.e. air-pollution control and renewable energy plant. **Trade:**Reduction or elimination of tariffs and NTBs. **Environment:** Assesment of whether a product has clear environmental end-uses, can be captured using a narrower product description, whether the non-environmental uses of a product poses an environmental risk and if not whether tthe environmental benefit warrants inclusion of the product as an environment good. Also an assessment of whether a product contributes to contribute to the 3Rs – reduce, reuse/recycle, and recover – or is otherwise beneficial from a life cycle consideration.	8-TACB					

Row No.	CTE Document	Date issued	Topic / Title	Proponent(s)	Proposal - Modality and T, E, D Rationale	Modality Code	T Score (max 3)	E Score (max 3)	D Score (max 3)	Total Score (+1 max 10)	Notes
	4 Submissions by Participants /Members										
1	4.4 Paragraph 31 (iii)										
54	JOB(06)/74	3 April 2006	Technical Discussions under Paragraph 31(iii) of the Doha Declaration - Japanese List of Environmental Goods (Air Pollution Control/Renewable Energy) - Non-Paper	Japan	**Non-paper submitting Japanese list of environmental goods relevant to air-pollution control and renewable energy. Trade:** Reduction or elimination of tariffs and NTBs on proposed goods. **Environment:** Clean-up of polluted air and relevance to climate-change mitigation.	1-Tariff 2-NTMs					
55	JOB(06)/70	30 March 2006	Technical Discussions under Paragraph 31(iii) of the Doha Declaration - Non-Paper	European Communities	**Non-paper to facilitate CTE SS technical discussions sorting sorting products nominated by EU into one of three baskets: (1) single environmental end use; (2) predominant environmental end use; (3) otherwise environmentally beneficial for the renewabl energy products (REP) category. Trade:**Reduction or elimination of tariffs and NTBs. **Environment:** Screening of degree of environmental end-use or environmental benefit of proposed renewable energy products.	8-TACB					
56	TN/TE/W/64	20 February 2006	Continued Work Under Paragraph 31(iii) of the Doha Declaration	United States	**Questions to help identify products for inclusion as environmental goods for trade liberalisation purposes. Trade:** Ensuring market access for environmental goods identified based on objective criteria. **Environment:** Includes questions to assess whether a product has a clear or obvious environmental benefit or end-use. **Development:**Includes questions to assess whether products included raise sustainable development concerns or are sensitive to delegations.	8-TACB					
57	TN/TE/W/62	14 October 2005	Integrated Proposal on Environmental Goods for Development	Argentina	**Proposes an integrated approach combining elements from previous approaches on liberalisation modalities that provide for the multilateral identification of categories of environmental projects and "environmental goods" that could be included in those projects. Trade:** Removal of tarffs and NTBs though a hybrid (Integrated) Approach. **Development:** Tariff and NTB reduction based to be multilaterally agreed and reflect S&DT with conditions of access to transfer of clean technology and local capacity building to be negotiated within the environmental project. **Environment:** Clear environmental categories and relevant goods to be defined making tariff liberalisation initaitive 'environmentally-credible.'	1-Tariff 2-NTMs 7-Technology 9-Dev					
58	TN/TE/W/60	19 September 2005	Procedural and Technical Aspects of the Environmental Project Approach	India	**Submission addressing procedural and practical aspects of the 'project apporach'. Trade:** Enables firms involved in projects to import required goods and services horozontally as well as vertically duty free across sectors. **Development:** Provides framework for tech-transfer by developing countries and increased capacity. This can eventualy translate into export opportunities. **Environment:** Due to selection of projects based on environmental objective, trade will have a direct and positive environmental impact.	8-TACB					

Row No.	CTE Document	Date Issued	Topic / Title	Proponent(s)	Proposal - Modality and T, E, D Rationale	Modality Code	T Score (max 3)	E Score (max 3)	D Score (max 3)	Total Score (+1 max 10)	Notes
	4 Submissions by Participants /Members										
1	4.4 Paragraph 31 (iii)										
59	TN/TE/W/59	8 July 2005	Environmental Goods for Development	Brazil	**A definition of environmental goods should cover products, such as natural fibres and colorants and other non-timber forest products, renewable energy, including ethanol and biodiesel. Such a definition would allowl mutually supportive outcomes and a triple win situation, i.e., trade promotion, environmental improvement and poverty alleviation.** Brazil proposes to adopt the UNCTAD approach on "environmentally preferable products" as a basis to develop a definition of environmental goods that encompasses the development dimension.**Trade:** Greater market access for EPPs such as biofuels. **Development:** contributes to poverty alleviation through income generation and job creation for local populations.. **Environment:** Beneficial impact of using biofuels as opposed to fossil fuels and longer-term beneficial environmental impact of poverty reduction.	8-TACB					
60	TN/TE/W/57	6 July 2005	Environmental Goods	Switzerland	**Submission puts forward Switzerland's list of environmental goods and proposes the use of the OECD definition for the environmental industry and for the identification of environmental goods as best suited for 'screening purpose' and as general reference point. Also proposes inclusion of EPPs based on end-use and disposal characteristics.Also sees the necessity for a process of regular review and updating of the agreed list of environmental goods, on the basis of the OECD definition and its respective main categories. Trade:** Market access for proposed list of environmental goods through removal of tariffs and non-tariff barriers. **Development:** EPPs are also of export interest to developing countries.**Environment:**The proposed definition captures all major environmental categories of goods proposed so far namely: (i) Pollution management (ii) resource management (iii) Cleaner technologies and products and (iv) Environmentally preferable products.	1-Tariff 2-NTMs					
61	and Corr.1	14 September 2005									
62	TN/TE/W/55	5 July 2005	Environmental Goods	Cuba	**Proposal on developing negotiating modalities that reflect developing country interests particulalry special and differential treatment. Also emphasises need to address NTBs, agricutural products and linkage of environmental goods with environmental services.**Need to ensure that the EGS negotiations fulfil the specific mandate of "enhancing the mutual supportiveness of trade and environment"as set forth in paragraph 31. **Trade:** Addressing NTBs to environmental goods and linkage to services. **Development:** Reflecting S&DT and developing country concerns.Environment:	3-NTMs 8-TACB 9-Dev					
63	TN/TE/W/56	5 July 2005	Submission on Environmental Goods	European Communities	**Submission of list of environmental goods by the EC which is negotiable and guiding principles and modalities. List is also open to further review as technologies develop. Trade:** Market access for proposed goods in the list through elimination of tariffs and non-tariff barriers. **Development**: Products included in the list include those Millennium Development Goals (in particular on access to safe water and sanitation)and also encompass categories of interest to all WTO Members including developing countries.**Environment:** Products included in the list contribute to the fulfilment of national and international environmental priorities including Multilateral Environmental Agreements, Agenda 21 and the WSSD Plan of Implementation.	1-Tariff 2-NTMs					

Row No.	CTE Document	Date Issued	Topic / Title	Proponent(s)	Proposal - Modality and T, E, D Rationale	Modality Code	T Score (max 3)	E Score (max 3)	D Score (max 3)	Total Score (+1 max 10)	Notes
	4 Submissions by Participants /Members										
1	4.4 Paragraph 31 (iii)										
64	TN/TE/W/52	4 July 2005	Initial List of Environmental Goods	United States	**Submission of initial list of environmental goods based on on end-use criteria (e.g., goods which are used to clean the environment or to contain or prevent pollution),** and does not rely on product distinctions based on process or production methods (PPM-based criteria) or end-use certificates. **Trade:** Market access through removal of tariffs and NTBs on proposed products in the list. **Environment**: includes column which conveys environmental relevance of each product included. Includes major environmental categories mentioned in OECD and APEC lists.	1-Tariff 2-NTMs					
65	TN/TE/W/54	4 July 2005	Structural Dimensions of the Environmental Project Approach	India	**Submission dealing with structural dimension of the Environmental project Approach, namely four principal aspects – 1) the EPA and environment and sustainable development, 2) the EPA and multi-lateral trading system, 3) the EPA and transfer of technology, and 4) the functioning of the Designated National Authority (DNA) under EPA.** All of these clarify the feasibility and the potential for the operational success of this approach. **Trade:** Streamlining and fast-tracking process of project approval for environmental goods and services by DNA vastly improving trade facilitation and would thus support the "win-win" strategy of negotiations on environmental goods and services. Building of domestic capacities and TBT compliance further boost market access for developing countries. **Development:** Tariff reduction for goods and trade-concessions for servcies to be based on S&DT and 'less than full-reciprocity' for developing countries.EPA approach also faciliattes transfer of technology. **Environment:** Criteria for environmental projects to benefit from trade libelraisation would be set by CTE-SS based on environment and sustainable development concerns and applied by DNA. EPA approach also facilities compliance with MEA objectives.	1-Tariff 8-TACB					
66	TN/TE/W/51	3 June 2005	An Alternative Approach for Negotiations under Paragraph 31(iii)	India	**Proposal highlights problems with the list approach and failures to address issues such as 'multiple-use', IPR protection of key technologies, lack of capacity among developing country SMEs, and adverse impacts of 'across the board' liberalisation on developing country SMEs and lack of synergy with environmental services liberalisation. Proposes environmental project approach (EPA) to deal with these issues. Trade:** Trade-liberalisation for EGS used in designated environmental projects including on NTBs as well as services. **Development:** Addresses capacity concerns of SMEs and can addresses issues of technology-transfer such as reduction, elimination or appropriate treatment of standards and licensing restrictions.**Environment:** Responsive to national environmental priorities as well as MEA objectives and based on environmental criteria set by CTESS and identified environmental benefits in each member country.	1-Tariff 2-NTMs 7-Technology 9-Dev					
67	TN/TE/W/48	18 February 2005	Initial List of Environmental Goods Proposed	Korea	**Initial list of environmental goods proposed by Korea based on environmental end-use and 'practicality' consdierations given the absence of a universally accepted definition. Trade:** Market access through removal of tariffs and NTBs on proposed products in the list. **Environment:** Inclusion of products based primarily on 'environmental' end-use criteria.	1-Tariff 2-NTMs					

Row No.	CTE Document	Date issued	Topic / Title	Proponent(s)	Proposal - Modality and T, E, D Rationale	Modality Code	T Score (max 3)	E Score (max 3)	D Score (max 3)	Total Score (+1 max 10)	Notes
	4 Submissions by Participants /Members										
1	4.4 Paragraph 31 (iii)										
68	TN/TE/W/47	17 February 2005	Market Access for Environmental Goods	European Communities	**Submission laying out EC's initial approach to negotiating para 31 (iii) including guiding principles, definition and additional modalities. Trade:** Proposes deeper cuts with tariff elimination as the final aim for agreed upon envrironmental goods for all members except LDCs. Also calls for addressing NTBs and parallel liberalisation of environmental services where appropriate. **Development:** Technical assistance for developing countries, different time-periods for tariff phase-outs. Welcomes developing country proposals of products of export interest. **Environment:**Proposes comprehensive definition of environmental goods must at the very least include the following two categories: (a) Goods used in pollution control and resource management; (b) goods that have a high environmental performance or low environmental impacts. Also goods that contribute to the fulfilment of national and internationally agreed environmental priorities.	1-Tariff 2-NTMs 8-TACB					
69	TN/TE/W/46	10 February 2005	Environmental Goods	New Zealand	**Proposal laying out modalities for negotiating environmental goods including the use of "reference points" which may be cited to initiate a discussion about the environmental credentials of a specific good and to use as a "screening tool" as an alternative to formally negotiating an agreed upon definition.** Such reference poinst could include but not limited to: - The OECD's definition of environmental industries; - APEC's conceptualization6 of environmental goods; and - approaches to environmental goods agreed through high quality and comprehensive regional or bilateral Free Trade Agreements Proposal also includes considerations to make the lists of environmental goods as "living lists." **Environment:** Ensuring greater environmental credibility of agreed upon environmental goods list.	8-TACB					
70	TN/TE/W/44	7 October 2004	Proposed Initial List of Environmental Goods	Chinese Taipei	**Initial list of environmental goods proposed by Chinese Taipei based on APEC list of products.** Suggestion of "direct-use" in pollution-control as a practical and effective criteria forMembers to use in negotiations, for identifying environmental goods in the category of pollution management. **Trade:** Market access through removal of tariffs and NTBs on proposed products in the list. **Environment:** Strong focus on 'pollution-control' products.	1-Tariff 2-NTMs					
71	and Corr.1	3 December 2004									

Row No.	CTE Document	Date issued	Topic / Title	Proponent(s)	Proposal - Modality and T, E, D Rationale	Modality Code	T Score (max 3)	E Score (max 3)	D Score (max 3)	Total Score (+1 max 10)	Notes
	4 Submissions by Participants /Members										
1	4.4 Paragraph 31 (iii)										
72	JOB(04)/98	16 July 2004	The Use of Detailed Categories in CTESS Discussions on the Liberalization of Environmental Goods - CTESS in Meeting of 22 June 2004 – Paragraph 31 (iii)	Canada	**Submission of categories of products for consideration under a possible 'core' and 'complementary' list of environmental goods.** The categories include: Air pollution control • Water pollution control • Solid/hazardous waste management • Remediation/clean-up of soil and water • Noise/vibration abatement • Environmental monitoring, analysis and assessment equipment • Potable water treatment • Recycling systems • Renewable energy plant • Heat/energy management • Soil conservation. **Trade:** Facilitating market-access for identified environmental goods. **Environment:** Considering individual environmental goods on their merits - as opposed to focussing exclusively on principles - allows for a better assessment of the potential environmental benefits offered by candidate goods.	1-Tariff 2-NTMs					
73				China	**Elaborates on broad modalities of liberalisation comprising conepts of a "common list" and a "development list". Trade:** Proposes reduction or elimination of environmental goods included in a "common list." **Development:** Proposes inclusion of products of export interest to developing countries and LDCs in common list. Exemption or lower-level of reduction commitments for developing and LDC members for products in "development list" to be derived from the broader "common list."Stresses need and importance of technology-transfer to developing and LDC members.	1-Tariff 2-NTMs 9-Dev					
74	TN/TE/W/42	6 July 2004	Environmental Goods at the CTESS Meeting of 22 June 2004								
75	TN/TE/W/38			United States	**Elaborates on broad modalities of liberalisation comprising conepts of a "core list" and a "complementary list." Core list would include products on which there is consensus that they constitute environmental goods. Complementary listproducts on which definitive consensus could not be reached but for which there is a high degree of acknowledgment that they can have significance for environmental protection, pollution prevention or remediation, and sustainability. Trade:** Elimination of tariffs on core list at earliest but no later than by 2010 and elimination of tariffs on a certain x percent of tariff lines in complementary list by 2010. **Environment:** Core list should include should fall into one of two categories: 1) environmental remediation or pollution prevention; or 2) "clean technologies." **Development:** To reflect less than full reciprocity, developing countries would be required to eliminate tariffs on a lesser percentage of products on the complementary list than the x percent that would apply to developed countries.	1-Tariff 2-NTMs 9-Dev					
76	TN/MA/W/18/Add .5	7 July 2003	Market Access for Non-Agricultural Products, US Contribution on an Environmental Goods Modality								
77	TN/TE/W/34			United States	**Information exchange:** Explains rationale and approach followed for the earlier APEC's liberalisation initative on environmental goods including practical considerations for tariff liberalisation. Also outlines different approached to defining environmental goods adopted by APEC and OECD. Also outlines reasons for Para 31 (iii) mandate including economic, environmental and sustainable development benefits.	8-TACB					
78	TN/MA/W/18/Add .4	19 June 2003	Liberalizing Environmental Goods in the WTO: Approaching the Definition Issue								
79	TN/TE/W/33			OECD Secretariat	NA						

Row No.	CTE Document	Date issued	Topic / Title	Proponent(s)	Proposal - Modality and T, E, D Rationale	Modality Code	T Score (max 3)	E Score (max 3)	D Score (max 3)	Total Score (+1 max 10)	Notes
	4 Submissions by Participants /Members										
1	4.4 Paragraph 31 (iii)										
80	WT/CTE/W/228	21 May 2003	OECD Joint Working Party on Trade and Environment: Environmental Goods: A Comparison of the APEC and OECD lists - Information Note			NA					
81	TN/TE/W/27	25 April 2003	Harmonized System (HS) Classification Codes of Gas-Related Goods	Qatar	**Puts forward harmonised system (HS) classifications for natural-gas related goods. Trade:** Elimination of tariffs and NTBs for proposed natural-gas related goods.**Environment:** Natural gas is propsoed as a cleaner and less-carbon intensive alternative to coal.	1-Tariff 2-NTMs					
82	TN/MA/W/33										
83	TN/TE/W/19	28 January 2003	Negotiations on Environmental Goods: Efficient, Lower-Carbon and Pollutant-Emitting Fuels and Technologies	Qatar	**Proposal attempts to define and assess the economic and environmental merits of natural-gas systems and other related efficient lower-carbon and pollutant-emitting fuels and technologies.** Proposes list of products be included in the OECD illustrative categories of environmental goods, Section B relating to cleaner technologies and products. **Trade:**Elimination of tariffs and NTBs and other energy-market distortions impeding market access for proposed natural-gas related goods. **Development:** Increased energy-efficiency in the economy.**Environment:** relevance of natural gas to meet GHG commitments as recognised under kyoto protocol and its relevance to the hydrogen economy. Other benefits include reduced toxic air pollution emissions and waste generation and improved air quality conditions and decreased adverse environmental impacts on human health, human welfare and on biodiversity.	1-Tariff 2-NTMs 3-SMs					
84	TN/MA/W/24										
85	and Corr.1	21 February 2003									
86	TN/TE/W/17	20 November 2002	Market Access for Non-Agricultural Products	Japan	**Puts forward preliminary specific list of environmental and proposes thoughts on modalities for liberalising environmental goods. Reduction of tariffs in this area to be treated as integral part of market access negotiations. Trade:** Elimination of tariffs on goods in proposed list and addressing of NTBs. **Environment:** Special consideration to be given to goods which have to be appropriately addressed in terms of global environment issues and the sustainable use of exhaustible natural resources.	1-Tariff 2-NTMs					
87	and Corr.1	25 November 2002									

Row No.	CTE Document	Date issued	Topic / Title	Proponent(s)	Proposal - Modality and T, E, D Rationale	Modality Code	T Score (max 3)	E Score (max 3)	D Score (max 3)	Total Score (+1 max 10)	Notes
	4 Submissions by Participants /Members										
1	4.4 Paragraph 31 (iii)										
88	TN/TE/W/14	9 October 2002	Environmental Goods	Qatar	**Proposes that technologies such as combined-cycle natural-gas-fired generation systems and advanced gas-turbine systems known for their energy efficiency and sustainable development potential must be subtitled and elaborated in the definition of environmental goods. Trade:** Promotes market access through elimination of tariffs and NTBs on Combined-cycle natural-gas-fired generation systems and Advanced-gas turbine systems (industrial and utility turbines). **Development:** Benefits human health, energy-efficiency and wider issues of sustainable development. **Environment:** Facilitates climate change mitigation controls air pollution Emissions and toxic waste generation .	1-Tariff 2-NTMs					
89	TN/TE/W/8	9 July 2002	Negotiations on Environmental Goods	United States	**Proposes modalities for negotiations including co-ordination between CTESS and NAMA, using APEC lists and OECD work to inform development of environmental goods lists and identifying NTBS as well as establishing a mechanism to deal with NTBs drawing upon previous analytical work including that undertaken by the OECD.**	8-TACB					
90	TN/TE/W/6G91:O 92	6 June 2002	Environmental Goods	New Zealand	**Information Exchange: Points to previous work that may help clarify the concept of environmental goods including APEC's sectoral liberalisation on environment covering (1) tariffs (2) services (3) non-tariff measures, and (4) economic and technical cooperation (Ecotech),use of the OECD definition of the environmental industry, illustrative product coverage and examples of trade barriers, environmental benefits and estimate of import levels for selected goods in APEC economies. Also emphasises close linkage between environmental goods and services and previous relevant work including by the WTO Secretariat, UNCTAD and OECD in this regard.**	8-TACB					

Environment and Trade Sectoral Discussions
(*See:* Master List of CTE6 Documents,
WT/CTE/INF/Rev.12, at Part 1.6 pp. 6 to 9, 29 Feb 2016)

A. **Agriculture (1998 – 2003)**
B. **Fisheries (1997 – 2006)**
C. **Energy Resources ((1998 – 2002, 2013, 2015)**
D. **Forestry Resources (1998 – 2003)**

A. Agriculture

Based on empirical studies conducted by the OECD, the FAO and the United Nations Conference on International Trade and Development ('UNCTAD'),[1] Members had, in the initial years of the CTE, taken note of the adverse effects of subsidization of agricultural products. The first submission made specifically on agriculture was in 1998 by Argentina.[2] This proposal raised non-trade concerns and noted that subsidization was closely linked to increased application of agro-chemicals, adoption of intensive animal production practice and overgrazing, degradation of natural resources and expansion of agricultural production into ecologically sensitive areas. While some Members considered a reduction of agricultural protection to be a "win-win" situation for trade and environment, others felt it was "inappropriate for the CTE to focus so narrowly on the agricultural sector." According to these Members, agricultural liberalization was best left to be discussed in the Agriculture Committee in the WTO, and they also expressed caution about drawing generalized conclusions on the environmental impact of agricultural support schemes.

Many WTO Members proposed solutions to remedy the complexity of the issue. Australia noted that there was scope to promote more sustainable agricultural policies in the context of the built-in agenda to the Uruguay Round results. Japan suggested that various inter-related factors, such as natural conditions and socio-economic circumstances in each country, contributed to environmental problems.[3] Japan's suggestions seemed to postulate that trade liberalization without appropriate environmental policies may negatively affect the environment. The EU argued that there is no automatic link between trade liberalization and environmental policy. It contended that pricing policies were not *a priori* environmentally efficient. The Republic of Korea proposed that an analytical and case-wise study be taken up to estimate the negative effects of trade-distorting agricultural measures. This proposal also noted that issues of food self-sufficiency and food security should be respected. Norway proposed that the multilateral trading system should offer incentives for the use of environmentally friendly products. It further noted that WTO rules should not encompass incentives for

1. *See* OECD, The Environmental Effects of Trade (1994); UNCTAD, Trade and Development Report (1995), UNCTAD/COM/35 (25 April 1995).
2. WTO CTE, Non-Trade Concerns in the Next Agricultural Negotiations (Submission by Argentina), WT/CTE/W/97 (10 August 1998).
3. WTO CTE, Annotated Bibliography of Selected Literature Concerning Compliance and Dispute Settlement in the WTO and in Multilateral Environmental Agreements, WT/CTE/W/197 (25 June 2001).

production and use of products that damage the environment. Besides this, Norway stated that trade liberalization should yield both economic and environmental benefits.[4] According to some Members, eliminating distortions and trade restrictions that affect commodity prices was a *sine qua non* for achieving environmental protection. Others argued that environmental protection would need to take development priorities into account. Therefore the discussions reflected the divergent views on agriculture.

As illustrative of the discussions that take place at the CTE, Chinese Taipei introduced its experience of organic agriculture. According to it, organic agriculture combined tradition, innovation and science and would be propitious to the environment. Developing and promoting organic agriculture would require the establishment of organic farmers' market, e-shops and franchised retail counters and organization of exhibitions promoting organic products. Chinese Taipei also stated that it had introduced the Agricultural Production and Certification Act in 2007, which introduced certification and accreditation management systems. As per the Act, inspection of the products was conducted on an annual basis, and major non-compliance would result in revocation of accreditation.

UNCTAD, UNEP and the International Trade Centre (ITC) were among those who provided overviews of their work on promoting organic agriculture.

Negotiations relating – directly or tangentially - to agriculture are often protracted given the economic, political and social sensitivities associated with the subject. Discussions at the CTE were no different. Statements by WTO members suggesting that trade policy regimes, not backed by sound environmental policy, could be detrimental to the environment was countered by other WTO members who considered that there should be no automaticity in linking the two issues. In the clash of norms, WTO members also recognized the importance of food security. Many WTO members also argued that discussions relating to agriculture at the CTE should not impinge countries' developmental aspirations. While there were some discussions on issues such as organic foods, the crux of the discussions remained stagnant in substance, due to the complexities involved relating to the sector.

B. Fisheries' subsidies

Discussions on fisheries subsidies started after the 1996 Singapore Ministerial Conference at the CTE. These discussions were built upon growing global concerns over fisheries resources being overused or over-exploited and that subsidies provided by governments to the fisheries sector were considered to be a part of the cause. The FAO's 1993 report noted that "the depletion of various fish stocks had occurred in virtually all coastal states throughout the world. Indeed [...] this is an inevitable outcome unless appropriate controls are adopted."[5] Appropriate controls included reducing global harvesting capacity and subsidies. Besides this report, concerns about

4. WTO CTE, Environmental Effects of Trade Liberalization in the Agriculture Sector (Submission by Norway), WT/CTE/W/100 (8 January 1999).
5. FAO Fisheries Department, *Marine Fisheries and the Law of the Sea: A Decade of Change* (Rome: FAO 1993).

the health of natural resources were also discussed in the 1995 Kyoto meeting on the Contribution of Sustainable Fisheries to Food Security and the 1995 United Nations Fish Stock Agreement. These agreements sought to introduce adjustments in the fishing industry since the natural resource was in stress.

The United States, in a 1997 submission, had noted that subsidies exacerbated problems of overcapacity and over-fishing. The United States called for the removal of fisheries subsidies which, according to it, would provide a double dividend to the environment and global economy.[6]

According to a note by the Secretariat dated November 1997, subsidies in the fisheries sector were primarily provided to reduce operating and capital costs of harvesting. Subsidies could be provided for, amongst other things, reducing operating costs, reducing fishing vessel construction and maintenance costs, reducing income-related expenses such as income tax (thereby conferring an indirect subsidy) and reducing vessel fuel costs. The note stated that determining the impact of subsidies would depend on how the subsidies are administered and monitored. For instance, subsidies could be given to reduce fleet capacity and enhance fish stocks. The EU at the time, agreed with the Secretariat that subsidies are not inherently good or bad for fish stocks.[7]

Iceland intervened with the Fisheries industry contributing to 18% of its GDP (as of 1997).[8] This was because fisheries subsidies, irrespective of whether they take the form of cost reduction or price support, encouraged increased fishing effort.[9]

New Zealand noted that states should support the exchange of scientific and technical information on issues related to the management of fishing capacity. It also noted that training and institutional strengthening should be encouraged and that financial, technical and other assistance must be provided to developing countries.[10] It recommended that new WTO rules on fisheries need to be considered.[11]

The United States made a detailed proposal on the types of subsidies that distort markets and are harmful to the environment. It categorized subsidies into: (a) Subsidies that reduce capital (fixed) and operating (variable) costs; and (b) Subsidies that

6. WTO CTE, Environmental and Trade Benefits of Removing Subsidies in the Fisheries Sector (Submission by the United States), WT/CTE/W/51(19 May 1997).
7. WTO CTE, European Community Comments on the Note by the Secretariat of the World Trade Organization's Committee on Trade and Environment - Environmental Benefits of Removing Trade Restrictions (Note from the European Community), WT/CTE/W/83 (10 June 1998); WTO CTE, Comments by the European Community on the Document of the Secretariat of the Committee on Trade and Environment (Note by the European Community), WT/CTE/W/99 (6 November 1998); Japan took a similar stance, *see* WTO CTE, Japan's Basic Position on the Fishery Subsidy Issue, Item 6 (Submission by Japan), WT/CTE/W/173 (23 October 2000).
8. WTO CTE, The Icelandic Fisheries Management System: A Market-Driven Sustainable Fisheries Regime (Submission by Iceland), WT/CTE/W/103 (25 January 1999).
9. WTO CTE, On the Environmental Impact of Fisheries Subsidies - A Short Report by the Icelandic Ministry of Fisheries - 1 February 1999 (Submission by Iceland), WT/CTE/W/111 (11 March 1999).
10. WTO CTE, Benefits of Eliminating Trade Distorting and Environmentally Damaging Subsidies in the Fisheries Sector (Submission by New Zealand), WT/CTE/W/121(28 June 1999).
11. WTO CTE, Subsidies in the Fisheries Sector: Update on Recent Work Conducted by New Zealand (Communication from New Zealand), WT/CTE/W/134 (24 February 2000).

support incomes and prices and the table below is based on the United States presentations.

Table A2.1: Environmentally Harmful Subsidies: USA Submission, WT/CTE/W/154 (July 4, 2000)

Subsidies That Reduce Capital (Fixed) and Operating (Variable) Costs	
Examples of Subsidy for Domestic Fisheries	**Description**
Government-Funded Commercially Applicable Research and Development	These types of subsidies reduce fixed and variable costs in both domestic and international fishing operations, noting that 90% of global capture fishery harvests are taken within the Exclusive Economic Zone ('EEZ').
Below market Government Loans and Loan Refinancing; Government Loan Guarantees; Forgiveness of Government-Funded Loans	These categories may reduce costs of capital which is a key item in a sector in which the costs of acquiring and financing a vessel play such a major role.
Investment Tax Credits; Income Tax Deferrals; Exemption from National Sales and Fuel Excise Taxes	These categories reduce income and sales taxes. The resulting profit margins encourage greater fishing efforts.
Government-Supported Marine Insurance at Below Market Rates	Risk-mitigating and cost-reducing that tends to promote fishing operations
Government Ownership/Management of Fishing Enterprises if Inconsistent with Market Terms; State Trading if Inconsistent with Market Terms and Customary Business Practices	These are relevant for countries with centrally controlled fisheries sectors.
Assistance to Shipbuilding when the Benefits Accrue Specifically to Fishers	This category is not a fisheries sector subsidy per se, but, to the degree that subsidies provided to shipyards assist the fishers who buy the vessels, this type should be considered.
Examples of Subsidy for International Fisheries	**Description**
Government-funded Foreign Access Payments; Government- Assistance to Foreign Fishery Joint Ventures; Government-supported Fishing Vessel Exports; Government-supported Below Market Risk Insurance for Foreign Fishery Investments	These types of subsidies explicitly promote international fisheries including operations on the high seas and in the EEZs of other coastal States, often supporting the operations of redundant vessels in ineffectively patrolled EEZ of developing countries.

Subsidies that support incomes and prices	
Domestic Price Support Programmes; Government Purchases for Above Market Remuneration	These are explicit price support programmes and have the general effect of promoting operations beyond an optimal point and sustaining marginal producers
Rebates on Certain Taxes on Inputs if the Finished Product is Exported; Government-Funded Export Subsidies	These are trade-promoting subsidies and do not appear to be widely practiced.
Sector-Specific Income Maintenance Programmes; Regional Economic Development, if effectively Fisheries Sector-Specific	These are sector-specific social assistance programmes which may be harmful when implemented in ways that effectively encourage fishers to remain active even when fishery resources are depleted.

Japan, in 2000, made a detailed comment on the United States' proposal. It voiced concern that it was not aware of any specific case in which fishery subsidies were a major cause of stock depletion. Giving the example of depletion of toothfish in the Antarctic Ocean and cod in Northwest Atlantic Ocean, it noted that factors other than fisheries subsidies such as lack of fisheries management and unregulated fishing activities were responsible. It said that WTO Members should be cautious in trying to reach a conclusion without having any concrete examples of the problem. Lastly, Japan also contended that discussions on subsidies should be discussed in the FAO or any other specialized fisheries fora.[12]

Among the various presentations made to the CTE, one of note was a workshop on fisheries subsidies[13] held on 12 February 2001 and attended by 60 governments and five IGOs including the WTO. Subsequently, the CTE prepared a summary of the meeting which was presented to Members on 15 March 2001. According to the note, opinions amongst countries differed over the relative importance of fisheries subsidies. Nonetheless, evidence indicated that subsidies contributed to overcapacity and depletion of fish stocks, particularly in the absence of appropriate management regimes.[14] The note identified that some convergence emerged towards the end of the meeting on the requirement of further analysis of the interaction between subsidies and fisheries management. The FAO also reported its activities related to fisheries subsidies in June 2001. The paper analysed existing regulations and data and concluded that more accurate information on the number and value of subsidies was needed before a quantitative analysis was initiated. To do this, the paper noted that there was a need to

12. WTO CTE, Japan's Basic Position on the Fishery Subsidy Issue (Submission by Japan), WT/CTE/W/173 (23 October 2000).
13. WTO CTE, UNEP Fisheries Subsidies Workshop: Chairman's Summary, Communication from UNEP, WT/CTE/W/187 (15 March 2001).
14. WTO CTE, UNEP Fisheries Subsidies Workshop: Chairman's Summary, Communication from UNEP, WT/CTE/W/187 (15 March 2001).

collect empirical knowledge about the impacts of subsidies on trade in fish and fisheries products.[15]

Many WTO Members welcomed the findings of the presentations made and reiterated that further discussions should take place at the CTE. Thailand observed that subsidies intended to improve the environment (also known as 'good subsidies') could also have a negative impact. For instance, subsidies to decommission fishing vessels on high seas could result in other fleets increasing their capacity, which would be harmful to fish-stock sustainability. Australia stressed that Members must give importance on this topic if "[...] there were to be balance overall on trade and environment at Doha." According to Australia, this was an opportunity to demonstrate that economic and environmental reforms could complement each other. Iceland was of the view that the existing WTO subsidies regime left much to be desired when it came to fisheries subsidies. It was of the opinion that the CTE must continue engaging Members on the topic until a solution is found. New Zealand felt that these presentations had raised more questions than resolve problems. However, it considered the CTE to be the correct forum for discussion.[16] Peru considered it important to remedy the effects of fisheries subsidies that contributed to overcapacity and over-fishing. It noted that some WTO Members, while proposing greater flexibility in WTO law to accommodate environmental protection, were reticent to adopt measures in the fisheries sector, which reflected a clear "win-win-win." Chile - a country with 5,000 miles coastline in which fisheries contributed substantially to the GDP - contended that subsidies were the exclusive competence of the WTO. Norway recalled that this issue was included in the CTE agenda because of a possible "win-win-win" outcome. Therefore, Norway reasoned that discussion should continue in the CTE and support discussions on fisheries subsidies in the Rules Committee of the WTO.

Motivated by the recognition that subsidies to the fishing industry have attracted increasing attention from researchers and policy makers, New Zealand, in March 2003, presented findings from a research paper that seemed to appear relevant to the discussions on fisheries subsidies.[17] After analyzing the existing subsidies regime based on limited available data, the paper concluded that:[18]

> [...] tentatively, that just under 50 per cent of the North Atlantic fisheries subsidies are benign, or neutral, in terms of their impact. We also conclude that just under 50 per cent are decidedly damaging, or are to be viewed, at best, with deep suspicion. The remainder, just over 5 per cent, we cannot classify on the basis of available information.
>
> There is wide acceptance of the view that subsidies used in vessel decommissioning (buyback) programs also have a positive impact on fisheries management and sustainability. By reducing fleet capacity, such subsidies will reduce economic waste in the fisheries and reduce pressure on the resource, or so the argument goes. We take sharp issue with this widely held view. Such subsidies, if

15. *See generally* WTO CTE, Communication from the FAO, WT/CTE/W/189 (18 June 2001).
16. WTO CTE, Report of the Meeting held on 29 April 2003, WT/CTE/M/33 (21 May 2003) at p. 19.
17. G.R. Munro and U.R. Sumalia, "Subsidies and their potential impact on the management of ecosystems of the North Atlantic," *in Fisheries Impacts on North Atlantic Ecosystems: Evaluations and Policy Explorations* (T. Pitcher, U.R. Sumalia & D. Pauli (eds.)) at p. 7 (2001).
18. *Ibid.*

> they come to be anticipated by the industry, can and will have a decidedly negative impact.
>
> Subsidies in fisheries, to the extent that their impact is negative, are seen as exacerbating the problems arising from the "common pool" nature of many capture fisheries. We do not question this claim. We do, however, raise the question of whether the subsidies would continue to have a negative impact if the characteristics of the fishery were removed, i.e. by the establishment of effective property rights. The answer is unquestionably yes.

In sum, the paper established that the addition of subsidies could destabilize the fish stocks even with the implementation of sound fisheries management regimes in place. New Zealand, however, introduced a note of caution that the study did not "really address market impact" given the narrow range of scenarios studied in the paper.

Reactions to the paper by the Members were varying with two distinct issues being raised. *First*, whether or not the CTE would play a role in ensuing discussions on fisheries subsidies. *Second*, whether the merits of the paper stood the test of real-life application. Regarding the first issues, Members were divided as to whether discussion on fisheries subsidies should continue at the CTE and whether such discussions would support the parallel discussions taking place in the Rules Negotiating Group. The EU noted, after assessing the contents of the paper, that the CTE should continue to examine fisheries subsidies in the context of paragraph 32 (i) of the Doha Declaration though the Rules Negotiating Group would be the forum for fisheries subsidies. Notably, this was in contrast to its earlier statement that the FAO was the correct forum for discussing this issue. The United States looked forward to discussing the issue of fisheries subsidies in the Rules Negotiating Group and also saw a continued role for CTE as enshrined in paragraph 32(i) of the Doha Declaration. Chile and Iceland raised concerns about the possibility of CTE becoming isolated with discussions taking place in the Rules Negotiating Group. Iceland, in particular, saw a greater role for the CTE in the discussions and stated that "the [CTE] would continue to play a progressive role in deepening the analysis of the implication of fisheries subsidies."[19]

On the issue of merits of the paper, the Republic of Korea pointed out that many more extraneous factors existed in real-life fisheries subsidies than those assessed in the paper. It reiterated that the main cause for the global fisheries problem was poor fisheries management which created a financial incentive to overfish. The Philippines noted that sound management was essential in reducing overcapacity. However, it also noted that subsidies could conceptually impede in the objective of reducing this overcapacity. Therefore, it concluded that no *a priori* assumption must be made regarding so-called "good" subsidies reducing livestock capacity. Japan was unconvinced by the findings of the paper that New Zealand presented of fisheries subsidies having damaging effects on the environment.[20]

Japan made two submissions regarding fisheries subsidies in 2003. The first was a proposal on the joint-issue of forest and fisheries products while the other was an

---

19. WTO CTE, Report of the Meeting held on 21 March 2002, WT/CTE/M/29 (7 May 2002) at p. 10.
20. *Id.* at p. 11.

independent evaluation of the relationship between fisheries subsidies and over-exploitation of fisheries resources. In the first proposal, Japan argued that Members must retain flexibility when determining the level of tariffs on fisheries products after having taken into account the level of fishery resources and the status of fishery management. Japan also stated that adequate technical and financial assistance must be granted as part of special and differential treatment to developing countries for the sustenance of fishery resource management. Regarding the fisheries subsidies issues, Japan asserted that no concrete cases had been provided to demonstrate that trade distortion caused by fisheries subsidies negatively affected the environment. Instead, Japan believed that comprehensive efforts must be made for attaining sustainable development of fisheries.[21]

In the second proposal, Japan cited three studies which indicated that coherence in fisheries management policies and subsidy policies would lead to a more environmentally sustainable outcome. The first was a study conducted by the OECD in 2000 that concluded that the negative effects of subsidies would be reduced substantially if subsidy policy and fisheries management policy were mutually supportive. For example, "when a subsidy for vessel construction was provided to fishing vessels engaged in a certain fishery, it was necessary to restrict the total fishing capacity of the fishery through regulations."[22] The second study was also conducted by the OECD in 2002, which observed that "the effects of subsidies on resources differed depending on the status of resource and management."

The third was an APEC study of 1999. As per this study, the "impact of subsidies was closely related to fishery management regimes and, therefore, [...] could not be discussed in isolation."[23] Based on these studies, Japan concluded that the "possible effects of subsidies on resources changed depending on the resource status and fishery management regime and the lack of effective fishery management created over-capacity even without subsidies." To substantiate its assertion, Japan provided the example of the skipjack tuna. Production of skipjack tuna had been on the increase since the 1950s when it was estimated at 20,000 metric tons. This production, through subsidies, reached 1.89 million metric tons in 2000.

It was reported by regional fishery management organizations (RFMOs) such as the Indian Ocean Tuna Commission that the stock status of skipjack tuna was strong and possessed a high reproductive potential. However, due to limited demand, the production was suppressed. According to Japan, this exemplified the logic that fisheries subsidies were unlikely to cause overexploitation if good management was present.[24]

The CTE witnessed continuing debate and concern over Japan's proposals, and many members regularly opposed Japan's position in the negotiations and discussions.

21. WTO CTE, Sustainable Development and the Trade of Forest and Fishery Products (Submission by Japan), WT/CTE/W/222 (6 February 2003).
22. WTO CTE, Report of the Meeting held on 29 April 2003, WT/CTE/M/33 (21 May 2003) at pp. 2 - 3.
23. *Ibid.*
24. WTO CTE, Analysis on the Relationship between Fisheries Subsidies and Over-Exploitation of Fisheries Resources (Submission by Japan), WT/CTE/W/226 (24 April 2003) at p. 2.

At the WTO, it was the forum provided by the CTE where the Member States engaged in earnest to discuss ways to discipline fisheries subsidies. These discussions were informed, fact-based and - once again - demonstrated the clash of environmental and trade norms. But this time, the subject was a global common: fish. Recognizing the seriousness of the issue, WTO Members decided to move to debate disciplines to regulate fisheries subsidies at the Rules Committee which, more specifically, dealt with the issue at hand. However, it was at the CTE that the Member States first debated the proposition of disciplining fisheries. In the process, many Member States had expressed and developed their divergent positions on the issue of identifying harmful fisheries subsidies during the early discussions at the CTE.

C. Energy

Much like agriculture, the number of discussions on the energy sector was limited in number and scope from 1995 until 2001. There was a three-year hiatus in discussions after Brazil had presented at the CTE its experience in ethanol fuel in September 1998.[25] In February 2001, the EU requested the CTE to update the list of environmentally harmful and trade-distorting measures and policies in energy markets based on recent works by the OECD and the International Energy Agency.[26] The CTE, in response to the request by the EU, prepared a paper which was presented in September 2001. Norway commented at length on the CTE paper. It agreed with most of the items highlighted in the paper. According to it,[27]

> [...] first, there were both good and bad subsidies; second, subsidy reform did not equal subsidy removal; third, subsidies had to be carefully targeted to have real environmental benefits because there was an array of measures in the energy sector that had trade-distortive as well as environmentally harmful effects; and fourth, certain taxes and subsidies were important for social and developmental objectives.

Saudi Arabia, in a paper dated September 2002, argued that the use of energy taxes within OECD countries unfairly discriminated against oil and petroleum products. The OECD, then, applied different tax rates on fossil fuels with oil being discriminated in comparison to other fuels. Saudi Arabia noted that a reform of these taxation policies should be based upon the carbon content; such a policy would be less damaging to oil-producing and exporting countries. Saudi Arabia also noted that subsidization of coal and nuclear energy should also be discouraged since "these protectionist approaches are inefficient, environmentally unsound."[28]

The discussion on energy became more specific over time with the introduction of topics such as hydropower, energy efficiency, natural gas, and carbon footprinting

25. WTO CTE, The Energy Sector: The Case of Alcohol Fuel (Ethanol) (Submission by Brazil), WT/CTE/W/98 (30 September 1998).
26. WTO CTE, Report of the Meeting held on 13 - 14 February 2001, WT/CTE/M/26 (30 March 2001).
27. WTO CTE, Environmental Benefits of Removing Trade Restrictions and Distortions: The Energy Sector - Item 6 of the Work Programme, WT/CTE/W/200 (18 September 2001).
28. WTO CTESS, Energy Taxation, Subsidies and Incentives in OECD Countries and their Economic and Trade Implications (Submission by Saudi Arabia), WT/CTE/W/215 (23 September 2002).

schemes, the latter one having been already covered in Chapter 5. Canada introduced the topic of hydropower at the CTE meeting of 6 October 2015.[29] According to Canada, hydropower had the potential to contribute to the greening of global electricity production. It could also complement other intermittent energy sources such as solar and wind to ensure a constant supply of low-carbon energy. According to Canada, hydropower, which accounted for 16% of global electricity generation, was the most used form of renewable energy. Since many Members were shifting to it as a form of energy generation, Canada introduced a monitoring tool called Hydropower Sustainability Assessment Protocol ('HSAP') which provided guidelines for the sustainability of hydropower plants. HSAP would ensure proper construction and maintenance of hydropower plants. This, in turn, would result in maximum energy outputs and minimal environmental impacts, thereby making hydroelectricity a reliable and economical source of energy. Canada also noted that as per HSAP methodology, large hydroelectric systems were more sustainable than smaller ones.

Discussions on energy efficiency are also more recent with the EU presenting its Energy Union strategy.[30] This strategy is focused on boosting energy security, creating a fully integrated internal energy market, improving energy efficiency, decarbonising the economy - not least by using more renewable energy - and supporting research, innovation and competitiveness. On energy efficiency, the Energy Union strategy covers five dimensions which are:[31]

> [...] (i) energy efficiency: a broad framework that had put in place targets for the EU members; (ii) energy performance of buildings; (iii) eco-design that had set minimum energy performance standards for products that were placed on the EU market; (iv) energy labelling; and (v) a framework to finance energy efficiency.

The EU also extended support to carbon accounting initiatives and noted that its citizens were interested in climate change issues which drive public and private efforts to build information on carbon footprints. Carbon accounting, according to the EU, also raised the possibilities of opening up new economic opportunities. Many other delegations participated and made presentations on similar experiences or their own initiatives.

The discussions, once again, demonstrated differences in opinion between WTO Members. While some supported the submissions, others questioned the *locus standi* of these submissions. In support of the submissions were EU and Australia who welcomed the sharing of information. Notwithstanding this view, Argentina stressed that both the Republic of Korea and Norway needed to explain how their schemes would contribute to sustainable development and avoid adverse effects on market access. Cuba argued that the CTE was mandated to discuss Member's experience of

29. WTO CTESS, Report of the Meeting held on 6 October 2015, WT/CTE/M/60 (3 September 2015).
30. WTO CTE, Report of the meeting held on 22 June 2015, WT/CTE/M/59 (3 September 2015) at ¶ 1.2. *See generally* European Union, European Strategy and Energy Union, available at https://ec.europa.eu/energy/en/topics/energy-strategy-and-energy-union (accessed on 30 November 2019);
31. *Ibid.*

implementing carbon footprinting and labelling schemes since they showed risks of barriers to trade for export products.

According to the Cuban delegation, the negative vote at the ISO on the draft of ISO 14067 which dealt with carbon footprints of producers demonstrated the chasm between existing measures being implemented and the circumstances of developing countries. India also criticized the sole focus on global warming without evaluating the adverse effects of products on other aspects such as resource depletion, soil, water and air pollution, or human health and safety. The Philippines opined that negotiations and commitments on carbon emissions were best dealt with at the UNFCCC and not the CTE. This view found support from some other WTO Members.

Thailand, Costa Rica, Switzerland and New Zealand also gave overviews of their domestic carbon footprinting legislations and strategies. Just to illustrate, New Zealand updated Members on its carbon footprint national strategy and reiterated its support for developing labelling schemes that were non-discriminatory against third-country trading partners.[32] Switzerland also informed Members that it had adopted a green economy plan that aimed at increasing information on the environmental impact of products such as transparency and private labelling schemes. Switzerland further stated that it would support the implementation of environmental schemes, including private labelling initiatives and elaboration of international standards, as a way to increase sustainable trade. In 2014, Switzerland expounded in greater detail the objectives of the green economy plan:[33]

> (i) resource efficiency in consumption and production; (ii) waste and raw material cycles; (iii) international engagement and "transversal instruments," namely the Cleantech Master plan and greener fiscal system; and (iv) explicit but flexible targets, follow-up, and reporting, including the integration of the notion of efficient and rational use of resources into legislative projects.

Argentina, however, felt that the concept of a green economy should be a voluntary tool for sustainable development. Venezuela, too, reiterated the need for further research and debate on the impacts of such measures on market access for developing countries. Bolivia rejected the general concept of a green economy altogether as it saw it as a means of appropriating and privatizing natural resources of developing countries, and preferred a flexible approach considering each country's national priorities and circumstances.[34]

Fragmented views of different WTO Members, thus, continued throughout the discussions on carbon footprint and policies related to GHG emissions. No consensus emerged regarding the methodology for quantification of captured carbon footprints. Further, there was a lack of reference since multilateral negotiations such as the one taking place at the UNFCCC were still discussing these issues. There is a submission submitted from January 2014 by the delegations of Venezuela, Egypt, Brazil, South Africa, Argentina, Angola on behalf of the African Group, Cuba, Bolivia, India, China,

32. WTO CTE, Report of the meeting held on 22 June 2015, WT/CTE/M/58 (23 March 2015).
33. WTO CTE, Report of the meeting held on 16 October 2013, WT/CTE/M/56 (31 January 2014) at ¶¶ 1.33 - 1.37.
34. *Id.* at ¶ 1.33.

and Lesotho on behalf of least developed countries ('LDC') Group.[35] These Members expressed their concern about certain topics being outside the mandate of DDA32(i). Further, they contended that many of the presentation topics on carbon footprinting were "available only at the last minute"[36]. This made effective participation difficult for many WTO Members, especially given the technical nature of discussions.

Discussions relating to energy were also caught in the conflict of norms. For example, to some WTO members, liberalizing the energy sector through the reduction of subsidies would result in a "double dividend" of both economic and environmental benefits. Other, however, believed that national decisions on energy choices included variables such as production, availability of energy sources, economic costs and social impacts on local population which should not be compromised. Recognizing these inherent challenges, WTO Member States, instead, started sharing positive national experiences of implementing clean energy and energy-efficient technologies. As a result, the CTE transitioned to an experience-sharing platform where WTO Members could interact with and learn from other WTO Members that implemented clean energy legislation.

D. Forestry

Initial discussions on forestry were limited to those that ensued upon Japan making three presentations between June 2002 and October 2003. The first broadly discussed issued of forest products with trade and environment. The second paper was a submission discussing fisheries and forestry-related environmental issues.[37] The third paper presented the bilateral cooperation between Japan and Indonesia in fighting illegal logging. It was upon submission of the third paper by Japan and Indonesia on illegal logging that led to the expansion of discussions on forestry.

The first paper reminded WTO Members that forests provided various public benefits. These included the mitigation of global warming and the conservation of biological diversity. It also recalled that forests are an exhaustible natural resource and could be depleted through mismanagement. It cited the FAO study titled *The State of the World's Forests 2001* where it was estimated that 9.4 million hectares of global forests had been lost in the past ten years (since 1990). Therefore, Japan was motivated to examine ways to contribute to the goal of sustainable forest management. Japan proposed export restriction and labelling as two possible solutions to tackle the issue. An example of export restriction was "when a certain country prohibits the export of unprocessed logs originating in designated national and state-owned regions of the country." As regards labelling, Japan proposed that WTO Members discuss solutions to introduce labelling requirements to forestry products. According to Japan, however, these labelling requirements should not become unnecessary obstacles to trade. Japan

35. *Id.* at ¶¶ 1.1 -1.3.
36. WTO CTE, Report of the Committee on Trade and Environment (2013), WT/CTE/20 (21 May 2013) at ¶ 4.
37. The fisheries part has already been discussed earlier in this section.

also proposed that WTO Members examine approaches from a trade perspective to reduce illegal logging.[38]

In the second paper - the reactions of which have been documented under the sub-heading of fisheries - proposed that Members can retain flexibility in determining appropriate levels of tariffs after taking into account factors such as the domestic production and consumption and the international supply and demand of the products.[39]

The third was a joint statement by Japan and Indonesia which had signed the "*Bilateral Cooperation between Japan and Indonesia in Combating Illegal Logging.*"[40] This agreement planned to include trade measures against illegally harvested timber and its products. However, the trade measures set in place would be compatible with WTO law, and a study to that effect would be initiated. The Republic of Korea and the EU welcomed this move by Japan and Indonesia.[41]

By 2012, illegal logging was widely recognized as a significant global problem. This was because of the widespread impact it had on forest degradation, climate change and loss of habitat and community livelihoods in developing timber economies. This impact also raised expansive discussions about global social and environmental costs. Australia explained its Illegal Logging Prohibition Bill of 2011 which sought to curb illegal logging by introducing a due diligence test on all timber products entering Australian markets that were sourced, both, domestically or imported. It also aimed at aligning the Bill with similar legislation in the United States and the EU. Australia further stated that it would continue its bilateral cooperation with Asia Pacific countries as an approach to combat illegal logging. After this, New Zealand described the approach it had adopted to stop illegal logging through a voluntary industry led-approach. This approach was tailored to suit the domestic market of New Zealand, which was, in global terms, a relatively small market for imported timber and wood products.

Through this approach, consumer awareness programs were introduced in 2010, which led to protest action from environmental NGOs. As a result, New Zealand's major importers and retailers of tropical timber voluntarily ceased importing and selling without verifying the legality of timber.[42]

The EU also discussed its Forest Law Enforcement, Governance and Trade (FLEGT) Plan. According to it, this plan was adopted in 2005 and introduced controls to timber imports into the EU from countries that signed the bilateral FLEGT voluntary partnership agreement (FLEGT VPA). Till 2012, EU had signed this agreement with Ghana, Cameroon and Congo and was in the process of either signing or negotiating

38. WTO CTE, Issues on Forestry Products Trade and Environment (Submission by Japan), WT/CTE/W/211 (11 June 2002) at p. 2.
39. *See generally* WTO CTE, Sustainable Development and the Trade of Forest and Fishery Products (Submission by Japan), WT/CTE/W/222 (6 February 2003).
40. WTO CTE, Bilateral Cooperation between Japan and Indonesia in Combating Illegal Logging (Communication from Japan), WT/CTE/W/233 (22 October 2003).
41. WTO CTE, Report of the Meeting held on 28 October 2003, WT/CTE/M/35 (19 November 2003).
42. WTO CTE, Bilateral Cooperation between Japan and Indonesia in Combating Illegal Logging (Communication from Japan), WT/CTE/W/233 (22 October 2003).

with Liberia, Central African Republic, Indonesia, Malaysia, Viet Nam, Gabon and the Democratic Republic of Congo. Further, the EU discussed a timber regulation that was adopted in October 2010, which prohibited illegal timber and its products in the EU internal market.[43]

Noteworthy interventions were made by the Philippines and India. The Philippines was concerned that the Australian legislation would create unintended impacts on legitimate exports by creating new restrictions. The Philippines also extended support to the delegation of India in wondering how illegal logging would fit the requirements under CTE's agenda set out in paragraph 32 (i) of Doha Ministerial Declaration. India noted that while Australia's legislation would benefit the environment, it would lead to a "win-loss" and not a "win-win-win" situation. In response, Australia explained that it brought up the topic since it had not been discussed in the CTE for some time. It also asserted that the proposed legislation promoted the trade of legal timber and restricting illegal timber which, according to it, was a "win-win-win" for trade, environment and development.[44]

Many submissions on legal regimes implemented to curb illegal logging were also presented in 2014. Indonesia discussed its forest management certification system, which was developed through multi-stakeholder consultations. This system served to function as a complementary mechanism to domestic law enforcement. Through this system, only forest concessionaires in possession of a sustainable forest management certificate granted by a national accredited body would be permitted to operate. Ghana also discussed its Timber Legality Program which banned logging in designated areas of ecological interest. Interestingly, both Ghana and Indonesia signed the EU FLEGT Voluntary Partnership Agreement (VPA).[45] Canada noted that the risk of exporting illegal timber originating in Canada was negligible because of rigorous legislative supervision. China elucidated its domestic legal regime and its efforts to establish mutual recognition certifications with other developing countries so as to ensure the legality of timber in trade.

In 2015, Malaysia and the Russian Federation provided an overview of their experiences in containing illegal logging. Malaysia implemented forest and timber certification processes; processes for verification of legality in response to legislation enacted by Australia, the United States and EU; introduced policies and legislation; and cooperated at regional and international levels. The process for verification of legality was particularly detailed since:[46]

> [...] Malaysia and Australia had jointly developed the Country specific guideline for Malaysia, which sought to provide guidance to Australian importers on the legality of imports of timber and timber products from Malaysia. Furthermore, Malaysia had made substantial progress in the negotiations of a Forest Law

43. *Ibid.*
44. WTO CTE, Report of the Meeting held on 14 November 2011, WT/CTE/M/53 (27 January 2012) at pp. 6 - 7.
45. *See generally* EU FLEGT, Voluntary Partnership Agreement, available at: http://www.euflegt.efi.int/vpa (accessed on 30 November 2019).
46. WTO CTE, Report of the Meeting held on 22 June 2015, WT/CTE/M/59 (3 September 2015) at p. 15.

Enforcement, Governance and Trade Voluntary Partnership Agreement ('FLEGT VPA') with the European Union. Pending the conclusion of these negotiations, Malaysia developed and implemented a Timber Legality Assurance System ('TLAS') for purposes of due diligence when exporting to the European Union. The FLEGT VPA was an important initiative that could contribute to combating illegal logging.

Malaysia also developed a National Action Plan for Combating Illegal Logging for a period of 2011-2015. This plan aimed at achieving "zero illegal logging." The Russian Federation also described domestic legislation that had led to a decrease in the number of illegal logging. It claimed that damage caused by illegal loggers decreased steadily since the implementation of legislation such as the Roundwood Act of 2013.[47] Mexico, Chinese Taipei and Chile also described the legal framework present in their respective jurisdictions that sought to stop illegal logging. Mexico enforced the Zero Tolerance for Illegal Logging Policy nationwide in 2011. This policy conducted inspection and surveillance at different stages of the forestry production chain. Chile regulated forest-related activities through Decree Law 701 dealing with the promotion of forestation and Law 20283 dealing with native forest recovery and development. Both these laws established procedures for compliance and penalties resulting from non-compliance. As per the laws, any logging activities that did not meet the prescribed plan by the National Forestry Agency were considered as illegal logging.[48]

The discussions and experience sharing in the CTE on Illegal Logging Trade have come a long way since Japan first submitted its paper to the CTE. Notably, while WTO members recognized that illegal logging needed to be curbed, no substantive proposals have been made to come up with new rules or disciplines.

Rather, WTO Members have used the CTE as a forum to raise awareness and queries on potential inconsistencies of WTO Member's domestic legislation with WTO rules and to underscore the importance of mitigating illegal logging, through various means, such as through bilateral initiatives and mutual recognition agreements. Perhaps, as in the Fish Subsidies discussions, the CTE discussions on illegal logging could serve as seeds towards a mandate to discipline illegal logging trade.

47. WTO CTE, Report of the Meeting held on 22 June 2015, WT/CTE/M/59 (3 September 2015) at p. 16.
48. WTO CTE, Report of the Meeting held on 23 October 2014, WT/CTE/M/58 (23 March 2015) at p. 6.

Annex 3

WTO CTESS, Report by the Chairman, Ambassador Manuel A. J. Teehankee, to the Trade Negotiations Committee, TN/TE/20, 21 April 2011

World Trade Organization

TN/TE/20
21 April 2011
(11-2083)

Committee on Trade and Environment
Special Session

TN/TE/20
pp. 1–46

COMMITTEE ON TRADE AND ENVIRONMENT IN SPECIAL SESSION
Report by the Chairman, Ambassador Manuel A. J. Teehankee, to the Trade Negotiations Committee

1. This report to the Trade Negotiations Committee (TNC) provides an update of progress made in the Committee on Trade and Environment in Special Session (CTESS) since my last written report to the TNC in March 2010.[1] It also aims at identifying areas that will require further attention from Members to bring negotiations to a successful conclusion on all three parts of the mandate in Paragraph 31 of the Doha Ministerial Declaration. The report reflects the work undertaken pursuant to the announcement by the Chairman of the TNC in November 2010 of an intensive work programme through the beginning of 2011 and complies with his guidance for draft texts to be developed so they may appear towards the end of the first quarter of 2011.

I. PARAGRAPHS 31(I) AND (II)

2. Paragraph 31(i) considers the relationship between existing WTO rules and specific trade obligations (STOs) set out in multilateral environmental agreements (MEAs). Paragraph 31(ii) considers procedures for regular information exchange between MEA secretariats and the relevant WTO committees, and the criteria for the granting of observer status.
3. I am pleased to report and attach a draft Ministerial Decision on Paragraphs 31(i) and 31(ii) in Annex I, while at the same time express caution that this is not an agreed text nor is it in complete or final form. Everything is conditional in the deepest sense and requires further engagement and deliberations in open-ended session, consistent with the bottom-up, Member-driven process, and our customary negotiating principles of inclusiveness and transparency.

1. As with TN/TE/19 (Report by the Chairman to the TNC, 22 March 2010), this report is circulated under the Chair's own responsibility and is without prejudice to the position of WTO Members in the negotiations.

4. The format is based on Members having converged on the idea of a combined outcome under Paragraphs 31(i) and 31(ii) in the format of a Ministerial Decision. There has been important work carried out in the CTESS, and the draft Ministerial Decision is an attempt to capture the progress made. The language in the draft Ministerial Decision is derived from Members' textual proposals and inputs of Members during the recent intensive process of consultations in varying configurations. In some instances, the textual language represents the Chairman's best perception of discussions and consultations held in the CTESS, particularly in the period of February and March 2011.
5. The draft Ministerial Decision includes square brackets in some places to highlight options, areas of divergence or aspects requiring focused discussion. Where possible, explanations of the debate are provided in footnotes. There are also some proposals which are contained in boxes in the draft Ministerial Decision or which are reflected in Annexes I.A or I.B which either have not yet been fully discussed in the CTESS or may still require considerable further work and discussion to arrive at a common textual formulation.

II. PARAGRAPH 31(III)

6. Paragraph 31(iii) of the Doha Ministerial Declaration considers the reduction or elimination of tariff and non-tariff barriers to trade in environmental goods and services. The format of an outcome under Paragraph 31(iii) is still open, although stated options and components have become clearer. The draft Ministerial Decision format of Paragraphs 31(i) and 31(ii) provides a point of reference.
7. On the identification of environmental goods, much work has been done since the circulation of the compilation of environmental goods of interest in my March 2010 Report to the TNC (TN/TE/19). Annex II.A to this report, which contains the reference universe of environmental goods of interest to Members, is based on HS-6 lines submitted by Members as they were reflected in Annex III of the March 2010 Report to the TNC, also JOB/TE/3/Rev.1 (5 January 2011) and any subsequent submissions. This compilation of Members' submissions is without prejudice to the outcome of the debate on whether the Committee should define what an environmental good is.
8. Annex II.A as well as document JOB/TE/3/Rev.1 (5 January 2011) are intended to be useful to Members across all approaches.[2] There are six

2. For instance, in the project approach, which identifies environmental activities, the reference universe contains various environmental categories or activities that may be relevant to the identified HS lines. In the request and offer, it can serve as a tool to indicate products of interest for requests and/or offers. In the combined approach, the required alpha or beta lines would be

broad categories under which goods have been submitted:[3] air pollution control, renewable energy, waste management and water treatment, environmental technologies, carbon capture and storage and others, and these categories are all indicated in the right column of Annex II.A.

9. A group of Members identified, on an illustrative basis, a number of tariff lines from the reference universe, and these are reflected in Annex II.B. Preliminary discussions on these goods showed that some of the goods included in this set could be considered by the membership as clear environmental goods, as long as they can be specifically identified in the HS classification by an ex-out or otherwise.
10. Over the years, the work on environmental goods identification has shown that a number of technical difficulties remain. Further work needs to be undertaken by delegations and their experts in this respect, including on the verification of HS description and the determination of ex-outs or sub-classifications. Such technical work should be done without prejudice to the approach and the final outcome.
11. Based on a review of all proposals on the table as reflected in the document TN/TE/INF/4/Rev.15 (28 March 2011) and subsequent submissions as well as the views of Members expressed in consultations on the structure of the outcome, there are still essentially four areas that will require Members' focused efforts to arrive at a draft outcome and modalities.[4] These are:
    A) Preambular Language;
    B) Coverage;
    C) Treatment of Tariffs and Non-Tariff Barriers, including Special and Differential Treatment; and
    D) Cross-Cutting and Development Elements.
12. Much discussion has occurred through the years on the above four areas and the following paragraphs review, without prejudging the final outcome, the options and elements discussed in the negotiating process. These are drawn from all the approaches and proposals, which all remain on the table.
13. On ***preambular language***, Members agree that a successful outcome of the negotiations under Paragraph 31 (iii) should deliver a triple-win in terms of trade, environment and development for WTO Members. First, the negotiations can benefit the environment by improving countries' ability to obtain high-quality environmental goods at low cost or by enhancing the

drawn from the reference universe submitted to the CTESS. In the hybrid approach, it could provide a basis for a self-selection by Members.

3. As reflected in Annex III of the March 2010 Report to the TNC and in document JOB/TE/3/Rev.1 (5 January 2011).
4. These proposals are reflected in document TN/TE/INF/4/Rev.15 (28 March 2011) and subsequent submissions. Members may also refer to document JOB/TE/20 which compiles the textual elements relevant to these four areas contained in Members' submissions under Paragraph 31(iii), from 2002 to date, and to a Secretariat Note compiling the various issues raised in Members' submissions under Paragraph 31(iii) in document JOB(07)/137 (17 September 2007).

ability to increase production, exports and trade in environmentally beneficial products.[5] This can directly improve the quality of life for citizens in all countries by providing a cleaner environment and better access to safe water, sanitation or clean energy.

14. The liberalization of trade in environmental goods and services can be beneficial for development by assisting developing countries in obtaining the tools needed to address key environmental priorities as part of their on-going development strategies.[6] Finally, trade wins because these products become less costly and efficient producers of such technologies can find new markets. In addition, liberalizing trade in environmental goods will encourage the use of environmental technologies, which can, in turn stimulate innovation and technology transfer.[7]
15. The primary area requiring delegations' urgent attention relates to agreeing on an approach to ***coverage***.[8] The two most recent proposals - a hybrid approach and combined approach - were put forward in an effort to bridge the various proposals on the table and could, therefore, provide a starting point for structured discussions on coverage.
16. ***Attached at Annex II*** is a summary of the potential structures of an outcome on coverage, based on all approaches on the table. Delegations need to engage and work on the concrete elements of coverage to which the treatment modalities would apply.
17. On ***treatment***, although the treatment modalities proposed to depend on the final structure considered, all proposals for options include a reduction of tariffs to zero for some products or a reduction including 0 for X and a 50 per cent cut after formula application and elimination of tariffs by certain set periods of time. During consultations, we have also touched on

5. TN/TE/W/34 (United States, 19 June 2003), para. 3; TN/TE/W/47 (European Communities, 17 February 2005), para. 5; TN/TE/W/50/Rev.1 (Canada, 4 July 2006), para. 13; TN/MA/W/70, TN/TE/W/65 (Canada, European Communities, New Zealand, Norway, Singapore, Switzerland, and the United States, 9 May 2006), para. 2.3; TN/TE/W/57 (Switzerland, 6 July 2005), para. 4; TN/TE/W/54 (India, 4 July 2005), para. 2.
6. TN/TE/W/55 (Cuba, 5 July 2005), para. 15; TN/TE/W/42 (China, 6 July 2004), para. 2; TN/TE/W/34 (United States, 19 June 2003), para. 3; TN/MA/W/70, TN/TE/W/65 (Canada, European Communities, New Zealand, Norway, Singapore, Switzerland, and the United States, 9 May 2006), para. 2.2; TN/TE/W/49/Suppl.1 (New Zealand, 16 June 2005), para. 17; JOB(06)/140 (Canada, the European Communities, New Zealand, Japan, Norway, the Separate Customs Territory of Taiwan, Penghu, Kinmen and Matsu, Switzerland, and the United States, 8 May 2006), para. 2; JOB(07)/146 (Brazil, 1 October 2007), para. 3; JOB/TE/17 (Bolivia, Venezuela, 24 March 2011), para. 3; JOB/TE/18 (SVEs, 1 April 2011), paras. 4-5; TN/TE/W/79 (China and India, 15 April 2011), para. 4.
7. TN/TE/W/34 (United States, 19 June 2003), para. 3; TN/MA/W/70, TN/TE/W/65 (Canada, European Communities, New Zealand, Norway, Singapore, Switzerland, and the United States, 9 May 2006), para. 2.2-2.3; TN/TE/W/47 (European Communities, 17 February 2005), para. 5; TN/TE/W/74 (Argentina, 23 November 2009), para. 2; JOB/TE/5 (Singapore, 23 June 2010), para. 2.
8. Delegations are referred to Annex II as well as the compilation of textual elements drawn from all proposals (JOB/TE/20) and also the Secretariat Note compiling the various issues raised under Paragraph 31(iii) in JOB(07)/137.

reducing and eliminating non-tariff barriers (NTBs) to trade in environmental goods and services. Members have noted the existence of NTBs in certain sectors and provided general ideas on how NTBs can be reduced, for instance, by increasing transparency. Some general ideas for an outcome on NTBs were proposed, including in relation to transparency.[9]

18. As regards ***special and differential treatment*** for developing countries, lesser reductions, implementation delays and other forms of flexibilities were discussed. Product exemptions, as well as the liberalization by developing country Members of a lesser number of tariff lines, have also been envisaged.[10] For least-developed country Members and small and vulnerable economies, additional flexibilities could be envisaged.[11]
19. There are a number of important ***cross-cutting elements*** of the mandate, and this relates to environmental services and to develop aspects, such as environmental technologies.
20. With respect to environmental services, the main work is occurring in the Committee on Trade in Services Special Session, and one option is to draft textual elements cross-referring to work there relating to enhanced commitments on environmental services. Another possibility would be that enhanced commitments on environmental services are associated with the environmental goods in the reference universe or categories or to an agreed set of environmental goods.[12]
21. Concerning environmental technologies, discussions have clearly highlighted the importance of these elements as being an integral part of an outcome.[13]

---

9. TN/TE/W/76 (Argentina and Brazil, 30 June 2010), Annex, para. 10.
10. JOB/TE/16 and Corr. 1 (Mexico, Chile, 11 March 2011), para. 12; TN/TE/W/42 (China, 6 July 2004), para. 6; TN/TE/W/76 (Argentina and Brazil, 30 June 2010), Annex, para. 7.
11. JOB/TE/18 (Small, Vulnerable Economies (SVEs), 1 April 2011), para. 5.
12. JOB(07)193/Rev.1 (European Communities, United States, 6 December 2007), para. 3.
13. See TN/TE/W/79 (China and India, 15 April 2011), which provides further ideas on these aspects. JOB/TE/17 (Bolivia, Venezuela, 24 March 2011), para. 13. See also Part D of JOB/TE/20.

TN/TE/20
pp 5–13

Annex I: Draft Ministerial Decision on Trade and Environment

INTRODUCTORY COMMENT

The mains points covered in the draft Ministerial Decision below and Annexes I.A and I.B are summarized as follows:

- Members provided specific textual proposals for *preambular language* as reflected in the draft Ministerial Decision, covering such aspects as the mandate, the objective of sustainable development, mutual supportiveness of trade and environment, recognition of the different bodies of international law, and the importance of technical assistance and capacity building. A number of delegations have proposed other preambular texts for inclusion in the draft outcome, focusing on coherence and mutual supportiveness of MEAs and the WTO Agreement in the context of international law.
- The draft Ministerial Decision reflects the observation of Members in the CTESS that an *STO set out in an MEA* is understood to be one that requires an MEA party to take, or refrain from taking, a particular trade action. The sense of the Members of the CTESS has been to ensure there is no prescriptiveness in the description of an STO, and a few Members have questioned the need at all for a definition of STOs.
- Substantially all Members agree that an outcome should highlight the importance of *coordination at the national level* in the negotiation and implementation of STOs in MEAs and the value of sharing of domestic experiences in this regard in the Committee on Trade and Environment (CTE). The draft Ministerial Decision includes a provision that the CTE shall provide a forum for continued sharing of individual Members' experiences. One suggestion, raised during small group consultations, relates to coordination at the international level.
- The basic elements on *information exchange* for inclusion in a final outcome—holding of information exchange sessions with MEA secretariats; access to documents; and collaboration between WTO and MEA secretariats - are long-established, as contained in Annex II of my March 2010 Report to the TNC.[1] These elements are reflected in specific textual provisions in the draft Ministerial Decision. Recent discussions among Members focused on the required level of detail in a final outcome and also whether information exchange sessions might be held not only in the CTE but also other relevant WTO committees.
- On *observer status*, consultations confirmed that two main issues remain in this area: (i) to arrive at a textual formulation that can facilitate appropriate MEA observer status in the CTE; and (ii) whether a decision may be included

1. TN/TE/19 (Report by the Chairman to the TNC, 22 March 2010).

in a final outcome relating to pending MEA applications for observership in the Committee. On the first issue, the draft Ministerial Decision includes a textual formulation. On the issue of granting of observership to some MEA secretariats with longstanding participation in the work of the CTE, different formulations have been discussed in the CTESS, and possible compromise language is reflected in the draft Ministerial Decision that will require further work among delegations.

- There is clear support and convergence that Members wish to deliver an outcome on *technical assistance and capacity building*. The draft Ministerial Decision reflects Members' proposals to give guidance to the CTE on the provision and development of technical assistance by the WTO Secretariat focused on the implementation of STOs set out in MEAs. In addition, there are proposals for the establishment of a group of experts on trade and environment to give advice on certain issues to developing country Members.[2] A provisional textual formulation is contained in the draft Ministerial Decision, and further textual proposals are reflected in Annex I.A. This is a topic area where the proponent groups and delegations need to network further amongst themselves and with the wider membership.
- On *dispute settlement*, regarding the relationship between existing WTO rules and STOs in MEAs, the draft Ministerial Decision contains suggested compromise language largely based on the Swiss non-mandatory approach.[3] Further textual proposals derived from Members ideas and consultations are contained in Annex I.B, relating to the use of experts, on which divergences continue to remain.

DRAFT MINISTERIAL DECISION ON TRADE AND ENVIRONMENT [DISCUSSION DRAFT BASED ON THE TEXTUAL PROPOSALS AND IDEAS OF MEMBERS WITH RESPECT TO PARAGRAPHS 31(I) AND 31(II)]

Ministers,

Recalling that:

- Paragraph 31(i) of the Doha Ministerial Declaration called for negotiations on the relationship between existing WTO rules and specific trade obligations (STOs) set out in multilateral environmental agreements (MEAs) and stated that the negotiations were to be limited in scope to the applicability of such existing WTO rules as among parties to the MEA in question, and were not to prejudice the WTO rights of any Member that is not a party to the MEA in question;
- Paragraph 31(ii) of the Doha Ministerial Declaration called for negotiations on procedures for regular information exchange between MEA secretariats and the relevant WTO committees, and the criteria for the granting of observer status; and

2. JOB(08)/38 (African Group, 8 May 2008); JOB/TE/14 (ACP Group, 7 March 2011)
3. TN/TE/W/77 (Switzerland, 4 November 2011).

- Pursuant to Paragraph 32 of the Doha Ministerial Declaration, the outcome of negotiations carried out under Paragraphs 31 (i) and 31 (ii) was to be compatible with the open and non-discriminatory nature of the multilateral trading system, not to add to or diminish the rights and obligations of Members under existing WTO Agreements, in particular the Agreement on the Application of Sanitary and Phytosanitary Measures, nor alter the balance of these rights and obligations, and was to take into account the needs of developing and least-developed countries;

Affirming our commitment to the objective of sustainable development, as stated in the Preamble to the Marrakesh Agreement Establishing the World Trade Organization (WTO Agreement), and our conviction as stated in Paragraph 6 of the Doha Ministerial Declaration that the aims of upholding and safeguarding an open and non-discriminatory multilateral trading system, and acting for the protection of the environment and the promotion of sustainable development can and must be mutually supportive;[4]

Recalling also the 1994 Marrakesh Ministerial Decision on Trade and Environment which considered that there should not be, nor need be, any policy contradiction between upholding and safeguarding an open, non-discriminatory and equitable multilateral trading system on the one hand, and acting for the protection of the environment, and the promotion of sustainable development on the other;[5]

[*Noting that the Vienna Convention on the Law of Treaties states that every treaty in force is binding upon the parties to it and must be performed by them in good faith;*][6]
[*Recognizing that both MEAs and the WTO Agreement are instruments of international law of equal standing between parties to the agreements, and that all provisions under international law should be implemented harmoniously and in good faith;*][7]

4. TN/TE/W/78 (United States, 14 February 2011), preamble; JOB/TE/19 (Australia, Mexico, United States, 1 April 2011), preamble; and JOB(08)/33 (Norway, 29 April 2008), para. 7, all refer to language in Paragraph 6 of the Doha Ministerial Declaration.
5. TN/TE/W/68 (European Union, 30 June 2006), preamble, includes language: "Reaffirming that MEAs and WTO rules contribute jointly to the international community's pursuit of shared objectives; and expressing our desire that trade and environment policies blend effectively to deliver sustainable development", that is reflective of the language in the Marrakesh Ministerial Decision.
6. Mexico as Friend of the Chair provided this formulation, which is yet to be fully discussed with the wider membership. The Chair notes Mexico has emphasized that this bridging formulation would be in lieu of other textual proposals concerning the relative standing of MEAs and WTO rules in international law.
7. JOB(08)/33 (Norway, 29 April 2008), para. 6; supported by the European Union.

> *Committed* to ensure coherence between international trade and environmental law in a mutually supportive way in order to continue to improve the architecture of international law to better cope with future challenges in an ever more interlinked world;[8]
>
> *Reaffirming* that MEAs constitute the response of the international community to environmental problems and play an instrumental role in reinforcing the individual and collective actions of all Members;[9]

Recognizing the importance of technical assistance and capacity building in the field of trade and environment to developing countries, in particular, the least-developed among them;

Noting the important work undertaken in the Committee on Trade and Environment in Special Session (CTESS) on Paragraphs 31(i) and 31(ii) of the Doha Ministerial Declaration;

Considering observations of Members in the CTESS that:

- A specific trade obligation (STO) set out in a multilateral environmental agreement (MEA) is understood to be one that requires an MEA Party to take, or refrain from taking, a particular trade action[10] [a trade-related action[11]];
- The relationship between WTO rules and STOs set out in MEAs is working well, and no formal disputes in the WTO have arisen challenging the implementation of an STO set out in an MEA;[12]

> - Until now STOs among parties to MEAs have not been contested in the WTO and should a situation arise of a WTO Member bringing such cases before the WTO, WTO rules would be applicable: observing also that STOs that are multilaterally negotiated, between parties and specific in nature are unlikely to be challenged in the WTO;[13]

8. Textual proposal made by Switzerland at the March 2011 consultations. This proposal requires discussion in the wider membership.
9. See TN/TE/W/68 (European Union, 30 June 2006), preamble; also highlighted by the European Union during the March 2011 consultations. The European Union further proposed to give recognition that "multilateral approaches to global environmental problems are to be strongly preferred."
10. The current formulation, pursuant to Members' preference, is descriptive of observations of Members in the CTESS and not a prescriptive definition.
11. Textual proposal made by Japan at the March 2011 consultations and in a Non-paper circulated by Japan at consultations on 21 March 2011 - indicating its preference for "a trade-related action" and its view "that both (1) the trade measures explicitly provided for as mandatory under an MEA, and (2) *"obligation de résultat"* provided for in an MEA in which the trade measures are not identified should be included in the scope of STOs, and the definition of STOs should leave room for "obligation de résultat" in the scope of STOs." Chinese Taipei also supported reference to "trade-related action".
12. JOB(08)/33 (Norway, 29 April 2008), para. 9; JOB/TE/19 (Australia, Mexico, United States, 1 April 2011), preamble.
13. JOB(08)/33 (Norway, 29 April 2008), and Corr.1 (5 November 2010), paras. 9, 10, 11 (combined).

- Efforts undertaken by Members at the domestic level to coordinate the views of all relevant government agencies and stakeholders when negotiating and implementing STOs [as well as WTO rules][14] [and also at the international level in terms of coordination between various governmental bodies and international organizations when addressing WTO matters related to MEAs,][15] have been helpful to enhancing the mutual supportiveness of trade and the environment;[16]
- Sharing of domestic experiences in the CTESS in negotiating and implementing STOs [as well as WTO rules][17] has provided useful insight into ways in which Members can work to promote mutually supportive trade and environment policies;

> - Several features in the design of STOs set out in MEAs have contributed to the positive relationship between such obligations and existing WTO rules such as, careful tailoring of STOs to meet a particular environmental objective, clarity of scope and application of STOs, certain procedures laid out in the MEA that rely on objective criteria and scientific input to make decisions, and other built in procedures in the MEA for changes to its scope that are inclusive, transparent and appropriately flexible;[18]

Ministers,

With a view to enhancing the mutual supportiveness of trade and the environment, hereby *decide* as follows:

1. Members are encouraged to coordinate at the domestic level among relevant government agencies [and with international organizations][19] when negotiating and implementing WTO rules and when negotiating and implementing STOs set out in MEAs, and to share domestic experiences in this regard in the Committee on Trade and Environment (CTE) [with a view to ensuring

14. The European Union and Switzerland have emphasized the need for two-way balance and have objected to language emphasizing only the negotiation and implementation of STOs in MEAs while not addressing WTO rules.
15. The bracketed language requires further discussion with the broader membership and is derived from the January to March 2011 consultations where the European Union had provided a textual proposal: "Coordination between various governmental bodies and international organizations when addressing WTO matters related to MEAs is useful in enhancing mutual supportiveness between trade and the environment".
16. In TN/TE/W/78 (United States, 14 February 2011) and JOB/TE/19 (Australia, Mexico, United States, 1 April 2011), a further phrase was proposed, reading (in JOB/TE/19): "...and have fostered compatibility between Members' international trade obligations and domestic implementation of STOs set out in MEAs." This aspect was considered by certain Members such as India and Norway as unnecessary or overly prescriptive.
17. See footnote 14 above.
18. TN/TE/W/78 (United States, 14 February 2011), JOB/TE/19 (Australia, Mexico, United States, 1 April 2011); some delegations (European Union, Switzerland, Norway, India, Chinese Taipei viewed the proposed tiret as either unbalanced, as it does not refer to features in WTO rules, or unnecessary or overly prescriptive.
19. See footnote 15 above.

coherence/compatibility with rights and obligations arising from WTO Agreements and from STOs in MEAs].[20]

2. The WTO Secretariat, on behalf of the CTE, shall:
   (a) cooperate and collaborate with MEA secretariats, including through: increased information exchange; as appropriate, document sharing and preparation; and enhanced trade and environment-related technical assistance and capacity building activities, particularly those related to the implementation of STOs set out in MEAs;
   (b) facilitate appropriate access by MEA secretariats to derestricted WTO documents on a reciprocal basis and make information from MEA secretariats available to WTO Members, including through the use of indexing and internet-based tools. Access to derestricted WTO documents by MEA secretariats shall be facilitated in accordance with the General Council Decision of 14 May 2002 on Procedures for the Circulation and Derestriction of WTO Documents (WT/L/452).[21]
3. While affirming that requests for observer status of international intergovernmental organizations are subject to the criteria and procedures set out in Annex 3 of the Rules of Procedure for Sessions of the Ministerial Conference and Meetings of the General Council (WT/L/161) the CTE shall, when examining requests for observer status from MEA secretariats, have particular regard to the following:[22]
   (a) the relevance of the MEA's scope of work to the Committee as well as the relevance of the Committee's scope of work to the MEA;[a]
   (b) the MEA secretariat's participation in the CTE and its prior contribution to WTO work, including workshops, capacity building activities and preparation of documents; and/or the mutual benefit that may accrue to the Committee and the MEA from the MEA secretariat's participation in meetings of the CTE.
   a. *Explanatory Note: Examples of relevance would be whether the MEA contains provisions that have potential implications for international trade*

20. TN/TE/W/2 (Argentina, 23 May 2002), and highlighted by Argentina in the March 2011 consultations. Some delegations (European Union, Norway) countered with the need for balance and two-way coherence in this paragraph.
21. As supported in Paragraph 31(ii) Drafting Group consultations in January and February 2011 by India, this proposed paragraph (2(b)) is drawn from Annex II of TN/TE/19 (Chairman's Report to the TNC, 22 March 2010).
22. TN/TE/W/78 (United States, 14 February 2011) and also Annex II of TN/TE/19 (Chairman's Report to the TNC, 22 March 2010) highlighted two other criteria derived from Annex 3 of the Rules of Procedure for Sessions of the Ministerial Conference and Meetings of the General Council (WT/L/161), namely (i) the MEA's membership, e.g., whether it broadly reflects the membership of WTO; and (ii) the reciprocity provided by the MEA to the WTO with respect to access to proceedings, documents, and other aspects of observers status. In consultations, various Members noted that the reference to "whether it broadly reflects the membership of WTO" went beyond Annex 3 of WT/L/161: concerning the reciprocity aspects, it was considered by various Members that these were already covered by Annex 3 of WT/L/161 and did not need to be highlighted.

or whether the WTO Committee's work covers aspects and rules that have potential implications for the environmental issues covered by the MEA.

4. The CTE shall grant observer status to MEA secretariats that have applied for such status in the Committee and have met the criteria set out in paragraph 3 above;[23]

The CTE shall grant observer status to the secretariats of the following MEAs, recognizing that all have applied for such status and have met the criteria and procedures set out in Annex 3 of the Rules of Procedure for Sessions of the Ministerial Conference and Meetings of the General Council: *(i) Basel Convention on the Control of Transboundary Movements of Hazardous Wastes and their Disposal; (ii) International Tropical Timber Organization; (iii) Montreal Protocol on Substances that Deplete the Ozone Layer; and (iv) Rotterdam Convention on the Prior Informed Consent Procedure for Certain Hazardous Chemicals and Pesticides in International Trade.*[24]

5. The CTE shall:
   (a) provide a forum to continue to share experiences of individual Members pursuant to paragraph 1 of this Decision with a view to enhancing the mutual supportiveness of trade and the environment;
   (b) hold information exchange sessions with MEA secretariats on a regular basis.[25] The sessions will provide an opportunity for two-way information exchanges between MEA and WTO secretariats and their respective memberships on topics of common interest;[26]

23. TN/TE/W/78 (United States, 14 February 2011), para 4, and JOB/TE/19 (Australia, Mexico, United States, 1 April 2011), para. 4, contained a textual proposal, drawn from language in Annex II of TN/TE/19 (Chairman's Report to the TNC, 22 March 2010): "Members shall also consider, in the event that they cannot reach a consensus with respect to a request from a particular MEA for permanent observer status to a WTO Committee, inviting the relevant MEA Secretariat to observe on a meeting-by-meeting basis, until a consensus on the request for permanent observer status can be reached." In consultations, some delegations expressed reservations on this proposal as it only reflects current practise which does not require a Ministerial Decision.
24. Canada as Friend of the Chair provided this formulation, which is yet to be fully discussed with the wider membership. In consultation with the CTE Secretariat, the Chair understands these are the four MEAs with pending observership requests and current *ad hoc* participation. In TN/TE/W/66 (European Union, 15 May 2006), and Drafting Group consultations, the European Union proposed the grant of observer status (automatic or by strong presumption) to MEAs with longstanding participation in the CTE.
25. In consultations, and as reflected in Annex II of TN/TE/19 (Chairman's Report to the TNC, 22 March 2010), India suggested specifying the information exchange sessions be held on an annual (or biennial) basis. Some delegations commented that the reference to "regular" would provide more flexibility to the Committee in the holding of the sessions.
26. In consultations held in the Drafting Group on Paragraph 31(ii) concerning information exchange sessions, a further suggestion was made by the European Union that upon request by other relevant WTO committees or MEA secretariats, these committees, in consultation with MEA secretariats, shall also hold information exchange sessions.

(c) oversee the provision and, as necessary, the development of technical assistance activities by the WTO Secretariat focused on the implementation of STOs set out in MEAs, drawing on the WTO Secretariat's knowledge of provisions of the WTO Agreement, as well as the relevant MEA secretariat's knowledge of particular STOs. The Committee shall ensure that such activities draw on experiences and expertise shared in the Committee on Trade and Environment pursuant to this Decision, and take into account, *inter alia*, the following important objectives:
   (i) maintenance of the independence of the respective secretariats;
   (ii) avoidance of duplication of resources and efforts; and
   (iii) consideration of developing countries, and in particular the least-developed among them, as recipients of technical assistance.

[(d) [Establish][Provide for the establishment of] a group of [2] experts on trade and environment to be elected [every three years] by the CTE based on criteria to be determined by the Committee, who shall be available on a priority basis to least-developed countries and developing countries as a complement to existing technical assistance mechanisms of the WTO.][27]

[(e) Provide for a flexible and expeditious procedure of a conciliatory and non-adjudicatory nature to assist Members with [potential] differences regarding the relationship between existing WTO rules and specific trade obligations of multilateral environmental agreements, through the offices of its Chair or a Friend of the Chair agreed upon by the parties.][28]

---

27. Proposed formulation drawn from various proposals and consultations.JOB(08)/38 (African Group, 8 May 2008), and JOB/TE/14 (ACP Group, 7 March 2011); see also Annex I.A on "Proposed Elements Relating to a Group of Experts."

28. TN/TE/W/77 (Switzerland, 4 November 2010), para 4. See also Annex I.B on "Proposed Elements on Dispute Settlement."

Annex I.A: Proposed Elements Relating to a Group of Experts[1]

Recommitting ourselves to protecting and preserving the environment and *recognizing* that the establishment of a specific, permanent technical assistance and capacity building instrument will assist developing country Members in strengthening the relationship between trade and environment regimes;[2]

1. The Committee on Trade and Environment (CTE) shall:
   - [Establish [and adequately fund][3] a "Group of Experts on Trade and Environment" (GETE)[4], drawing on experience from technical assistance mechanisms and other expert groups in the WTO and other organizations.][5]
   - [Establish a permanent group of independent experts on trade and environment composed of [x] highly qualified persons who shall be elected by the CTE.][6]
2. The Group of Experts (GETE) shall:
   - [Assist Members in terms of the implementation of specific trade obligations (STOs) under multilateral environmental agreements (MEAs).][7]
   - [Be available for consultations by any Member on the linkages between specific trade obligations (STOs) as laid out in multilateral environmental agreements (MEAs) and the WTO as a complement to existing technical assistance mechanisms of the WTO, with priority for LDCs and developing countries.][8]
   - [Assist in the provision of technical assistance and capacity building relating to multilateral environmental agreements (MEAs) with trade provisions, the negotiation of climate change-related MEAs with specific trade obligations (STOs), and environmental subsidies that affect international trade with developing countries, with priority for LDCs, SIDS and SVEs.][9]

---

1. The full proposals containing additional aspects can be consulted in JOB(08)/38 (African Group, 8 May 2008), and JOB/TE/14 (ACP Group, 7 March 2011).
2. JOB/TE/14 (ACP Group, 7 March 2011), para (a), and JOB(08)/38 (African Group, 8 May 2008), para. 6.
3. JOB/TE/14 (ACP Group, 7 March 2011), para. (e).
4. JOB(08)/38 (African Group, 8 May 2008), para. 7; JOB/TE/14 (ACP Group, 7 March 2011), para. (e).
5. JOB(08)/38 (African Group, 8 May 2008) also comments in para 8: "This expertise could also be drawn from international organizations such as the World Customs Organization (WCO), UNCTAD, UNEP and other organizations which provide technical assistance to Members."
6. Textual proposal by Pakistan from January 2011 small group consultations; circulated for information in a Chair's non-paper on Technical Assistance and Capacity Building at 21 March 2011 Chair's Consultations. The textual proposal makes reference in particular to the idea that the experts will be elected by the CTE and one shall be replaced each year.
7. JOB(08)/38 (African Group, 8 May 2008), para. 8.
8. Proposed textual suggestion by Pakistan from January 2011 small group consultations.
9. Drawn from JOB/TE/14 (ACP Group, 7 March 2011), para (e).

Annex I.B: Proposed Elements on Dispute Settlement

The Committee on Trade and Environment (CTE) shall:

- [Encourage Members, involved in formal consultations pursuant to Article 4 of the Understanding on Rules and Procedures Governing the Settlement of Disputes relating to a dispute regarding the relationship between existing WTO rules and multilateral environmental agreements (MEAs), to draw on the expertise of experts in the area at issue.][1]
- [[Encourage Members,] [Require Members,][2] who are parties to a dispute regarding the relationship between existing WTO rules and a specific trade obligation contained in a multilateral environmental agreement, to seek the advice of experts on the MEA in question; the Committee shall encourage as well disputing Members [to agree] [to request] that the dispute panel hearing their dispute utilize the procedures under Article 13 of the Understanding on Rules and Procedures Governing the Settlement of Disputes to seek advice and information in relation to the MEA in question.][3]

1. Drawn from TN/TE/W/77 (Switzerland, 4 November 2010), para. 4.
2. In TN/TE/W/68 (European Union, 30 June 2006), para. 3 the European Union proposed mandatory language with respect to WTO panels seeking expertise of MEAs: Para 3(c) reads: "Where a WTO panel examines issues with an environmental content, relating to a particular MEA, the panel shall call for and defer to, in the relevant points, the expertise of the MEA in question."
3. Proposal drawn from suggestions in TN/TE/W/77 (Switzerland, 4 November 2011), and TN/TE/W/68 (European Union, 30 June 2006).

ANNEX II: STRUCTURE OF THE OUTCOME ENVIRONMENTAL GOODS COVERAGE UNDER PARAGRAPH 31(III)

INTRODUCTORY COMMENT

1. The coverage approaches necessarily focus on how Members can agree on an environmentally credible universe of products to which the treatment modalities could apply.[1]
2. One proposal focuses on identifying environmental goods on the basis of environmental projects,[2] with the broad criteria for designating such projects decided by the CTE using the six broad categories included in the attached reference universe.[3] Goods under such projects would qualify for specified concessions for the duration of the project.
3. Another proposal focuses on a request and offer process that would allow each Member to propose those items it considers are environmental goods and for which it is prepared to assume liberalization commitments.[4] A certain number of "offer rounds" would be established following a strict timeline. It remains open whether Members contemplate this process to be a one-time process or a continuous process of progressive liberalization.
4. According to a submission presented during the recent intensification of negotiations, there would be two lists, one for developed and one for developing country Members with both being self-selected from the reference universe and subject to an agreed *alpha* minimum number of tariff lines for developed country Members and a *beta* minimum number of tariff lines for developing country Members, with *alpha* being greater in number than *beta*.[5]
5. The idea of developing two lists had been put forward by two proposals in the past. In one of these proposals, there would be a *core list* of environment products[6] that could deliver an ambitious and significant outcome.[7] In addition, there will be a *complementary list* on which consensus could not be reached from which Members would have to self-select a certain *x* per cent of tariff lines.[8]

---

1. Part B of JOB/TE/20 provides a comprehensive overview of textual elements on coverage modalities, as derived from Members submissions. Members may also refer to a secretariat note compiling the various issues raised in Mambers' submissions to the CTESS under Paragraph 31(iii) from 2002-2007 circulated in JOB(07)/137 on 17 September 2007.
2. JOB(07)/77 (Argentina and India, 6 June 2007).
3. See Annex II.A.
4. JOB(07)/146 (Brazil, 1 October 2007); JOB(09)/184 (Brazil, 15 December 2009); TN/TE/W/76 (Argentina, Brazil, 30 June 2010).
5. JOB/TE/16 and Corr. 1 (Mexico, Chile, 11 March 2011).
6. TN/TE/W/38 (United States, 7 July 2003), para. 3.
7. See for instance the "Convergence Set" composed of 153 entries submitted by a group of Members in document JOB(09)/132 (Canada, the European Communities, Japan, Korea, New Zealand, Norway, the Separate Customs Territory of Taiwan, Penghu, Kinmen and Matsu, Switzerland and the United States, 9 October 2009).
8. TN/TE/W/38 (United States, 7 July 2003), paras. 3, 5.

6. According to another proposal, there would be a *common list* for all Members, which comprises specific product lines that constitute environmental goods.[9] The second list would be a *development list* which could comprise products selected from the common list by developing countries for an exemption or a lower level of tariff treatment.
7. In an effort to combine the various elements of all proposals on the table, the *hybrid* approach includes the following components: (i) an agreed core list[10] which would comprise a targeted set of environmental goods on which all Members would take commitments; (ii) a complementary self-selected list: developed countries would individually select a number of environmental products for tariff elimination and developing countries are encouraged to participate; (iii) as a complement to the common core list and complementary lists, products would be identified through a request/offer process, the outcome of which would be multilateralized in accordance with the MFN principle; and (iv) environmental projects could be used to identify lines for inclusion in the common core list, the complementary self-selected list or the request-offer list[11] or by unilateral liberalization if used in environmental projects.

OVERALL STRUCTURE[12]

I. PREAMBULAR LANGUAGE
II. COVERAGE
III. TREATMENT OF TARIFFS AND NON-TARIFF BARRIERS, INCLUDING SPECIAL AND DIFFERENTIAL TREATMENT
IV. CROSS-CUTTING AND DEVELOPMENT ELEMENTS

II. COVERAGE: POTENTIAL STRUCTURES OF OUTCOME ON COVERAGE

A. HYBRID APPROACH[13]

(i) an agreed *core list* of environmental goods drawn from the reference universe in Annex II.A. on which all Members would take commitments;
(ii) a *complementary self-selected list*:
- developed countries would individually select a number of environmental products for tariff elimination
- developing countries are encouraged to participate;

9. TN/TE/W/42 (China, 6 July 2004), paras. 5-6.
10. A group of Members identified, on an illustrative and starting-point basis, 26 tariff lines drawn from the reference universe. Preliminary discussions showed that some of the goods included in this set could be considered by the membership as clear environmental goods, as long as they can be specifically identified in the HS classification by an ex-out or otherwise. See Annex II.B.
11. JOB/TE/15 (Australia; Colombia; Hong Kong, China; Norway; and Singapore, 8 March 2011).
12. Proposed textual elements derived from Members' submissions relating to these four areas are contained in JOB/TE/20.
13. JOB/TE/15 (Australia; Colombia; Hong Kong, China; Norway; and Singapore, 8 March 2011).

(iii) *request/offer process* as a complement to the common core list and complementary lists, the outcome of which would be multilateralized in accordance with the MFN principle; and
(iv) *environmental projects* used to identify lines for inclusion in the common core list, the complementary self-selected list or the request-offer list or by unilateral liberalization if used in environmental projects.

B. ALPHA BETA COMBINED APPROACH[14]
(i) Alpha - developed Members self-select Alpha goods from the reference universe in Annex II.A.;
(ii) Beta - developing Members self-select Beta goods from the reference universe in Annex II.A.;
(iii) Alpha greater than Beta - subject to an agreed Alpha minimum number of tariff lines for developed country Members and a Beta minimum number of tariff lines for developing country Members, with Alpha being greater in number than Beta;
(iv) products not covered by the individual Member's self-selected list could be committed under a *request and offer* process on a voluntary basis.

C. CORE/COMMON LIST WITH COMPLEMENTARY LIST/DEVELOPMENT LIST

A Core or Common List of goods for all Members multilaterally agreed.[15]

The agreed set of goods would be subject to periodic review under some form of the review mechanism.[16]

In addition to goods included in the core list, developed Members would self-select a number of products comprising a complementary list.[17]

Goods on which there is a strong acknowledgement of environmental credential, but no consensus, could constitute a complementary list, of which Members must self-select a certain x per cent of tariff lines.[18]

A development list of products selected by developing countries. SVEs and LDCs that could be exempted from, or subject to lesser commitments.[19]

D. IDENTIFICATION THROUGH REQUEST & OFFER

A bilateral Request and Offer process would be used to identify goods of environmental interest to Members, followed by a certain number of "offer rounds" held over a specified period of time, subsequently multilateralized.[20]

14. JOB/TE/16 and Cor. 1 (Mexico, Chile, 11 March 2011). SVEs (JOB/TE/18, 1 April 2011).
15. TN/TE/W/38 (United States, 7 July 2003); TN/TE/W/42 (China, 6 July 2004); JOB/TE/15 (Australia; Colombia; Hong Kong, China; Norway and Singapore, 8 March 2011).
16. JOB(09)/132 (Canada, the European Communities, Japan, Korea, New Zealand, Norway, the Separate Customs Territory of Taiwan, Penghu, Kinmen and Matsu, Switzerland, and the United States, 27 April 2007).
17. JOB/TE/15 (Australia; Colombia; Hong Kong, China; Norway and Singapore, 8 March 2011).
18. TN/TE/W/38 (United States, 7 July 2003); TN/TE/W/34 (United States, 19 June 2003).
19. TN/TE/W/42 (China, 6 July 2004).
20. JOB(07)/146 (Brazil, 1 October 2007); JOB(09)/184 (Brazil, 15 December 2009); JOB/TE/15 (Australia; Colombia; Hong Kong, China; Norway and Singapore, 8 March 2011).

Sample request and offer modality:[21]

Step 1. "A list is presented containing: six digit HS code of product with an indication of whether the request applies to the full six digit or part of it; [the] description of product; [an] indication of environmental goods category the good is believed to fall in; [an] indication of reason why the good is believed to be 'environmental'."
Step 2. "[The] requested country provides ... data on requested list, containing: [an] identification of national tariff code, at tariff line level, that corresponds to the description of requested good, with an "ex" indication in case it is an "ex out"; [a] full description of national tariff code; import data by national tariff line, average 200X/200X, with discrimination of all suppliers; bound rate; final rate after application of modalities."
Step 3. "[The] requesting country presents revised request list in national tariff codes of requested country."
Step 4. "[The] requested country presents offer lists to requesting countries containing: national tariff code; full description of national tariff code; import data by national tariff line, average 200X/200X, from requesting country; bound rate; final rate after application of modalities; offer expressed as final rate. Rate would be the same as final rate if no additional liberalization offer is made for the product."
Step 5. "[One week of] bilateral negotiations would take place in Geneva, [to be followed by another week of bilateral negotiations (with one week interval in between the two negotiating weeks).]"
Step 6. "Each requested country presents [then] its list with the result of negotiations to be multilateralized, containing: national tariff code; full description of national tariff code; bound rate; final rate after application of modalities; negotiated offer expressed as final rate (< to the final rate)."
Step 7. "[A] collective Evaluation Meeting [will take place.]"
Step 8. "[The final Schedules are presented] with the incorporation of the concessions, [without] "environmental good" marking or specification."

E. IDENTIFICATION THROUGH INTEGRATED-PROJECT APPROACH

The Integrated-Project approach would agree and define environmental projects, as well as environmental activities or categories, to be carried out by designated national entities, for which goods utilized in the activities could qualify for concessions.[22]

21. JOB(09)/184 (Brazil, 15 December 2009).
22. TN/TE/W/62 (Argentina, 14 October 2005); Job(07)/77 (Argentina and India, 6 June 2007); TN/TE/W/51 (India, 3 June 2005); TN/TE/W/67 (India, 13 June 2006); TN/TE/W/60 (India, 19 September 2005); TN/TE/W/54 (India, 4 July 2005).

ANNEX II.A: REFERENCE UNIVERSE OF ENVIRONMENTAL GOODS: OFFICIAL HS DESCRIPTIONS

1. The following HS lines include Members' submissions of environmental goods of interest as contained in Annex III of the Report by the Chairman to the TNC Report (TN/TE/19, March 2010) updated in JOB/TE/3/Rev.1 (5 January 2011) and any subsequent submissions. The environmental categories and sub-categories, as submitted by the Members, are reflected in the right column. This compilation should be considered as work in progress and may be updated in light of future submissions tabled by Members.
2. This table is based on the HS2002 classification at the 6-digit level. Descriptions are reproduced from the World Customs Organization, *Harmonized commodity description and coding system*, Brussels, 2002.
3. All product codes submitted under previous versions of the HS classification (e.g. HS1992 codes) have been converted to HS2002 codes.[1]
4. It should be noted that HS2002 official code descriptions do not always match descriptions provided by Members in their submissions. Some Members have identified the entire HS6 line while other Members have tried to be more specific (including by using sub-classification and/or ex-outs) to facilitate the identification of environmental goods of interest.
5. Accuracy and technical verification of the descriptions and HS codes contained in this document as well as the technical description if any, of ex-outs, will need to be undertaken by the environment and customs experts and it is expected that individual delegations will prepare draft technical descriptions and/or sub-classifications or ex-outs in their draft schedules for review and verification with other delegations.
6. The environmental categories and sub-categories as reflected in Annex III of the Report by the Chairman to the TNC Report (TN/TE/19, 22 March 2010) updated in JOB/TE/3/Rev.1 (5 January 2011) are indicated in the right column. They are as follows:
   - Air Pollution Control

1. The following HS1992 codes have been replaced with their equivalent HS2002 codes: 250310 and 250390 replaced with 250300; 291430 replaced with 291431; 291441 and 291449 replaced with 291440; 730420 replaced with 730421; 840611 replaced with 840610; 840619 replaced with 840681; 902520 replaced with 902580. Product submissions at the 4-digit HS level, for the purposes of this table, have been replaced with their 6-digit subheadings: 4707 has been replaced with 470710, 470720,470730, and 470790; 8506 has been replaced with 850610, 850630, 850640, 850650, 850660, 850680, and 850690 (note that the 6-digit HS code 850680 was also submitted individually by another Member); 9030 has been replaced with 903010, 903020, 903031, 903039, 903040, 903082, 903083, 903089, and 903090 (note that the 6-digit HS codes 903010, 903020, 903031, 903039, 903083, 903089, and 903090 were also submitted individually by another Member). The HS codes 841518, 841861, and 841869 were initially submitted as one, these product codes have been reflected separately for the purposes of this table. The HS codes 761190 and 841160 could not be found and were therefore not reflected in this table. Two other products descriptions were submitted, with HS codes to be determined. These were: LED lamp (LED light bulb etc.) and lighting and Energy efficient liquid crystal displays which conform to the energy efficiency standard and are so certified by the authority in destination country.

- Renewable Energy
- Waste Management and Water Treatment
  - Clean-Up Or Remediation of Soil and Water
  - Management of Solid and Hazardous Waste and Recycling Systems
  - Waste Management, Recycling and Remediation
  - Waste Water Management and Potable Water Treatment
- Environmental Technologies
  - Gas Flaring Emission Reduction
  - Efficient Consumption of Energy Technologies
  - Cleaner or More Resource-Efficient Technologies and Products
  - Energy Efficiency
  - Environmental Monitoring, Analysis and Assessment Equipment
  - Heat and Energy Management
  - Natural Risk Management
  - Noise and Vibration Abatement
- Carbon Capture and Storage
- Others
  - Environmentally Preferable Products based on End-Use or Disposal Characteristics
  - Natural Resources Protection
  - Renewable Products and Energy Source
  - Resources and Pollution Management
  - Others

	HS 2002 CODE	*HS CODE DESCRIPTION*	*CATEGORY(IES)*
	2503	**Sulphur of all kinds, other than sublimed sulphur, precipitated sulphur and colloidal sulphur.**	
1	250300	– Sulphur of all kinds, other than sublimed sulphur, precipitated sulphur and colloidal sulphur.	**Environmental Technologies, Carbon Capture and Storage,** Efficient Consumption of Energy Technologies
	2710	**Petroleum oils and oils obtained from bituminous minerals, other than crude; preparations not elsewhere specified or included, containing by weight 70% or more of petroleum oils or of oils obtained from bituminous minerals, these oils being the basic constituents of the preparations; waste oils**	
2	271011	– Light oils and preparations	**Others,** Environmentally Preferable Products based on End-Use or Disposal Characteristics
3	271019	– Others	**Others,** Environmentally Preferable Products based on End-Use or Disposal Characteristics
	2711	**Petroleum gases and other gaseous hydrocarbons**	

	HS 2002 CODE	*HS CODE DESCRIPTION*	*CATEGORY(IES)*
4	271111	– Natural gas, liquefied	**Environmental Technologies, Carbon Capture and Storage,** Gas Flaring Emission Reduction, Efficient Consumption of Energy Technologies **Others,** Environmentally Preferable Products based on End-Use or Disposal Characteristics
5	271112	– Propane, liquefied	**Environmental Technologies, Carbon Capture and Storage,** Gas Flaring Emission Reduction, Efficient Consumption of Energy Technologies **Others,** Environmentally Preferable Products based on End-Use or Disposal Characteristics
6	271113	– Butanes, liquefied	**Environmental Technologies, Carbon Capture and Storage** **Others,** Environmentally Preferable Products based on End-Use or Disposal Characteristics
7	271114	– Ethylene, propylene, butylene & butadiene, liquefied	**Environmental Technologies, Carbon Capture and Storage,** Gas Flaring Emission Reduction, Efficient Consumption of Energy Technologies
8	271119	– Other liquefied	**Environmental Technologies, Carbon Capture and Storage,** Gas Flaring Emission Reduction, Efficient Consumption of Energy Technologies
9	271121	– Natural gas, in gaseous state	**Environmental Technologies, Carbon Capture and Storage,** Gas Flaring Emission Reduction, Efficient Consumption of Energy Technologies **Others,** Environmentally Preferable Products based on End-Use or Disposal Characteristics
10	271129	– Other in gaseous state	**Environmental Technologies, Carbon Capture and Storage,** Gas Flaring Emission Reduction, Efficient Consumption of Energy Technologies
	2818	**Artificial corundum, whether or not chemically defined; aluminum oxide; aluminum hydroxide**	
11	281810	– Artificial corundum, whether or not chemically defined	**Environmental Technologies, Carbon Capture and Storage,** Gas Flaring Emission Reduction, Efficient Consumption of Energy Technologies
12	281820	– Aluminum oxide, other than artificial corundum	**Environmental Technologies, Carbon Capture and Storage,** Gas Flaring Emission Reduction, Efficient Consumption of Energy Technologies
13	281830	– Aluminum hydroxide	**Environmental Technologies, Carbon Capture and Storage,** Gas Flaring Emission Reduction, Efficient Consumption of Energy Technologies
	2909	**Ethers, ether-alcohols, ether-phenols, ether-alcohol-phenols, alcohol peroxides, ether peroxides, ketone peroxides (whether or not chemically defined), and their halogenated, sulphonated, nitrated or nitrosated derivatives**	
14	290911	– Acyclic ethers and their halogenated, sulphonated, nitrated or nitrosated derivatives: Diethyl ether	**Environmental Technologies, Carbon Capture and Storage,** Gas Flaring Emission Reduction, Efficient Consumption of Energy Technologies **Others,** Environmentally Preferable Products based on End-Use or Disposal Characteristics
15	290919	– Acyclic ethers and their halogenated, sulphonated, nitrated or nitrosated derivatives: Other	**Environmental Technologies, Carbon Capture and Storage,** Gas Flaring Emission Reduction, Efficient Consumption of Energy Technologies

	HS 2002 CODE	*HS CODE DESCRIPTION*	*CATEGORY(IES)*
16	290920	– Cyclanic, cyclenic or cycloterpenic ethers and their halogenated, sulphonated, nitrated or nitrosated derivatives	**Environmental Technologies, Carbon Capture and Storage,** Gas Flaring Emission Reduction, Efficient Consumption of Energy Technologies
17	290930	– Aromatic ethers and their halogenated, sulphonated, nitrated or nitrosated derivatives	**Environmental Technologies, Carbon Capture and Storage,** Gas Flaring Emission Reduction, Efficient Consumption of Energy Technologies
18	290941	– Ether-Alcohols and their halogenated, sulphonated, nitrated or nitrosated derivatives: 2,2'- Oxydiethanol (diethylene glycol, digol)	**Environmental Technologies, Carbon Capture and Storage,** Gas Flaring Emission Reduction, Efficient Consumption of Energy Technologies
19	290942	– Ether-Alcohols and their halogenated, sulphonated, nitrated or nitrosated derivatives: Monomethyl ethers of ethylene glycol/of diethylene glycol	**Environmental Technologies, Carbon Capture and Storage,** Gas Flaring Emission Reduction, Efficient Consumption of Energy Technologies
20	290943	– Ether-Alcohols and their halogenated, sulphonated, nitrated or nitrosated derivatives: Monobutyl ethers of ethylene glycol/of diethylene glycol	**Environmental Technologies, Carbon Capture and Storage,** Gas Flaring Emission Reduction, Efficient Consumption of Energy Technologies
21	290944	– Ether-Alcohols and their halogenated, sulphonated, nitrated or nitrosated derivatives: Other monoalkylethers of ethylene glycol or of diethylene glycol	**Environmental Technologies, Carbon Capture and Storage,** Gas Flaring Emission Reduction, Efficient Consumption of Energy Technologies
22	290949	– Ether-alcohols & their halogenated/sulphonated/nitrated/nitrosated derivatives: Others	**Environmental Technologies, Carbon Capture and Storage,** Gas Flaring Emission Reduction, Efficient Consumption of Energy Technologies
23	290950	– Ether-phenols, ether-alcohol-phenols and their halogenated, sulphonated, nitrated or nitrosated derivatives	**Environmental Technologies, Carbon Capture and Storage,** Gas Flaring Emission Reduction, Efficient Consumption of Energy Technologies
24	290960	– Alcohol peroxides, ether peroxides, ketone peroxides and their halogenated, sulphonated, nitrated or nitrosated derivatives	**Environmental Technologies, Carbon Capture and Storage,** Gas Flaring Emission Reduction, Efficient Consumption of Energy Technologies
	2914	**Ketones and quinones, whether or not with other oxygen function, and their halogenated, sulphonated, nitrated or nitrosated derivatives**	
25	291411	– Acyclic ketones without other oxygen function: Acetone	**Environmental Technologies, Carbon Capture and Storage,** Gas Flaring Emission Reduction, Efficient Consumption of Energy Technologies
26	291412	– Acyclic ketones without other oxygen function: Butanone (methyl ethyl ketone)	**Environmental Technologies, Carbon Capture and Storage,** Gas Flaring Emission Reduction, Efficient Consumption of Energy Technologies
27	291413	– Acyclic ketones without other oxygen function: 4-Methylpentan-2-one (methyl isobutyl ketone)	**Environmental Technologies, Carbon Capture and Storage,** Gas Flaring Emission Reduction, Efficient Consumption of Energy Technologies
28	291419	– Acyclic ketones without other oxygen function: Others	**Environmental Technologies, Carbon Capture and Storage,** Gas Flaring Emission Reduction, Efficient Consumption of Energy Technologies
29	291421	– Cyclanic, cyclenic or cycloterpenic ketones without other oxygen function: Camphor	**Environmental Technologies, Carbon Capture and Storage,** Gas Flaring Emission Reduction, Efficient Consumption of Energy Technologies
30	291422	– Cyclanic, cyclenic or cycloterpenic ketones without other oxygen function: Cyclohexanone & methylcyclohexanones	**Environmental Technologies, Carbon Capture and Storage,** Gas Flaring Emission Reduction, Efficient Consumption of Energy Technologies
31	291423	– Cyclanic, cyclenic or cycloterpenic ketones without other oxygen function: Ionones & methylionones	**Environmental Technologies, Carbon Capture and Storage,** Gas Flaring Emission Reduction, Efficient Consumption of Energy Technologies

	HS 2002 CODE	*HS CODE DESCRIPTION*	*CATEGORY(IES)*
32	291429	– Cyclanic/cyclenic/cycloterpenic ketones without other oxygen function: Other	**Environmental Technologies, Carbon Capture and Storage,** Gas Flaring Emission Reduction, Efficient Consumption of Energy Technologies
33	291431	– Aromatic ketones without other oxygen function: Phenylacetone (phenylpropan-2-one)	**Environmental Technologies, Carbon Capture and Storage,** Gas Flaring Emission Reduction, Efficient Consumption of Energy Technologies
34	291440	– Ketone-alcohols & ketone-aldehydes	**Environmental Technologies, Carbon Capture and Storage,** Gas Flaring Emission Reduction, Efficient Consumption of Energy Technologies
35	291450	– Ketone-phenols and ketones with other oxygen function	**Environmental Technologies, Carbon Capture and Storage,** Gas Flaring Emission Reduction, Efficient Consumption of Energy Technologies
36	291461	– Quinones: Anthraquinone	**Environmental Technologies, Carbon Capture and Storage,** Gas Flaring Emission Reduction, Efficient Consumption of Energy Technologies
37	291469	– Quinones: Other	**Environmental Technologies, Carbon Capture and Storage,** Gas Flaring Emission Reduction, Efficient Consumption of Energy Technologies
38	291470	– Halogenated, sulphonated, nitrated or nitrosated derivatives	**Environmental Technologies, Carbon Capture and Storage,** Gas Flaring Emission Reduction, Efficient Consumption of Energy Technologies
	3824	**Prepared binders for foundry molds or cores; chemical products and preparations of the chemical or allied industries (including those consisting of mixtures of natural products), not elsewhere specified or included**	
39	382490	– Other	**Waste Management and Water Treatment,** WWM **Renewable Energy,** Renewable Products and Energy Source
	3902	**Polymers of propylene or of other olefins, in primary forms.**	
40	390210	– Polypropylene	**Environmental Technologies, Carbon Capture and Storage,** Efficient Consumption of Energy Technologies
41	390220	– Polyisobutylene	**Environmental Technologies, Carbon Capture and Storage,** Efficient Consumption of Energy Technologies
42	390230	– Propylene copolymers	**Environmental Technologies, Carbon Capture and Storage,** Efficient Consumption of Energy Technologies
43	390290	– Other	**Environmental Technologies, Carbon Capture and Storage,** Efficient Consumption of Energy Technologies
	3907	**Polyacetals, other polyethers and epoxide resins, in primary forms; polycarbonates, alkyd resins, polyallyl esters and other polyesters, in primary forms.**	
44	390799	– Other polyesters: Other	**Renewable Energy,** Renewable Products and Energy Source
	3909	**Amino-resins, phenolic resins and polyurethanes, in primary forms**	

	HS 2002 CODE	*HS CODE DESCRIPTION*	*CATEGORY(IES)*
45	390910	– Urea resins; thiourea resins	**Environmental Technologies, Carbon Capture and Storage,** Efficient Consumption of Energy Technologies
46	390920	– Melamine resins	**Environmental Technologies, Carbon Capture and Storage,** Efficient Consumption of Energy Technologies
47	390930	– Other amino-resins	**Environmental Technologies, Carbon Capture and Storage,** Efficient Consumption of Energy Technologies
48	390940	– Phenolic resins	**Environmental Technologies, Carbon Capture and Storage,** Efficient Consumption of Energy Technologies
49	390950	– Polyurethanes	**Environmental Technologies, Carbon Capture and Storage,** Efficient Consumption of Energy Technologies
	3911	**Petroleum resins, coumarone-indene resins, polyterpenes, polysulphides, polysulphones and other products specified in Note 3 to this Chapter, not elsewhere specified or included, in primary forms.**	
50	391110	– Petroleum resins, coumarone, indene or coumarone-indene resins and polyterpenes	**Environmental Technologies, Carbon Capture and Storage,** Efficient Consumption of Energy Technologies
51	391190	– Other	**Environmental Technologies, Carbon Capture and Storage,** Efficient Consumption of Energy Technologies
	3912	**Cellulose and its chemical derivatives, not elsewhere specified or included, in primary forms**	
52	391211	– Cellulose acetates; non-plasticised	**Environmental Technologies, Carbon Capture and Storage,** Efficient Consumption of Energy Technologies
53	391212	– Cellulose acetates, plasticised	**Environmental Technologies, Carbon Capture and Storage,** Efficient Consumption of Energy Technologies
54	391220	– Cellulose nitrates (including collodions)	**Environmental Technologies, Carbon Capture and Storage,** Efficient Consumption of Energy Technologies
55	391231	– Cellulose ethers: Carboxymethylcellulose & its salts	**Environmental Technologies, Carbon Capture and Storage,** Efficient Consumption of Energy Technologies
56	391239	– Cellulose ethers: Other	**Environmental Technologies, Carbon Capture and Storage,** Efficient Consumption of Energy Technologies
57	391290	– Other	**Environmental Technologies, Carbon Capture and Storage,** Efficient Consumption of Energy Technologies
	3920	**Other plates, sheets, film, foil and strip, of plastics, non-cellular and not reinforced, laminated, supported or similarly combined with other materials**	
58	392010	– Of polymers of ethylene	**Waste Management and Water Treatment,** Management of Solid and Hazardous Waste and Recycling Systems

	HS 2002 CODE	HS CODE DESCRIPTION	CATEGORY(IES)
	4016	**Other articles of vulcanized rubber other than hard rubber**	
59	401699	– Other: Other	**Renewable Energy,** Renewable Products and Energy Source
	4504	**Agglomerated cork (with or without a binding substance)**	
60	450410	– Blocks, plates, sheets and strip; tiles of any shape; solid cylinders, including discs	**Environmental Technologies,** Noise and Vibration Abatement
	4601	**Plaits and similar products of plaiting materials, whether or not assembled into sTRIPS; plaiting materials, plaits and similar products of plaiting materials, bound together in parallel strands or woven, in sheet form, whether or not being finished artic**	
61	460120	– Mats, matting and screens of vegetable materials	**Waste Management and Water Treatment,** Waste Management, Recycling and Remediation
	4707	**Recovered (waste and scrap) paper or paperboard**	
62	470710	– Recovered (waste & scrap) unbleached kraft paper/paperboard/corrugated paper/paperboard	**Renewable Energy, R**enewable Products and Energy Source
63	470720	– Other paper or paperboard made mainly of bleached chemical	**Renewable Energy, R**enewable Products and Energy Source
64	470730	– Paper or paperboard made mainly of me-chanical pulp (for example, newspapers, journals and similar printed matter)	**Renewable Energy, R**enewable Products and Energy Source
65	470790	– Other, including unsorted waste and scrap	**Renewable Energy, R**enewable Products and Energy Source
	5303	**Jute and other textile bast fibers (excluding flax, true hemp and ramie), raw or processed but not spun; tow and waste of these fibers (including yarn waste and garneted stock)**	
66	530310	– Jute and other textile bast fibers, raw or retted	**Others,** Environmentally Preferable Products based on End-Use or Disposal Characteristics
	5304	**Sisal and other textile fibers of the genus Agave, raw or processed but not spun; tow and waste of these fibers (including yarn waste and garneted stock) .**	
67	530410	– Sisal and other textile fibers of the genus Agave, raw	**Others,** Environmentally Preferable Products based on End-Use or Disposal Characteristics
68	530490	– Other	**Others,** Environmentally Preferable Products based on End-Use or Disposal Characteristics
	5603	**Nonwovens, whether or not impregnated, coated, covered or laminated**	
69	560314	– Of man-made filaments: Weighing more than 150 g/m^2;	**Waste Management and Water Treatment,** Waste Water Management and Potable Water Treatment
	5607	**Twine, cordage, ropes and cables, whether or not plaited or braided and whether or not impregnated, coated, covered or sheathed with rubber or plastics**	
70	560710	– Of jute or other textile bast fibers of heading 53.03	**Others,** Environmentally Preferable Products based on End-Use or Disposal Characteristics

	HS 2002 CODE	*HS CODE DESCRIPTION*	*CATEGORY(IES)*
71	560721	– Of sisal or other textile fibers of the genus Agave: Binder or baler twine	Environmentally Preferable Products based on End-Use or Disposal Characteristics
	5608	**Knotted netting of twine, cordage or rope; made up fishing nets and other made up nets, of textile materials**	
72	560811	– Of man-made textile materials: Made up fishing nets	**Others,** Natural Resources Protection
73	560890	– Other	Natural Resources Protection
	6305	**Sacks and bags, of a kind used for the packing of goods**	
74	630510	– Of jute or of other textile bast fibers of heading 53.03	**Others,** Environmentally Preferable Products based on End-Use or Disposal Characteristics
	6910	**Ceramic sinks, wash basins, wash basin pedestals, baths, bidets, water closet pans, flushing cisterns, urinals and similar sanitary fixtures**	
75	691010	– Of porcelain or china	**Waste Management and Water Treatment,** Waste Water Management and Potable Water Treatment
	7019	**Glass fibers (including glass wool) and articles thereof (for example, yarn, woven fabrics)**	
76	701931	– Thin sheets (voiles), webs, mats, mattresses, boards and similar nonwoven products: Mats	**Environmental Technologies,** Heat and Energy Management
	7303	**Tubes, pipes and hollow profiles, of cast iron**	
77	730300	– Tubes, pipes & hollow profiles of cast iron	**Waste Management and Water Treatment,** Waste Water Management and Potable Water Treatment **Environmental Technologies, Carbon Capture and Storage,** Efficient Consumption of Energy Technologies
	7304	**Tubes, pipes and hollow profiles, seamless, of iron (other than cast iron) or steel**	
78	730410	– Line pipe of a kind used for oil or gas pipelines	**Environmental Technologies, Carbon Capture and Storage,** Efficient Consumption of Energy Technologies
79	730421	– Casing, tubing and drill pipe, of a kind used in drilling for oil or gas: Drill Pipe	**Environmental Technologies, Carbon Capture and Storage,** Efficient Consumption of Energy Technologies
80	730431	– Other, of circular cross-section, of iron or non-Alloy steel: Cold-drawn or cold-rolled (cold-reduced)	**Waste Management and Water Treatment,** Waste Water Management and Potable Water Treatment **Environmental Technologies, Carbon Capture and Storage,** Efficient Consumption of Energy Technologies
81	730439	– Other, of circular cross-section, of iron or non-Alloy steel: Other	**Waste Management and Water Treatment,** Waste Water Management and Potable Water Treatment **Environmental Technologies, Carbon Capture and Storage,** Efficient Consumption of Energy Technologies

	HS 2002 CODE	*HS CODE DESCRIPTION*	*CATEGORY(IES)*
82	730441	– Other, of circular cross-section, of stainless steel: Cold-drawn or cold-rolled (cold-reduced)	**Waste Management and Water Treatment,** Waste Water Management and Potable Water Treatment **Environmental Technologies, Carbon Capture and Storage,** Efficient Consumption of Energy Technologies
83	730449	– Other, of circular cross-section, of stainless steel: Other	**Waste Management and Water Treatment,** Waste Water Management and Potable Water Treatment **Environmental Technologies, Carbon Capture and Storage,** Efficient Consumption of Energy Technologies
84	730451	– Other, of circular cross-section, of other alloy steel: Cold-drawn or cold-rolled (cold-reduced)	**Waste Management and Water Treatment,** Waste Water Management and Potable Water Treatment **Environmental Technologies, Carbon Capture and Storage,** Efficient Consumption of Energy Technologies
85	730459	– Other, of circular cross-section, of other alloy steel: Other	**Waste Management and Water Treatment,** Waste Water Management and Potable Water Treatment **Environmental Technologies, Carbon Capture and Storage,** Efficient Consumption of Energy Technologies
86	730490	– Other	**Waste Management and Water Treatment,** Waste Water Management and Potable Water Treatment **Environmental Technologies, Carbon Capture and Storage,** Efficient Consumption of Energy Technologies
	7305	**Other tubes and pipes (for example, welded, riveted or similarly closed), having circular cross sections, the external diameter of which exceeds 406.4 mm, of iron or steel**	
87	730511	– Line pipe of a kind used for oil or gas pipelines: Longitudinally submerged arc welded	**Environmental Technologies, Carbon Capture and Storage,** Efficient Consumption of Energy Technologies
88	730512	– Line pipe of a kind used for oil or gas pipelines: Other, longitudinally welded	**Environmental Technologies, Carbon Capture and Storage,** Efficient Consumption of Energy Technologies
89	730519	– Line pipe of a kind used for oil or gas pipelines: Other	**Environmental Technologies, Carbon Capture and Storage,** Efficient Consumption of Energy Technologies
90	730520	– Casing of a kind used in drilling for oil or gas	**Environmental Technologies, Carbon Capture and Storage,** Efficient Consumption of Energy Technologies
91	730531	– Other, welded: Longitudinally welded	**Environmental Technologies, Carbon Capture and Storage,** Efficient Consumption of Energy Technologies
92	730539	– Other, welded: Other	**Environmental Technologies, Carbon Capture and Storage,** Efficient Consumption of Energy Technologies
93	730590	– Other	**Environmental Technologies, Carbon Capture and Storage,** Efficient Consumption of Energy Technologies

	HS 2002 CODE	*HS CODE DESCRIPTION*	*CATEGORY(IES)*
	7306	**Other tubes, pipes and hollow profiles (for example, open seam or welded, riveted or similarly closed), of iron or steel**	
94	730610	– Line pipe of a kind used for oil or gas pipelines	**Environmental Technologies, Carbon Capture and Storage,** Efficient Consumption of Energy Technologies
95	730620	– Casing and tubing of a kind used in drilling for oil or gas	**Environmental Technologies, Carbon Capture and Storage,** Efficient Consumption of Energy Technologies
96	730630	– Other, welded, of circular cross-section, of iron or non-Alloy steel	**Waste Management and Water Treatment,** Waste Water Management and Potable Water Treatment **Environmental Technologies, Carbon Capture and Storage,** Efficient Consumption of Energy Technologies
97	730640	– Other, welded, of circular cross-section, of stainless steel	**Waste Management and Water Treatment,** Waste Water Management and Potable Water Treatment **Environmental Technologies, Carbon Capture and Storage,** Efficient Consumption of Energy Technologies
98	730650	– Other, welded, of circular cross-section, of other alloy steel	**Waste Management and Water Treatment,** Waste Water Management and Potable Water Treatment **Environmental Technologies, Carbon Capture and Storage,** Efficient Consumption of Energy Technologies
99	730660	– Other, welded, of non-circular cross-section	**Waste Management and Water Treatment,** Waste Water Management and Potable Water Treatment **Environmental Technologies, Carbon Capture and Storage,** Efficient Consumption of Energy Technologies
100	730690	– Other	**Waste Management and Water Treatment,** Waste Water Management and Potable Water Treatment **Environmental Technologies, Carbon Capture and Storage,** Efficient Consumption of Energy Technologies
	7307	**Tube or pipe fittings (for example, couplings, elbows, sleeves), of iron or steel**	
101	730711	– Cast fittings: Of non-malleable cast iron	**Environmental Technologies, Carbon Capture and Storage,** Efficient Consumption of Energy Technologies
102	730719	– Cast fittings: Other	**Environmental Technologies, Carbon Capture and Storage,** Efficient Consumption of Energy Technologies
103	730721	– Other, of stainless steel: Flanges	**Environmental Technologies, Carbon Capture and Storage,** Efficient Consumption of Energy Technologies
104	730722	– Other, of stainless steel: Threaded elbows, bends and sleeves	**Environmental Technologies, Carbon Capture and Storage,** Efficient Consumption of Energy Technologies
105	730723	– Other, of stainless steel: Butt welding fittings	**Environmental Technologies, Carbon Capture and Storage,** Efficient Consumption of Energy Technologies

	HS 2002 CODE	*HS CODE DESCRIPTION*	*CATEGORY(IES)*
106	730729	– Other, of stainless steel: Other	**Environmental Technologies, Carbon Capture and Storage,** Efficient Consumption of Energy Technologies
107	730791	– Other: Flanges	**Environmental Technologies, Carbon Capture and Storage,** Efficient Consumption of Energy Technologies
108	730792	– Other: Threaded elbows, bends & sleeves	**Environmental Technologies, Carbon Capture and Storage,** Efficient Consumption of Energy Technologies
109	730793	– Other: Butt welding fittings	**Environmental Technologies, Carbon Capture and Storage,** Efficient Consumption of Energy Technologies
110	730799	– Other: Other	**Environmental Technologies, Carbon Capture and Storage,** Efficient Consumption of Energy Technologies
	7308	**Structures (excluding prefabricated buildings of heading 94.06) and parts of structures (for example, bridges and bridge sections, lock gates, towers, lattice masts, roofs, roofing frameworks, doors and windows and their frames and thresholds for doors, shutters, balustrades, pillars and columns), of iron or steel; plates, rods, angles, shapes, sections, tubes and the like, prepared for use in structures, of iron or steel**	
111	730820	– Towers & lattice masts	**Renewable Energy,** Renewable Energy **Renewable Energy,** Renewable Products and Energy Source
	7309	**Reservoirs, tanks, vats and similar containers for any material (other than compressed or liquefied gas), of iron or steel, of a capacity exceeding 300 l, whether or not lined or heat insulated, but not fitted with mechanical or thermal equipment.**	
112	730900	– Reservoirs, tanks, vats and similar containers for any material (other than compressed or liquefied gas), of iron or steel, of a capacity exceeding 300 l, whether or not lined or heat-insulated, but not fitted with mechanical or thermal equipment.	**Waste Management and Water Treatment,** Waste Water Management and Potable Water Treatment **Environmental Technologies, Carbon Capture and Storage,** Efficient Consumption of Energy Technologies
	7310	**Tanks, casks, drums, cans, boxes and similar containers, for any material (other than compressed or liquefied gas), of iron or steel, of a capacity not exceeding 300 l, whether or not lined or heat-insulated, but not fitted with mechanical or thermal equipment**	
113	731010	– Of a capacity of 50 liters or more	**Waste Management and Water Treatment,** Waste Water Management and Potable Water Treatment **Environmental Technologies, Carbon Capture and Storage,** Efficient Consumption of Energy Technologies
114	731021	– Of a capacity of less than 50 liters: Cans which are to be closed by soldering or crimping	**Environmental Technologies, Carbon Capture and Storage,** Efficient Consumption of Energy Technologies

	HS 2002 CODE	*HS CODE DESCRIPTION*	*CATEGORY(IES)*
115	731029	– Of a capacity of less than 50 liters: Other	**Waste Management and Water Treatment,** Waste Water Management and Potable Water Treatment **Environmental Technologies, Carbon Capture and Storage,** Efficient Consumption of Energy Technologies
	7311	**Containers for compressed or liquefied gas, of iron or steel**	
116	731100	– Containers for compressed or liquefied gas, of iron or steel	**Environmental Technologies, Carbon Capture and Storage,** Efficient Consumption of Energy Technologies
	7321	**Stoves, ranges, grates, cookers (including those with subsidiary boilers for central heating), barbecues, braziers, gas-rings, plate warmers and similar non-electric domestic appliances, and parts thereof, of iron or steel.**	
117	732111	– Cooking appliances and plate warmers:	**Environmental Technologies,** Cleaner or More Resource Efficient Technologies and Products
118	732190	– Parts	**Environmental Technologies,** Cleaner or More Resource Efficient Technologies and Products
	7324	**Sanitary ware and parts thereof, of iron or steel**	
119	732490	– Other, including parts	**Waste Management and Water Treatment,** Waste Water Management and Potable Water Treatment **Environmental Technologies, Carbon Capture and Storage,** Efficient Consumption of Energy Technologies
	7325	**Other cast articles of iron or steel**	
120	732510	– Of non-malleable cast iron	**Waste Management and Water Treatment,** Waste Water Management and Potable Water Treatment
	7326	**Other articles of iron or steel**	
121	732690	– Other.	**Waste Management and Water Treatment,** Waste Water Management and Potable Water Treatment
	7611	**Aluminum reservoirs, tanks, vats and similar containers, for any material (other than compressed or liquefied gas), of a capacity exceeding 300 l, whether or not lined or heat-insulated, but not fitted with mechanical or thermal equipment**	
122	761100	– Aluminum reservoirs, tanks, vats & similar containers, for any material (other than compressed or liquefied gas), of a capacity exceeding 300 l, whether or not lined or heat-insulated, but not fitted with mechanical or thermal equipment	**Renewable Energy,** Renewable Energy **Environmental Technologies, Carbon Capture and Storage,** Efficient Consumption of Energy Technologies
	7612	**Aluminum casks, drums, cans, boxes and similar containers (including rigid or collapsible tubular containers), for any material (other than compressed or liquefied gas), of a capacity not exceeding 300 l, whether or not lined or heat-insulated, but not fitted with mechanical or thermal equipment.**	

	HS 2002 CODE	*HS CODE DESCRIPTION*	*CATEGORY(IES)*
123	761290	– Other	**Waste Management and Water Treatment,** Management of Solid and Hazardous Waste and Recycling Systems
	7613	**Aluminum containers for compressed or liquefied gas**	
124	761300	– Aluminum containers for compressed or liquefied gas	**Environmental Technologies, Carbon Capture and Storage,** Efficient Consumption of Energy Technologies
	8402	**Steam or other vapor generating boilers (other than central heating hot water boilers capable also of producing low pressure steam); super-heated water boilers**	
125	840211	– Steam or other vapor generating boilers: Watertube Boilers With a Steam Production > 45 t per hour	**Environmental Technologies, Carbon Capture and Storage,** Efficient Consumption of Energy Technologies
126	840212	– Steam or other vapor generating boilers: Watertube boilers with a steam production not > 45 t per hour	**Environmental Technologies, Carbon Capture and Storage,** Efficient Consumption of Energy Technologies
127	840219	– Steam or other vapor generating boilers: Other vapor generating boilers, including hybrid boilers	**Environmental Technologies, Carbon Capture and Storage,** Efficient Consumption of Energy Technologies **Waste Management and Water Treatment,** Management of Solid and Hazardous Waste and Recycling Systems
128	840220	– Super-heated Water Boilers	**Environmental Technologies, Carbon Capture and Storage,** Efficient Consumption of Energy Technologies
129	840290	– Parts	**Environmental Technologies, Carbon Capture and Storage,** Efficient Consumption of Energy Technologies **Waste Management and Water Treatment,** Management of Solid and Hazardous Waste and Recycling Systems **Waste Management and Water Treatment,** Waste Management, Recycling and Remediation
	8403	**Central heating boilers other than those of heading 84.02.**	
130	840310	– Boilers	**Environmental Technologies, Carbon Capture and Storage,** Efficient Consumption of Energy Technologies
131	840390	– Parts	**Environmental Technologies, Carbon Capture and Storage,** Efficient Consumption of Energy Technologies
	8404	**Auxiliary plant for use with boilers of heading 84.02 or 84.03 (for example, economizers, super-heaters, soot removers, gas recoverers); condensers for steam or other vapor power units**	
132	840410	– Auxiliary plant for use with boilers of heading 84.02 or 84.03	**Waste Management and Water Treatment,** Waste Management, Recycling and Remediation **Waste Management and Water Treatment,** Management of Solid and Hazardous Waste and Recycling Systems **Environmental Technologies, Carbon Capture and Storage,** Efficient Consumption of Energy Technologies

	HS 2002 CODE	*HS CODE DESCRIPTION*	*CATEGORY(IES)*
133	840420	– Condensers for steam or other vapor power units	**Air Pollution Control** **Environmental Technologies, Carbon Capture and Storage,** Efficient Consumption of Energy Technologies
134	840490	– Parts	**Air Pollution Control** **Environmental Technologies, Carbon Capture and Storage,** Efficient Consumption of Energy Technologies
	8405	**Producer gas or water gas generators, with or without their purifiers; acetylene gas generators and similar water process gas generators, with or without their purifiers**	
135	840510	– Producer gas or water gas generators, with or without their purifiers; acetylene gas generators and similar water process gas generators, with or without their purifiers	**Air Pollution Control** **Renewable Energy,** Renewable Energy **Waste Management and Water Treatment,** Waste Water Management and Potable Water Treatment **Environmental Technologies, Carbon Capture and Storage,** Efficient Consumption of Energy Technologies
136	840590	– Parts	**Environmental Technologies, Carbon Capture and Storage,** Efficient Consumption of Energy Technologies
	8406	**Steam turbines and other vapor turbines**	
137	840610	– Turbines for marine propulsion	**Environmental Technologies, Carbon Capture and Storage,** Efficient Consumption of Energy Technologies
138	840681	– Other turbines of an output exceeding 40MW	**Environmental Technologies, Carbon Capture and Storage,** Efficient Consumption of Energy Technologies **Renewable Energy,** Renewable Energy
139	840682	– Other turbines of an output not exceeding 40 MW	**Renewable Energy,** Renewable Energy
140	840690	– Parts	**Renewable Energy,** Renewable Energy **Environmental Technologies, Carbon Capture and Storage,** Efficient Consumption of Energy Technologies
	8407	**Spark-ignition reciprocating or rotary internal combustion piston engines**	
141	840790	– Other Engines	**Environmental Technologies, Carbon Capture and Storage,** Efficient Consumption of Energy Technologies
	8408	**Compression-ignition internal combustion piston engines (diesel or semi-diesel engines)**	
142	840890	– Other Engines	**Environmental Technologies, Carbon Capture and Storage,** Efficient Consumption of Energy Technologies
	8409	**Parts suitable for use solely or principally with the engines of heading 84.07 or 84.08**	
143	840991	– Other: suitable for use solely or principally with the engines of heading 84.07 or 84.08.	**Environmental Technologies, Carbon Capture and Storage,** Efficient Consumption of Energy Technologies **Environmental Technologies, Carbon Capture and Storage,** Noise and Vibration Abatement

	HS 2002 CODE	*HS CODE DESCRIPTION*	*CATEGORY(IES)*
144	840999	– Other	**Air Pollution Control** **Environmental Technologies, Carbon Capture and Storage,** Efficient Consumption of Energy Technologies **Environmental Technologies, Carbon Capture and Storage,** Noise and Vibration Abatement
	8410	**Hydraulic turbines, water wheels, and regulators therefor**	
145	841011	– Hydraulic turbines and water wheels of a power not exceeding 1,000 kW .	**Renewable Energy,** Renewable Energy **Environmental Technologies, Carbon Capture and Storage,** Efficient Consumption of Energy Technologies
146	841012	– Hydraulic Turbines and Water Wheels, Power 1, 000-10, 000kw	**Environmental Technologies, Carbon Capture and Storage,** Efficient Consumption of Energy Technologies
147	841013	– Hydraulic Turbines, Water Wheels, of a Power Exceeding 10, 000kw	**Environmental Technologies, Carbon Capture and Storage,** Efficient Consumption of Energy Technologies
148	841090	– Parts, including regulators	**Renewable Energy,** Renewable Energy **Environmental Technologies, Carbon Capture and Storage,** Efficient Consumption of Energy Technologies
	8411	**Turbo-jets, turbo-propellers and other gas turbines**	
149	841111	– Turbo-jets of a Thrust Not Exceeding 25kn	**Environmental Technologies, Carbon Capture and Storage,** Efficient Consumption of Energy Technologies
150	841112	– Turbo-jets of a Thrust Exceeding 25kn	**Environmental Technologies, Carbon Capture and Storage,** Efficient Consumption of Energy Technologies
151	841121	– Turbo-propellers of a Power Not Exceeding 1, 100kW	**Environmental Technologies, Carbon Capture and Storage,** Efficient Consumption of Energy Technologies
152	841122	– Turbo-propellers of a Power Exceeding 1, 100kW	**Environmental Technologies, Carbon Capture and Storage,** Efficient Consumption of Energy Technologies
153	841181	– Other gas turbines of a power not exceeding 5,000 kW	**Renewable Energy,** Renewable Energy **Environmental Technologies, Carbon Capture and Storage,** Efficient Consumption of Energy Technologies **Others,** Environmentally Preferable Products based on End-Use or Disposal Characteristics
154	841182	– Other gas turbines of a power exceeding 5,000 kW	**Renewable Energy,** Renewable Energy **Environmental Technologies, Carbon Capture and Storage,** Efficient Consumption of Energy Technologies **Others,** Environmentally Preferable Products based on End-Use or Disposal Characteristics
155	841191	– Parts of Turbo-jets or Turbo-propellers	**Environmental Technologies, Carbon Capture and Storage,** Efficient Consumption of Energy Technologies **Others,** Environmentally Preferable Products based on End-Use or Disposal Characteristics
156	841199	– Parts: Other	**Environmental Technologies, Carbon Capture and Storage,** Efficient Consumption of Energy Technologies
	8412	**Other engines and motors**	

	HS 2002 CODE	*HS CODE DESCRIPTION*	*CATEGORY(IES)*
157	841210	– Reaction Engines Other than Turbo-jets	**Environmental Technologies, Carbon Capture and Storage,** Efficient Consumption of Energy Technologies
158	841221	– Hydraulic Power Engines and Motors, Linear Acting (cylinders)	**Environmental Technologies, Carbon Capture and Storage,** Efficient Consumption of Energy Technologies
159	841229	– Other Hydraulic Power Engines and Motors	**Environmental Technologies, Carbon Capture and Storage,** Efficient Consumption of Energy Technologies
160	841231	– Pneumatic Power Engines and Motors, Linear Acting (cylinders)	**Environmental Technologies, Carbon Capture and Storage,** Efficient Consumption of Energy Technologies
161	841239	– Other Pneumatic Power Engines and Motors	**Environmental Technologies, Carbon Capture and Storage,** Efficient Consumption of Energy Technologies
162	841280	– Other	**Environmental Technologies, Carbon Capture and Storage,** Efficient Consumption of Energy Technologies **Renewable Energy,** Renewable Products and Energy Source
163	841290	– Parts	**Environmental Technologies, Carbon Capture and Storage,** Efficient Consumption of Energy Technologies **Renewable Energy,** Renewable Products and Energy Source
	8413	**Pumps for liquids, whether or not fitted with a measuring device; liquid elevators**	
164	841311	– Pumps fitted or designed to be fitted with a measuring device: Pumps for Dispensing Fuel or Lubricants of the type used in filling-stations or in garages	**Environmental Technologies, Carbon Capture and Storage,** Efficient Consumption of Energy Technologies
165	841319	– Other Pumps fitted or designed to be fitted with a measuring device	**Environmental Technologies, Carbon Capture and Storage,** Efficient Consumption of Energy Technologies
166	841320	– Hand pumps, other than those of subheading 8413.11 or 8413.19	**Waste Management and Water Treatment,** Waste Water Management and Potable Water Treatment **Environmental Technologies, Carbon Capture and Storage,** Efficient Consumption of Energy Technologies
167	841330	– Fuel, Lubricating or Cooling Medium Pumps for internal combustion piston engines	**Environmental Technologies, Carbon Capture and Storage,** Efficient Consumption of Energy Technologies
168	841340	– Concrete Pumps	**Environmental Technologies, Carbon Capture and Storage,** Efficient Consumption of Energy Technologies
169	841350	– Other reciprocating positive displacement pumps	**Waste Management and Water Treatment,** Waste Water Management and Potable Water Treatment **Environmental Technologies, Carbon Capture and Storage,** Efficient Consumption of Energy Technologies

	HS 2002 CODE	*HS CODE DESCRIPTION*	*CATEGORY(IES)*
170	841360	– Other rotary positive displacement pumps	**Waste Management and Water Treatment,** Waste Water Management and Potable Water Treatment **Environmental Technologies, Carbon Capture and Storage,** Efficient Consumption of Energy Technologies
171	841370	– Other Centrifugal Pumps	**Waste Management and Water Treatment,** Waste Water Management and Potable Water Treatment **Environmental Technologies, Carbon Capture and Storage,** Efficient Consumption of Energy Technologies
172	841381	– Other pumps	**Waste Management and Water Treatment,** Waste Water Management and Potable Water Treatment **Environmental Technologies, Carbon Capture and Storage,** Efficient Consumption of Energy Technologies
173	841382	– Liquid Elevators	**Environmental Technologies, Carbon Capture and Storage,** Efficient Consumption of Energy Technologies
174	841391	– Parts of Pumps	**Environmental Technologies, Carbon Capture and Storage,** Efficient Consumption of Energy Technologies
175	841392	– Parts of Liquid Elevators	**Environmental Technologies, Carbon Capture and Storage,** Efficient Consumption of Energy Technologies
	8414	**Air or vacuum pumps, air or other gas compressors and fans; ventilating or recycling hoods incorporating a fan, whether or not fitted with filters**	
176	841410	– Vacuum pumps	**Air Pollution Control** **Environmental Technologies, Carbon Capture and Storage,** Efficient Consumption of Energy Technologies
177	841430	– Compressors of a kind used in refrigerating equipment	**Air Pollution Control**
178	841440	– Air compressors mounted on a wheeled chassis for towing.	**Air Pollution Control** **Other,** Resources and Pollution Management
179	841459	– Fans: other	**Air Pollution Control**
180	841480	– Other	**Air Pollution Control** **Environmental Technologies, Carbon Capture and Storage,** Efficient Consumption of Energy Technologies **Environmental Technologies,** Noise and Vibration Abatement
181	841490	– Parts	**Air Pollution Control** **Environmental Technologies, Carbon Capture and Storage,** Efficient Consumption of Energy Technologies **Other,** Resources and Pollution Management
	8415	**Air conditioning machines, comprising a motor-driven fan and elements for changing the temperature and humidity, including those machines in which the humidity cannot be separately regulated**	

	HS 2002 CODE	*HS CODE DESCRIPTION*	*CATEGORY(IES)*
182	841510	– Window or wall types, self-contained or "split-system"	**Environmental Technologies,** Energy Efficiency
183	841581	– Others: incorporating a refrigerating unit & a valve for reversal of the cooling or heat cycle (reversible heat pumps)	**Environmental Technologies,** Energy Efficiency
	8416	**Furnace burners for liquid fuel, for pulverized solid fuel or for gas; mechanical stokers, including their mechanical grates, mechanical ash dischargers and similar appliances**	
184	841610	– Furnace Burners for Liquid Fuel	**Environmental Technologies, Carbon Capture and Storage,** Gas Flaring Emission Reduction, Efficient Consumption of Energy Technologies
185	841620	– Other Furnace Burners, Including Combination Burners	**Environmental Technologies, Carbon Capture and Storage,** Gas Flaring Emission Reduction, Efficient Consumption of Energy Technologies **Others,** Environmentally Preferable Products based on End-Use or Disposal Characteristics
186	841630	– Mechanical Stokers, including their Mechanical Grates, Mechanical Ash Dischargers and similar appliances	**Environmental Technologies, Carbon Capture and Storage,** Gas Flaring Emission Reduction, Efficient Consumption of Energy Technologies
187	841690	– Parts	**Environmental Technologies, Carbon Capture and Storage,** Gas Flaring Emission Reduction, Efficient Consumption of Energy Technologies
	8417	**Industrial or laboratory furnaces and ovens, including incinerators, non-electric**	
188	841780	– Other	**Waste Management and Water Treatment,** Management of Solid and Hazardous Waste and Recycling Systems **Environmental Technologies, Carbon Capture and Storage,** Gas Flaring Emission Reduction, Efficient Consumption of Energy Technologies
189	841790	– Parts	**Waste Management and Water Treatment,** Management of Solid and Hazardous Waste and Recycling Systems **Environmental Technologies, Carbon Capture and Storage,** Gas Flaring Emission Reduction, Efficient Consumption of Energy Technologies
	8418	**Refrigerators, freezers and other refrigerating or freezing equipment, electric or other; heat pumps other than air conditioning machines of heading 84.15**	
190	841810	– Combined refrigerator-freezers, fitted with separate external doors	**Environmental Technologies,** Energy Efficiency
191	841821	– Household type refrigerators of compression-type	**Environmental Technologies,** Energy Efficiency
192	841830	– Freezers of the chest type, not exceeding 800 l capacity	**Environmental Technologies,** Energy Efficiency
193	841840	– Freezers of the upright type, not exceeding 900 l capacity	**Environmental Technologies,** Energy Efficiency
194	841861	– Other refrigerating or freezing equipment, heat pumps: Compression-type units whose condensers are heat exchangers	**Renewable Energy,** Renewable Energy
195	841869	– Other refrigerating or freezing equipment heat pumps: Parts	**Renewable Energy,** Renewable Energy
	8419	**Machinery, plant or laboratory equipment**	

	HS 2002 CODE	*HS CODE DESCRIPTION*	*CATEGORY(IES)*
196	841919	– Instantaneous or storage water heaters, non-electric: Other	**Renewable Energy,** Renewable Energy
197	841939	– Other dryers	**Waste Management and Water Treatment,** Waste Water Management and Potable Water Treatment **Environmental Technologies, Carbon Capture and Storage,** Gas Flaring Emission Reduction, Efficient Consumption of Energy Technologies
198	841940	– Distilling/rectifying plant	**Waste Management and Water Treatment,** Management of Solid and Hazardous Waste and Recycling Systems **Environmental Technologies, Carbon Capture and Storage,** Gas Flaring Emission Reduction, Efficient Consumption of Energy Technologies **Others,** Others
199	841950	– Heat exchange units	**Renewable Energy,** Renewable Energy **Environmental Technologies, Carbon Capture and Storage,** Gas Flaring Emission Reduction, Efficient Consumption of Energy Technologies **Environmental Technologies,** Heat and Energy Management
200	841960	– Machinery for liquefying air or other gases	**Air Pollution Control** **Environmental Technologies, Carbon Capture and Storage,** Gas Flaring Emission Reduction, Efficient Consumption of Energy Technologies
201	841989	– Other machinery, plant and equipment: Other	**Air Pollution Control** **Environmental Technologies, Carbon Capture and Storage,** Gas Flaring Emission Reduction, Efficient Consumption of Energy Technologies **Others,** Others
202	841990	– Parts	**Renewable Energy,** Renewable Energy **Environmental Technologies, Carbon Capture and Storage,** Gas Flaring Emission Reduction, Efficient Consumption of Energy Technologies
	8420	**Calendering or other rolling machines, other than for metals or glass, and cylinders therefor**	
203	842010	– Calendering or Other Rolling Machines	**Environmental Technologies, Carbon Capture and Storage,** Efficient Consumption of Energy Technologies
204	842091	– Parts: Cylinders	**Environmental Technologies, Carbon Capture and Storage,** Efficient Consumption of Energy Technologies
205	842099	– Parts: Other	**Environmental Technologies, Carbon Capture and Storage,** Efficient Consumption of Energy Technologies
	8421	**Centrifuges, including centrifugal dryers; filtering or purifying machinery and apparatus, for liquids or gases**	
206	842119	– Other: Centrifuges, including centrifugal dryers	**Waste Management and Water Treatment,** Clean Up Or Remediation of Soil and Water **Environmental Technologies, Carbon Capture and Storage,** Efficient Consumption of Energy Technologies

	HS 2002 CODE	*HS CODE DESCRIPTION*	*CATEGORY(IES)*
207	842121	– Filtering or purifying machinery and apparatus for liquids: for filtering or purifying water	**Waste Management and Water Treatment,** Waste Water Management and Potable Water Treatment **Environmental Technologies, Carbon Capture and Storage,** Efficient Consumption of Energy Technologies
208	842123	– Filtering or purifying machinery and apparatus for liquids: Oil or Petrol-filters for Internal Combustion Engines	**Environmental Technologies, Carbon Capture and Storage,** Gas Flaring Emission Reduction, Efficient Consumption of Energy Technologies
209	842129	– Filtering or purifying machinery and apparatus for liquids: Other	**Waste Management and Water Treatment,** Waste Water Management and Potable Water Treatment **Environmental Technologies, Carbon Capture and Storage,** Gas Flaring Emission Reduction, Efficient Consumption of Energy Technologies
210	842131	-Filtering or purifying machinery and apparatus for gases: Intake Air Filters for Internal Combustion Engines	**Environmental Technologies, Carbon Capture and Storage,** Gas Flaring Emission Reduction, Efficient Consumption of Energy Technologies
211	842139	– Filtering or purifying machinery and apparatus for gases: Other	**Air Pollution Control** **Environmental Technologies, Carbon Capture and Storage,** Gas Flaring Emission Reduction, Efficient Consumption of Energy Technologies
212	842191	– Parts of centrifuges, including centrifugal dryers.	**Waste Management and Water Treatment,** Clean Up Or Remediation of Soil and Water **Environmental Technologies, Carbon Capture and Storage,** Gas Flaring Emission Reduction, Efficient Consumption of Energy Technologies
213	842199	– Parts: Other	**Waste Management and Water Treatment,** Waste Water Management and Potable Water Treatment **Environmental Technologies, Carbon Capture and Storage,** Gas Flaring Emission Reduction, Efficient Consumption of Energy Technologies
	8422	**Dish washing machines; machinery for cleaning or drying bottles or other containers; machinery for filling, closing, sealing or labelling bottles, cans, boxes, bags or other containers; machinery for capsuling bottles, jars, tubes and similar containers; other packing or wrapping machinery (including heat-shrink wrapping machinery); machinery for aerating beverages**	
214	842220	– Machinery for cleaning or drying bottles or other containers.	**Waste Management and Water Treatment,** Management of Solid and Hazardous Waste and Recycling Systems
215	842290	– Parts.	**Waste Management and Water Treatment,** Management of Solid and Hazardous Waste and Recycling Systems
	8428	**Other lifting, handling, loading or unloading machinery**	
216	842833	– Continuous-action elevators and conveyors, for goods or materials: Other, belt type.	**Waste Management and Water Treatment,** Waste Water Management and Potable Water Treatment
	8429	**Self-propelled bulldozers, angledozers, graders, levellers, scrapers, mechanical shovels, excavators, shovel loaders, tamping machines and road rollers**	

	HS 2002 CODE	HS CODE DESCRIPTION	CATEGORY(IES)
217	842940	– Tamping machines and road rollers.	**Waste Management and Water Treatment,** Management of Solid and Hazardous Waste and Recycling Systems
	8462	**Machine-tools (including presses) for working metal by forging, hammering or die-stamping; machine-tools (including presses) for working metal by bending, folding, straightening, flattening, shearing, punching or notching; presses for working metal or metal carbides**	
218	846291	– Other: Hydraulic presses.	**Waste Management and Water Treatment,** Management of Solid and Hazardous Waste and Recycling Systems
	8465	**Machine-tools (including machines for nailing, stapling, gluing or otherwise assembling) for working wood, cork, bone, hard rubber, hard plastics or similar hard materials**	
219	846596	– Other: Splitting, slicing or paring machines	**Waste Management and Water Treatment,** Management of Solid and Hazardous Waste and Recycling Systems
220	846599	– Other machine tools not elsewhere specified or included	**Waste Management and Water Treatment,** Management of Solid and Hazardous Waste and Recycling Systems
	8466	**Parts and accessories suitable for use solely or principally with the machines of headings 84.56 to 84.65, including work or tool holders, self-opening dieheads, dividing heads and other special attachments for machine-tools; tool holders for any type of tool for working in the hand**	
221	846694	– Other: for machines of heading 84.62 to 84.63.	**Waste Management and Water Treatment,** Management of Solid and Hazardous Waste and Recycling Systems
	8471	**Automatic data processing machines and units thereof; magnetic or optical readers, machines for transcribing data onto data media in coded form and machines for processing such data, not elsewhere specified or included**	
222	847130	– Portable digital automatic data processing machines, weighing not more than 10 kg, consisting of at least a central processing unit, a keyboard and a display	**Environmental Technologies,** Energy Efficiency
223	847160	– Input or output units, whether or not containing storage units in the same housing	**Environmental Technologies,** Energy Efficiency
224	847170	– Storage units	**Environmental Technologies,** Energy Efficiency
	8474	**Machinery for sorting, screening, separating, washing, crushing, grinding, mixing or kneading earth, stone, ores or other mineral substances, in solid (including powder or paste) form; machinery for agglomerating, shaping or molding solid mineral fuels, ceramic paste, unhardened cements, plastering materials or other mineral products in powder or paste form; machines for forming foundry molds of sand**	

	HS 2002 CODE	*HS CODE DESCRIPTION*	*CATEGORY(IES)*
225	847410	– Sorting, Screening, Separating or Washing Machines	**Environmental Technologies, Carbon Capture and Storage,** Efficient Consumption of Energy Technologies
226	847420	– Crushing or Grinding Machines	**Waste Management and Water Treatment,** Management of Solid and Hazardous Waste and Recycling Systems **Environmental Technologies, Carbon Capture and Storage,** Efficient Consumption of Energy Technologies
227	847431	– Mixing or kneading machines: Concrete or Mortar Mixers	**Environmental Technologies, Carbon Capture and Storage,** Efficient Consumption of Energy Technologies
228	847432	– Mixing or kneading machines: Machines for Mixing Mineral Substances With Bitumen	**Environmental Technologies, Carbon Capture and Storage,** Efficient Consumption of Energy Technologies
229	847439	– Other Mixing or Kneading Machines	**Environmental Technologies, Carbon Capture and Storage,** Efficient Consumption of Energy Technologies
230	847480	– Other machinery	**Environmental Technologies, Carbon Capture and Storage,** Efficient Consumption of Energy Technologies
231	847490	– Parts	**Environmental Technologies, Carbon Capture and Storage,** Efficient Consumption of Energy Technologies
	8477	**Machinery for working rubber or plastics or for the manufacture of products from these materials, not specified or included elsewhere in this Chapter**	
232	847710	– Injection-molding Machines	**Environmental Technologies, Carbon Capture and Storage,** Efficient Consumption of Energy Technologies
233	847720	– Extruders	**Environmental Technologies, Carbon Capture and Storage,** Efficient Consumption of Energy Technologies
234	847730	– Blow Molding Machines	**Environmental Technologies, Carbon Capture and Storage,** Efficient Consumption of Energy Technologies
235	847740	– Vacuum Molding Machines and Other Thermoforming Machines	**Environmental Technologies, Carbon Capture and Storage,** Efficient Consumption of Energy Technologies
236	847751	– Other machinery for molding or otherwise forming: For Molding or Retreading Pneumatic Tyres or for molding otherwise forming inner tubes	**Environmental Technologies, Carbon Capture and Storage,** Efficient Consumption of Energy Technologies
237	847759	– Other machinery for molding or otherwise forming: Other	**Environmental Technologies, Carbon Capture and Storage,** Efficient Consumption of Energy Technologies
238	847780	– Other Machinery	**Environmental Technologies, Carbon Capture and Storage,** Efficient Consumption of Energy Technologies
239	847790	– Parts	**Environmental Technologies, Carbon Capture and Storage,** Efficient Consumption of Energy Technologies

	HS 2002 CODE	*HS CODE DESCRIPTION*	*CATEGORY(IES)*
	8479	**Machines and mechanical appliances having individual functions, not specified or included elsewhere in this Chapter**	
240	847920	– Machinery for the extraction or preparation of animal or fixed vegetable fats or oils	**Renewable Energy,** Renewable Products and Energy Source
241	847982	– Other machines and mechanical appliances: Mixing, kneading, crushing, grinding, screening, sifting, homogenizing, emulsifying or stirring machines	**Waste Management and Water Treatment,** Management of Solid and Hazardous Waste and Recycling Systems
242	847989	– Other machinery for molding or otherwise forming: Other	**Air Pollution Control** **Waste Management and Water Treatment,** Management of Solid and Hazardous Waste and Recycling Systems **Renewable Energy,** Renewable Products and Energy Source
243	847990	– Parts	**Waste Management and Water Treatment,** Management of Solid and Hazardous Waste and Recycling Systems
	8481	**Taps, cocks, valves and similar appliances for pipes, boiler shells, tanks, vats or the like, including pressure-reducing valves and thermostatically controlled valves**	
244	848110	– Pressure-reducing valves	**Waste Management and Water Treatment,** Waste Water Management and Potable Water Treatment **Environmental Technologies, Carbon Capture and Storage,** Efficient Consumption of Energy Technologies **Others,** Resources and Pollution Management
245	848120	– Valves for oleohydraulic or pneumatic transmissions	**Waste Management and Water Treatment,** Waste Water Management and Potable Water Treatment **Environmental Technologies, Carbon Capture and Storage,** Efficient Consumption of Energy Technologies **Others,** Resources and Pollution Management
246	848130	– Check (non-return) valves	**Waste Management and Water Treatment,** Waste Water Management and Potable Water Treatment **Environmental Technologies, Carbon Capture and Storage,** Efficient Consumption of Energy Technologies **Others,** Resources and Pollution Management
247	848140	– Safety or relief valves	**Waste Management and Water Treatment,** Waste Water Management and Potable Water Treatment **Environmental Technologies, Carbon Capture and Storage,** Efficient Consumption of Energy Technologies **Others,** Resources and Pollution Management
248	848180	– Other appliances	**Waste Management and Water Treatment,** Waste Water Management and Potable Water Treatment **Environmental Technologies, Carbon Capture and Storage,** Efficient Consumption of Energy Technologies

	HS 2002 CODE	HS CODE DESCRIPTION	CATEGORY(IES)
249	848190	– Parts	**Waste Management and Water Treatment,** Waste Water Management and Potable Water Treatment **Environmental Technologies, Carbon Capture and Storage,** Efficient Consumption of Energy Technologies
	8482	**Ball or roller bearings**	
250	848210	– Ball Bearings	**Environmental Technologies, Carbon Capture and Storage,** Efficient Consumption of Energy Technologies
251	848220	– Tapered Roller Bearings, Including Cone and Tapered Roller Assemblies	**Environmental Technologies, Carbon Capture and Storage,** Efficient Consumption of Energy Technologies
252	848230	– Spherical Roller Bearings	**Environmental Technologies, Carbon Capture and Storage,** Efficient Consumption of Energy Technologies
253	848240	– Needle Roller Bearings	**Environmental Technologies, Carbon Capture and Storage,** Efficient Consumption of Energy Technologies
254	848250	– Other Cylindrical Roller Bearings	**Environmental Technologies, Carbon Capture and Storage,** Efficient Consumption of Energy Technologies
255	848280	– Other Bearings, Including Combined Ball or Roller Bearings	**Environmental Technologies, Carbon Capture and Storage,** Efficient Consumption of Energy Technologies
256	848291	– Parts: Balls, Needles and Rollers	**Environmental Technologies, Carbon Capture and Storage,** Efficient Consumption of Energy Technologies
257	848299	– Parts: Other	**Environmental Technologies, Carbon Capture and Storage,** Efficient Consumption of Energy Technologies
	8483	**Transmission shafts (including cam shafts and crank shafts) and cranks; bearing housings and plain shaft bearings; gears and gearing; ball or roller screws; gear boxes and other speed changers, including torque converters; flywheels and pulleys, including pulley blocks; clutches and shaft couplings (including universal joints)**	
258	848340	– Gears, gearing (excluding toothed wheels, chain sprockets and other transmission elements presented separately); ball or roller screws; gear boxes, other speed changers, including torque converters	**Renewable Energy,** Renewable Energy
	8483	**Transmission shafts (including cam shafts and crank shafts) and cranks; bearing housings and plain shaft bearings; gears and gearing; ball or roller screws; gear boxes and other speed changers, including torque converters; flywheels and pulleys, including pulley blocks; clutches and shaft couplings (including universal joints)**	
259	848360	– Clutches & shaft couplings (incl. universal joints)	**Renewable Energy,** Renewable Energy
	8501	**Electric motors and generators (excluding generating sets)**	

	HS 2002 CODE	*HS CODE DESCRIPTION*	*CATEGORY(IES)*
260	850161	– AC generators (alternators), of an output not exceeding 75 kVA	**Renewable Energy,** Renewable Energy
261	850162	– AC generators (alternator), of an output exceeding 75 kVA but not exceeding 375 kVA	**Renewable Energy,** Renewable Energy
262	850163	– AC generators (alternator), of an output exceeding 375 kVA but not exceeding 750 kVA	**Renewable Energy,** Renewable Energy
263	850164	– AC generators (alternator), of an output exceeding 750 kVA	**Renewable Energy,** Renewable Energy
	8502	**Electric generating sets and rotary converters**	
264	850231	– Other generating sets - wind-powered	**Renewable Energy,** Renewable Energy **Renewable Energy,** Renewable Products and Energy Source
265	850239	– Other generating sets: other	**Renewable Energy,** Renewable Energy
	8503	**Parts suitable for use solely or principally with the machines of heading 85.01 or 85.02**	
266	850300	– Parts suitable for use solely or principally with the machines of heading 85.01 or 85.02.	**Renewable Energy,** Renewable Energy **Environmental Technologies, Carbon Capture and Storage,** Efficient Consumption of Energy Technologies
	8504	**Electrical transformers, static converters (for example, rectifiers) and inductors**	
267	850410	– Ballasts for Discharge Lamps or Tubes	**Environmental Technologies, Carbon Capture and Storage,** Efficient Consumption of Energy Technologies
268	850421	– Liquid Dielectric Transformers, having a power handling capacity not Exceeding 650kVA	**Environmental Technologies, Carbon Capture and Storage,** Efficient Consumption of Energy Technologies
269	850422	– Liquid Dielectric Transformers having a power handling capacity exceeding 650 kVA but not exceeding-10, 00kVA	**Environmental Technologies, Carbon Capture and Storage,** Efficient Consumption of Energy Technologies
270	850423	– Liquid Dielectric Transformers having a power handling capacity exceeding 10, 000kVA	**Environmental Technologies, Carbon Capture and Storage,** Efficient Consumption of Energy Technologies
271	850431	– Other Transformers, Having a Power Handling Capacity Not Exceeding 1kVA	**Environmental Technologies, Carbon Capture and Storage,** Efficient Consumption of Energy Technologies
272	850432	– Other Transformers, Having a Power Handling Capacity Exceeding 1kVA But Not Exceeding 16kVA	**Environmental Technologies, Carbon Capture and Storage,** Efficient Consumption of Energy Technologies
273	850433	– Other Transformers, having a power handling capacity exceeding 16kVA But Not Exceeding 500kVA	**Environmental Technologies, Carbon Capture and Storage,** Efficient Consumption of Energy Technologies
274	850434	– Other Transformers, Having a Power Handling Capacity Exceeding 500kVA	**Environmental Technologies, Carbon Capture and Storage,** Efficient Consumption of Energy Technologies
275	850440	– Static converters	**Renewable Energy,** Renewable Energy **Environmental Technologies, Carbon Capture and Storage,** Efficient Consumption of Energy Technologies
276	850450	– Other Inductors	**Environmental Technologies, Carbon Capture and Storage,** Efficient Consumption of Energy Technologies

	HS 2002 CODE	*HS CODE DESCRIPTION*	*CATEGORY(IES)*
277	850490	– Parts	**Environmental Technologies, Carbon Capture and Storage,** Efficient Consumption of Energy Technologies
	8505	**Electro-magnets; permanent magnets and articles intended to become permanent magnets after magnetization; electro-magnetic or permanent magnet chucks, clamps and similar holding devices; electromagnetic couplings, clutches and brakes; electro-magnetic lifting heads**	
278	850511	– Permanent Magnets and Magnetized Articles, intended to become permanent magnets after magnetization, of metal	**Environmental Technologies, Carbon Capture and Storage,** Efficient Consumption of Energy Technologies
279	850519	– Permanent Magnets and Magnetized Articles intended to become permanent magnets after magnetization, other	**Environmental Technologies, Carbon Capture and Storage,** Efficient Consumption of Energy Technologies
280	850520	– Electromagnetic Couplings, Clutches and Brakes	**Environmental Technologies, Carbon Capture and Storage,** Efficient Consumption of Energy Technologies
281	850530	– Electromagnetic Lifting Heads	**Environmental Technologies, Carbon Capture and Storage,** Efficient Consumption of Energy Technologies
282	850590	– Other, including parts	**Waste Management and Water Treatment,** Management of Solid and Hazardous Waste and Recycling Systems **Environmental Technologies, Carbon Capture and Storage,** Efficient Consumption of Energy Technologies
	8506	**Primary cells and primary batteries**	
283	850610	– Primary cells & primary batteries, manganese dioxide	**Renewable Energy,** Renewable Products and Energy Source
284	850630	– Primary cells & primary batteries, mercuric oxide	**Renewable Energy,** Renewable Products and Energy Source
285	850640	– Primary cells & primary batteries, silver oxide	**Renewable Energy,** Renewable Products and Energy Source
286	850650	– Primary cells & primary batteries, lithium	**Renewable Energy,** Renewable Products and Energy Source
287	850660	– Primary cells & primary batteries, air-zinc	**Renewable Energy,** Renewable Products and Energy Source
288	850680	– Other Primary cells & primary batteries	**Renewable Energy,** Renewable Products and Energy Source **Renewable Energy,** Renewable Energy **Environmental Technologies, Carbon Capture and Storage,** Efficient Consumption of Energy Technologies
289	850690	– Parts	**Renewable Energy,** Renewable Products and Energy Source
	8507	**Electric accumulators, including separators therefor, whether or not rectangular (including square)**	
290	850720	– Other lead - Acid accumulators	**Renewable Energy,** Renewable Energy
291	850740	– Nickel-iron	**Renewable Energy,** Renewable Energy

	HS 2002 CODE	*HS CODE DESCRIPTION*	*CATEGORY(IES)*
292	850780	– Other accumulators	**Renewable Energy,** Renewable Energy **Environmental Technologies,** Energy Efficiency **Others,** Environmentally Preferable Products based on End-Use or Disposal Characteristics
293	850790	– Parts	**Others,** Environmentally Preferable Products based on End-Use or Disposal Characteristics
	8509	**Electro-mechanical domestic appliances, with self-contained electric motor**	
294	850980	– Other appliances	**Environmental Technologies,** Cleaner or More Resource-Efficient Technologies and Products
	8511	**Electrical ignition or starting equipment of a kind used for spark-ignition or compression-ignition internal combustion engines (for example, ignition magnetos, magneto-dynamos, ignition coils, sparking plugs and glow plugs, starter motors); generators (for example, dynamos, alternators) and cut-outs of a kind used in conjunction with such engines.**	
295	851140	– Starter Motors and Dual Purpose Starter-generators	**Environmental Technologies, Carbon Capture and Storage,** Efficient Consumption of Energy Technologies
296	851150	– Other Generators	**Environmental Technologies, Carbon Capture and Storage,** Efficient Consumption of Energy Technologies
297	851180	– Other Equipment	**Environmental Technologies, Carbon Capture and Storage,** Efficient Consumption of Energy Technologies
298	851190	– Parts	**Environmental Technologies, Carbon Capture and Storage,** Efficient Consumption of Energy Technologies
	8514	**Industrial or laboratory electric furnaces and ovens (including those functioning by induction or dielectric loss); other industrial or laboratory equipment for the heat treatment of materials by induction or dielectric loss.**	
299	851410	– Resistance heated furnaces & ovens	**Waste Management and Water Treatment,** Management of Solid and Hazardous Waste and Recycling Systems **Environmental Technologies, Carbon Capture and Storage,** Gas Flaring Emission Reduction, Efficient Consumption of Energy Technologies
300	851420	– Furnaces & ovens functioning by induction/dielectric loss	**Waste Management and Water Treatment,** Management of Solid and Hazardous Waste and Recycling Systems **Environmental Technologies, Carbon Capture and Storage,** Gas Flaring Emission Reduction, Efficient Consumption of Energy Technologies
301	851430	– Other Furnaces and Ovens	**Waste Management and Water Treatment,** Management of Solid and Hazardous Waste and Recycling Systems **Environmental Technologies, Carbon Capture and Storage,** Gas Flaring Emission Reduction, Efficient Consumption of Energy Technologies

	HS 2002 CODE	*HS CODE DESCRIPTION*	*CATEGORY(IES)*
302	851440	– Other equipment for the heat treatment of materials by induction or dielectric loss	**Environmental Technologies, Carbon Capture and Storage,** Gas Flaring Emission Reduction, Efficient Consumption of Energy Technologies
303	851490	– Parts	**Waste Management and Water Treatment,** Management of Solid and Hazardous Waste and Recycling Systems
	8516	**Electric instantaneous or storage water heaters and immersion heaters; electric space heating apparatus and soil heating apparatus; electro-thermic hair-dressing apparatus (for example, hairdryers, hair curlers, curling tong heaters) and hand dryers; electric smoothing irons; other electro-thermic appliances of a kind used for domestic purposes; electric heating resistors, other than those of heading 85.45**	
304	851629	– Electric space heating apparatus and electric soil heating apparatus; other	**Waste Management and Water Treatment,** Clean Up Or Remediation of Soil and Water
	8517	**Electrical apparatus for line telephony or line telegraphy, including line telephone sets with cordless handsets and telecommunication apparatus for carrier-current line systems or for digital line systems; videophones**	
305	851711	– Telephone sets; videophones: Line telephone sets with cordless handsets	**Environmental Technologies,** Energy Efficiency
306	851721	– Facsimile machines	**Environmental Technologies,** Energy Efficiency
307	851730	– Telephonic or telegraphic switching apparatus	**Environmental Technologies,** Energy Efficiency
308	851750	– Other apparatus, for carrier-current line systems or for digital line systems	**Environmental Technologies,** Energy Efficiency
	8518	**Microphones and stands therefor; loudspeakers, whether or not mounted in their enclosures; headphones and earphones, whether or not combined with a microphone, and sets consisting of a microphone and one or more loudspeakers; audio-frequency electric amplifiers; electric sound amplifier sets**	
309	851840	– Audio-frequency electric amplifiers	**Environmental Technologies,** Energy Efficiency
	8520	**Magnetic tape recorders and other sound recording apparatus, whether or not incorporating a sound reproducing device**	
310	852090	– Other	**Environmental Technologies,** Energy Efficiency
	8521	**Video recording or reproducing apparatus, whether or not incorporating a video tuner**	
311	852190	– Other	**Environmental Technologies,** Energy Efficiency
	8522	**Parts and accessories suitable for use solely or principally with the apparatus of headings 85.19 to 85.21**	
312	852210	– Pick-up cartridges	**Environmental Technologies,** Energy Efficiency

	HS 2002 CODE	*HS CODE DESCRIPTION*	*CATEGORY(IES)*
	8523	**Prepared unrecorded media for sound recording or similar recording of other phenomena, other than products of Chapter 37**	
313	852390	– Other	**Environmental Technologies,** Energy Efficiency
	8525	**Transmission apparatus for radio-telephony, radio-telegraphy, radio-broadcasting or television, whether or not incorporating reception apparatus or sound recording or reproducing apparatus; television cameras; still image video cameras and other video camera recorders; digital cameras**	
314	852540	– Still image video cameras and other video camera records; digital cameras	**Environmental Technologies,** Energy Efficiency
	8526	**Radar apparatus, radio navigational aid apparatus and radio remote control apparatus**	
315	852691	– Other: Radio navigational aid apparatus	**Environmental Technologies,** Energy Efficiency
	8528	**Reception apparatus for television, whether or not incorporating radio-broadcast receivers or sound or video recording or reproducing apparatus; video monitors and video projectors**	
316	852812	– Reception apparatus for television, whether or not incorporating radiobroadcast receivers or sound or video recording or reproducing apparatus: Color	**Environmental Technologies,** Energy Efficiency
317	852821	– Video monitors: Color	**Environmental Technologies,** Energy Efficiency
318	852830	– Video projectors	**Environmental Technologies,** Energy Efficiency
	8536	**Electrical apparatus for switching or protecting electrical circuits, or for making connections to or in electrical circuits (for example, switches, relays, fuses, surge suppressors, plugs, sockets, lamp-holders, junction boxes), for a voltage not exceeding 1,000 volts**	
319	853661	– Lamp-holders, plugs and sockets: Lamp holders	**Environmental Technologies,** Energy Efficiency
	8537	**Boards, panels, consoles, desks, cabinets and other bases, equipped with two or more apparatus of heading 85.35 or 85.36, for electric control or the distribution of electricity, including those incorporating instruments or apparatus of Chapter 90, and numerical control apparatus, other than switching apparatus of heading 85.17**	
320	853710	– For a voltage not exceeding 1,000 V	**Renewable Energy,** Renewable Energy
	8539	**Electric filament or discharge lamps, including sealed beam lamp units and ultra-violet or infra-red lamps; arc-lamps**	
321	853949	– Ultra-violet or infra-red lamps; arc-lamps: Other	**Waste Management and Water Treatment,** Waste Water Management and Potable Water Treatment

	HS 2002 CODE	*HS CODE DESCRIPTION*	*CATEGORY(IES)*
	8541	**Diodes, transistors and similar semiconductor devices; photosensitive semiconductor devices, including photovoltaic cells whether or not assembled in modules or made up into panels; light emitting diodes; mounted piezo-electric crystals**	
322	854140	– Photosensitive semiconductor devices, including photovoltaic cells whether or not assembled in modules or made up into panels; light-emitting diodes.	**Renewable Energy,** Renewable Energy **Renewable Energy,** Renewable Products and Energy Source
	8543	**Electrical machines and apparatus, having individual functions, not specified or included elsewhere in this Chapter**	
323	854389	– Other machines and apparatus: Other	**Waste Management and Water Treatment,** Waste Water Management and Potable Water Treatment
324	854390	– Parts	**Waste Management and Water Treatment,** Waste Water Management and Potable Water Treatment
	8702	**Motor vehicles for the transport of ten or more persons, including the driver**	
325	870210	– With compression-ignition internal combustion piston engine (diesel or semi-diesel)	**Air Pollution Control**
326	870290	– Other	**Air Pollution Control** **Renewable Energy,** Renewable Energy
	8703	**Motor cars and other motor vehicles principally designed for the transport of persons (other than those of heading 87.02), including station wagons and racing cars**	
327	870321	– Other vehicles, with spark-ignition internal combustion: of a cylinder capacity not exceeding 1,000 cc	**Air Pollution Control** **Renewable Energy,** Renewable Energy
328	870322	– Other vehicles, with spark-ignition internal combustion: of a cylinder capacity exceeding 1,000 cc but not exceeding 1,500 cc	**Air Pollution Control** **Renewable Energy,** Renewable Energy
329	870323	– Other vehicles, with spark-ignition internal combustion: of a cylinder capacity exceeding 1,500 cc but not exceeding 3,000 cc	**Air Pollution Control** **Renewable Energy,** Renewable Energy
330	870324	– Other vehicles, with spark-ignition internal combustion: of a cylinder capacity exceeding 3,000 cc	**Air Pollution Control** **Renewable Energy,** Renewable Energy
331	870331	– Other vehicles, with compression-ignition internal combustion piston engine (diesel or semi-diesel): of a cylinder capacity not exceeding 1,500 cc	**Air Pollution Control** **Renewable Energy,** Renewable Energy
332	870332	– Other vehicles, with compression-ignition internal combustion piston engine (diesel or semi-diesel): of a cylinder capacity exceeding 1,500 cc but not exceeding 2,500 cc	**Air Pollution Control** **Renewable Energy,** Renewable Energy
333	870333	– Other vehicles, with compression-ignition internal combustion piston engine (diesel or semi-diesel): of a cylinder capacity exceeding 2,500 cc	**Air Pollution Control** **Renewable Energy,** Renewable Energy
334	870390	– Other	**Air Pollution Control** **Renewable Energy,** Renewable Energy
	8704	**Motor vehicles for the transport of goods**	

	HS 2002 CODE	*HS CODE DESCRIPTION*	*CATEGORY(IES)*
335	870410	– Dumpers designed for off-highway use	**Air Pollution Control** **Renewable Energy,** Renewable Energy
336	870421	– Other, with compression-ignition internal combustion piston engine (diesel or semi-diesel):, g.v.w. not exceeding 5 tonnes	**Air Pollution Control** **Renewable Energy,** Renewable Energy
337	870422	– Other, with compression-ignition internal combustion piston engine (diesel or semi-diesel):, g.v.w. not exceeding 5 tonnes but not exceeding 20 tonnes	**Air Pollution Control** **Renewable Energy,** Renewable Energy
338	870423	– Other, with compression-ignition internal combustion piston engine (diesel or semi-diesel):, g.v.w. exceeding 20 tonnes	**Air Pollution Control** **Renewable Energy,** Renewable Energy
339	870431	– Other, with spark-ignition internal combustion piston engine: g.v.w. not exceeding 5 tonnes	**Air Pollution Control** **Renewable Energy,** Renewable Energy
340	870432	– Other, with spark-ignition internal combustion piston engine: g.v.w. exceeding 5 tonnes	**Air Pollution Control** **Renewable Energy,** Renewable Energy
341	870490	– Other	**Air Pollution Control** **Renewable Energy,** Renewable Energy
	8705	**Special purpose motor vehicles, other than those principally designed for the transport of persons or goods (for example, breakdown lorries, crane lorries, fire fighting vehicles, concrete mixer lorries, road sweeper lorries, spraying lorries, mobile workshops, mobile radiological units)**	
342	870510	– Crane lorries	**Air Pollution Control** **Renewable Energy,** Renewable Energy
343	870520	– Mobile drilling derricks	**Air Pollution Control** **Renewable Energy,** Renewable Energy
344	870530	– Fire fighting vehicles	**Air Pollution Control** **Renewable Energy,** Renewable Energy
345	870540	– Concrete-mixer lorries (concrete-mixers)	**Air Pollution Control** **Renewable Energy,** Renewable Energy
346	870590	– Other	**Air Pollution Control** **Renewable Energy,** Renewable Energy
	8711	**Motorcycles (including mopeds) and cycles fitted with an auxiliary motor, with or without side-cars; side-cars**	
347	871110	– With reciprocating internal combustion piston engine of a cylinder capacity not exceeding 50 cc.	**Air Pollution Control** **Renewable Energy,** Renewable Energy
348	871120	– With reciprocating internal combustion piston engine of a cylinder capacity exceeding 50 cc but not exceeding 250cc.	**Air Pollution Control** **Renewable Energy,** Renewable Energy
349	871130	– With reciprocating internal combustion piston engine of a cylinder capacity exceeding 250 cc but not exceeding 500cc.	**Air Pollution Control** **Renewable Energy,** Renewable Energy
350	871140	– With reciprocating internal combustion piston engine of a cylinder capacity exceeding 500 cc but not exceeding 800cc.	**Air Pollution Control** **Renewable Energy,** Renewable Energy
351	871150	– With reciprocating internal combustion piston engine of a cylinder capacity exceeding 800 cc.	**Air Pollution Control** **Renewable Energy,** Renewable Energy

	HS 2002 CODE	HS CODE DESCRIPTION	CATEGORY(IES)
	8907	**Other floating structures (for example, rafts, tanks, coffer-dams, landing-stages, buoys and beacons)**	
352	890790	– Other	**Waste Management and Water Treatment,** Clean Up Or Remediation of Soil and Water
	9001	**Optical fibers and optical fiber bundles; optical fiber cables other than those of heading 85.44; sheets and plates of polarizing material; lenses (including contact lenses), prisms, mirrors and other optical elements, of any material, unmounted, other than such elements of glass not optically worked**	
353	900190	– Other	**Renewable Energy,** Renewable Energy
	9002	**Lenses, prisms, mirrors and other optical elements, of any material, mounted, being parts of or fittings for instruments or apparatus, other than such elements of glass not optically worked**	
354	900290	– Other	**Renewable Energy,** Renewable Energy
	9015	**Surveying (including photogrammetrical surveying), hydrographic, oceanographic, hydrological, meteorological or geophysical instruments and appliances, excluding compasses; rangefinders**	
355	901510	– Rangefinders	**Environmental Technologies, Carbon Capture and Storage,** Efficient Consumption of Energy Technologies
356	901520	– Theodolites and tachymeters (tacheometers)	**Environmental Technologies, Carbon Capture and Storage,** Efficient Consumption of Energy Technologies
357	901530	– Levels	**Environmental Technologies, Carbon Capture and Storage,** Efficient Consumption of Energy Technologies **Environmental Technologies,** Environmental Monitoring, Analysis and Assessment Equipment
358	901540	– Photogrammeterical surveying instruments and appliances	**Environmental Technologies, Carbon Capture and Storage,** Efficient Consumption of Energy Technologies **Environmental Technologies,** Natural Risk Management
359	901580	– Other instruments and appliances	**Environmental Technologies, Carbon Capture and Storage,** Efficient Consumption of Energy Technologies **Environmental Technologies,** Natural Risk Management
360	901590	– Parts and accessories	**Environmental Technologies, Carbon Capture and Storage,** Efficient Consumption of Energy Technologies **Environmental Technologies,** Natural Risk Management
	9024	**Machines and appliances for testing the hardness, strength, compressibility, elasticity or other mechanical properties of materials (for example, metals, wood, textiles, paper, plastics)**	

	HS 2002 CODE	*HS CODE DESCRIPTION*	*CATEGORY(IES)*
361	902410	– Machines and appliances for testing metals	**Environmental Technologies, Carbon Capture and Storage,** Efficient Consumption of Energy Technologies
362	902480	– Other machines and appliances	**Environmental Technologies, Carbon Capture and Storage,** Efficient Consumption of Energy Technologies
363	902490	– Parts and accessories	**Environmental Technologies, Carbon Capture and Storage,** Efficient Consumption of Energy Technologies
	9025	**Hydrometers and similar floating instruments, thermometers, pyrometers, barometers, hygrometers and psychrometers, recording or not, and any combination of these instruments**	
364	902511	– Thermometers and pyrometers, not combined with other instruments: Liquid-filled, for direct reading	**Environmental Technologies, Carbon Capture and Storage,** Efficient Consumption of Energy Technologies
365	902519	– Thermometers and pyrometers, not combined with other instruments: Other	**Environmental Technologies, Carbon Capture and Storage,** Efficient Consumption of Energy Technologies
366	902580	– Other instruments	**Environmental Technologies, Carbon Capture and Storage,** Efficient Consumption of Energy Technologies
367	902590	– Parts and accessories	**Environmental Technologies, Carbon Capture and Storage,** Efficient Consumption of Energy Technologies
	9026	**Instruments and apparatus for measuring or checking the flow, level, pressure or other variables of liquids or gases (for example, flow meters, level gauges, manometers, heat meters), excluding instruments and apparatus of heading 90.14, 90.15, 90.28 or 90.32**	
368	902610	– For measuring or checking the flow or level of liquids	**Air Pollution Control** **Environmental Technologies,** Environmental Monitoring, Analysis and Assessment Equipment
369	902620	– For measuring or checking pressure	**Environmental Technologies, Carbon Capture and Storage,** Gas Flaring Emission Reduction, Efficient Consumption of Energy Technologies **Environmental Technologies,** Environmental Monitoring, Analysis and Assessment Equipment
370	902680	– Other instruments or apparatus	**Environmental Technologies, Carbon Capture and Storage,** Gas Flaring Emission Reduction, Efficient Consumption of Energy Technologies **Environmental Technologies,** Environmental Monitoring, Analysis and Assessment Equipment
371	902690	– Parts and accessories	**Environmental Technologies, Carbon Capture and Storage,** Gas Flaring Emission Reduction, Efficient Consumption of Energy Technologies **Environmental Technologies,** Environmental Monitoring, Analysis and Assessment Equipment

	HS 2002 CODE	*HS CODE DESCRIPTION*	*CATEGORY(IES)*
	9027	**Instruments and apparatus for physical or chemical analysis (for example, polarimeters, refractometers, spectrometers, gas or smoke analysis apparatus); instruments and apparatus for measuring or checking viscosity, porosity, expansion, surface tension or the like; instruments and apparatus for measuring or checking quantities of heat, sound or light (including exposure meters); microtomes**	
372	902710	– Gas or smoke analysis apparatus	**Environmental Technologies,** Environmental Monitoring, Analysis and Assessment Equipment
373	902720	– Chromatographs and electrophoresis instruments	**Environmental Technologies,** Environmental Monitoring, Analysis and Assessment Equipment
374	902730	– Spectrometers, spectrophotometers and spectrographs using optical radiations (UV, visible, IR)	**Environmental Technologies,** Environmental Monitoring, Analysis and Assessment Equipment
375	902740	– Exposure meters	**Environmental Technologies,** Environmental Monitoring, Analysis and Assessment Equipment
376	902750	– Other instruments and apparatus using optical radiations (UV, visible, IR)	**Environmental Technologies,** Environmental Monitoring, Analysis and Assessment Equipment
377	902780	– Other instruments and apparatus	**Environmental Technologies,** Environmental Monitoring, Analysis and Assessment Equipment
378	902790	– Microtomes; parts and accessories	**Environmental Technologies,** Environmental Monitoring, Analysis and Assessment Equipment
	9028	**Gas, liquid or electricity supply or production meters, including calibrating meters therefor**	
379	902810	– Gas meters	**Environmental Technologies, Carbon Capture and Storage,** Gas Flaring Emission Reduction, Efficient Consumption of Energy Technologies **Others,** Resources and Pollution Management **Environmental Technologies,** Heat and Energy Management
380	902820	– Liquid meters	**Environmental Technologies, Carbon Capture and Storage,** Efficient Consumption of Energy Technologies **Environmental Technologies,** Heat and Energy Management
381	902830	– Electricity meters	**Environmental Technologies, Carbon Capture and Storage,** Efficient Consumption of Energy Technologies **Environmental Technologies,** Heat and Energy Management
382	902890	– Parts and accessories	**Environmental Technologies, Carbon Capture and Storage,** Efficient Consumption of Energy Technologies **Environmental Technologies,** Heat and Energy Management

	HS 2002 CODE	*HS CODE DESCRIPTION*	*CATEGORY(IES)*
	9030	**Oscilloscopes, spectrum analyzers and other instruments and apparatus for measuring or checking electrical quantities, excluding meters of heading 90.28; instruments and apparatus for measuring or detecting alpha, beta, gamma, X-ray, cosmic or other ionizing radiations**	
383	903010	– Instruments and apparatus for measuring or detecting ionizing radiations.	**Environmental Technologies,** Environmental Monitoring, Analysis and Assessment Equipment
384	903020	– Cathode-ray oscilloscopes and cathode-ray oscillographs.	**Environmental Technologies,** Environmental Monitoring, Analysis and Assessment Equipment
385	903031	– Other instruments and apparatus, for measuring or checking voltage, current, resistance or power, without a recording device: Multimeters.	**Environmental Technologies,** Environmental Monitoring, Analysis and Assessment Equipment
386	903039	– Other instruments and apparatus, for measuring or checking voltage, current, resistance or power, without a recording device: Other.	**Environmental Technologies,** Environmental Monitoring, Analysis and Assessment Equipment
387	903040	– Other instruments and apparatus, specially designed for telecommunications (for example, cross-talk meters, gain measuring instruments, distortion factor meters, psophometers)	**Environmental Technologies,** Environmental Monitoring, Analysis and Assessment Equipment
388	903082	– Other instruments and apparatus: for measuring or checking semiconductor wafers or devices	**Environmental Technologies,** Environmental Monitoring, Analysis and Assessment Equipment
389	903083	– Other instruments and apparatus: Other, with a recording device	**Environmental Technologies,** Environmental Monitoring, Analysis and Assessment Equipment
390	903089	– Other instruments and apparatus: Other	**Environmental Technologies,** Environmental Monitoring, Analysis and Assessment Equipment
391	903090	– Parts and accessories	**Environmental Technologies,** Environmental Monitoring, Analysis and Assessment Equipment
	9031	**Measuring or checking instruments, appliances and machines, not specified or included elsewhere in this Chapter; profile projectors**	
392	903110	– Machines for balancing mechanical parts	**Environmental Technologies,** Environmental Monitoring, Analysis and Assessment Equipment **Environmental Technologies, Carbon Capture and Storage,** Efficient Consumption of Energy Technologies **Environmental Technologies,** Noise and Vibration Abatement
393	903120	– Test benches.	**Environmental Technologies,** Environmental Monitoring, Analysis and Assessment Equipment

	HS 2002 CODE	HS CODE DESCRIPTION	CATEGORY(IES)
394	903130	– Profile projectors.	**Environmental Technologies,** Environmental Monitoring, Analysis and Assessment Equipment **Environmental Technologies, Carbon Capture and Storage,** Efficient Consumption of Energy Technologies
395	903140	– Other optical instruments and appliances	**Environmental Technologies,** Environmental Monitoring, Analysis and Assessment Equipment **Environmental Technologies, Carbon Capture and Storage,** Efficient Consumption of Energy Technologies
396	903149	– Other optical instruments and appliances: Other	**Environmental Technologies,** Environmental Monitoring, Analysis and Assessment Equipment
397	903180	– Other instruments, appliances and machines.	**Environmental Technologies,** Environmental Monitoring, Analysis and Assessment Equipment **Environmental Technologies, Carbon Capture and Storage,** Efficient Consumption of Energy Technologies
398	903190	– Parts and accessories	**Environmental Technologies,** Environmental Monitoring, Analysis and Assessment Equipment **Environmental Technologies, Carbon Capture and Storage,** Efficient Consumption of Energy Technologies
	9032	**Automatic regulating or controlling instruments and apparatus**	
399	903210	– Thermostats	**Environmental Technologies,** Environmental Monitoring, Analysis and Assessment Equipment **Environmental Technologies, Carbon Capture and Storage,** Gas Flaring Emission Reduction, Efficient Consumption of Energy Technologies
400	903220	– Manostats.	**Environmental Technologies,** Environmental Monitoring, Analysis and Assessment Equipment **Environmental Technologies, Carbon Capture and Storage,** Gas Flaring Emission Reduction, Efficient Consumption of Energy Technologies
401	903281	– Other instruments and apparatus: Hydraulic or pneumatic	**Environmental Technologies,** Environmental Monitoring, Analysis and Assessment Equipment **Environmental Technologies, Carbon Capture and Storage,** Gas Flaring Emission Reduction, Efficient Consumption of Energy Technologies
402	903289	– Other instruments and apparatus: Other	**Environmental Technologies,** Environmental Monitoring, Analysis and Assessment Equipment **Environmental Technologies, Carbon Capture and Storage,** Gas Flaring Emission Reduction, Efficient Consumption of Energy Technologies **Renewable Energy,** Renewable Energy

	HS 2002 CODE	*HS CODE DESCRIPTION*	*CATEGORY(IES)*
403	903290	– Parts and accessories	**Environmental Technologies,** Environmental Monitoring, Analysis and Assessment Equipment **Environmental Technologies, Carbon Capture and Storage,** Gas Flaring Emission Reduction, Efficient Consumption of Energy Technologies
	9033	**Parts and accessories (not specified or included elsewhere in this Chapter) for machines, appliances, instruments or apparatus of Chapter 90**	
404	903300	– Parts and accessories (not specified or included elsewhere in this chapter) for machines, appliances	**Environmental Technologies, Carbon Capture and Storage,** Gas Flaring Emission Reduction, Efficient Consumption of Energy Technologies **Environmental Technologies,** Environmental Monitoring, Analysis and Assessment Equipment
	9405	**Lamps and lighting fittings including searchlights and spotlights and parts thereof, not elsewhere specified or included; illuminated signs, illuminated name-plates and the like, having a permanently fixed light source, and parts thereof not elsewhere specified or included**	
405	940510	– Chandeliers and other electric ceiling or wall lighting fittings, excluding those of a kind used for lighting public open spaces or thoroughfares	**Environmental Technologies,** Energy Efficiency
406	940520	– Electric table, desk, bedside or floor-standing lamps	**Environmental Technologies,** Energy Efficiency
407	940540	– Other electric lamps and lighting fittings	**Environmental Technologies,** Energy Efficiency
	9507	**Fishing rods, fishhooks and other line fishing tackle; fish landing nets, butterfly nets and similar nets; decoy birds (other than those of heading 92.08 or 97.05) and similar hunting or shooting requisites**	
408	950720	– Fish-hooks, whether or not snelled.	**Others,** Natural Resources Protection

Annex II.B: Sample Core List of Environmental Goods by Official HS 2002 Descriptions

1. The following HS lines have been identified and drawn from JOB/TE/3/Rev.1 (See Annex II.B hereof) by a number of Members[1], as a ***starting point*** for discussion in the CTESS towards a credible core list of environmental goods, without prejudice to the final outcome.
2. This table is based on the HS2002 classification at the 6-digit level. Descriptions are reproduced from the World Customs Organization, *Harmonized commodity description and coding system*, Brussels, 2002. It should be noted that HS2002 official code descriptions do not always match descriptions provided by Members in their submissions. Some Members have identified the entire HS6 line while other Members have tried to be more specific (including by using ex-outs) to facilitate the identification of environmental goods of interest.
3. Accuracy and technical verification of the descriptions and HS codes contained in this document as well as the technical description if any, of ex-outs, will need to be undertaken by the environment and customs experts and it is expected that individual delegations will prepare draft technical descriptions and/or sub-classifications or ex-outs in their draft schedules for review and verification with other delegations.

	HS 2002 CODE	*HS CODE DESCRIPTION*	*CATEGORY(IES)*
	4601	**Plaits and similar products of plaiting materials, whether or not assembled into sTRIPS; plaiting materials, plaits and similar products of plaiting materials, bound together in parallel strands or woven, in sheet form, whether or not being finished artic**	
1	460120	– Mats, matting and screens of vegetable materials	**Waste Management and Water Treatment,** Waste Management, Recycling and Remediation
	7308	**Structures (excluding prefabricated buildings of heading 94.06) and parts of structures (for example, bridges and bridge sections, lock gates, towers, lattice masts, roofs, roofing frameworks, doors and windows and their frames and thresholds for doors, shutters, balustrades, pillars and columns) of iron or steel; plates, rods, angles, shapes, sections, tubes and the like, prepared for use in structures, of iron or steel**	
2	730820	– Towers & lattice masts	**Renewable Energy,** Renewable Energy **Renewable Energy,** Renewable Products and Energy Source

1. Based on Room document circulated on 17 March 2011 without prejudice by Australia; Colombia; Hong Kong, China; Norway; and Singapore.

	HS 2002 CODE	*HS CODE DESCRIPTION*	*CATEGORY(IES)*
	7321	**Stoves, ranges, grates, cookers (including those with subsidiary boilers for central heating), barbecues, braziers, gas rings, plate warmers and similar non-electric domestic appliances, and parts thereof, of iron or steel**	
3	732111	– Cooking appliances and plate warmers: For gas fuel or for both gas and other fuels.	**Environmental Technologies,** Cleaner or More Resource-Efficient Technologies and Products
	7324	**Sanitary ware and parts thereof, of iron or steel**	
4	732490	– Other, including parts	**Waste Management and Water Treatment,** Waste Water Management and Potable Water Treatment **Environmental Technologies, Carbon Capture and Storage,** Efficient Consumption of Energy Technologies
	8402	**Steam or other vapor generating boilers (other than central heating hot water boilers capable also of producing low-pressure steam); superheated water boilers**	
5	840290	– Parts	**Environmental Technologies, Carbon Capture and Storage,** Efficient Consumption of Energy Technologies **Waste Management and Water Treatment,** Management of Solid and Hazardous Waste and Recycling Systems **Waste Management and Water Treatment,** Waste Management, Recycling and Remediation
	8404	**Auxiliary plant for use with boilers of heading 84.02 or 84.03 (for example, economizers, super-heaters, soot removers, gas recoverers); condensers for steam or other vapor power units**	
6	840410	– Auxiliary plant for use with boilers of 84.02 or 84.03	**Waste Management and Water Treatment,** Waste Management, Recycling and Remediation **Waste Management and Water Treatment,** Management of Solid and Hazardous Waste and Recycling Systems **Environmental Technologies, Carbon Capture and Storage,** Efficient Consumption of Energy Technologies
	8405	**Producer gas or water gas generators, with or without their purifiers; acetylene gas generators and similar water process gas generators, with or without their purifiers**	
7	840510	– Producer gas or water gas generators, with or without their purifiers; acetylene gas generators and similar water process gas generators, with or without their purifiers	**Air Pollution Control** **Renewable Energy,** Renewable Energy **Waste Management and Water Treatment,** Waste Water Management and Potable Water Treatment **Environmental Technologies, Carbon Capture and Storage,** Efficient Consumption of Energy Technologies
	8406	**Steam turbines and other vapor turbines**	
8	840681	– Turbines for marine propulsion: Of an output exceeding 40 MW	**Renewable Energy,** Renewable Energy
	8409	**Parts suitable for use solely or principally with the engines of heading 84.07 or 84.08**	

	HS 2002 CODE	*HS CODE DESCRIPTION*	*CATEGORY(IES)*
9	840999	– Other: other	**Air Pollution Control** **Environmental Technologies, Carbon Capture and Storage,** Efficient Consumption of Energy Technologies **Environmental Technologies, Carbon Capture and Storage,** Noise and Vibration Abatement
	8410	**Hydraulic turbines, water wheels, and regulators therefor**	
10	841011	– Hydraulic turbines and water wheels of a power not exceeding 1,000 kW.	**Renewable Energy,** Renewable Energy **Environmental Technologies, Carbon Capture and Storage,** Efficient Consumption of Energy Technologies
11	841012	– Hydraulic Turbines and Water Wheels, Power 1, 000-10, 000kw	**Environmental Technologies, Carbon Capture and Storage,** Efficient Consumption of Energy Technologies
12	841090	– Hydraulic turbines, water wheels, and regulators; parts, including regulators	**Renewable Energy,** Renewable Energy **Environmental Technologies, Carbon Capture and Storage,** Efficient Consumption of Energy Technologies
	8411	**Turbo-jets, turbo-propellers and other gas turbines**	
13	841181	– Other gas turbines of a power not exceeding 5,000 kW	**Renewable Energy,** Renewable Energy **Environmental Technologies, Carbon Capture and Storage,** Efficient Consumption of Energy Technologies **Others,** Environmentally Preferable Products based on End-Use or Disposal Characteristics
14	841182	– Other gas turbines of a power exceeding 5,000 kW	**Renewable Energy,** Renewable Energy **Environmental Technologies, Carbon Capture and Storage,** Efficient Consumption of Energy Technologies **Others,** Environmentally Preferable Products based on End-Use or Disposal Characteristics
	8418	**Refrigerators, freezers and other refrigerating or freezing equipment, electric or other; heat pumps other than air conditioning machines of heading 84.15**	
15	841861	– Other refrigerating or freezing equipment; heat pumps: Compression-type units whose condensers are heat exchangers	**Renewable Energy,** Renewable Energy
	8419	**Machinery, plant or laboratory equipment, whether or not electrically heated (excluding furnaces, ovens and other equipment of heading 85.14), for the treatment of materials by a process involving a change of temperature such as heating, cooking, roasting**	
16	841919	– Instantaneous or storage water heaters, non-electric: Other	**Renewable Energy,** Renewable Energy
17	841950	– Heat exchange units	**Renewable Energy,** Renewable Energy **Environmental Technologies, Carbon Capture and Storage,** Gas Flaring Emission Reduction, Efficient Consumption of Energy Technologies **Environmental Technologies,** Heat and Energy Management
	8479	**Machines and mechanical appliances having individual functions, not specified or included elsewhere in this Chapter**	

	HS 2002 CODE	*HS CODE DESCRIPTION*	*CATEGORY(IES)*
18	847989	– Other machines and mechanical appliances: Other	**Air Pollution Control** **Waste Management and Water Treatment,** Management of Solid and Hazardous Waste and Recycling Systems **Renewable Energy,** Renewable Products and Energy Source
	8502	**Electric generating sets and rotary converters**	
19	850231	– Other generating sets: Wind-powered	**Renewable Energy,** Renewable Energy **Renewable Energy,** Renewable Products and Energy Source
	8504	**Electrical transformers, static converters (for example, rectifiers) and inductors**	
20	850410	– Ballasts for discharge lamps or tubes	**Environmental Technologies, Carbon Capture and Storage,** Efficient Consumption of Energy Technologies
	8537	**Boards, panels, consoles, desks, cabinets and other bases, equipped with two or more apparatus of heading 85.35 or 85.36, for electric control or the distribution of electricity, including those incorporating instruments or apparatus of Chapter 90, and numerical control apparatus, other than switching apparatus of heading 85.17**	
21	853710	– For a voltage not exceeding 1,000V	**Renewable Energy,** Renewable Energy
	8541	**Diodes, transistors and similar semiconductor devices; photosensitive semiconductor devices, including photovoltaic cells whether or not assembled in modules or made up into panels; light emitting diodes; mounted piezo-electric crystals**	
22	854140	– Photosensitive semiconductor devices, including photovoltaic cells whether or not assembled in modules or made up into panels; light-emitting diodes.	**Renewable Energy,** Renewable Energy **Renewable Energy,** Renewable Products and Energy Source
	9001	**Optical fibers and optical fiber bundles; optical fiber cables other than those of heading 85.44; sheets and plates of polarizing material; lenses (including contact lenses), prisms, mirrors and other optical elements, of any material, unmounted, other than such elements of glass not optically worked**	
23	900190	– Other	**Renewable Energy,** Renewable Energy
	9002	**Lenses, prisms, mirrors and other optical elements, of any material, mounted, being parts of or fittings for instruments or apparatus, other than such elements of glass not optically worked**	
24	900290	– Other	**Renewable Energy,** Renewable Energy

	HS 2002 CODE	*HS CODE DESCRIPTION*	*CATEGORY(IES)*
	9027	**Instruments and apparatus for physical or chemical analysis (for example, polarimeters, refractometers, spectrometers, gas or smoke analysis apparatus); instruments and apparatus for measuring or checking viscosity, porosity, expansion, surface tension or the like; instruments and apparatus for measuring or checking quantities of heat, sound or light (including exposure meters); microtomes**	
25	902730	– Spectrometers, spectrophotometers and spectrographs using optical radiations (UV, visible, IR)	**Environmental Technologies,** Environmental Monitoring, Analysis and Assessment Equipment
	9032	**Automatic regulating or controlling instruments and apparatus**	
26	903210	– Thermostats	**Environmental Technologies,** Environmental Monitoring, Analysis and Assessment Equipment **Environmental Technologies, Carbon Capture and Storage,** Gas Flaring Emission Reduction, Efficient Consumption of Energy Technologies
27			
28			
29			
30			
31			
32			
33			
34			
35			
36			

Bibliography

Books and Articles

Abi-Saab, Georges. "Progressive Development of the Principles and Norms of International Law Relating to the New International Economic Order." In *UN Doc. A/39/504/Add.1*, 28-111. New York: United Nations, 1984.

Aceves, William J. "Institutionalist Theory and International Legal Scholarship." *American University International Law Review* 12, no. 2 (1997): 227-266.

Ala'i, Padideh. "From the Periphery to the Center? The Evolving WTO Jurisprudence on Transparency and Good Governance." *Journal of International Economic Law* 11 (2008): 779–802.

Ala'i, Padideh. "Transparency in International Economic Relations and the Role of the WTO" (co-author with Matthew D'Orsi), in *Research Handbook on Transparency: Comparative Approaches* (Edwards Elgar Publishing, Padideh Ala'i & Robert Vaughn eds., 2014).

Ala'i, Padideh. *Research Handbook on Transparency: Comparative Approaches* (co-edit with Robert Vaughn), Edwards Elgar Publishing, 2014. Using comparative approaches, the Handbook provides a framework for considering the diverse goals of transparency and explores the complexity of circumstances and values that transparency considers.

Ala'i, Padideh. "Origins of GATT/WTO" in *International Trade Law and the WTO* (Federation Press, Carr, Alam and Bhuiyan eds., 2013).

Ala'i, Padideh. "From the Periphery to the Centre? The Evolving WTO Jurisprudence on Transparency and Good Governance." in *Redesigning the WTO for the Twenty-First Century* (Wilfrid Laurier University Press, The Center for International Governance Innovation, and IDRC (Canada), 2010.

Andonova, Liliana & Manfred Elsig. "Informal International Public Policy Making—A Conceptual View from International Relations." Background Paper, Research Workshop on Defining and classifying IIPPMs, at the IIPPM Mapping the Action and Testing Concepts of Accountability and Effectiveness Conference of the Centre for Trade and Economic Integration, The Graduate Institute of Geneva, Geneva, June 24-25, 2010.

Armitage, David. "The Fifty years' Rift: Intellectual History and International Relations." *Modern Intellectual History* 1, no. 1 (2004): 97-109.

Arsanjani, Mahnoush H. *International Regulation of Internal Resources: A Study of Law and Policy (Virginia Legal Studies)*. Virginia: Univ. of Virginia Press, 1981.

Ashford, Nicolas A., & Charles C. Caldart. *Environmental Law, Policy, and Economics: Reclaiming the Environmental Agenda*. Cambridge, MA (USA): The MIT Press, 2008.

Ashford, Nicholas A. *Technology, Globalization & Sustainability: Co-optimizing Competitiveness, Employment, and Environment through Technological Change and Trade.* Cambridge, MA (USA): The MIT Press, 2005.

Ashford, Nicholas A & Charles C. Caldart. *Technology, Law, and the Working Environment*. Washington, D.C.: Island Press, 1996.

Auty, Richard. *Sustaining Development in Mineral Economies: The Resource Curse Thesis*. Oxford: Routledge, 1993.

Baker, Roozbeh. 'Customary International Law in the 21st Century: Old Challenges and New Debates', *European Journal of International Law* 21 no. 1., 2010

Barnett, Harold J. & Chandler Morse. *Scarcity and Growth: The Economics of Natural Resource Availability*. Baltimore, MD: Johns Hopkins University Press for Resources for the Future, 1963.

Barrett, Scott. *Environment and Statecraft: The Strategy of Environmental Treaty-Making*. Oxford, UK: Oxford University Press, 2006.

Barrett, Scott. "Climate Change and International Trade: Lessons on their Linkage from International Environmental Agreements." Background Paper, Round Table 6, at the conference Climate Change, Trade and Competitiveness: Issues for the WTO of the Centre for Trade and Economic Integration, The Graduate Institute of Geneva, Geneva, June 16-18, 2010.

Bernasconi-Osterwalder, et al. *Environment and Trade: A Guide to WTO Jurisprudence*. London: Earthscan, 2006.

Bernstein, Steve. 'Legitimacy in Intergovernmental and Non-state Global Governance', *Review of International Political Economy* 18, no. 1.

Besada, Hany & Shannon Kindornay, eds. *Multilateral Development Cooperation in a Changing Global Order*. Basingstoke, UK: Palgrave Macmillan, 2013.

Biukovic, Liljana. "Selective Adaptation of WTO Transparency Norms and Local Practices in China and Japan." *Journal of International Economic Law* 11, no. 1 (2008): 751–777.

Bodansky, Daniel. *The Art and Craft of International Environmental Law*. Reprint edition. Cambridge, MA (USA): Harvard University Press, 2011.

Bodansky, Daniel. "Legitimacy in International and International Relations." In *Interdisciplinary Perspectives on International Law and International Relations: The State of the Art*, edited by Jeffrey L. Dunoff, and Mark A. Pollack. Cambridge University Press, 2013.

Bonneuil, Christophe & Les Levidow. "How Does the World Trade Organization Know? The Mobilization and Staging of Scientific Expertise in the GMO Trade Dispute." *Social Studies of Science* 42, no. 1 (2011): 75–100.

Breton, Albert, et al, eds. *Environmental Governance and Decentralisation*. Northampton, MA: Edward Elgar Publishing Ltd, 2007.

Brunnee, Jutta & Stephen Toope. "Interactional International Law: An Introduction". *International Theory* 3, no. 2 (2011).

Bulte, Erwin H & Edward B. Barbier. "Trade and Renewable Resources in a Second Best World: An Overview." *Environmental and Resource Economics* 30, no. 4 (2005): 423-464.

Calster, Geert Van & Denise Prevost, eds. *Research Handbook on Environment, Health and the WTO (Research Handbooks on the WTO Series) (Elgar Original Reference)*. Northampton, MA: Edward Elgar Publishing, 2013.

Campbell, C. J. & J.H. Laherrere. "The End of Cheap Oil". *Scientific American* (March 1998): 78-83.

Campling, Liam & Elizabeth Havice, "Mainstreaming Environment and Development at the World Trade Organization? Fisheries Subsidies, the Politics of Rule-Making, and the Elusive 'Triple Win'" *Journal of Environment and Planning* 45 (2013): 835.

Chang, Howard. "Toward a Greener GATT: Environmental Trade Measures and the Shrimp-Turtle Case." *Southern California Law Review* 74 (2000): 31-47.

Charnovitz, Steve. "The NAFTA Environmental Side Agreement: Implications for Environmental Cooperation, Trade Policy, and American Treaty Making". *Temple International and Comparative Law* 257 (1994).

Charnovitz, Steve. "A Critical Guide to the WTO's Report on Trade and Environment." *Arizona Journal International and Competition Law* 14 (1997): 341–370.

Charnovitz, Steve. "World Trade and the Environment: A Review of the New WTO Report". *Georgetown International Environmental Law Review* 12 (1999-2000): 523.

Charnovitz, Steve. "The WTO's Environmental Progress." *Journal of International Economic Law* 10, no. 3 (2007): 685-706.

Charnovitz, Steve. "The Path of World Trade Law in the 21st Century". *World Scientific Studies in International Economics* 37 (2015).

Chayes, Abram & Antonia Handler Chayes. *The New Sovereignity: Compliance with International Regulatory Agreements*. Cambridge, MA (USA): Harvard University Press, 1995.

Chayes, Abram & Antonia Handler Chayes. "On Compliance". *International Organization* 47, no. 2 (1993): 175-205.

Chayes, Abram, Antonia Handler & Ronald Mitchell. "Managing Compliance: A Comparative Perspective". In *Engaging Countries: Strengthening Compliance with International Environmental Accords*, edited by Edith Brown Weiss & Harold Jacobson, Cambridge, MA (USA): MIT Press.

Cheng, Bin. *General Principles of Law as Applied by International Courts and Tribunals*. Cambridge, UK: Cambridge University Press, 2006.

Clement, Merideth O., et al. *Who Protects the Ocean? Environment and Development of the Law of the Sea*. Eagan, MN: West Publishing Company, 1975.

Coimbra, José Duarte. "Global Administrative Law: A New Branch of Law or a Quest for an Academic Grail—A Comment on Ana Gouveia Martins." e-Pública [online] 2, no. 3 (2015): 204-214

Collier, Paul & Anthony Venables. "International Rules for Trade in Natural Resources." *Journal of Globalization and Development* 1, no. 1 (2010): 1.

Corrales, Werner. *The EPAs and Sustainable Development: Benchmarks for Pro-development Monitoring of the Negotiations*. Brussels and Geneva: ICTSD APRODEV, May 2005.

Corrales, Werner. *Competitiveness Revisited: A Policy Approach for Achieving Development Objectives in the Economic, Social and Environmental Spheres*. Geneva: UNCTAD,2003.

Corrales, Werner. "Basic Concepts and Proposals in the Trade-Supported Stategies for Sustainable Development (TSDS)." Supporting Paper, Capacity Building Workshop on Sustainable Development, Investment and Intellectual Property, UN-ECLAC, Costa Rica, May 2007.

Criddle, Evan & Evan Fox-Decent. "A Fiduciary Theory of Jus Cogens", *Yale Journal of International Law* 2, no. 34 (2009).

Damassa, Thomas. *World Resources Institute Carbon Dioxide Inventory Report for Calendar Years 2006 & 2007*. Washington D.C.: World Resources Institute, December 2008.

Dasgupta, Partha S. & Geoffrey Heal. *Economic Theory and Exhaustible Resources*. Welwyn, UK: James Nisbet and Co., 1979.

Dasgupta, Partha S. & Geoffrey Heal. "The Optimal Depletion of Exhaustible Resources." *The Review of Economic Studies* 41 (1974): 3-28.

Demortain, David. "Standardising Through Concepts: The Power of Scientific Experts in International Standard Setting." *Science and Public Policy* 35, no. 6 (2008): 391-402.

Devarajan, Shantayanan & Anthony C. Fisher. "Hotelling's 'Economics of Exhaustible Resources': Fifty Years Later". *Journal of Economic Literature* 19 (March 1981): 75–73.

Edenhofer, Ottmar, et al., eds. *IPCC Special Report on Renewable Energy Sources and Climate Change Mitigation*. Cambridge University Press, 2011.

Ehrlich, Paul R. *The Population Bomb*. New York: Ballantine Books, 1968.

Elsig, Manfred, Hoekman, Bernard and Joost Pauwelyn, *Thinking about the Performance of the World Trade Organization: A Discussion Across Disciplines*, EUI Working Papers, RSCAS 2016/13, 2016.

Elsig, Manfred, 'The World Trade Organization at Work: Performance in a Member-Driven Milieu'. Review of International Organizations, 2010, 5:345-363.

Fehr, Ernst & Andreas Leibbrandt. "Cooperativeness and Impatience in the Tragedy of the Commons." IZA Discussion Paper no. 3625, University of Zurich, 2008.

Fischer, Carolyn, Sandra Hoffman & Yutaka Yoshino. *Multilateral Trade Agreements and Market-Based Environmental Policies*, May 2002, Discussion Paper 02-28, Resources for the Future Publication.

Fitzmaurice, Magnolia. "History of Article 38 of the State of International Court of Justice." Queen Mary School of Law Legal Studies Research Paper No. 232/2016.

French, Duncan. *International Law and Policy of Sustainable Development*. Huffington, New York: Juris Publishing, Inc., 2005.

Gareau, Brian J. *From Precaution to Profit: Contemporary Challenges to Environmental Protection in the Montreal Protocol (Yale Agrarian Studies Series)*. New Haven, CT: Yale University Press, 2013.

Gaudet, G. "Natural Resource Economics under the Rule of the Hotelling." *Canadian Journal of Economics* 40 (2007): 1033–1059.

Giddens, Anthony. *The Politics of Climate Change*. Cambridge, UK: Polity Press, 2009.

Gray, Kevin & Craig N. Murphy, eds. *Rising Powers and the Future of Global Governance (ThirdWorlds)*. Oxford: Routledge, 2013.

Guruswamy, Lakshman D., et al. *International Environmental Law and World Order: A Problem-Oriented Coursebook (American Casebook Series)*. 2 edn. St. Paul, MN: West Group, 1999.

Gutner, Tamar & Alexander Thompson. "The Politics of IO performance: A Framework". *The Review of International Organizations* 5 (Springer Publications, 2010).

Guzman, Andrew. "Saving Customary International Law". *Michigan Journal of International Law* 27, no. 1 (2005).

Haas, Peter M. & John A. Hird, eds. *Controversies in Globalization: Contending Approaches to International Relations*. 2nd edn. Thousand Oaks, CA: CQ Press, 2012.

Haas, Peter M., Marc A. Levy & Robert O. Keohane, eds. *Institutions for the Earth: Sources of Effective International Environmental Protection (Global Environmental Accord: Strategies for Sustainability and Institutional Innovation)*. Cambridge, MA (USA): The MIT Press, 1993.

Hardin, Gareth. 'Tragedy of the Commons', *Science* 162 (1968):1243-1248.

Hartwick, John M. "Intergenerational Equity and the Investing of Rents from Exhaustible Resources." *American Economic Review* 9, no. 2 (December 1977): 972-74.

Hickel, Jason & Gorgio Kallis, "Is Green Growth Possible?". New Political Economy 25, no. 1 (2019).

Hirsch, Robert L., Roger Bezdek & Robert Wendling. *Peaking of world Oil Production: Impacts, Mitigation and Risk Management*. Morgantown, WV: National Energy Technology Laboratory, 2005.

Hodos, George H. *Show Trials: Stalinist Purges in Eastern Europe, 1948-1954*. Westport, CN: Praeger, 1987.

Hoel, M. "Resource Extraction, Uncertainty, and Learning." *The Bell Journal of Economics* 9, no. 2 (Autumn 1978): 642–645.

Horn, Henrik, Petros Mavroidis & Erik Wijkström. "In the Shadow of the DSU: Addressing Specific Trade Concerns in the WTO SPS and TBT Committees." *Journal of World Trade* 47, no. 4 (2013): 729–760.

Hotelling, Harold. "The Economics of Exhaustible Resources." *The Journal of Political Weekly* 39, no. 2 (April 1931):137-175.

Howse, Robert. "The Appellate Body Rulings in the Shrimp/Turtle Case: A New Legal Baseline for the Trade and Environment Debate". *Columbia Journal of Environmental Law* 27 (2002): 491–521.

Hubbert, M. King. "Nuclear Energy and the Fossil Fuels." Paper, spring meeting of the Southern District division of Production, American Petroleum Institute, San Antonio, TX, March 7-9, 1956.

Intergovernmental Panel on Climate Change. *Climate Change: The IPCC Response Strategies*. Geneva: IPCC, 1990.

Intergovernmental Panel on Climate Change. *Second Assessment: Climate Change 1995*. Geneva: IPCC, 1995.

Jackson, John H. *Restructuring the GATT System*. London: Royal Institute of International Affairs, 1990.

Jasanoff, Sheila. "Ordering Knowledge, Ordering Society." In *States of Knowledge: The Co-production of Science and Social Order*, edited by Sheila Jasanoff. Oxford: Routledge, 2006.

Jasanoff, Sheila. "Science and Norms in Global Environmental Regimes." In *Earthly Goods: Environmental Change and Social Justice*, edited by Fen Osler Hampson and Judith Reply. Ithaca, NY: Cornell University Press, 1996.

Jennings, Robert. "The Role of the International Court of Justice in the Development of International Environmental Law". *Review of European, Comparative and International Environmental Law* 1, no. 3 (September 1992): 240–244

Jha, Veena. *Environmental Priorities and Trade Policy for Environmental Goods: A Reality Check*. Issue Paper No. 7. Geneva: ICTSD, 2008.

Johnstone, Ian. "Law-Making by International Organizations: Perspectives from IL/IRTheory." In *Interdisciplinary Perspectives on International Law and International Relations: The State of the Art*, edited by Jeffrey L.Dunoff, and Mark A. Pollack.Cambridge University Press, 2013.

Johnstone, Ian. "Security Council Deliberations: The Power of the Better Argument." *European Journal of International Law* 13, no. 3 (2003): 437-480.

Jones, Kent. *The Doha Blues: Institutional Crisis and Reform in the WTO*. Oxford University Press, 2009.

Kennedy, David. "Challenging Expert Rule: The Politics of Global Governance." *Sydney Journal of International Law* 27 (2005): 5-28.

Keohane, Robert O. *After Hegemony: Cooperation and Discord in the World Political Economy*. Princeton, NJ: Princeton Press, 1984.

Keohane, Robert O (ed.). "Neoliberal Institutionalism: A Perspective on World Politics." In *International Institutions and State Power: Essays in International Relations Theory*. Boulder, CO: Westview Press Inc., April 1989.

Keohane, Robert O. "International Institutions: Two Approaches." *International Studies Quarterly* 32 (1988): 379-396.

Kingsbury, Benedict. "The Concept of Law in Global Administrative Law." *European Journal of International Law* 20 (2009): 23

Kingsbury, Benedict, Nico Krisch & Richard Stewart. "The Emergence of Global Administrative Law, Introduction: The Unnoticed Rise of Global Administrative Law." *Law and Contemporary Problems* 68 no. 15 (2005).

Kiss, Alexandre. *Droit international de l'environnement (Etudes internationales) (French Edition)*. Paris: A. Pedone, 1989.

Kiss, Alexandre. "The International Protection of the Environment". In *The Structure and Process of International Law: Essays in Legal Philosophy, Doctrine and Theory*, edited by Ronald St. J. MacDonald and Douglas Johnston. The Hague: Martinus Nijhoff Publishers, 1983.

Kiss, Alexandre. Hague Yearbook of International Law/Annuaire De La Haye de droit international. Martinus Nijhoff Publishers, 1998.

Klabbers, Jan. "Jurisprudence in International Trade Law—Article XX of GATT." *Journal of World Trade* 26, no. 2 (1992): 63–94.

Knox, John H. "The Judicial Resolution of the Conflict Between Trade and the Environment." *Harvard Environmental Law Review* 28 (2004): 1-78.

Knuchel, Sevrine. "State Immunity and the Promise of Jus Cogens". *Northwestern Journal of International Human Rights Law* 9, no. 2 (2011).

Koh, Kheng-Lian, ed. *ASEAN Environmental Law, Policy and Governance: Selected Documents, (Volume II)*. Singapore: World Scientific Publishing Company, 2013.

Koh, Kheng-lian, ed. *ASEAN Environmental Law, Policy and Governance: Selected Documents, (Volume I)*. Singapore: World Scientific Publishing Company, 2009.

Krishna-Hensel, Sai Felicia, ed. *Order and Disorder in the International System (Global Interdisciplinary Studies Series)*. Surrey, UK: Ashgate, 2013.

Krugman, Paul. "The Narrow Moving Band, the Dutch Disease, and the Competitive Consequences of Mrs. Thatcher, Notes on Trade in the Presence of Dynamic Scale Economies." *Journal of Development Economics* 27 (1987): 41–55.

Kupchan, Charles A., et al. *Power in Transition: The Peaceful Change of International Order*. Tokyo: United Nations University Press, 2001.

Kurtz, Jürgen. "Normative Interactions." *The Foundations of International Investment Law: Bringing Theory into Practice*, Eds. Zachary Douglas, Joost Pauwelyn and Jorge E. Viñuales, Oxford University Press.

Lang, Andrew. *World Trade Law After Neoliberalism (Reimagining the Global Economic Order)*. Oxford, UK: Oxford University Press, 2011.

Lang, Andrew & Joanne Scott. "The Hidden World of WTO Governance." *European Journal of International Law* 20 (2009): 575–614.

Levy, Marc A., Oran R. Young, and Martin Zürn. *The Study of International Regimes*. Laxenburg, Austria: International Institute for Applied Systems Analysis, 1996.

Levy, Marc A. "International Co-operation to Combat Acid Rain." In *Green Globe Yearbook of International Cooperation on Environment and Development*, edited by Helge Ole Bergesen, Georg Parmann, and Øystein B. Thommessen. Oxford, UK: Oxford University Press, 1995.

Linklater, Andrew. *Men and Citizens in the Theory of International Relations, 2nd edition*. London: MacMillan Press, 1990.

Low, Patrick, Gabrielle Marceau & Julia Reinaud. "The Interface Between the Trade and Climate Change Regimes: Scoping the Issues." *Staff Working Paper ERSD-2011-1*. Geneva: WTO, 2011.

Lugg, Amy & Mark Hong, eds. *Energy Issues in the Asia-Pacific Region*. Singapore: Institute of Southeast Asian Studies, 2010.

Maloney, Michael & Robert McCormick. "A Positive Theory of Environmental Quality Regulation." *Journal of Law and Economics* 25, no. 1 (April 1982): 99-123.

Malthus, Thomas Robert. *An Essay on the Principle of Population*. London: John Murray, 1826. Also available online at http://www.econlib.org/library/Malthus/malPlong11.html.

Marchetti Juan & Martin Roy. *The TiSA Initiative: An Overview of Market Access issues*. Geneva: WTO, 2013.

Marhold, Anna. "The World Trade Organization and Energy: Fuel for Debate." *European Society of International Law (ESIL) Reflection* 2, no. 8 (September 30, 2013): 1–6.

McCormick, Rachel. "A Qualitative Analysis of the WTOs Role on Trade and Environment Issues". *Global Environmental Politics* 6, no. 1 (February 2006): 102–124.

Meadows, Donella H., et al. *The Limits to Growth: A Report for the Club of Rome's Project on the Predicament of Mankind*. New York: Universe Books, 1974.

Monkelbaan, Joachim. *Governance for the Sustainable Development Goals: Exploring an Integrative Framework of Theories, Tools, and Competencies*. Singapore: Springer, 2019.

Munro, G.R. and U.R. Sumalia. "Subsidies and Their Potential Impact on the Management of Ecosystems of the North Atlantic." In *Fisheries Impacts on North Atlantic Ecosystems: Evaluations and Policy Explorations*, edited by Pitcher Tony, Sumalia, Ussif Rashid& Pauli Daniel at p. 7 (Fisheries Centre Report, 2001).

Mytelka, Lynn. "Technology Transfer Issues in Environmental Goods and Services: An Illustrative Analysis of Sectors Relevant to Air-pollution and Renewable Energy." *Issue Paper No. 6*. Geneva: ICTSD, 2007.

Neumayer, Eric, "A Missed Opportunity: The Stern Review on Climate Change Fails to Tackle the Issue of Non-substitutable Loss of Natural Capital." *Global Environmental Change* 17 (2007): 297–301.

Newman, Abraham & David Zaring. "Regulatory Networks: Power, Legitimacy, and Compliance." In *Interdisciplinary Perspectives on International Law and International Relations: The State of the Art*, edited by Jeffrey L. Dunoff, and Mark A. Pollack. Cambridge, UK: Cambridge University Press, 2013.

Nobel Prize. "The Prize in Economic Sciences 2009—Advanced Information." *Nobelprize.org*. http://www.nobelprize.org/nobel_prizes/economic-sciences/laureates/2009/advanced.html (accessed December 1, 2019).

Nordhaus, William D. "Resources as a Constraint on Growth." *American Economic Review* 64, no. 2 (May 1974): 22–26.

Nowrot, Karsten. "Governance and Internatonal Law." *Beiträge Zum Transationalen Wirtschaftsrecht* 33 (November 2004): 1–34.

Ostrom, Elinor. *Governing the Commons: The Evolution of Institutions for Collective Action*. Cambridge, UK: Cambridge University Press, 1990.

Ostrom, Elinor. "Rational Choice Theory and Institutional Analysis: Toward Complementarity." *The American Political Science Review* 85, no. 1 (1991): 237-243.

Ostrom, Elinor. "Prize Lecture: Beyond Markets and States: Polycentric Governance of Complex Economic Systems." *Nobelprize.org*. https://www.nobelprize.org/prizes/economic-sciences/2009/ostrom/lecture/; *See also* "Beyond Markets and States: Polycentric Governance of Complex Economic Systems." Workshop in Political Theory and Policy Analysis, Indiana University, and Center for the Study of Institutional Diversity, Arizona State University, Tempe, AZ, December 8, 2009.

Oxenford, Matthew. *Rethinking the WTO's Role in a Digital, Divided World.* Chatham House: Royal Institute of International Affairs (2019).

Oxford Martin School. *Now for the Long Term: The Report of the Oxford Martin Commission for Future Generations.* Oxford, UK: Oxford Martin School, October 2013.

Pauwelyn, Joost., Ramses Wessel and Jan Wouters, eds. *Informal International Lawmaking.* Oxford, UK: Oxford University Press, 2012.

Pauwelyn, Joost. *Conflict of Norms in Public International Law: How WTO Law Relates to Other Rules of International Law.* Cambridge, UK: Cambridge University Press, 2003.

Pfluger, Andrew. "Why the Montreal Protocol Is Not a Template for Multilateral Environmental Agreements: An Examination of why China and India Ratified." *Middle States Geographer* 43 (2010): 96-103.

Pigou, A.C., *The Economics of Welfare.* London: MacMillan 1920.

Pindyck, R.S. "The Optimal Exploration and Production of Non-Renewable Resources." *Journal of Political Economy* 86, no. 5 (October 1978): 841-861.

Raustiala, Kal. "Institutional Proliferation and the International Legal Order." In *Interdisciplinary Perspectives on International Law and International Relations: The State of the Art*, edited by Jeffrey L. Dunoff, and Mark A. Pollack. Cambridge University Press, 2013.

Raustiala, Kal. 'The Architecture of International Cooperation: Trangovernmental Networks and the Future of International Law". *Virginia Journal of International Law* 43 (2002-2003): 1.

Read, Robert. "Process and Production Methods and the Regulation of International Trade." In *The WTO and the Regulation of International Trade: Recent Trade Disputes Between the European Union and the United States*, edited by Nicolas Perdikis and Robert Read. Northampton, MA: Edward Elgar Pub, 2005.

Reynolds, D.B. "The Mineral Economy: How Prices and Costs Can Falsely Signal Decreasing Scarcity." *Ecological Economics* 31 (1999): 155-66.

Ricardo, David. *On the Principles of Political Economy and Taxation.* London: John Murray, 1821.

Rolland, Sonia E. *Development at the WTO (International Economic Law Series).* Oxford University Press, 2012.

Sands, Philippe, Jacqueline Peel & Ruth MacKenzie. *Principles of International Environmental Law.* Cambridge University Press, 2012.

Sachs, Jeffrey D. & Warner, Andrew M. *Natural Resource Abundance and Economic Growth.* Working Paper 5398. National Bureau of Economic Research, 1995.

Shaffer, Gregory & Pollack, Mark. 'Hard vs. Soft Law: Alternatives, Complements and Antagonists in International Governance'. *Minnesota Law Review* (2010).

Shelton, Dinah. *Soft Law in Handbook of International Law.* Routledge Press, 2008.

Singer, Clifford E. *Energy And International War: From Babylon to Baghdad and Beyond (World Scientific Series on Energy and Resource Economics).* Singapore: World Scientific Publishing Company, 2008.

Singh, Nagendra. *The Role and Record of the International Court of Justice*. Martinus Nijhoff Publishers, 1989.

Slaughter, Anne-Marie, 'The Accountability of Government Networks', *Indiana Journal of Global Legal Studies* 8 no. 2 (2001).

Slaughter, Anne-Marie. *A New World Order*. Princeton, NJ: Princeton University Press, 2004.

Slaughter, Anne-Marie. "International Law and International Relations Theory: Twenty Years Later." In *Interdisciplinary Perspectives on International Law and International Relations: The State of the Art*, edited by Jeffrey L.Dunoff, and Mark A. Pollack. Cambridge, UK: Cambridge University Press, 2013.

Slaughter, Anne-Marie. "International Relations, Principal Theories." In *The Max Planck Encyclopedia of International Law*, edited by Rüdiger Wolfrum. Oxford, UK: Oxford University Press, 2011.

Slaughter, Anne-Marie. "The Real New World Order." *Foreign Affairs* 76, no. 5 (September-October 1997): 183-197.

Solow, Robert M. "On the Intergenerational Allocation of Natural Resources." *The Scandinavian Journal of Economics* 88, no. 1 (March 1986): 141-149.

Solow, Robert M. "The Economics of Resources or the Resources of Economics." *The American Economic Review* 64, no. 2 (May 1974): 1-14.

Solow, R.M. "Intergenerational Equity and Exhaustible Resources." *The Review of Economic Studies* 41 (1974): 29-45.

Stein, Arthur. "Neoliberal Institutionalism." Chapter II. In *The Oxford Handbook of International Relations*, edited by Christian Reus-Smit and Duncan Snidal. Oxford, UK: Oxford University Press, 2008.

Steinberg, Richard H. "Trade-Environment Negotiations in the EU, NAFTA, and WTO: Regional Trajectories of Rule Development." *American Journal of International Law* 91, no. 2 (April 1997): 231-267.

Stern, Nicholas. *Stern Review on the Economics of Climate Change*. Cambridge, UK: Cambridge University Press, 2007.

Stewart, Richard, Badin and Michelle Ratton Sanchez. *The World Trade Organization and Global Administrative Law*. IILJ Working Paper 2009/7 (Global Administrative Law Series).

Stiglitz, J.E. 'What Is the Role of the State?', In *Escaping the Resource Curse*, edited by Humphreys, Sachs, and Stiglitz. New York: Columbia University Press, 2007.

Stiglitz, J.E. "Monopoly and the Rate of Extraction of Exhaustible Resources." *American Economic Review* 66, no. 4 (September 1976): 655-661.

Tarasofsky, Richard G. 'The WTO Committee on Trade and Environment: Is it Making a Difference?'. In *The Max Planck Yearbook of United Nations Law*, edited by Jochen Frowein and Rüdiger Wolfrum. New York: Springer, 1999.

Teehankee, Manuel A.J. "The WTO China Raw Materials Case: Reigniting the Debate on Coherence and Conflict Between Free Trade Theory and Resource Economics." *Teri GALT* 6, no. 1 & 2 (2012): 10-16.

The Royal Swedish Academy of Sciences. "Economic Governance: The Organization of Cooperation." *The Price in Economic Sciences 2009: Information to the Pubic* (October 12, 2009): 1-5.

Townsend, David J. and Charnovitz, Steve. "Preventing Opportunistic Uncompliance by WTO Members." *Journal of International Economic Law* 14, no. 2 (2011): 437-468.

Uhlmann, Eva M. Kornicker. "State Community Interests, Jus Cogens and Protection of the Global Environment: Developing Criteria for Preemptory Norms". *Georgetown International Environmental Law Review* 11 (1998-1999).

United Nations Development Programme. *Case Studies of Sustainable Development in Practice: Triple-wins for Sustainable Development*. New York: UNDP, June 2012.

Utton, Albert E., and Ludwik A. Teclaff, eds. *Transboundary Resources Law (Westview Special Studies in Natural Resources and Energy Management)*. New York: Westview Press, 1987.

Van Grasstek, Craig. *The History and Future of the WTO. Geneva: WTO*, 2013.

Verdier, Pierre-Hugues. 'Transnational Regulatory Networks and Their Limits'. *Yale Journal of International Law* 34 (2009).

Viñuales, Jorge E. *Foreign Investment and the Environment in International Law.* Cambridge University Press, 2012.

Viñuales, Jorge E. "The Environment Breaks into Investment Disputes." In *International Investment Law*, edited by Marc Bungenberg, Jörn Griebel, Stephan Hobe, and August Reinisch. Munich/London: C.H. Beck/Hart/Nomos, 2012.

Viñuales, Jorge E. "The Resource Curse—A Legal Perspective." *Global Governance* 17 (2011): 197-212.

Visgilio, Gerald R. and Diana M. Whitelaw, eds. *Acid in the Environment: Lessons Learned and Future Prospects*. New York: Springer, 2006.

Vogel, David. "The WTO, International Trade and Environmental Protection: European and American Perspectives." *Roman Schuman Centre Working Papers no. 2002/34*. Florence: European University Institute, 2002.

Von Moltke, Konrad. "The World Trade Organization and the Environment: What Must Change?" *PSIO Occasional Paper*. Geneva: Graduate Institute, 1996.

Vossenaar, Rene. "Climate-Related Single-Use Environmental Goods." *ICTSD Issue Paper No. 13*. Geneva: ICTSD, 2010.

Vossenaar, Rene. *The APEC List of Environmental Goods: An analysis of the Outcome and Expected Impact*. Geneva: ICTSD, 2013.

Vossenaar, Rene. *Reducing Import Tariffs for Environmental Goods: The APEC Experience*. Geneva: ICTSD, 2016.

Vranes, Erich. *Trade and the Environment: Fundamental Issues in International and WTO Law (International Economic Law)*. Oxford, UK: Oxford University Press, 2009.

Watson, James. *The WTO and the Environment: Development of Competence beyond Trade*. Oxford: Routledge, 2013.

Weinstein, Michael M. and Steve Charnovitz. "The Greening of the WTO." *Foreign Affairs*, November-December 2001. http://www.foreignaffairs.com/articles/57426/ichael-m-weinstein-and-steve-charnovitz/the-greening-of-the-wto.

Weitzman, Martin L. "A Review of the Stern Review on the Economics of Climate Change." *Journal of Economic Literature* 45, no. 3 (September 2007): 703-724.

Weisburd, Mark. *Failing of International Court of Justice*. Oxford, UK: Oxford University Press, 2016.

Weiss, Edith Brown. *The Evolution of International Environmental Law*. Washington, DC: Georgetown University Centre of Law Publication, 9 September 2016.

Wilke, Marie. "Feed in Tariffs for Renewable Energy and WTO Subsidy Rules." *Issue Paper No. 4*. Geneva: ICTSD, November 2011.

Wilkinson, Rorden, & James Scott, eds. *Trade, Poverty, Development: Getting Beyond the WTO's Doha Deadlock (Global Institutions)*. Oxford: Routledge, 2012.

Winkler, Harald and Andrew Marquard. "Analysis of the Economic Implications of a Carbon Tax." *Journal of Energy in Southern Africa* 22, no. 1 (February 2011): 55-68.

Winquist, Tina. *Trade in Domestically Prohibited Goods*. Geneva: IISD Publication, 1999.

Wolfe, Robert. Letting the Sun Shine in at the WTO: How Transparency Brings the Trading System to Life (March 6, 2013). World Trade Organization, Staff Working Paper ERSD-2013-03, March 2013. Available at SSRN: https://ssrn.com/abstract=2229741 or http://dx.doi.org/10.2139/ssrn.2229741.

World Bank. *International Trade & Climate Change: Economic, Legal, and Institutional Perspectives*. Washington, D.C.: World Bank, 2008.

World Bank. *China: Promoting a Circular Economy*. Washington, D.C.: World Bank, 2009.

World Trade Organization. *World Trade Report 2010: Trade in Natural Resources*. Geneva: WTO, 2010.

World Trade Organization & United Nations Environment Programme. *WTO-UNEP Report: Trade and Climate Change*. Geneva: WTO, 2009.

World Trade Organization. Nordström, Håkan and Vaughan, Scott. *Special Study 4 (1999): Trade and Environment*. Geneva: WTO, 1999.

World Trade Organization. *Future of the WTO*. Geneva: WTO, 2005.

Young, Oran R. *International Governance: Protecting the Environment in a Stateless Society*. Ithaca, NY: Cornell University Press, 1994.

Yu, Vicente Paolo III. *WTO Negotiating Strategy on Environmental Goods and Services for Asian Developing Countries*. Geneva: ICTSD, 2007.

Zaring, David. 'International Law by Other Means: The Twilight Existence of International Financial Regulatory Organizations.' *Texas International Law Journal* 33 (1998): 281.

Zurn, Michael, Andre Nollkaemper & Randy Peerenboom, eds. *Rule of Law Dynamics: In an Era of International and Transnational Governance*. Cambridge, UK: Cambridge University Press, 2012.

Zimmermann, Andreas, et al. *The Statute of the International Court of Justice: A Commentary*. Oxford, UK: Oxford University Press, 2013.

International Instruments: Cases, Documents Treaties

International Convention relating to the Simplification of Customs Formalities, Geneva, November 3, 1923, 30 L.N.T.S. 371.

Convention for the Abolition of Import and Export Prohibitions and Restrictions, Geneva, November 8, 1927, 97 L.N.T.S. 393.

Factory At Chorzów, Germany v Poland, Judgment, Claim for Indemnity, Merits, Judgment No 13, (1928) PCIJ Series A No 17, ICGJ 255 (PCIJ 1928), September 13, 1928, League of Nations.

General Agreement on Tariffs and Trade, Geneva, October 30, 1947, 61 Stat. A-11, 55 U.N.T.S. 194.

General Assembly, Integrated Economic Development and Trade Agreements (A/RES/6/523), January 12, 1952.

International Convention for the Protection of New Varieties of Plants Convention 1991 Act of 2 December 1961 [as revised in Geneva on November 10, 1972, October 23, 1978 and March 19, 1991] 815 U.N.T.S. 89.

General Assembly, Permanent Sovereignty over Natural Resources (A/RES/17/1803), December 14, 1962.

General Assembly, Permanent Sovereignty over Natural Resources (A/RES/21/2158), November 25, 1966.

General Assembly, Development of Natural Resources (A/RES/21/2173), December 6, 1966.

General Assembly, Declaration on Social Progress and Development in the Social (A/RES/24/2542), December 11, 1969.

Conference on Human Environment, *Report of the U.N. Conference on the Human Environment* (A/Conf.48/14/Rev. 1), June 16, 1972 [Stockholm Declaration].

Convention on International Trade in Endangered Species of Fauna and Flora, Lausanne, Switzerland, March 3, 1973, 993 U.N.T.S. 243.

General Assembly, Declaration on the Establishment of a New International Economic Order (A/RES/S-6/3201), May 1, 1974.

General Assembly, Charter of Economic Rights and Duties of States (A/RES/29/3281), December 12, 1974.
General Assembly, Other Methods and Means Available Within the United Nations System for Improving the Effective Enjoyment of Human Rights and Fundamental Freedoms (A/RES/32/130), December 16, 1977.
General Assembly, World Charter for Nature (A/RES/37/7), October 28, 1982.
Report of the Secretary General, Progressive Development of the Principles and Norms of International Law Relating to the New International Economic Order (A/39/504/Add.1), October 23, 1984.
General Assembly, Declaration on the Right to Development (A/RES/41/128), December 4, 1986.
Report of the World Commission on Environment and Development, "Our Common Future," Annex in Development and International Co-operation: Environment (A/42/427), August 4, 1987 [Brundtland Report].
Protocol on Substances that Deplete the Ozone Layer to the Vienna Convention for the Protection of the Ozone Layer, September 16, 1987, 1522 U.N.T.S. 3. [Montreal Protocol].
Vienna Convention for the Protection of the Ozone Layer, March 22, 1985, 26 I.L.M. 1516, 1513 U.N.T.S. 293, entered into force September 22, 1988.
Basel Convention on the Control of Transboundary Movements of Hazardous Wastes and their Disposal, March 22, 1989, 1673 U.N.T.S. 57; 28 I.L.M. 657.
Helsinki Declaration on the Protection of the Ozone Layer, May 2, 1989; 29 I.L.M. 1335.
United Nations Framework Convention on Climate Change, May 9, 1992, 1771 U.N.T.S. 107; 31 I.L.M. 849.
Convention on Biological Diversity, Rio de Janeiro, June 5, 1992, 1760 U.N.T.S. 79, 31 I.L.M. 818.
General Assembly, Agenda 21: Programme of Action for Sustainable Development (A/Conf.151/26), June 14, 1992.
United Nations Rio Declaration on Environment and Development, June 14, 1992, UN Doc. A/CONF.151/26 (vol. I), 31 ILM 874 (1992).
Certain Phosphate Lands in Nauru, Nauru v Australia, Preliminary Objections, Judgment, [1992] ICJ Rep 240, ICGJ 91 (ICJ 1992), June 22, 1992, International Court of Justice [ICJ].
North American Free Trade Agreement, December 17, 1992, 32 I.L.M. 289.
North American Agreement on Environmental Cooperation, September 14, 1993; 32 ILM 1482.
Ministerial Decision on Trade and Environment, MTN.TNC/MIN (94)/1/Rev.1, as part of Marrakesh Agreement Establishing the World Trade Organization, April 14, 1994, 1867 U.N.T.S. 133 (I-31874, 1995); 33 I.L.M. 1267.
Marrakesh Agreement Establishing the World Trade Organization, April 15, 1994, 1867 U.N.T.S. 154 (I-31874, 1995); 33 I.L.M. 1144.
Convention on Biological Diversity, Conference of Parties Decision III/17, UNEP/CBD/COP/DEC/III/9, 1996.

Gabčikovo-Nagymaros Project, Hungary v Slovakia, Judgment, Merits, ICJ GL No 92, [1997] ICJ Rep 7, [1997] ICJ Rep 88, (1998) 37 ILM 162, ICGJ 66 (ICJ 1997), September 25, 1997, International Court of Justice [ICJ].

Kyoto Protocol to the United Nations Framework Convention on Climate Change, December 11, 1997, 2303 U.N.T.S. 148.

Commission on Human Rights, *Study on the Current State of Progress in the Implementation of the Right to Development Submitted by Mr. Arjun K. Sengupta, Independent Expert, Pursuant to Commission Resolution1998/72 and General Assembly Resolution 53/155* (E/CN.4/1999/WG.18/2), July 27, 1999.

Cartagena Protocol on Biosafety to the Convention on Biological Diversity, January 29, 2000, 2226 U.N.T.S. 208.

General Assembly, United Nations Millennium Declaration (A/RES/55/2), September 8, 2000.

General Assembly, Promotion of a Democratic and Equitable International Order (A/RES/55/107), March 14, 2001.

Convention on Biological Diversity, Bonn Guidelines on Access to Genetic Resources and Fair and Equitable Sharing of the Benefits Arising out of their Utilization, CBD Conference of Parties 6 Decision VI/24, UNEP/CBD/COP/6/20, 2002.

Commission on Human Rights, Working Group on the Right to Development. *Implementing the Right to Development in the Current Global Context* (E/CN.4/2004/WG.18/2), February 17, 2004.

GATT and WTO Documents

GATT Secretariat, Industrial Pollution Control and International Trade, L/3538, June 9, 1971.

GATT Council, Minutes of the Meeting held in the Palais des Nations, Geneva, on October 6-7, 1971, C/M/73, October 19, 1971.

GATT Council, Industrial Pollution Control, November 9-10, 1971, C/W/194/Rev.1, November 9, 1971.

GATT Council, Minutes of the Meeting held in the Palais des Nations, Geneva, on November 9, 1971, C/M/74, November 17, 1971.

GATT Trade Negotiations Committee, Communication from Austria, Finland, Iceland, Norway, Sweden and Switzerland, MTN.TNC/W/47, December 3, 1990.

GATT Council, Minutes of the Meeting held in the Centre William Rappard on February 6, 1991, C/M/247, March 5, 1991.

GATT Council, Minutes of the Meeting held in the Centre William Rappard on April 24, 1991, C/M/249, May 22, 1991.

WTO Agreement on the Application of Sanitary and Phytosanitary Measures, April 15, 1994, 1867 U.N.T.S. 493, entered into force January 1, 1995 [SPS Agreement].

WTO Agreement on Technical Barriers to Trade, April 15, 1994, 1868 U.N.T.S. 120, entered into force January 1, 1995 [TBT Agreement].

WTO Agreement on Trade-related Aspects of Intellectual Property, April 15, 1994, 1869 U.N.T.S. 299, entered into force January 1, 1995 [TRIPS Agreement].

WTO Council for Trade in Services, Decision on Trade in Services and the Environment, S/L/4, April 4, 1995.

WTO Committee on Technical Barriers to Trade, WTO CTE, Note on Negotiating History of the Coverage of the Agreement on Technical Barriers to Trade with Regard to Labelling Requirements, Voluntary Standards, and Processes and Production Methods Unrelated to Product Characteristics, WT/CTE/W/10; G/TBT/W/11, August 29, 1995.

WTO Committee on Technical Barriers to Trade, Draft Minutes of the Meeting Held on October 20, 1995, G/TBT/W/55, November 22, 1995.

WTO Committee on Technical Barriers to Trade, Decisions and Recommendations Adopted by the Committee since January 1, 1995, G/TBT/1/Rev.3, March 28, 1996.

WTO Ministerial Conference (1st Session Singapore December 9–13, 1996), Ministerial Declaration, WT/MIN(96)/DEC; 36 I.L.M. 218 (1997).

WTO General Council, Preparations for the 1999 Ministerial Conference, Focus and Priorities of the New Round of Services Negotiations, Communication from Hong Kong, China, S/C/W/112, June 22, 1999.

WTO Committee on Specific Commitments, Communication from the European Communities and their Members, Classification Issues in the Environmental Sector, S/CSC/W/25, September 28, 1999.

WTO Council for Trade in Service Special Session, Communication from the United States—Environmental Services, S/CSS/W/25, December 18, 2000.

WTO Council for Trade in Services Special Session, Communication from the European Communities and their Members—GATS 2000: Environmental Services, S/CSS/W/38, December 22, 2000.

WTO Council for Trade in Services Special Session, Communication from Canada, Initial Negotiating Proposal on Environmental Services, S/CSS/W/51, March 14, 2001.

WTO Council for Trade in Services Special Session, Communication from Switzerland—GATS 2000: Environmental Services, S/CSS/W/76, May 4, 2001.

WTO Council for Trade in Services Special Session, Negotiating Proposal (Communication from Kenya, Negotiating Proposal), S/CSS/W/109, September 26, 2001.

WTO Ministerial Conference (4th Session Doha November 9–14, 2001), Ministerial Declaration, WT/MIN(01)/DEC/1, November 20, 2001.

WTO Committee on Technical Barriers to Trade, Minutes of the Meeting of November 10-11, 2011, G/TBT/M/55, February 9, 2002.

WTO Committee on Technical Barriers to Trade, Labelling and Requirements of the Agreement on Technical Barriers to Trade (Communication from Canada), G/TBT/W/174, March 12, 2002.

WTO Council for Trade in Services Special Session, Communication from Colombia, Negotiating Proposal on Environmental Services, S/CSS/W/121, March 22, 2002.

WTO Council for Trade in Services Special Session, Communication from Cuba, Negotiating Proposal on Environmental Services, S/CSS/W/142, March 22, 2002.

WTO Council for Trade-Related Aspects of Intellectual Property Rights, Review of Article 27.3(b) (Communication by the European Communities and their Members), IP/C/W/383, October 17, 2002.

WTO Council for Trade in Services Special Session, Report by the Chairman to the Trade Negotiations Committee, TN/S/23, November 28, 2005.

WTO Council for Trade-Related Aspects of Intellectual Property Rights, Minutes of Meeting Held in the Centre William Rappard on 25—26 and 28 October, 29 November and 6 December 2006, IP/C/M/49, October 31, 2006.

WTO Ministerial Decision of 17 December 2011 on Preferential Treatment to Services and Service Suppliers of Least-Developed Countries, WT/L/847, December 19, 2011.

WTO Committee on Technical Barriers to Trade, Notification (China), G/TBR/N/CHN/1211, July 18, 2017.

WTO Committee on Technical Barriers to Trade, China—Chinese Environmental Protection Control Standards for Imported Solid Waste as Raw Materials (Statement by the United States to the Committee on Technical Barriers to Trade), G/TBT/W/468, March 27, 2018.

GATT and WTO Cases

Brazil – Measures Affecting Imports of Retreaded Tyres, WT/DS332/AB/R, adopted December 17, 2007, DSR 2007:IV, 1527.

Canada – Certain Measures Affecting the Renewable Energy Generation Sector / Canada – Measures Relating to the Feed-in Tariff Program, WT/DS412/AB/R / WT/DS426/AB/R, adopted May 24, 2013.

Canada – Certain Measures Affecting the Renewable Energy Generation Sector / Canada – Measures Relating to the Feed-in Tariff Program, WT/DS412/R / WT/DS426/R / and Add.1, adopted May 24, 2013.

China – Measures Related to the Exportation of Rare Earths, Tungsten, and Molybdenum, WT/DS431/R; WT/DS432/R; WT/DS433/R, adopted August 29, 2014.

China – Measures Related to the Exportation of Rare Earths, Tungsten, and Molybdenum, WT/DS431/AB/R; WT/DS432/AB/R; WT/DS433/AB/R, adopted August 29, 2014.

China – Measures Related to the Exportation of Various Raw Materials, WT/DS394/AB/R / WT/DS395/AB/R, WT/DS398/AB/R, adopted February 22, 2012.

China – Measures Related to the Exportation of Various Raw Materials, WT/DS394/R / WT/DS395/R / WT/DS398/R / and Corr.1, adopted February 22, 2012.

European Communities – Measures Affecting Asbestos and Asbestos Containing Products, WT/DS135/AB/R, adopted April 5, 2001, DSR 2001:VII, 3243.

European Communities – Measures Concerning Meat and Meat Products (Hormones), WT/DS26/AB/R, WT/DS48/AB/R, adopted February 13, 1998, DSR 1998:I, 135.

United States – Import Prohibition of Certain Shrimp and Shrimp Products, WT/DS58/AB/R, adopted November 6, 1998, DSR 1998:VII, 2755.

United States – Import Prohibition of Certain Shrimp and Shrimp Products – Recourse to Article 21.5 of the DSU by Malaysia, WT/DS58/AB/RW, adopted November 21, 2001, DSR 2001:XIII, 6481.

United States – Measures Affecting the Production and Sale of Clove Cigarettes, WT/DS406/AB/R, adopted April 24, 2012.

United States - Measures Concerning the Importation, Marketing and Sale of Tuna and Tuna Products, WT/DS381/AB/R, adopted June 13, 2012.

United States - Measures Concerning the Importation, Marketing and Sale of Tuna and Tuna Products, WT/DS381/R, adopted June 13, 2012.

United States - Prohibition of Imports of Tuna and Tuna Products from Canada, L/5198, adopted February 22, 1982, BISD 29S/91.

United States - Restrictions on Imports of Tuna, DS21/R, September 3, 1991, unadopted, BISD 39S/155.

United States - Restrictions on Imports of Tuna, DS29/R, June 16, 1994, unadopted, reprinted in 33 ILM 839 (1994).

United States - Standards for Reformulated and Conventional Gasoline, WT/DS2/AB/R, adopted May 20, 1996, DSR 1996:I, 3.

GATT GEMIT, WTO CTE, WTO CTESS Documents

CTE CTESS Master Lists

CTE, Selective Bibliography on Trade and Environment, WT/CTE/W/49, May 16, 1997; WT/CTE/W/49/Add.1, October 7, 2002.

CTESS, Committee on Trade and Environment (CTESS) List of Documents, TN/TE/INF/4/Rev.16, May 3, 2013.

CTE, Committee on Trade and Environment (CTE) List of Documents, WT/CTE/INF/5/Rev.12, February 29, 2016.

GEMIT Documents

GATT Ministerial Work, Export of Domestically Prohibited Goods, BISD 29S/19, 1982.

GATT GEMIT, Report by the Chairman of the Working Group on Domestically Prohibited Goods and Other Hazardous Substances, L/6872, July 2, 1991.

GATT GEMIT, Trade Provisions contained in Multilateral Environmental Agreements, TRE/W/1, April 29, 1992.

GATT GEMIT, Agenda Item 2: Multilateral Transparency of National Environmental Regulations, TRE/W/2, September 4, 1992; TRE/W/7, March 3, 1993; TRE/W/14, March 10, 1993.

GATT GEMIT, Agenda Item 3: Packaging and Labelling Requirements, TRE/W/3, September 29, 1992; TRE/W/9, March 10, 1993; TRE/W/12, June 14, 1993.

GATT GEMIT, Multilateral Transparency of National Environmental Regulations likely to have Trade Effects (Submission by the EC), TRE/W/4, November 16, 1992.

GATT GEMIT, GATT and the Trade Provisions of Multilateral Environmental Agreements, TRE/W/5, November 17, 1992.

GATT GEMIT, Environmental Packaging and Labelling Activities in the United States (Submission by the United States), TRE/W/6, December 11, 1992.

GATT GEMIT, Agenda Item 1: Trade Provisions contained in Existing Multilateral Environmental Agreements vis-à-vis GATT Principles and Provisions,

TRE/W/16, September 2, 1993; TRE/W/17, September 7, 1993; TRE/W/18, October 1, 1993.

GATT GEMIT, GATT and International Environmental Agreements (IEAs) (Submission by Austria), TRE/W/19, October 1, 1993.

GATT GEMIT, Border Tax Adjustment, TRE/W/20, January 11, 1994.

GATT GEMIT, Unnecessary Obstacles to International Trade, TRE/W/21, January 17, 1994.

CTE CTESS Chairman Reports, Annual Reports, Meeting Reports, Annotated Agendas

CTE

Summary of Activities of the Committee on Trade and Environment (1995) Presented by the Chairman, WT/CTE/W/17, December 12, 1995.

Result of the Stocktaking Exercise Adopted at the May 28–29, 1996 CTE Meeting, WT/CTE/W/33, June 4, 1996.

1996 CTE Report "Singapore Report", WT/CTE/1, November 12, 1996.

Reports of the Meetings (1995-2019), WT/CTE/M/1 through to WT/CTE/M/67, March 6, 1995–October 24, 2019.

Report of the CTE (1997 to 2019), WT/CTE/2 through to WT/CTE/26, November 26, 1997-December 9, 2019.

CTESS

Statement by the Chairperson of the Special Session of the Committee on Trade and Environment (CTESS) to the Trade Negotiation Committee (TNC) (Meeting on March 22, 2002), TN/TE/1, April 12, 2002.

Summary Report on the First Meeting of the CTESS (2002), TN/TE/R1, April 19, 2002.

Annotated Agenda on the Meeting of June 11–12, 2002, JOB (02)/54, June 6, 2002.

Statement by the Chairperson of the CTESS to the TNC (Meeting of June 11-12, 2002), TN/TE/2, July 4, 2002.

Summary Report on the MEA Information Session on Paragraph 31 (ii) of the Doha Declaration—November 12, 2002, TN/TE/R/4, January 21, 2003.

Annotated Agenda of the Meeting of February 12–13, 2003, JOB (03)/15, February 3, 2003.

Draft Annotated Agenda for the Meeting (May 2003—July 2006), JOB (03)/78 through to JOB (06)/219, April 24, 2003—July 3, 2006.

Reports by the Chairperson of the CTESS to the TNC (2004–2008), TN/TE/3 through to TN/TE/18, December 2, 2002—July 18, 2008.

Report by the Chairman, Ambassador Manuel A.J. Teehankee, to the TNC for the purpose of the TNC stocktaking exercise, TN/TE/19, March 22, 2010.

Report by the Chairman, Ambassador Manuel A.J. Teehankee, to the TNC, TN/TE/20, April 21, 2011.

Textual Elements Derived from Member's Submissions under Paragraph 31 (iii), JOB/TE/20, April 21, 2011.

Summary Report on Meeting of the CTESS (2nd to 23rd), TN/TE/R/2 through to TN/TE/R/23, July 25, 2002—May 3, 2013.

International Organization and MEA Secretariat Papers

UNCTAD, UNCTAD Expert Meeting on Strengthening Capacities in Developing Countries to Develop their Environmental Services Sector, Communication from UNCTAD, WT/CTE/W/96, August 3, 1998.

WTO, Nordström, Håkan and Vaughan, Scott. Special Study 4 (1999): Trade and Environment. Geneva: WTO, 1999.

WTO and UNEP, Joint Note on Compliance and Dispute Settlement Provisions in the WTO and in Multilateral Environmental Agreements, WT/CTE/W/191, June 6, 2001.

UNEP, UNEP High-Level Meeting on Developing Mutually Supportive Trade and Environment Policies—Berlin, WT/CTE/W/198, June 25, 2001.

UN, United Nations Consolidated List of Products whose Consumption and/or Sale have been Banned, Withdrawn, Submission by the UN Secretariat, WT/CTE/W/194, June 26, 2001.

UNEP, UNEP Meeting on Compliance, Enforcement and Dispute Settlement in Multilateral Environmental Agreements and the WTO, WT/CTE/W/199, July 20, 2001.

UNEP, MEA Secretariats and WTO, MEA Information Session on Technical Assistance, Capacity Building and Enhancing Information Exchange—Input from the World Trade Organization, UNEP and MEA Secretariats, WT/CTE/W/209, June 5, 2002.

UNEP, Enhancing Synergies and Mutual Supportiveness of MEAS and the WTO—A Synthesis Report, Contribution by UNEP, WT/CTE/W/213, June 12, 2002.

WTO and UNEP, WTO-UNEP Report: Trade and Climate Change. Geneva: WTO, 2009.

CTE/CTE Secretariat Working Documents

CTE

Item 4: The Provisions of the Multilateral Trading with Respect to the Transparency of Trade Measures, WT/CTE/W/5, March 23, 1995.

Description of International Agreements and Instruments Dealing With Trade in Domestically Prohibited Goods and Other Substances, Note by the Secretariat, WT/CTE/W/6, March 31, 1995.

Environment and TRIPS, WT/CTE/W/8, June 8, 1995.

Note on Negotiating History of the Coverage of the Agreement on Technical Barriers to Trade with Regard to Labelling Requirements, Voluntary Standards, and Processes and Production Methods Unrelated to Product Characteristics, WT/CTE/W/10; G/TBT/W/11, August 29, 1995.

Factors Affecting Transfer of Environmentally-Sound Technology, WT/CTE/W/22, February 21, 1996.

The Effects of Environmental Measures on Market Access especially in relation to Developing Countries in particular to the Least Developed amongst them, Note by the Secretariat, WT/CTE/W/26, March 26, 1996.

Item 7: Domestically Prohibited Goods, Assessment of the Product Coverage in Specific International Instruments, Note by the Secretariat, WT/CTE/W/29, May 14, 1996.

A Review of the Information Available in the World Trade Organization on the Export of Domestically Prohibited Goods, Note by the Secretariat, WT/CTE/W/43, April 22, 1997.

Note on Taxes and Charges for Environmental Purposes—Border Tax Adjustment, WT/CTE/W/47, May 2, 1997.

The Convention on Biological Diversity and the Agreement on Trade-Related Aspects of Intellectual Property Rights, WT/CTE/W/50, May 20, 1997.

Note on the Relationship between the Convention on Biological Diversity (CBD) and the Agreement on the Trade-Related Aspects of Intellectual Property Rights (TRIPS); with focus on Article 27.3 (b), WT/CTE/W/125, October 5, 1999.

Note on Information Relevant to the Consideration of the Market Access effects of Eco-Labelling Schemes, WT/CTE/W/150, June 29, 2000.

Clarification of the Relationship between the WTO and Multilateral Environmental Agreements, WT/CTE/W/168, October 19, 2000.

GATT/World Trade Organization Dispute Settlement Practice relating to GATT Article XX, Paragraphs (b), (d) and (g), WT/CTE/W/203, March 8, 2002.

Discussion Paper on Environmental Effects of Services Trade Liberalization, Note by the Secretariat, WT/CTE/W/218, October 3, 2002.

Environmental Issues Raised in the Services Negotiations, Statement by Mr. A. Hamid Mamdouh—30 April 2003—Paragraph 51, WT/CTE/GEN/11, April 16, 2003.

Note on Environmental Requirements and Market Access: Recent Work in OECD and UNCTAD, WT/CTE/W/244, December 8, 2006.

List of Environmental Reviews ("Notifications"), WT/CTE/W/245, June 4, 2007.

Central Registry of Notifications (CRN), Note by the Secretariat, WT/CTE/W/34, August 5, 2007.

Matrix on Trade Measures Pursuant to Selected MEAs, Note by the Secretariat, WT/CTE/W/160/Rev.1 through to WT/CTE/W/160/Rev.8, June 14, 2001—October 9, 2017.

Environmental Database (2001—2019), WT/CTE/EDB/1 though to WT/CTE/EDB/18, June 13, 2002—November 12, 2019.

CTESS

Synthesis of Submissions on Environmental Goods, Informal Note by the Secretariat, JOB (05)/57/Rev.1., July 4, 2005.

Revision of the Synthesis of Submissions on Environmental Goods in TN/TE/W/63, November 17, 2005, JOB (07)/137, September 17, 2007.

Note on Eco-Labelling: Overview of Current Work in Various International Foras, JOB/TE/9, September 29, 2010.

Reference Universe of Environmental Goods: Official HS Description (Based on Compilation of Submissions under paragraph 31 (iii) of Doha relevant to the CTESS Work Programme, JOB/TE/3, March 22, 2010); JOB/TE/3/Rev.1, January 5, 2011.

Matrix on Trade-Related Measures Pursuant to Selected MEAs, WT/CTE/W/160/Rev.5; TN/TE/S/5/Rev.3, June 15, 2011.

WTO Member Submissions

ACP Group, Technical Assistance and Capacity Building Activities in 2002—Paragraph 33, WT/CTE/W/216, September 30, 2002.

African Group, Proposal for the Establishment of a Group of Experts on Trade and Environment, JOB (08)/38, May 8, 2008.

Argentina and India, Integrated Approach to Paragraph 31(iii), JOB (07)/77, June 6, 2007.

Argentina, Integrated Proposal on Environmental Goods for Development, TN/TE/W/62, October 14, 2005.

Argentina, The Doha Round and Climate Change, TN/TE/W/74, November 23, 2009.

ASEAN, The Relationship between the Provisions of the Multilateral Trading System and Trade Measures for Environmental Purposes, including those Pursuant to Multilateral Environmental Agreements (MEAs), WT/CTE/W/39, July 24, 1996.

Australia and Argentina, Proposal for an Outcome on Trade and Environment Concerning Paragraph 31 (i) of the Doha Ministerial Declaration, TN/TE/W/72/Rev.1, May 7, 2007.

Australia, Colombia, Hong Kong, China, Norway and Singapore, A Hybrid Approach to the Liberalization of Environmental Goods under Paragraph 31(iii), JOB/TE/15, March 8, 2011.

Bangladesh, Trade in Domestically Prohibited Goods, WT/CTE/W/141, June 15, 2000.

Brazil, Environmental Goods for Development, JOB (07)/146, October 1, 2007.

Canada, Canada's Initial List of Environmental Goods Paragraph 31(iii), TN/TE/W/50, June 2, 2005.

Chile and Mexico, Combined approach for environmental goods, JOB/TE/16, March 11, 2011.

Chile, Communication from Chile, WT/CTE/W/2, February 16, 1995.

China and India, WTO negotiations on environmental goods and services—Addressing the development dimension for a "triple-win" outcome, TN/TE/W/79, April 15, 2011.

Cuba, Communication from Cuba—Paragraph 31 (iii), TN/TE/W/73, July 9, 2008.

European Communities, Labelling for Environment Purposes (Submission by EC), WT/CTE/W/208, June 3, 2002.

European Communities, Market Access for Environmental Goods, TN/TE/W/47, February 17, 2005.

European Communities, Resolving the Relationship between WTO Rules and Multilateral Environmental Agreements, WT/CTE/W/170, October 19, 2000.

European Communities, Switzerland and United States, Market Access for Non-agricultural Products, TN/TE/W/65, May 9, 2005.

European Communities, The Relationship between MEAS and World Trade Organization Agreements: Set out in MEAs (Submission by the European Communities), TN/TE/W/31, May 14, 2003.

European Union, Circular Economy in the European Union: Achievements under the 2015-2019 Circular Economy Action Plan, RD/CTE/164, November 25, 2019.

India, An Alternative Approach for Negotiations under Paragraph 31(iii), TN/TE/W/51, June 3, 2005.

India, Cluster on Market Access, the Relationship between the TRIPS Agreement and the Convention on Biodiversity, WT/CTE/W/65, September 29, 1997.

India, Structural Dimensions of the Environmental Project Approach, TN/TE/W/54, July 4, 2005.

India, WTO Council for Trade-Related Aspects of Intellectual Property Rights, Protection of Biodiversity and Traditional Knowledge, WT/CTE/W/156; IP/C/W/198, July 14, 2000.

Japan, Market Access for Non-Agricultural Products, TN/TE/W/17, November 20, 2002.

Mexico and Chile, Combined Approach for Environmental Goods, JOB/TE/16, March 11, 2011.

Mexico and Chile, Combined Approach for Environmental Goods, JOB/TE/16/Corr.1, March 21, 2011.

New Zealand, Environmental Goods (Submission by New Zealand), TN/TE/W/46, June 6, 2002.

New Zealand, Item 1: The Relationship between the provisions of the Multilateral Trading System and Trade Measures for Environmental Purposes, including those pursuant to Multilateral Environmental Agreements (MEAs), WT/CTE/W/20, February 15, 1996.

Nigeria and Senegal, Communication from the Delegations of Nigeria and Senegal—Domestically Prohibited Goods, WT/CTE/W/11, September 14, 1995.

Peru, Peru's Experience of the Protection of Traditional Knowledge and Access to Genetic Resources, WT/CTE/W/176, October 27, 2000.

Plurinational State of Bolivia and the Bolivarian Republic of Venezuela, Elements for ensuring a sustainable development outcome under paragraph 31 (iii) of the Doha Ministerial Declaration, JOB/TE/17, March 24, 2011.

Qatar, Negotiating Group on Market Access Harmonized System (HS) Classification Codes of Gas-Related Goods, TN/TE/W/27, April 25, 2003.

Qatar, Negotiations on Environmental Goods, TN/TE/W/19, January 28, 2003.

Republic of Korea, Initial List of Environmental Goods Proposed, TN/TE/W/48, February 18, 2005.

Saudi Arabia, Technology Dissemination, WT/CTE/W/247, October 29, 2010.

Separate Customs Territory of Taiwan and Matsu, Proposed Initial List of Environmental Goods, TN/TE/W/44, October 7, 2004.

Separate Customs Territory of Taiwan, Penghu, Kinmen and Matsu, Identification of Multilateral Environmental Agreements (MEAs) and Specific Trade Obligations (STOs), TN/TE/W/35 Rev.1, July 3, 2003.

Separate Customs Territory of Taiwan, Penghu, Kinmen and Matsu, The Relationship between WTO Rules and Specific Trade Obligations Set Out in MEAs, TN/TE/W/36, July 3, 2003.

Singapore, Promoting Mutual Supportiveness between Trade and Climate Change Mitigation Actions: Carbon-Related Border Tax Adjustments, WT/CTE/W/248, March 30, 2011.

Small, Vulnerable Economies Group, Views of the Small Vulnerable Economies on the Negotiation of Paragraph 31 (iii) of the Doha Ministerial Declaration—Communication from the Small, Vulnerable Economies, JOB/TE/18, April 1, 2011.

Switzerland, Clarification of the Relationship between the WTO and MEA, WT/CTE/W/168, October 19, 2000.

Switzerland, Clarification of the Relationship between the WTO and Multilateral Environmental Agreements, WT/CTE/W/168, October 19, 2000.

Switzerland, Labelling for Environment Purposes, WT/CTE/W/219, October 14, 2002.

Switzerland, The Relationship between the Provisions of the Multilateral Trading System and Multilateral Environmental Agreements, WT/CTE/W/139, June 8, 2000.

United States, Circular Economy and the WTO, RD/CTE/153, November 19, 2019.

United States, Cluster on MEAs, Response of India to Comments by United States, WT/CTE/W/65; WT/CTE/W/85, July 7, 1998.

United States, Draft decision for an outcome under Doha paragraphs 31(i) and 31(ii), TN/TE/W/78, February 14, 2011.

United States, Liberalization of Trade in Environmental Services and the Environment, WT/CTE/W/70, November 21, 1997.

United States, Liberalizing Environmental Goods in the World Trade Organization, TN/TE/W/34, June 19, 2003.

United States, Market Access for Non-Agricultural Products—Contribution Environmental Goods Modality (Addendum), TN/TE/W/38, July 7, 2003.

United States, Negotiating Group on Market Access—Initial List of Environmental Goods, TN/TE/W/52, July 4, 2005.

United States, Paragraph 33 of the Doha Declaration, WT/CTE/W/227, April 29, 2003.

Index

1. Emmanuel T. Laryea, *Paperless Trade: Opportunities, Challenges and Solutions,* 2002 (ISBN 90-411-9897-0).
2. Xiang Gao, *The Fraud Rule in the Law of Letters of Credit: A Comparative Study,* 2002 (ISBN 90-411-9898-9).
3. Yuwa Wei, *Comparative Corporate Governance: A Chinese Perspective,* 2003 (ISBN 90-411-9908-X).
4. Ross P. Buckley (ed.), *The WTO and the Doha Round: The Changing Face of World Trade,* 2003 (ISBN 90-411-9947-0).
5. Bradley J. Condon, Joyce C. Sadka & Tapen Sinha (eds), *Insurance Regulation in North America: Integrating American, Canadian and Mexican Markets,* 2003 (ISBN 90-411-2301-6).
6. Jan Hoogmartens, *EC Trade Law Following China's Accession to the WTO,* 2004 (ISBN 90-411-2301-6).
7. Yang Guohua, Bryan Mercurio & Li Yongjie, *WTO Dispute Settlement Understanding: A Detailed Interpretation,* 2005 (ISBN 90-411-2361-X).
8. Jan Job de Vries Robbé, Paul U. Ali, *Securitisation of Derivatives and Alternative Asset Classes, Yearbook,* 2005 (ISBN 90-411-2375-X).
9. Markus W. Gehring, Marie-Claire Cordonier Segger, *Sustainable Development in World Trade Law,* 2005 (ISBN 90-411-2366-0).
10. Yann Aubin & Arnaud Idiart, *Export Control Law and Regulations Handbook: A Practical Guide to Military and Dual-Use Goods Trade Restrictions and Compliance,* 2007 (ISBN 90-411-2601-5).
11. Henry Kibet Mutai, *Compliance with International Trade Obligations: The Common Market for Eastern and Southern Africa,* 2007 (ISBN 978-90-411- 2664-1).
12. Yong-Shik Lee, *Economic Development through World Trade: A Developing World Perspective,* 2007 (ISBN 978-90-411-2681-8).
13. Yanning Yu, *Circumvention and Anti-Circumvention Measures: The Impact on Anti-Dumping Practice in International Trade,* 2007 (ISBN 978-90-411- 2686-3).
14. Ross Buckley, Vai Io Lo & Laurence Boulle, *Challenges to Multilateral Trade: The Impact of Bilateral, Preferential and Regional Agreements,* 2008 (ISBN 978-90-411-2711-2).
15. K.D. Raju, *World Trade Organization Agreement on Anti-dumping: A GATT/ WTO and Indian Jurisprudence,* 2008 (ISBN 978-90-411-2780-8).
16. Xiaochen Wu, *Anti-dumping Law and Practice in China,* 2008 (ISBN 978-90-411-2790-7).
17. Amin Alavi, *Legalization of Development in the WTO: Between Law and Politics,* 2008 (ISBN 978-90-411-2795-2).
18. Henrik Andersen, *EU Dumping Determinations and WTO Law,* 2009 (ISBN 978-90-411-2827-0).

19. Sherzod Shadikhodjaev, *Retaliation in the WTO Dispute Settlement System*, 2009 (ISBN 978-90-411-2811-9).
20. Yi Shin Tang, *The International Trade Policy for Technology Transfers: Legal and Economic Dilemmas on Multilateralism versus Bilateralism*, 2009 (ISBN 978-90-411-2825-6).
21. Reem Anwar Ahmed Raslan, *Antidumping: A Developing Country Perspective*, 2009 (ISBN 978-90-411-3128-7).
22. Pietro Poretti, *The Regulation of Subsidies within the General Agreement on Trade in Services of the WTO: Problems and Prospects*, 2009 (ISBN 978-90- 411-3162-1).
23. Esther Lam, *China and the WTO: A Long March towards the Rule of Law*, 2009 (ISBN 978-90-411-3144-7).
24. Jorge Alberto Huerta-Goldman, *Mexico in the WTO and NAFTA: Litigating International Trade Disputes*, 2009 (ISBN 978-90-411-3169-0).
25. Laurence Boulle, *The Law of Globalization: An Introduction*, 2009 (ISBN 978-90-411-2828-7).
26. Daniel Lovric, *Deference to the Legislature in WTO Challenges to Legislation*, 2010 (ISBN 978-90-411-3145-4).
27. Gregory W. Bowman, Nick Covelli, David A. Gantz & Ihn Ho Uhm, *Trade Remedies in North America*, 2010 (ISBN 978-90-411-2840-9).
28. Madalina Diaconu, *International Trade in Gambling Services*, 2010 (ISBN 978-90-411-3248-2).
29. Mohamed Ramadan Hassanien, *United States Bilateral Free Trade Agreements: Consistencies or Conflicts with Norms in the Middle East?*, 2010 (ISBN 978-90-411-3281-9).
30. Marie-Claire Cordonier Segger, Markus W Gehring & Andrew Newcombe, *Sustainable Development in World Investment Law*, 2011 (ISBN 978-90- 411-3166-9).
31. Nellie Munin, *Legal Guide to GATS*, 2010 (ISBN 978-90-411-2824-9).
32. Thomas G. Kelch, *Globalization and Animal Law: Comparative Law, International Law and International Trade*, 2011 (ISBN 978-90-411-3338-0).
33. Yann Aubin & Arnaud Idiart (eds), *Export Control Law and Regulations Handbook: A Practical Guide to Military and Dual-Use Goods Trade Restrictions and Compliance*, Third Edition, 2016 (ISBN 978-90-411-5443-9).
34. Yulia Selivanova (ed.), *Regulation of Energy in International Trade Law: WTO, NAFTA and Energy Charter*, 2011 (ISBN 978-90-411-3264-2).
35. Germano Franceschin & Francesco Misuraca, *India: Commercial Law, Customs and Taxation*, 2011 (ISBN 978-90-411-2836-2).
36. Humberto Zúñiga Schroder, *Harmonization, Equivalence and Mutual Recognition of Standards in WTO Law*, 2011 (ISBN 978-90-411-3657-2).

37. Kati Kulovesi, *The WTO Dispute Settlement System: Challenges of the Environment, Legitimacy and Fragmentation*, 2011 (ISBN 978-90-411- 3406-6).
38. Martín Molinuevo, *Protecting Investment in Services: Investor-State Arbitration versus WTO Dispute Settlement*, 2012 (ISBN 978-90-411-3827-9).
39. Joachim Åhman, *Trade, Health, and the Burden of Proof in WTO Law*, 2012 (ISBN 978-90-411-3825-5).
40. Umair Hafeez Ghori, *Global Textiles and Clothing Trade: Trade Policy Perspectives*, 2012 (ISBN 978-90-411-3875-0).
41. Yenkong Ngangjoh Hodu, *Theories and Practices of Compliance with WTO Law*, 2012 (ISBN 978-90-411-3228-4).
42. Dan Wei & Fernando M. Furlan, *Brazil in World Trade: Contingent Protection Measures*, 2012 (ISBN 978-90-411-3335-9).
43. Jorge A. Huerta-Goldman, Antoine Romanetti & Franz X. Stirnimann (eds), *WTO Litigation, Investment Arbitration, and Commercial Arbitration*, 2013 (ISBN 978-90-411-4686-1).
44. Gilles Muller, *Liberalization of Trade in Legal Services*, 2013 (ISBN 978-90-411-4853-7).
45. Christian Struck, *Product Regulations and Standards in WTO Law*, 2014 (ISBN 978-90-411-4950-3).
46. Gonzalo Villalta Puig, *Economic Relations between Australia and the European Union: Law and Policy*, 2014 (ISBN 978-90-411-3405-9).
47. Maurizio Gambardella, Davide Rovetta & Simon van Cutsem, *Remission and Repayment of Customs Duties in the EU*, 2014 (ISBN 978-90-411-4764-6).
48. Lisa Spagnolo, *CISG Exclusion and Legal Efficiency*, 2014 (ISBN 978-90-411-5407-1).
49. Dennis Ndonga, *Single Windows and Trade Facilitation: A Tool for Development*, 2015 (ISBN 978-90-411-5834-5).
50. Malebakeng Agnes Forere, *The Relationship of WTO Law and Regional Trade Agreements in Dispute Settlement: From Fragmentation to Coherence*, 2015 (ISBN 978-90-411-6274-8).
51. Julien Chaisse & Jiaxiang Hu (eds), *International Economic Law and the Challenges of the Free Zones*, 2019 (ISBN 978-94-035-0893-1).
52. Boris Praštalo, *Uniformity in the Application of the CISG: Analysis of the Problem and Recommendations for the Future*, 2020 (ISBN 978-94-035-2072-8).
53. Manuel A.J. Teehankee, *Trade and Environment Governance at the World Trade Organization Committee on Trade and Environment*, 2020 (ISBN 978-94-035-2202-9).

www.ingramcontent.com/pod-product-compliance
Ingram Content Group UK Ltd.
Pitfield, Milton Keynes, MK11 3LW, UK
UKHW020230290926
15470UKWH00002B/449

9 789403 522029